The COLORFUL CAPE FEAR

A coloring book for lovers of
Cape Fear History
by
Jack E. Fryar, Jr.

Great for Children AND Adults!
Works Best With Colored Pencils & Crayons!

Published in the United States of America by Dram Tree Books

10 9 8 7 6 5 4 3 2 1

Dram Tree Books
P.O. Box 7183
Wilmington, N.C. 28406
www.dramtreebooks.com
dramtreebooks@gmail.com

Introduction

When you live in a place that has four centuries of great history like the Cape Fear, the stories you can tell are endless. But teaching kids about that history can be a tough job. Generally speaking, I have found you have to have a little history before you can really appreciate history. Still, there are ways. In writing books for general readers, I try to make sure I am always telling a story - true, factually accurate, but a story nonetheless. Then there are the titles I have written in our *Young Reader's Series of North Carolina History* that use lots color, pictures, and minimal text to introduce young people to our past. But I am always on the lookout for new ways to tell the stories that tell our story as North Carolinians and people who call the Cape Fear home. So why not a coloring book!

Kids love coloring. Lots of adults do too, even if they won't admit it. So what could be better than a coloring book that spotlights the great history that surrounds us in southeastern North Carolina? While I'm not an artist, I have managed to accumulate a ton of pictures over the years from reenactments, historic sites, and illustrations I've used in other books. Finding an app that takes those pictures and converts them to coloring book pages made doing this book an easy choice.

I hope you (and your kids) enjoy it, and that maybe you will learn a little bit of Cape Fear history too!

Jack E. Fryar, Jr.
October 2025

THE EARLY DAYS

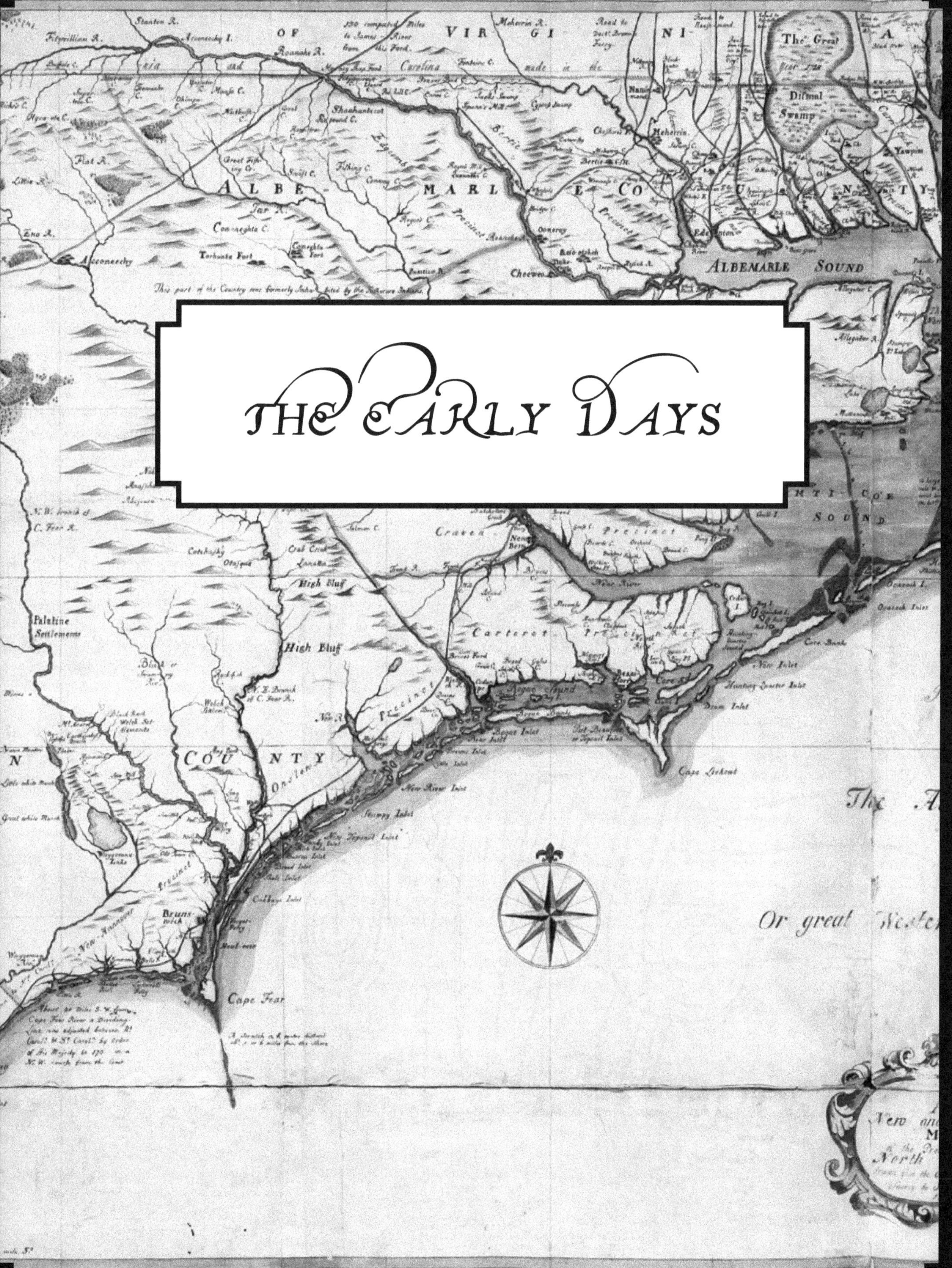

First sighting of Cape Fear...

Giovanni de Verrazano was the first European to sight Cape Fear, crossing the Atlantic and making landfall there in 1524. Verrazano did not come ashore, but his account of the voyage recalled seeing native peoples on the sandy beaches of what would become southeastern North Carolina. Verrazano sailed a bit further south before turning north to explore the coast as far as what is now Nova Scotia, before returning to Europe with news of his discoveries. Giovanni de Verrazano was just one of the many Europeans who would investigate the newfound land along the New World's eastern shore, including what came to be called North America.

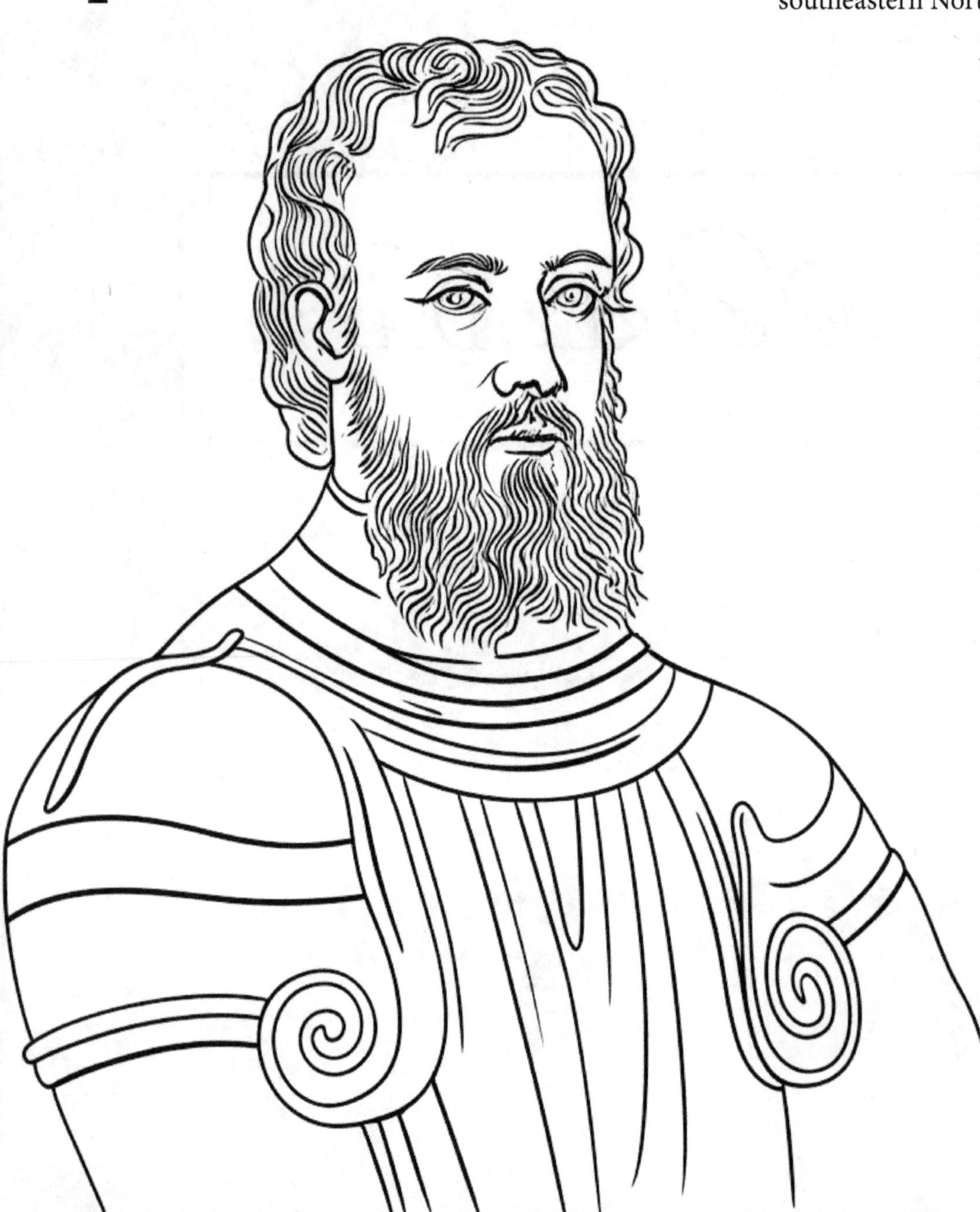

Charles Towne on the Cape Fear...

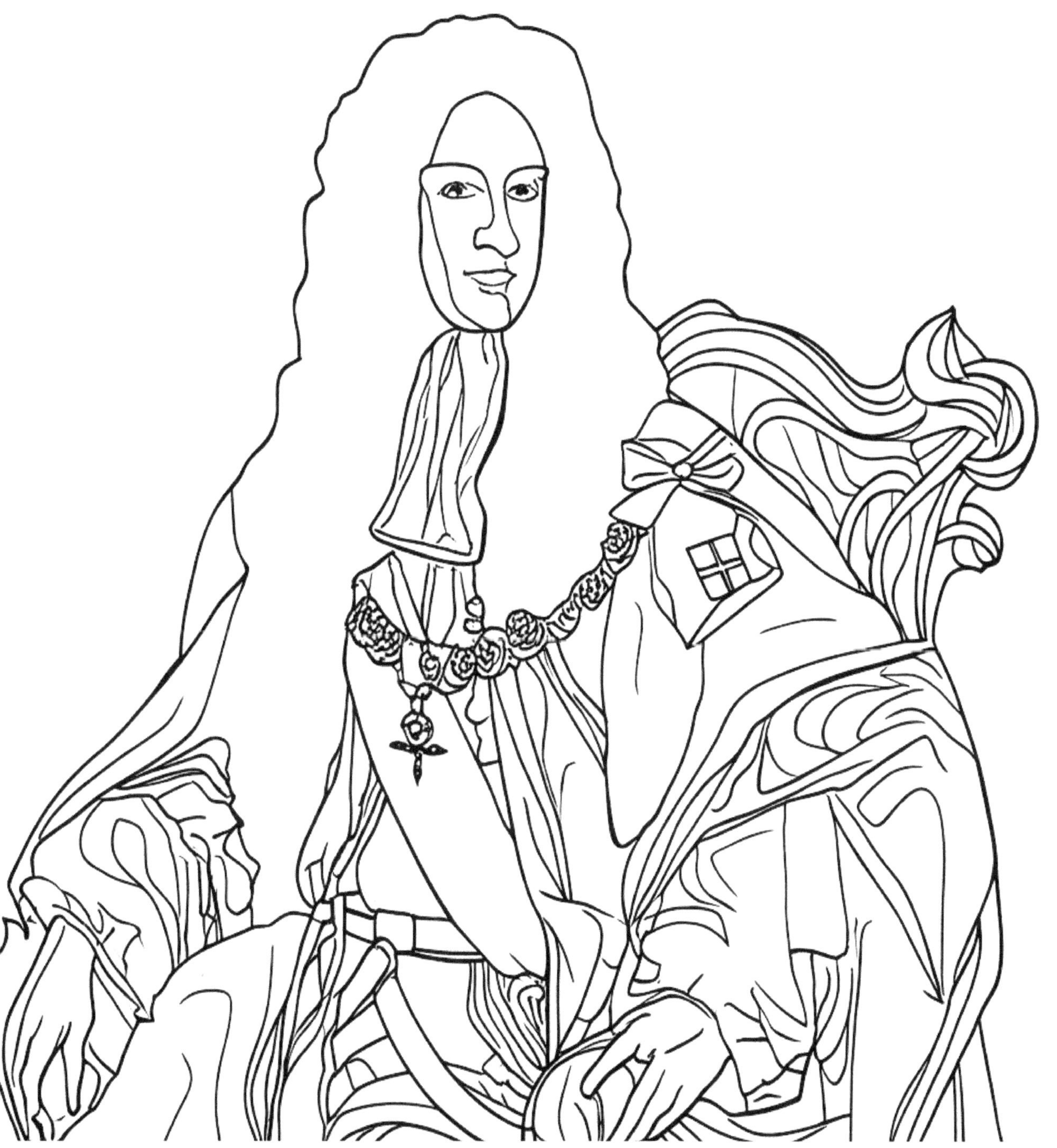

The restoration of the English monarchy came in 1660, when King Charles II returned from exile and reclaimed his crown in London. Charles was restored to his throne through the efforts of eight loyal men. The king rewarded those eight men with a grant of land in North America that they would call Carolina, after their king. The new Lords Proprietors of Carolina set out to plant colonies in their New World grant, and let it be known that they were looking for people to make the journey.

The Lords Proprietors of Carolina...

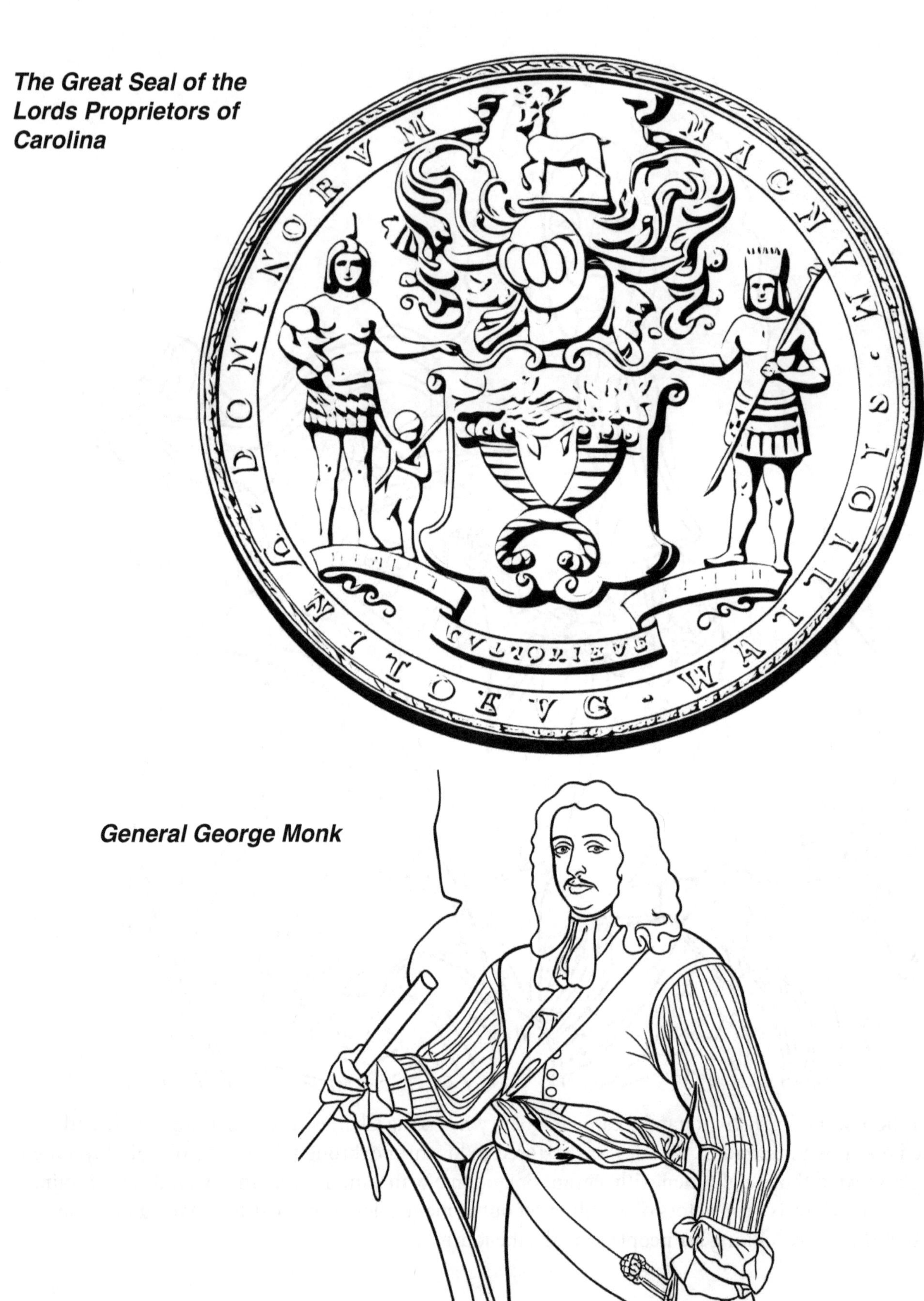

The Great Seal of the Lords Proprietors of Carolina

General George Monk

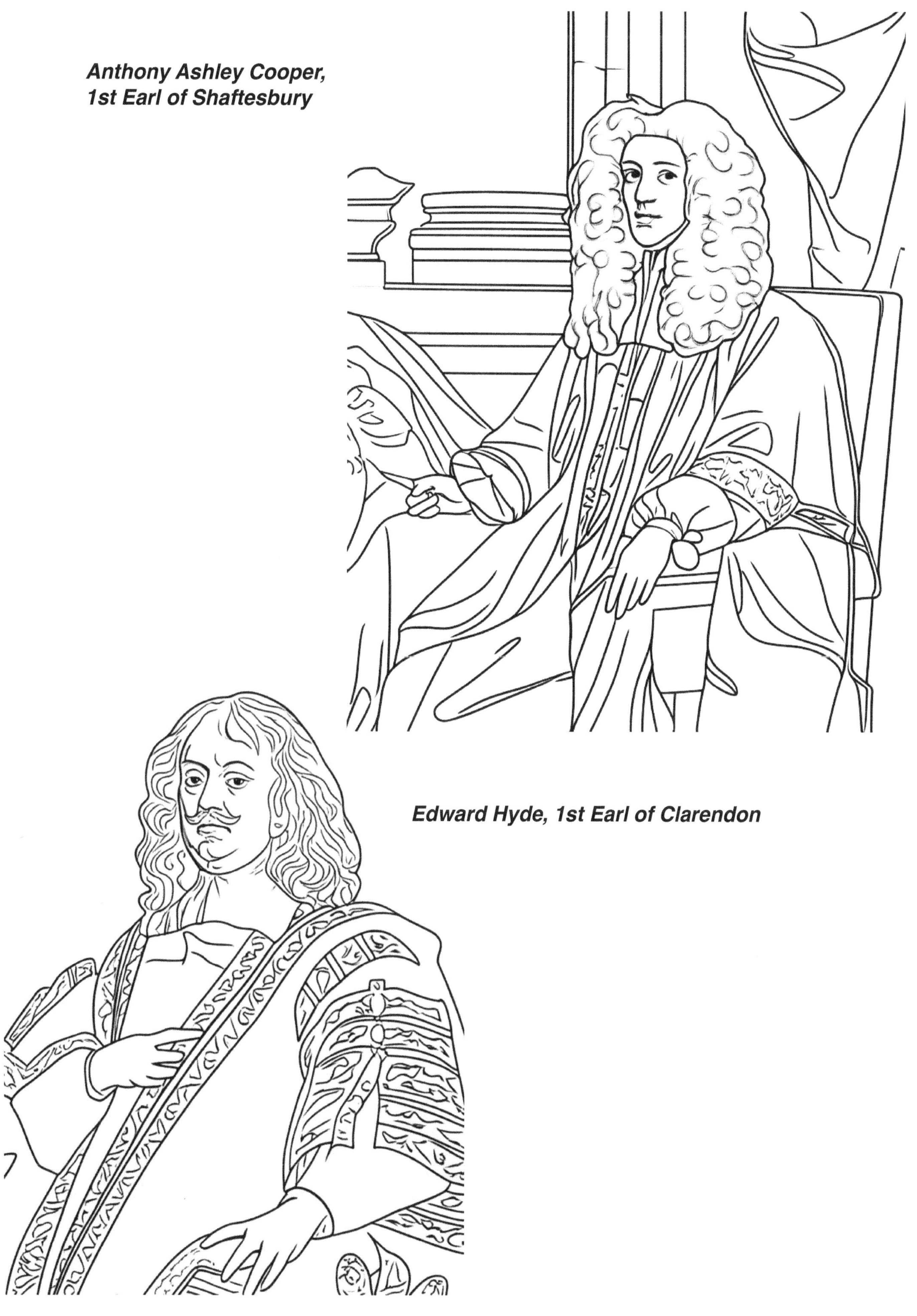

Anthony Ashley Cooper, 1st Earl of Shaftesbury

Edward Hyde, 1st Earl of Clarendon

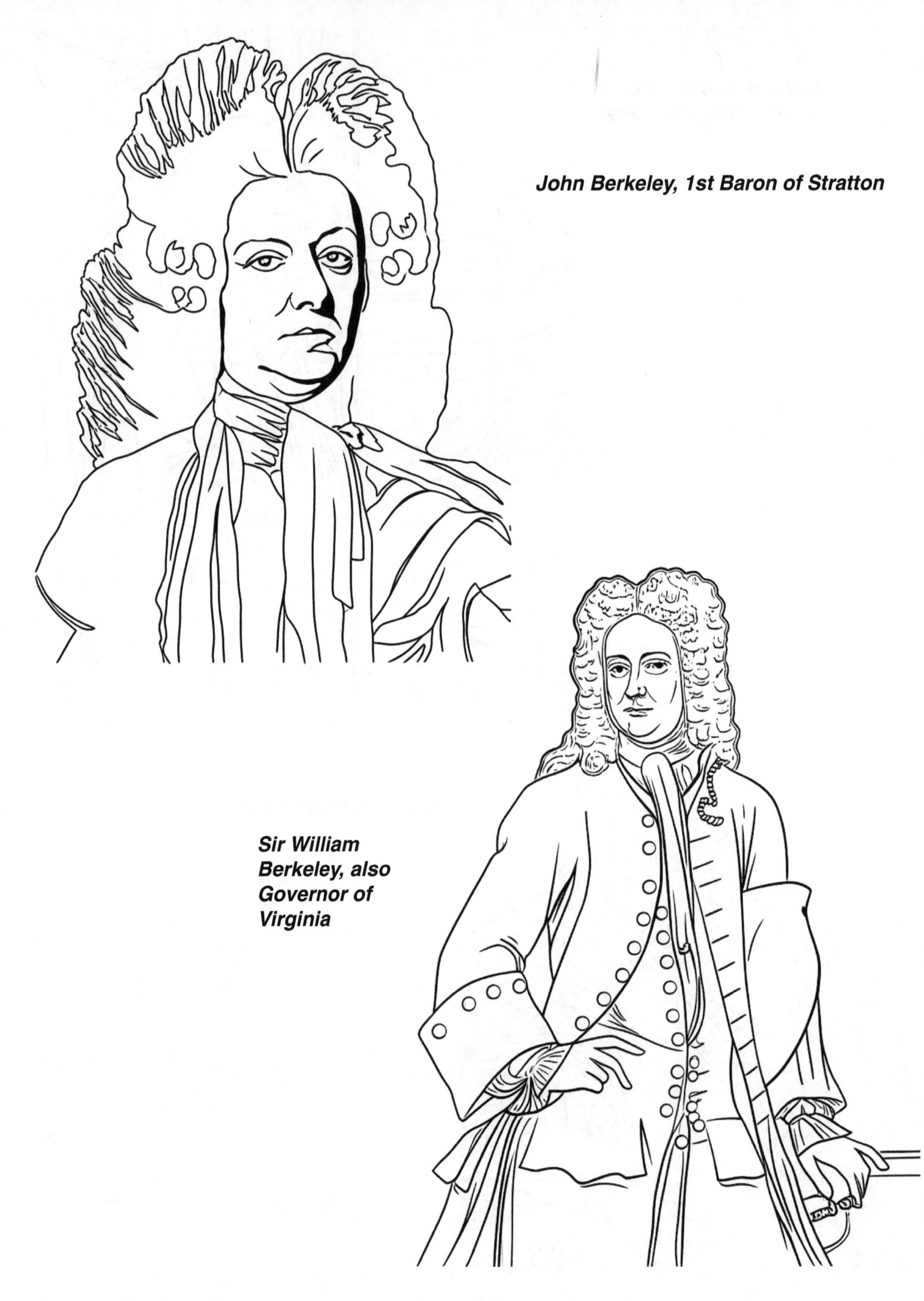

John Berkeley, 1st Baron of Stratton

Sir William Berkeley, also Governor of Virginia

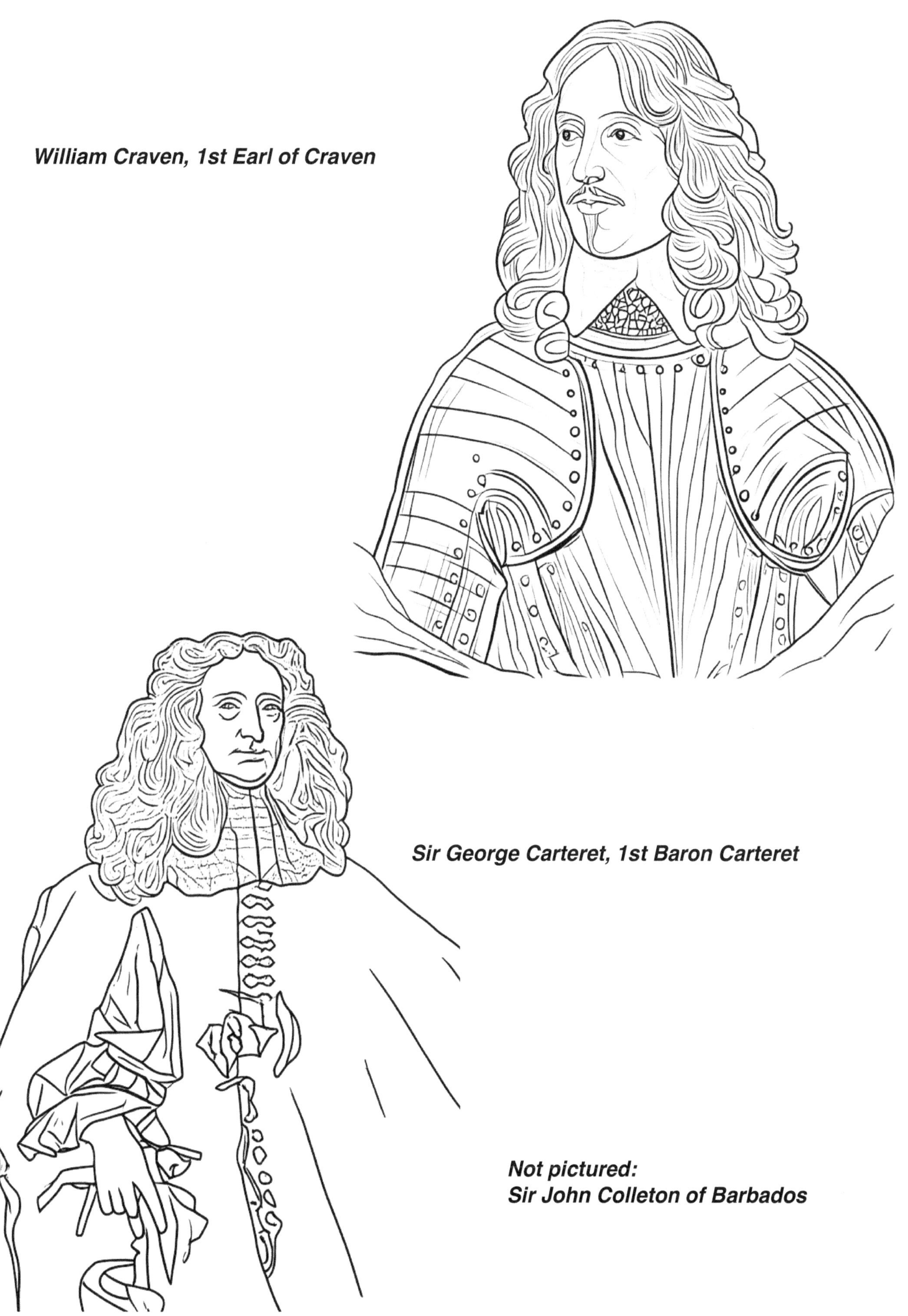
William Craven, 1st Earl of Craven
Sir George Carteret, 1st Baron Carteret
Not pictured:
Sir John Colleton of Barbados

The Company of Barbadian Advenurers...

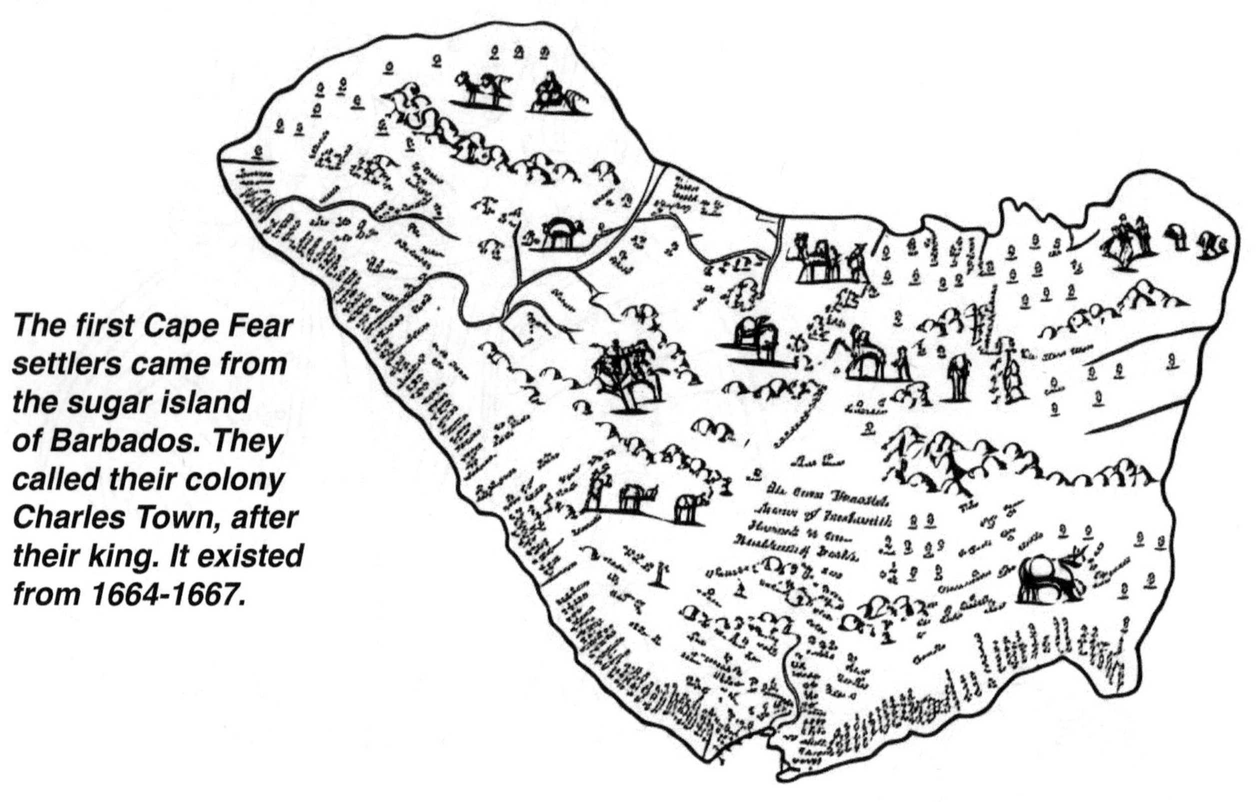

The first Cape Fear settlers came from the sugar island of Barbados. They called their colony Charles Town, after their king. It existed from 1664-1667.

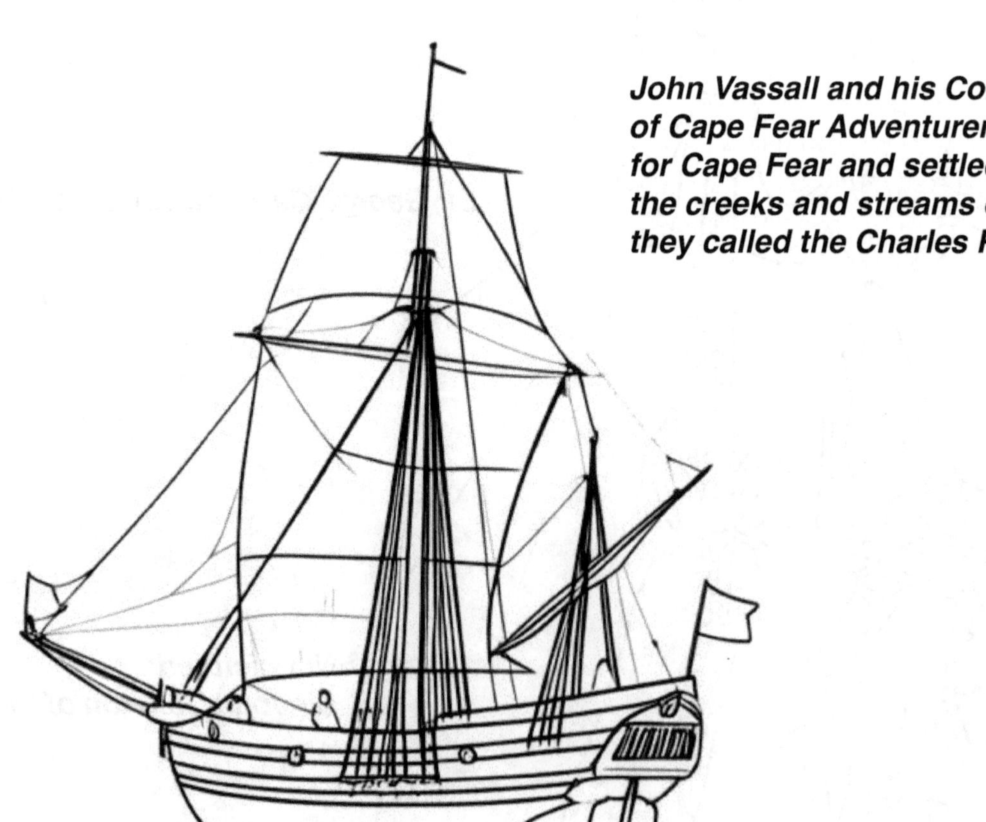

John Vassall and his Company of Cape Fear Adventurers sailed for Cape Fear and settled along the creeks and streams of what they called the Charles River.

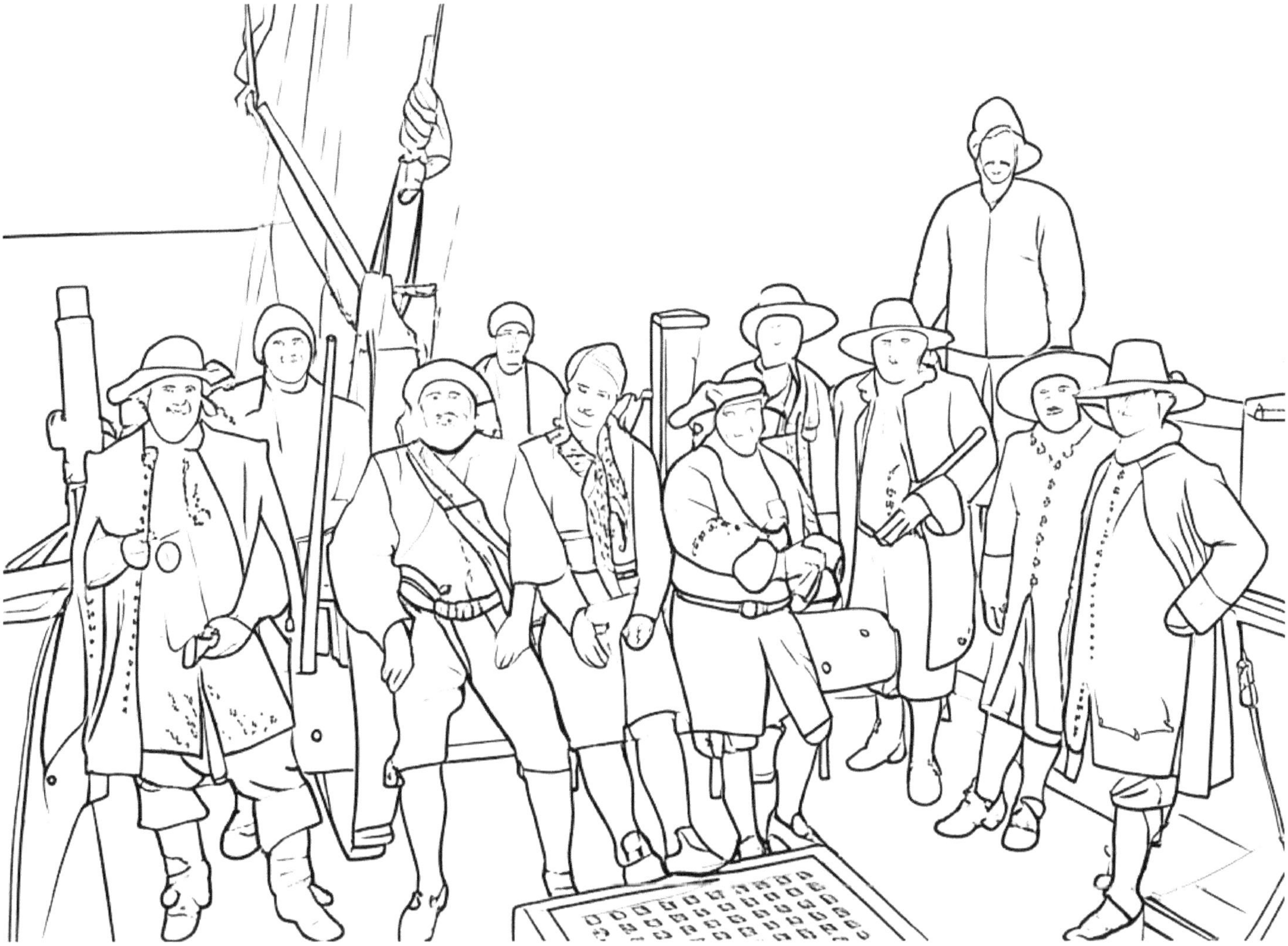

Barbadian Adventurers (above) and Puritans from Massachusetts (below) established a colony along the waterways of the Cape Fear that at its peak numbered as many as 800 people. The colony was centered around a central compound just north of modern Town Creek, and across from a village of local Native Americans just south of the creek.

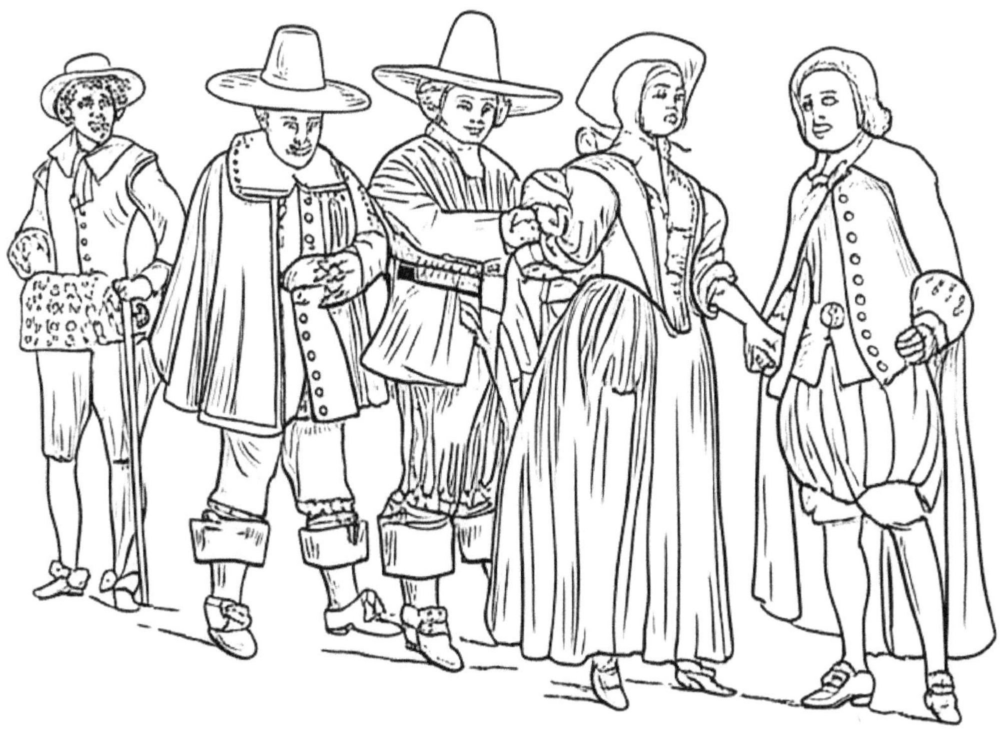

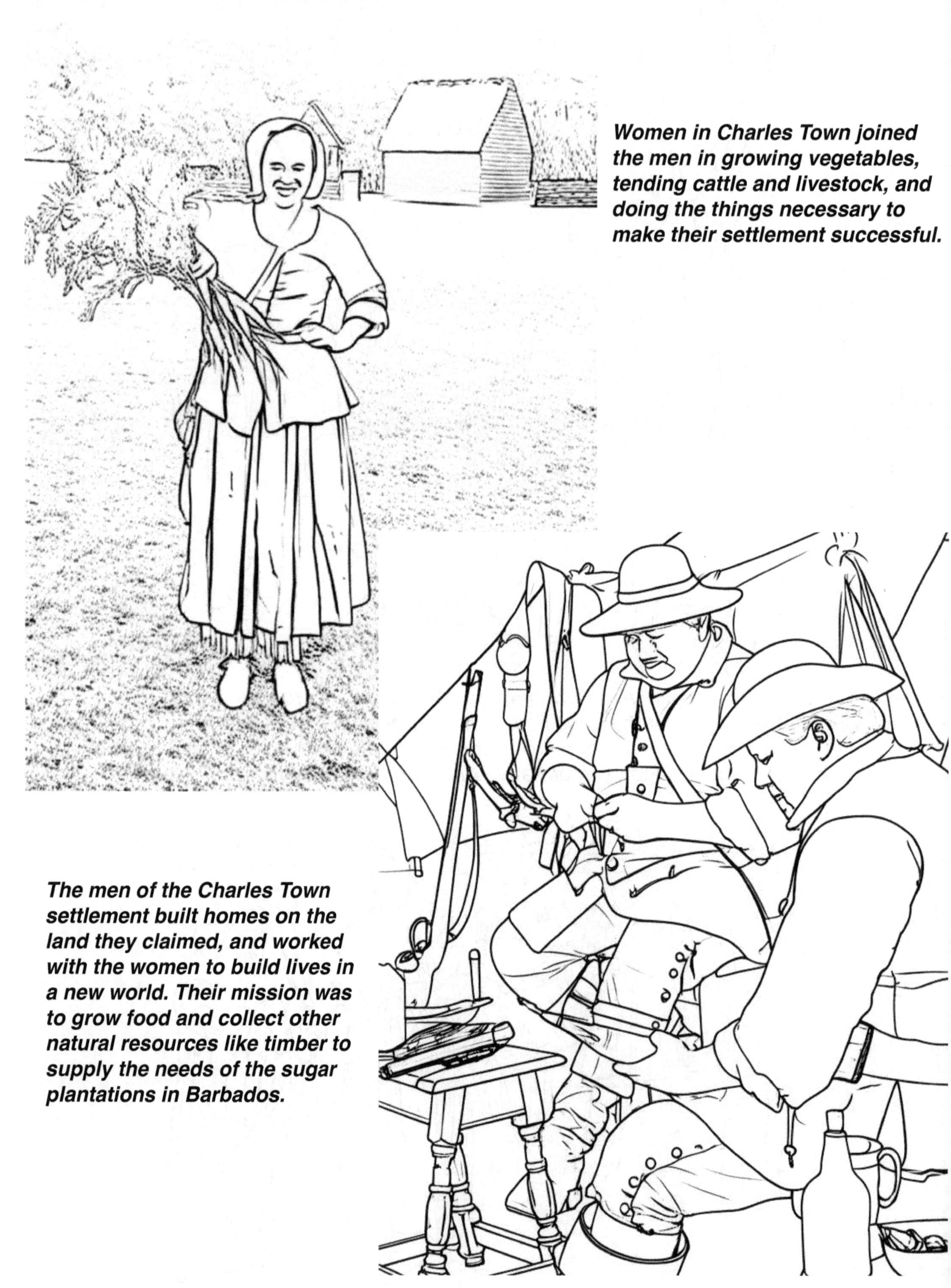

Women in Charles Town joined the men in growing vegetables, tending cattle and livestock, and doing the things necessary to make their settlement successful.

The men of the Charles Town settlement built homes on the land they claimed, and worked with the women to build lives in a new world. Their mission was to grow food and collect other natural resources like timber to supply the needs of the sugar plantations in Barbados.

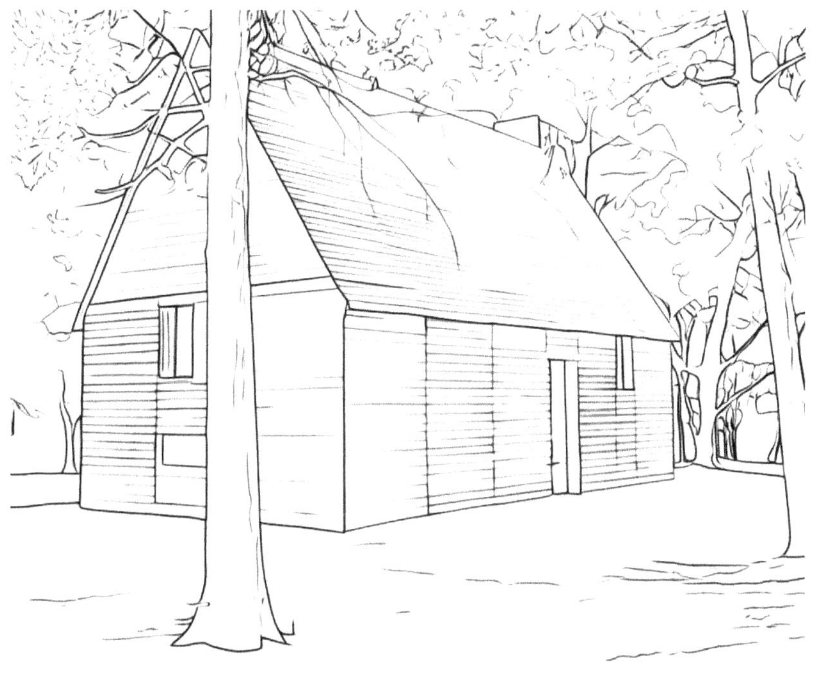

Charles Town settlers built simple timber and log houses like the one pictured here.

The houses usually had one large room with a big fireplace to provide heat and to cook with.

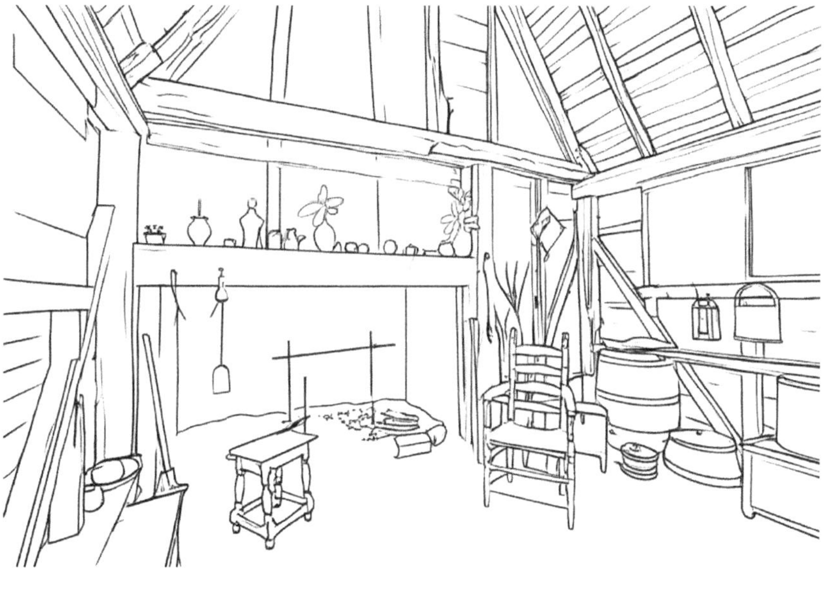

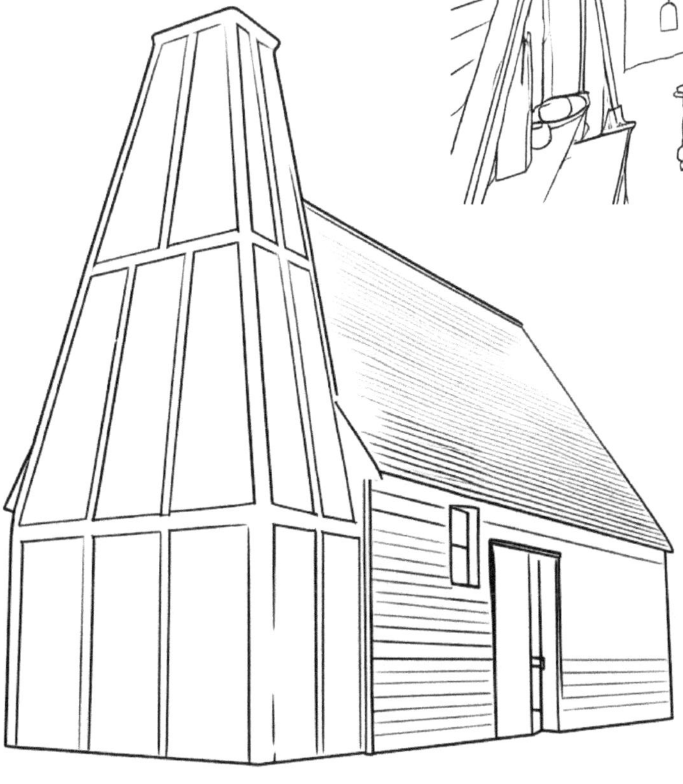

The fireplaces channeled the smoke up large chimneys like this one.

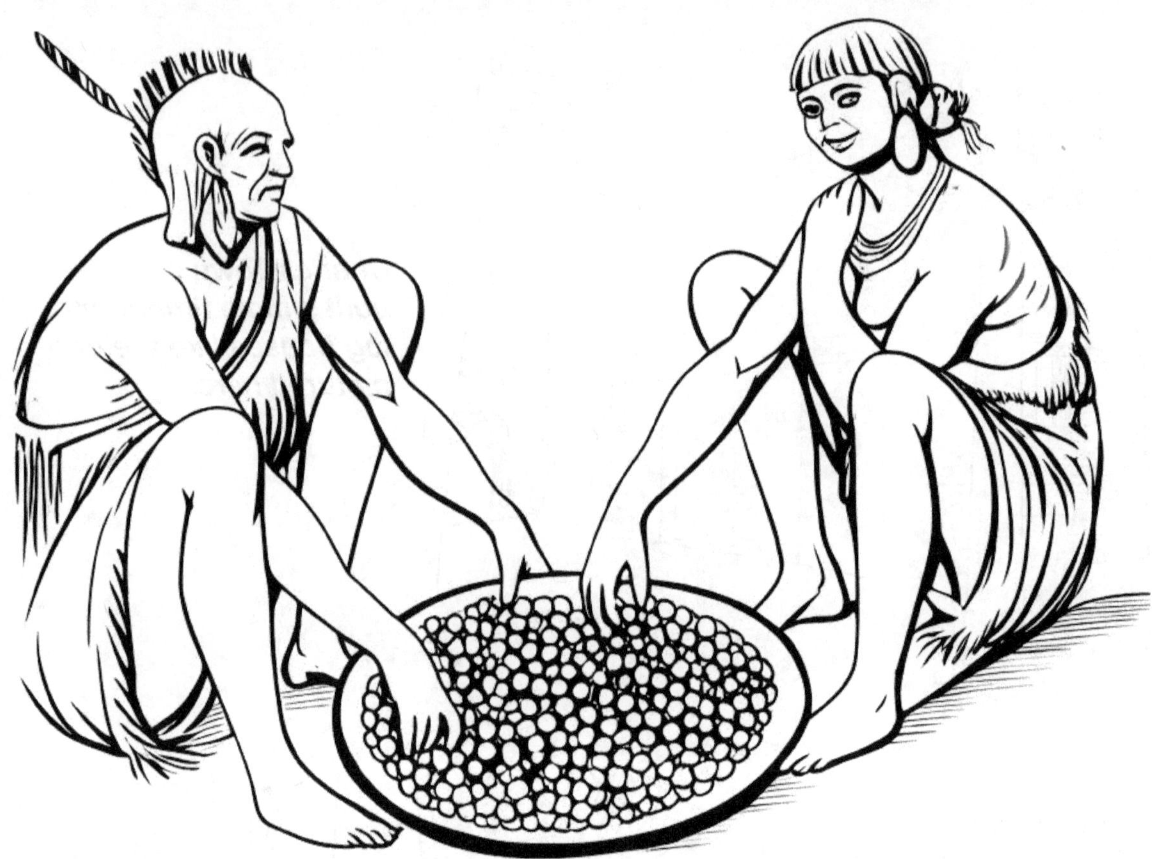

The Charles Town settlers found their native neighbors on the other side of Town Creek to be friendly and industrious. Relations with the native people were good until the colonists began kidnapping Indian children to "Christianize" them. In reality, the children were made slaves.

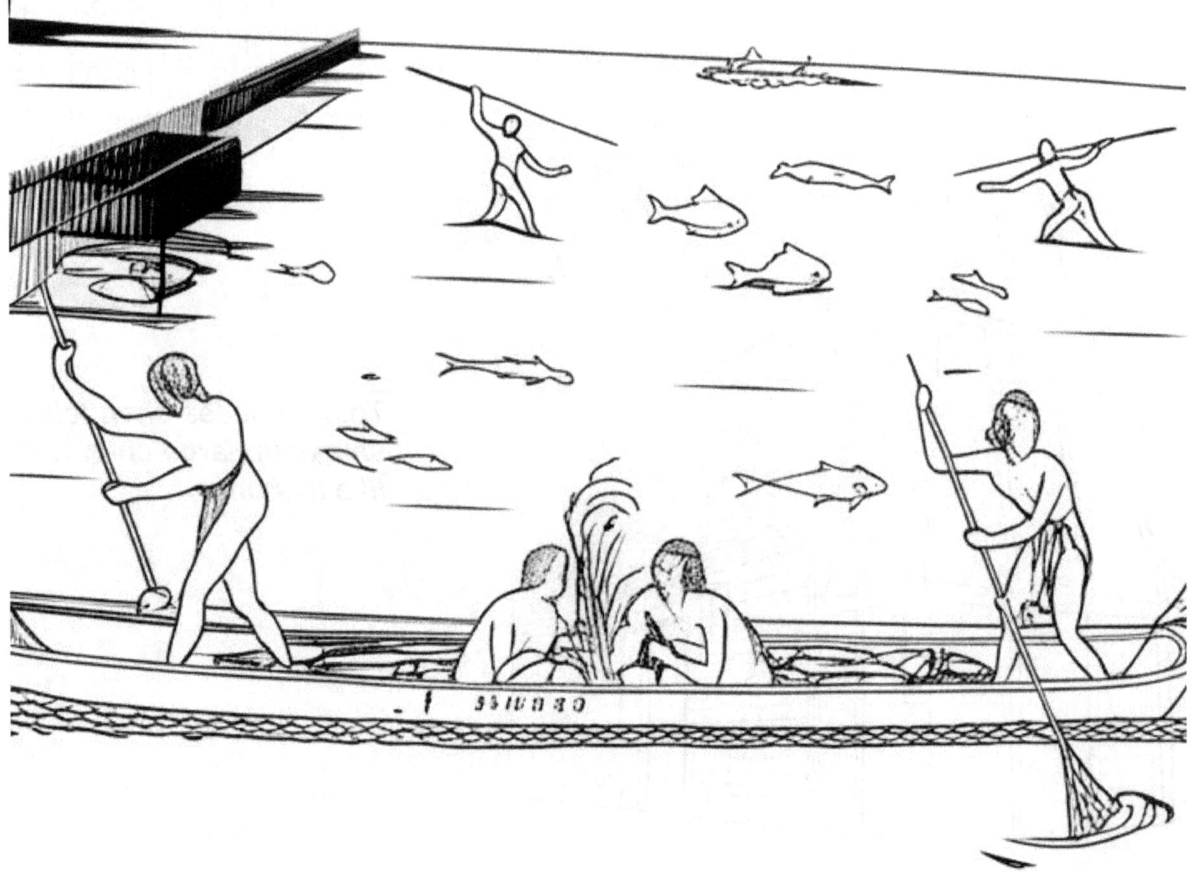

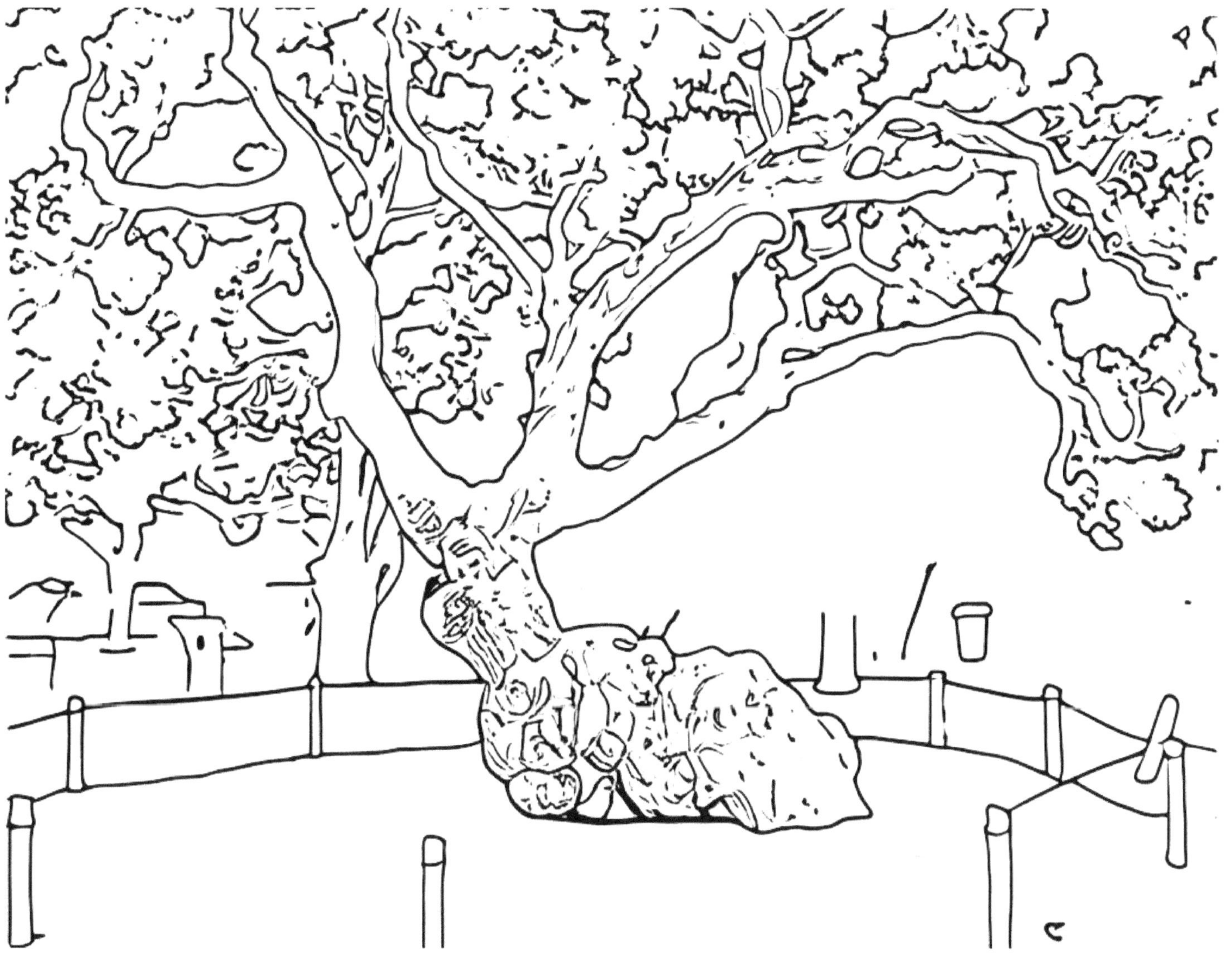

This tree in Southport, N.C. was intentionally bent and twisted in this manner by native peoples to serve as a trail guide pointing visiting people from the interior towards nearby beaches and oyster beds.

The Pirates...

With 300 miles of mostly empty coastline, North Carolina was a favorite hideout for pirates like Blackbeard and Stede Bonnet in the first decade of the 18th century. Bonnet was captured across from modern Southport in the Battle of the Sandbars, after a running fight with two British sloops of war in 1718. Colonel William Rhett took Bonnet and his crew to Charleston and hanged them on the order of Judge Nicholas Trott.

Stede Bonnet, the "Gentleman Pirate."

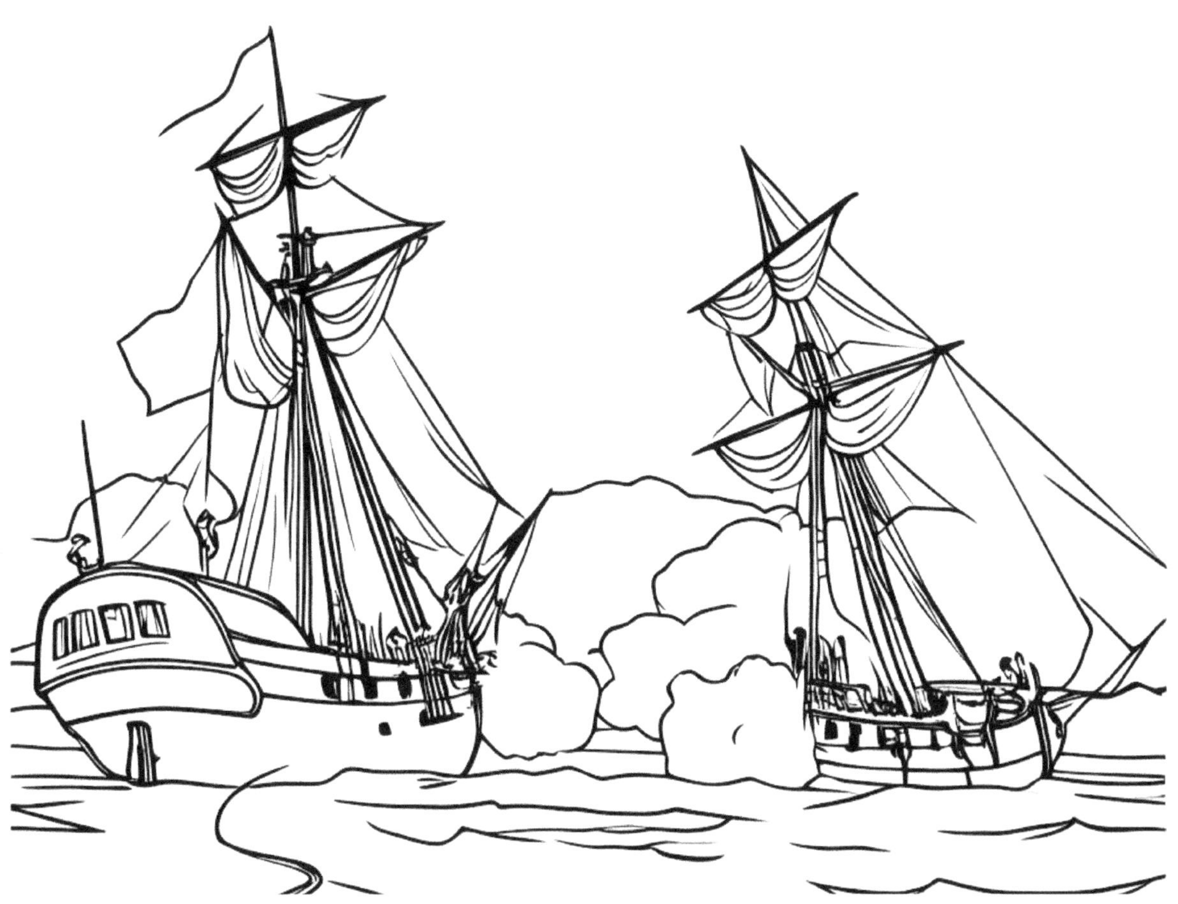

Bonnet's ship, the* Revenge*, and Col. Rhett's two sloops, ran aground on a falling tide across from modern Southport. They hammered each other until the tide came in again and Rhett gained the upper hand (above). There were casualties aboard all three vessels before the fight ended (below).

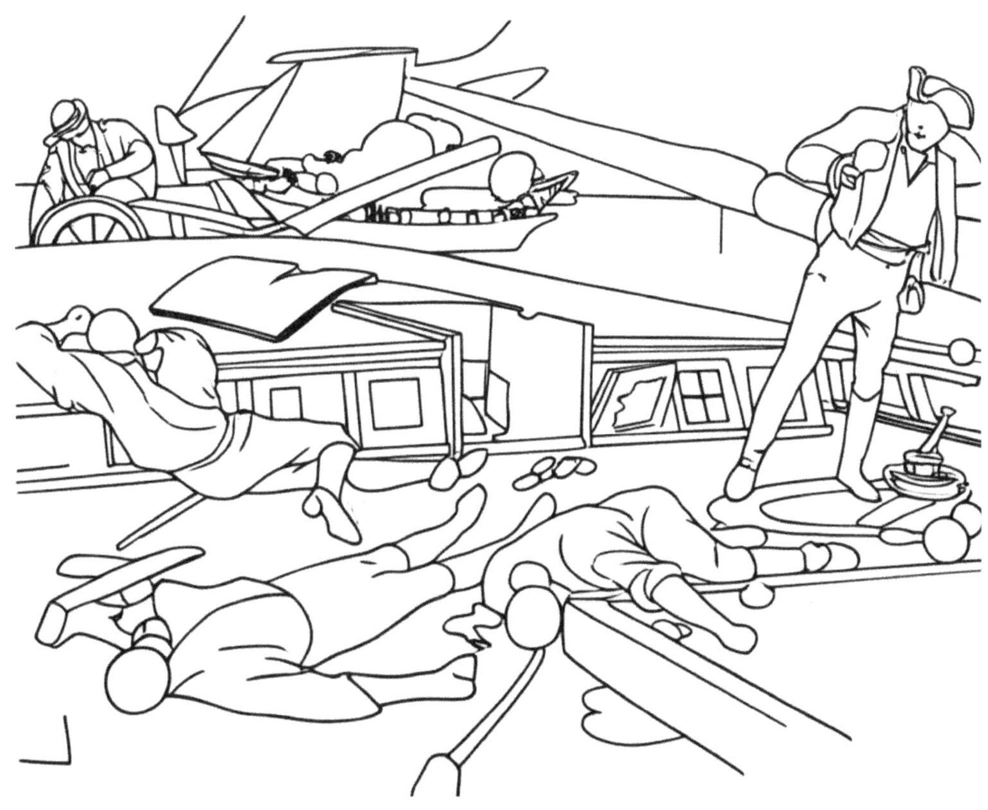

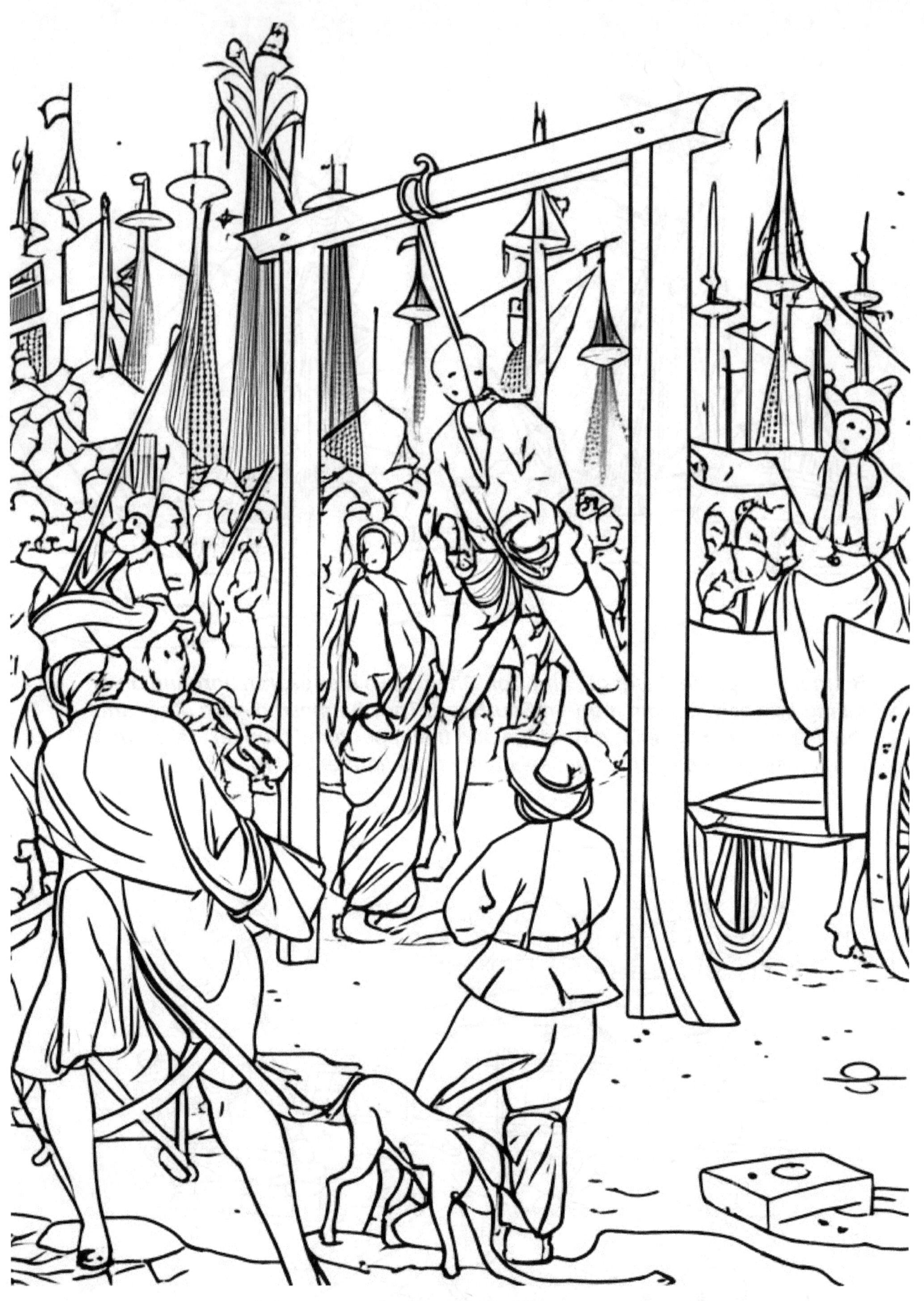

Though he escaped captivity once, Bonnet was soon recaptured. He was hanged at White Point in Charleston, then buried below the high tide mark on Sullivan's Island.

SOUTHPORT, BALD HEAD, AND OAK ISLAND

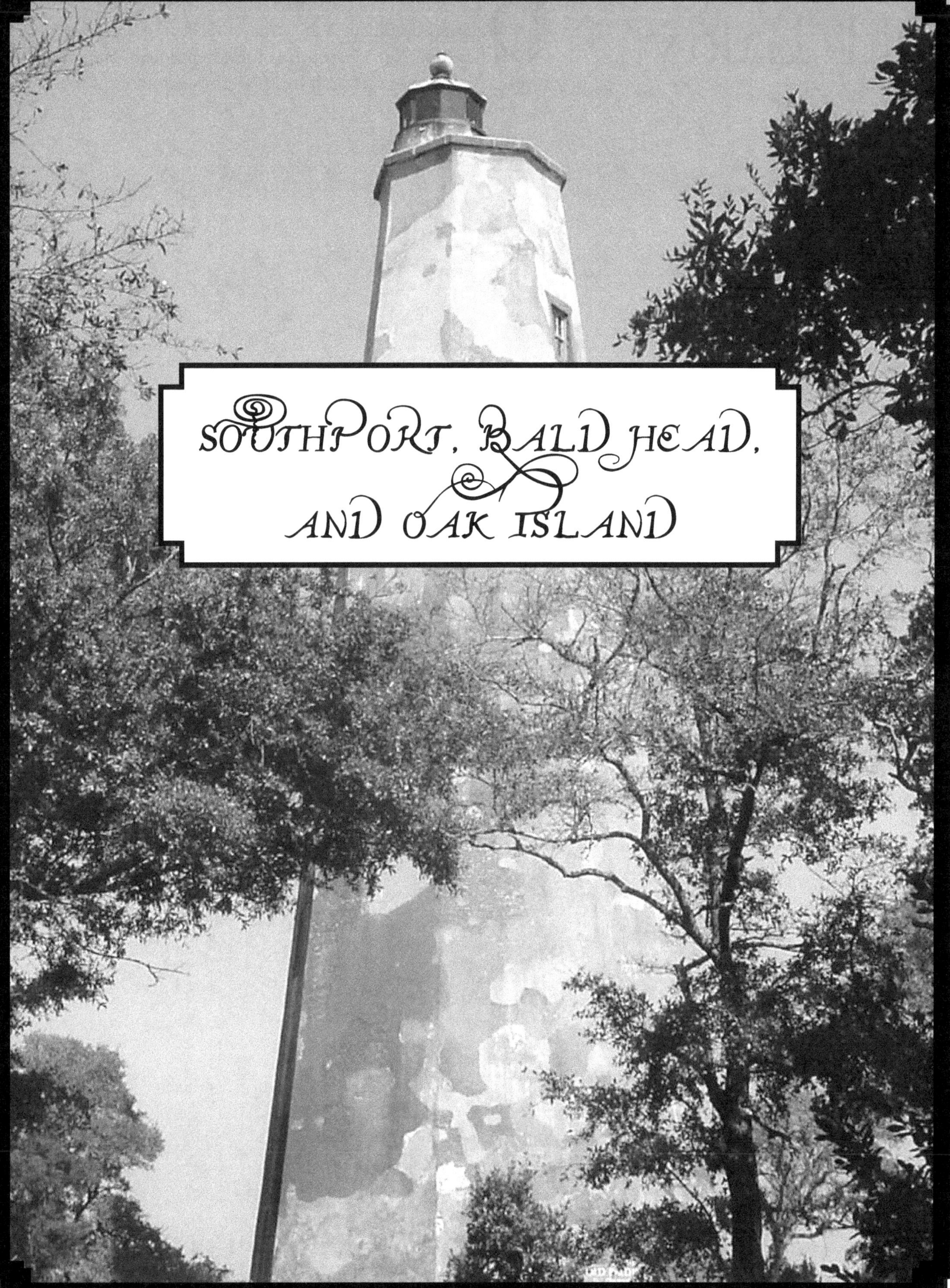

Old Baldy...

On a treacherous coast like Cape Fear, lighthouses served to guide ships around the dangerous Frying Pan Shoals. Old Baldy is North Carolina's oldest lighthouse. The original wooden lighthouse was built in 1794. The current light replaced it in 1816.

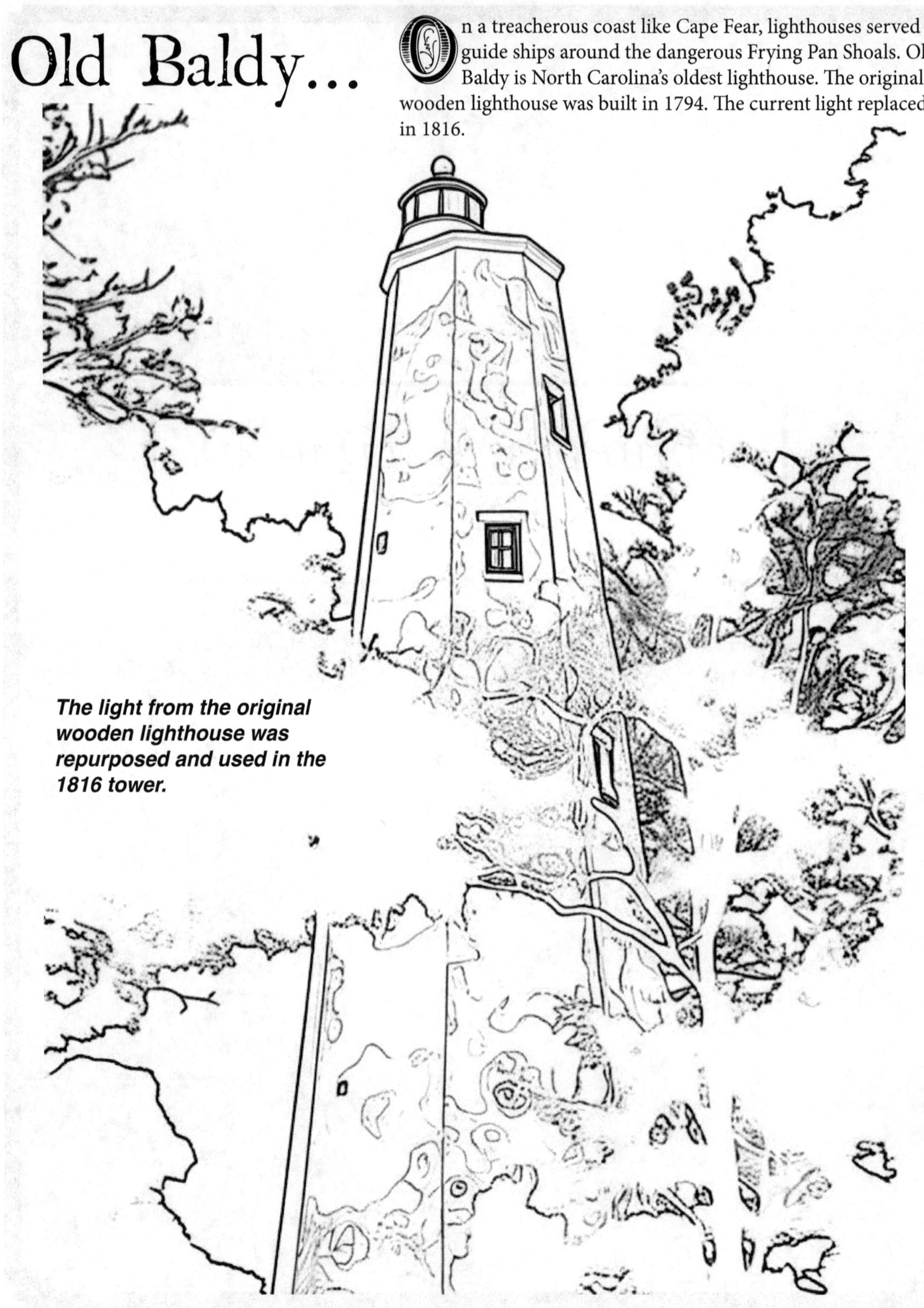

The light from the original wooden lighthouse was repurposed and used in the 1816 tower.

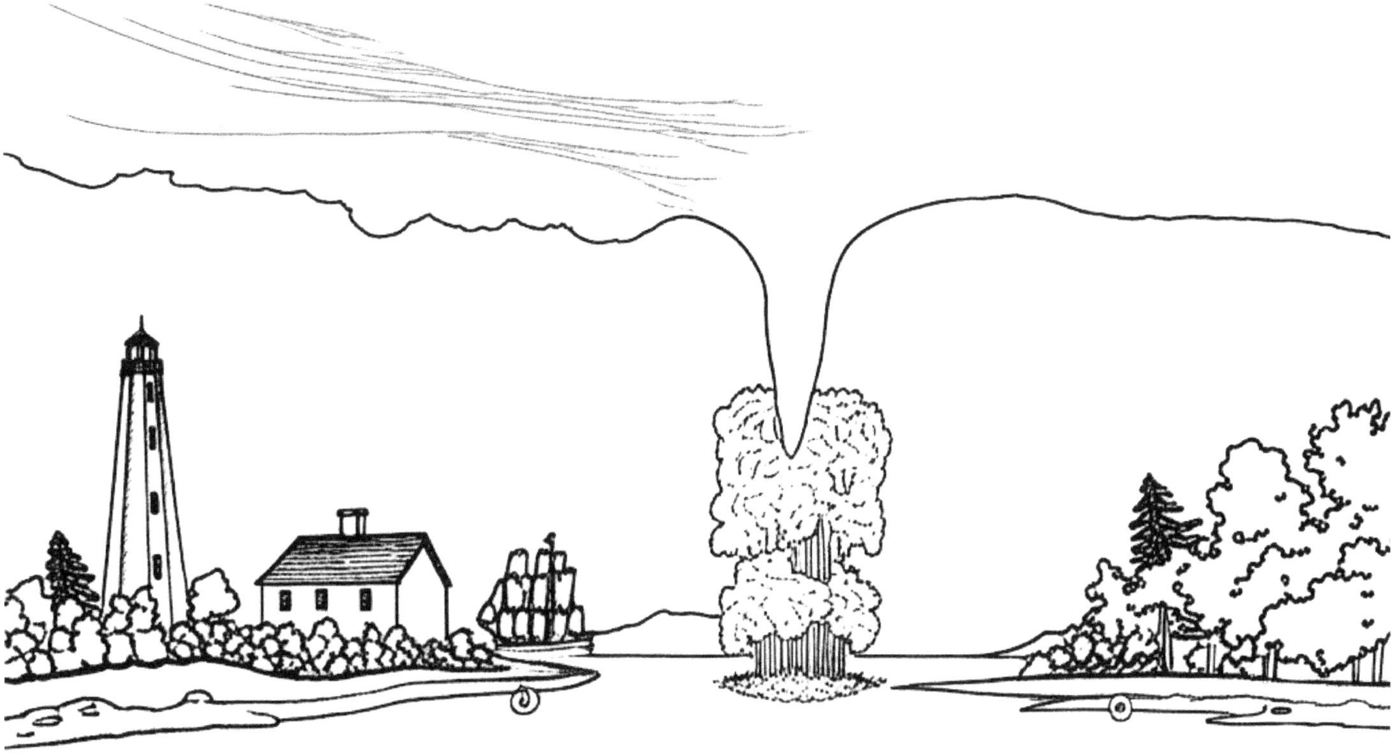

A waterspout churns in Old Inlet between Old Baldy and Oak Island (above). The drawing is taken from the oldest know illustration of the lighthouse.

Bald Head Island was owned by Langrave Thomas Smith (right), originally of Goose Creek, S.C. The island was granted to Smith by the Lords Proprietors of Carolina, and was known as Smith Island until the name was officially changed to Bald Head Island in the 20th Century.

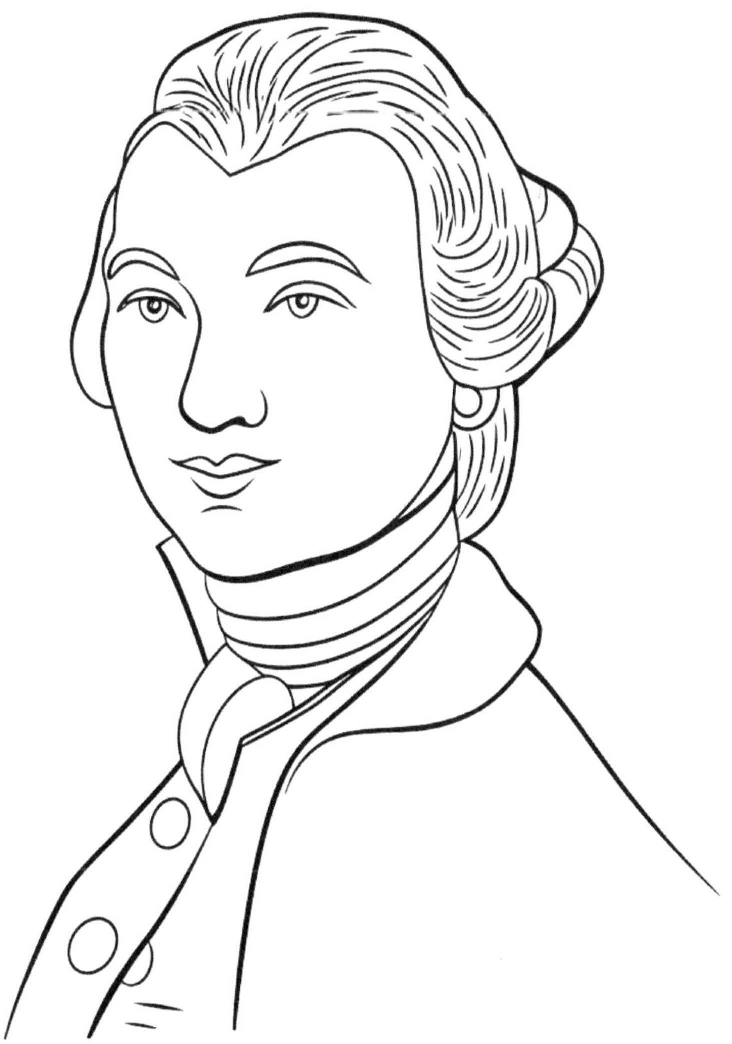

Landgrave Thomas Smith

Lighthouses & Lifesaving Stations...

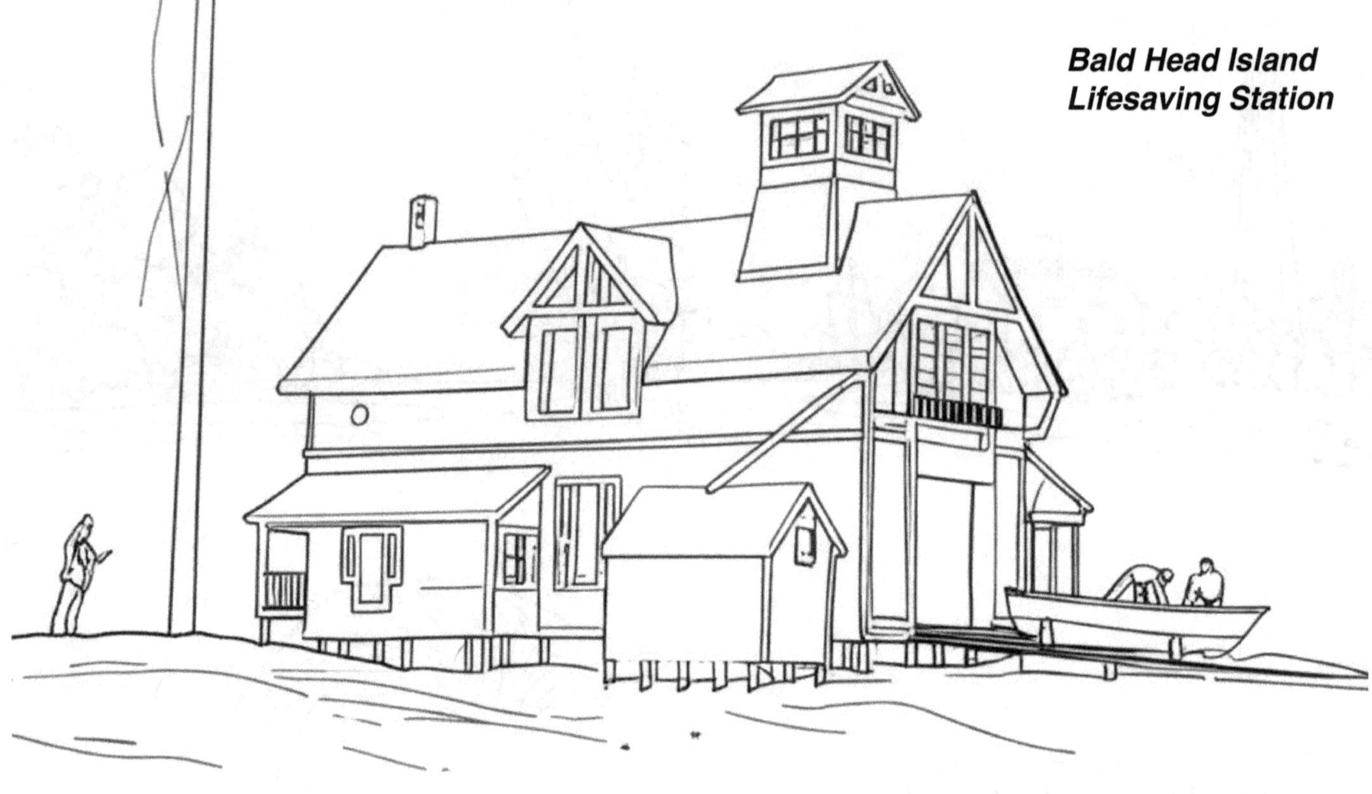

Bald Head Island Lifesaving Station

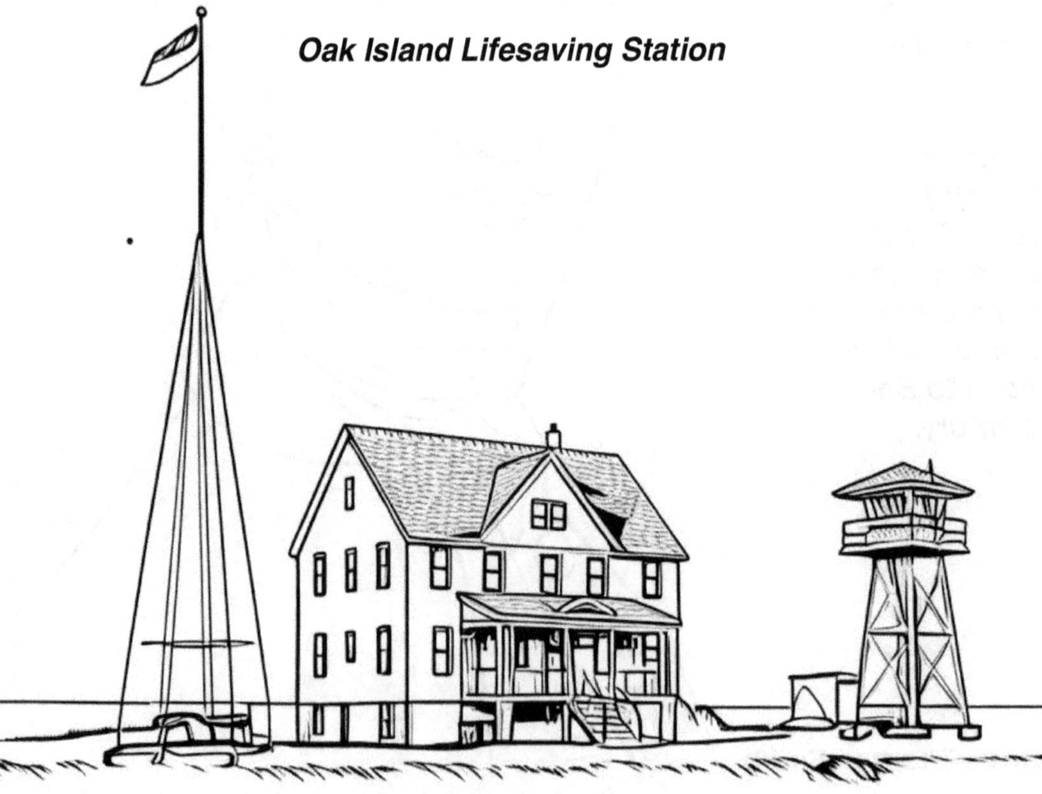

Oak Island Lifesaving Station

Lifesaving stations along the North Carolina coast stretched from the Outer Banks to Cape Fear. The two stations on Oak Island and Bald Head were ready at a moments notice to race into the surf to save ships and mariners that ran afoul of Frying Pan Shoals, and later, German U-boats.

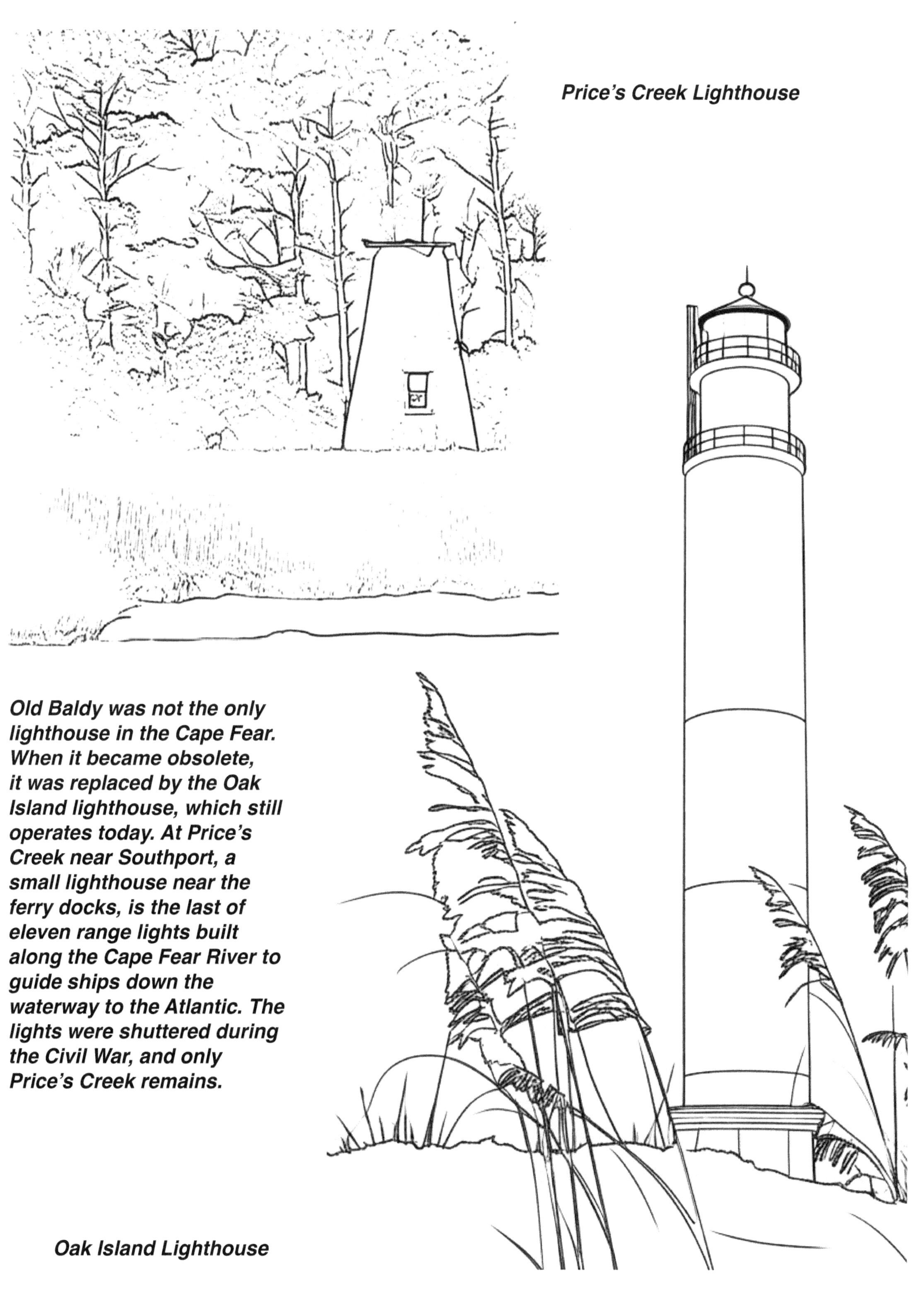

Price's Creek Lighthouse

Old Baldy was not the only lighthouse in the Cape Fear. When it became obsolete, it was replaced by the Oak Island lighthouse, which still operates today. At Price's Creek near Southport, a small lighthouse near the ferry docks, is the last of eleven range lights built along the Cape Fear River to guide ships down the waterway to the Atlantic. The lights were shuttered during the Civil War, and only Price's Creek remains.

Oak Island Lighthouse

Southport...

The Old Brunswick Jail in Southport (below), used until the 1970s.

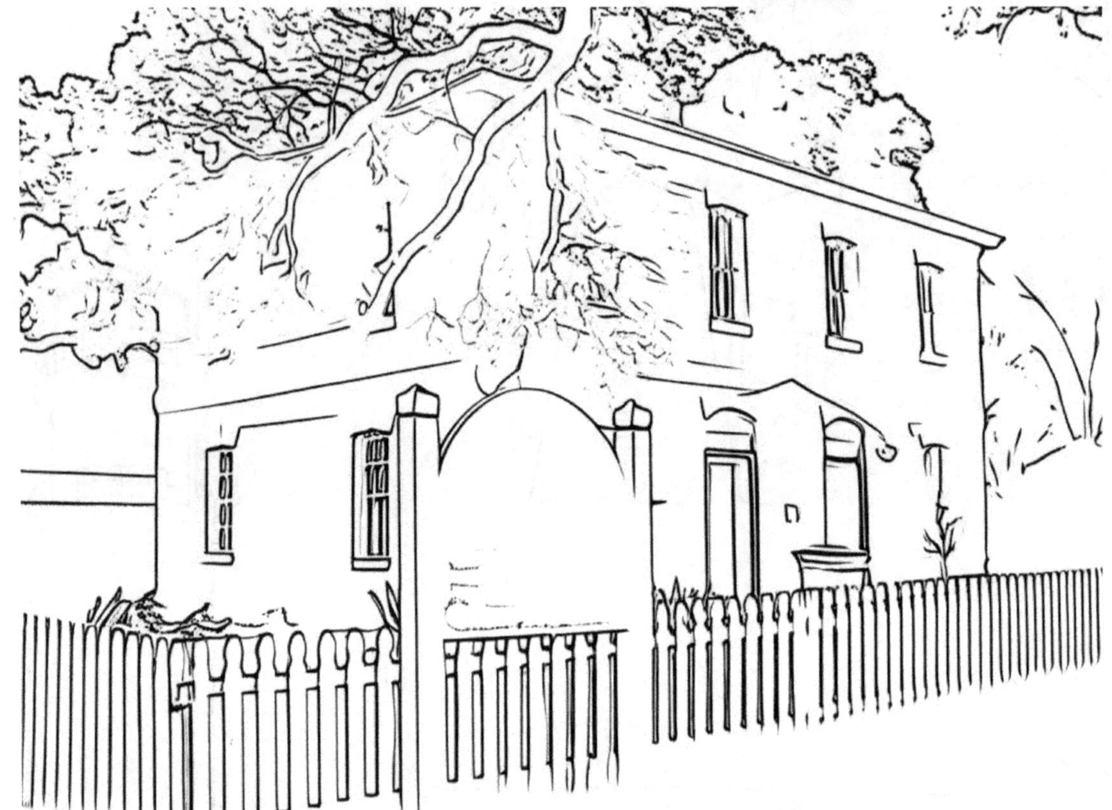

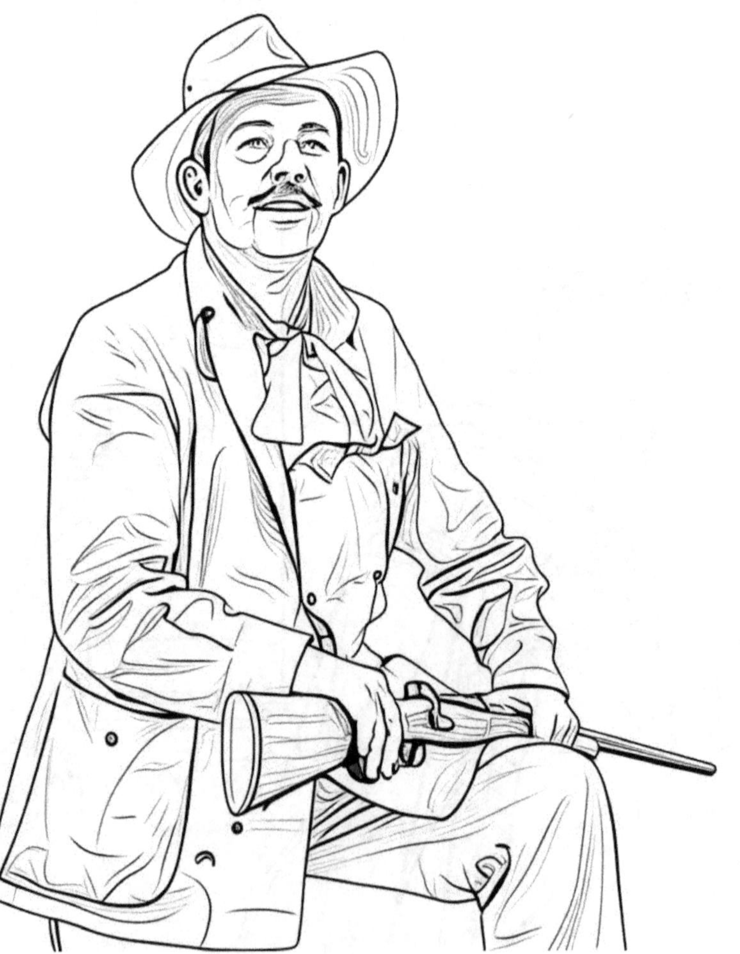

Though it was incorporated as Smithville in 1792, people had been living in what is now Southport for much longer. River pilots stationed themselves close to Fort Johnston to go aboard visiting ships and guide them up the Cape Fear to the ports at Brunswick and Wilmington. The town was built on land owned by Gov. Benjamin Smith, a descendant of Landgrave Thomas Smith, who owned not just Bald Head Island, but also plantations all along the west bank of the river. The most prominent of those is now the site of the town of Navassa. It was also home to author Robert Ruark, whose work and style compares favorably to that of Ernest Hemingway.

Robert Ruark

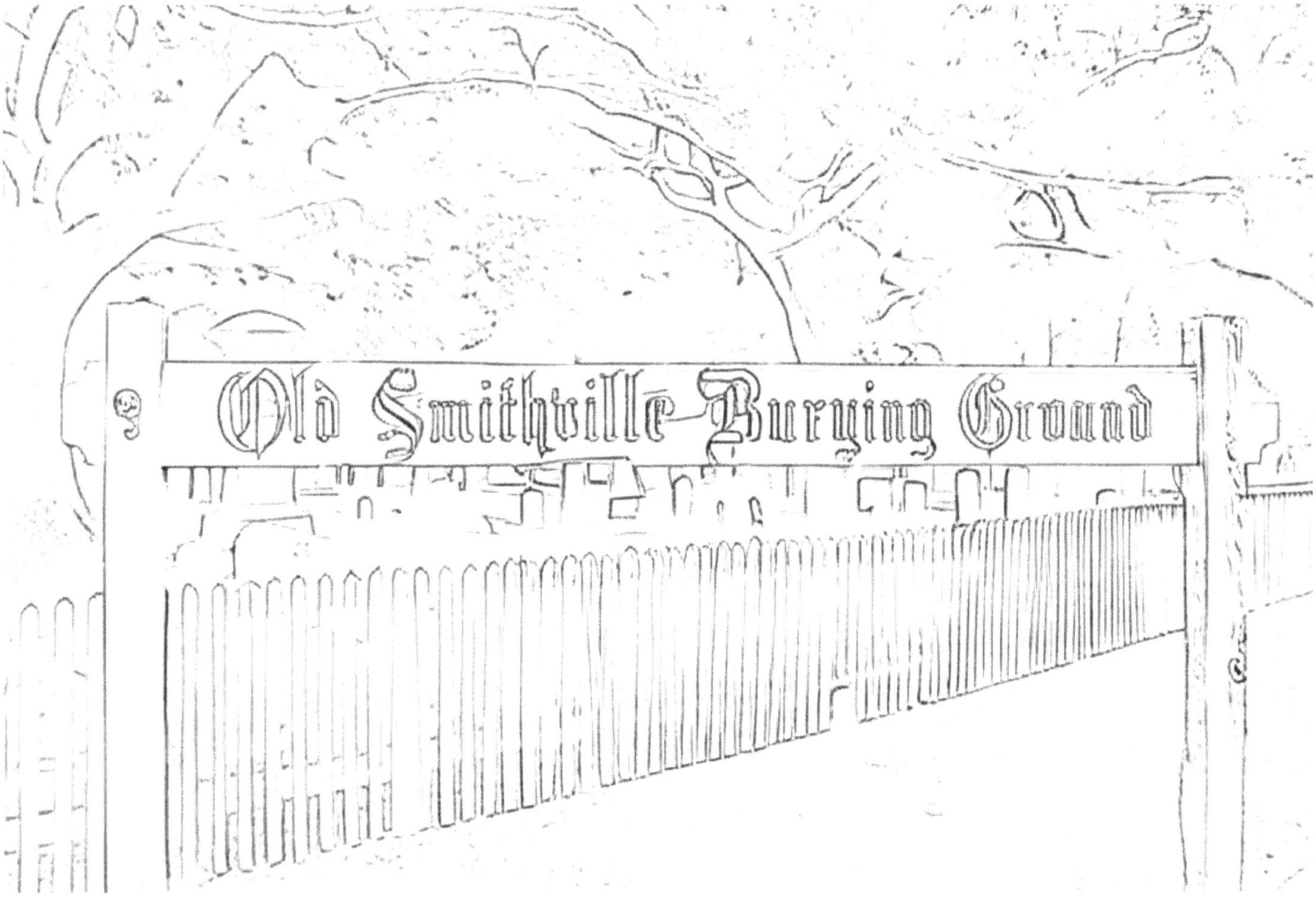

The Old Smithville Burying Ground in Southport is one of the most historic cemeteries in the area, the final resting place of many of the Cape Fear's most notable people. The Whittler's Bench (below), was a longtime landmark on the Southport riverfront until a hurricane destroyed it in the 2000s.

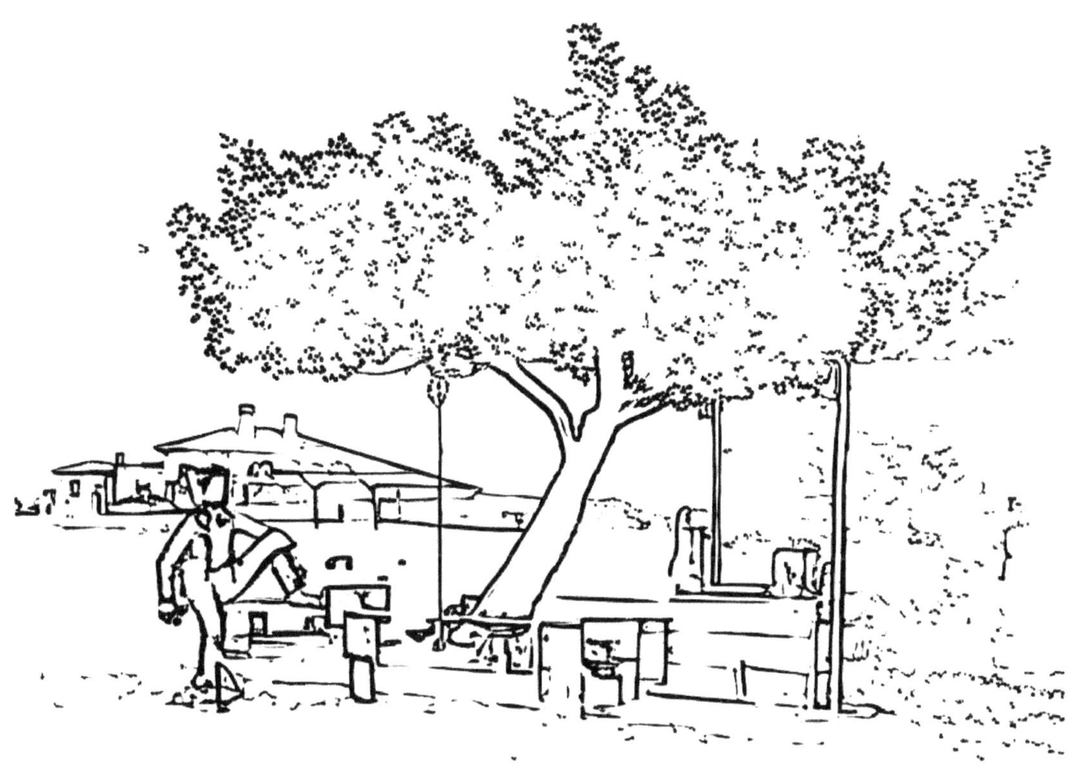

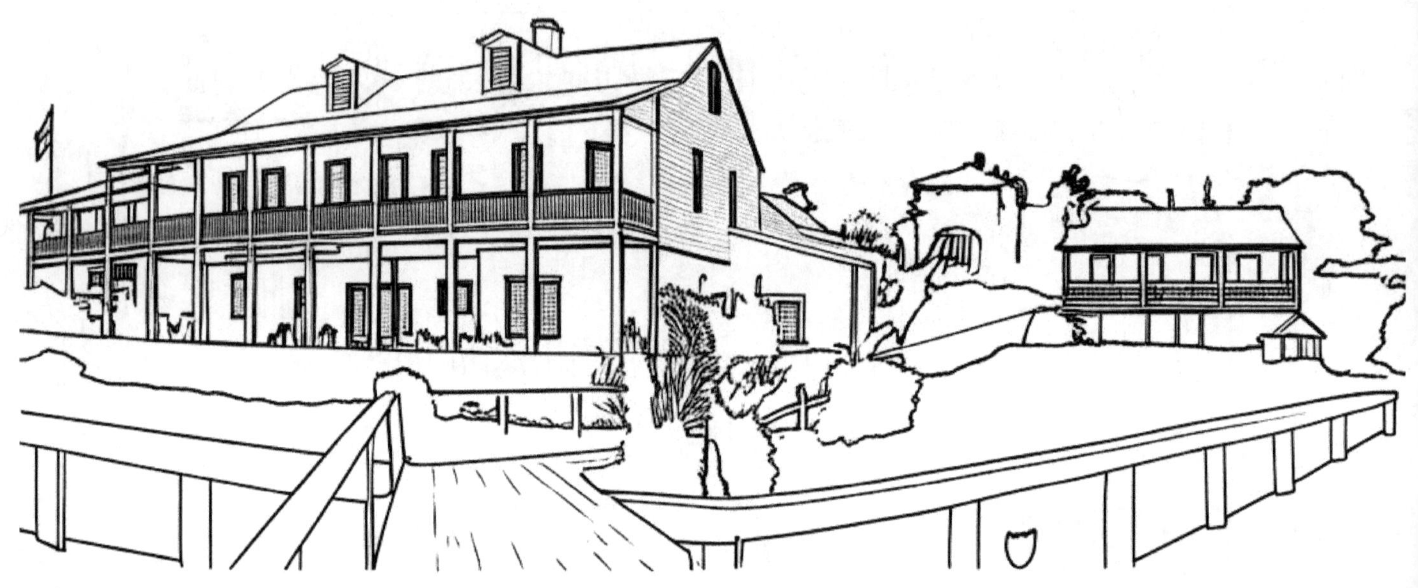

Kate Stuart's boarding house on the Cape Fear River at Southport provided meals and beds to travelers for decades. One of the most colorful characters of the lower Cape Fear, Stuart was a leading citizen of the town all of her life.

Fort Caswell...

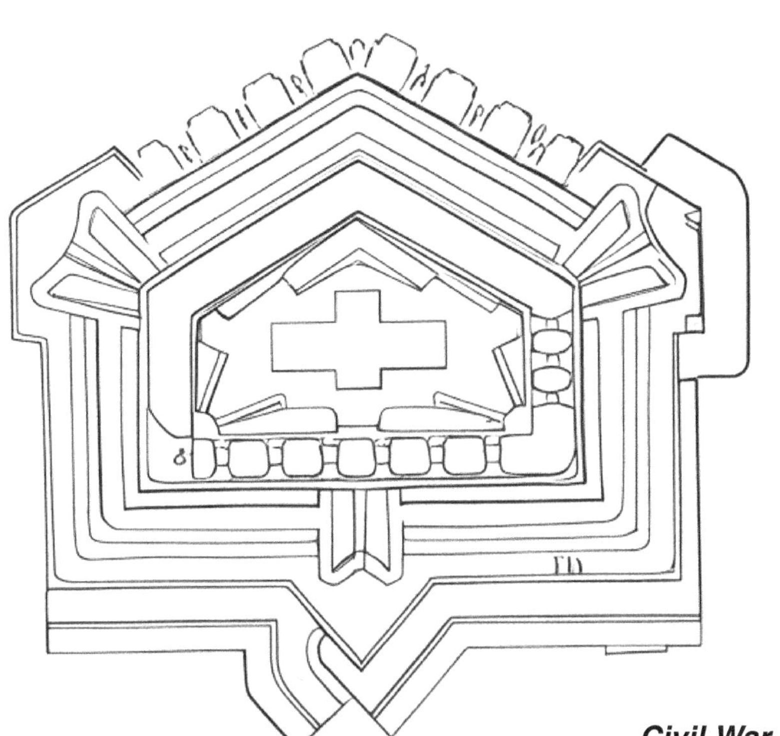

Fort Caswell on Oak Island began its life as one of a series of masonry forts Congress ordered built along the American coast in the wake of the War of 1812. By the time of the Civil War, it figured prominently in the Cape Fear defenses the Confederacy erected to guard the important port at Wilmington. The fort served through World War II before being retired as an active duty military installation, and was eventually sold to the Southern Baptist Association. The church uses it as a retreat now, where campers can enjoy a day at the beach.

Civil War-era plans of Fort Caswell (left).

Soldiers muster on the parade ground at Fort Caswell during World War I.

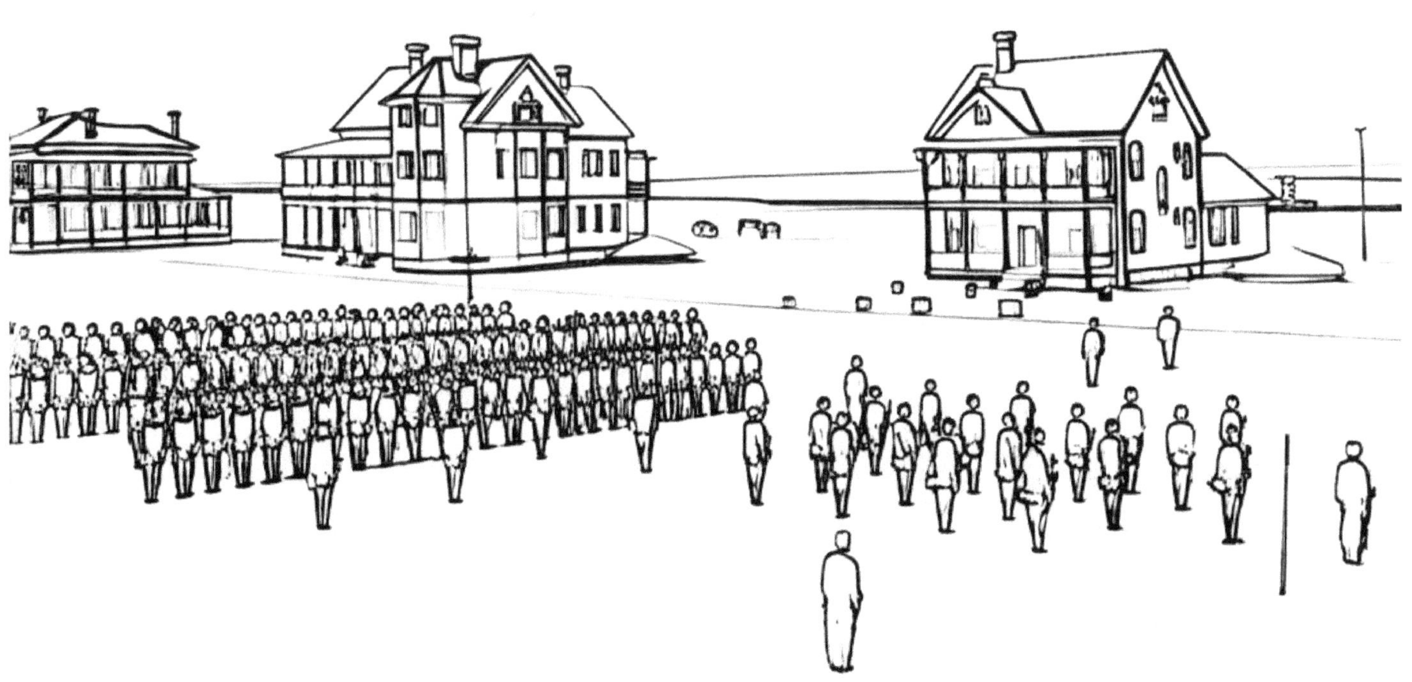

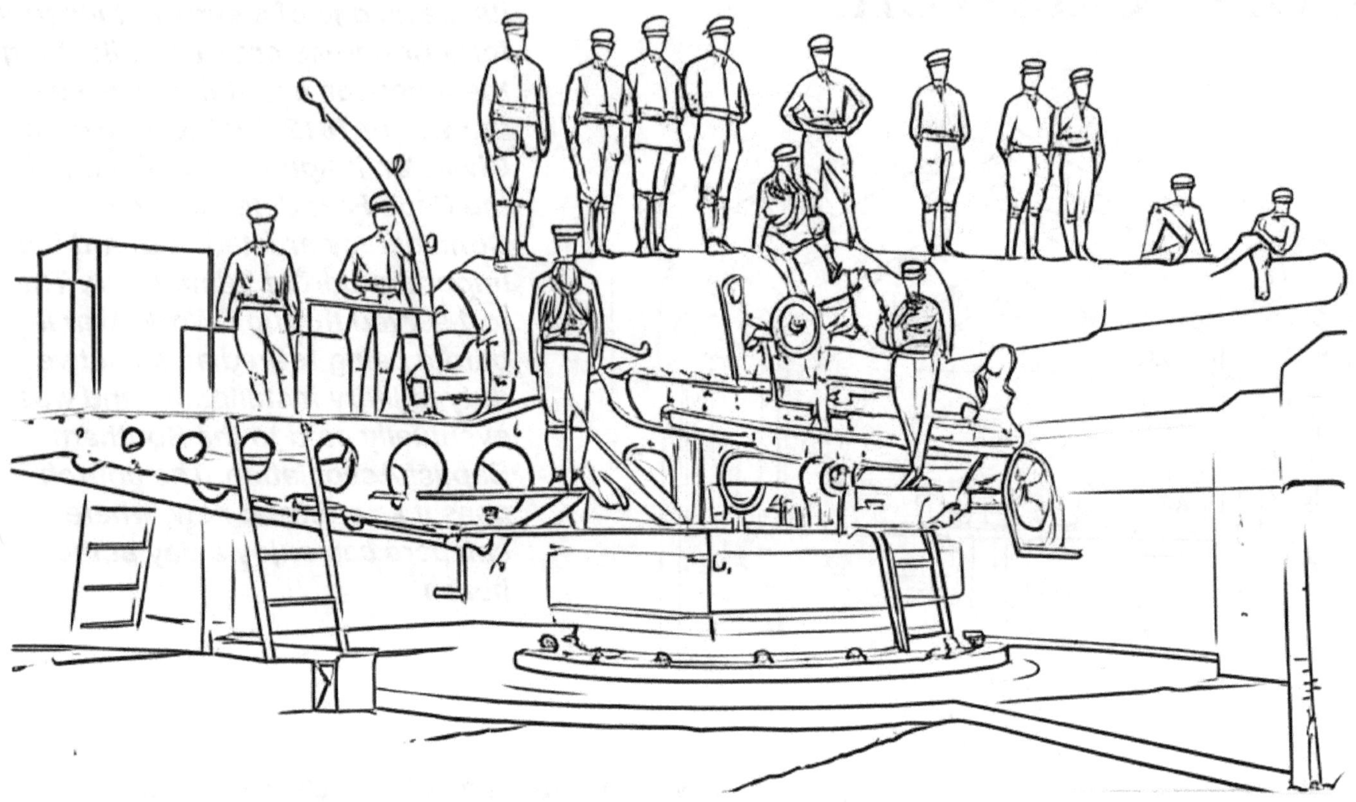

World War I soldiers of a coastal artillery company at Fort Caswell pose with a howitzer cannon (above) and a 3" mortar (below).

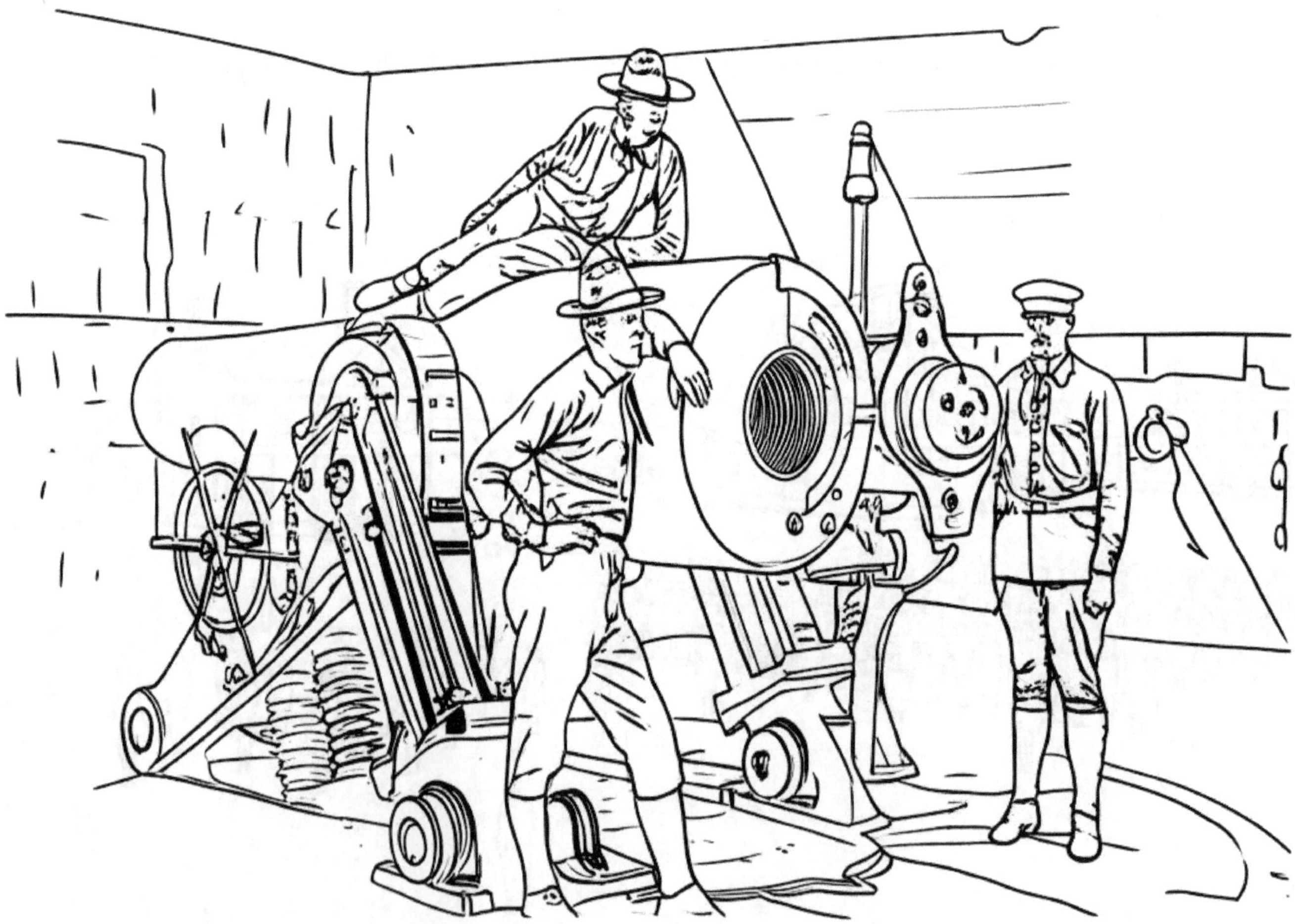

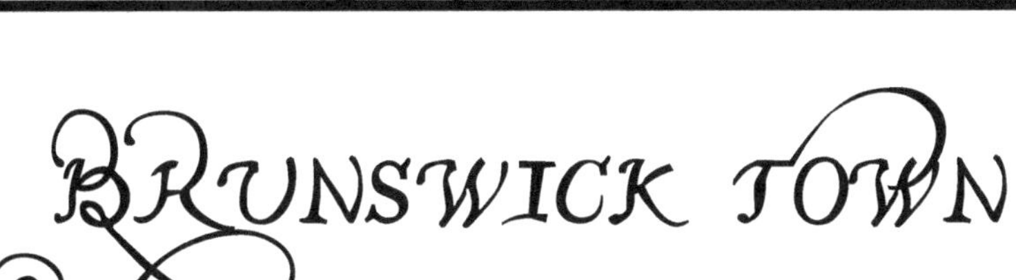
BRUNSWICK TOWN
CAPE FEAR RIVER
PLAN of the Town and
BRUNSWICK
in Brunswick County.
NORTH CAROLINA
REFERENCE.
A, Church. B, Court House
D, His Excellency Governor
and Plantation.
Survey'd & Drawn in April 1769 By

Cape Fear's First Port...

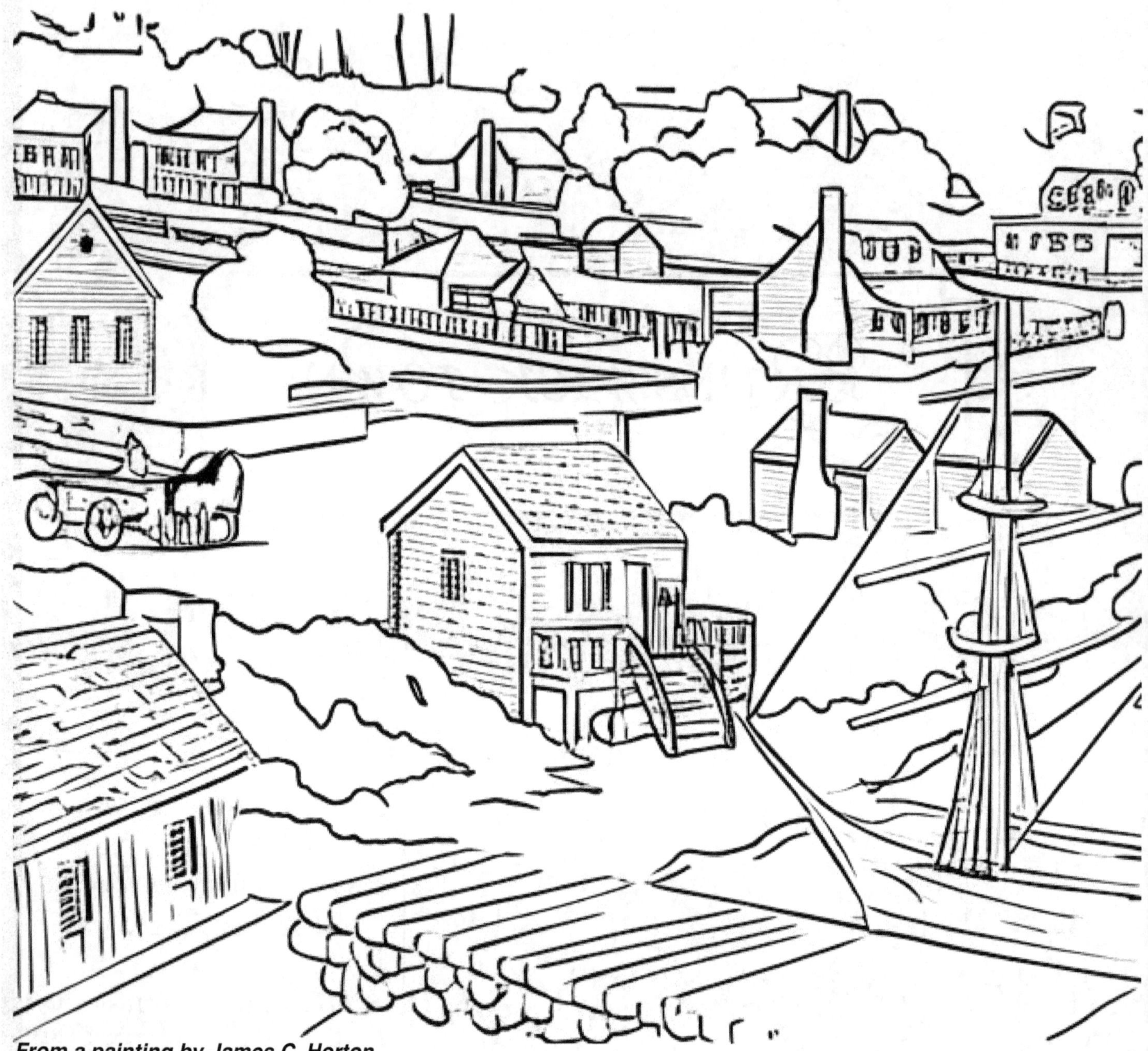

From a painting by James C. Horton

Brunswick Town was the first permanent settlement in the Cape Fear, established a half century after Charles Towne was abandoned. The town was founded by the Moore family of Goose Creek, S.C. The Moore family became wealthy power brokers in southeastern North Carolina and their town, located several miles above Old Inlet, became the official port of entry for vessels calling on the Cape Fear. Royal governors Arthur Dobbs and William Tryon both resided at Brunswick in their stately Russelborough home, just north of the town limits. The town was home to the only North Carolinian to serve on the Supreme Court of the United States, Alfred Moore. Brunswick was raided by Spanish privateers in 1748, and sacked by the British in 1776. St. Philips Anglican Church, one of the first two Cape Fear churches, is located at Brunswick. During the Civil War, Confederates consrtucted Fort Anderson over roughly half the footprint of the old colonial town. After the fort fell in February 1865, newly freed slaves used the grounds of the fort as a Freedmen's colony for a while. Today a state historic site, Brunswick Town/Fort Anderson is one of the most historic places in the state.

Artifacts found at Brunswick include a bottle seal bearing the name of William Dry (right). Dry served as Port Collector during the Stamp Act crisis of 1765, and was a prominent merchant of the lower Cape Fear. After Royal Governor William Tryon moved from Russelborough to his new "palace" in New Bern, Dry bought the house and lived there himself.

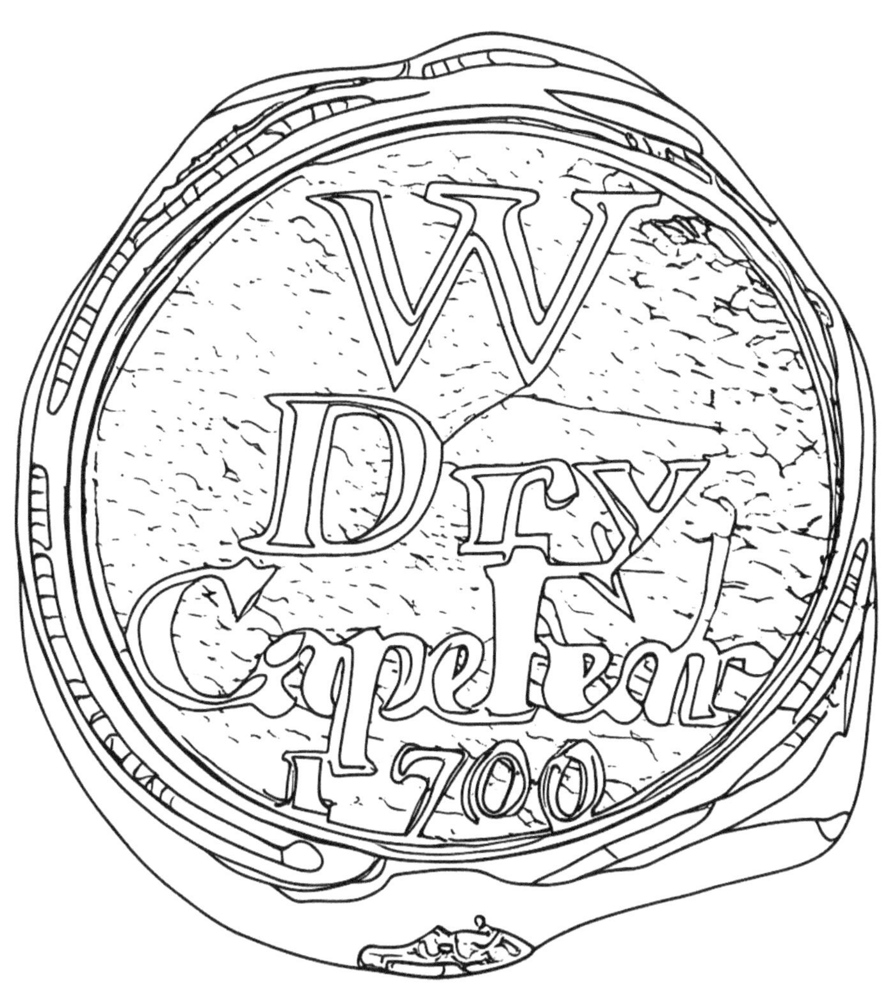

As a port, Brunswick had access to goods imported from all over the world. That included fine Delftware tiles like the one depicted below. The image comes from a tile found by archaeologists at Brunswick, and shows the scene seen here, painted in blue on a white glazed base.

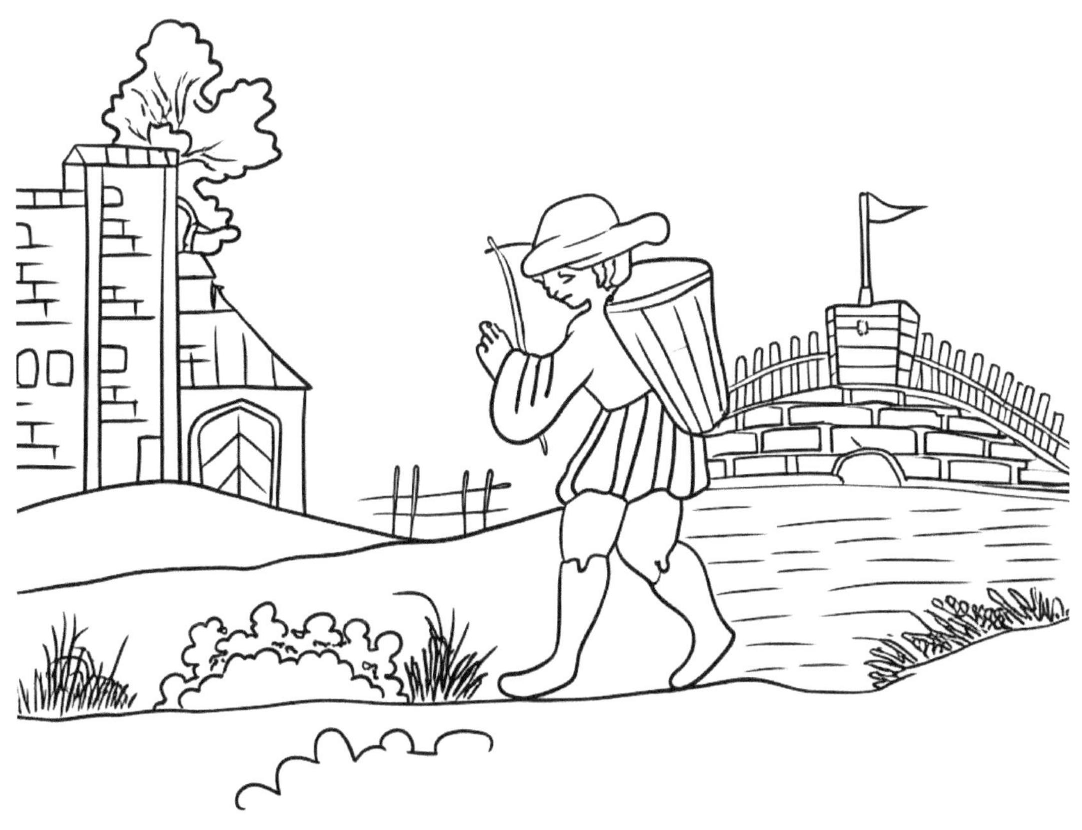

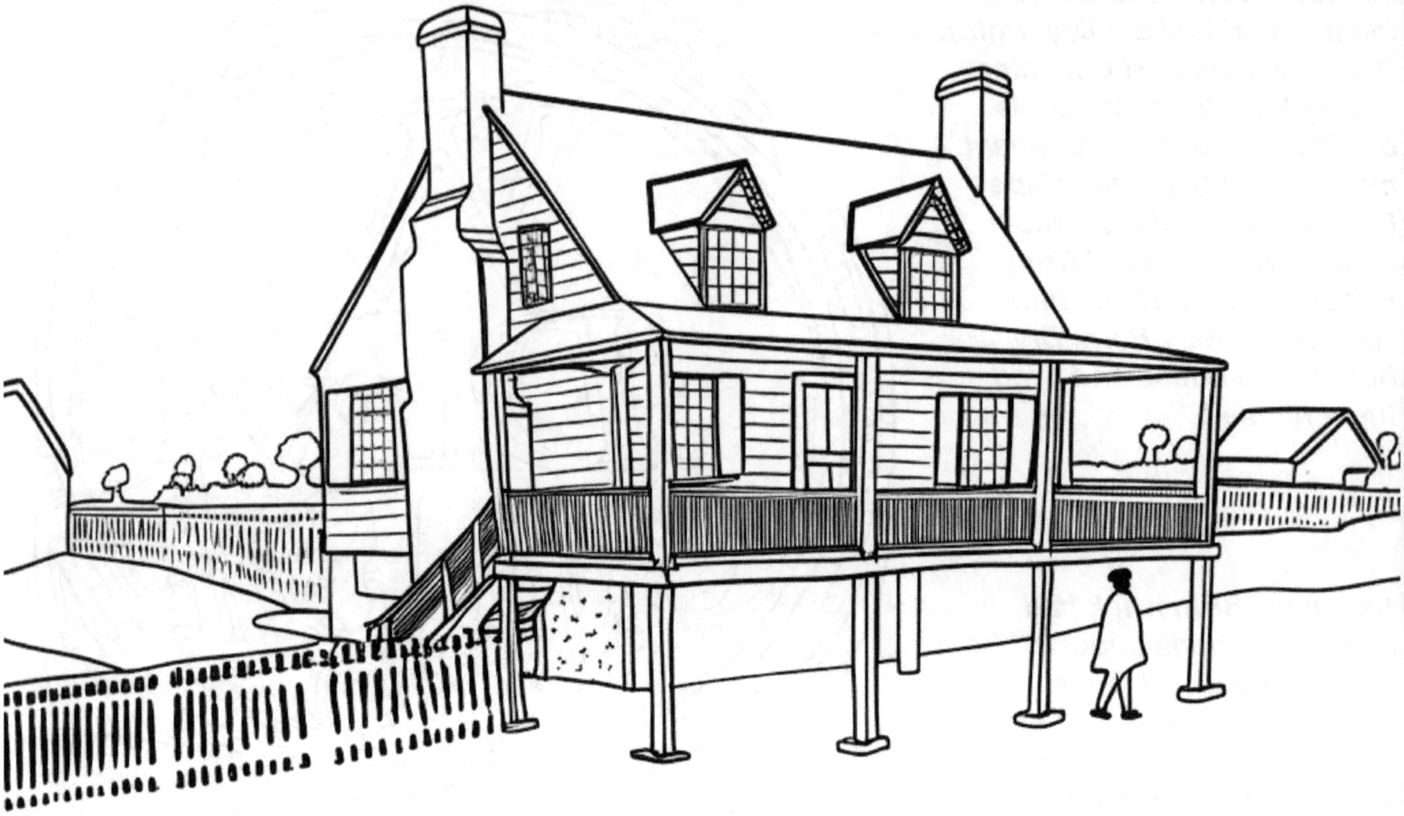

Houses in Brunswick Town took advantage of stones used as ballast by visiting ship to build solid foundations for their homes (below). The stones were held together with a concrete-like substance called tapia, made from lime, sand, and ground up oyster shells. The concoction proved to be surprisingly durable. The architectural drawing above is representative of the style of homes that were built at Brunswick.

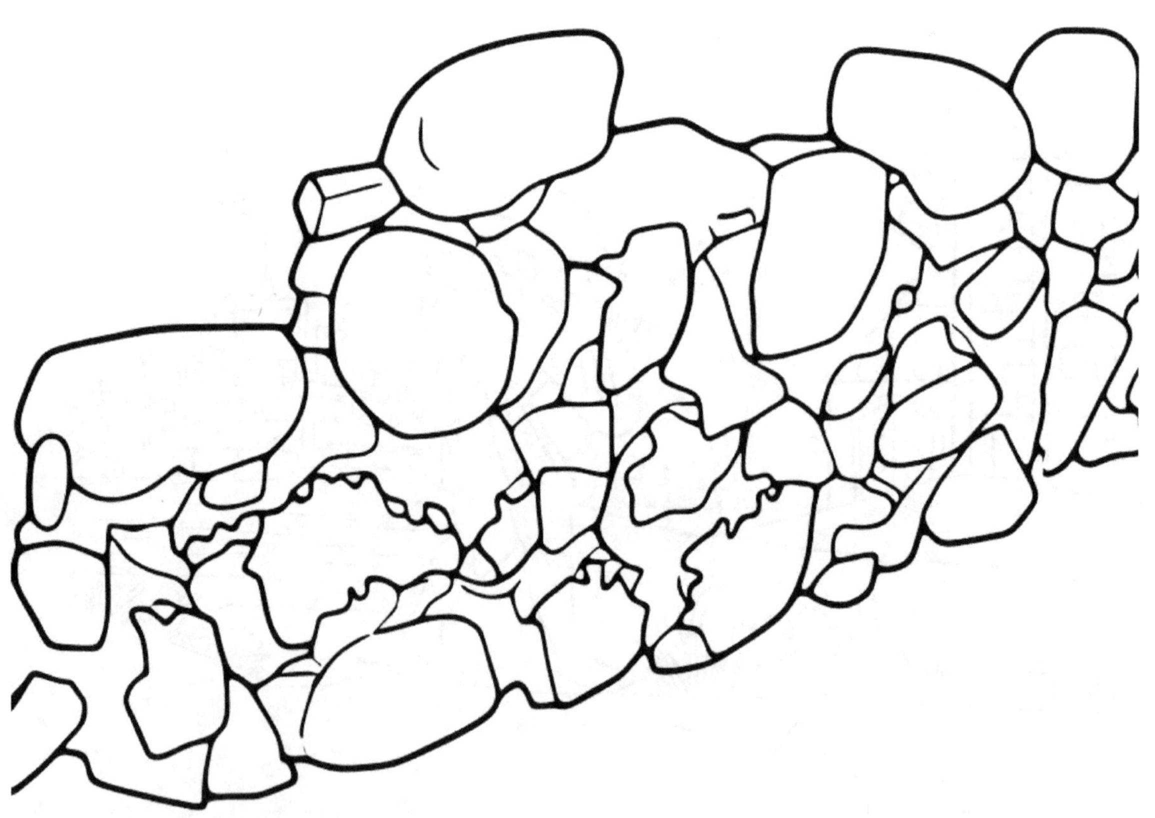

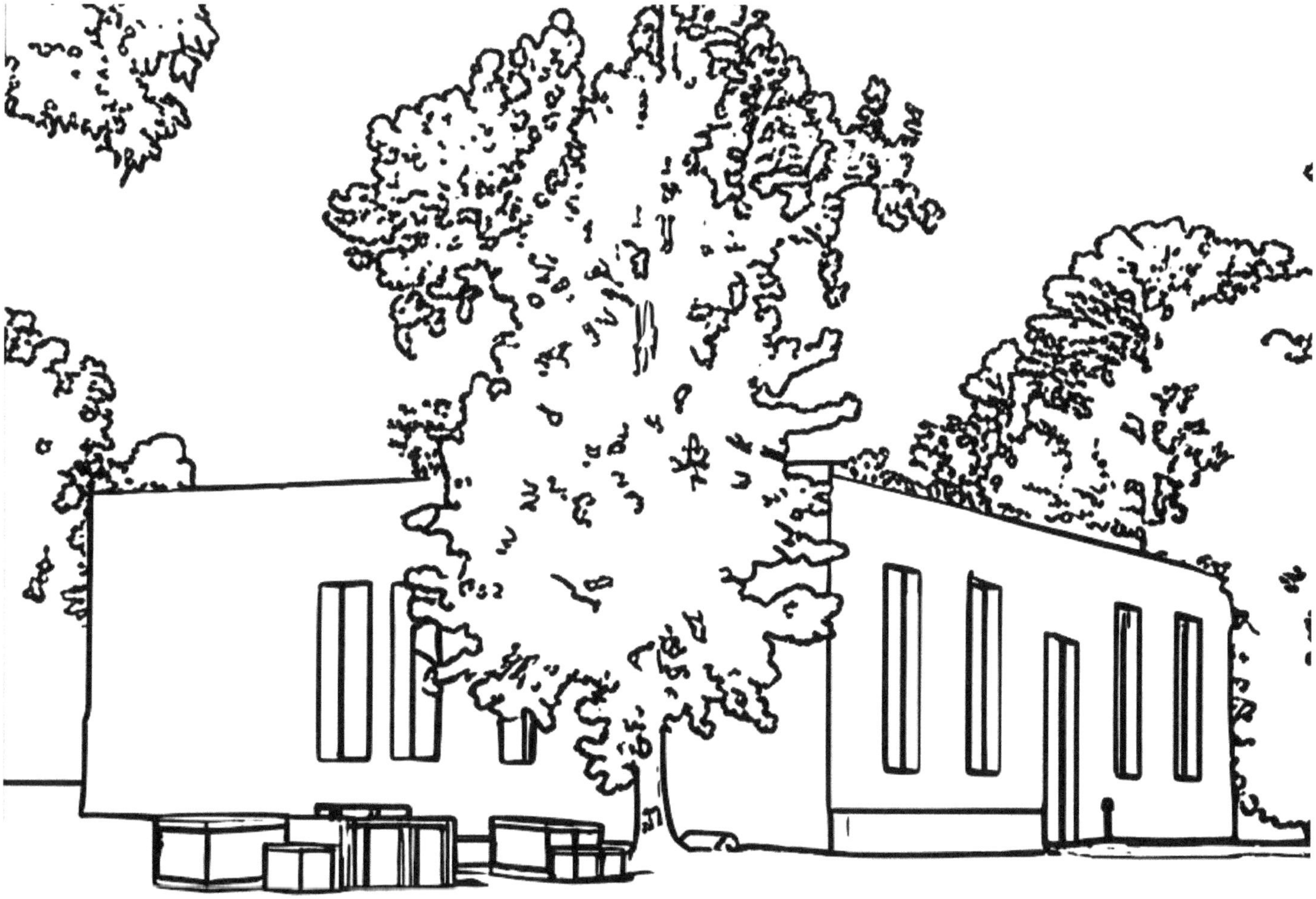

St. Philips Anglican Church as it was intended to look upon completion (below), and as it looks today at Brunswick Town . The church was one of two built after the Spanish Raid of 1748. When one of the Spanish ships exploded, the colony's general assembly ordered that proceeds from the ship's salvage go to building St. Philips and St. James Anglican Church in Wilmington.

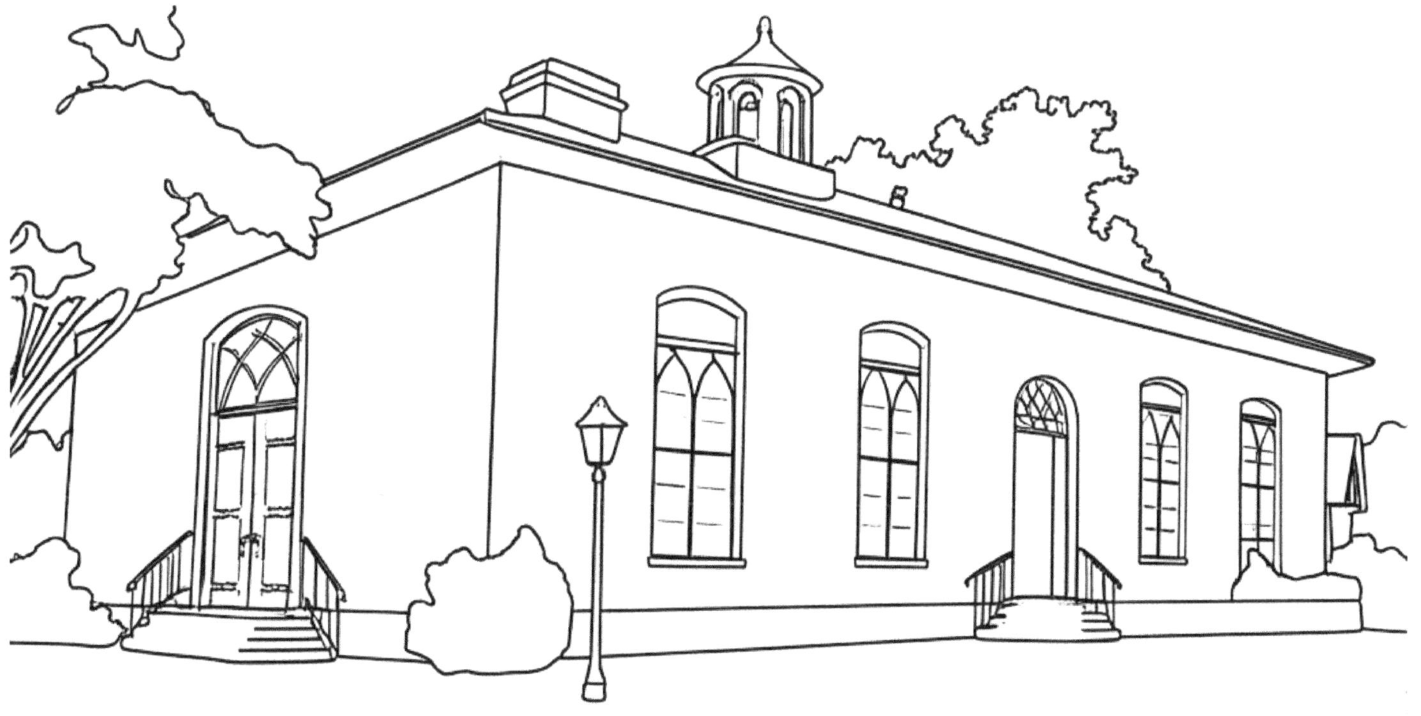

Notable Residents of Brunswick

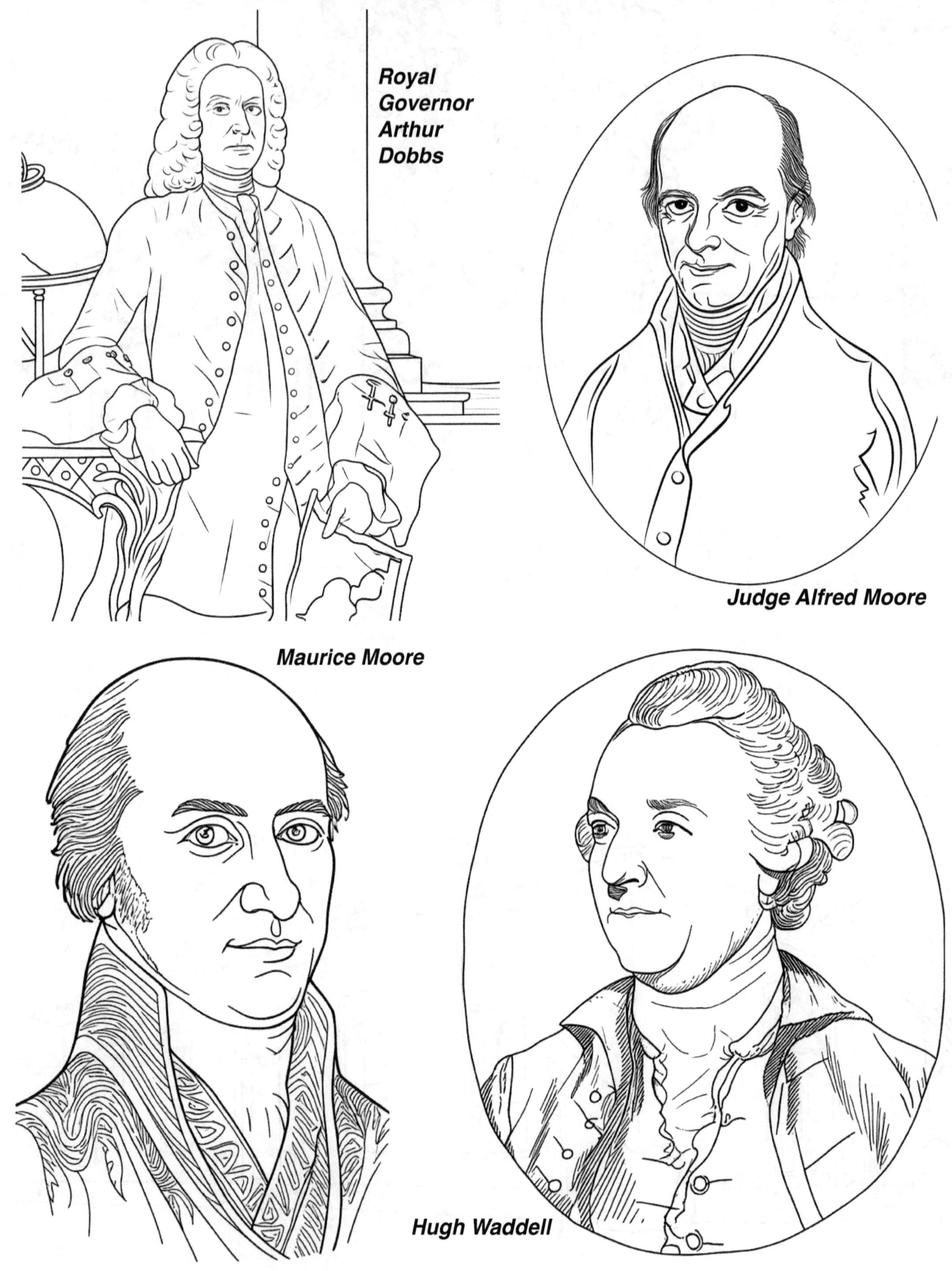

The Spanish Raid

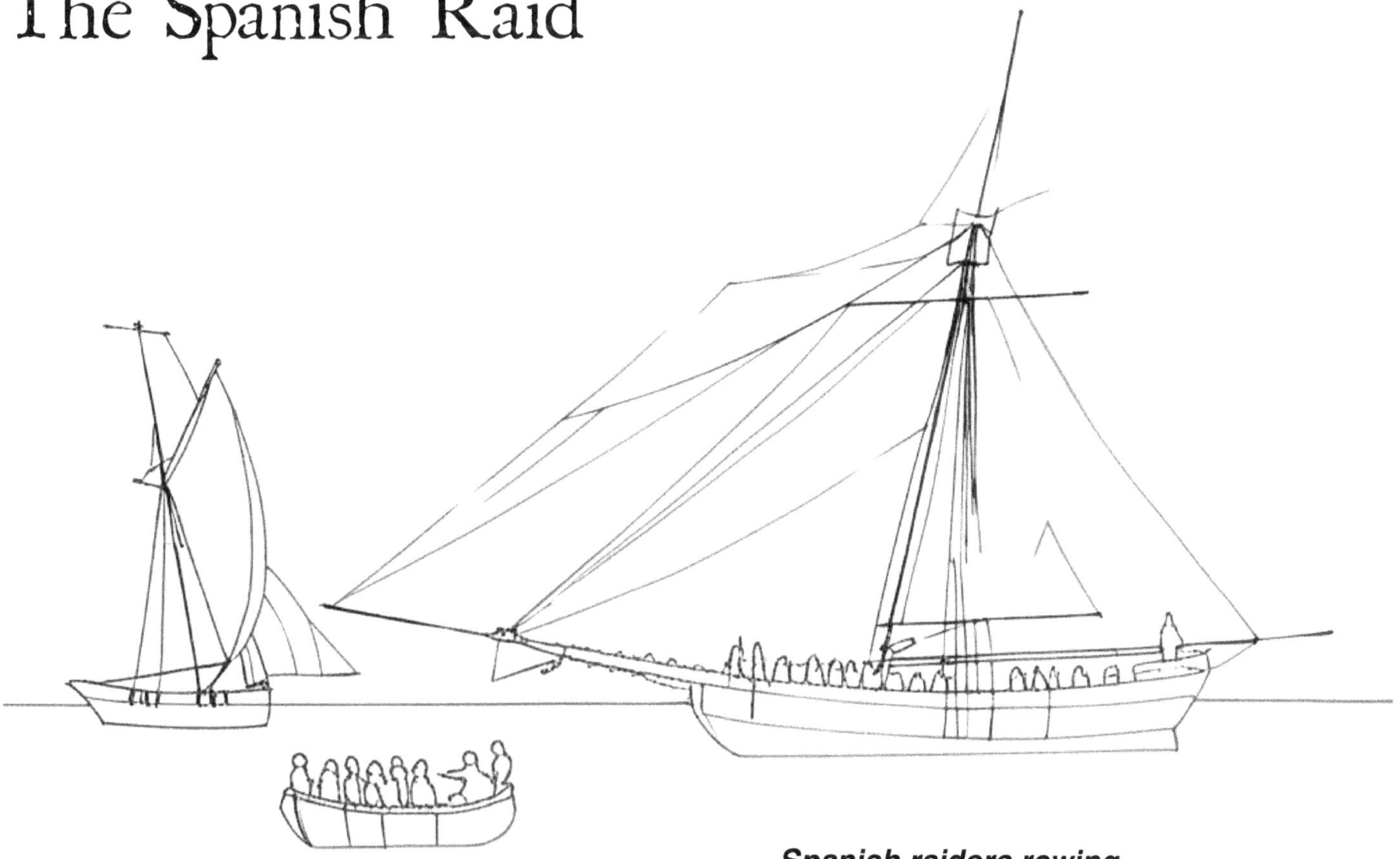

Spanish raiders rowing ashore after Brunswick was abandoned by its residents.

In 1748, during the War of Jenkins' Ear, Spanish privateers raided Brunswick and looted the town. Surprised residents fled as the Spanish pillaged their homes and businesses at will. Soon, though, militiamen from Brunswick and Wilmington rallied and a great battle ensued. The Spanish withdrew to their ships and shelled the town until their flagship, called La Fortuna, *exploded. The Spanish fled, and residents salvaged what they could from the ship. In modern times, a cannon believed to have been aboard* La Fortuna *has been recovered and is on display at Brunswick Town Fort Anderson State Historic Site. In the summer of 2025, archaeologists from East Carolina University found the remains of the ship itself and raised it for preservation.*

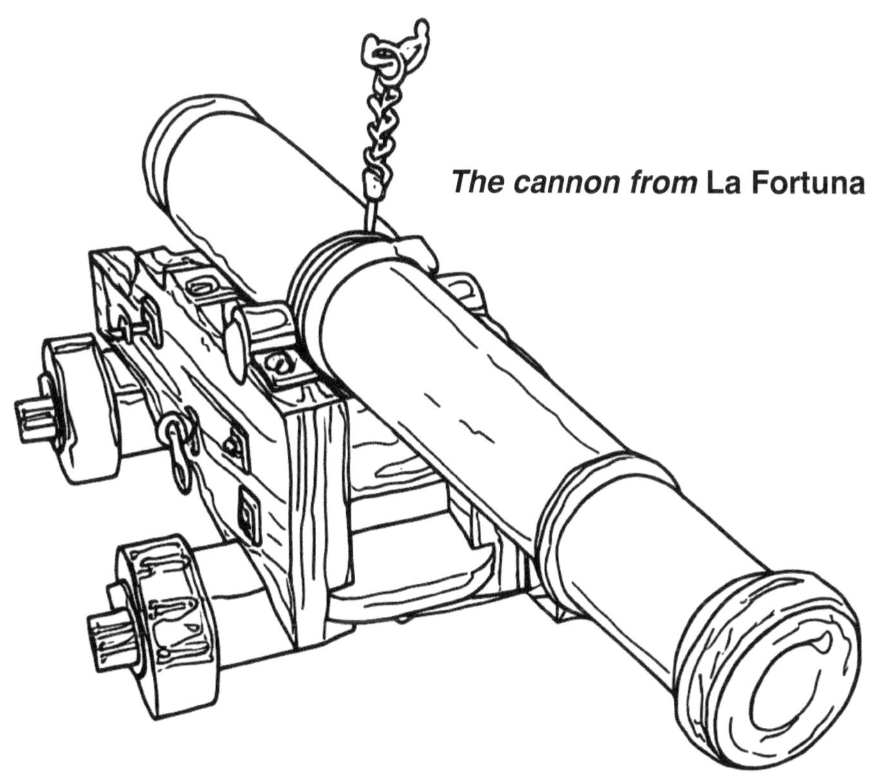

The cannon from La Fortuna

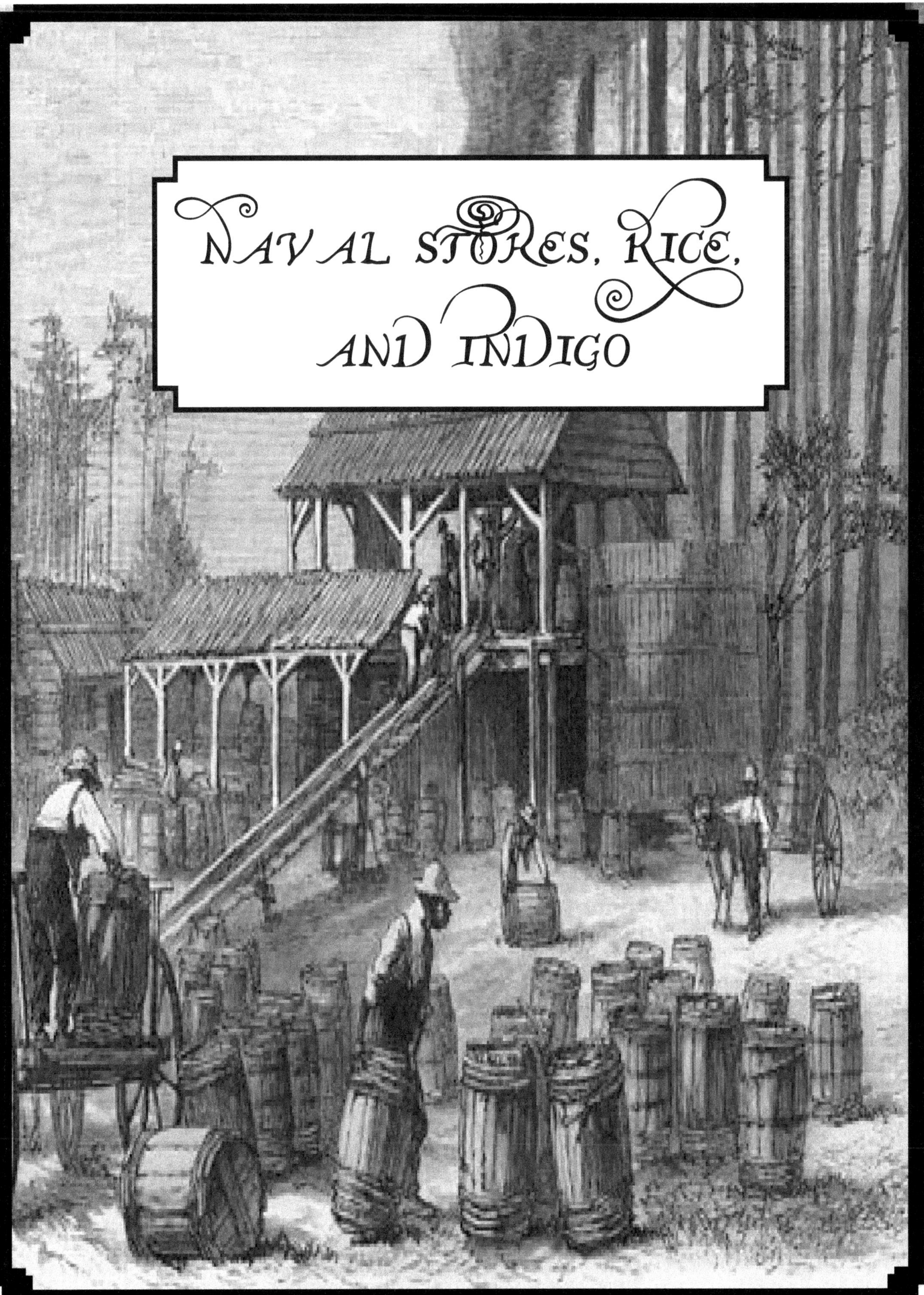
NAVAL STORES, RICE,
AND INDIGO

Naval Stores...

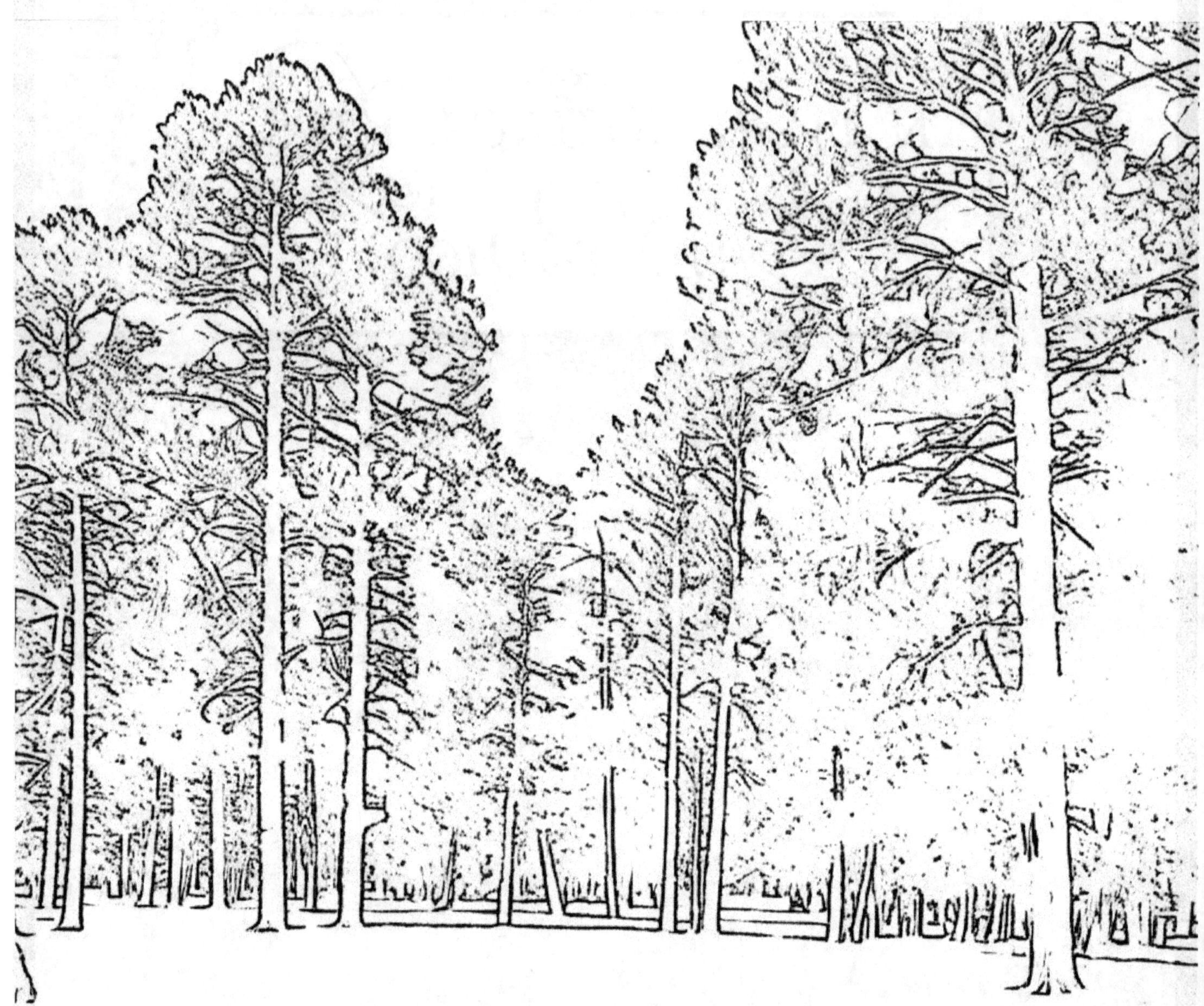

The plentiful longleaf pine trees of southeastern North Carolina provided the colonists who called it home with their first cash crop, the naval stores produced from the rosin extracted from them. The tar, pitch, and turpentine manufactured from the longleaf sap was used to keep Great Britain's navy and merchant fleet afloat. The Cape Fear became the largest exporter of naval stores in the world, making it a vital supplier for the Royal Navy. Naval stores would remain a major source of income for the people of southeastern North Carolina until after steamships made sailing vessels obsolete.

To extract the sap of the long-leaf pine, bark was stripped to expose the tree itself. Then, grooves were cut into the tree at angles, resembling a cat's whiskers. A bucket was placed underneath the slashes to catch the sap as it flowed from the cuts and down the tree trunk. When one set of cuts dried up, new ones were cut and the process repeated until the tree was played out. Once everything could be extracted from it, the tree could be cut down and used to make lumber for building and construction.

Workers gathering pine sap in barrels for shipment to distilleries (below).

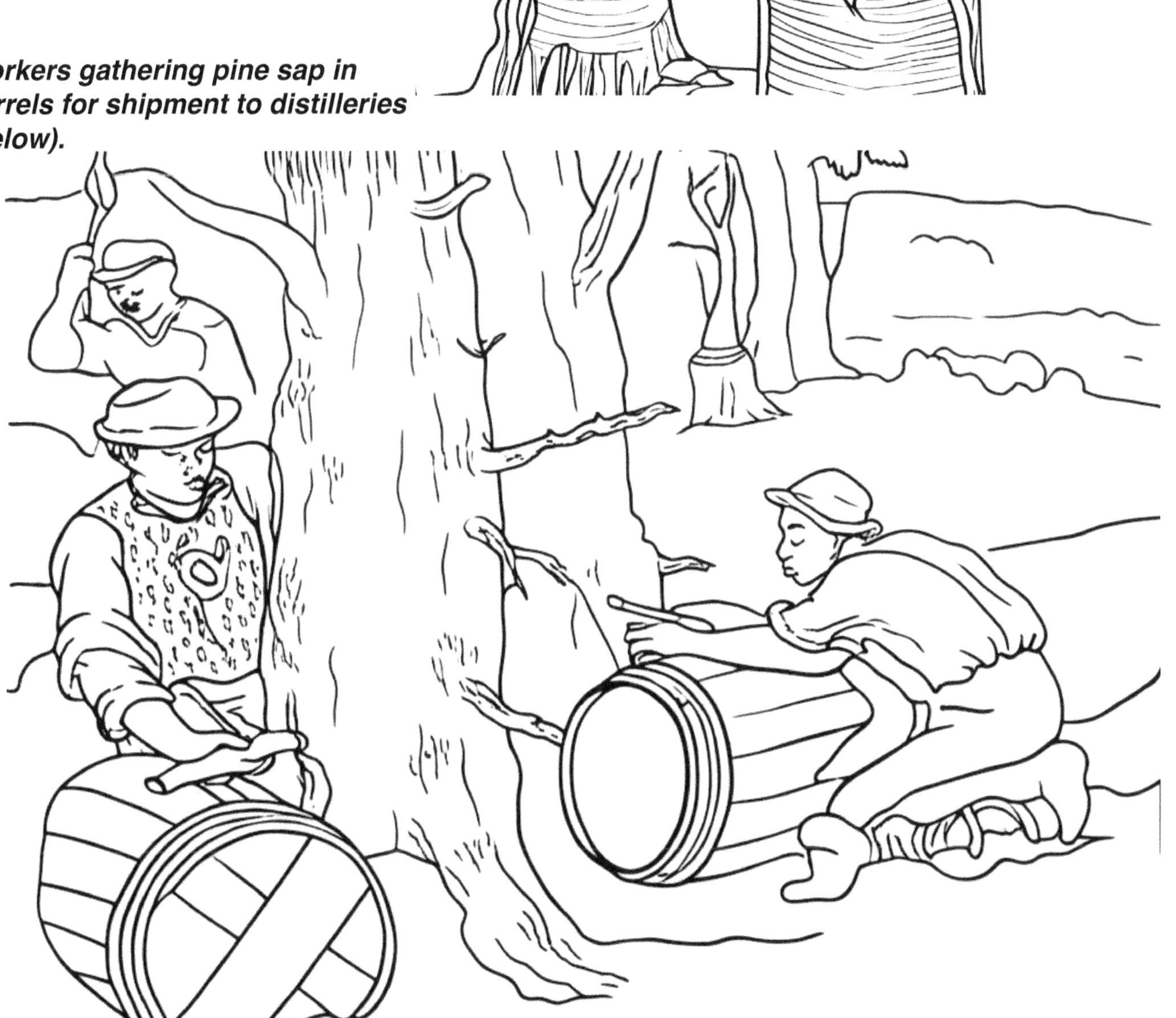

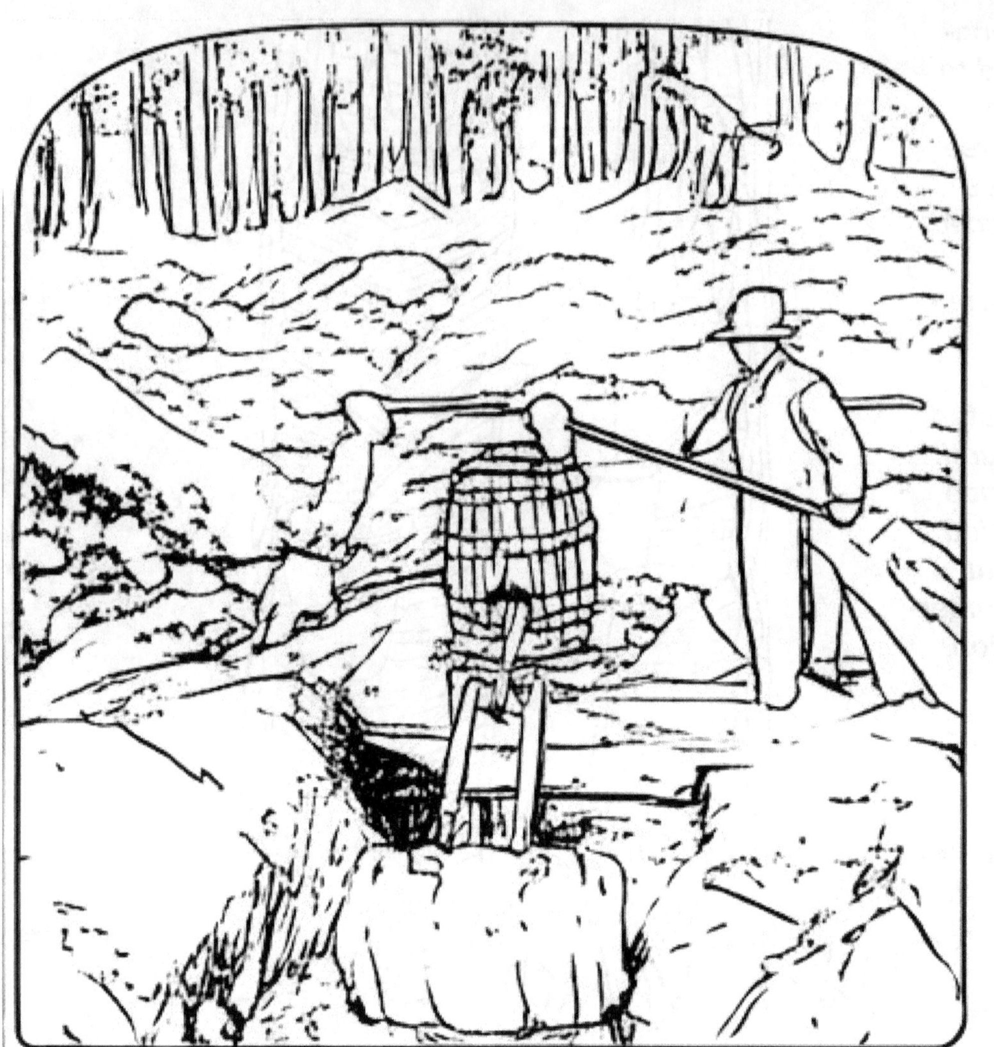

The process of extracting tar and pitch from longleaf pine rosin invloved boiling it down and exposing it to high heat to produce the final products. Southeastern North Carolina woods are dotted with depressions where earthen kilns once did the work of manufacturing the valuable tar that coated a ship's ropes against the weather and sun, pitch that sealed the planking of wooden ships against leaks, and turpentine that was used in a number of ways, including as paint thinner.

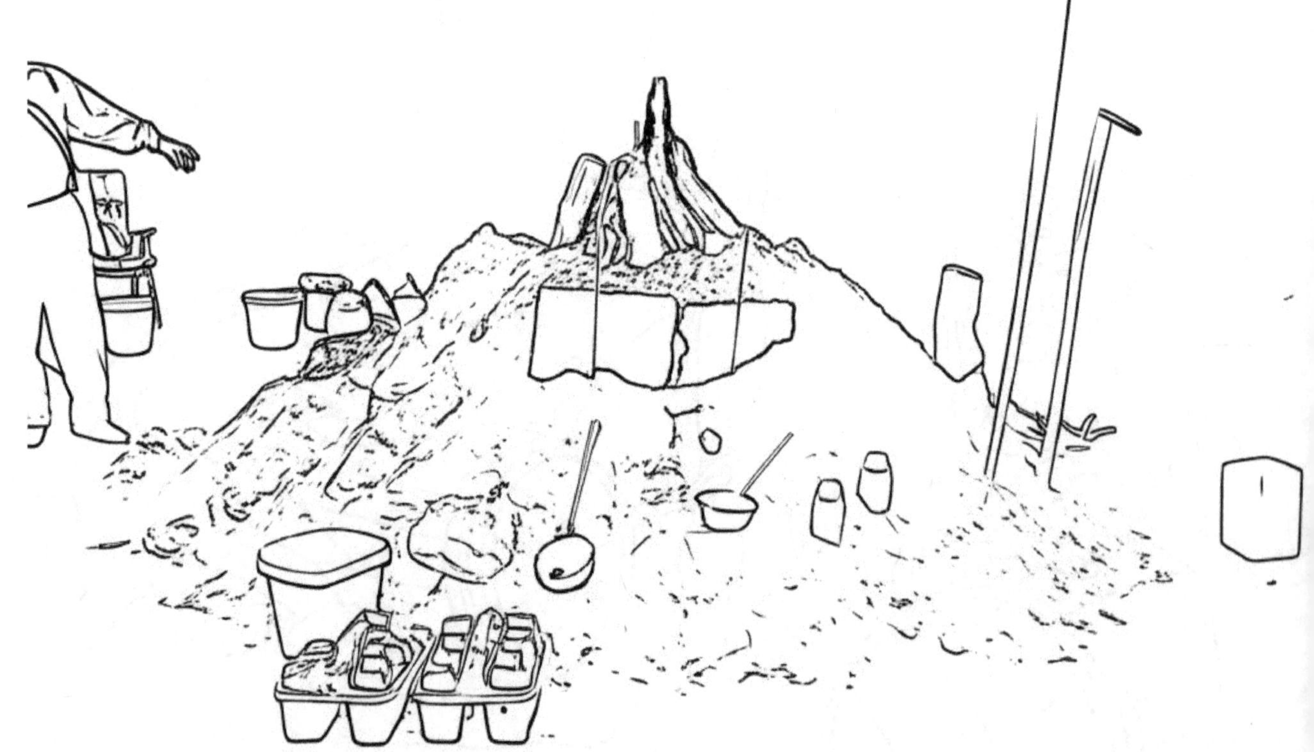

Naval stores distilleries used to exist throughout the North Carolina pine forests.

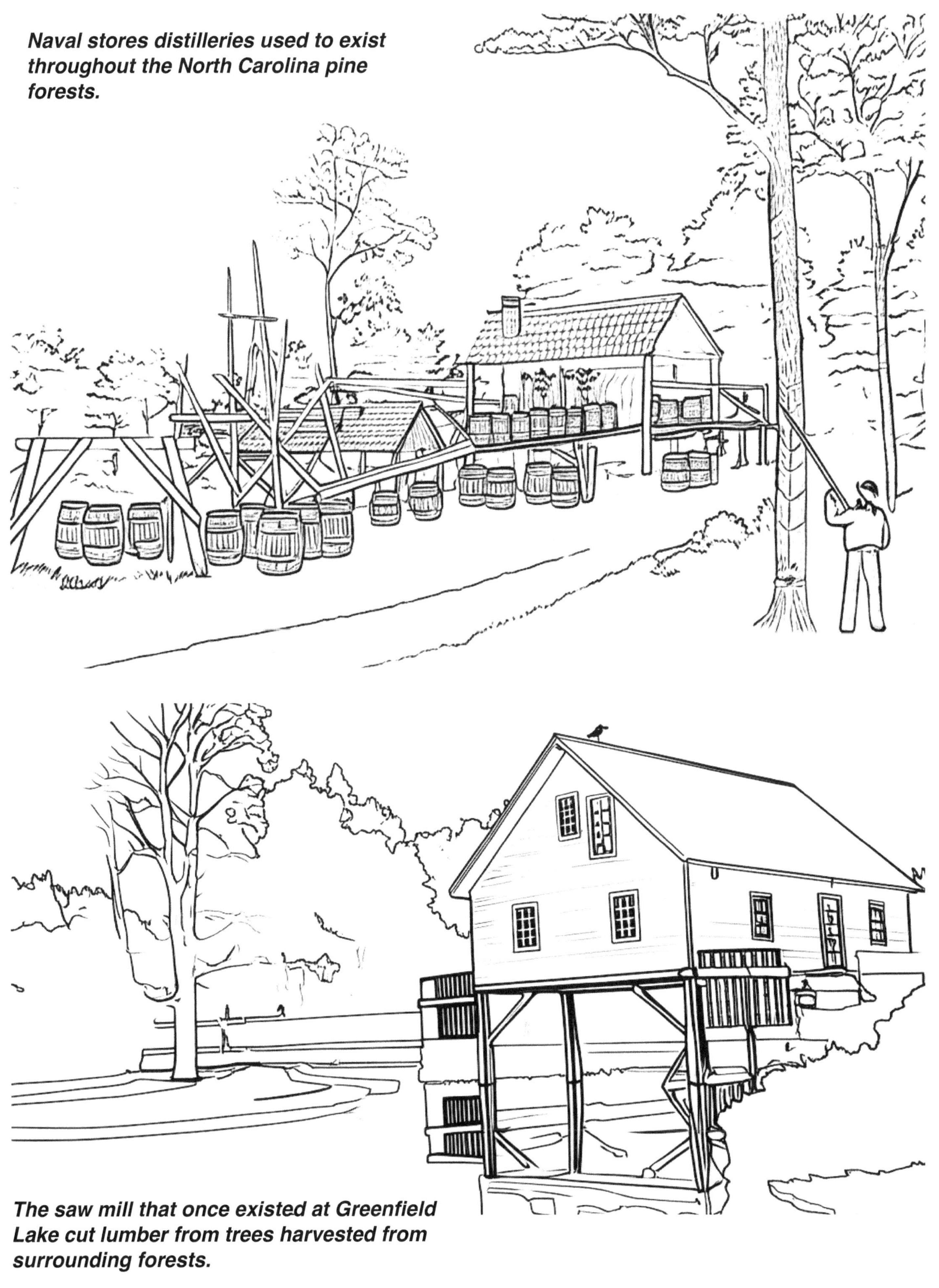

The saw mill that once existed at Greenfield Lake cut lumber from trees harvested from surrounding forests.

Naval stores waiting to be loaded aboard a steam boat at the Worth & Worth docks in Wilmington in the early 1900s.

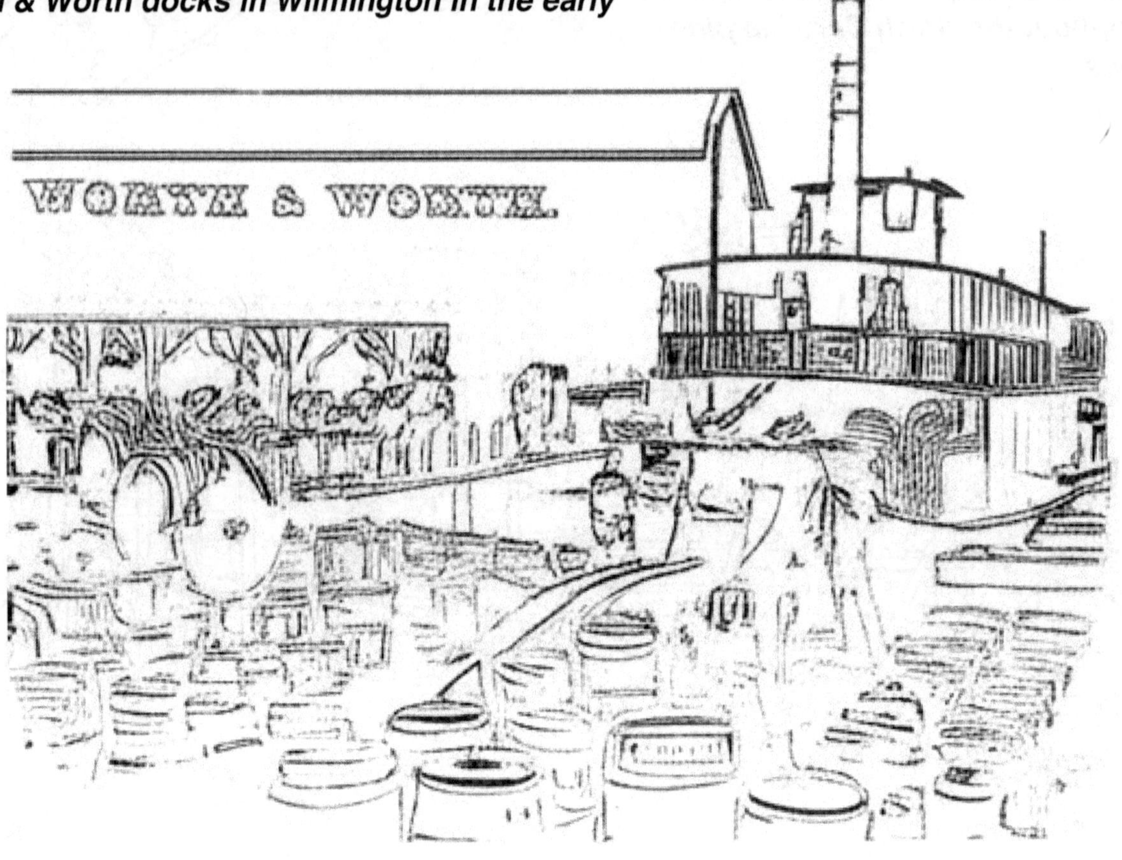

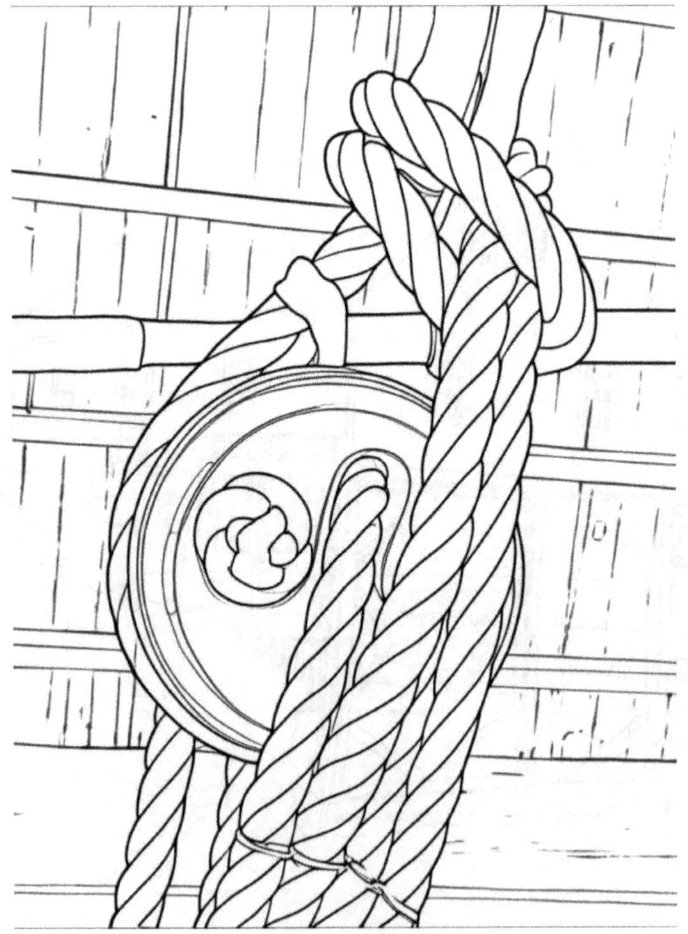

Tar from longleaf pines was used aboard ships to weatherproof the ropes that operated the sails.

Sailing ships were intricate machines that were the workhorses of the British Empire. Those ships allowed that empire to span the globe. It was naval stores, especially from southeastern North Carolina, that kept those ships afloat.

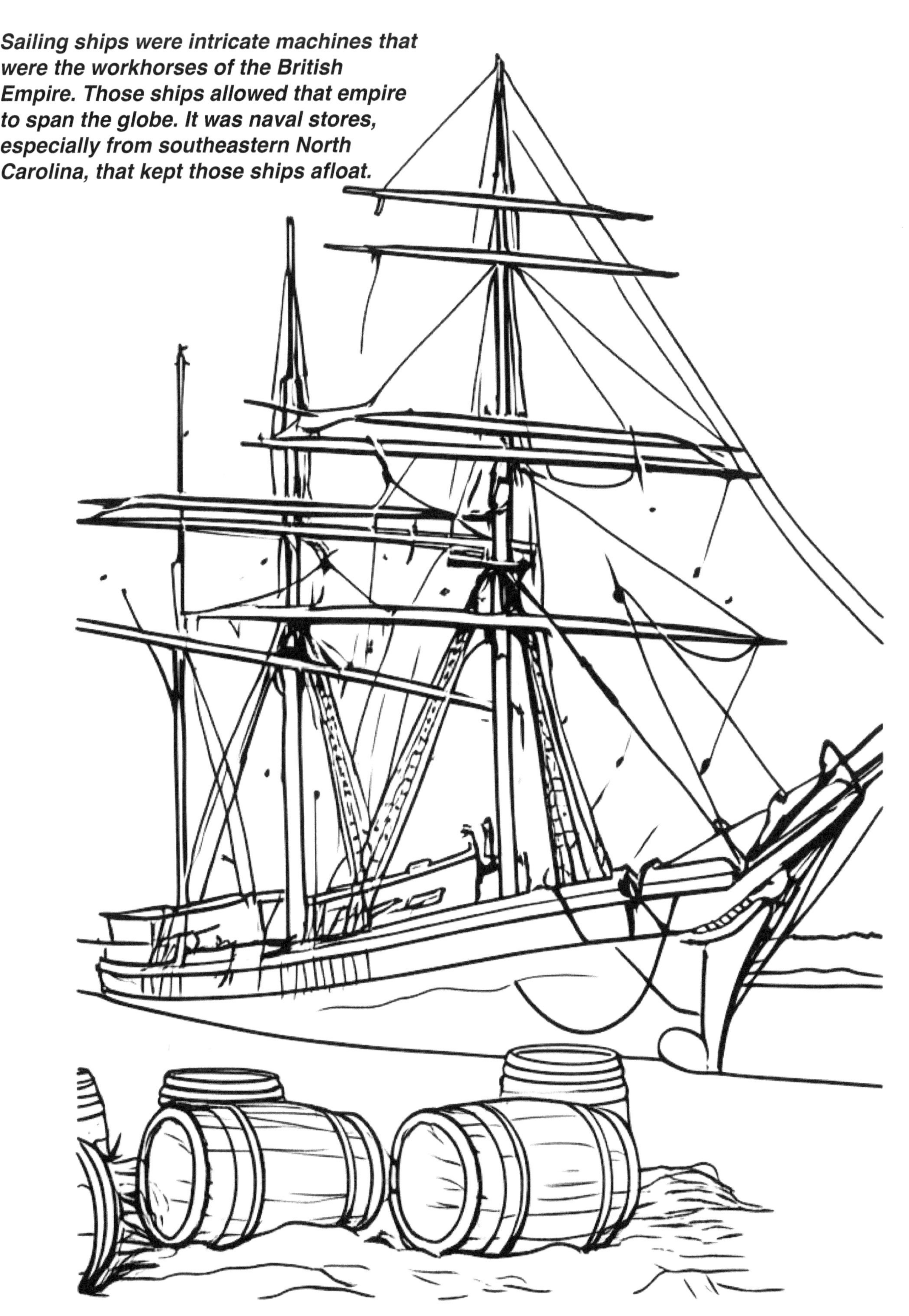

Rice...

While naval stores were the Cape Fear's first cash crop, rice soon surpassed it in profitability. Because the Cape Fear River is a tidal river with ample fresh water, it was perfect to grow the lowcountry rice made popular around Charleston and the South Carolina coast. The Cape Fear River marked the northern-most boundary of rice cultivation in the United States.

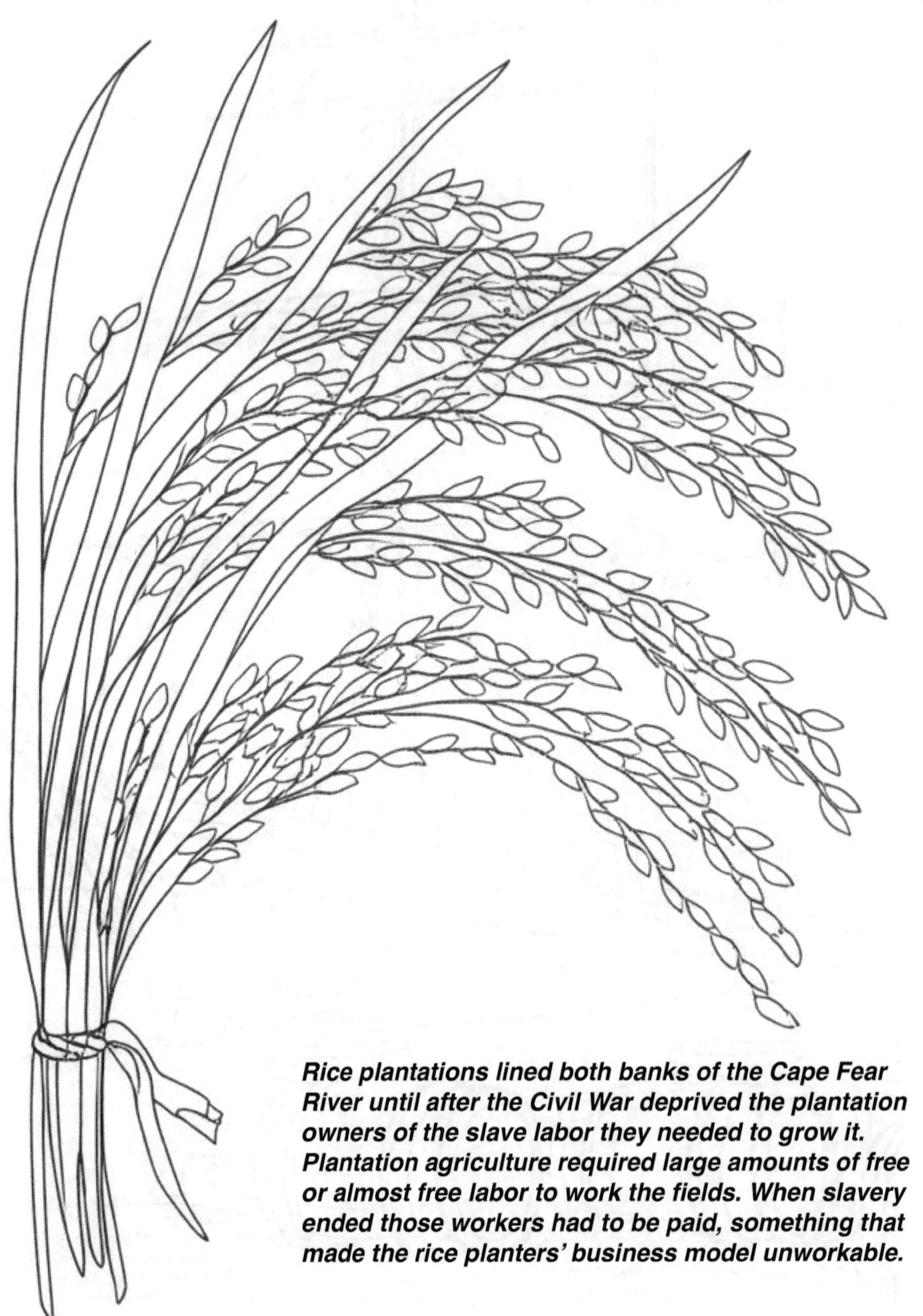

Rice plantations lined both banks of the Cape Fear River until after the Civil War deprived the plantation owners of the slave labor they needed to grow it. Plantation agriculture required large amounts of free or almost free labor to work the fields. When slavery ended those workers had to be paid, something that made the rice planters' business model unworkable.

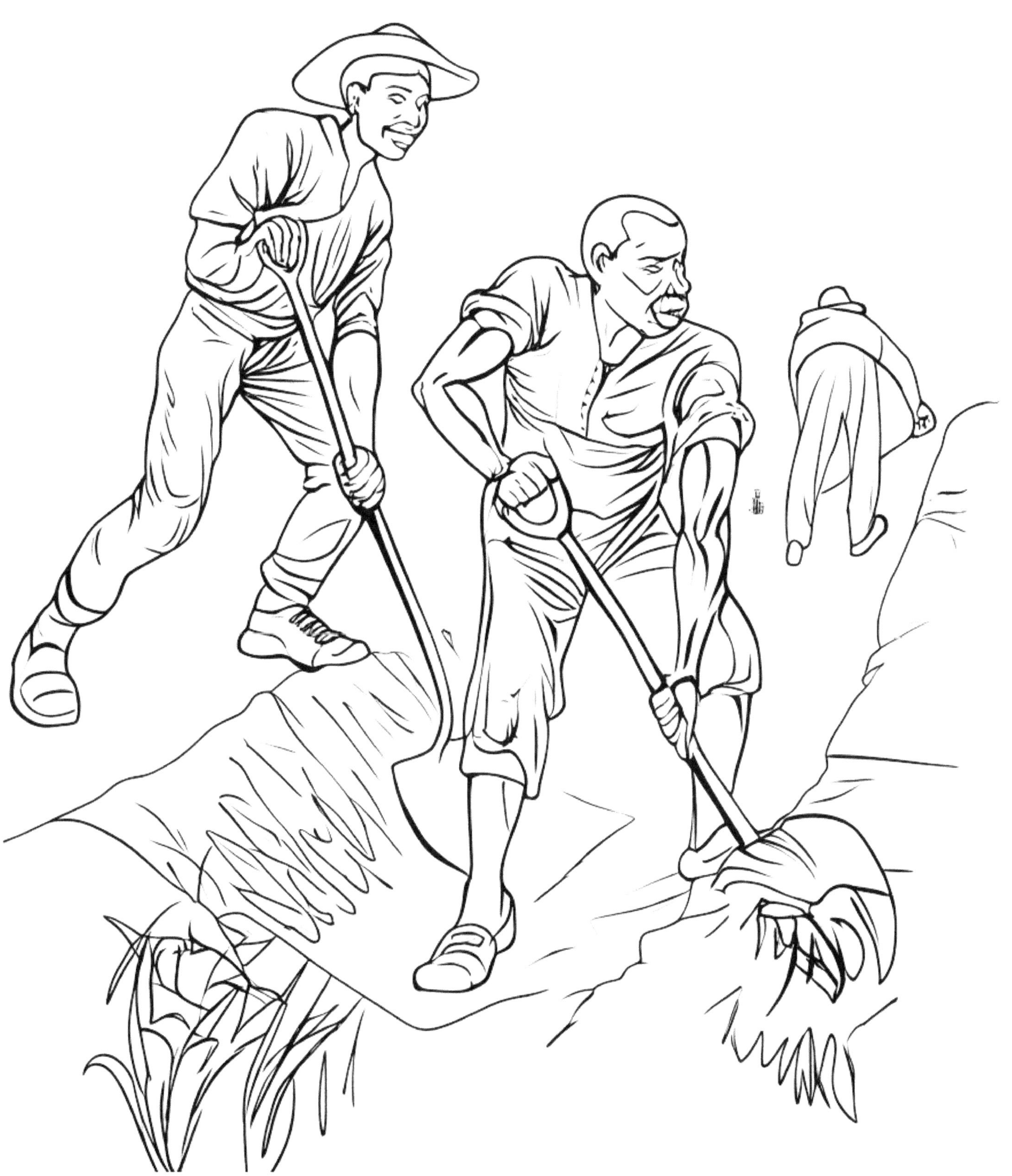

Enslaved African Americans labored to prep rice fields for planting. The first step was to clear a field close to the river and dig ditches for irrigation.

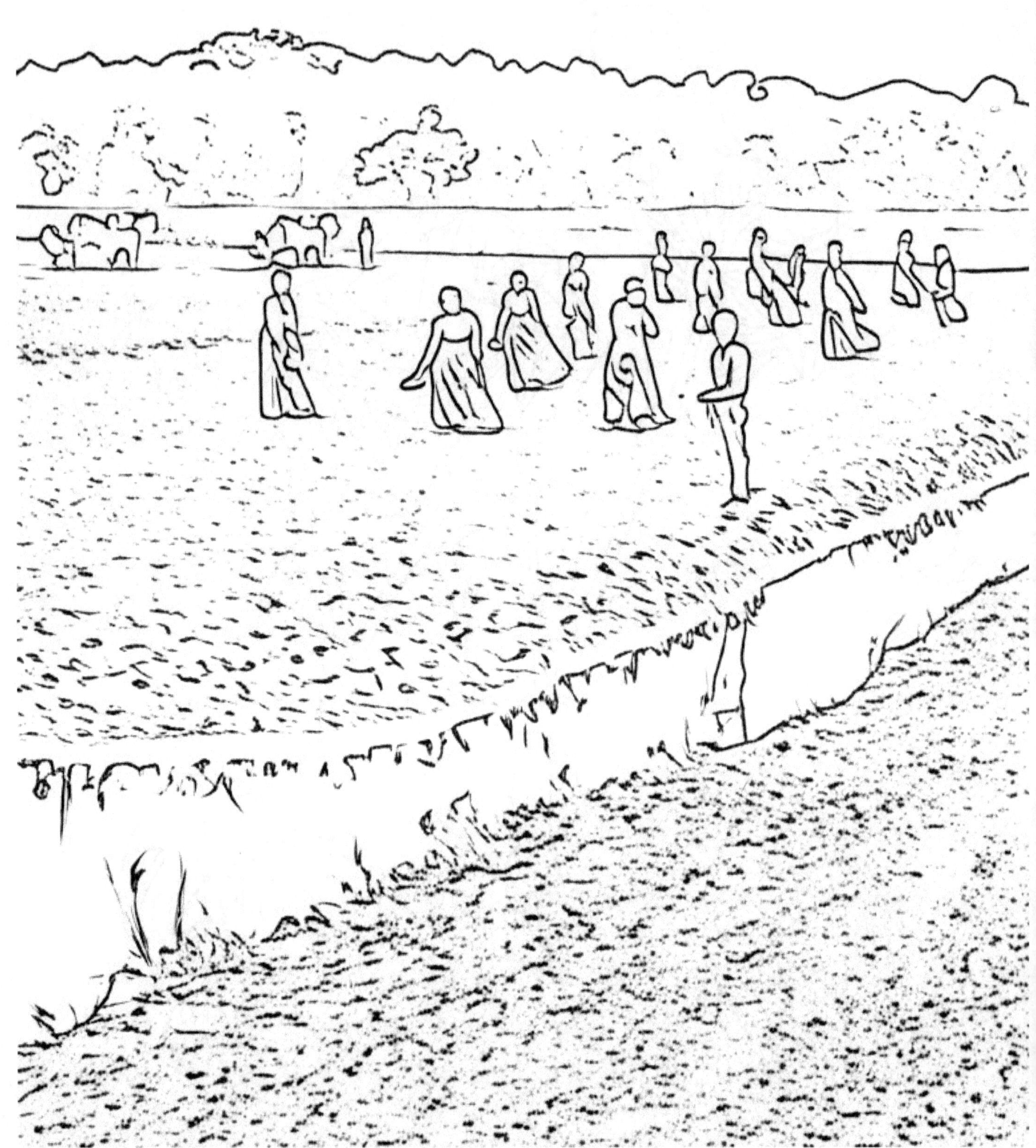

Enslaved field workers planted young rice plants on the higher ground between the irrigation ditches.

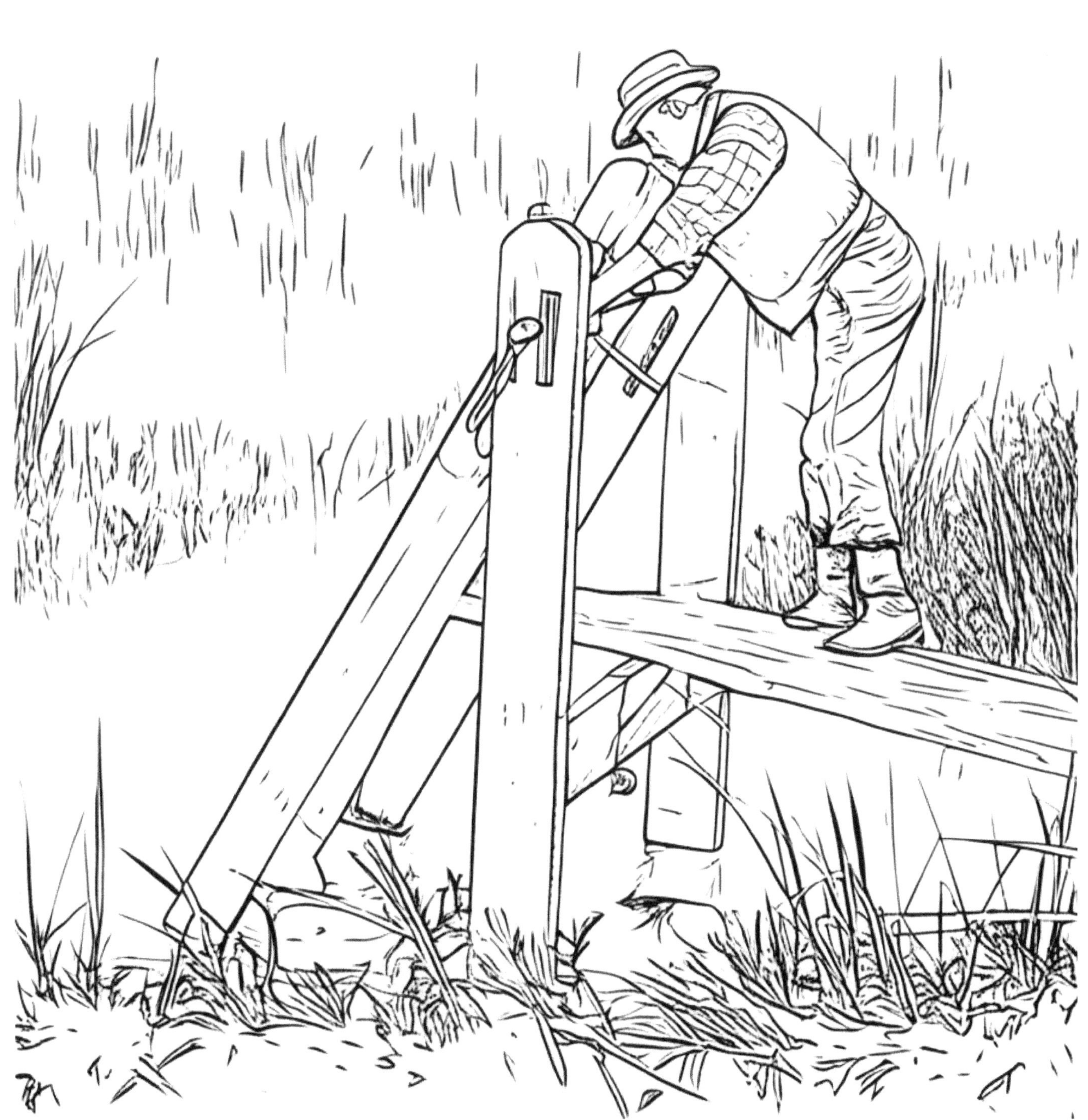

Flood gates allowed fresh water from the Cape Fear River to cover the young plants. When they reached a certain height, the floodgates were opend again and the fields were drained.

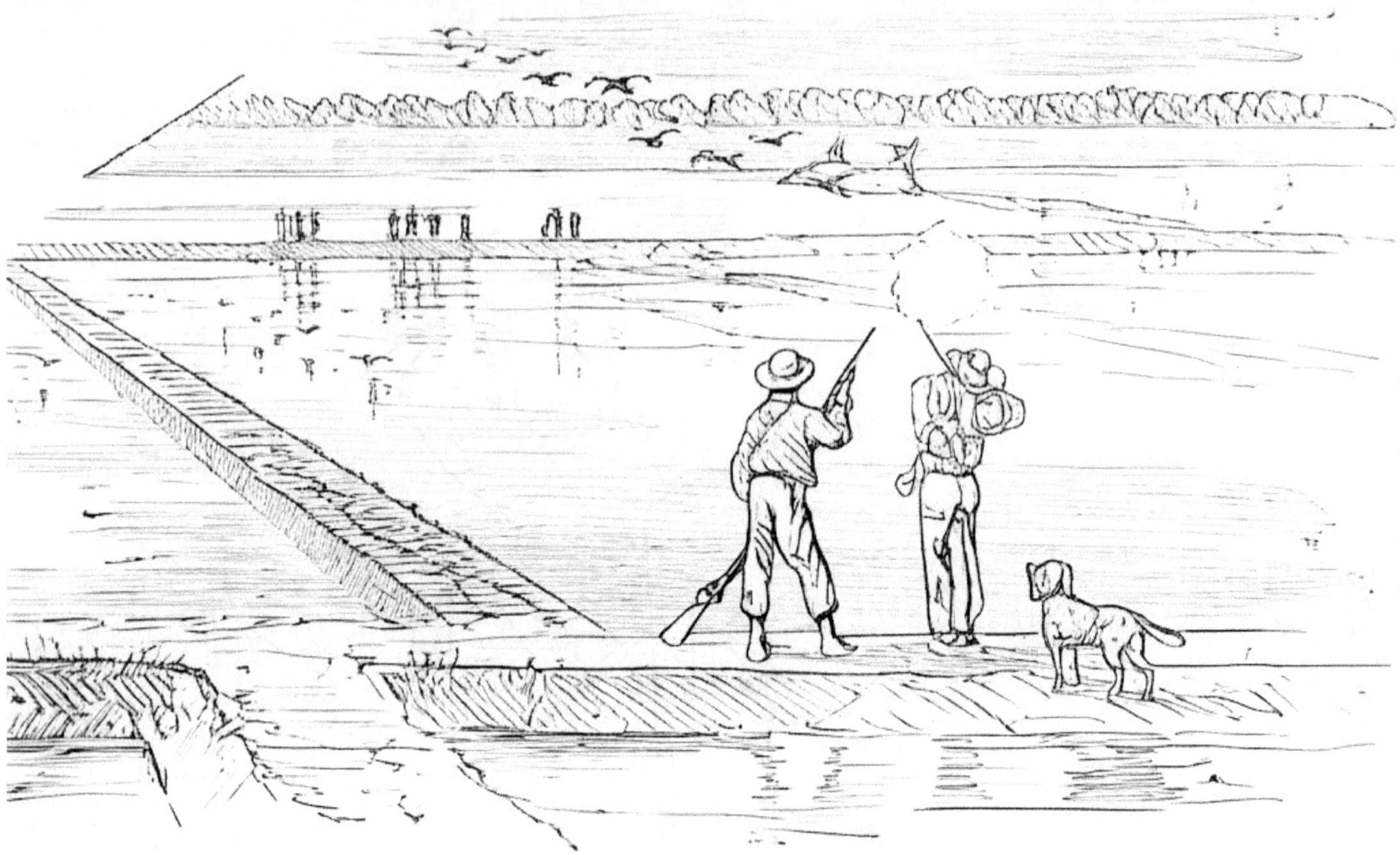

In the above image, a plantation owner hunts from atop the dikes surrounding the flooded rice fields. Below, field workers tend the maturing rice plants after the fields have been drained of the protective water that previously covered them while they were young.

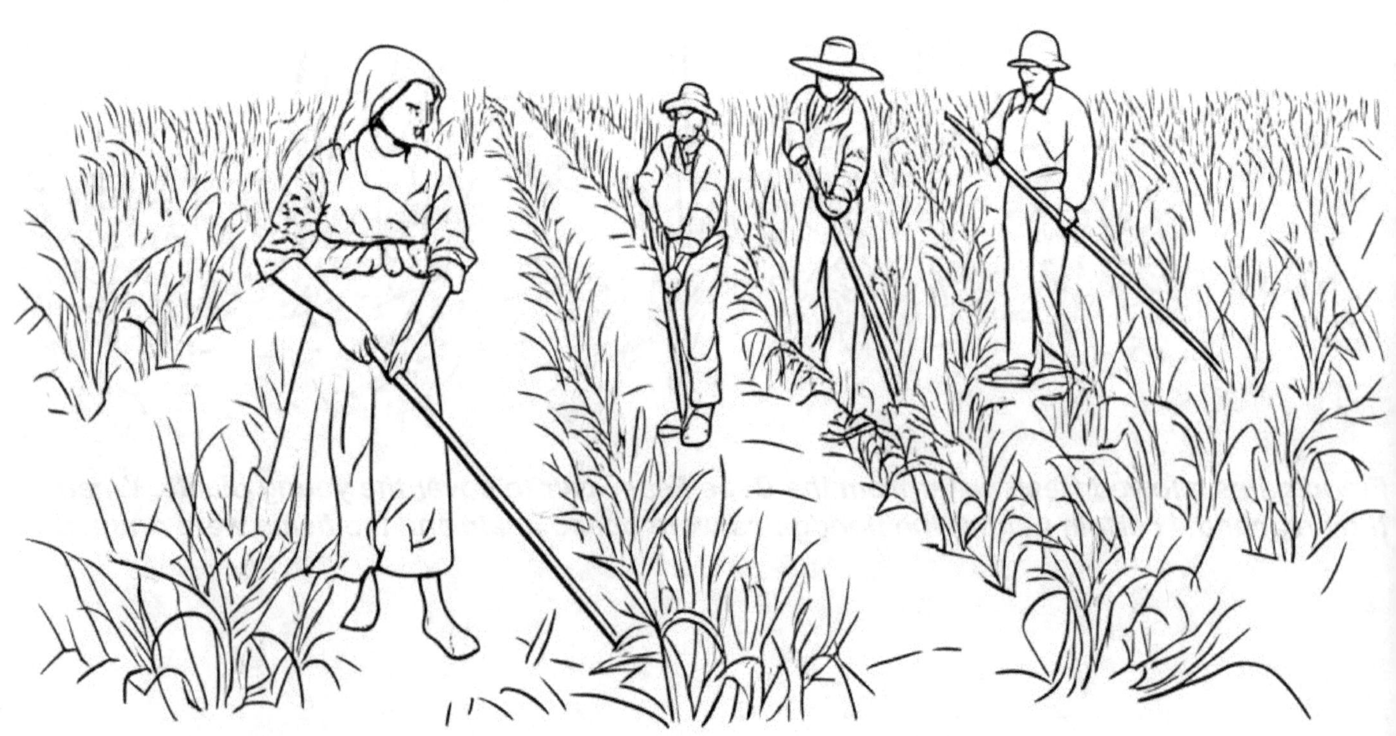

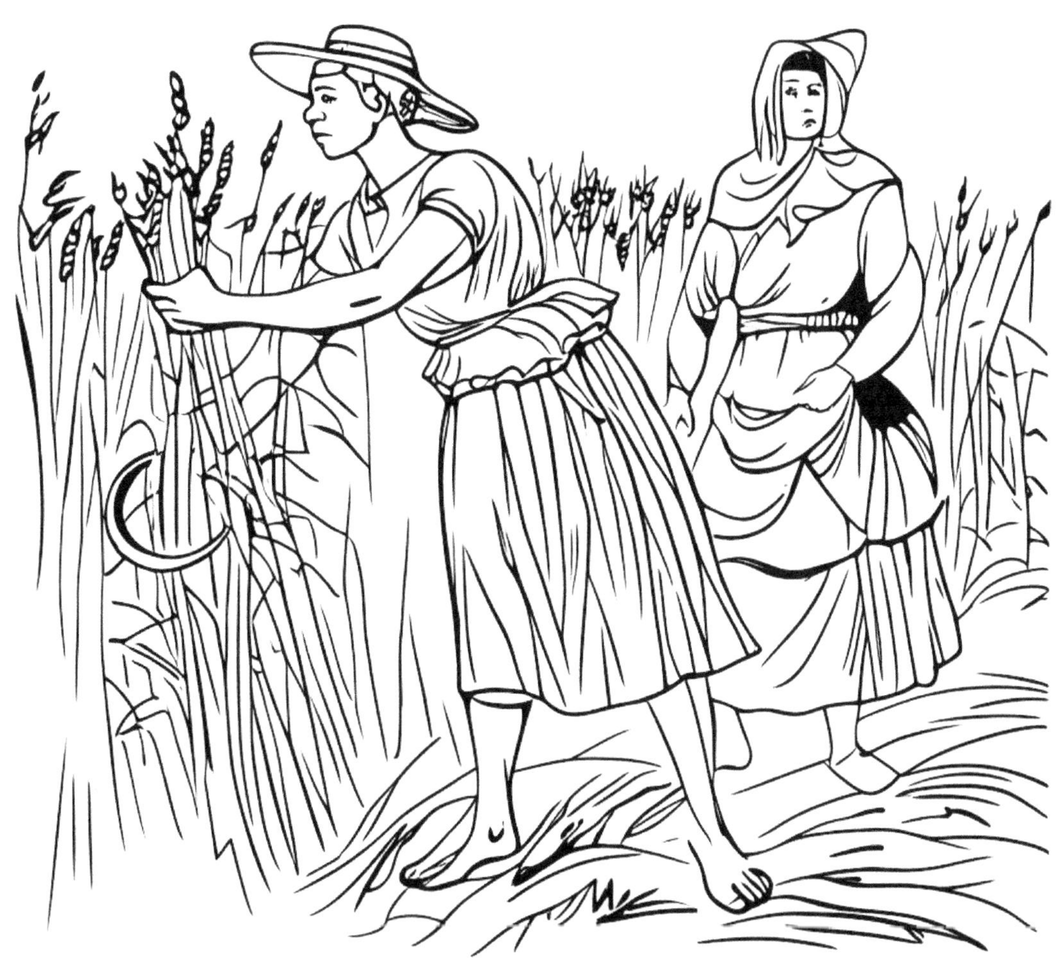

When rice reached its maturity, workers would cut the stalks and bundle them for threshing to separate the rice grains.

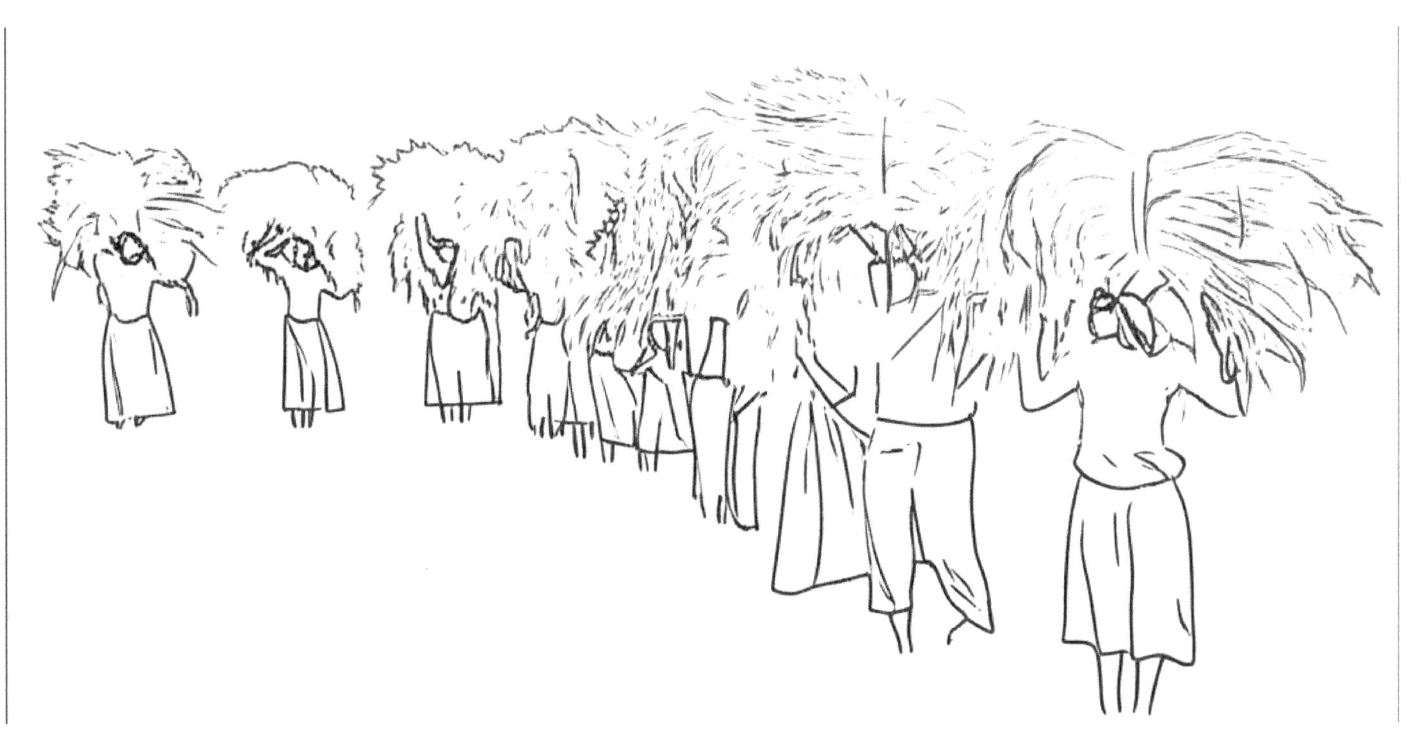

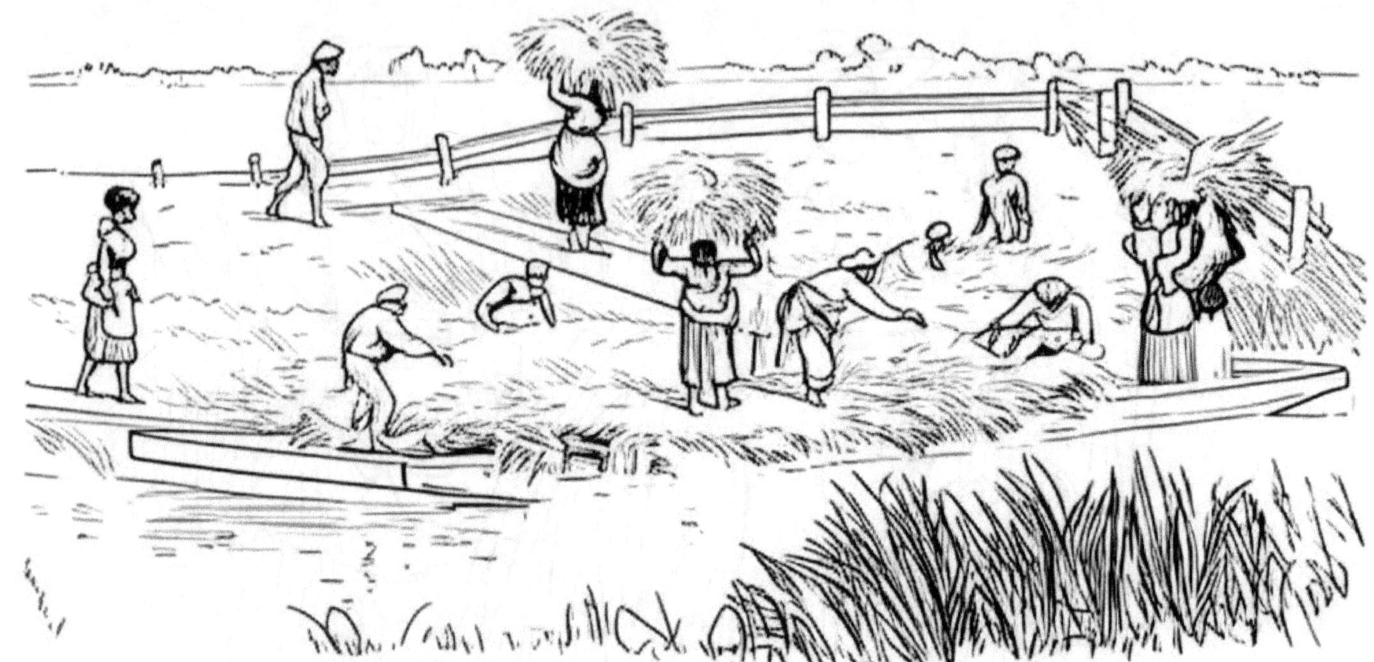

In the above image, workers unload a barge carrying bundled rice stalks. Below, women pound the rice to seperate the grains from the feathery tops that held them.

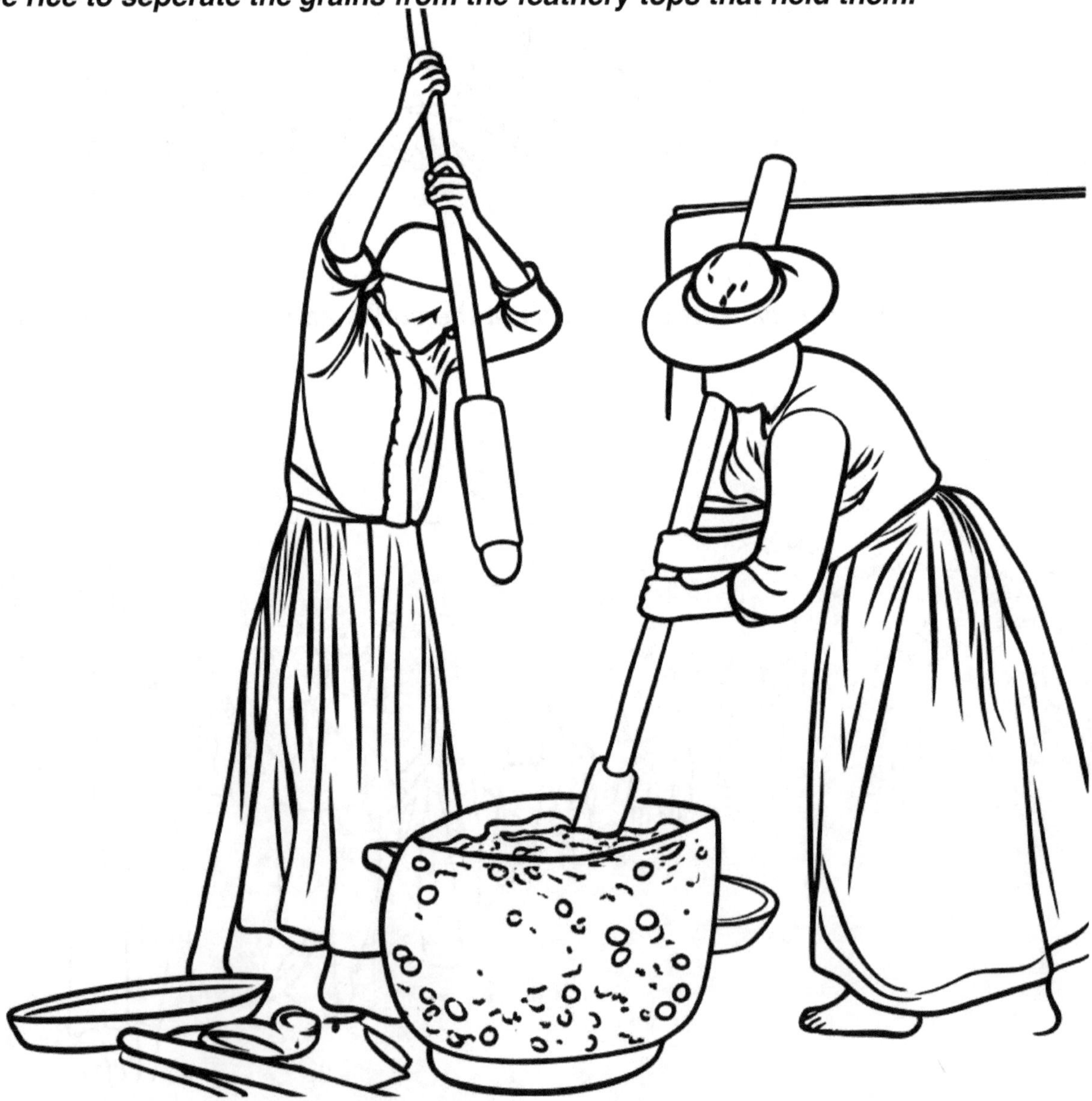

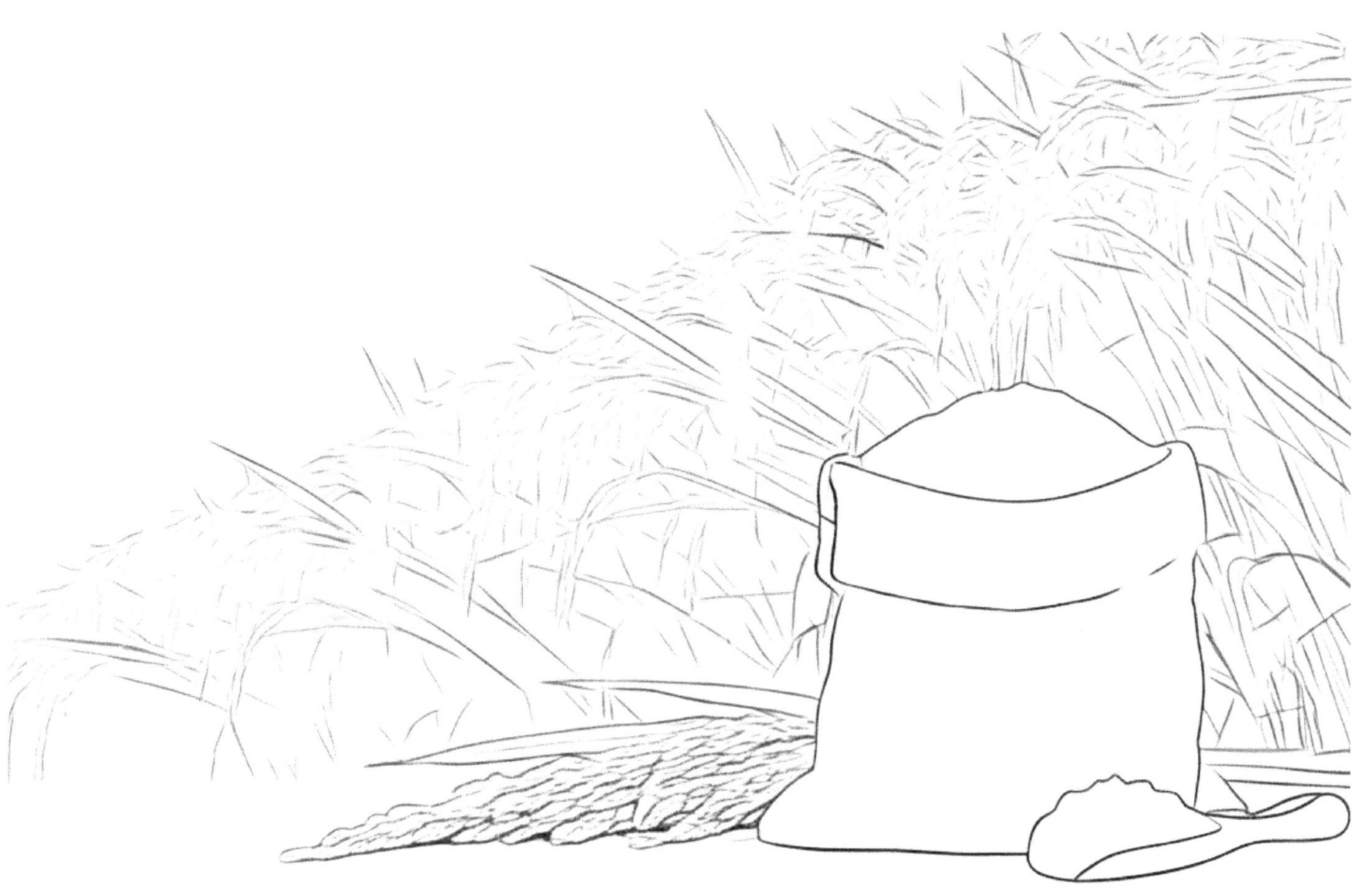

Rice proved to be an eduring source of income for planters in southeastern North Carolina. It was said that the rice grown here was so distinct that one could tell the difference between rice grown on the Brunswick County side of the Cape Fear River, versus that grown on the New Hanover County side. The great rice plantations like Orton fell into decline after the Civil War when the emancipation of the slaves made it unprofitable to follow the plantation agriculture business model.

Indigo...

Cape Fear planters experimented with growing indigo as a cash crop, but they never achieved the success with it that they did with naval stores and rice. Indigo is a plant that produces a rich blue color that was used in garment manufacture.

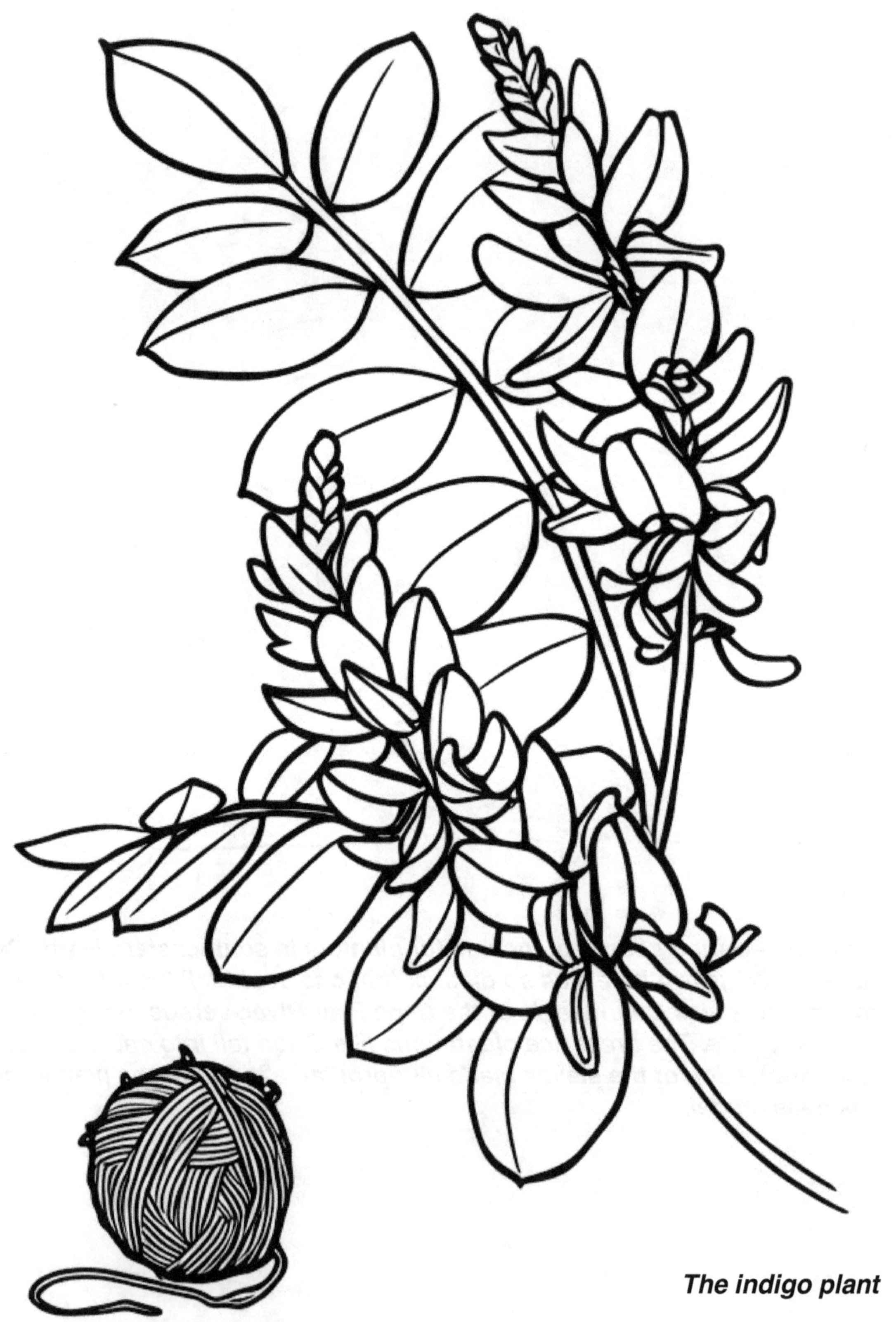

The indigo plant

This drawing illustrates the process for making blue dye out of indigo plants. The plants are harvested and bundled, then put into vats where they are crushed into a paste that is heated to produce the rich blue color that was so valuable to cloth merchants.

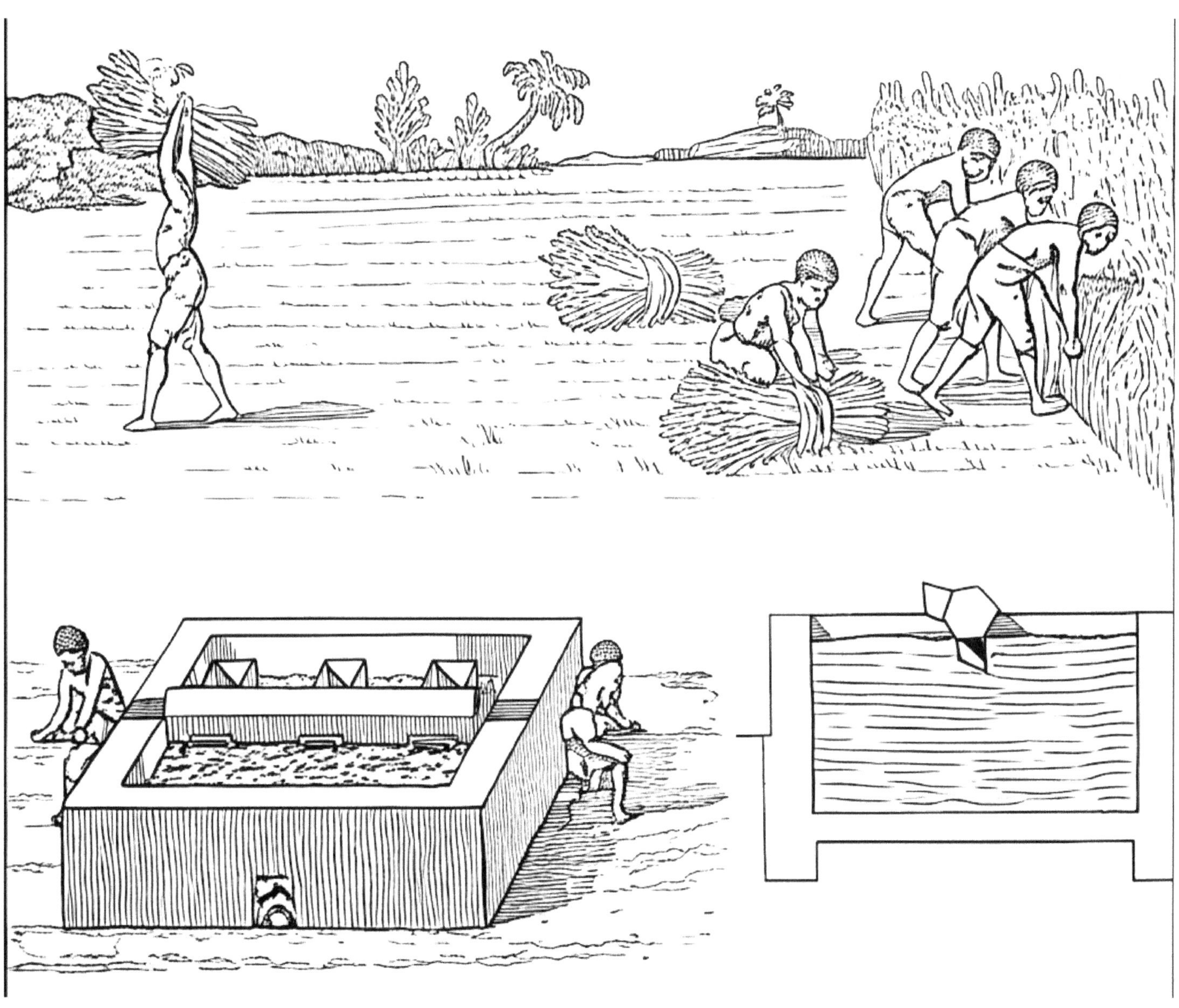

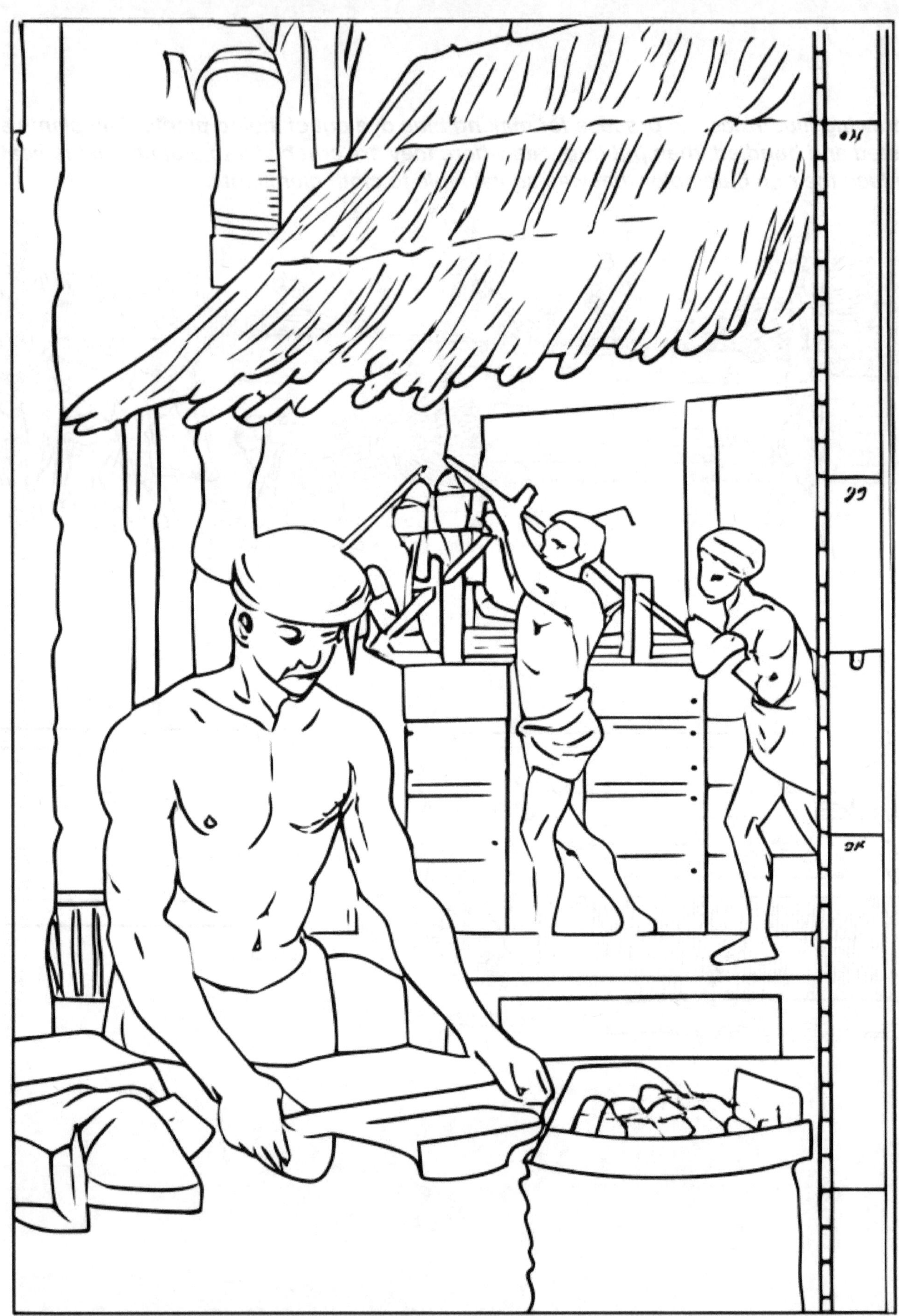

As with rice and naval stores, enslaved workers provided the labor to grow, harvest, and process indigo plants into blue dye.

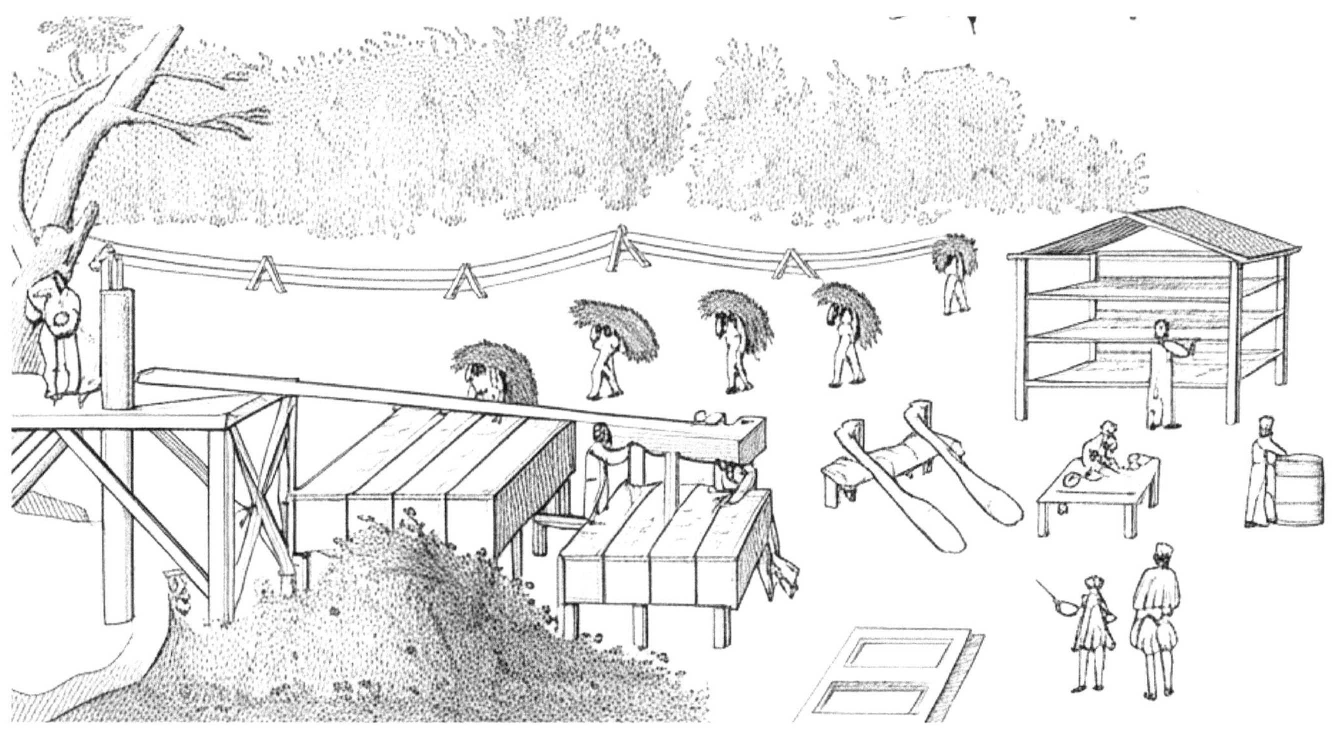

Two more illustrations showing the indigo dye making process. These images show large scale production of indigo as it was done on Caribbean islands like Barbados and Jamaica. The process on the Cape Fear would have been similar, but probably on a smaller scale. Indigo never became as profitable as other cash crops, so Cape Fear planters eventually abandoned it.

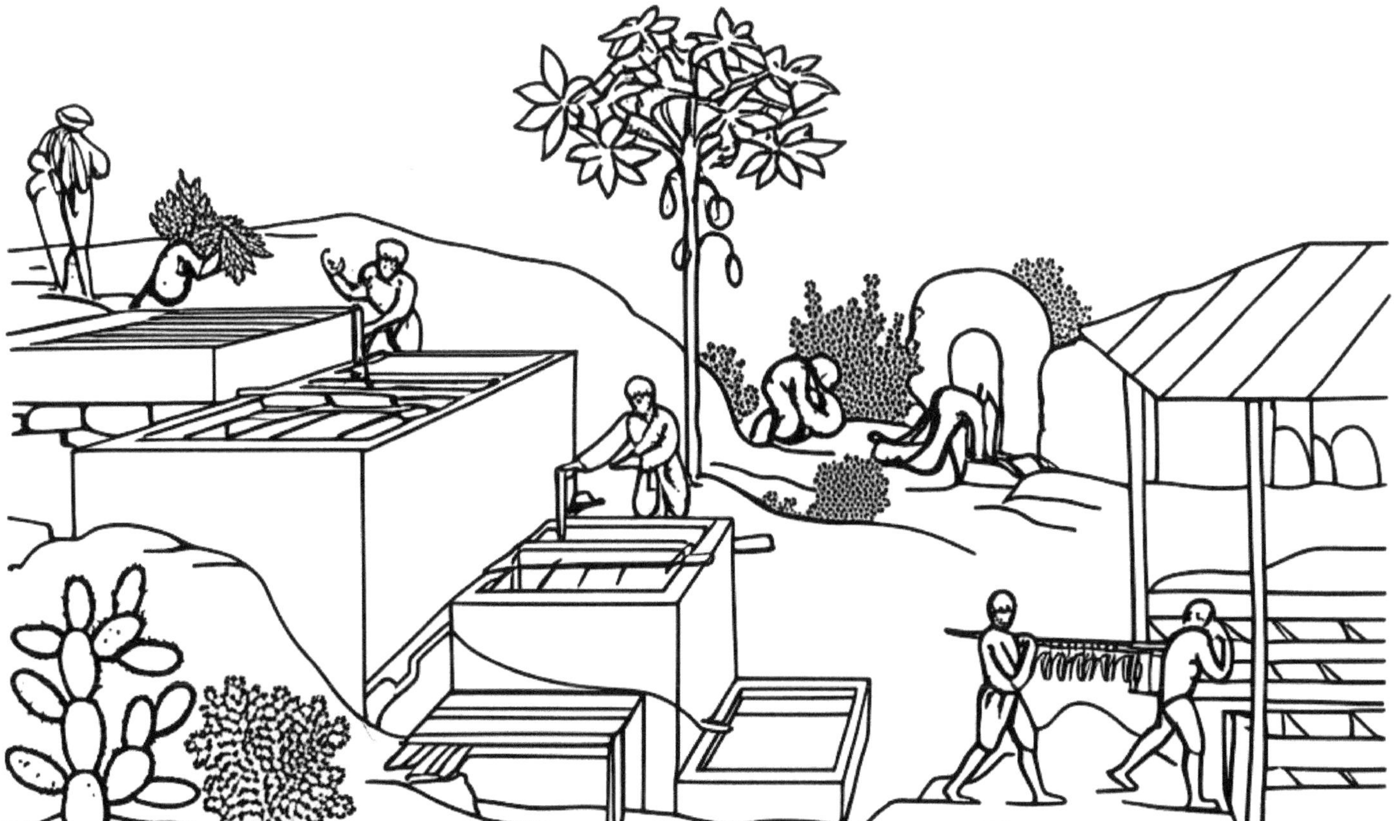

WILMINGTON WATERFRONT

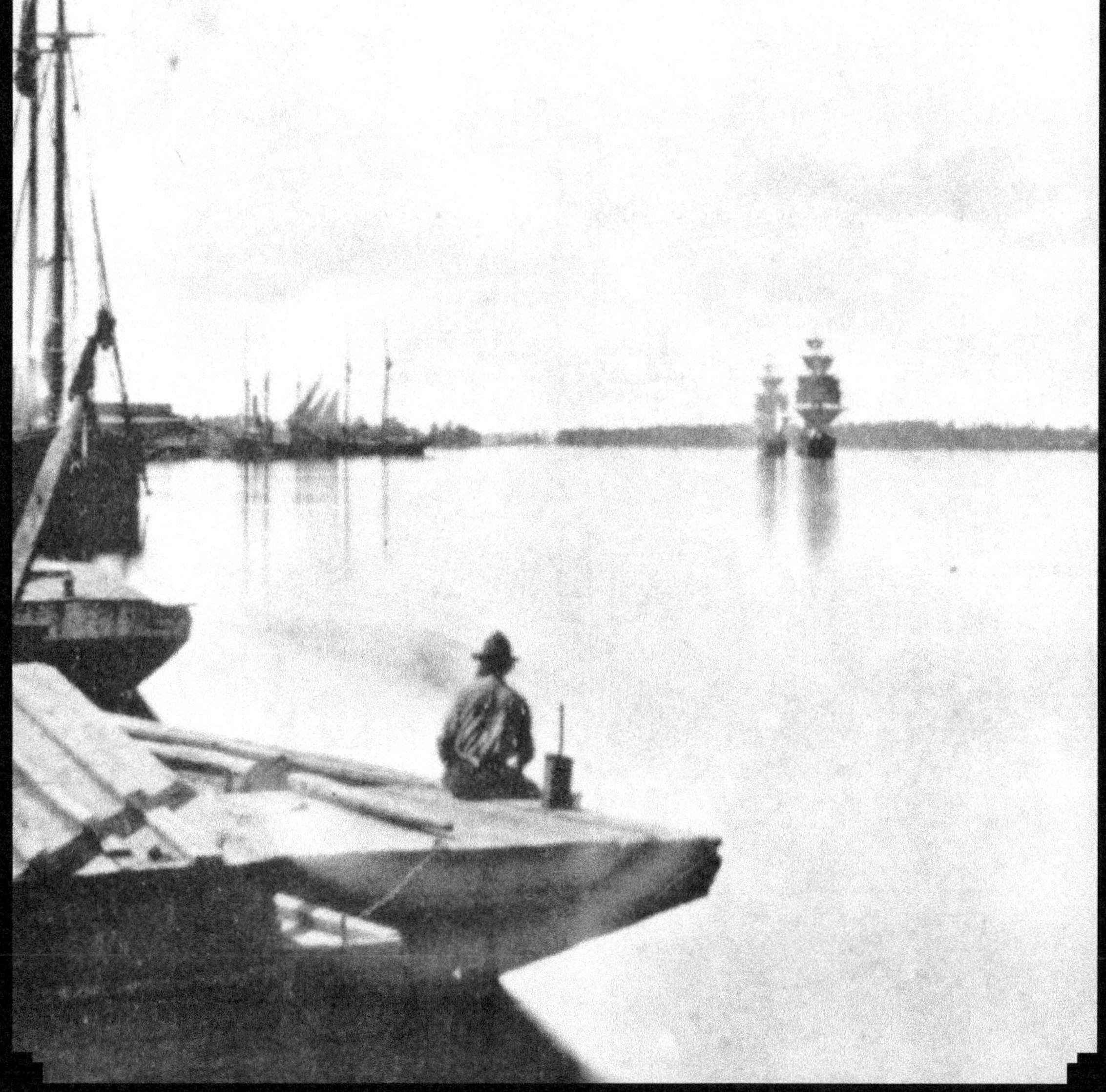

On the River...

The Cape Fear River is the artery that carries the life blood of southeastern North Carolina. For centuries, life for the people of the region has always centered around the river and its surrounding waterways.

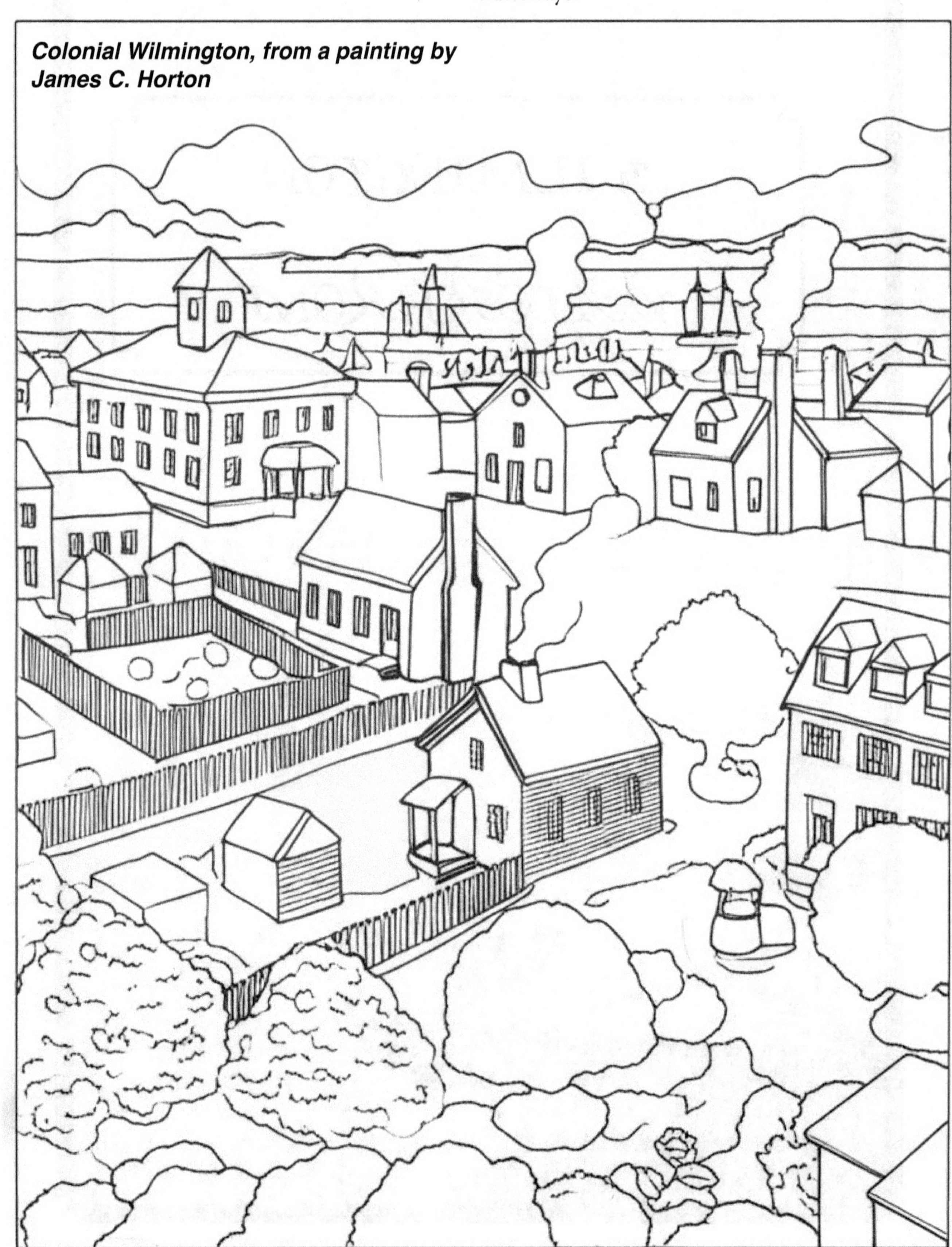

Colonial Wilmington, from a painting by James C. Horton

This image from 1900 shows a Cape Fear River so flat that it mirrors the reflections of the tall ships making their way to and from the docks at Wilmington.

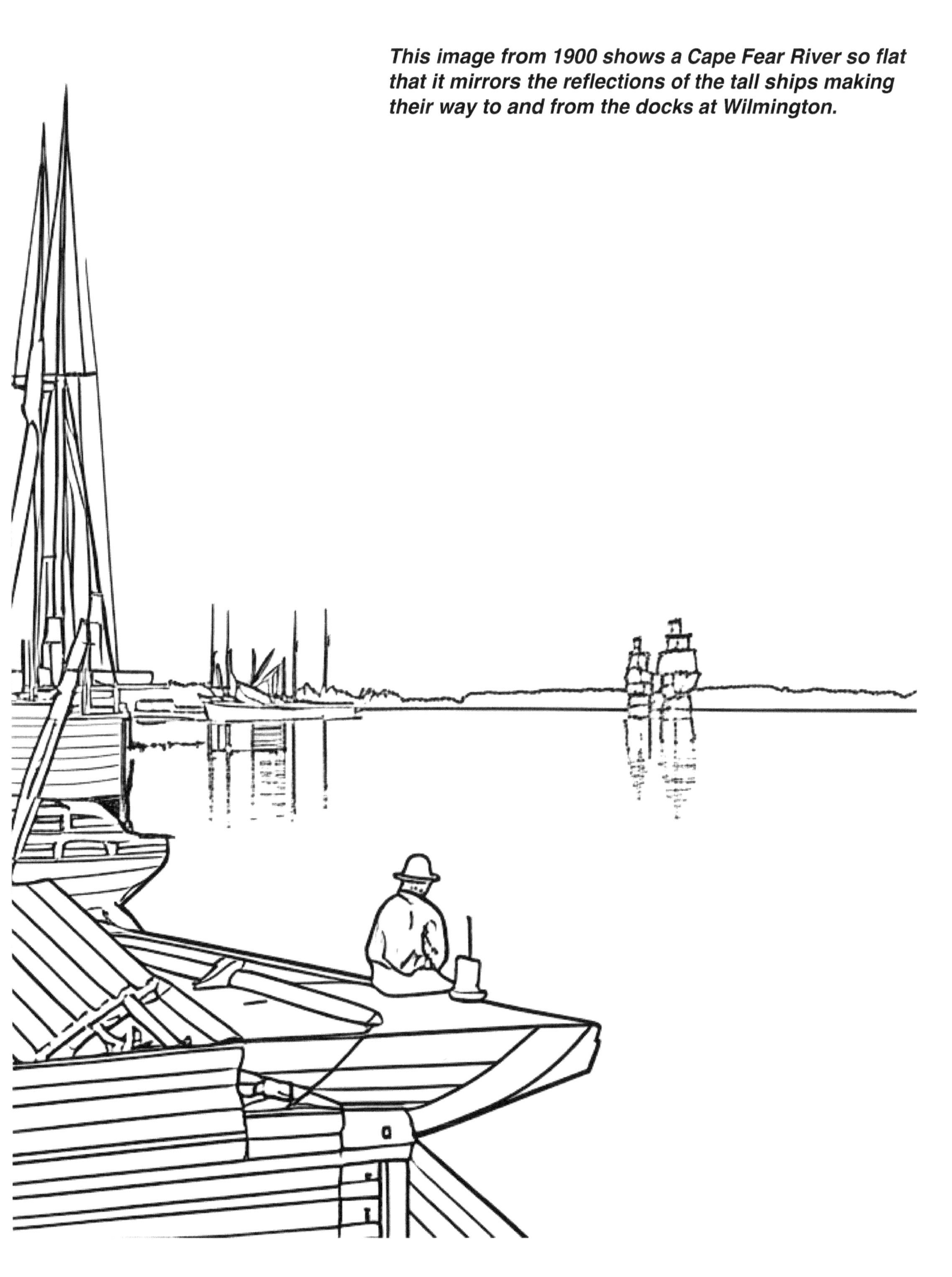

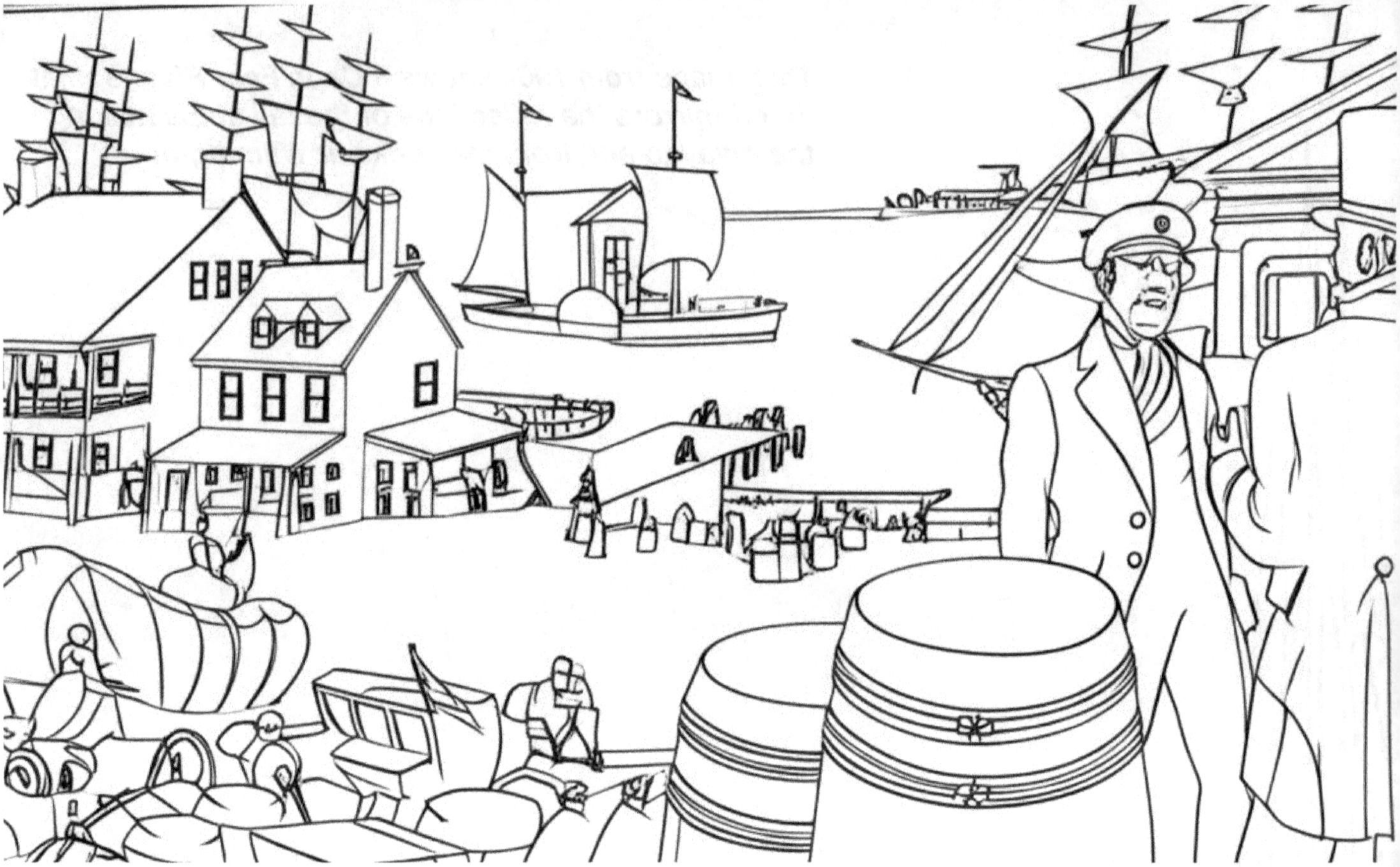

The Wilmington waterfront was once a bustliing commercial center where cargoes destined for far away places were loaded onto ships, while imported cargo was unloaded and either carted away for land-bound merchants, or loaded onto river steamers for destinations further up the Cape Fear like Fayetteville.

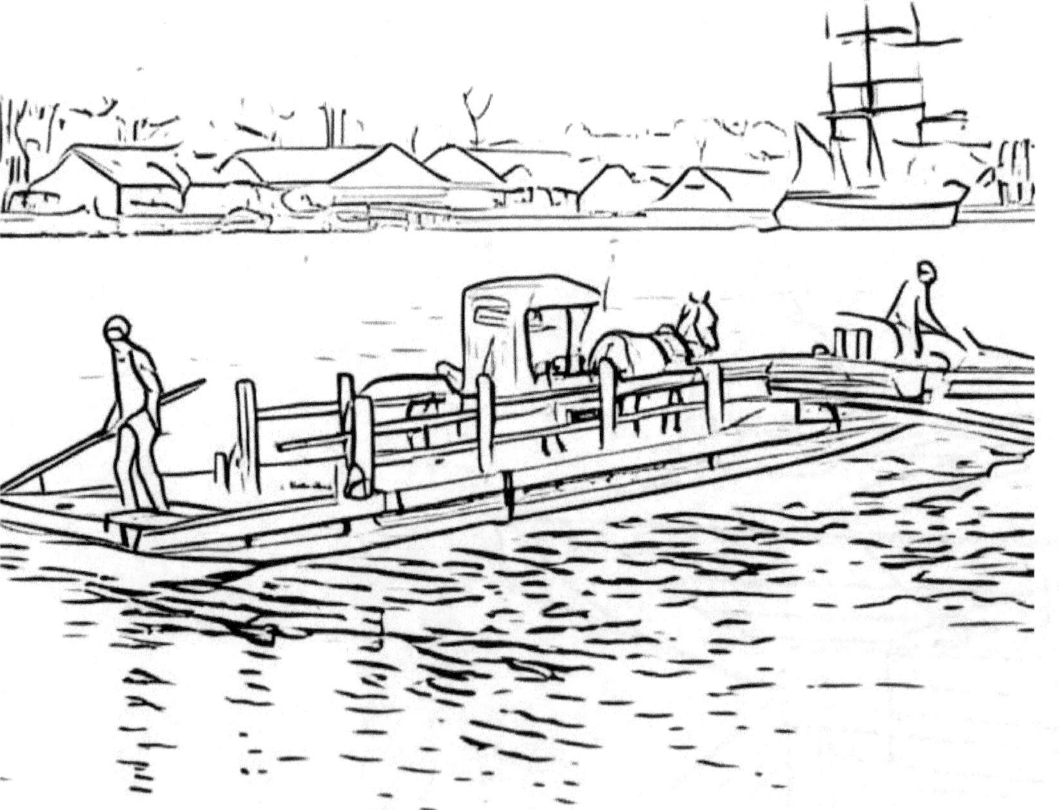

Until the completion of the Thomas S. Rhodes Bridge in the early 20th century, the only way to cross the Cape Fear River was by ferry (left).

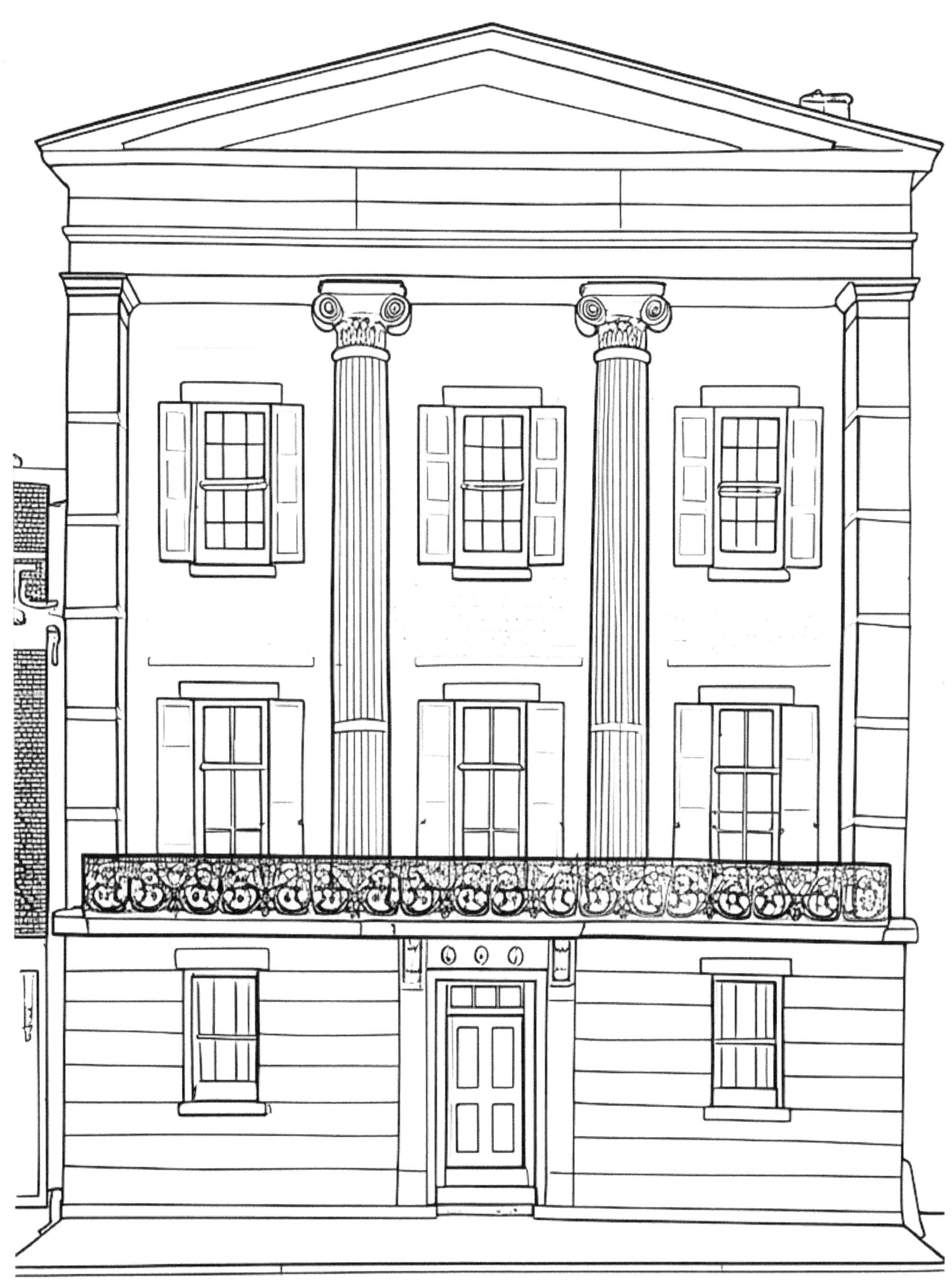

At the corner of Market and Water Streets once stood the U.S. Customs House. When the Alton Lennon Federal Building was built to replace it, architects intentionally designed the new building to resemble the facade of the old Customs House.

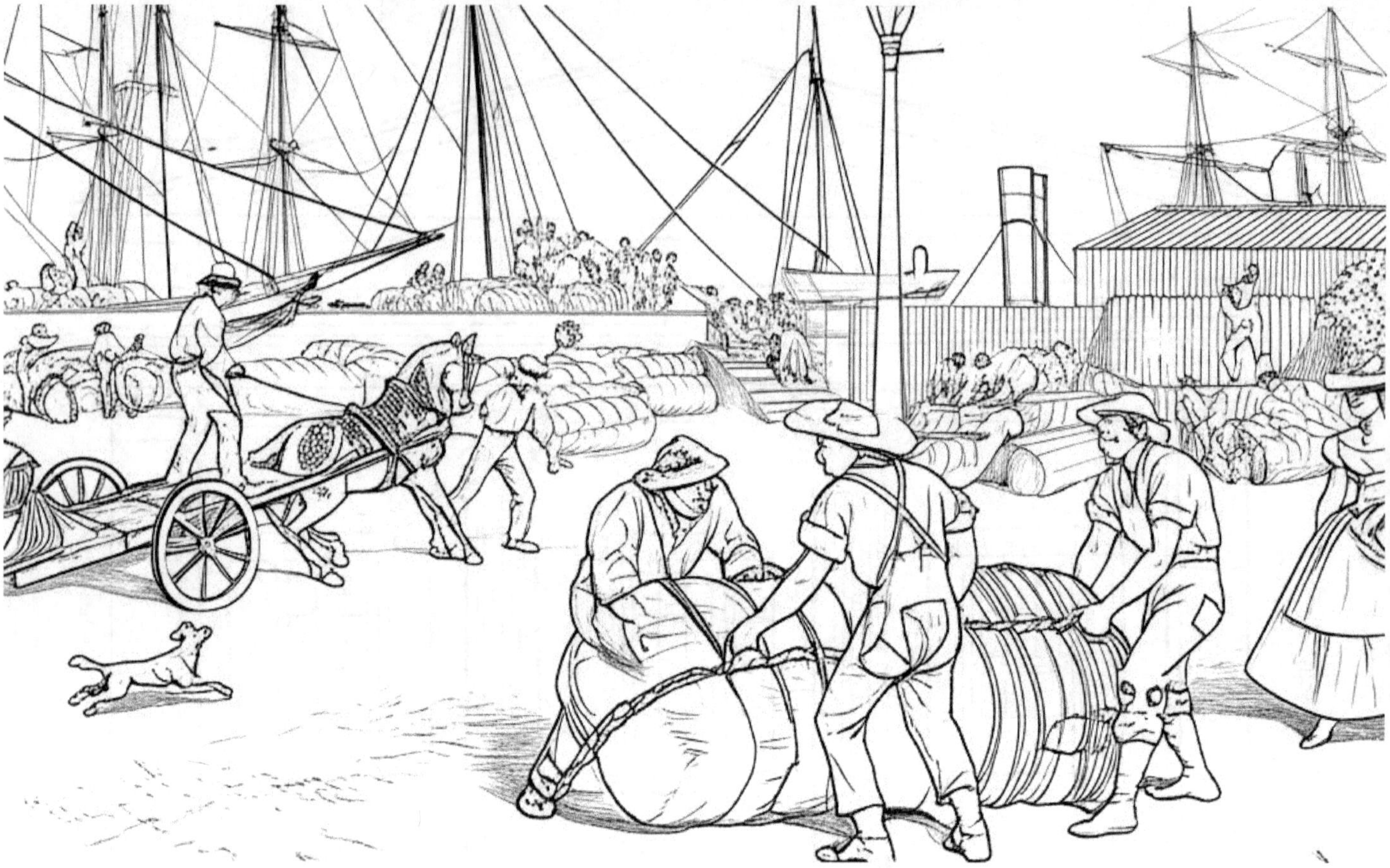

More scenes of Wilmington's working waterfront. The first depicts cotton being loaded onto ships during the Civil War era (above). The other shows Wilmington in the earlier Antebellum Era (below).

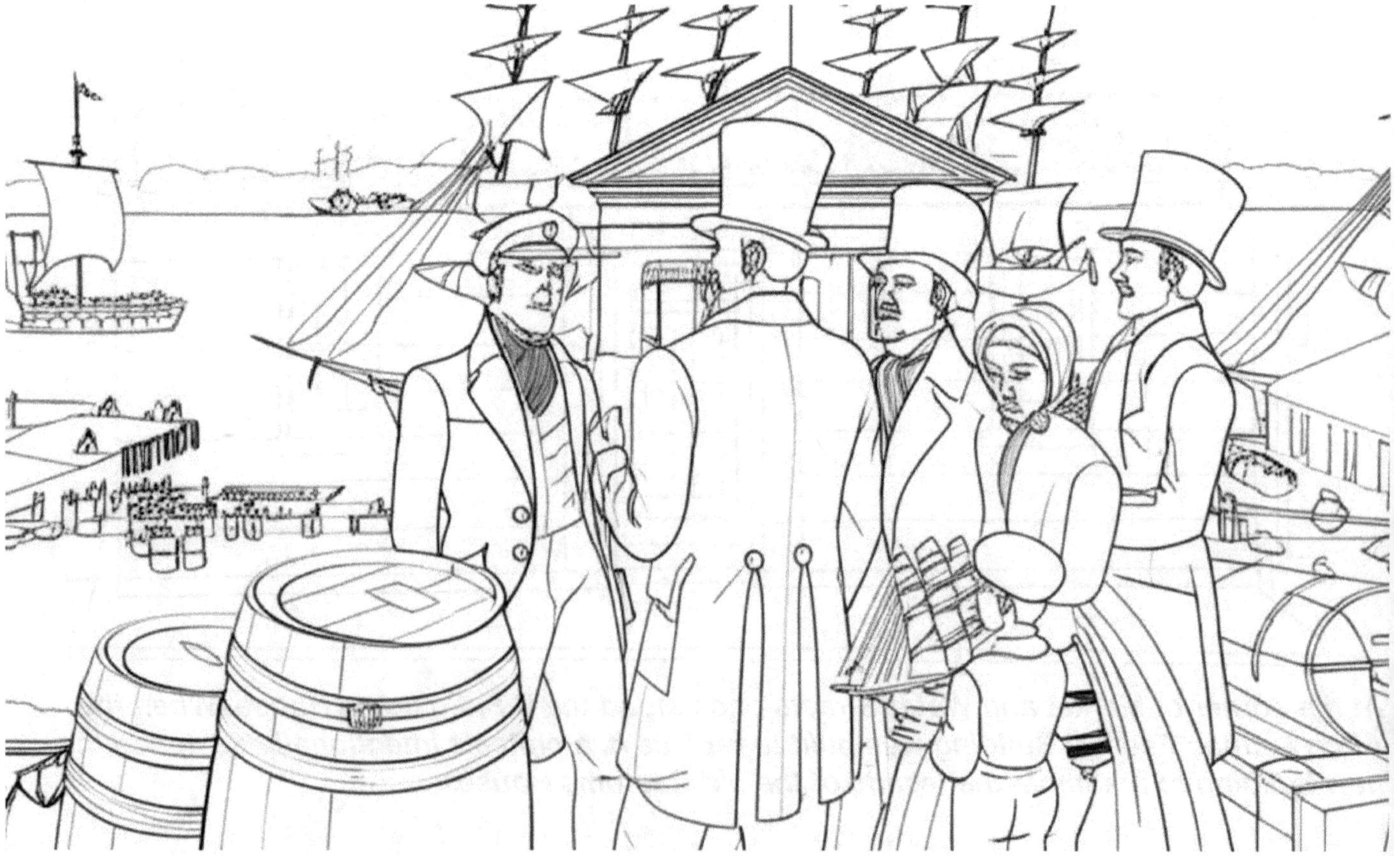

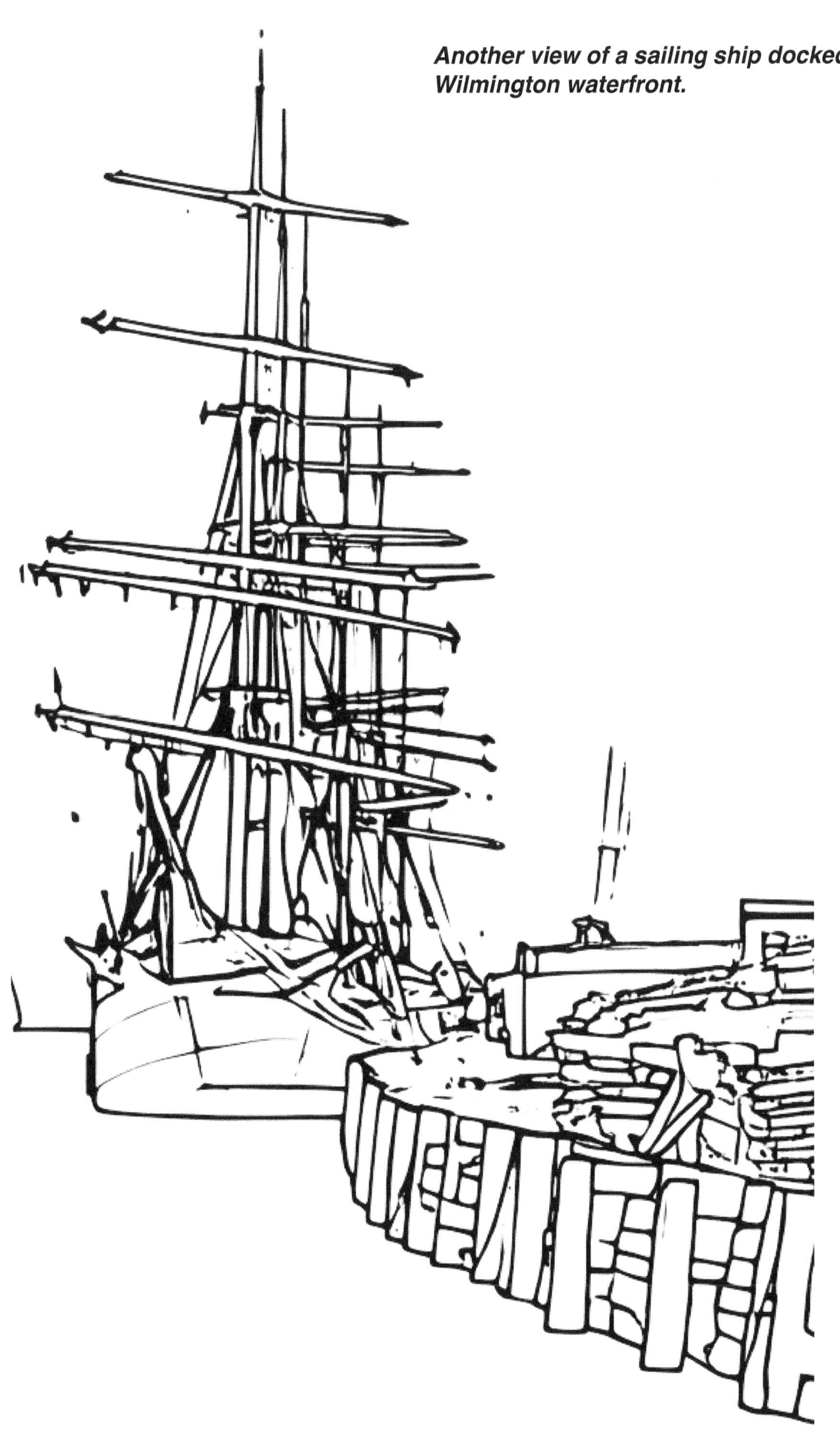

Another view of a sailing ship docked at the Wilmington waterfront.

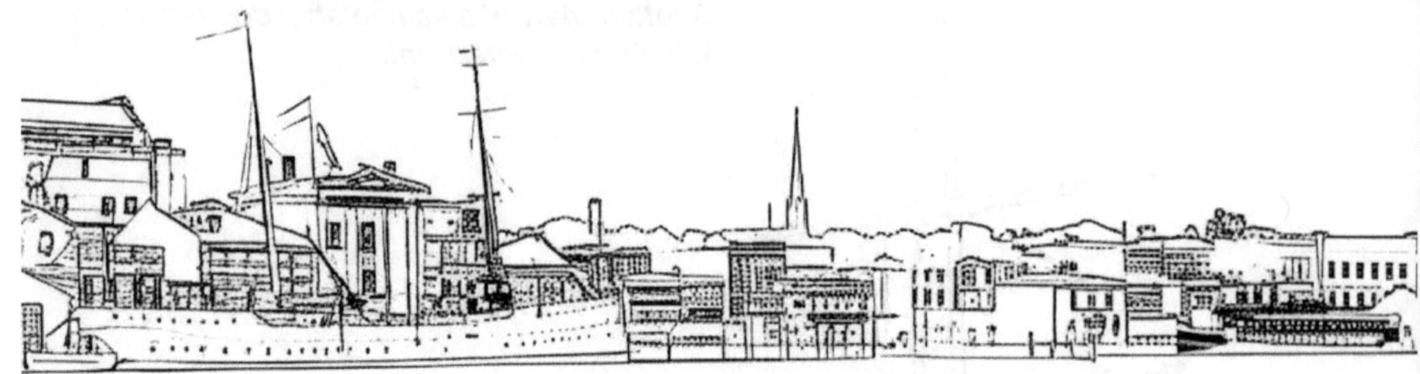

Two views of Wilmington's waterfront in the early 1900s. Notice the U.S. Revenue Cutter docked in front of the Customs House, and the many buildings and warehouses that occupied what is now Water Street. Unlike today, businesses existed along the riverfront on Eagles Island too, catering to marine trades like shipbuilding and shipping.

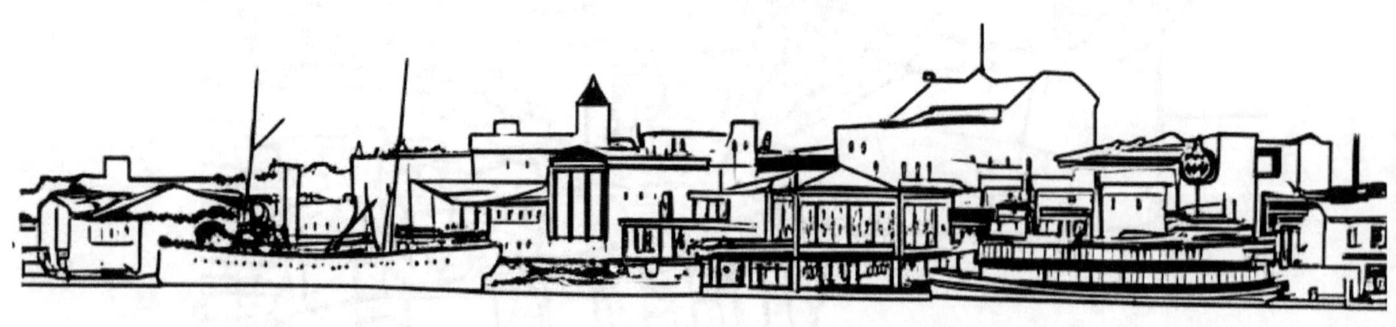

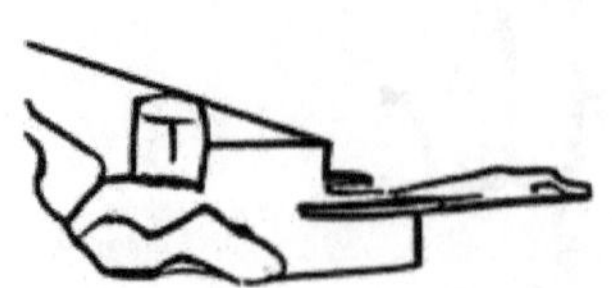

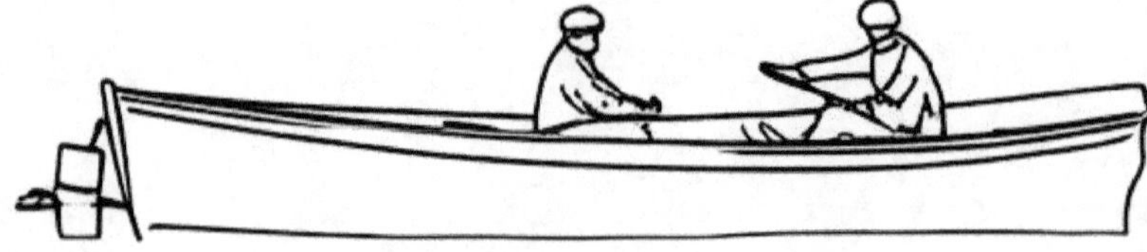

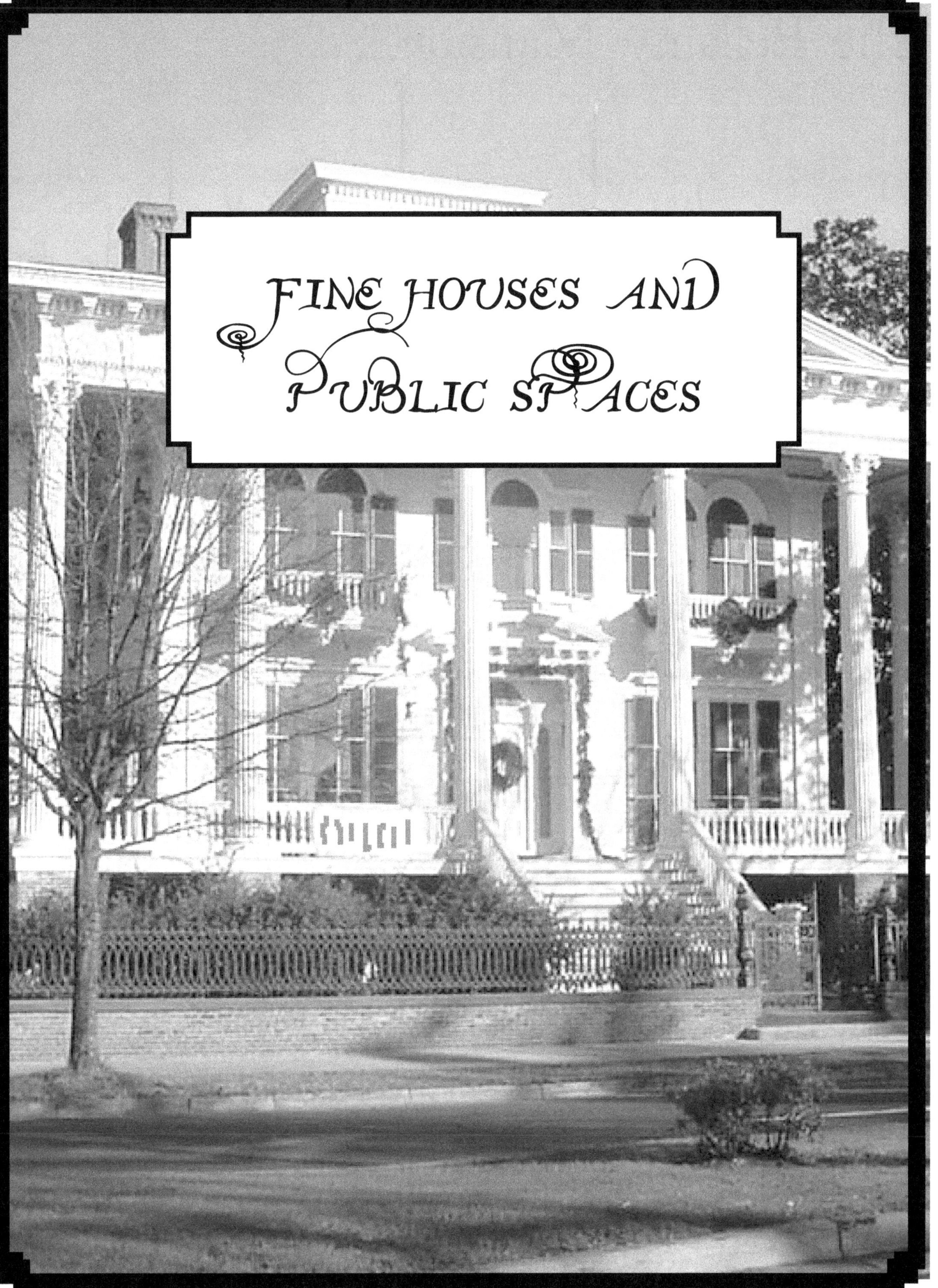

Fine Houses and Public Spaces

The Bellamy Mansion...

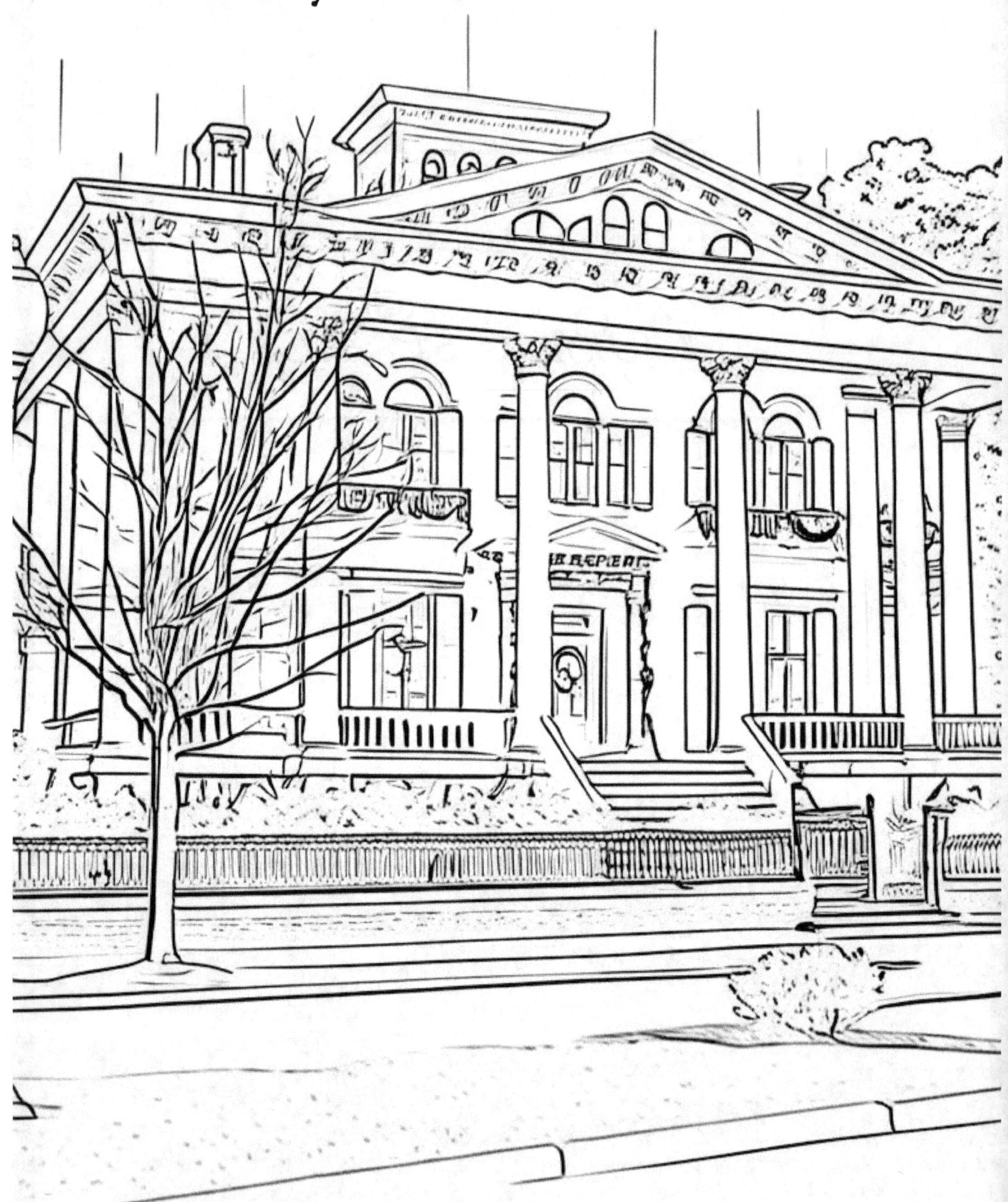

The Bellamy Mansion is an iconic landmark in downtown Wilmington, located at the corner of Fifth and Market Streets.

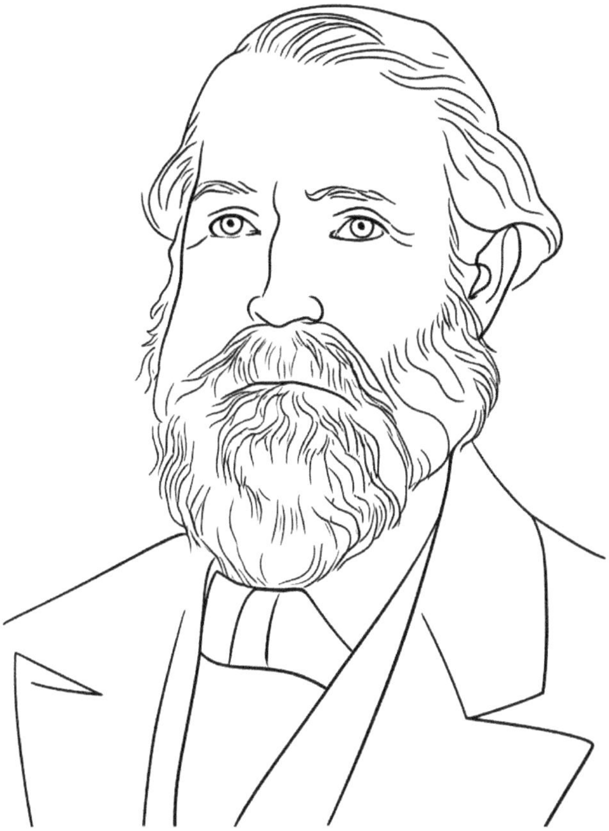

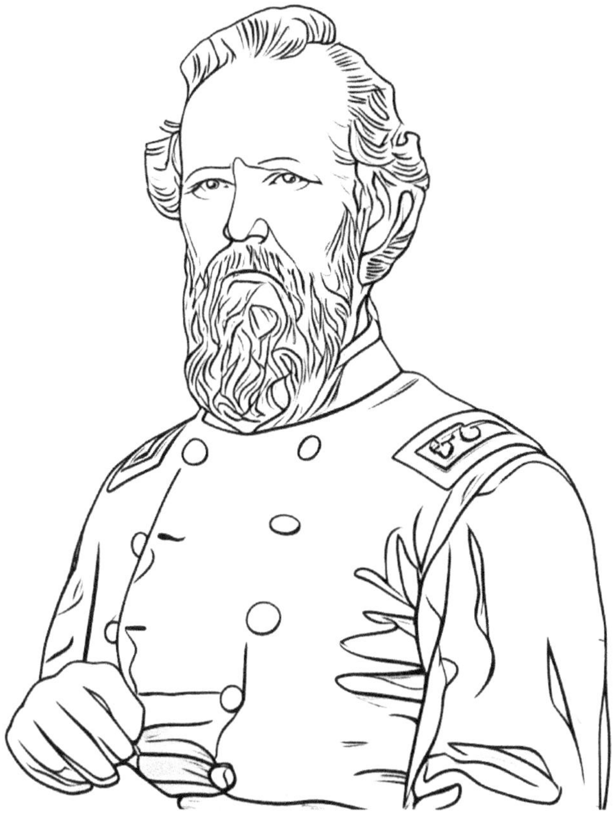

Built by Dr. John D. Bellamy (top left) on the eve of the Civil War, the Bellamy Mansion is one of Wilmington's best examples of antebellum architecture. The house and grounds are a landmark in the city, open for tours and telling the story of the Wilmington before, during, and after the Civil War. Dr. Bellamy was an ardent supporter of secession, so when the war ended he had to travel to Washington, D.C. to personally make the loyalty oath in front of President Andrew Johnson before he was allowed to reclaim his confiscated property, including the mansion. In the meantime, Union Gen. Joseph P. Hawley commandeered the house and used it as a headquarters for troops occupying the city, and the Freedman's Bureau that helped newly freed slaves find their way in a radically different world.

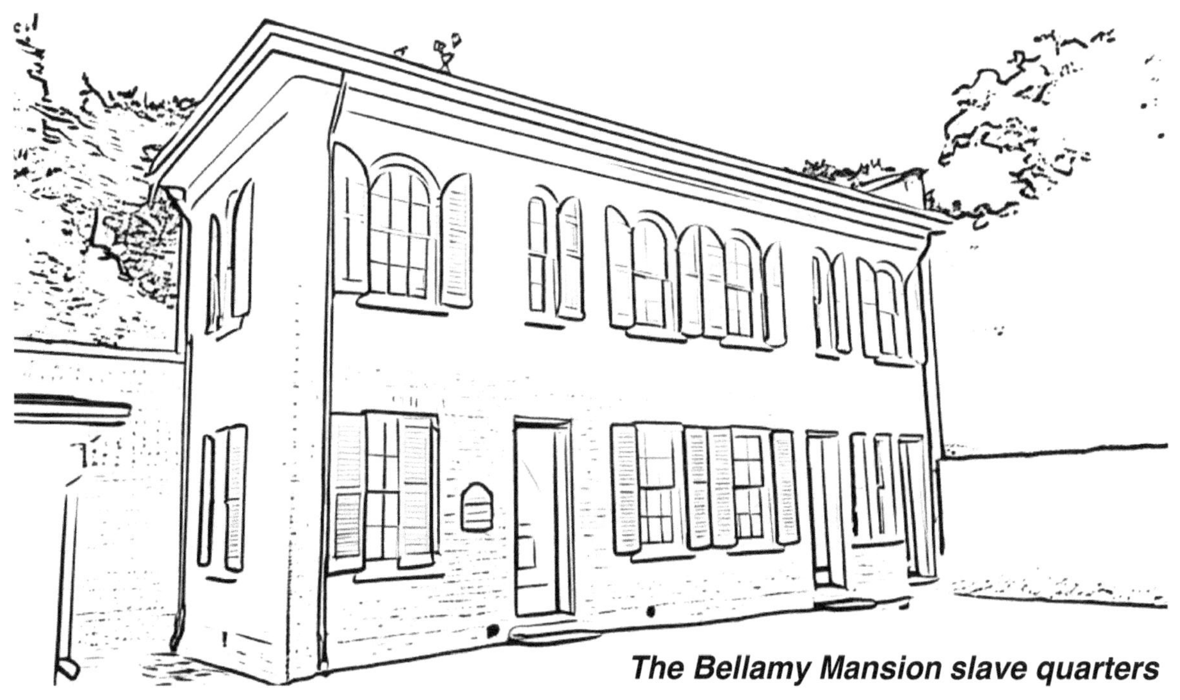

The Bellamy Mansion slave quarters

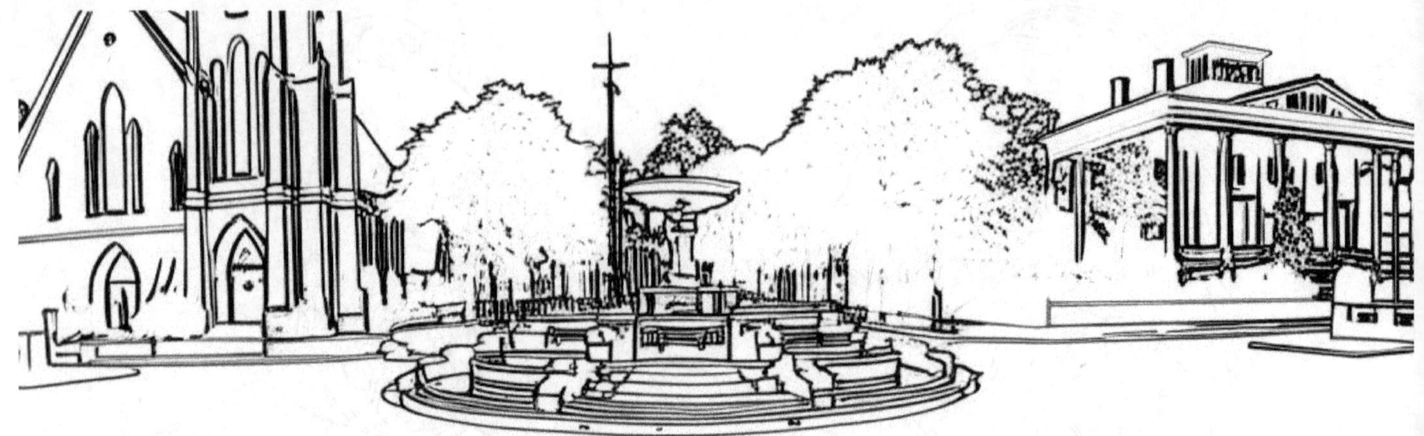

The Bellamy Mansion sits at one of the most historical intersections in Wilmington. Across the street is First Baptist Church, built in the 1850s. In the center of the intersection is the Kenan Fountain, a decorative piece of civic sculpture presented to the city by railroad magnate William Rand Kenan in 1921.

The Burgwin-Wright House...

The Burgwin-Wright House was built by merchant and planter John Burgwin in 1770. Burgwin built his fine house atop the ballast stone walls of the old city jail. The three story structure, pictured here in a sketch by Benson J. Lossing from the 1850s, is one of just four buildings dating from the colonial days left in Wilmington.

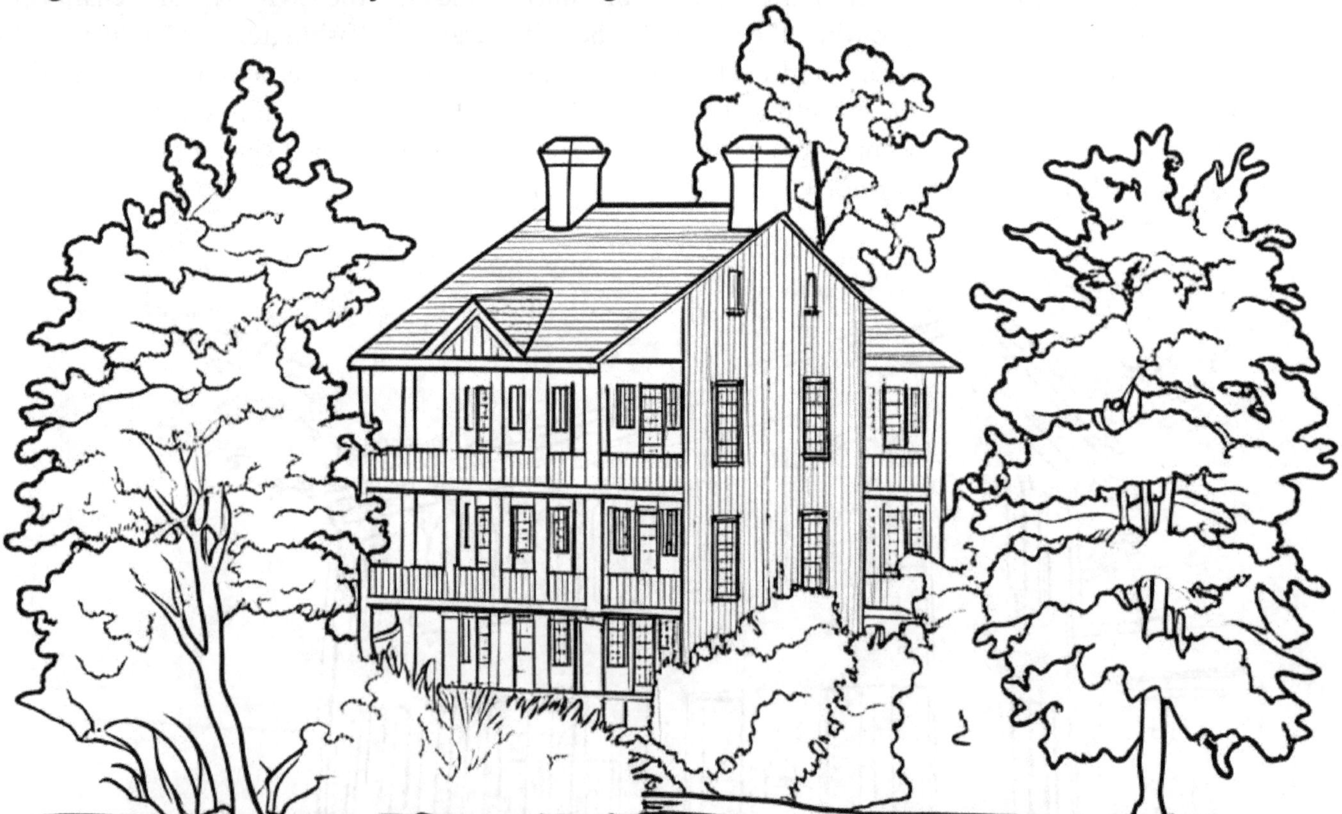

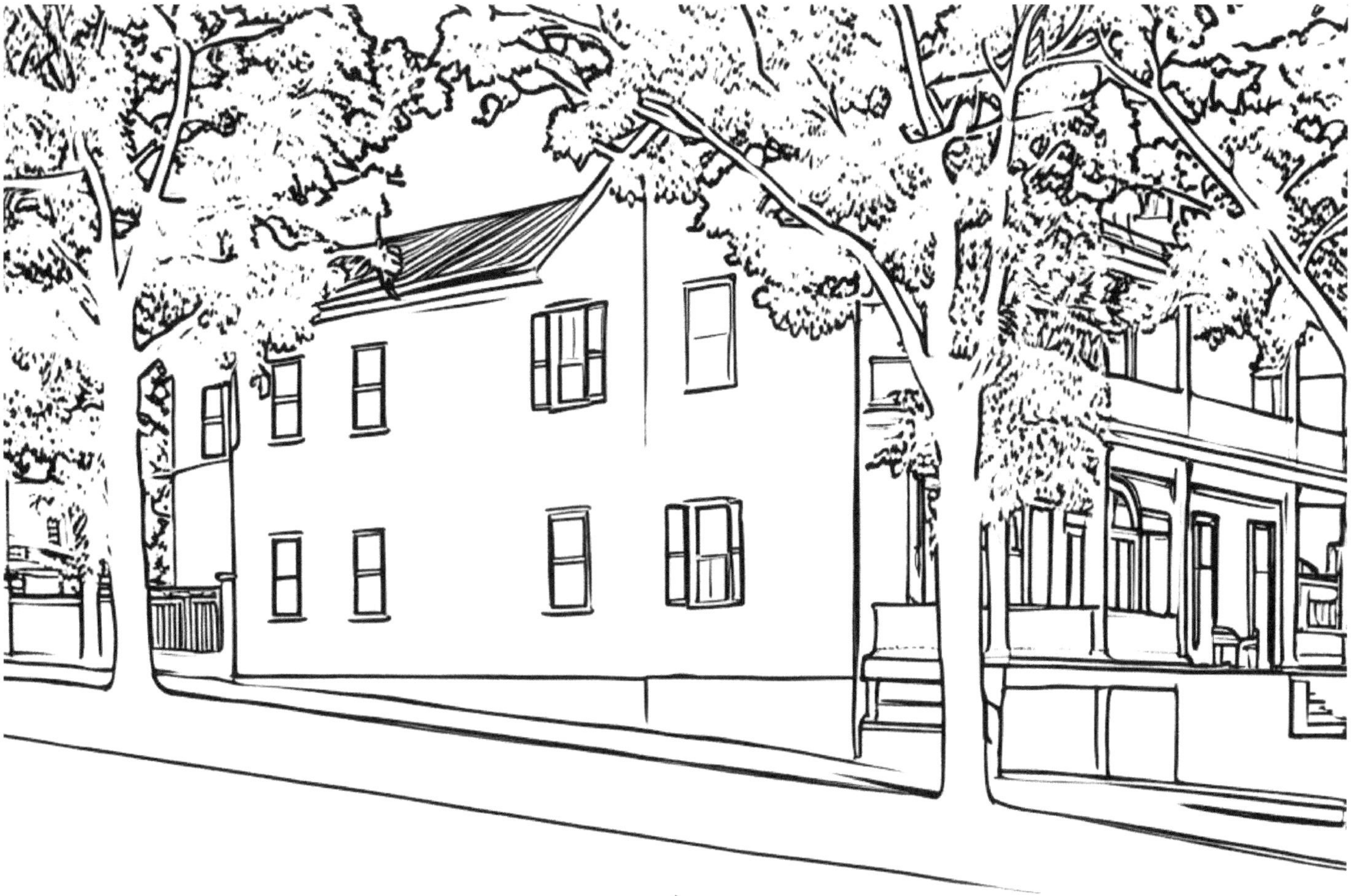

The above view of the Burgwin-Wright House from 1900 shows the side of the house along Third Street. John Burgwin (right), was an English merchant and planter who moved to Wilmington from Charleston, S.C. in the 1750s. Burgwin married Margaret Haynes and eventually inherited Castle Haynes from her family. John Burgwin also owned a plantation called The Hermitage on Prince George's Creek. A loyalist in the war for American independence, Burgwin left Wilmington for what he said were medical reasons and stayed in England for the rest of the war, except for a short visit in 1777. After the war was over, Burgwin and his family moved back to Wilmington permanently in 1784. He was well thought of enough that he was allowed to reclaim his property, unlike most loyalists who had their holdings confiscated and sold off.

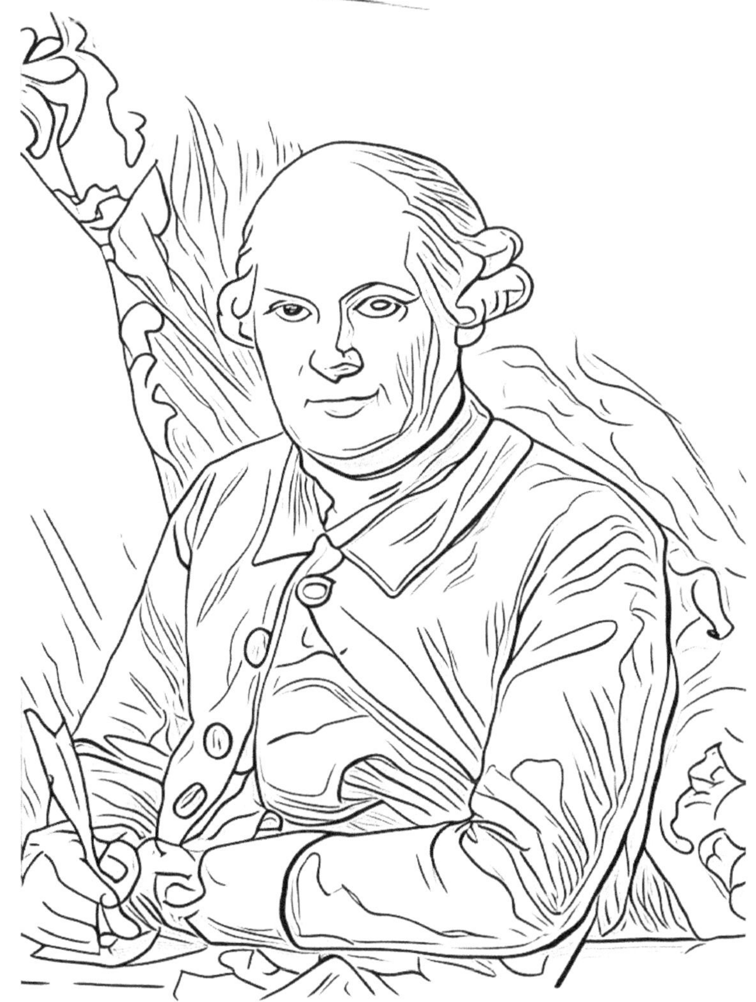

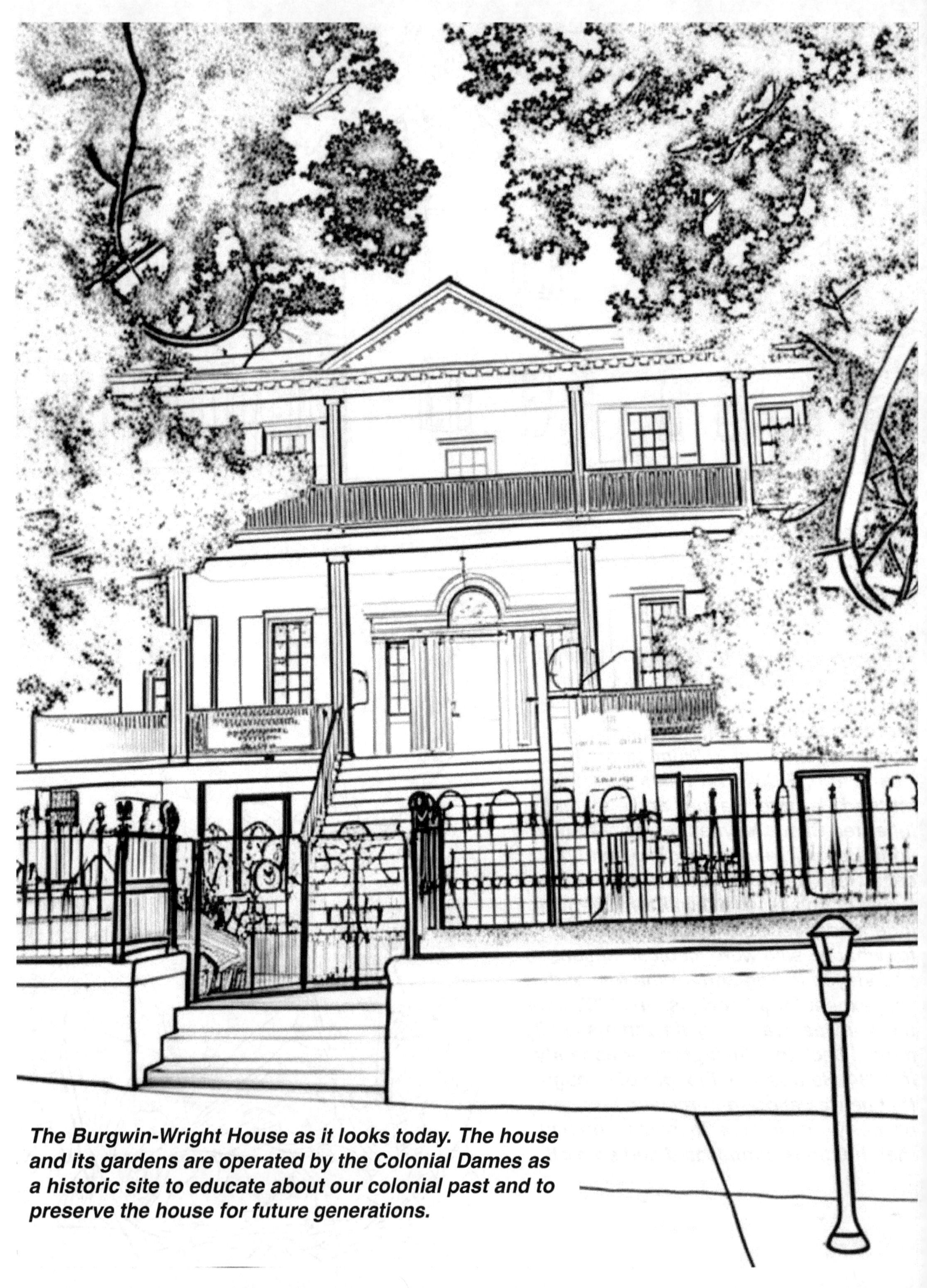

The Burgwin-Wright House as it looks today. The house and its gardens are operated by the Colonial Dames as a historic site to educate about our colonial past and to preserve the house for future generations.

The Latimer House

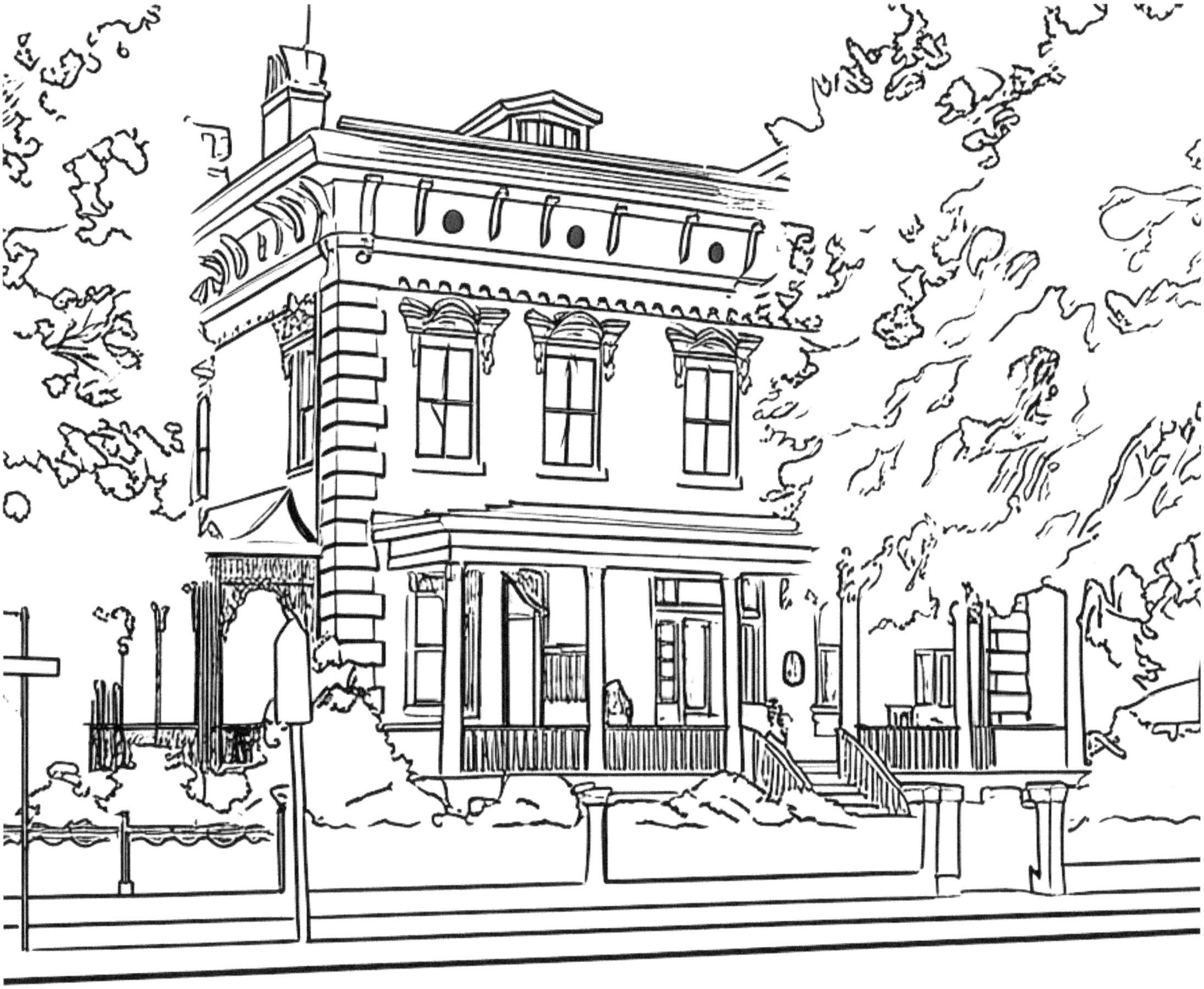

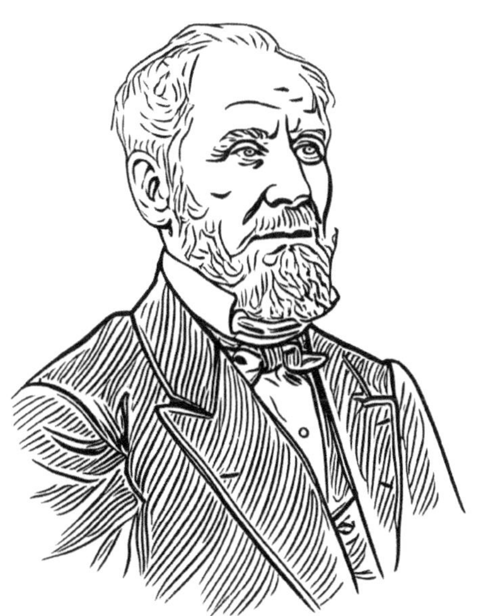

Zebulon Latimer (left) moved to Wilmington after the Civil War to take advantage of the business opportunities created by the devastation of the conflict. He built his Italianate-style home in 1852. Latimer quickly became a leading citizen and merchant, making his money in dry goods, railroads, and naval stores. His home at the corner of Third and Orange Streets is now a museum house that tells the story of the Latimer family and the lower Cape Fear. The Latimer House is the headquarters of the Lower Cape Fear Historical Society.

Clarendon & Orton Plantations

Clarendon Plantation is one of the oldest plantations that still exists along the Cape Fear River, dating from 1728.

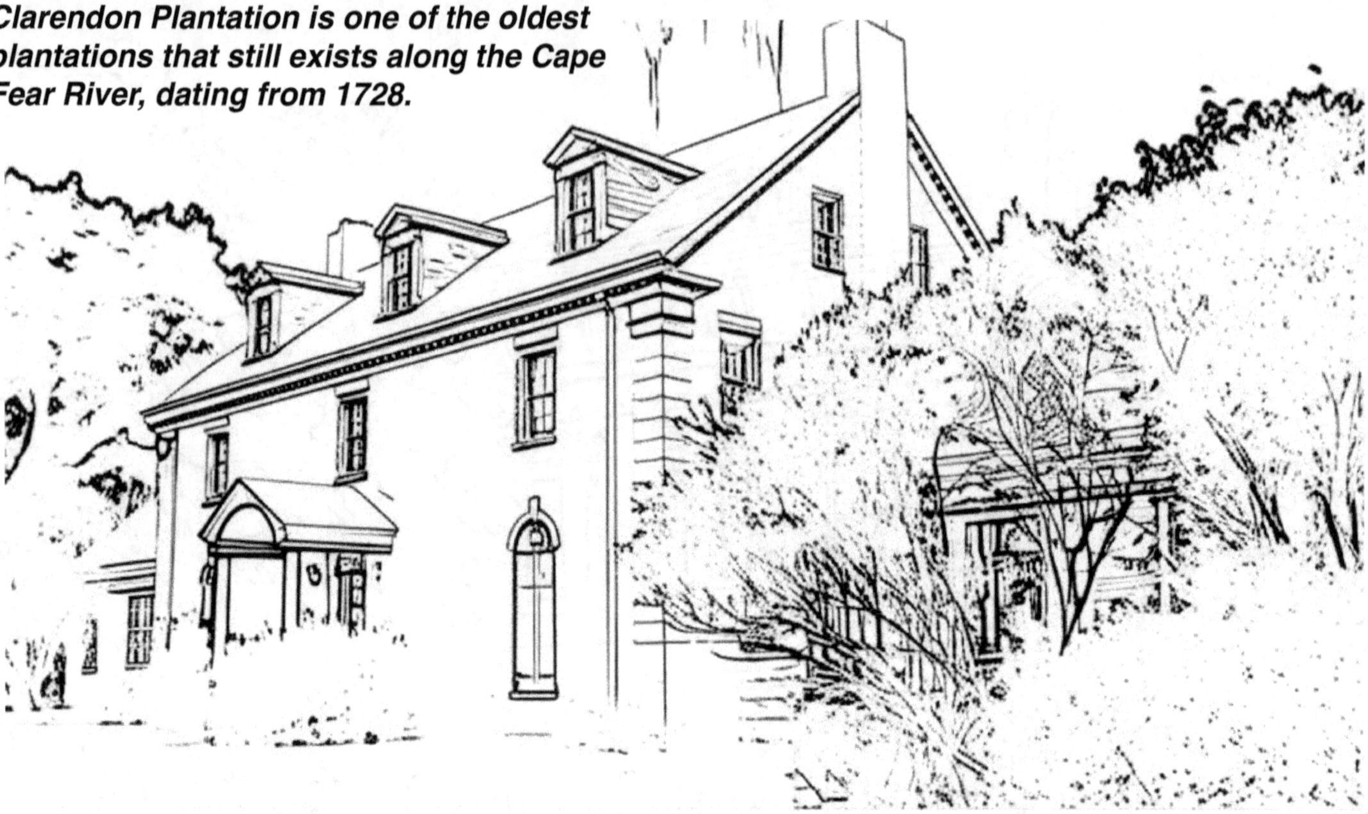

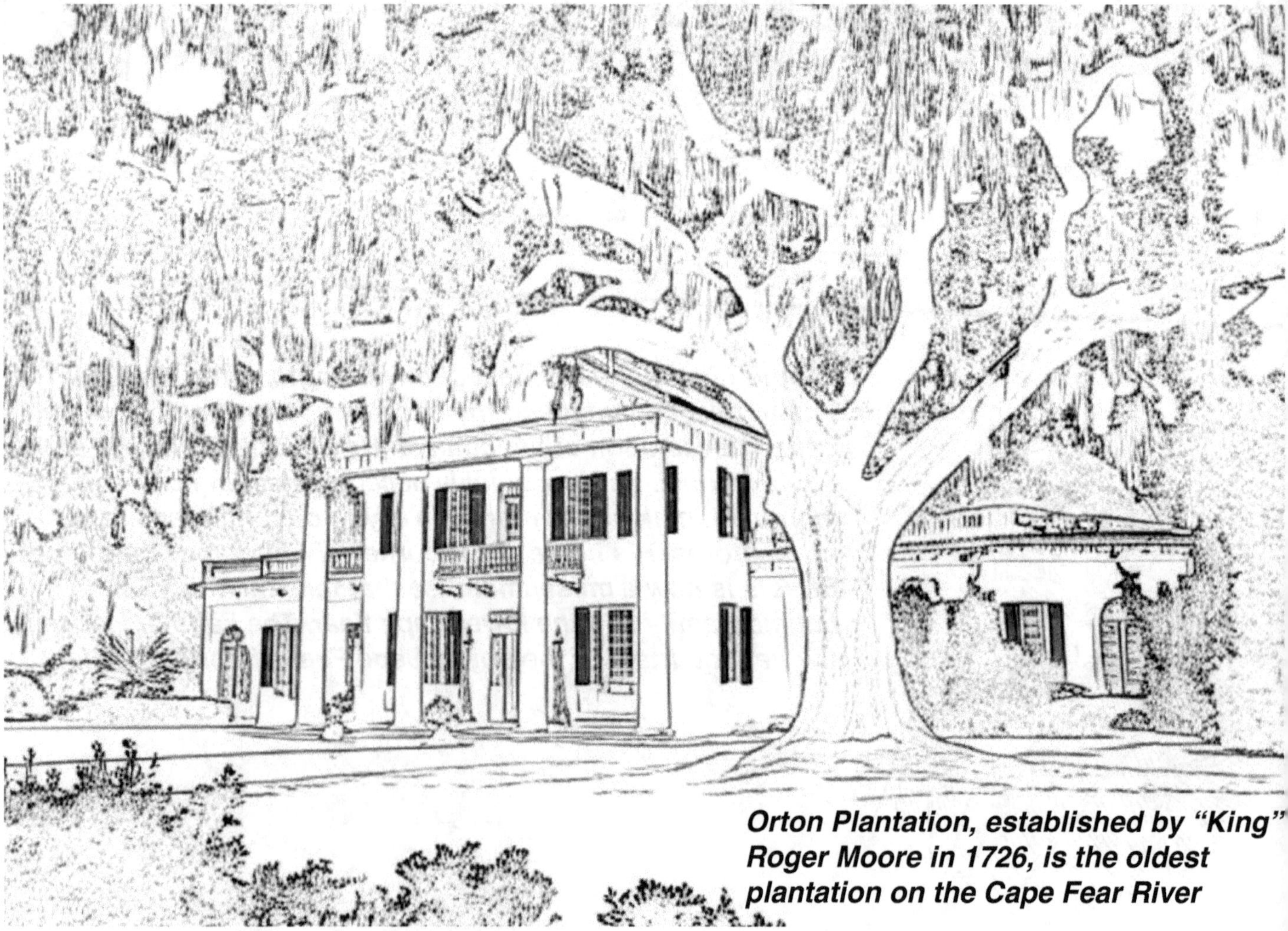

Orton Plantation, established by "King" Roger Moore in 1726, is the oldest plantation on the Cape Fear River

Poplar Grove Plantation

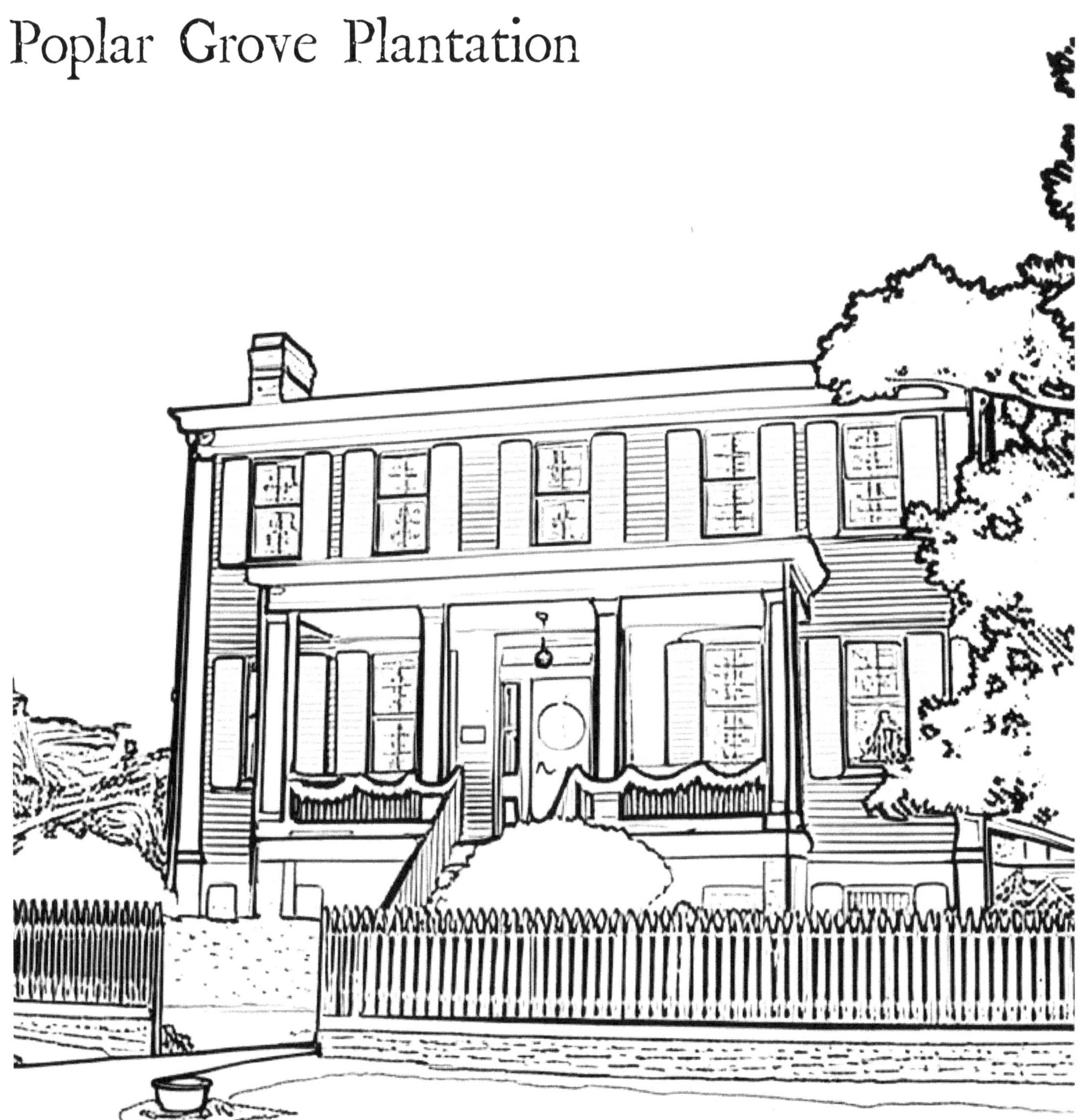

The Scotts Hill land that Poplar Grove Plantation is on was originally owned by Revolutionary War patriot Cornelius Harnett, Jr. The plantation was later owned by the Foy family, and grew peanuts and other crops. One of the Foy men was the one of only two casualties that Patriot forces suffered at the Battle of Moores Creek in 1776. James Foy, Sr. was wounded in the hand.

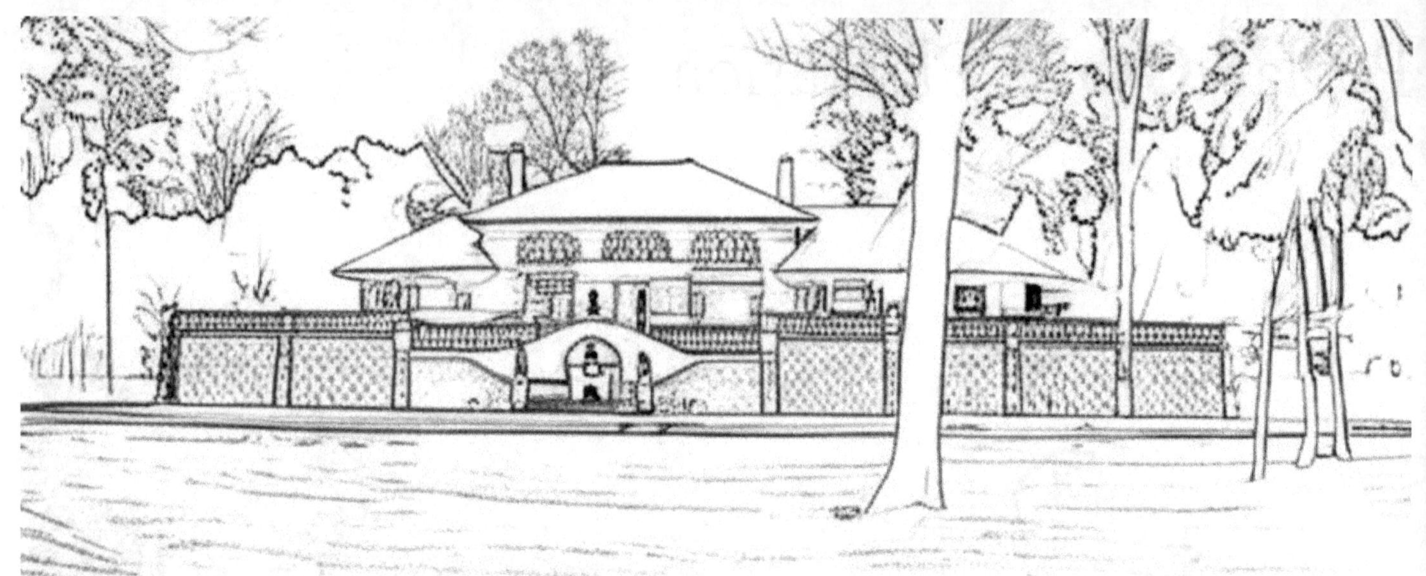

Railroad investor and industrialist J. Pembroke Jones was raised by a maternal aunt in Wilmington, N.C., but during the Gilded Age he and his wife, Sarah, rose to prominence among upper class northern elites by virtue of their entertaining acumen. On the land that Landfall now occupies, Jones built what he called a "hunting lodge" that was far more elaborate than most people's homes. The grounds included pools and fountains, and a pergola (pictured below). The Jones estate was the scene of some of the grandest parties ever thrown in the Cape Fear, with celebrities and notables attending from as far away as New York City, Boston, and Newport. It is said that the phrase, "keeping up with the Joneses" refers to the trendsetting Pembroke and Sarah.

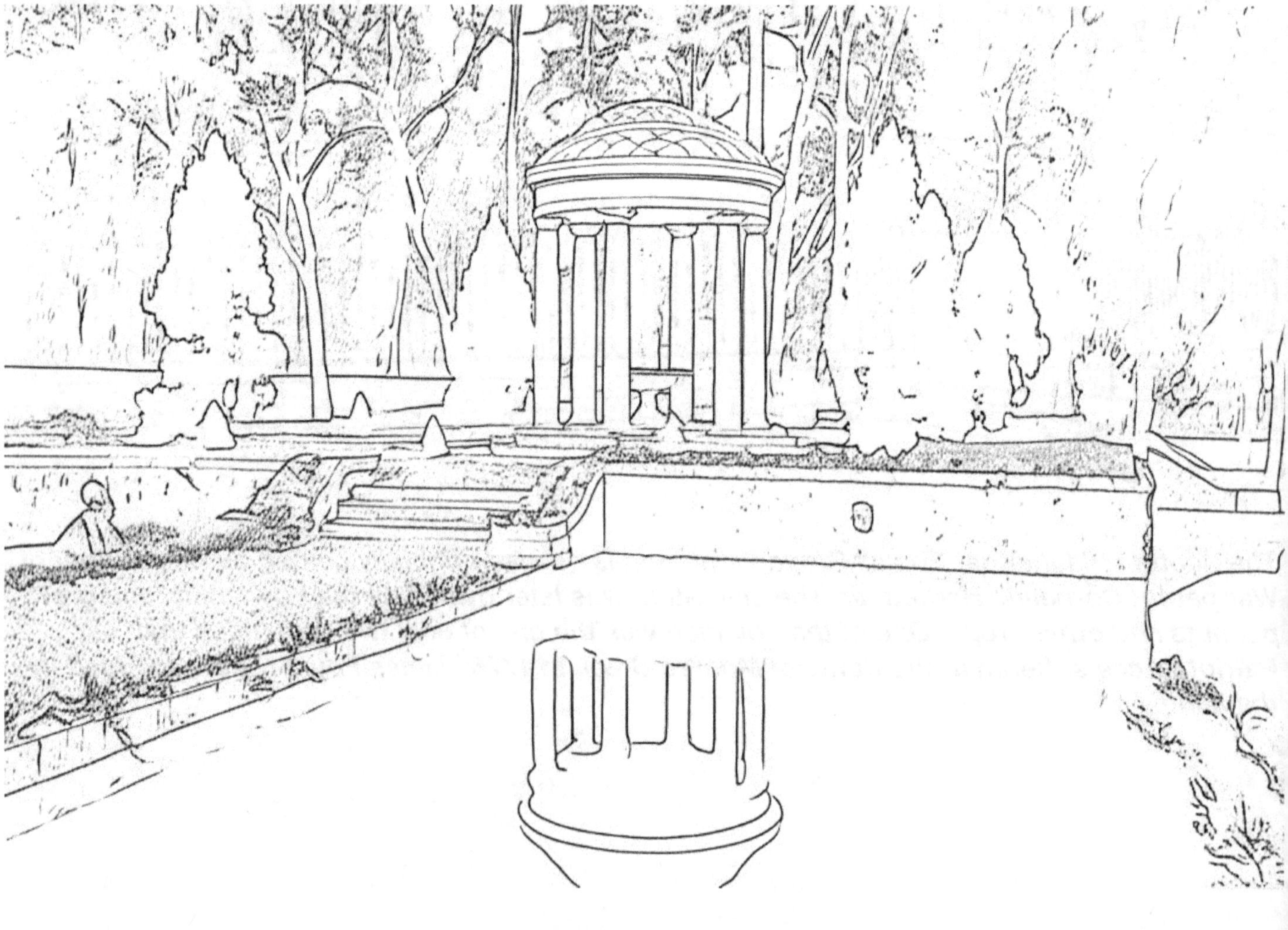

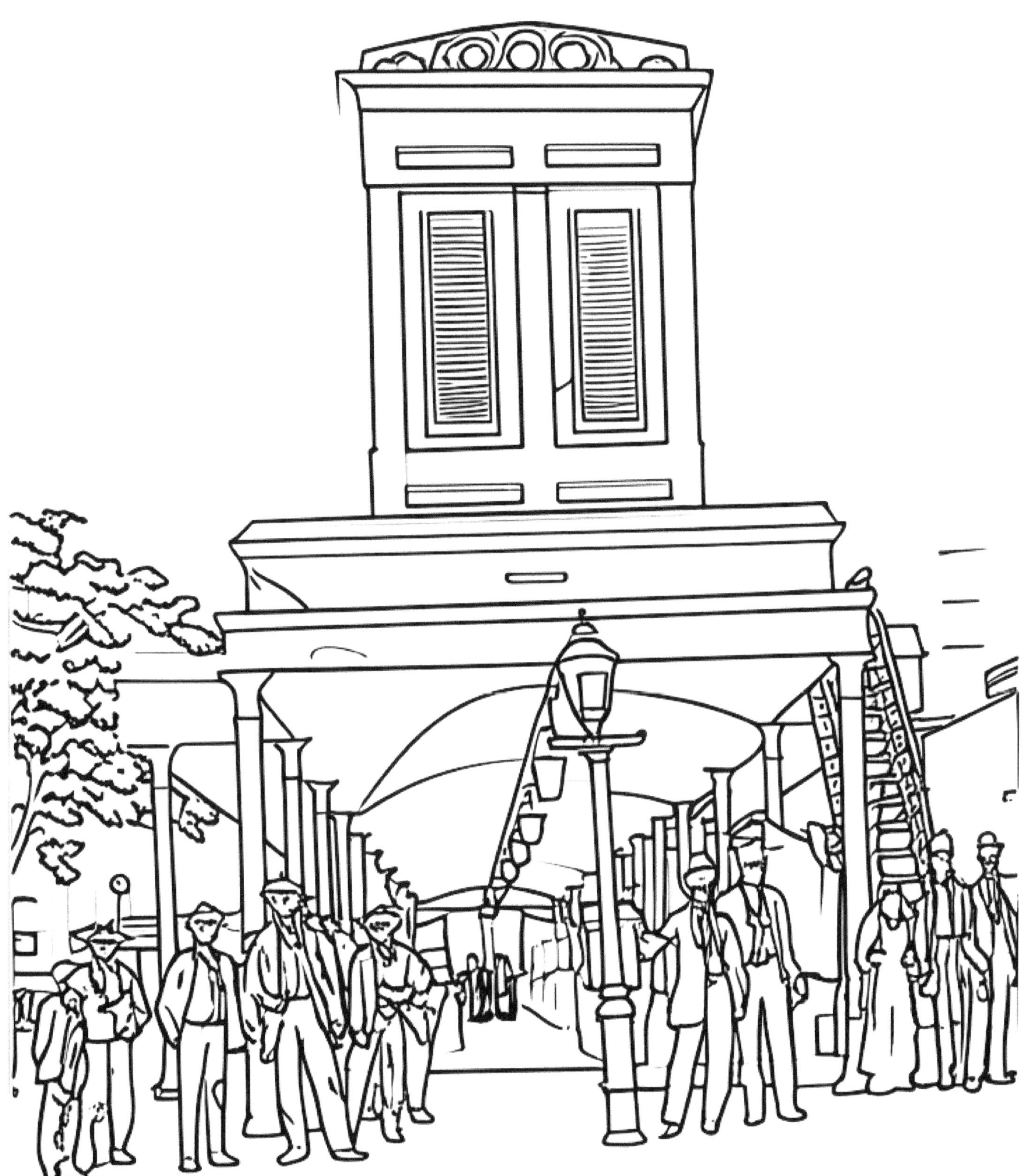

The Old Market House used to sit in the middle of Market Street between Front and Water Streets. An open air market where farmers and vendors could display their wares to their customers, the building also was the site of slave auctions before 1865.

Thalian Hall

Thalian Hall is one of the most historic theaters in the nation, housing what is believed to be the country's first amateur theatrical group, the Thalian Association.

Thalian Hall as seen in 1899.

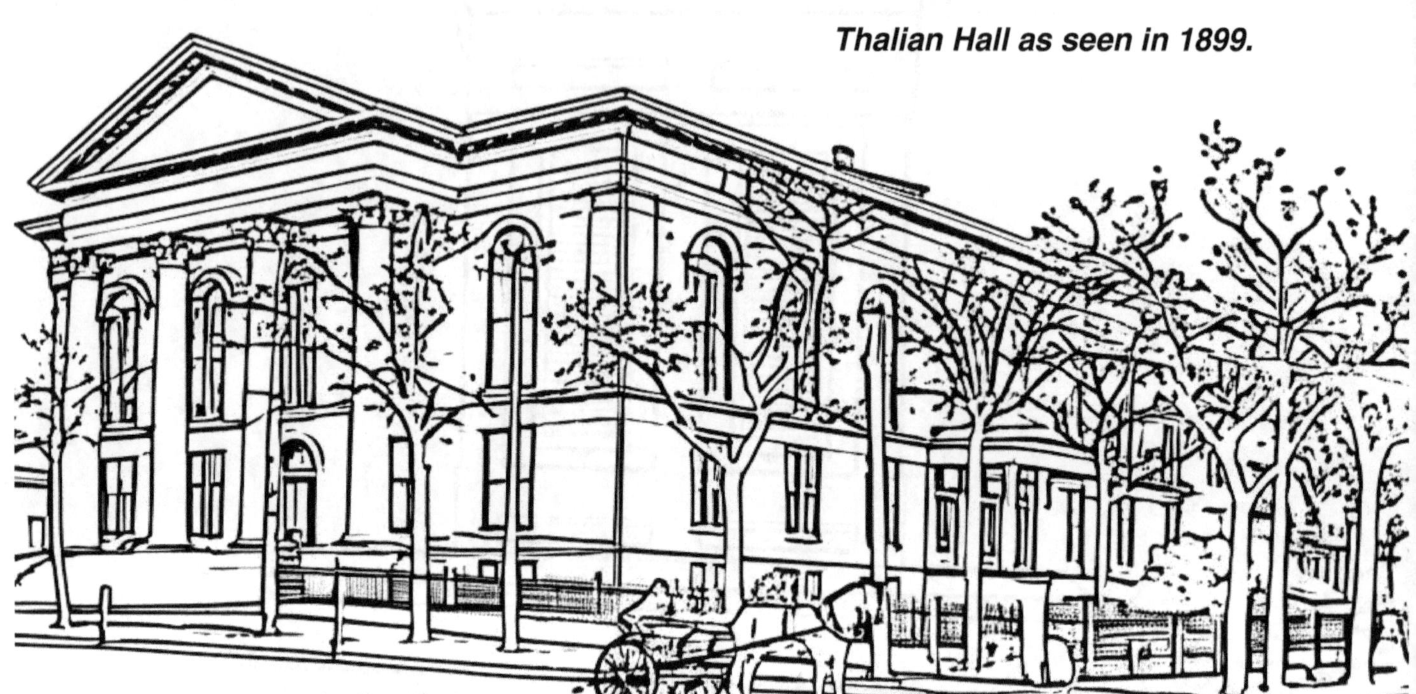

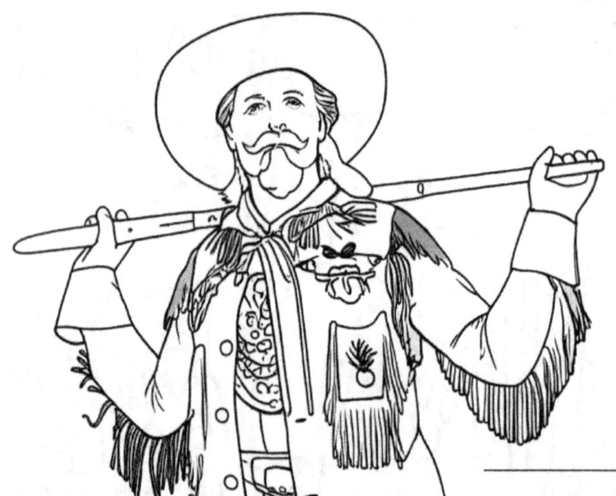

The theater shared space with the Wilmington City Hall until 2025, when the city offices and Council Chamber moved to the site of the former PPD building by the river.

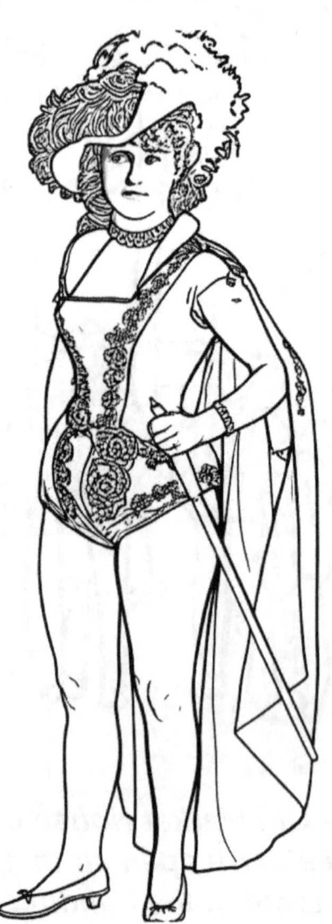

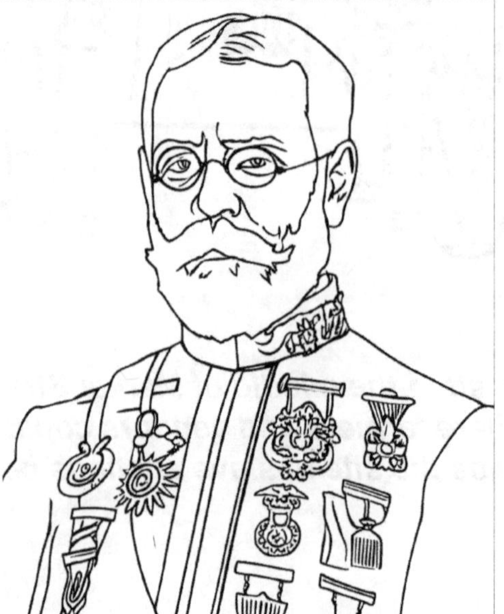

Among the many notable performers who walked the stage at Thalian Hall are William F. "Buffalo Bill" Cody (above), march composer and director of the U.S. Marine Corps Band John Phillip Sousa (right), and the "Swedish Nightingale" Jenny Lind (far right).

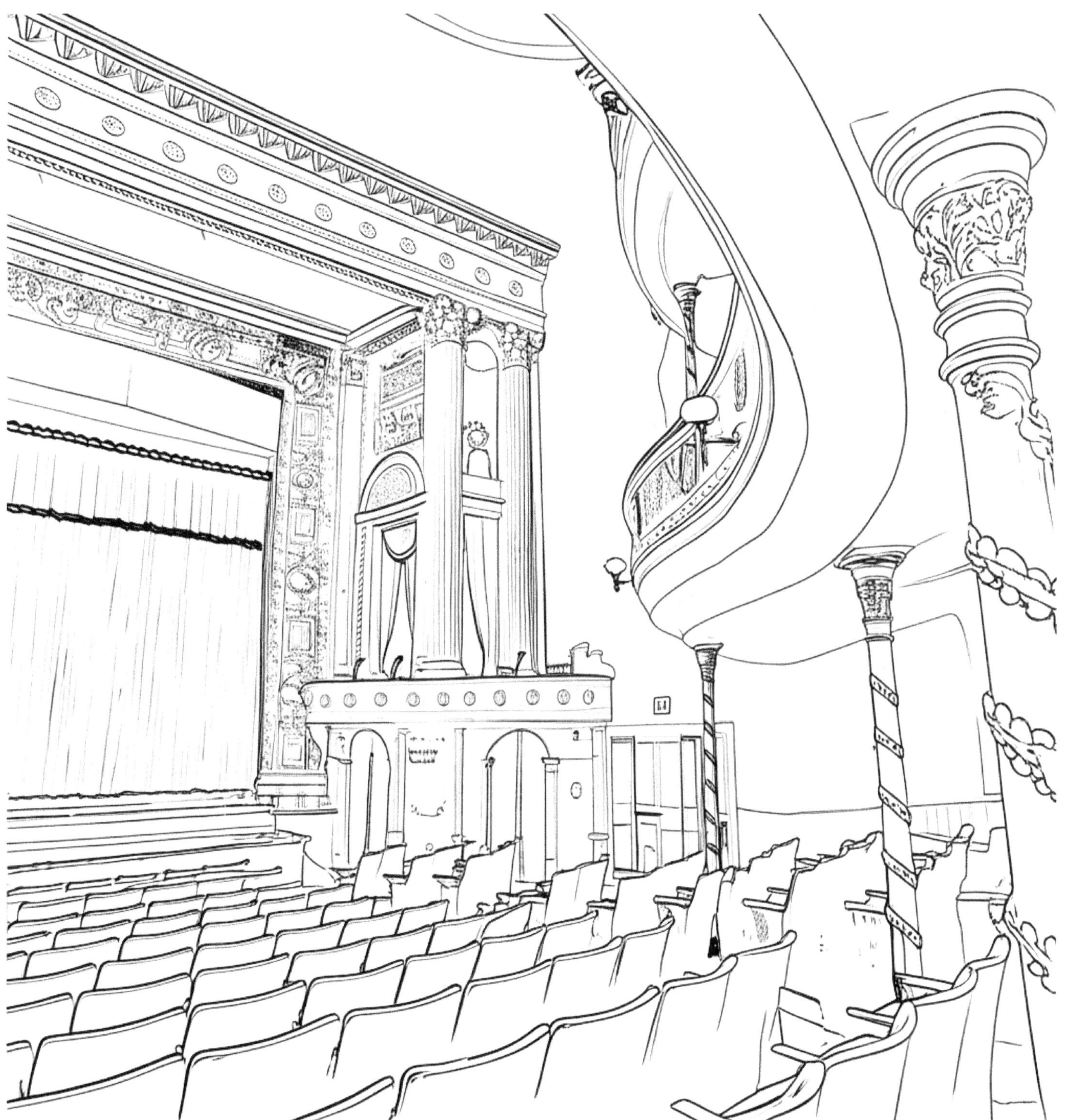

The ornate interior of Thalian Hall is a throwback to the entertainment palaces of days gone by, when going to the theater was an event.

At the Movies

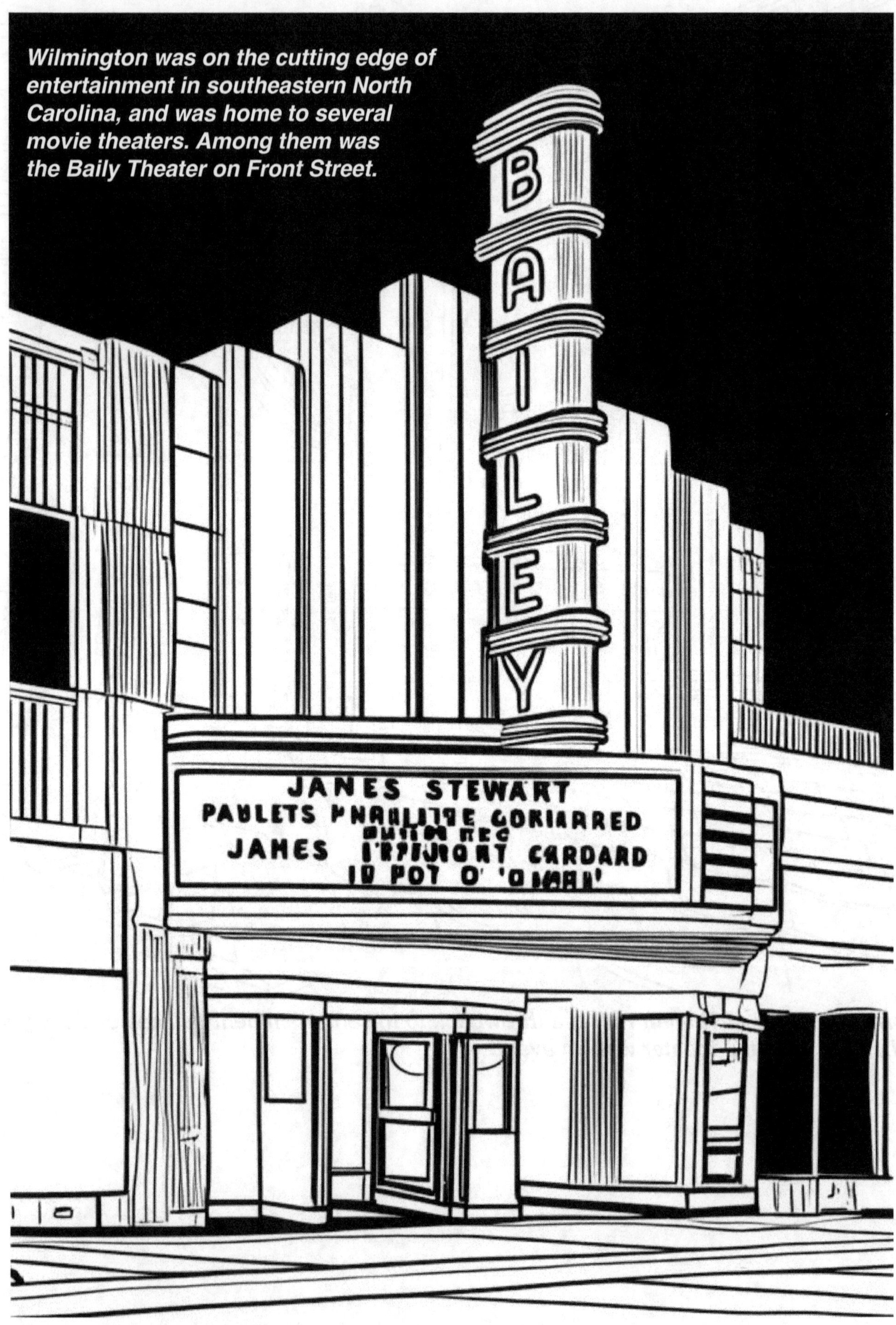

Wilmington was on the cutting edge of entertainment in southeastern North Carolina, and was home to several movie theaters. Among them was the Baily Theater on Front Street.

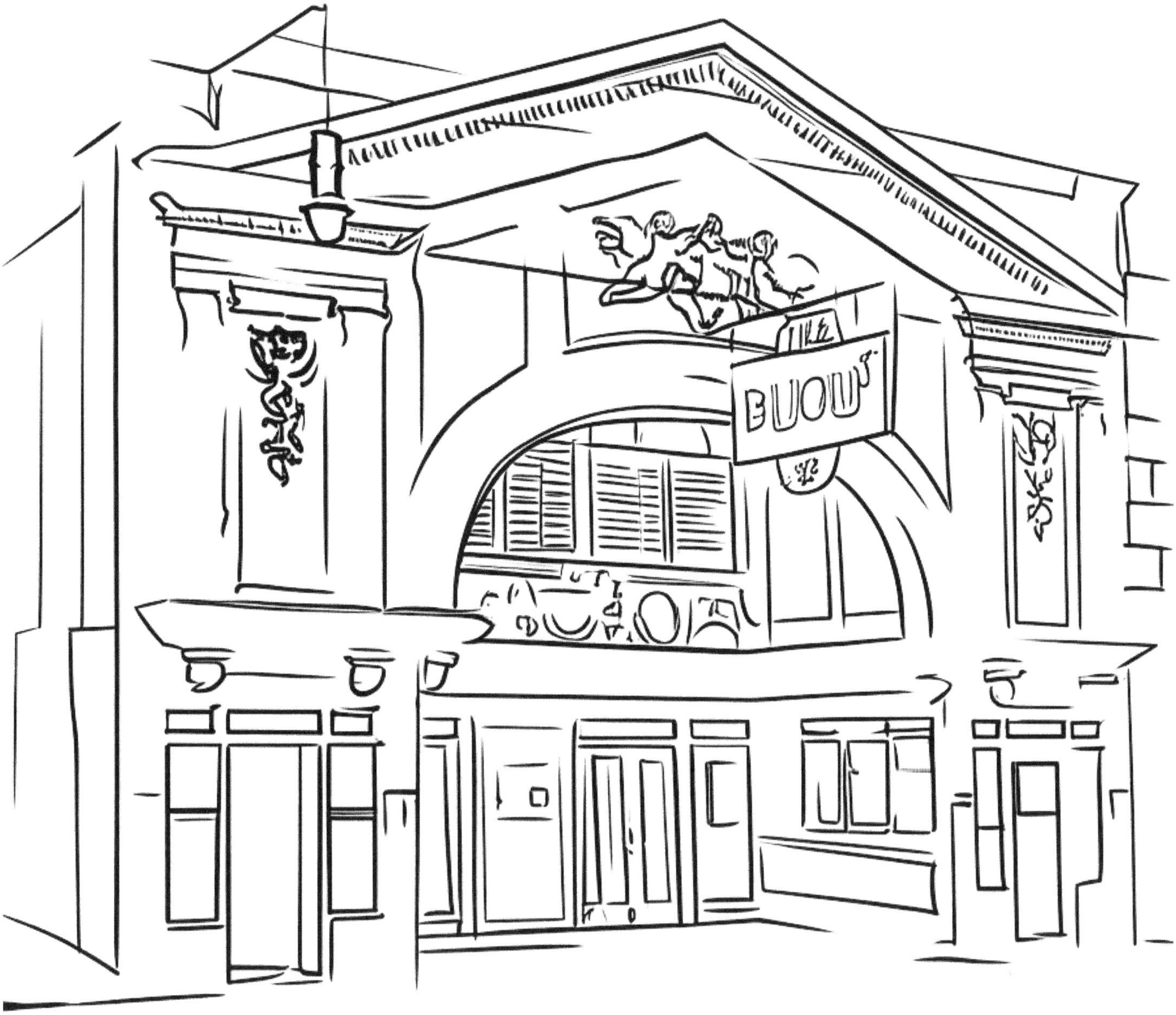

There is only a park to recall the Bijou theater now, but it once was a center of activity on North Front Street. Originally housed in a big tent in 1904, by 1912 a building had replaced the temporary shelter. It closed somewhere around 1956 and was later torn down. Drive-In theaters like the Starway and Skyline rounded out Wilmington's movie scene.

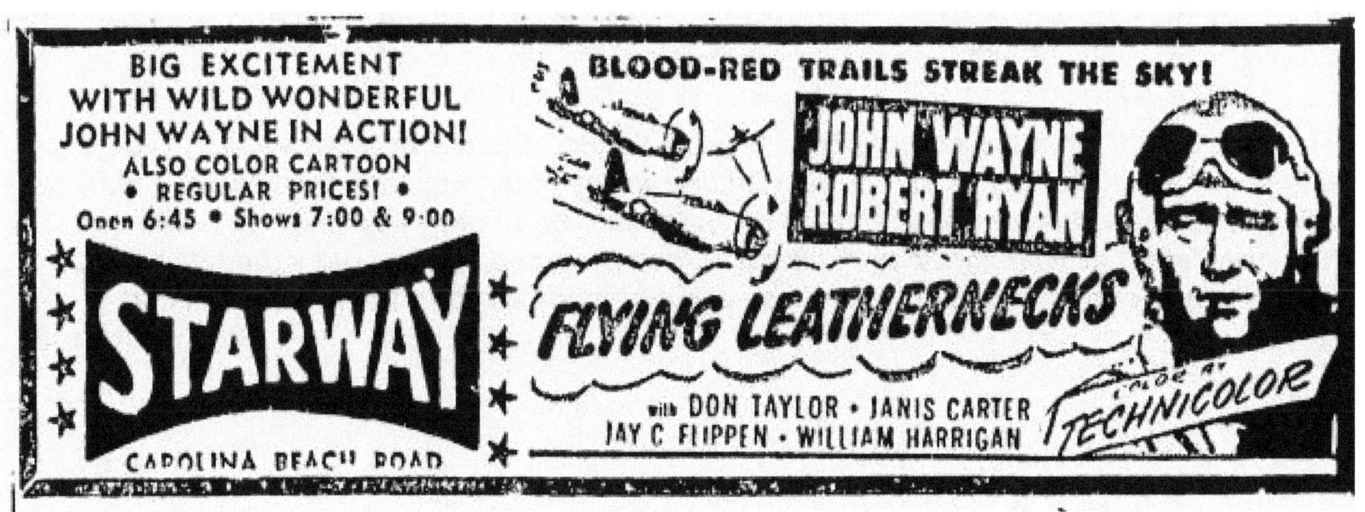

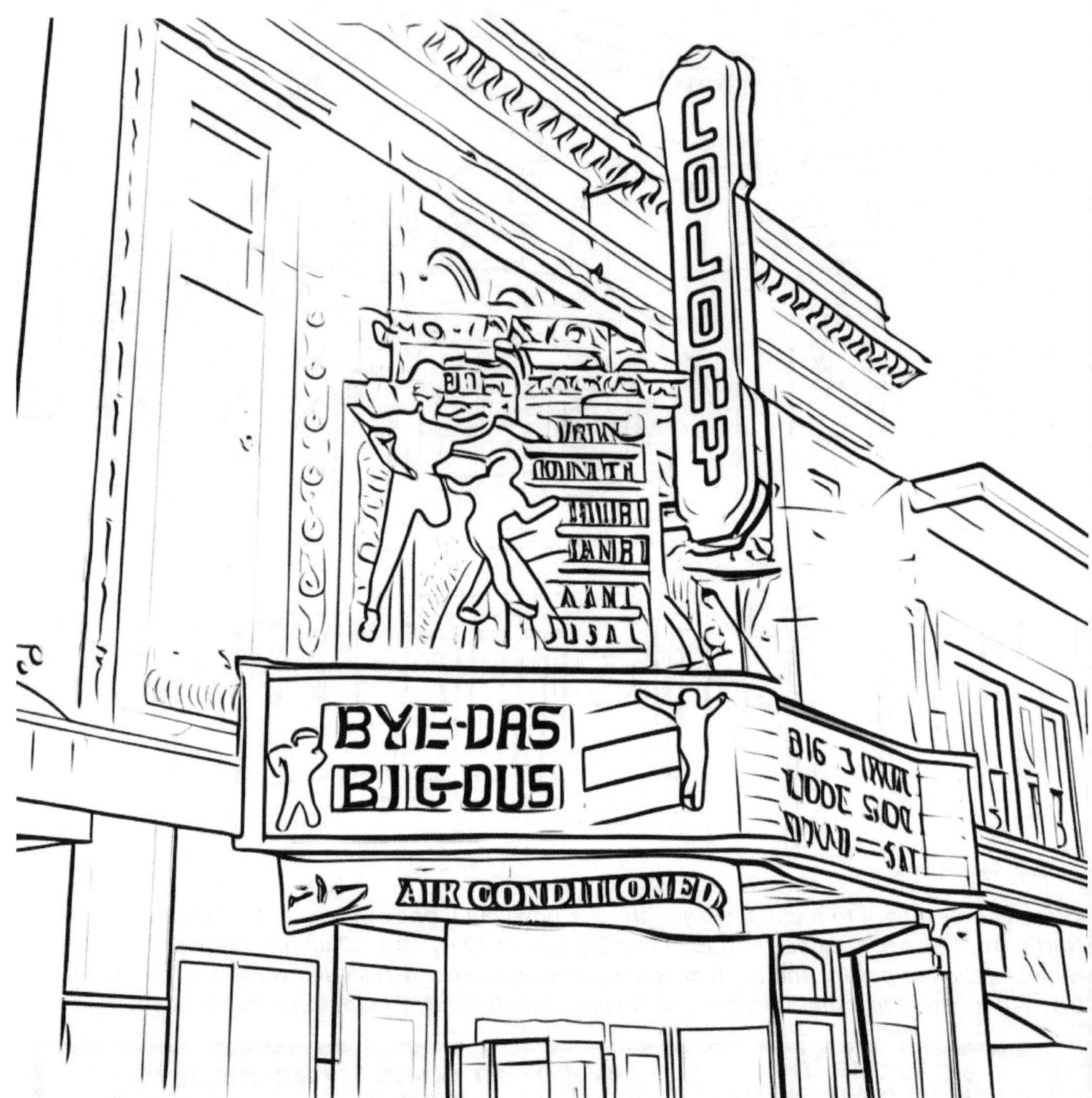

There is an empty lot at the corner of Market and Second Streets now where the Colony theater used to be. As late as the 1970s it had Saturday matinees showing Disney films and holding prize drawings for youngsters in attendance. The Colony was another of the old school theaters that Wilmington had, with a screen mounted over an old vaudeville stage, thick red velvet curtains, and ornate woodwork that made a trip to the movies special.

Healing Places...

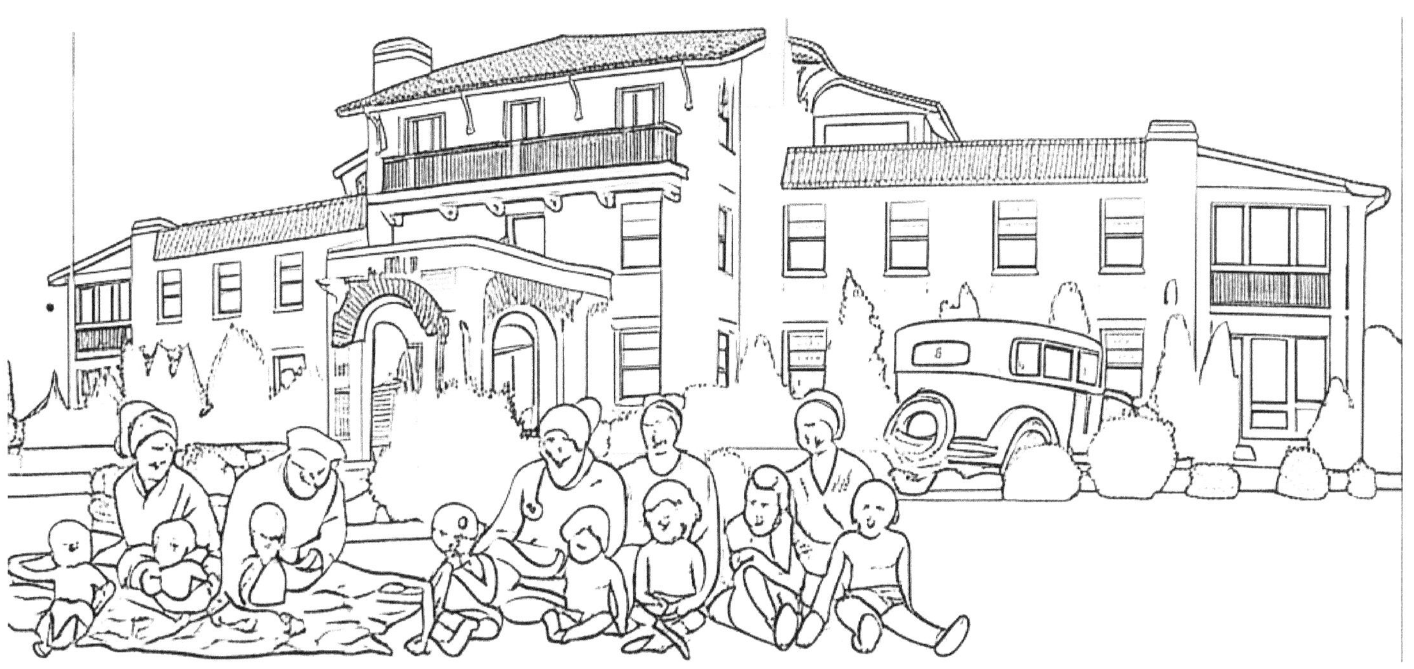

Babies Hospital sat at the foot of the Wrightsville Beach drawbridge, a landmark and revered institution since Dr. J. Buren Sidbury opened it in 1920. The hospital specialized in pediatric care and was open until 1978. When it closed as a hospital, the building was converted into offices, until it was torn down in 2004.

Community Hospital was the medical center for African American residents of Wilmington during the days of segregation. Located between Dawson and Wooster Streets, the hospital closed once desegregation eliminated the need for it.

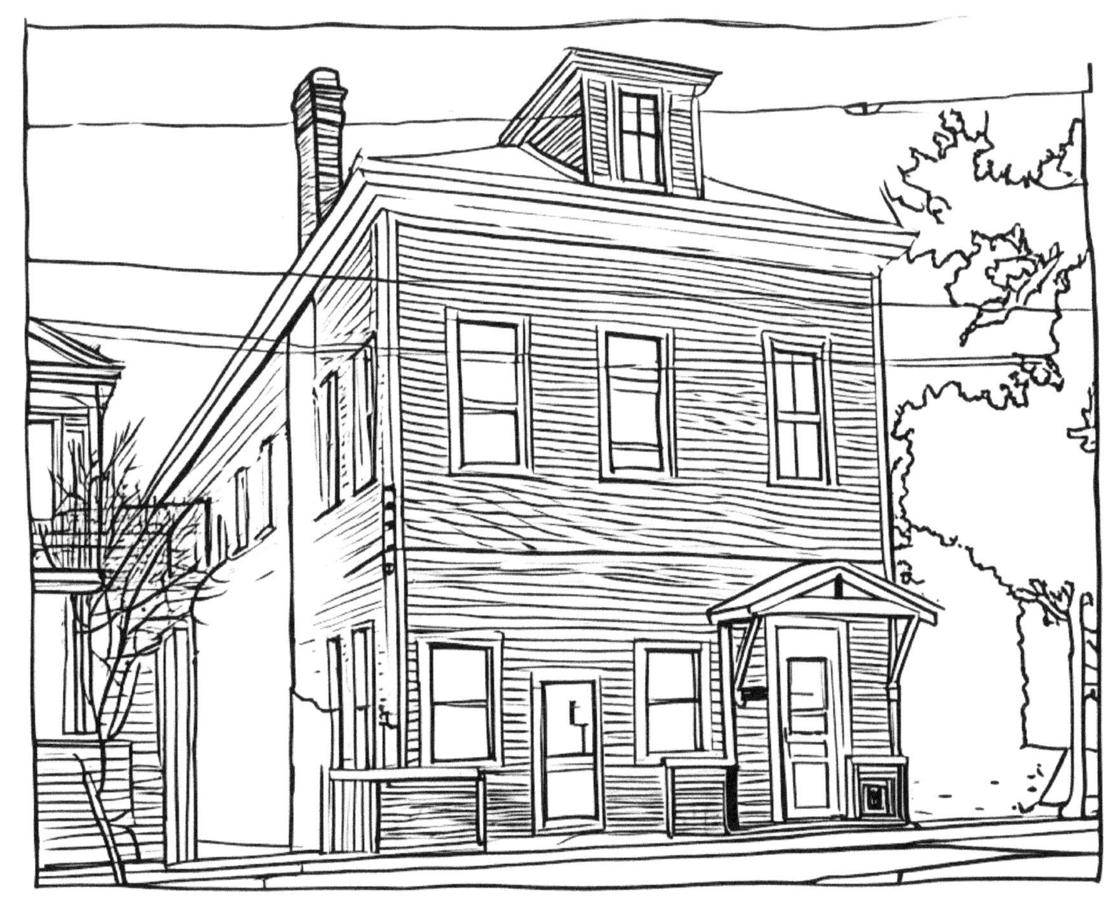

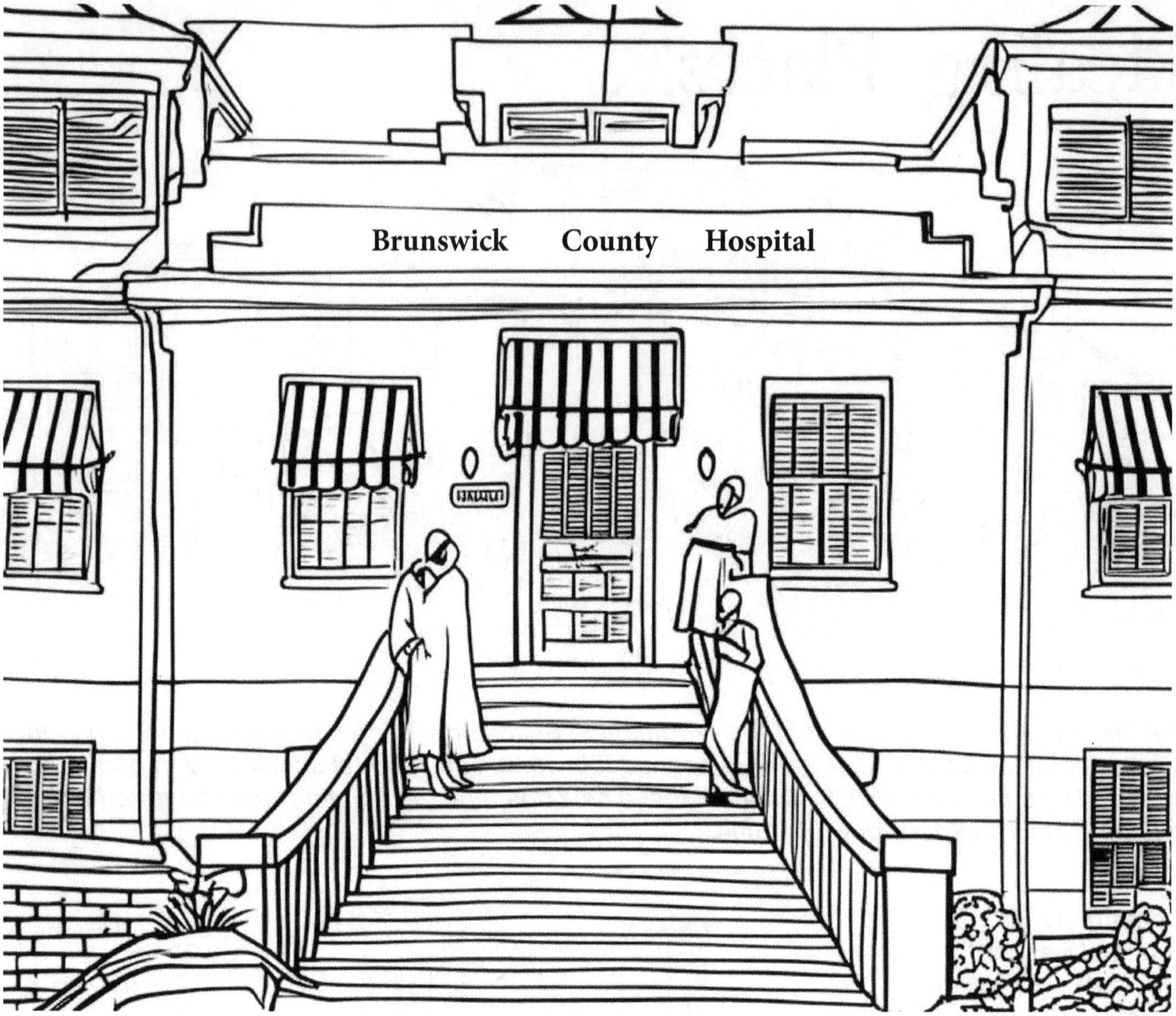

Dr. J. Arthur Dosher (right) opened his hospital in Southport, N.C. in 1930 as Brunswick County Hospital (above). Nine years later it was renamed to honor him. The hospital has served the southern part of Brunswick County every since. In one memorable event, survivors of the S.S. John D. Gill *were transfered to the care of Dosher Hospital after being torpedoed by a German U-boat off Cape Fear in World War II.*

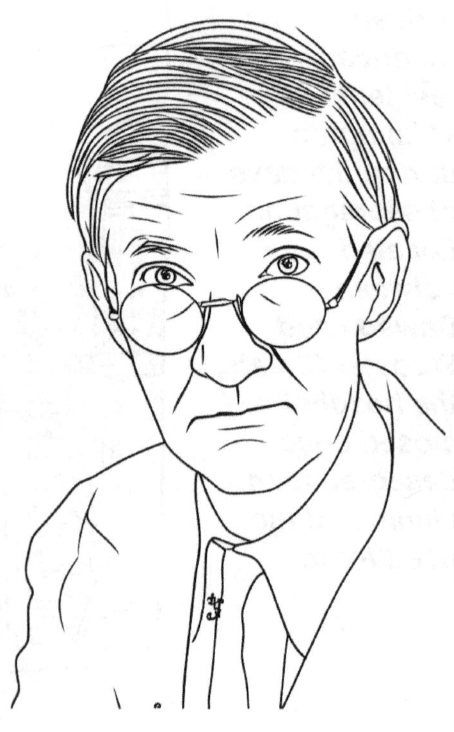

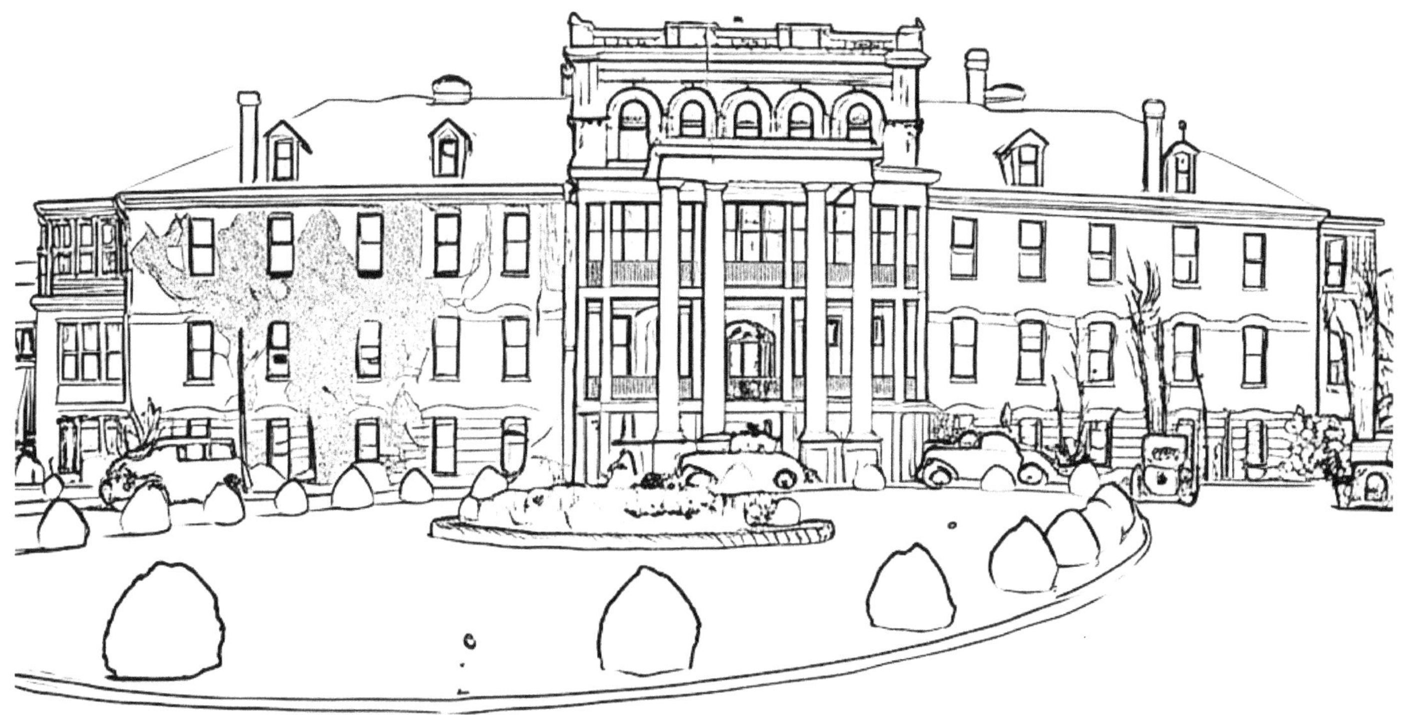

James Walker Memorial Hospital (above) was also a nursing college in North Wilmington. The hospital was founded in 1901 and treated patients for the next 66 years. When the hospital was torn down, a wing was retained for nursing student residences. Today it is used as low income housing. Wilmington's Marine Hospital (below) treated seamen and civilians from the 1850s until after the Civil War.

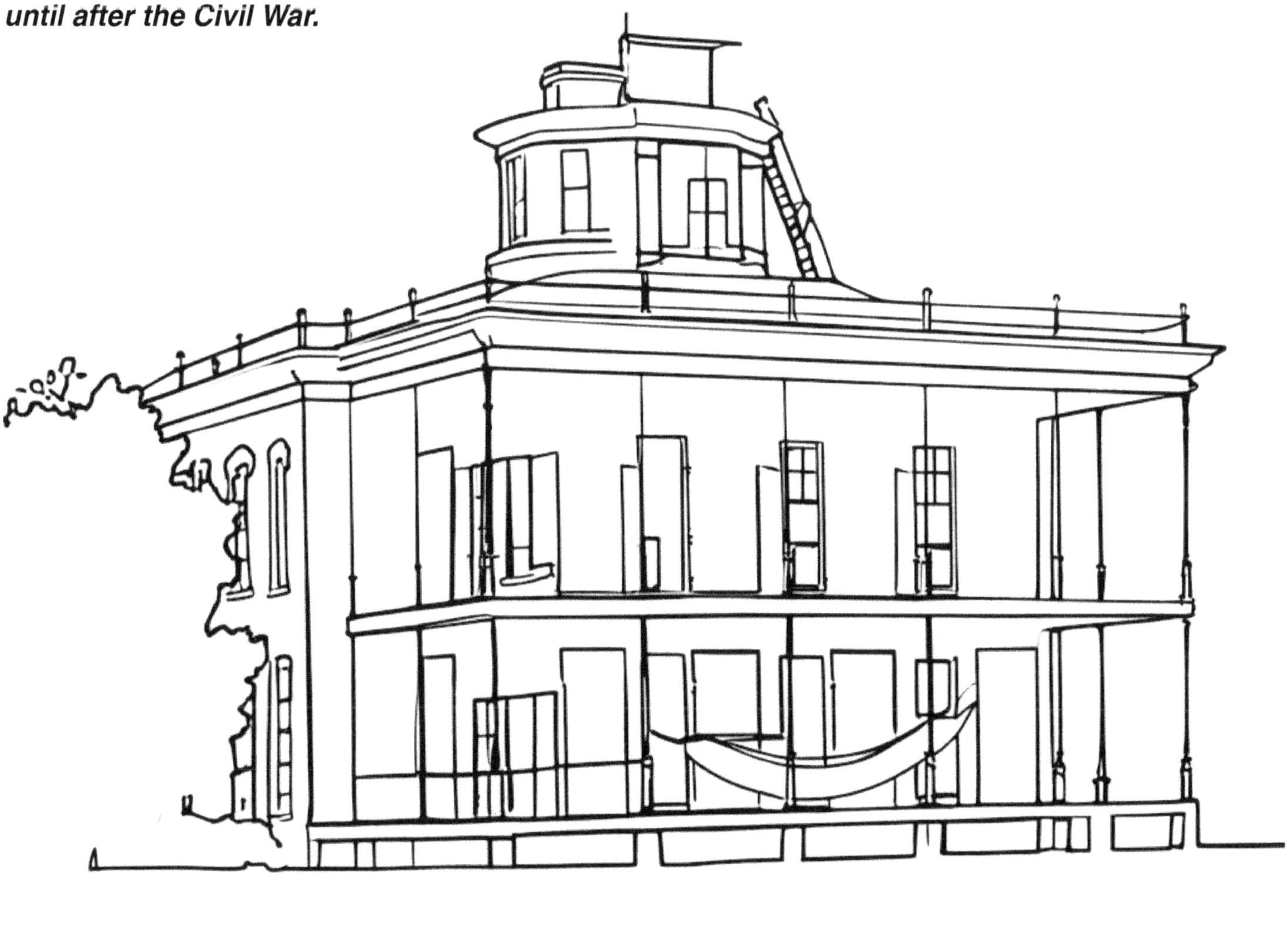

Houses of Faith...

Wilmington's first church was St. James Anglican Church, which sat in the middle of the intersection of Fourth and Market Streets (right). That building was used as a stable by the British who occupied the town in 1781. The current building at Third and Market Streets was completed in 1840. Union forces used the new building as a hospital after Wilmington fell in 1865.

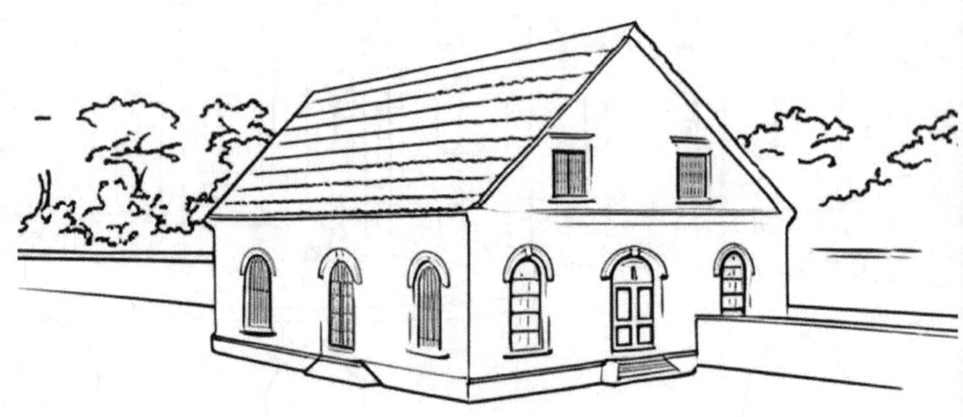

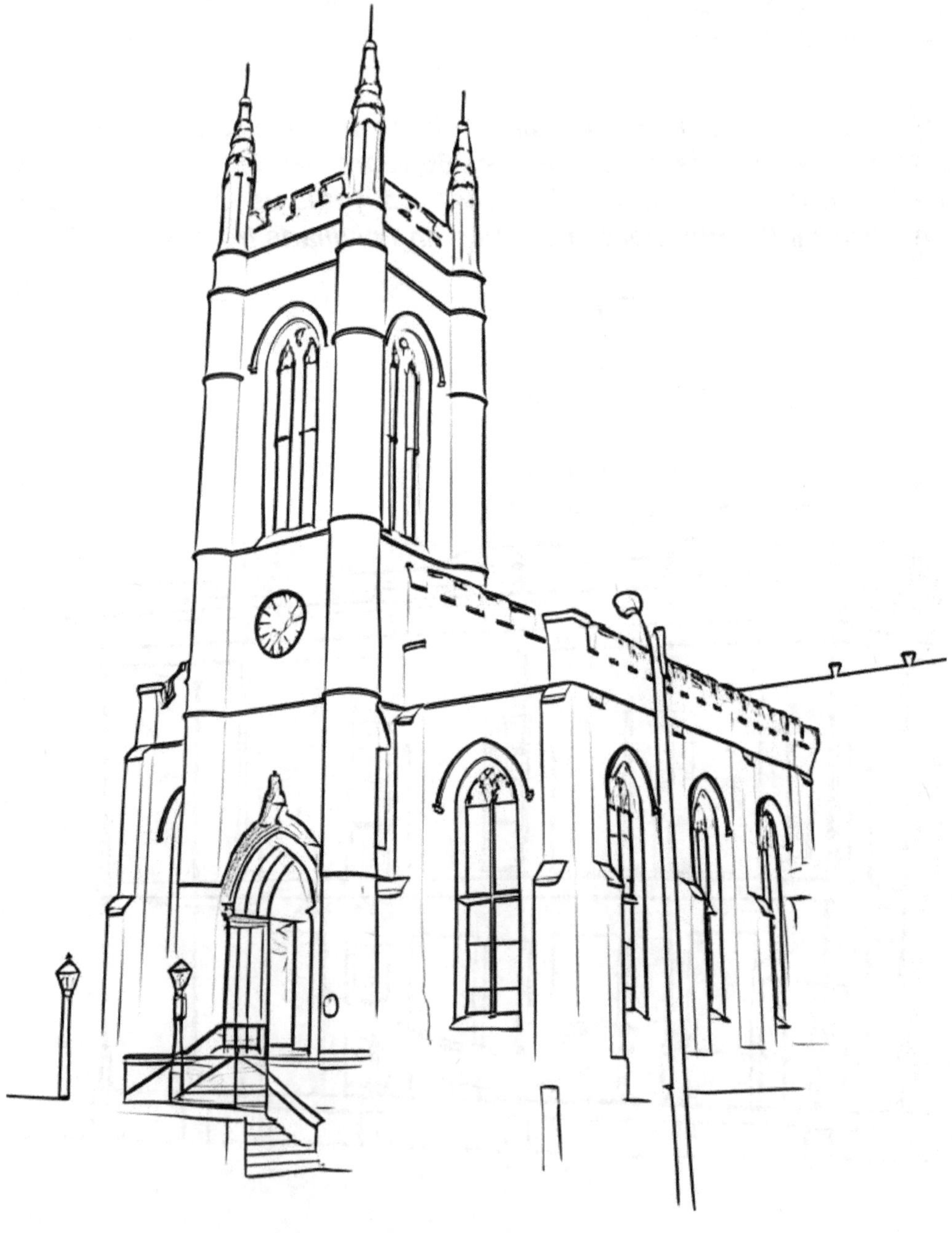

Funds to build St. James were secured through the auction of salvaged material and goods from the Spanish privateer **La Fortuna** ***that attacked Brunswick Town in 1748. One of the things salvaged from aboard the ship was a painting,*** **Ecce Homo** ***(Latin for*** **Behold the Man*****). The painting (opposite page) still hangs in the sanctuary of the current church (left).***

“Ecce Homo,” or “Behold the Man”

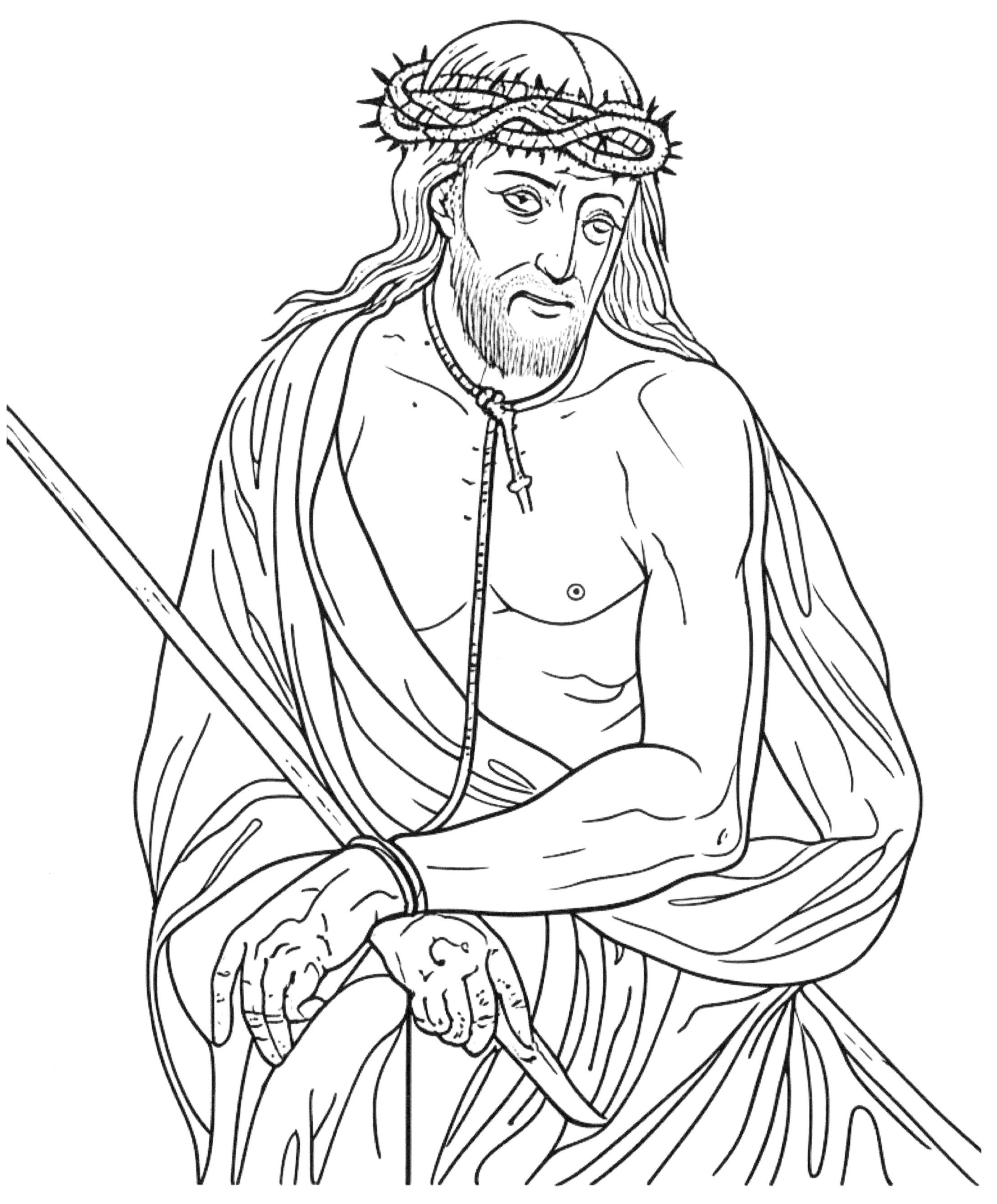

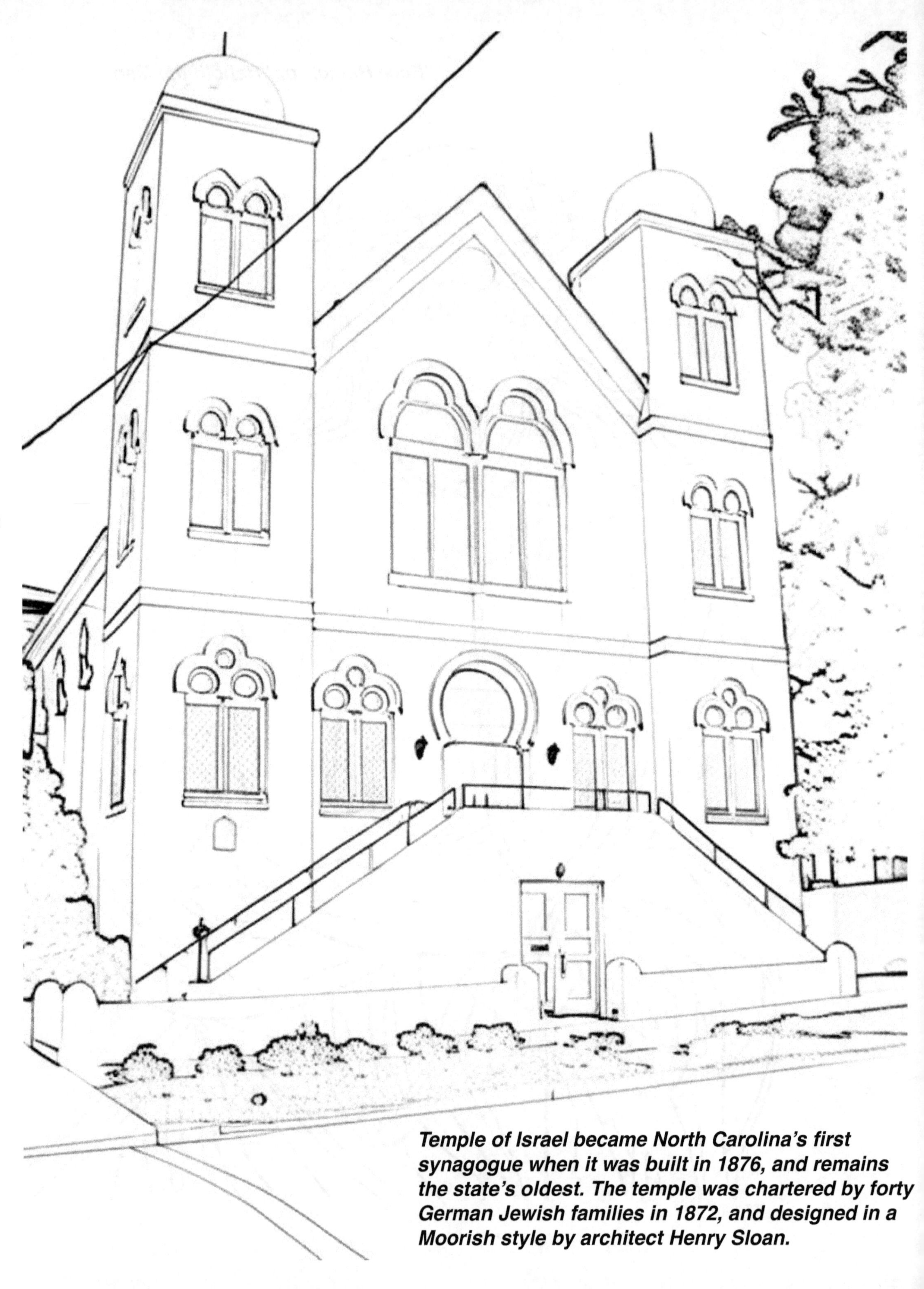

Temple of Israel became North Carolina's first synagogue when it was built in 1876, and remains the state's oldest. The temple was chartered by forty German Jewish families in 1872, and designed in a Moorish style by architect Henry Sloan.

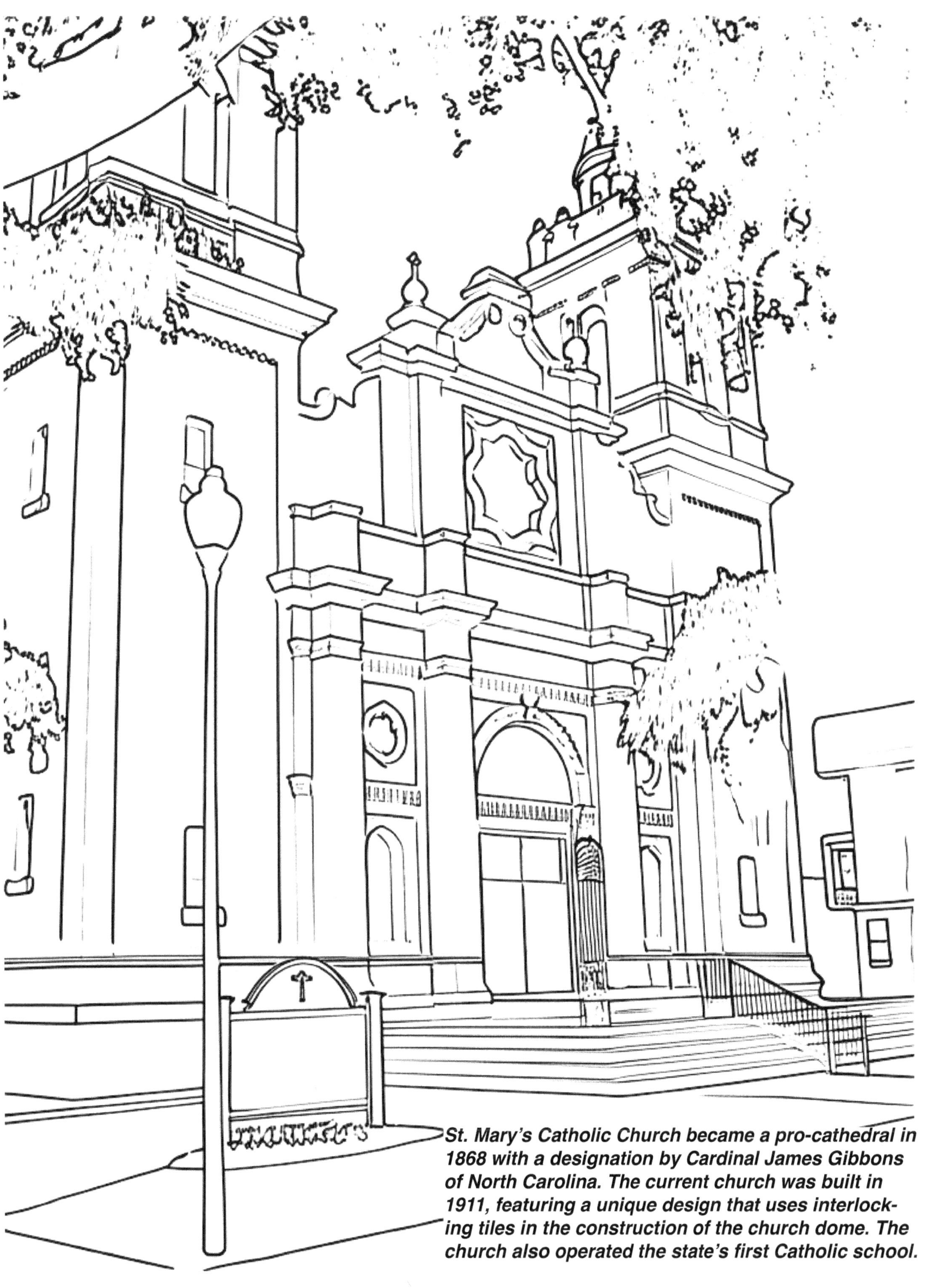

St. Mary's Catholic Church became a pro-cathedral in 1868 with a designation by Cardinal James Gibbons of North Carolina. The current church was built in 1911, featuring a unique design that uses interlocking tiles in the construction of the church dome. The church also operated the state's first Catholic school.

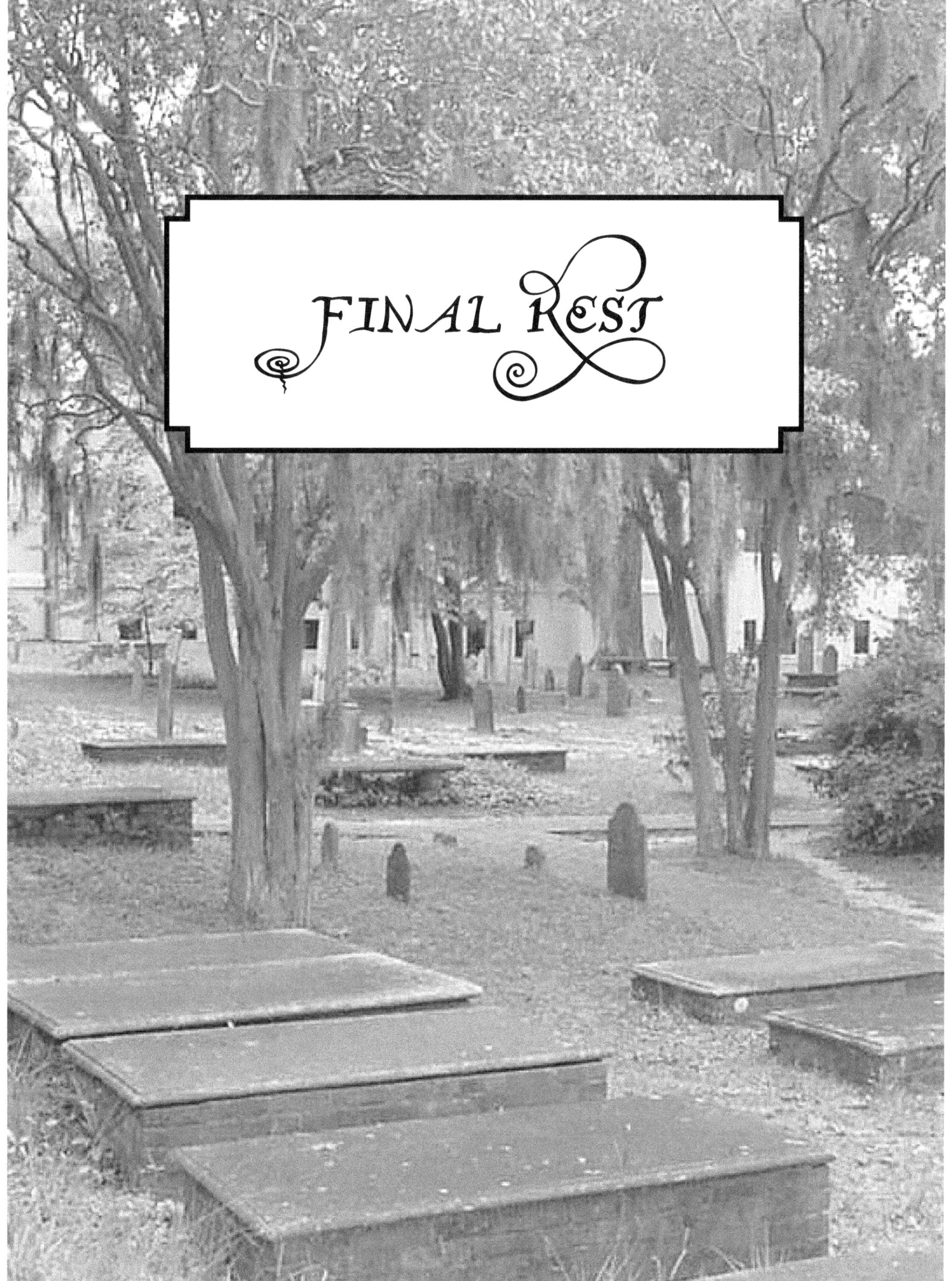

Final Rest

St. James Graveyard

St. James Graveyard, behind the church at Fourth and Market Streets, holds the graves of some of the oldest residents of Wilmington and the lower Cape Fear. The graves there date back to colonial days, and include people like Cornelius Harnett, Jr. and Thomas Godfrey.

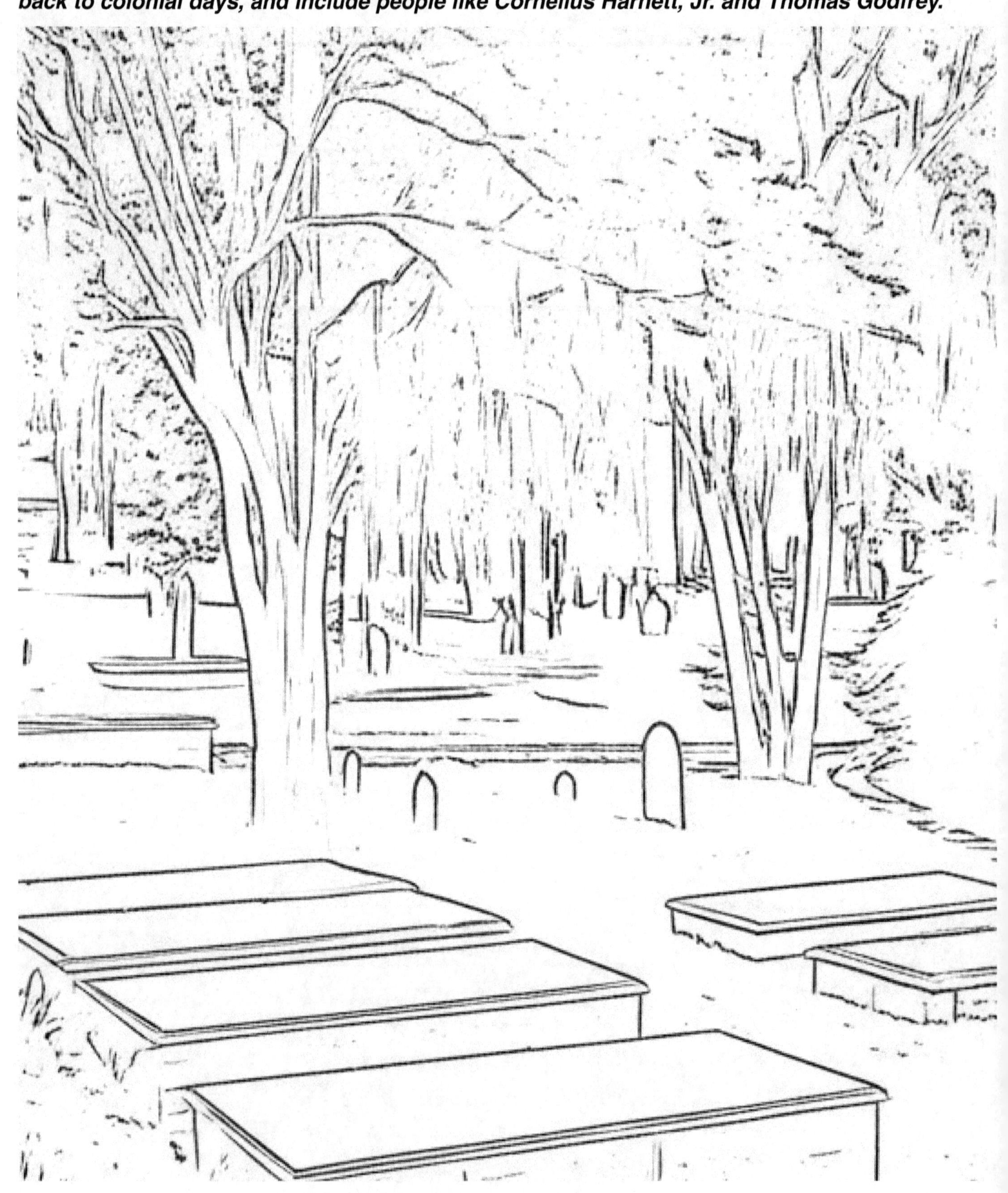

Philadelphian Thomas Godfrey (right) is buried in the St. James Graveyard. Godfrey is credited with authoring the play, "The Prince of Parthia," the first theatrical production to be penned by an American and performed in the colonies.

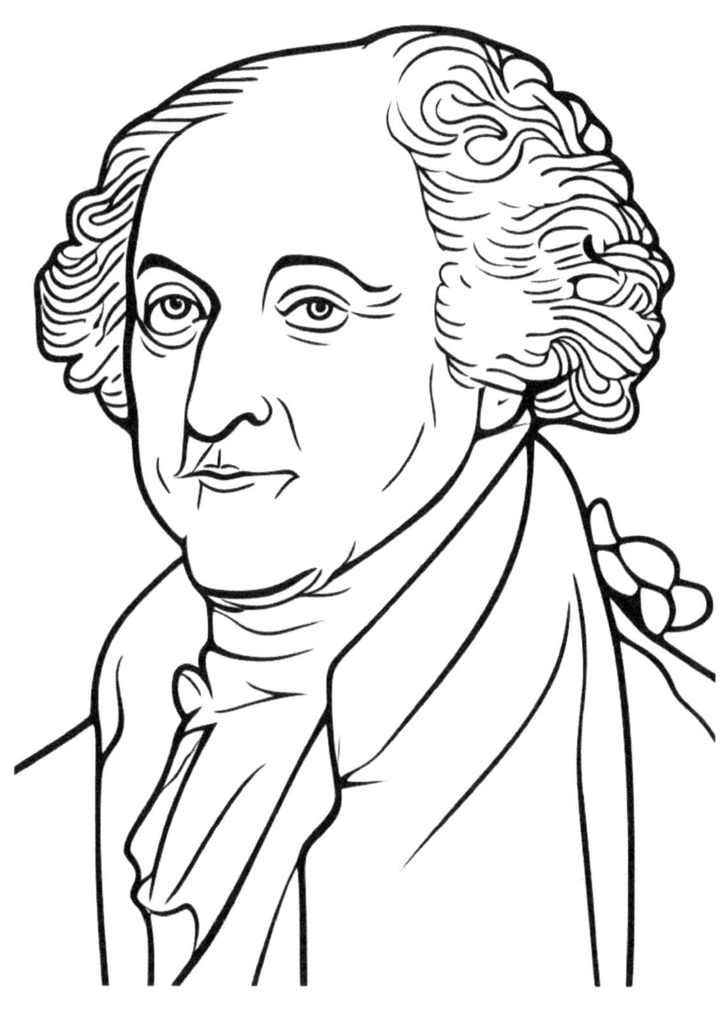

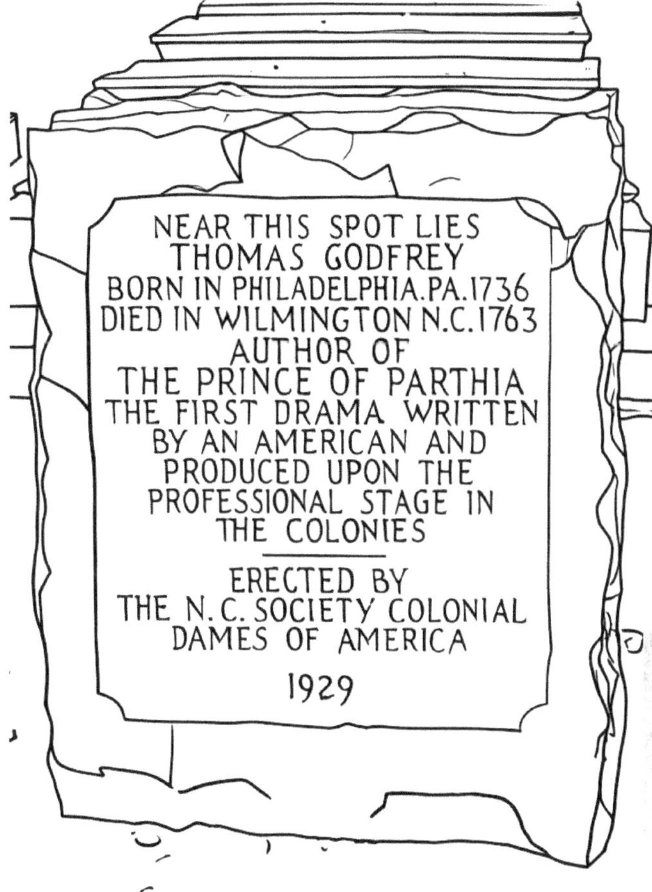

The newspaper announcement to the right advertises a production of Godfrey's "The Prince of Parthia."

Schooner Charming Nancy, J. Mullowny to Halifax.

By Authority.

NEVER PERFORMED BEFORE.

By the AMERICAN COMPANY,

At the NEW THEATRE, in *Southwark,* On *FRIDAY*, the *Twenty-Fourth* of *April*, will be presented, A TRAGEDY written by the late ingenious Mr. *Thomas Godfrey*, of this city, called the

PRINCE *of* PARTHIA.

The PRINCIPAL CHARACTERS by Mr. HALLAM, Mr. DOUGLASS, Mr. WALL, Mr. MORRIS, Mr. ALLYN, Mr. TOMLINSON, Mr. BROAD-BELT, Mr. GREVILLE, Mrs. DOUGLASS, Mrs. MORRIS, Miss WAINWRIGHT, and Miss CHEER.

To which will be added, A *Ballad Opera* called

The CONTRIVANCES,

To begin exactly at *Seven* o'Clock.--*Vivant Rex & Regina.*

Oakdale Cemetery

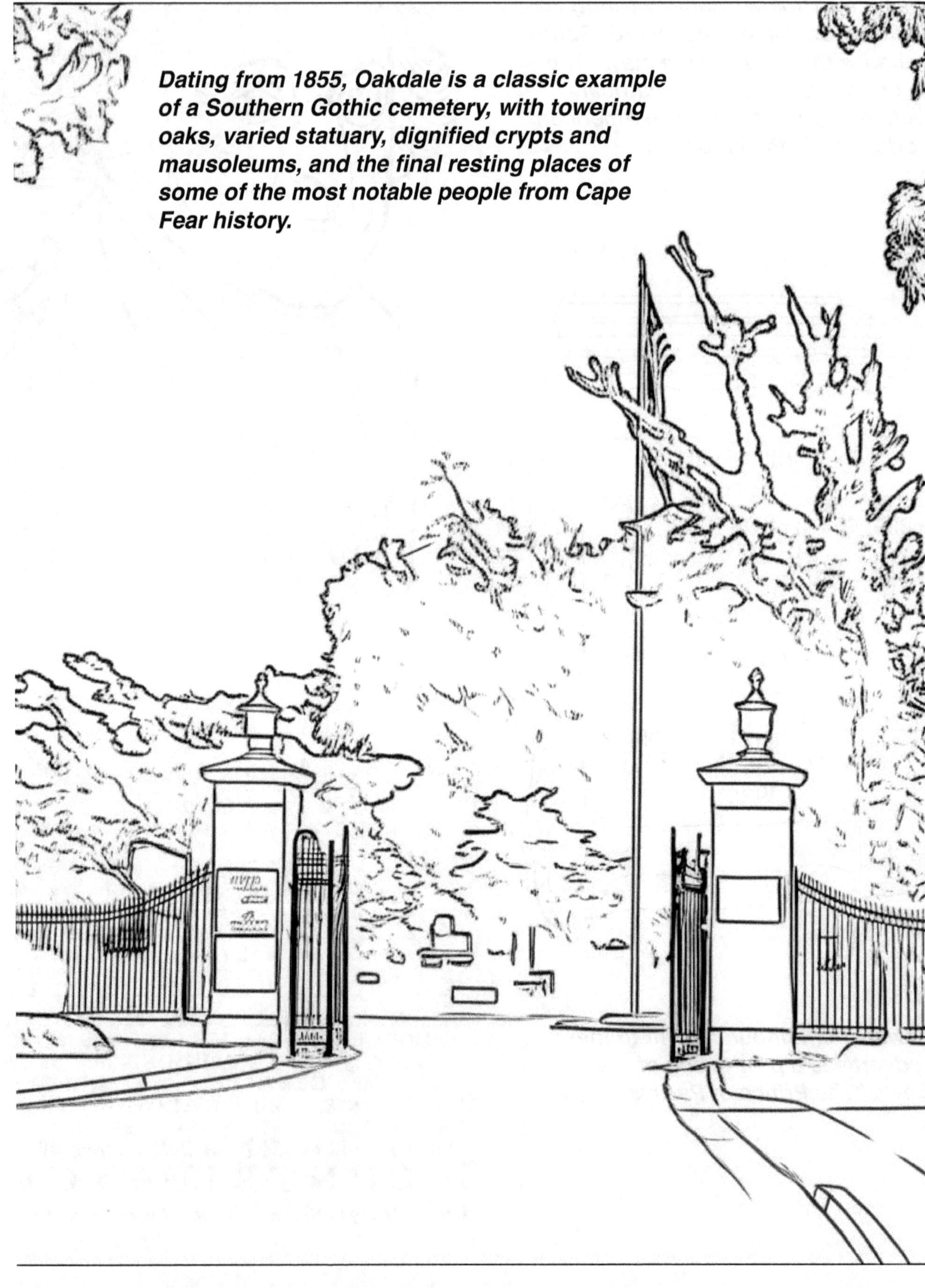

Dating from 1855, Oakdale is a classic example of a Southern Gothic cemetery, with towering oaks, varied statuary, dignified crypts and mausoleums, and the final resting places of some of the most notable people from Cape Fear history.

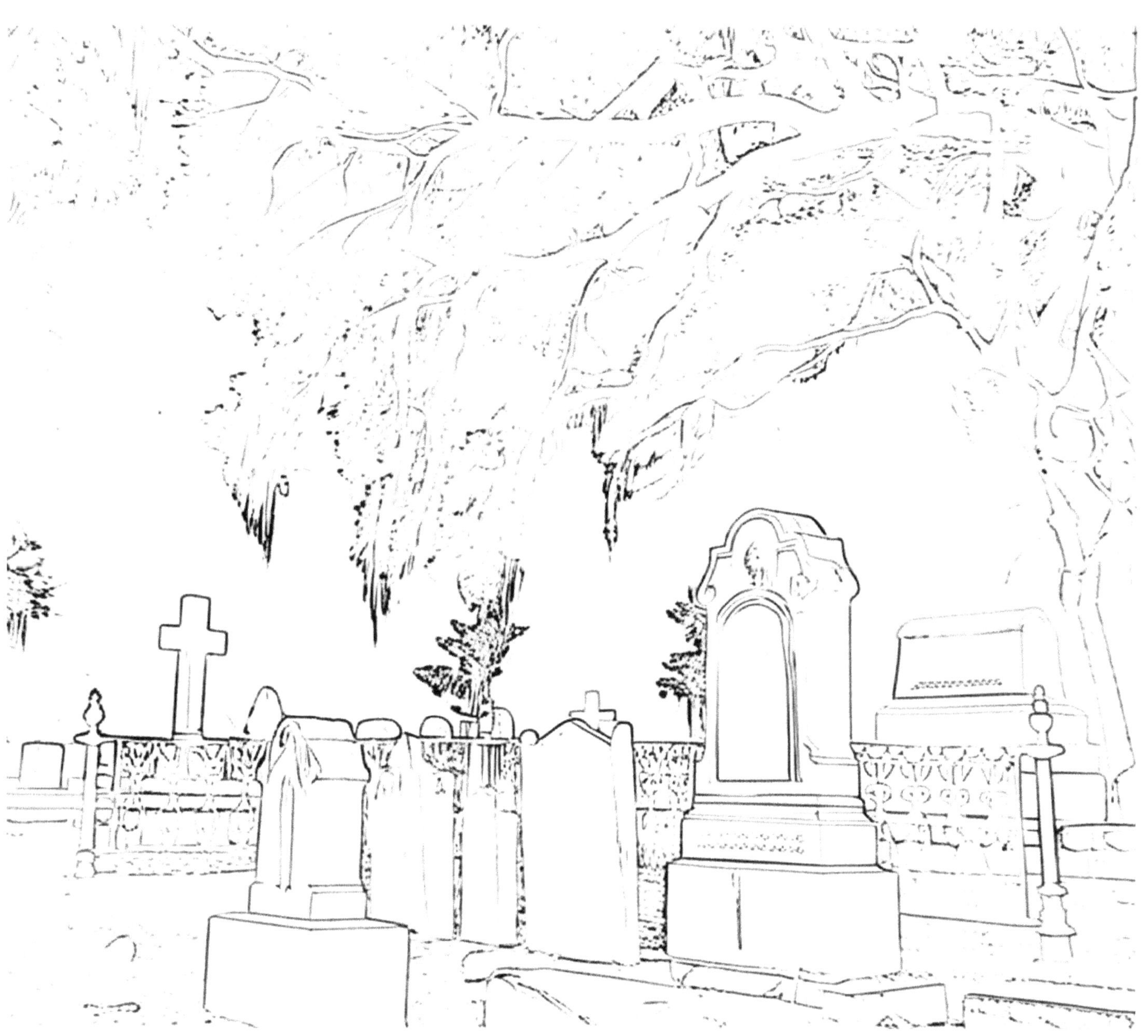

It is hard to imagine a more peaceful place to spend eternity than Oakdale Cemetery. A casual stroll through the grounds reveals gravesites with tombstones that tell fascinating stories about Wilmngton's past and the people who lived - and died - here.

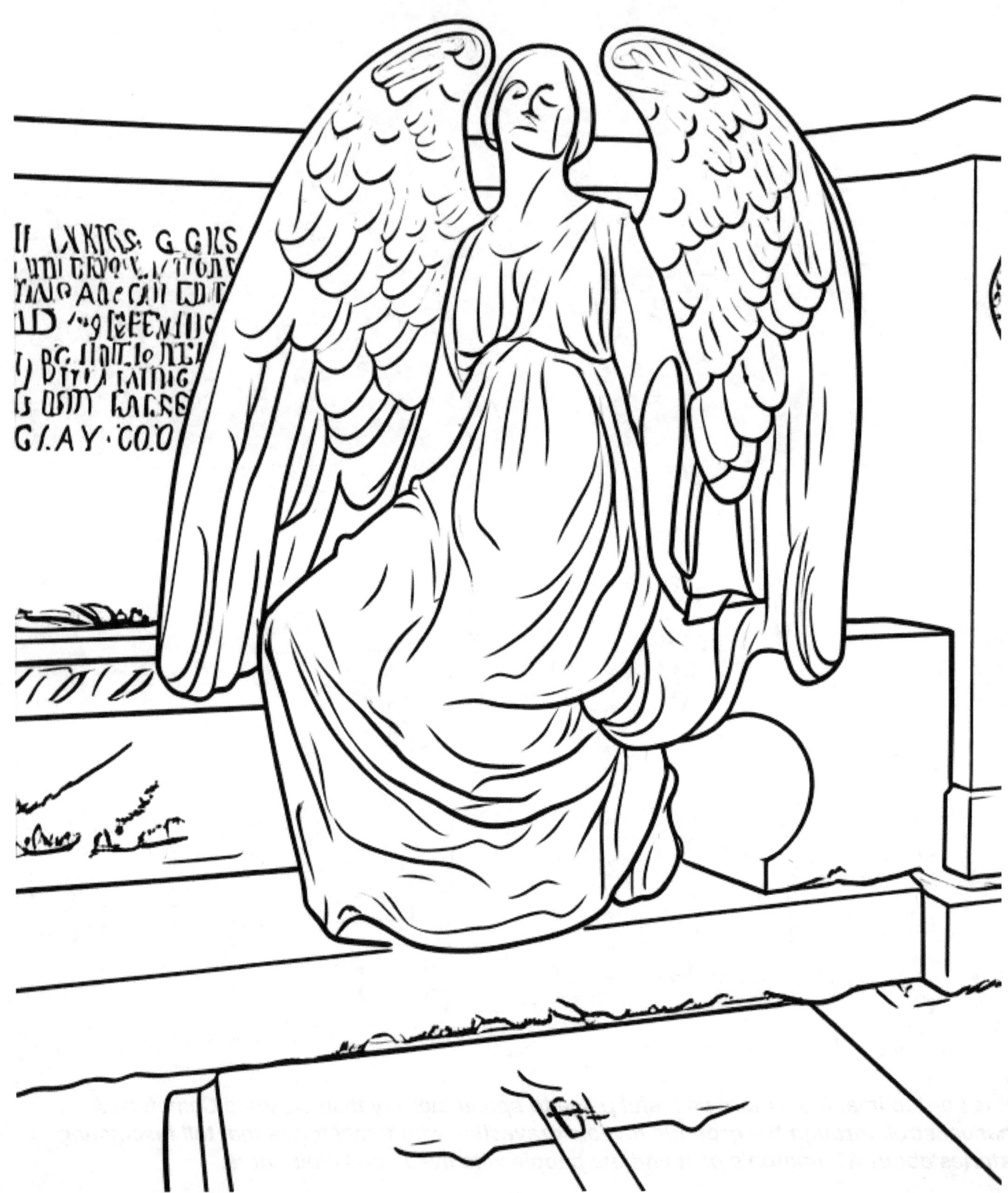

Oakdale holds fine examples of the art of remembrance, with statues, intricate wrought iron fences, and plots decorated to deliver a message about the people interred there.

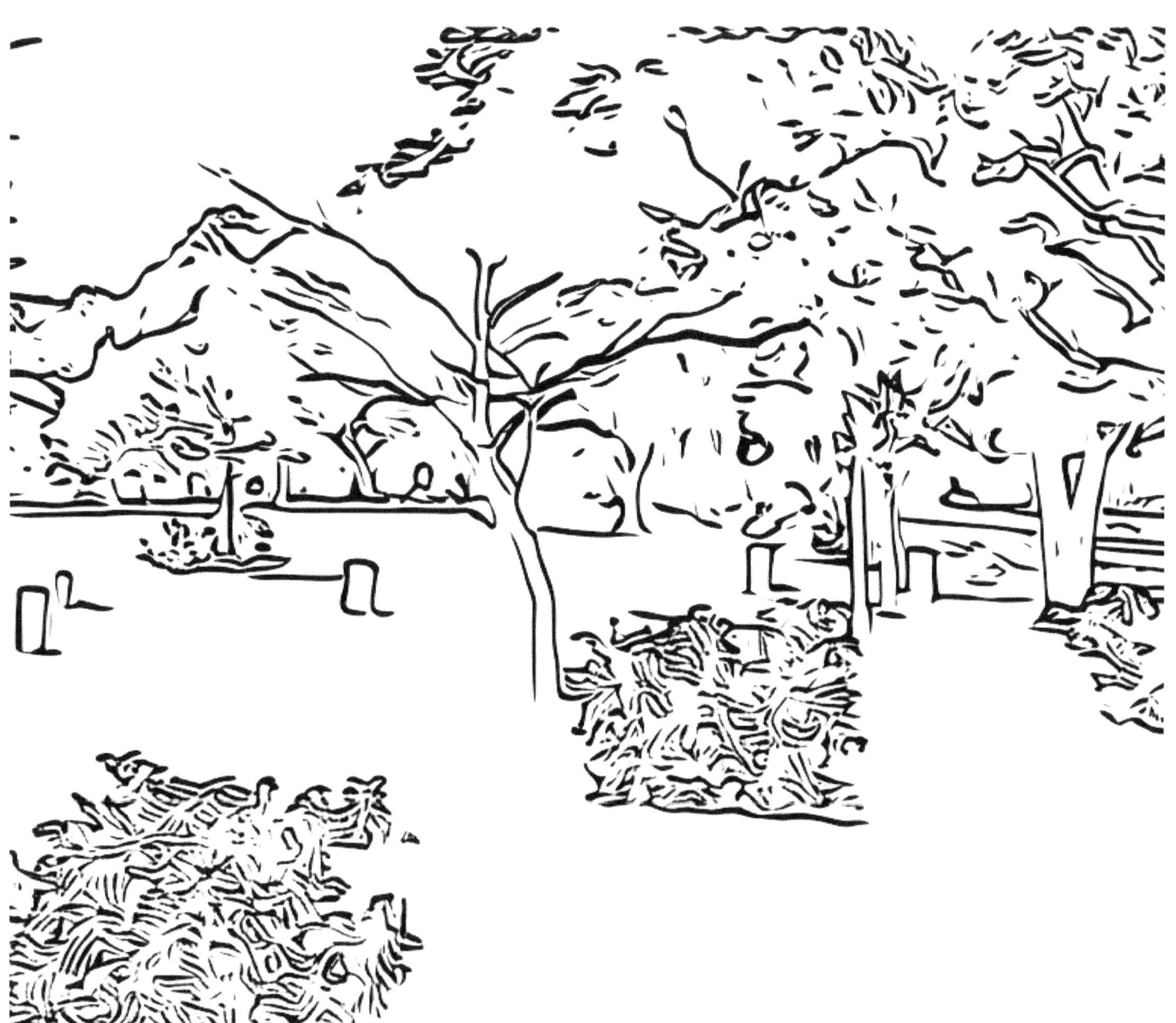

Among the first people buried at Oakdale are victims of the 1862 yellow fever epidemic that killed off a third of the city during the Civil War. People were dying so fast that officials were not able to keep up with the names of those who died. A mass grave was dug in Oakdale, where cartloads of bodies were dropped off for burial. Young John D. Bellamy recalled playing in the front yard of his family's mansion at Fifth and Market Streets and seeing wagonloads of the dead passing by on the way to Oakdale.

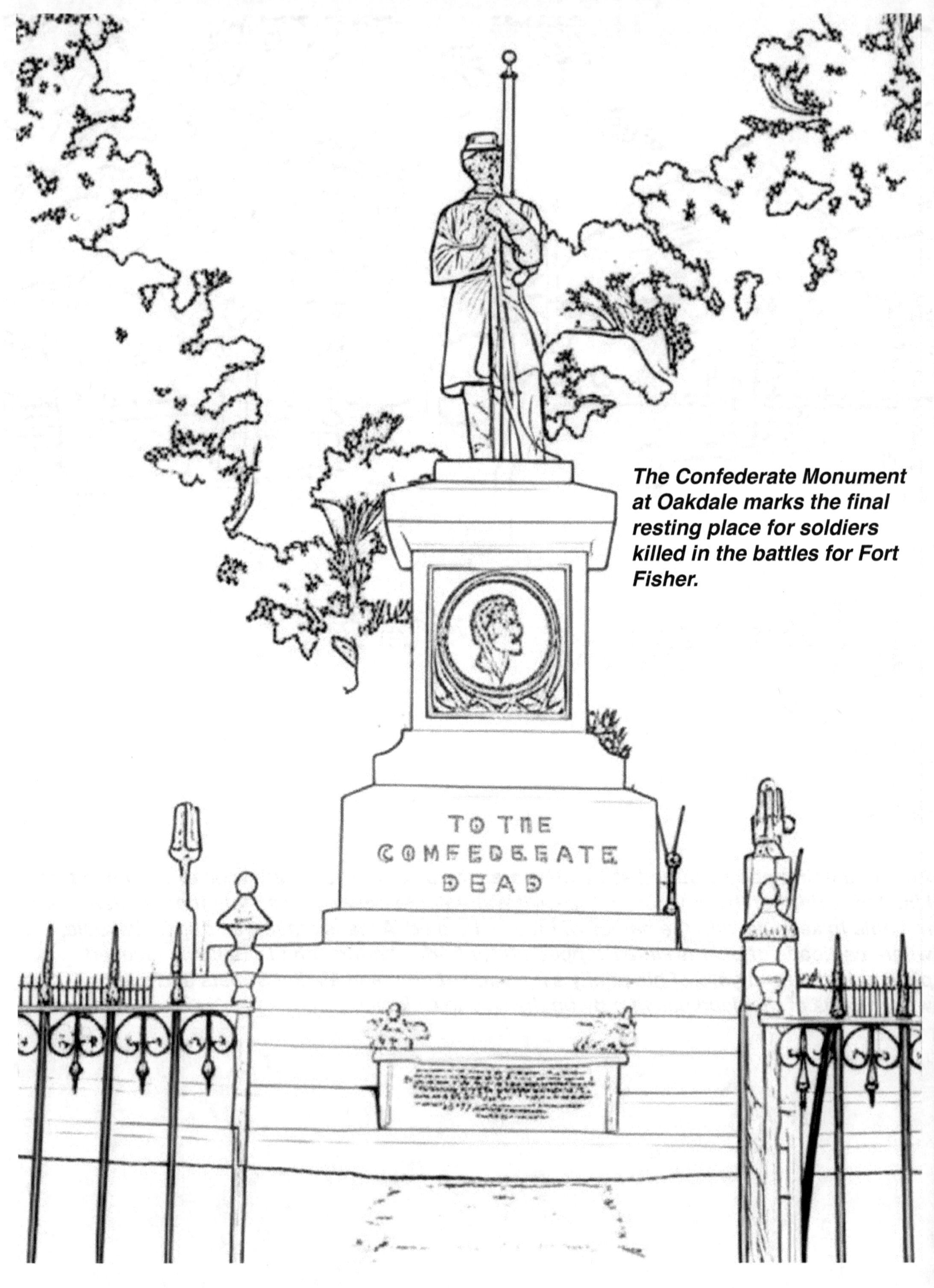

The Confederate Monument at Oakdale marks the final resting place for soldiers killed in the battles for Fort Fisher.

Pine Forest Cemetery

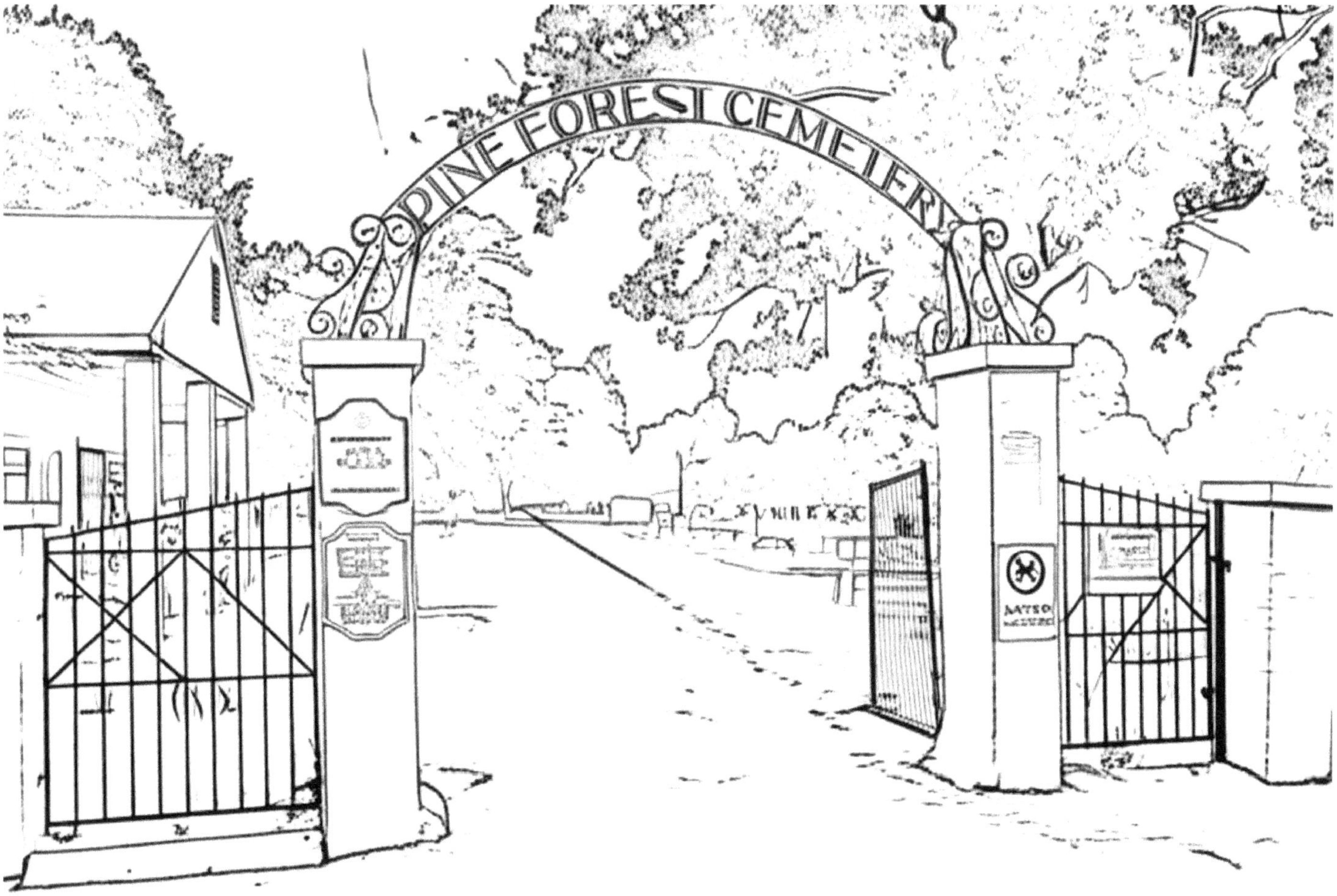

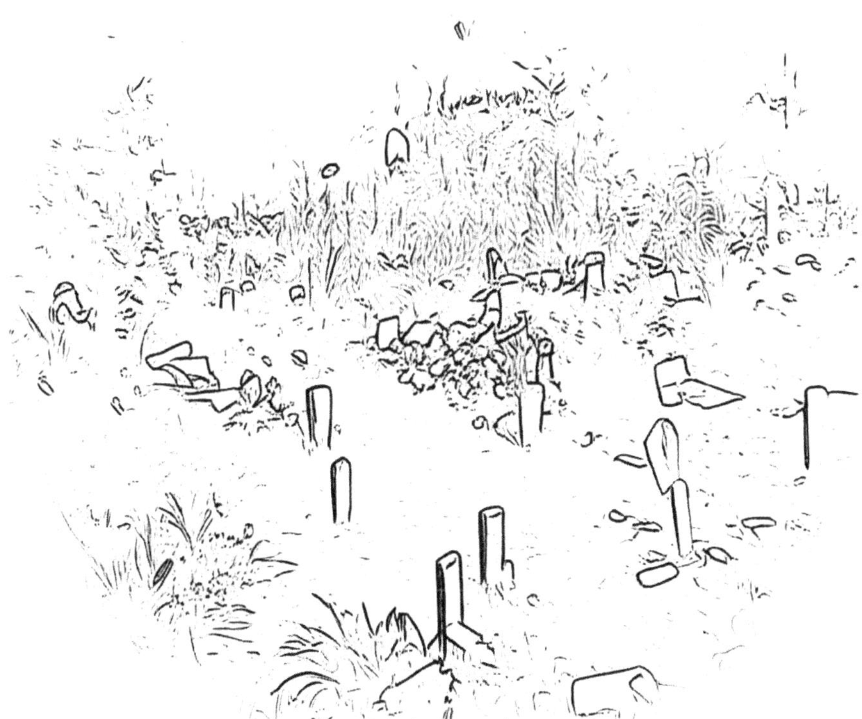

Next to Oakdale is Pine Forest Cemetery, where African American residents of Wilmington were laid to rest. The segregation of the Jim Crow era prohibited Blacks from being buried inthe same cemetery as whites, so Pine Forest was created to serve the Black community. It holds the remains of several notable African American residents of Wilmington, including Dr. James F. Shober.

Wilmington National Cemetery

Wilmington National Cemetery was built to bury the dead from the battles for Fort Fisher. Confederate troops who were mistakenly buried there were moved to Oakdale when the error was discovered. Veterans from every war since 1865 are buried in the Wilmington National Cemetery.

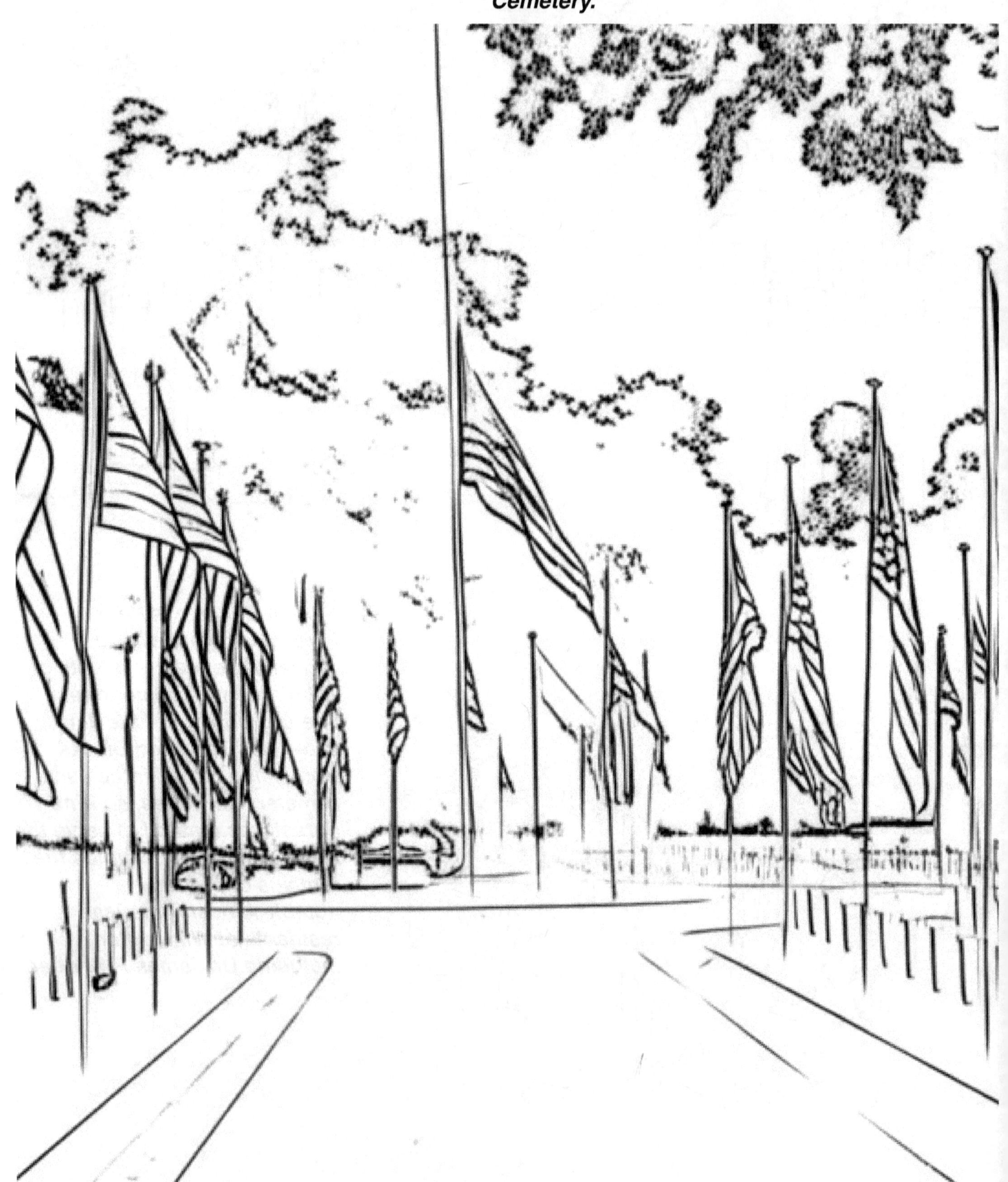

Union forces offered a bounty for the bodies of U.S. soldiers brought for burial at the new national cemetery. Enterprising locals began stripping the bodies of Confederate dead and passing them off as Union bodies. When the ruse was discovered, the Confederates were dug up and buried elsewhere. Many of the bodies were unknown when buried (right). The bandstand at the cemetery is the central place where commemorations of our veteran dead are held.

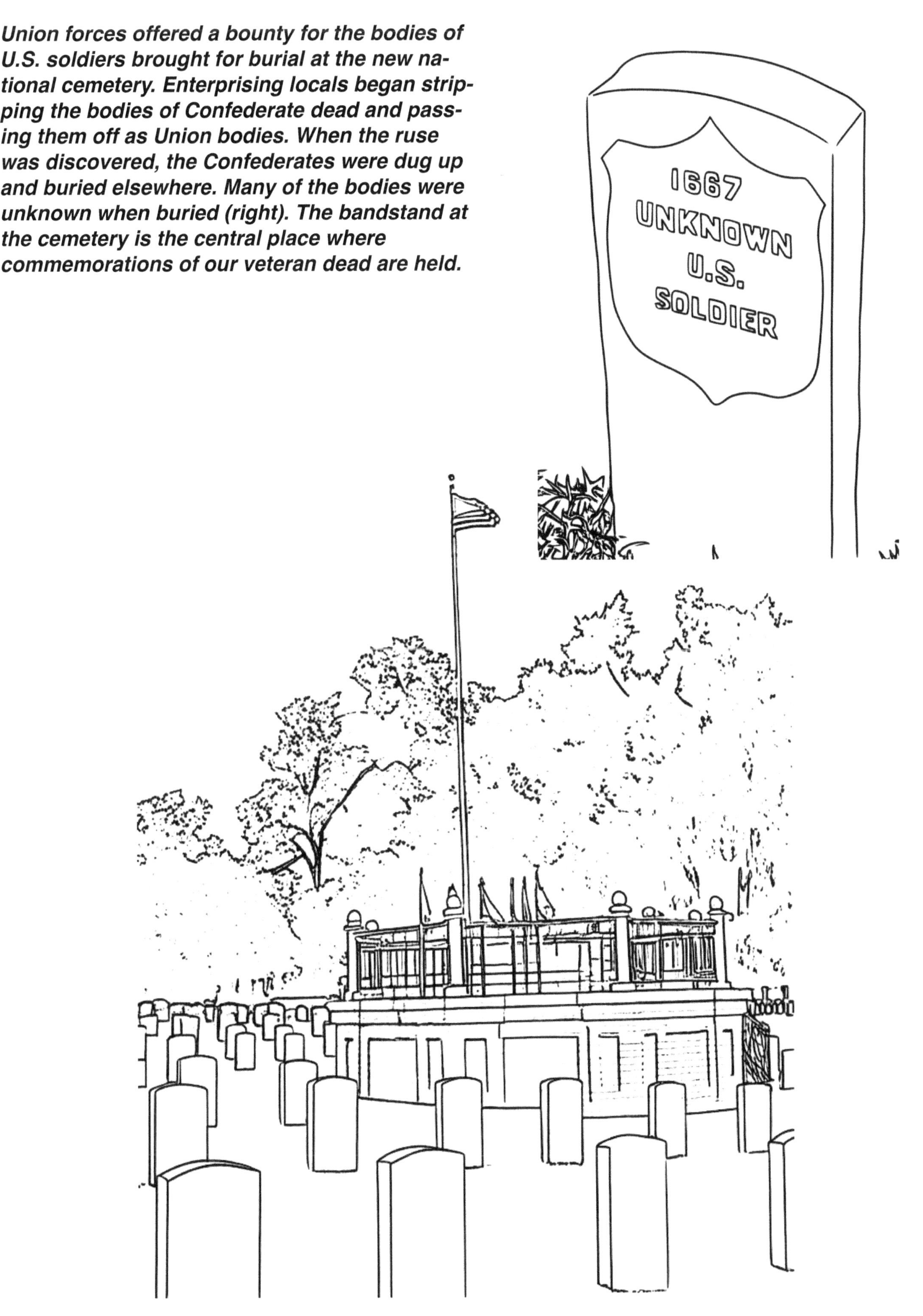

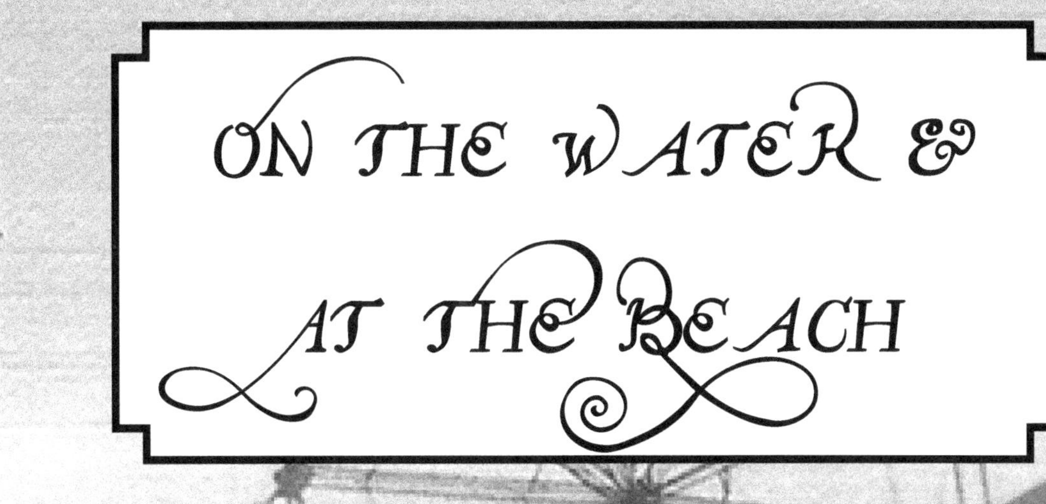
ON THE WATER &
AT THE BEACH

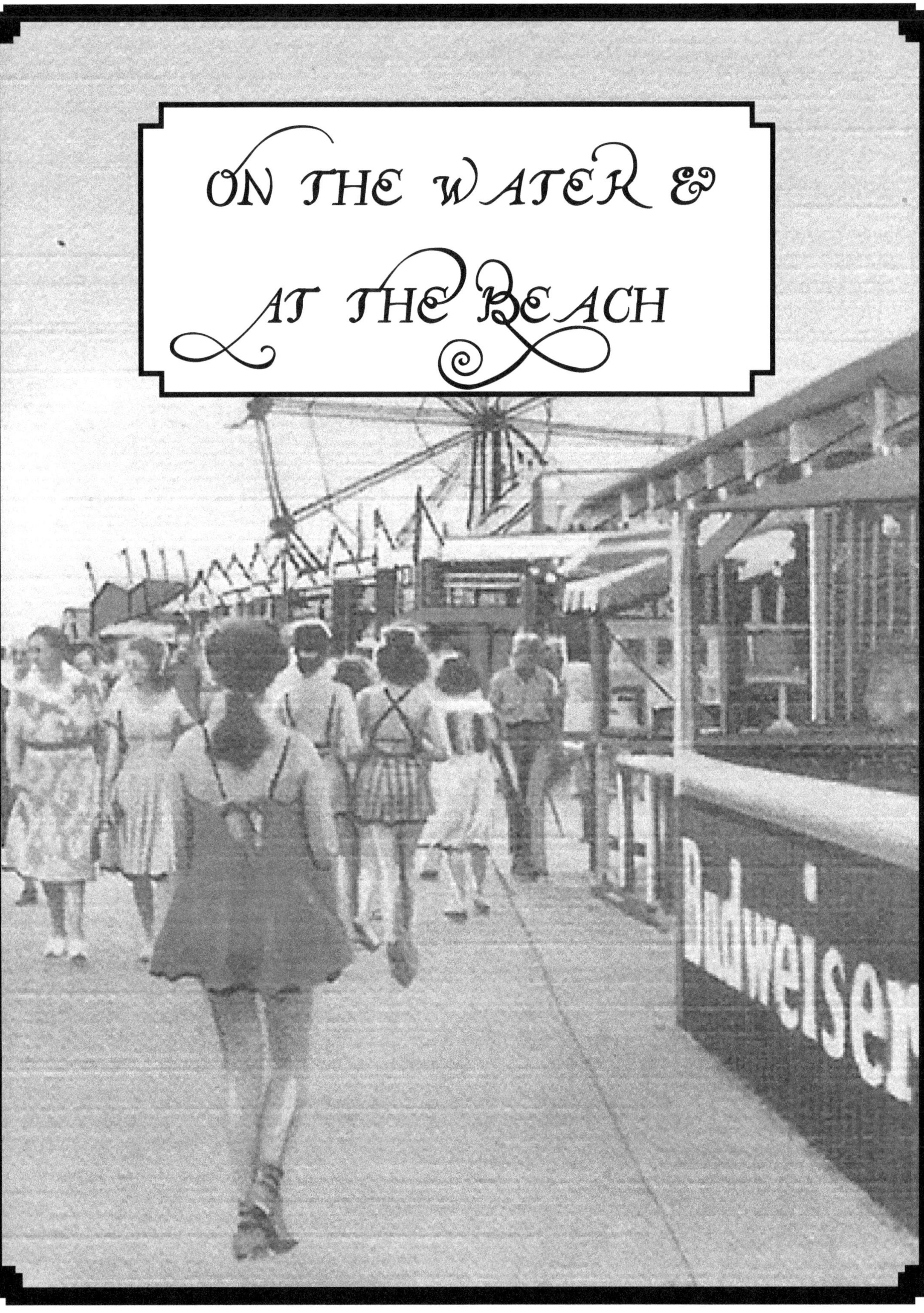

The Water for Work and Play

Where people lives dictates what life is like there. In the Cape Fear, our closeness to water has shaped the lives of the people who call it home.

Early Cape Fear settlers had no roads to travel on, so they used the waterways instead. The rivers, creeks, and streams made for fast transport of people and goods that simply could not be achieved over land.

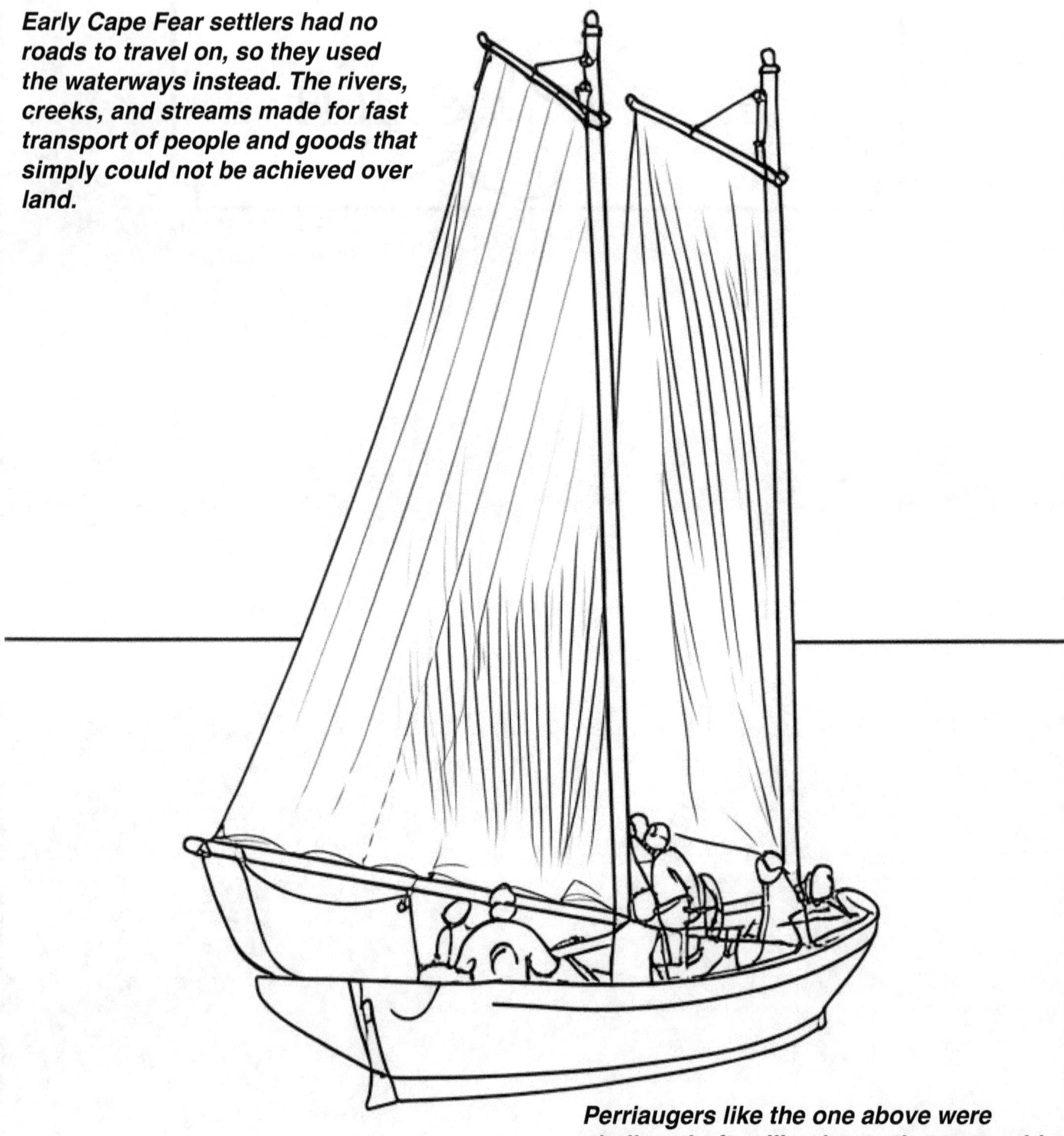

Perriaugers like the one above were shallow draft sailing boats that were wide and widely seen on the Cape Fear River, moving people between plantations and towns like Wilmington and Brunswick.

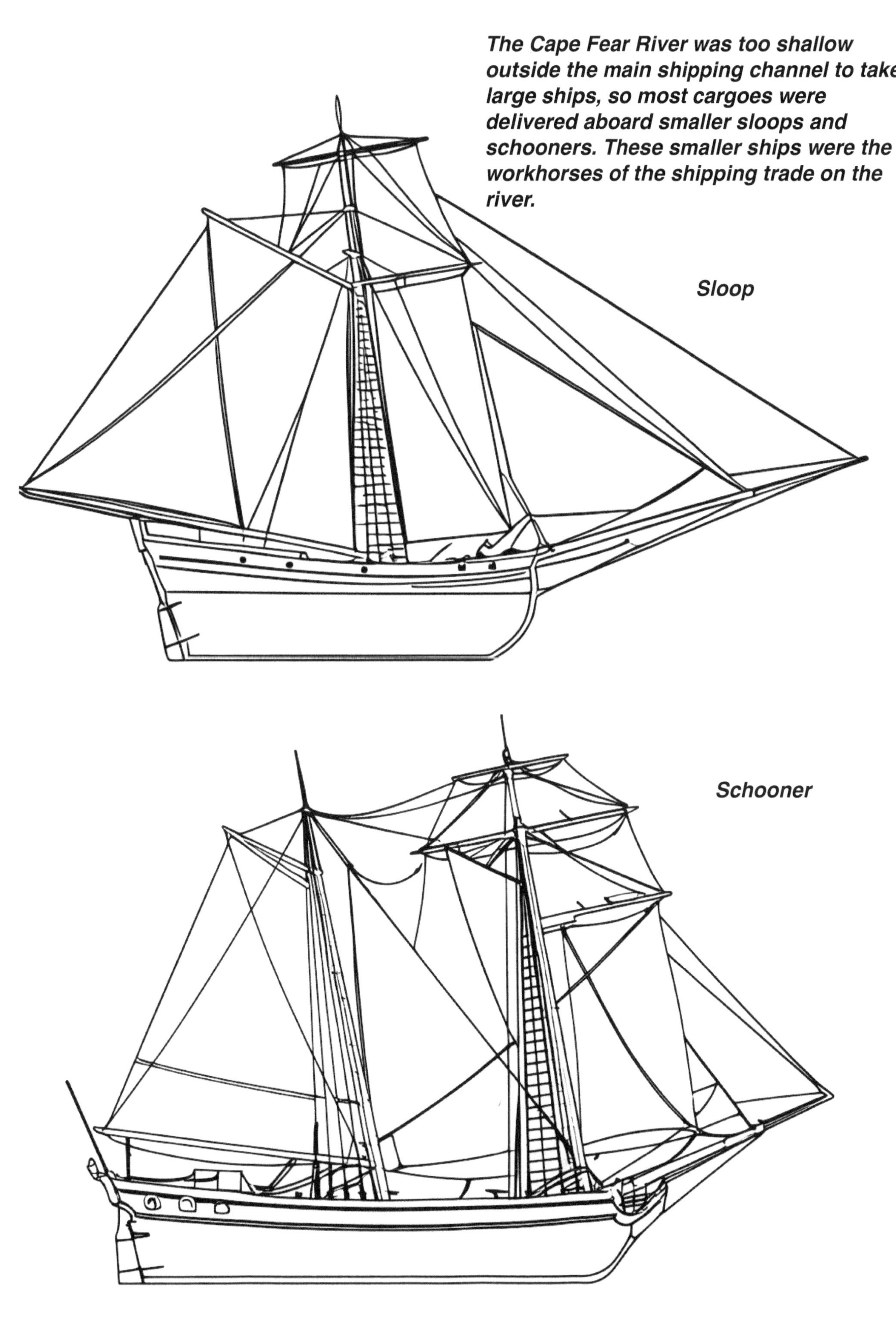

The Cape Fear River was too shallow outside the main shipping channel to take large ships, so most cargoes were delivered aboard smaller sloops and schooners. These smaller ships were the workhorses of the shipping trade on the river.

Steam replaces Sail

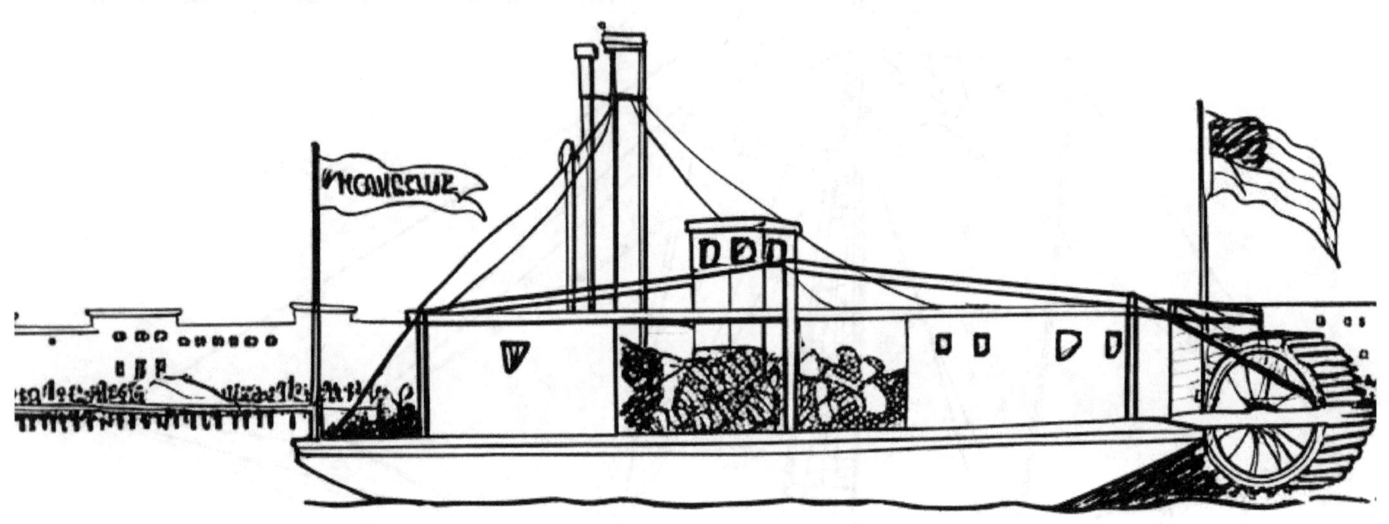

Captain Otway Burns (below) made his reputation as a privateer during the War of 1812, during which he and his ship, the Snap Dragon*, captured many British prizes. But he was also on the cutting edge of marine technology, embracing steam power as a means pf propelling a ship. Burns designed and built the first steamship on the Cape Fear River, the* Prometheus *(above).*

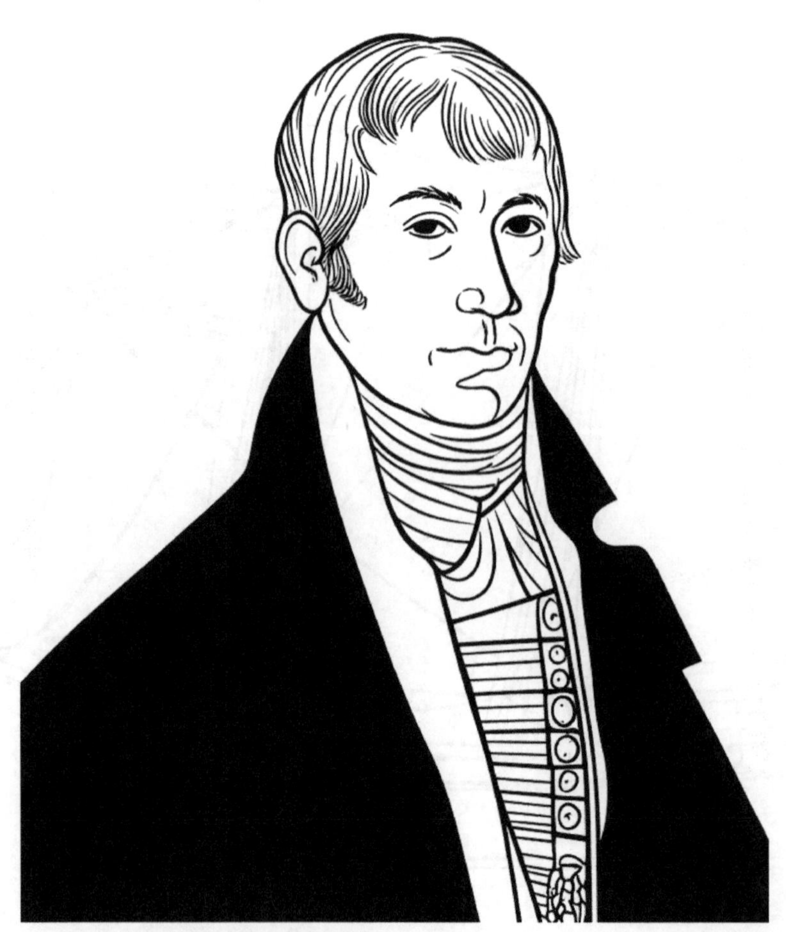

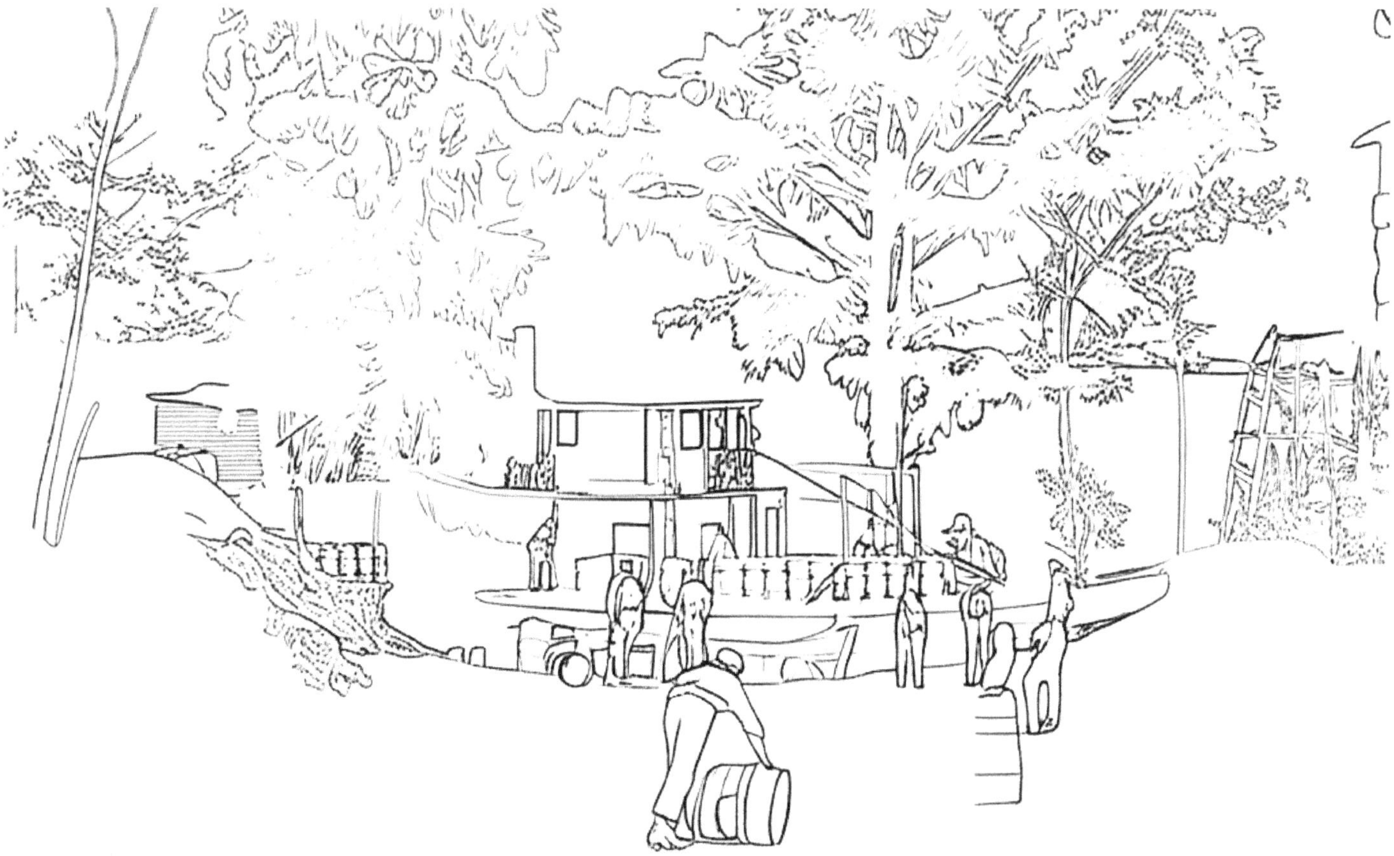

Steam boats carried goods like naval stores, cotton, tobacco, and more from upriver plantations to the port at Wilmington in the 1800s. In the above picture, workers load barrels of tar, pitch, and turpentine onto a river steamer. A loaded steamer (below) makes its way from Fayetteville to Wilmngton to deliver its cargo for shipment aboard ocean going vessels.

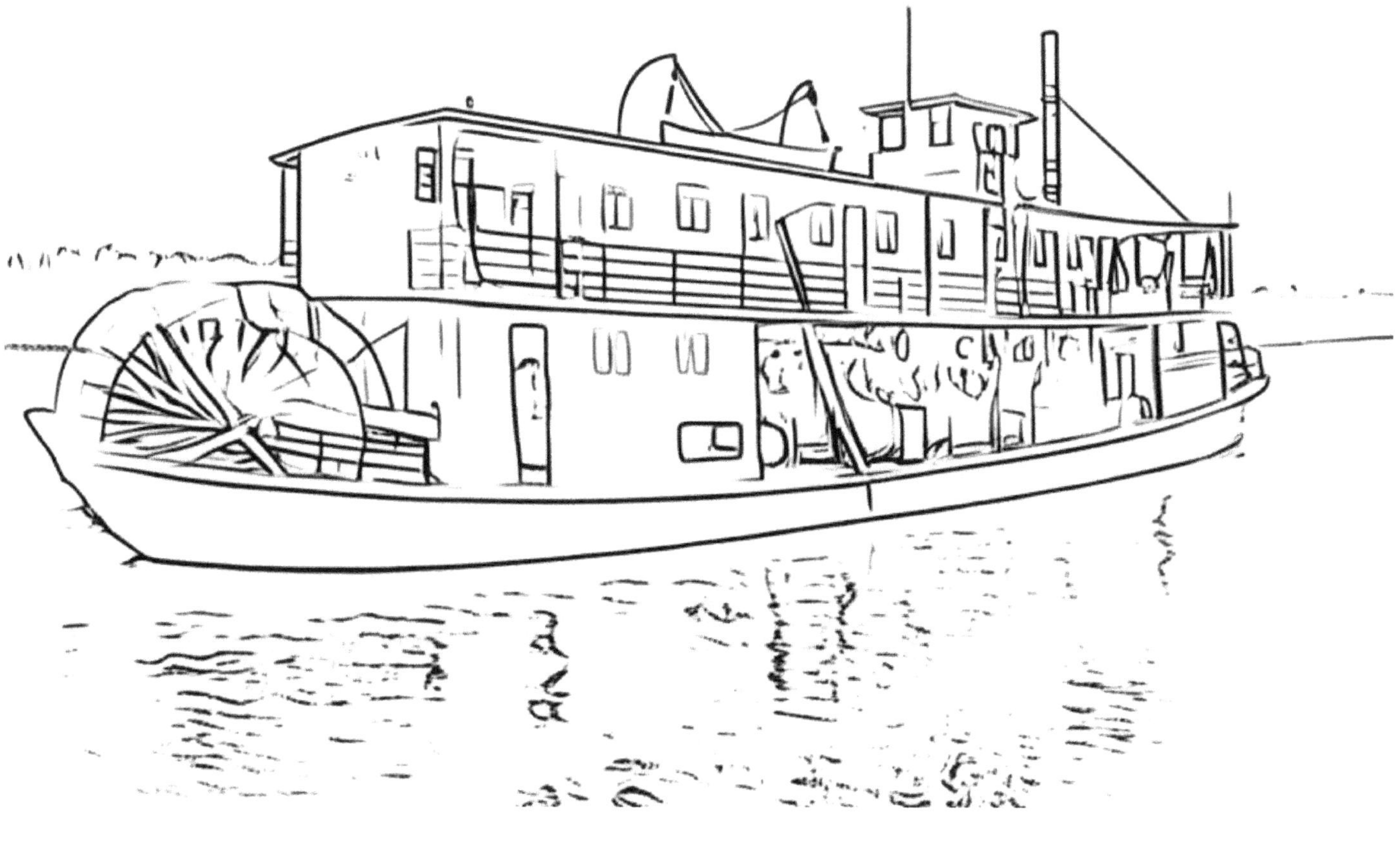

Arriving in the River

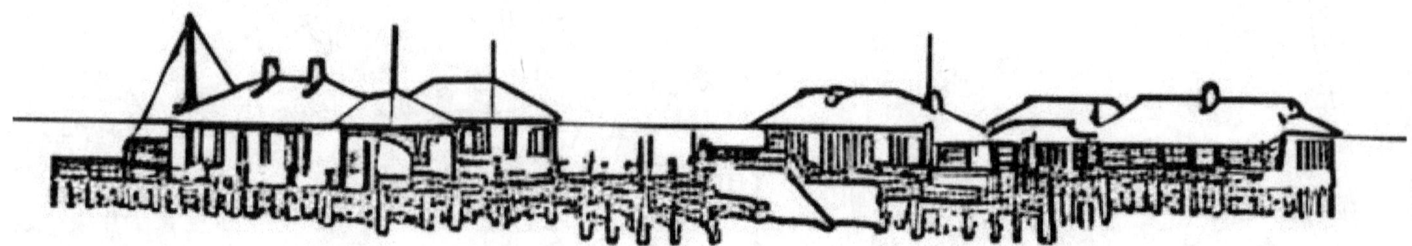

Arriving in the Cape Fear was just one part of the journey to safe harbor. The quarantine station in the river at Southport (above) made sure no vessels brought in dangerous sickness that could infect the local population. Ships also paused to take on pilots at Southport (below) to guide them up the ever shifting Cape Fear River channel to the safety of the port at Wilmington.

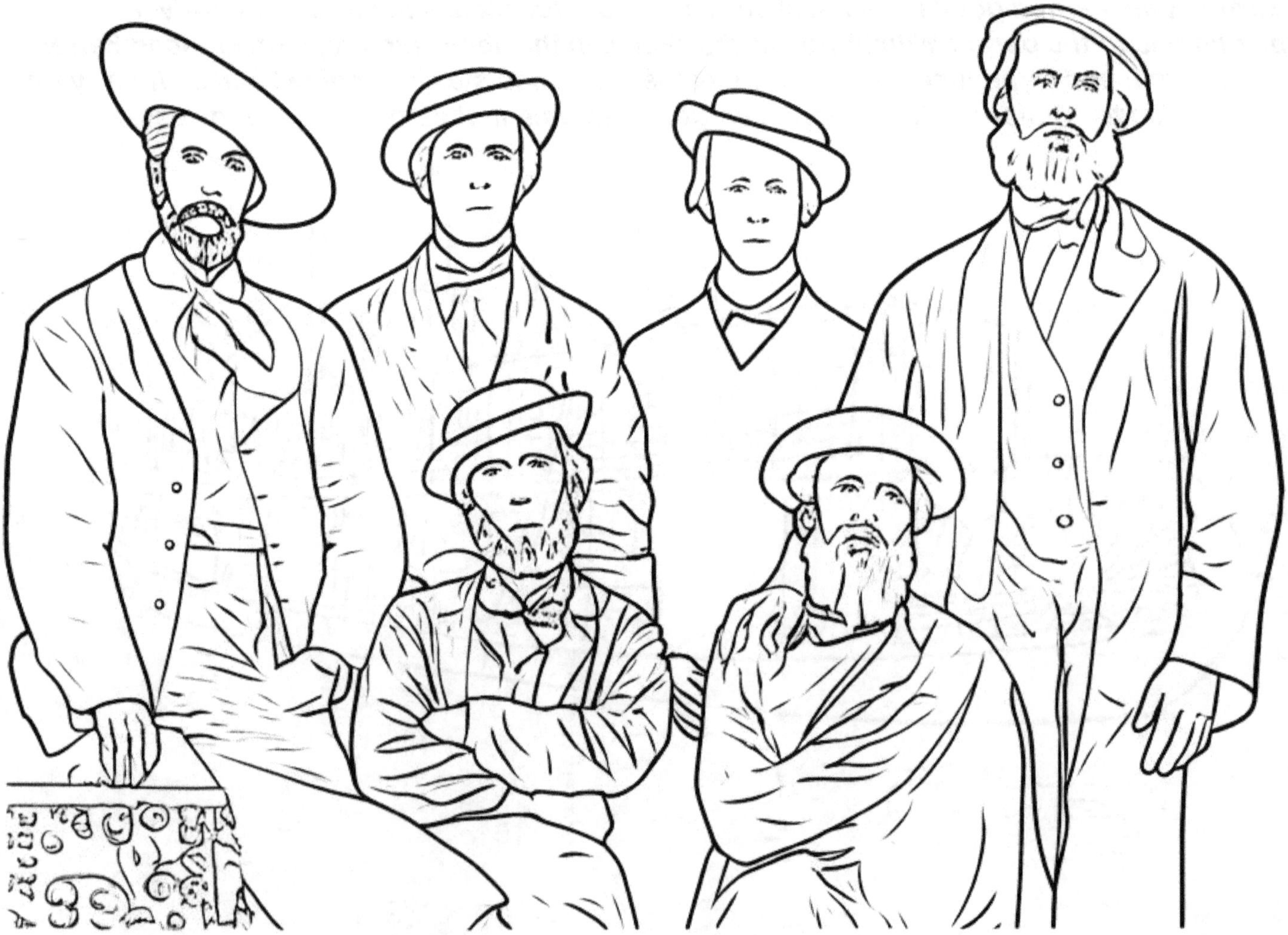

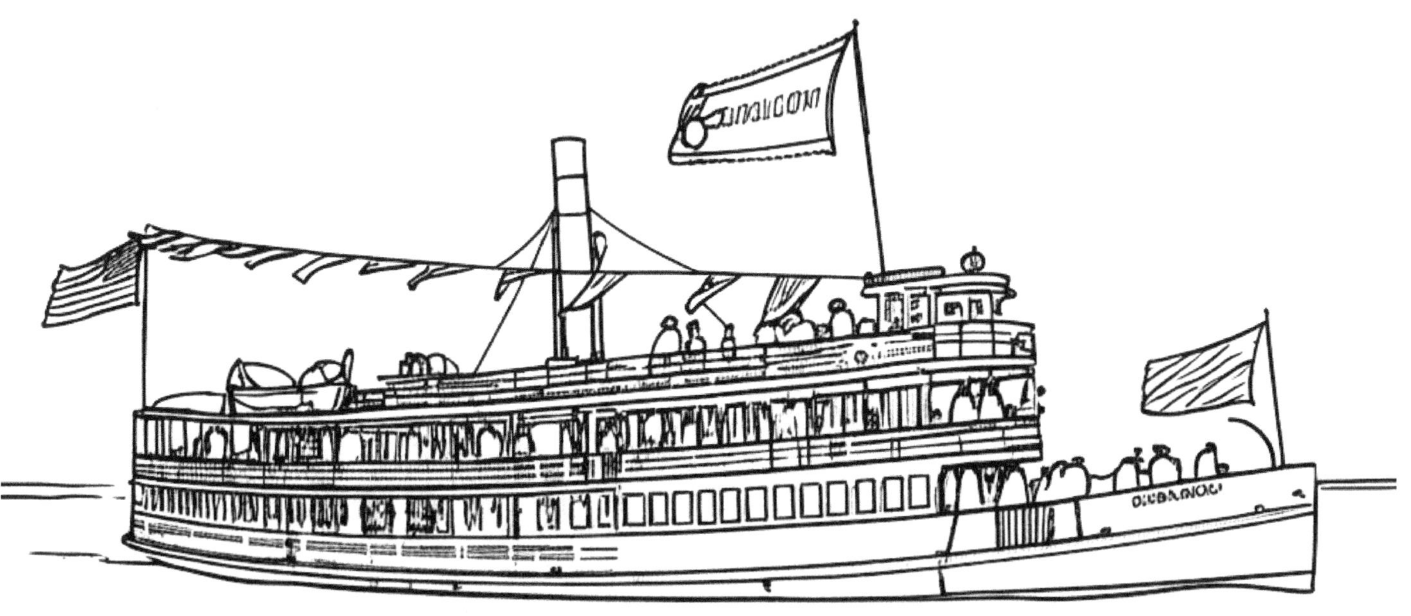

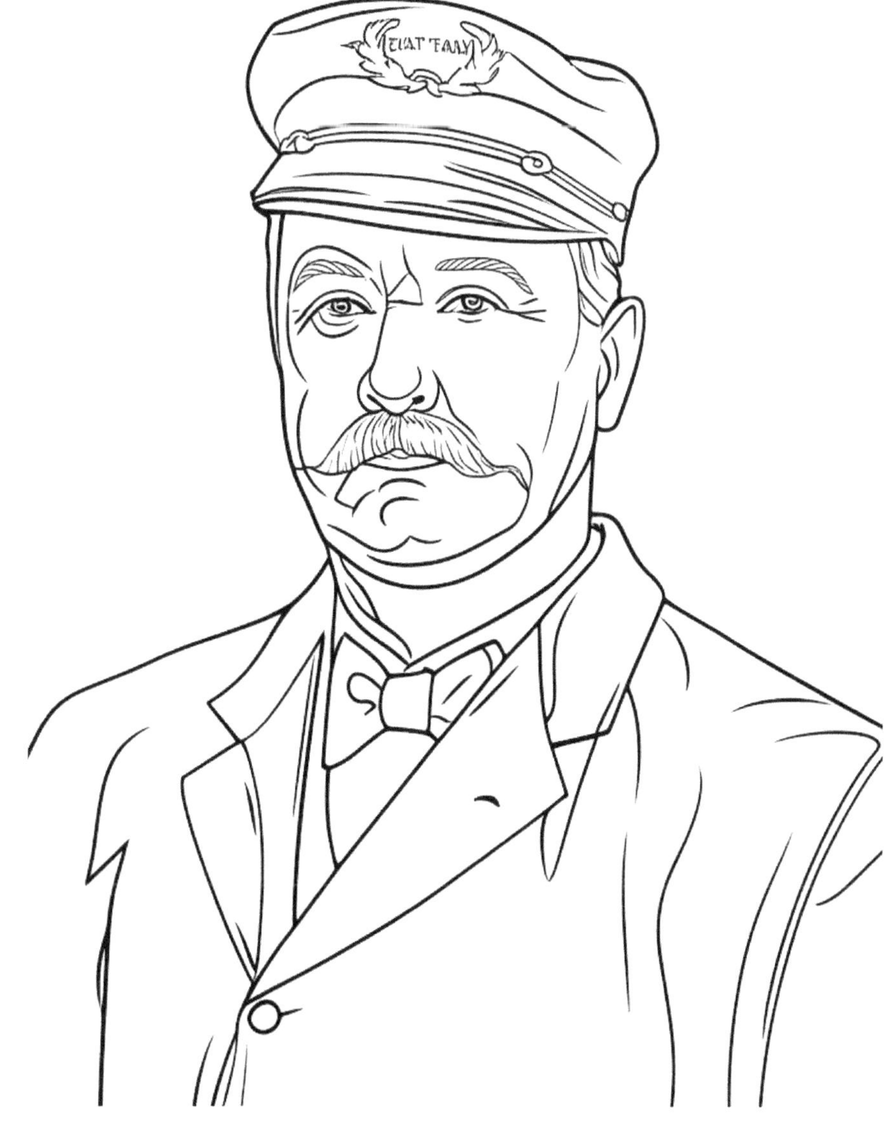

Captain John Harper (right) and his steam ship* Wilmington *(above) ferried people from the town of the same name 30 miles upriver down to Southport or to Carolina Beach for beach outings.

The Days of Lumina

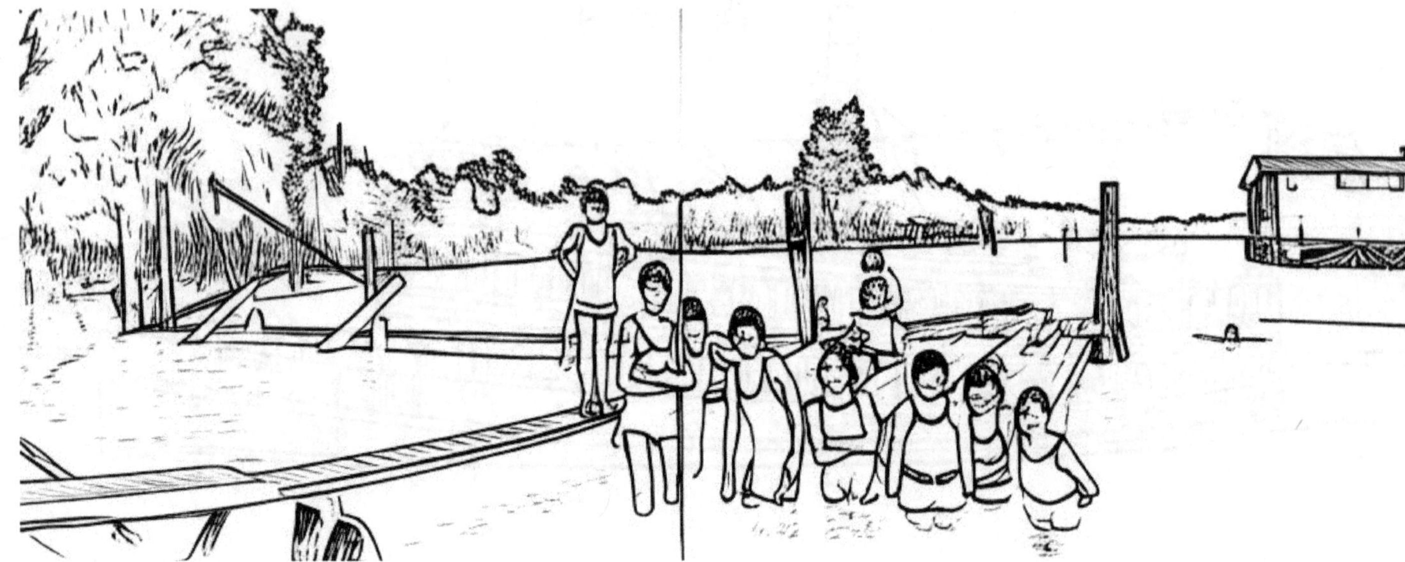

Greenfield Lake, built on what was once the colonial rice plantation of Dr. Samuel Green, was a place that people who did not have a way to get to the beach could enjoy a fun day swimming and boating (above).

But for those who could, trolleys (below) carried customers from Wilmington to Wrightsville Beach to enjoy the sun, surf, and attractions like Lumina Pavilion.

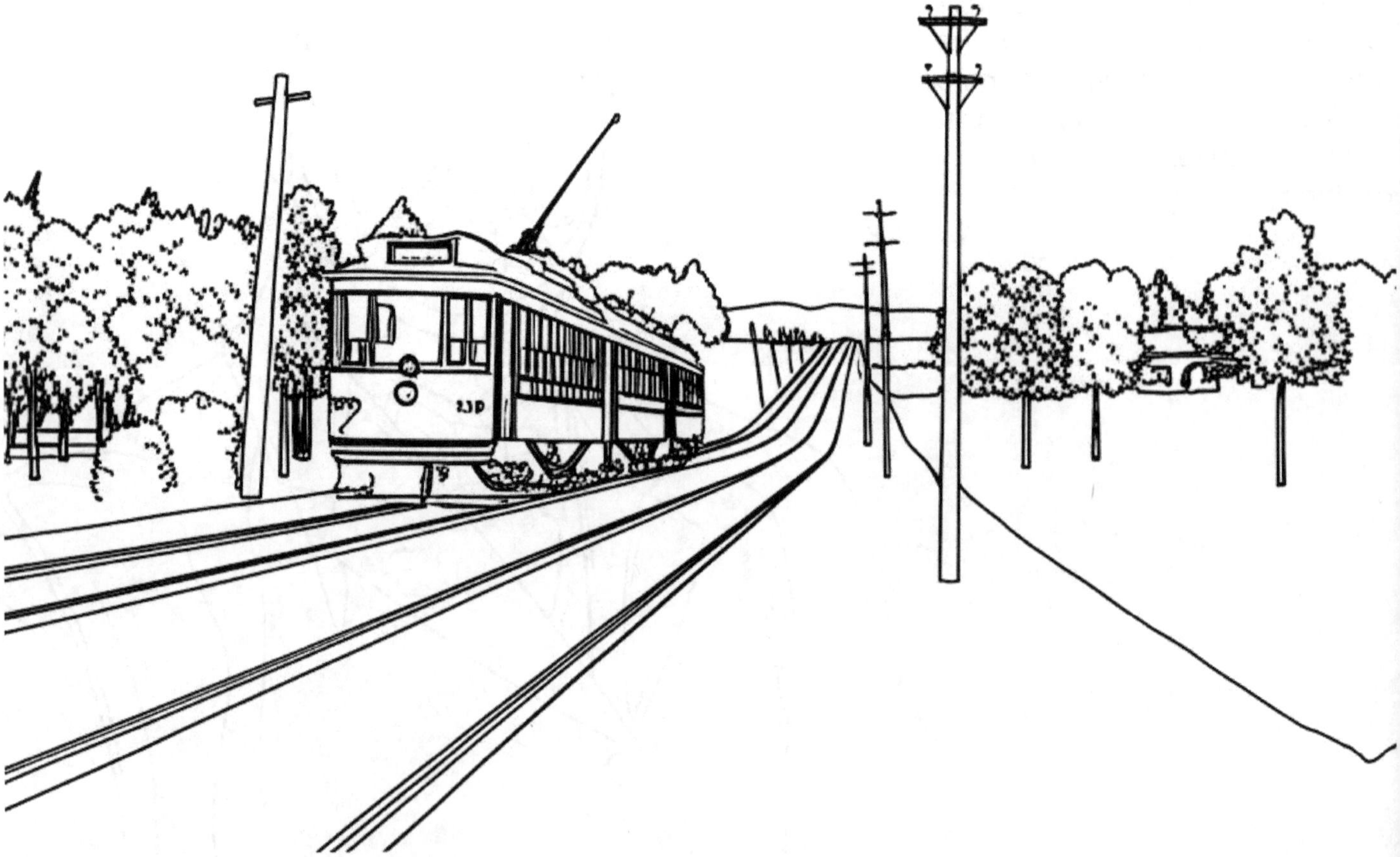

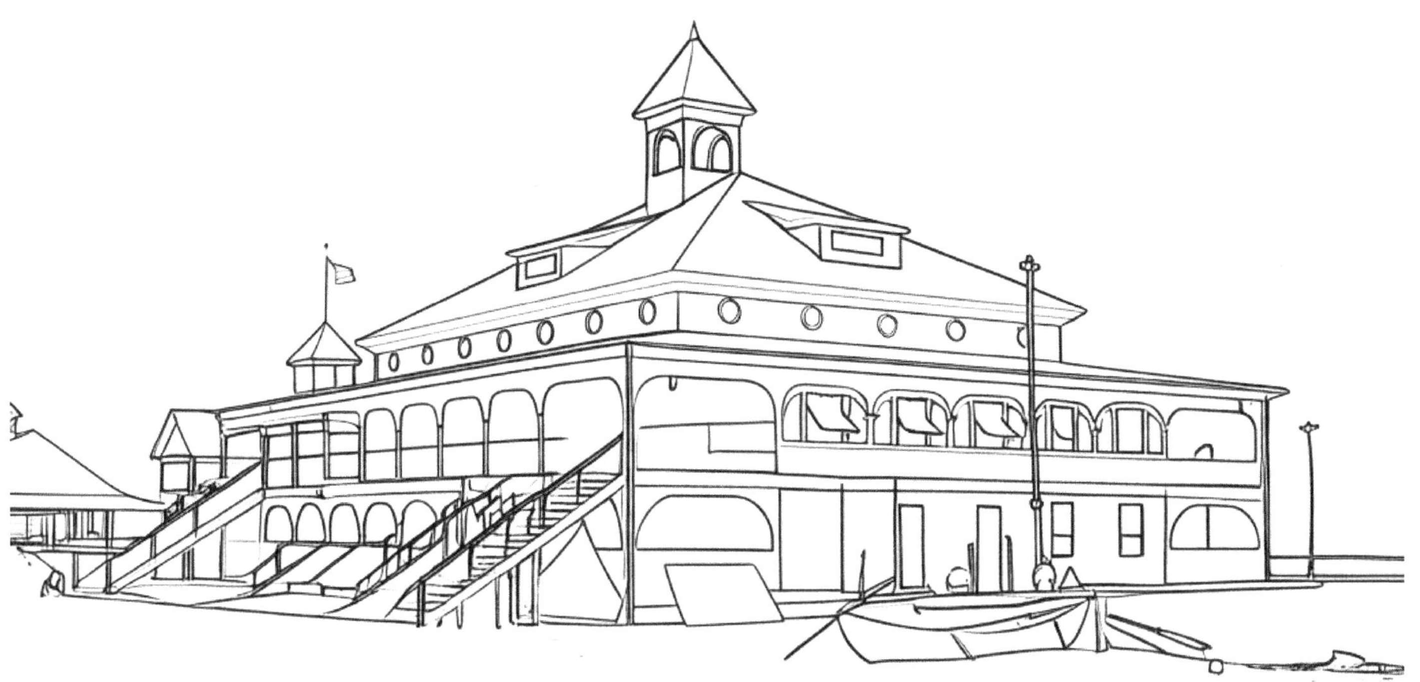

Wrightsville Beach's Lumina Pavilion (above) was a destination to hear big bands, enjoy dances (below), watch movies on the beach, and much more. It was an iconic building on the beach until it fell into disrepair and was demolished by 1970.

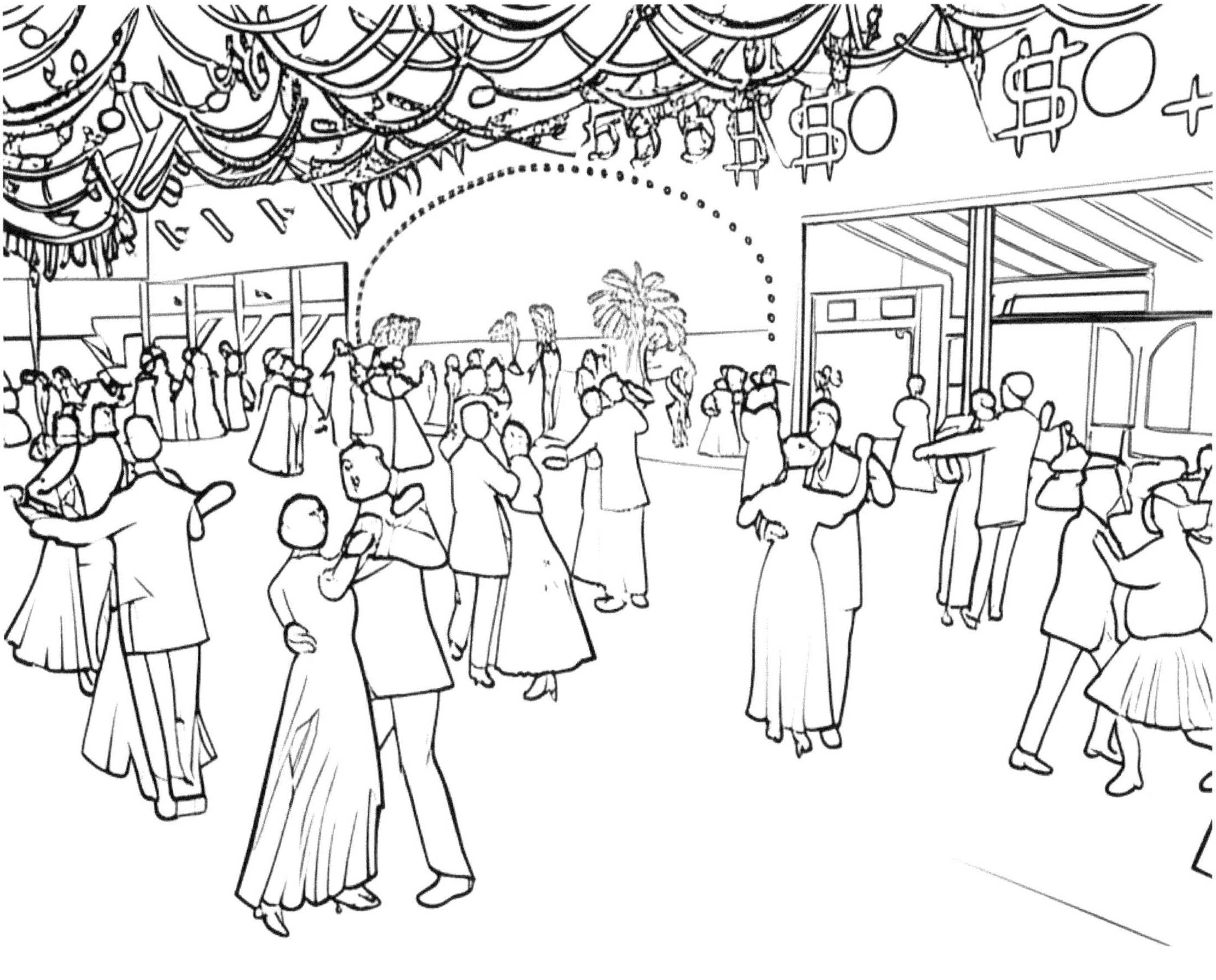

Putting the Pleasure in the Island

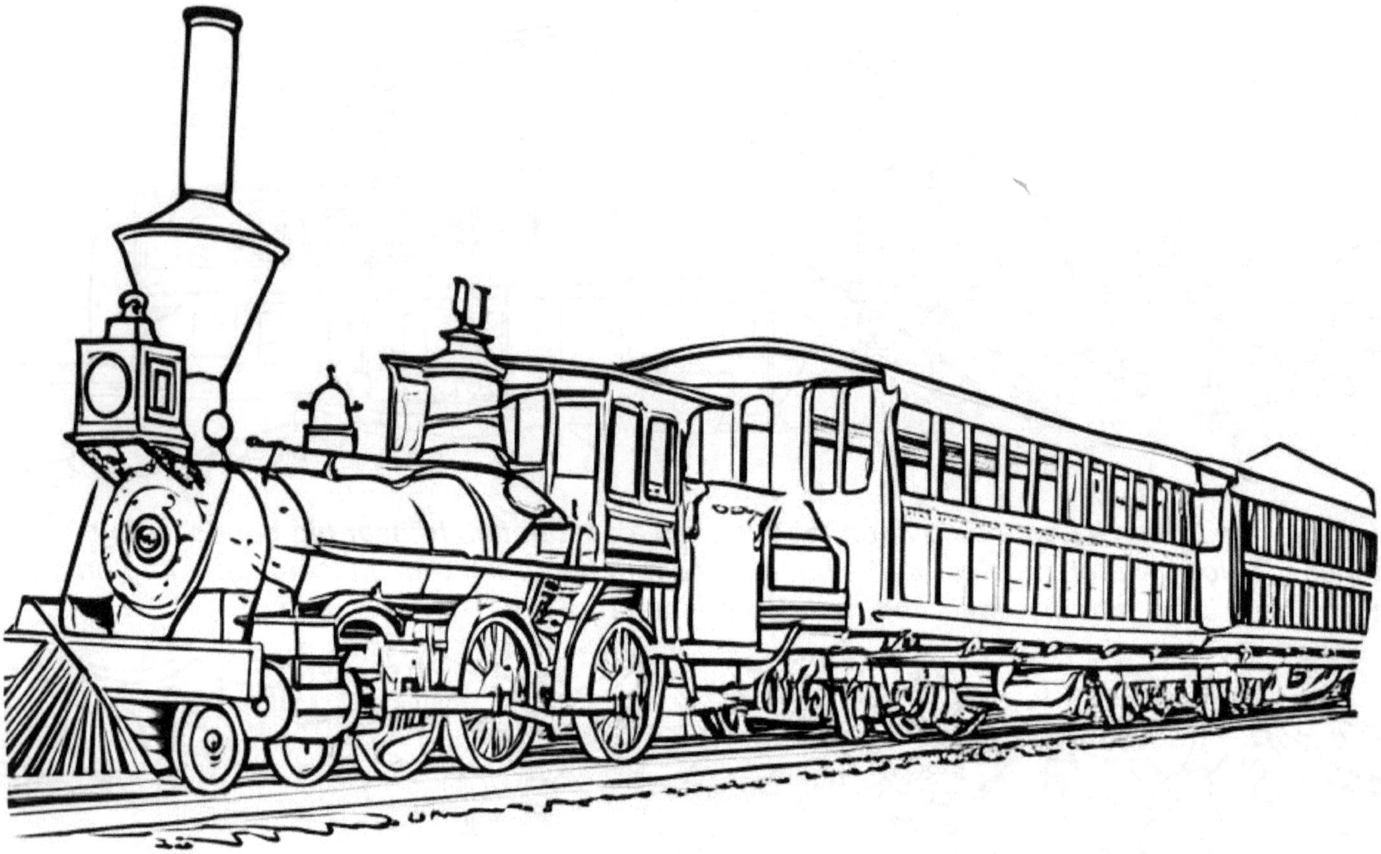

After Capt. John Harper's steamer Wilmington *delivered visitors to the river side of Carolina Beach, the Shoofly Train (above) carted them across the sands to the ocean side to enjoy their day at the beach. Riders loaded up at a small station near modern Snow's Cut (below) to make the journey.*

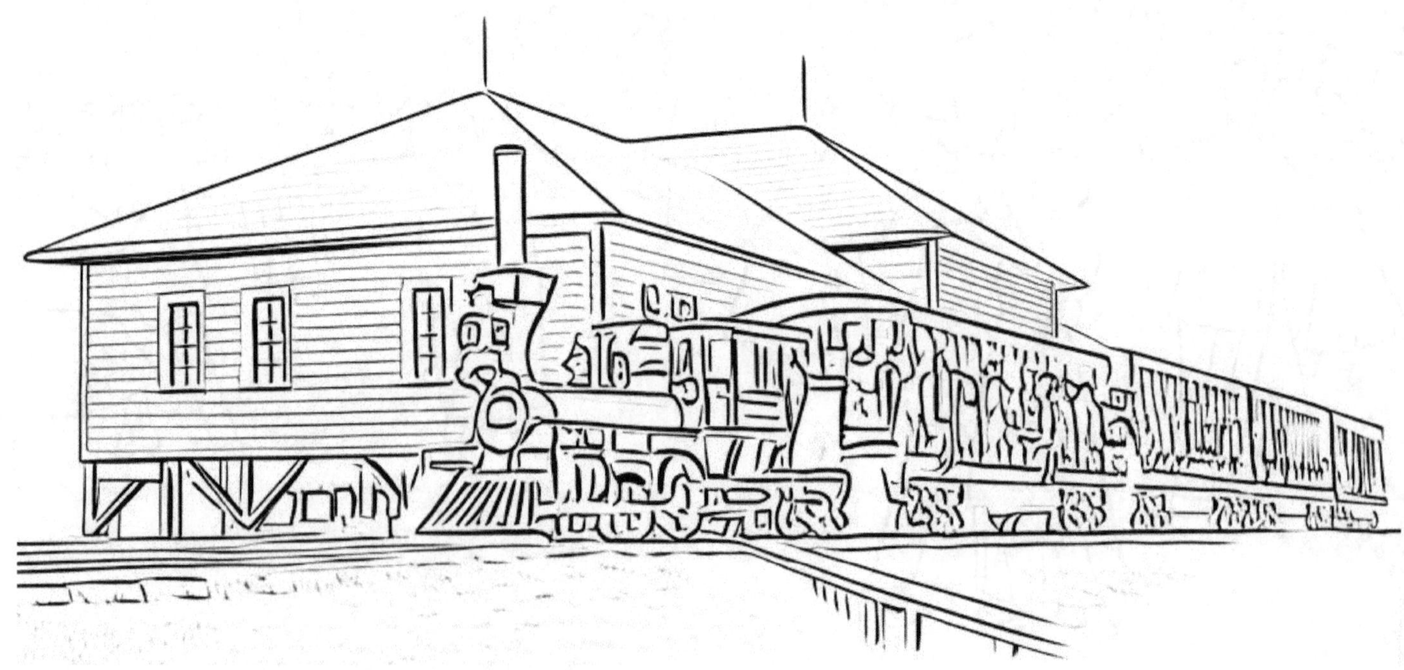

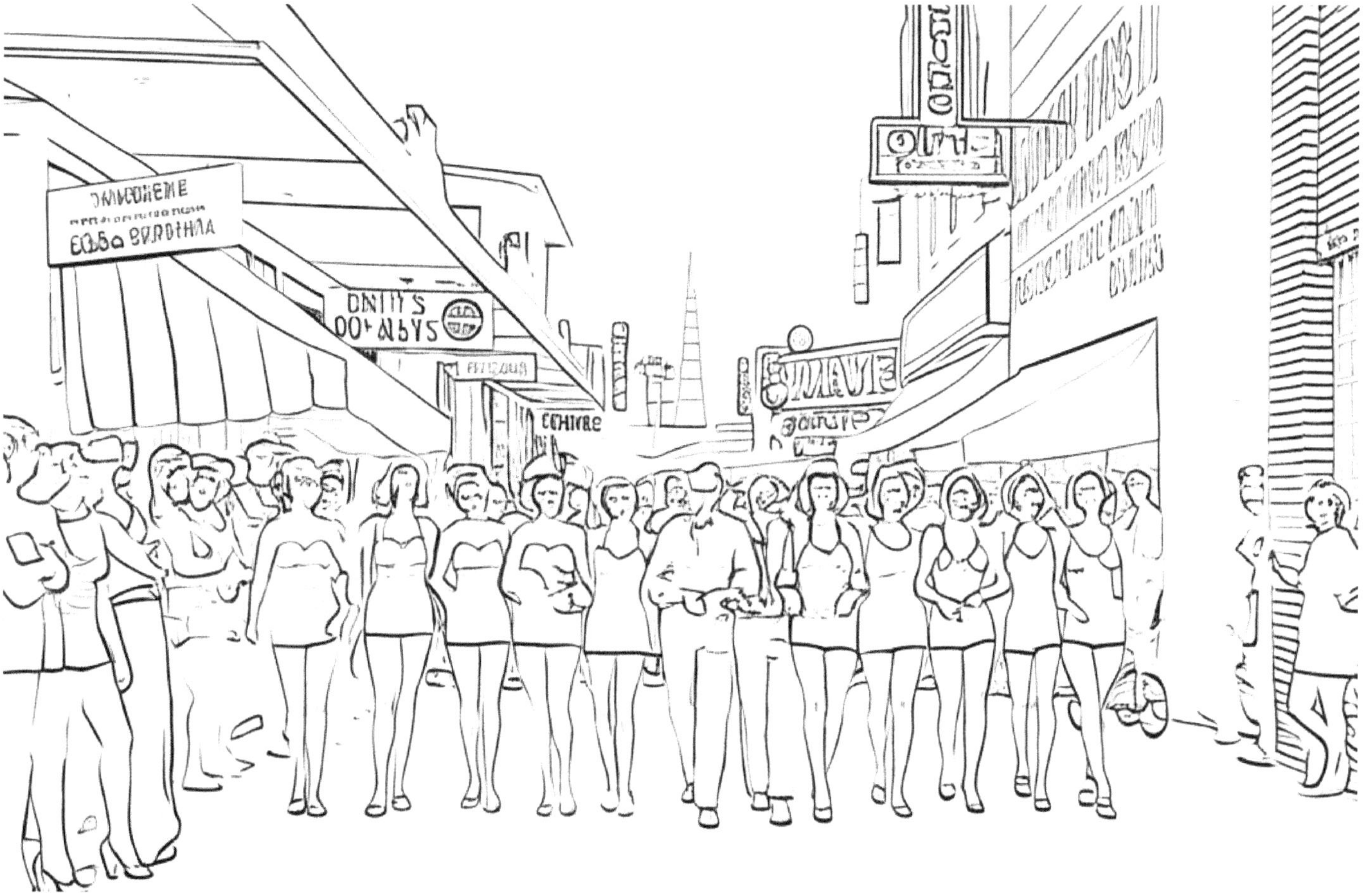

The Carolina Beach boardwalk has been the center of activity at least as far back as the 1940s, when bathing beauties like the ones above drew soldiers from surrounding bases looking for companionship and fun. With amusement park rides and white beaches close by, the boardwalk has provided fun times for generations.

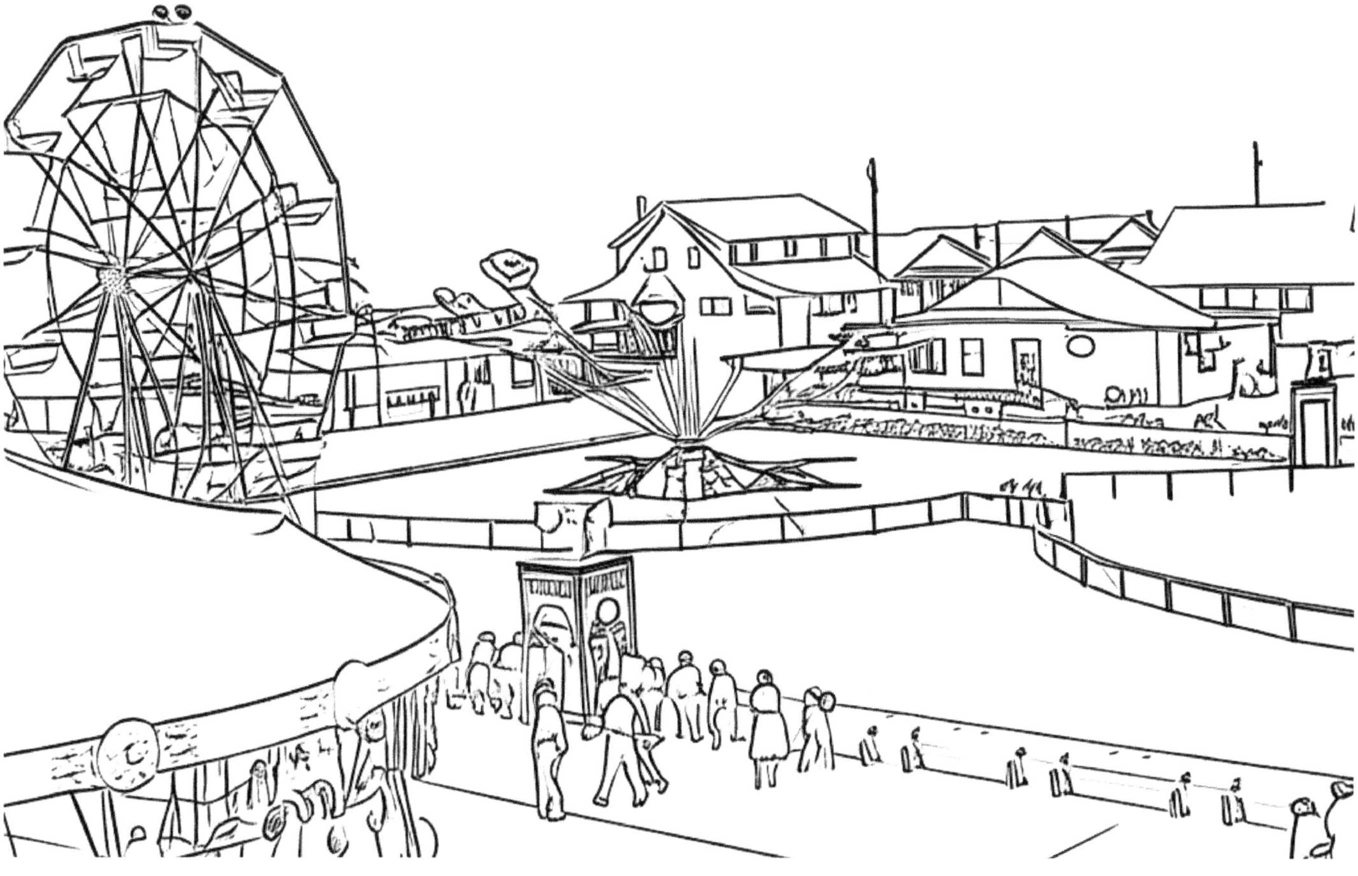

Segregated Seas & Sun

Seabreeze and other segregated beaches provided African Americans with opportunities to enjoy the sun and surf at a time when races did not mix.

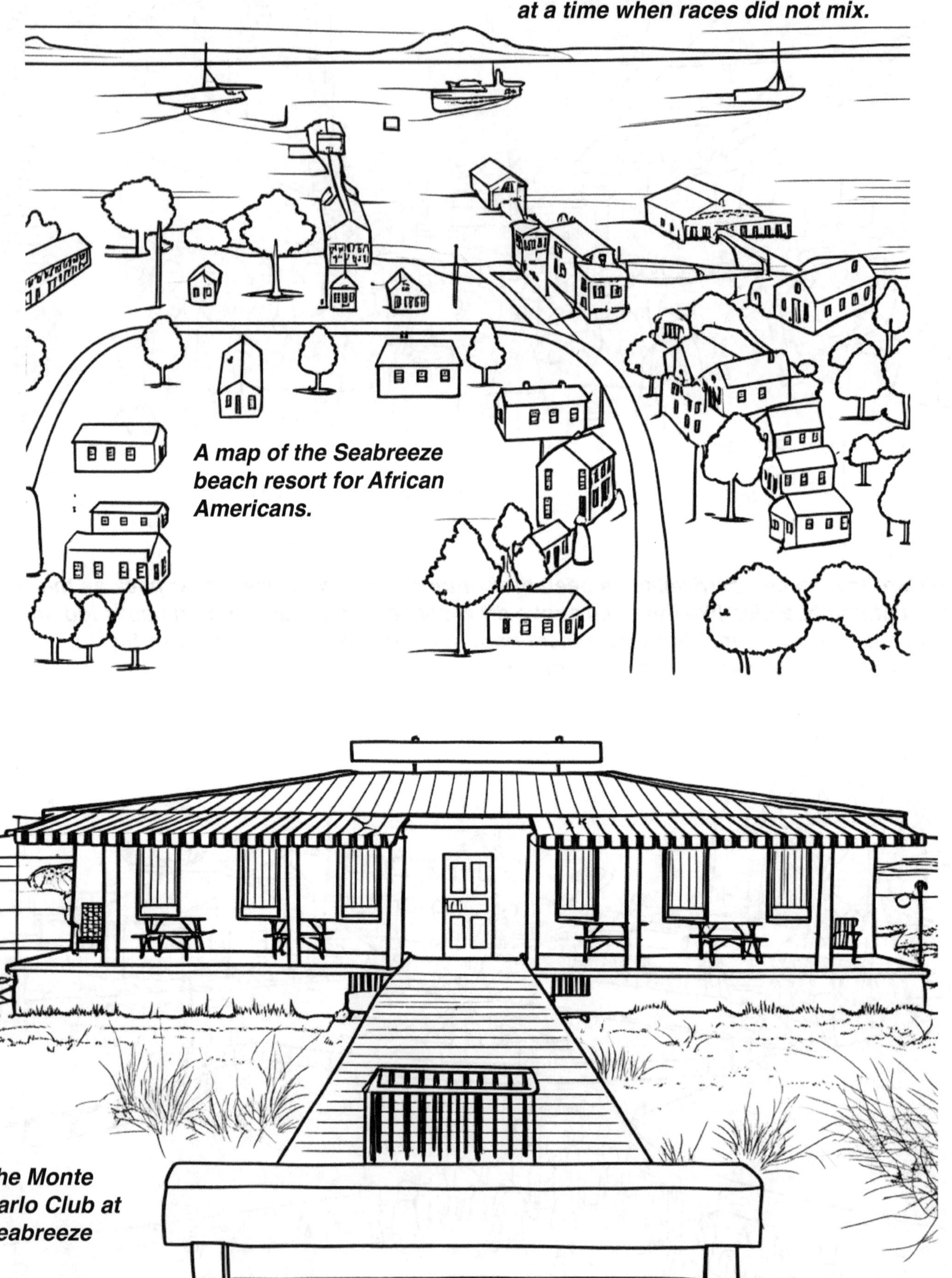

A map of the Seabreeze beach resort for African Americans.

The Monte Carlo Club at Seabreeze

Seabreeze was a place where Black families (right) could have a pleasant time at the beach without worrying about the Jim Crow society that reigned in the South. Segregated beaches were the rule, just as segregation applied to all other aspects of life in North Carolina between 1877 aand 1965.

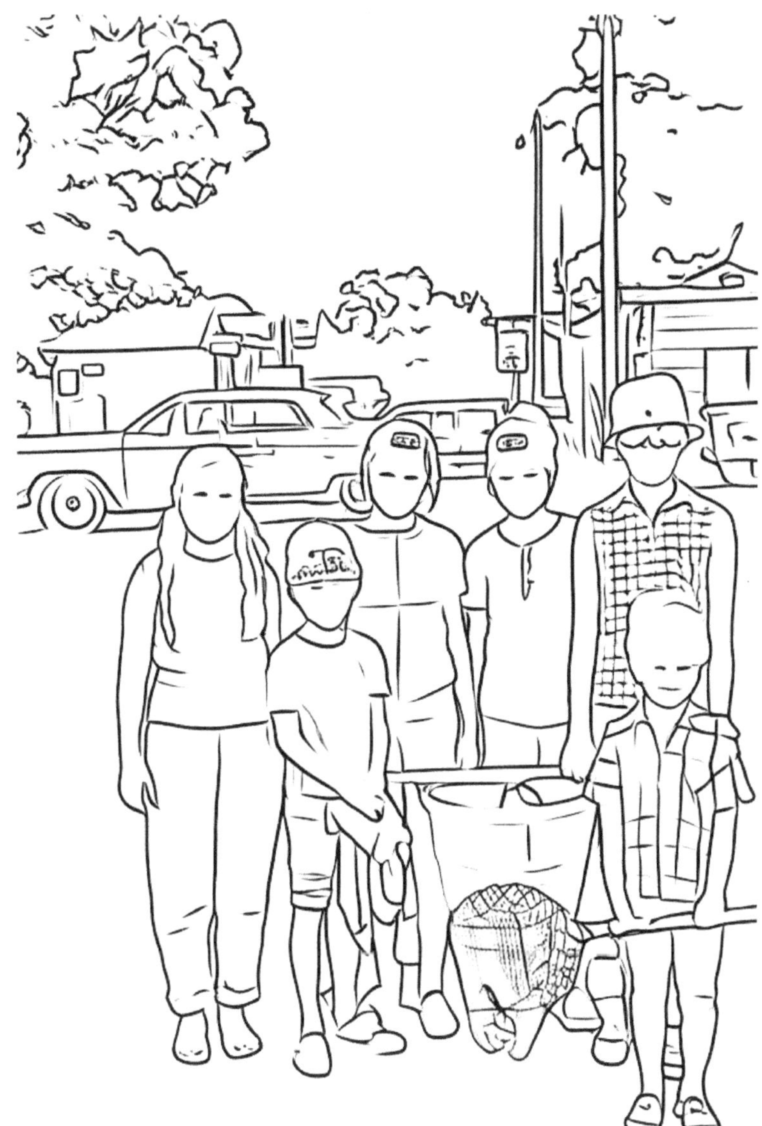

African Americans came from all over the South to enjoy Seabreeze and other segregated beaches.

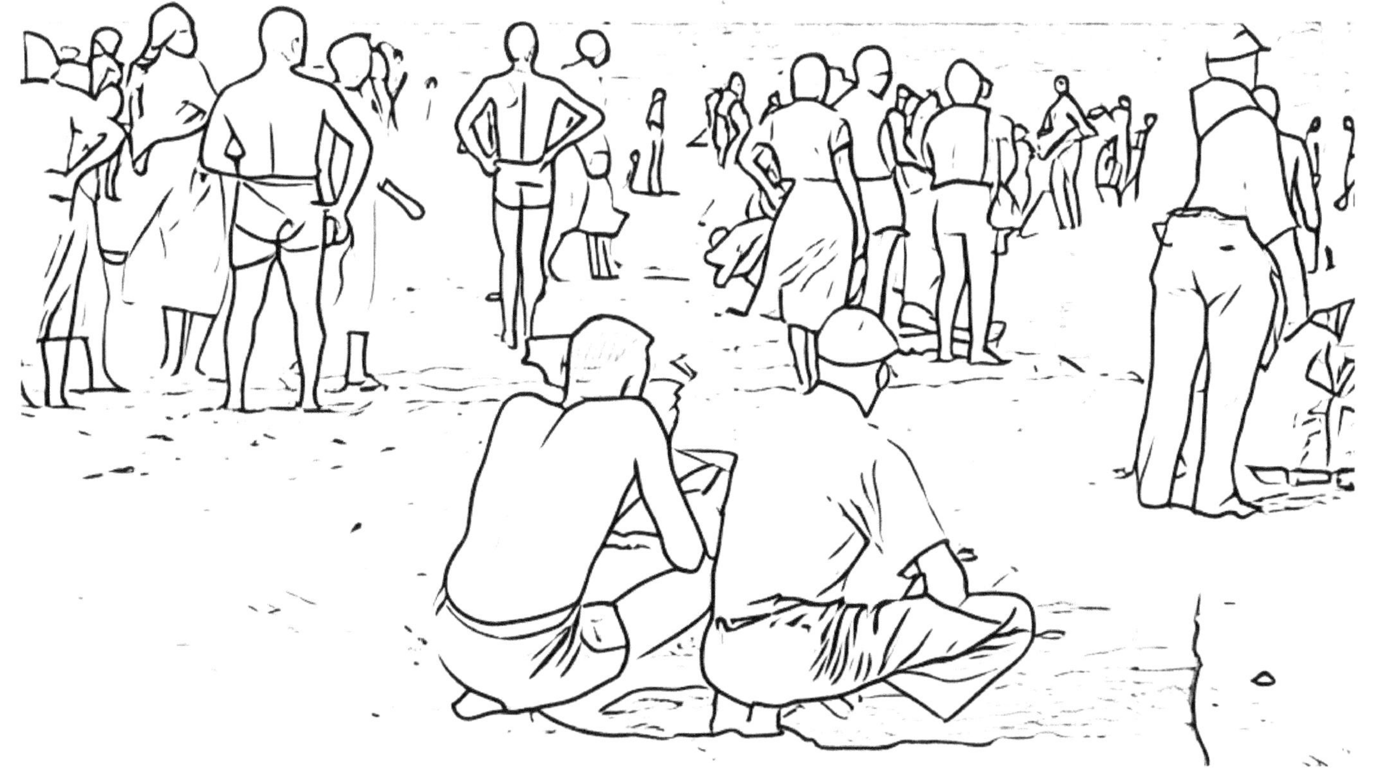

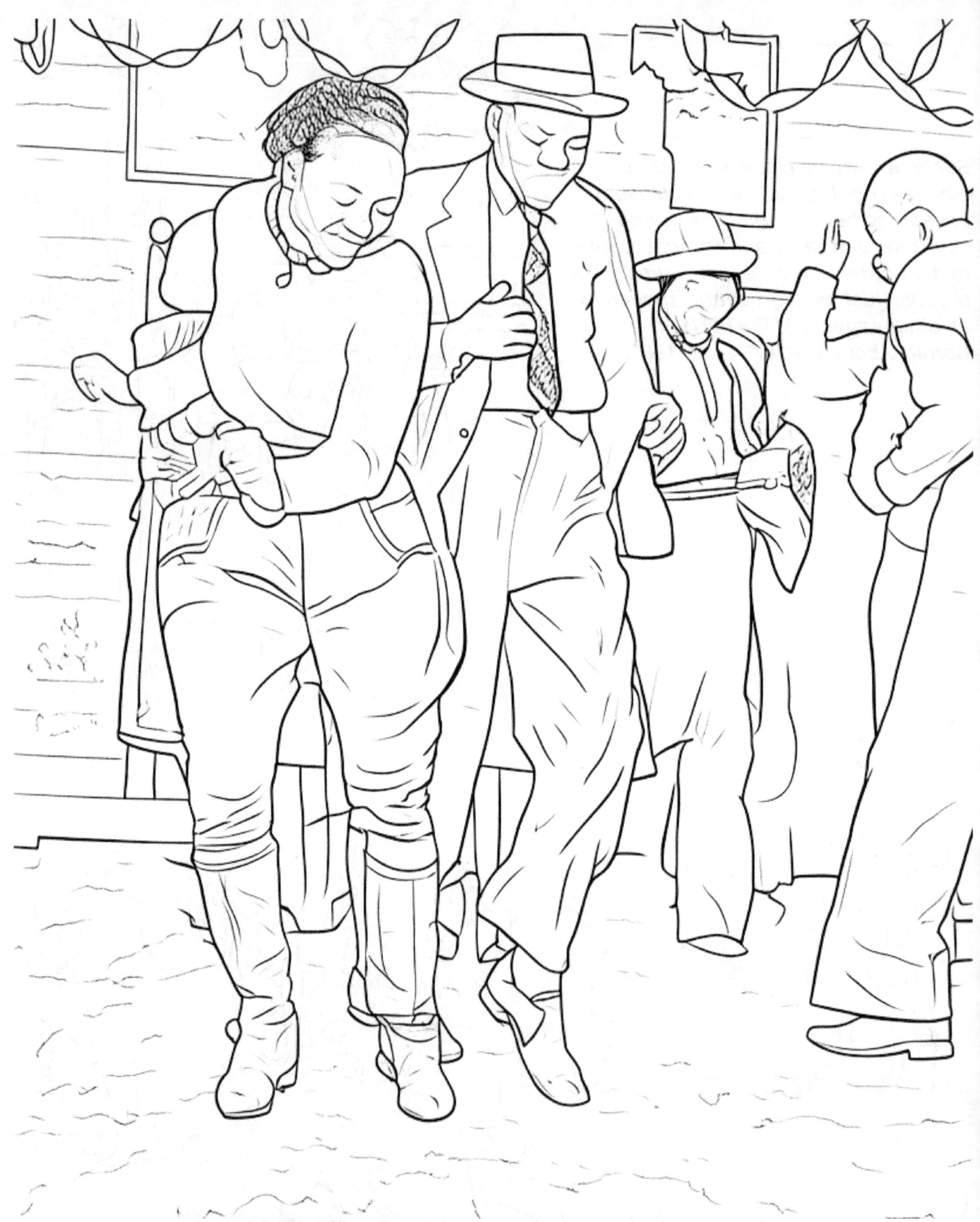

Clubs like the Monte Carlo at Seabreeze offered a wide range of entertainments for African Americans, including dancing. It was at Seabreeze that dances like the shag were born.

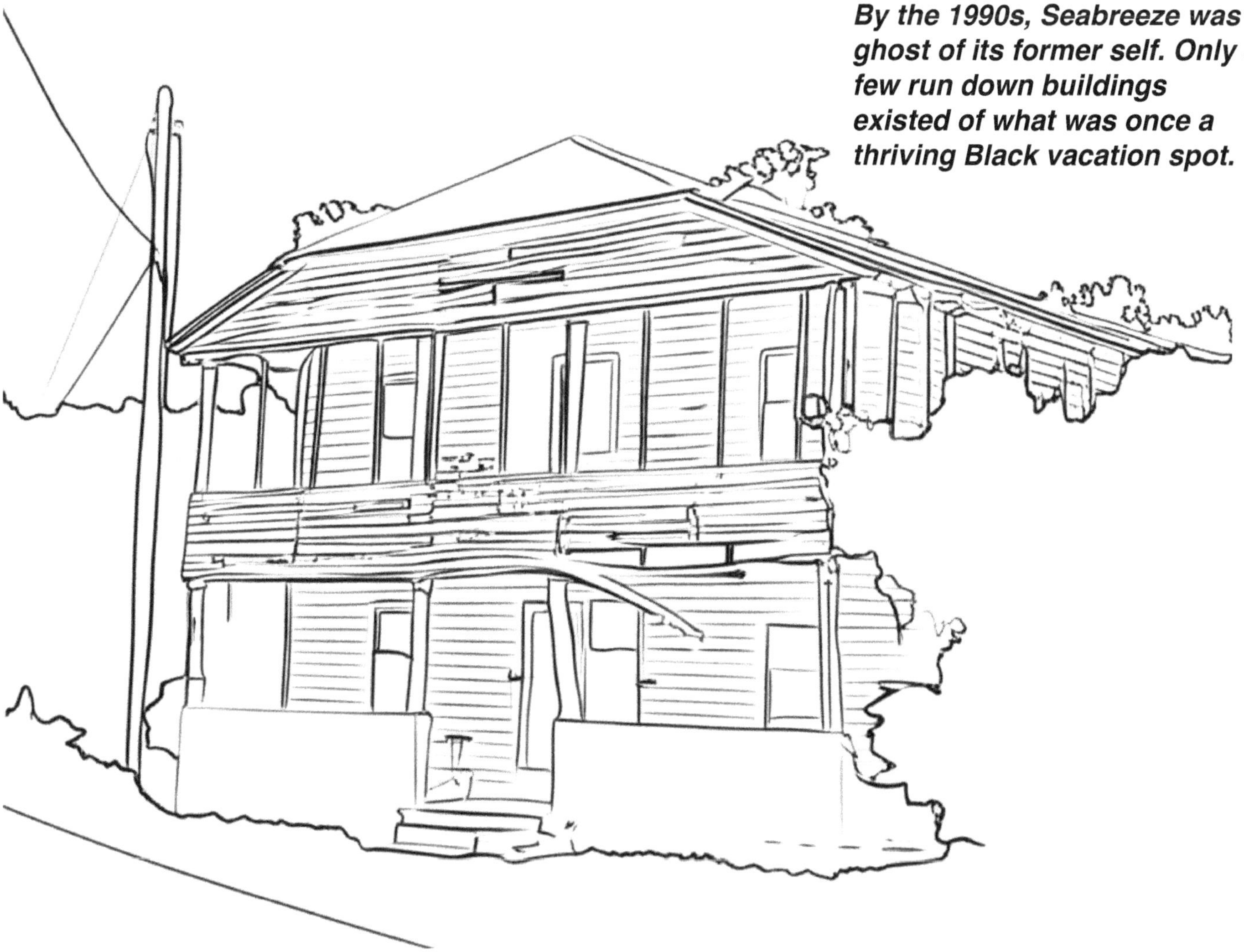

By the 1990s, Seabreeze was a ghost of its former self. Only a few run down buildings existed of what was once a thriving Black vacation spot.

Wrightsville's Shell Island

The north end of Wrightsville Beach boasted a Black beach of its own. Shell Island was designated for use by African Americans just as Seabreeze was.

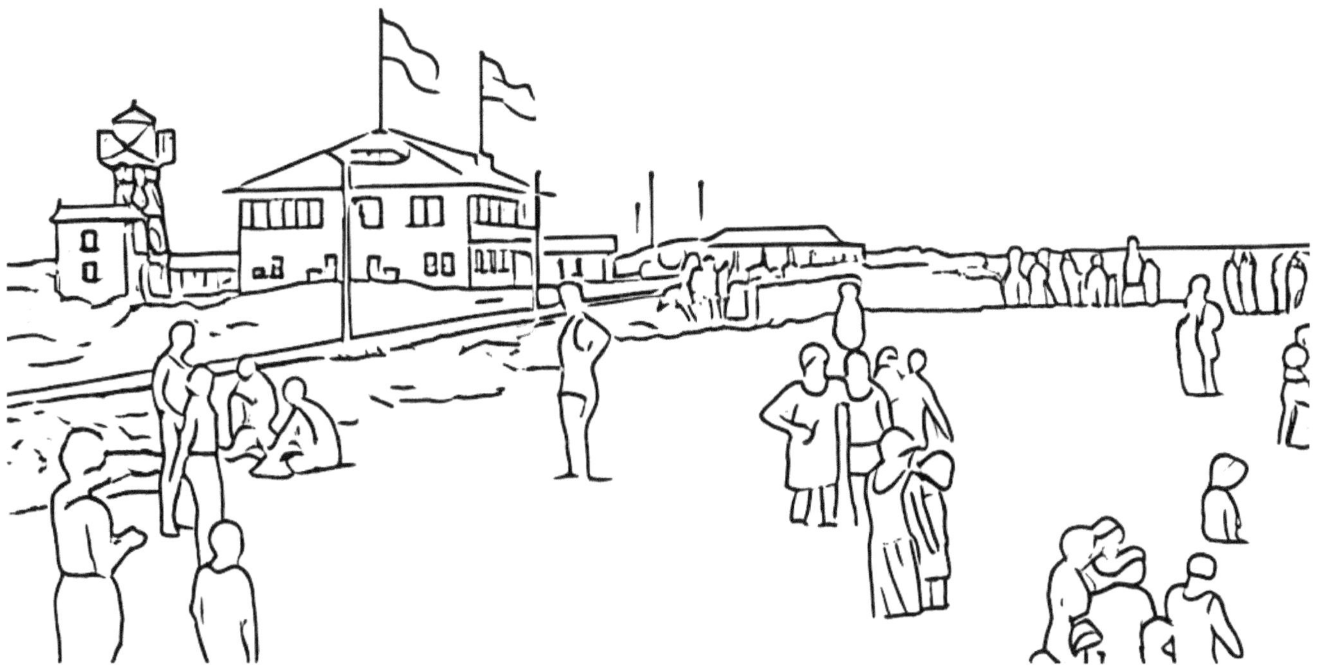

Shipbuilding for Liberty

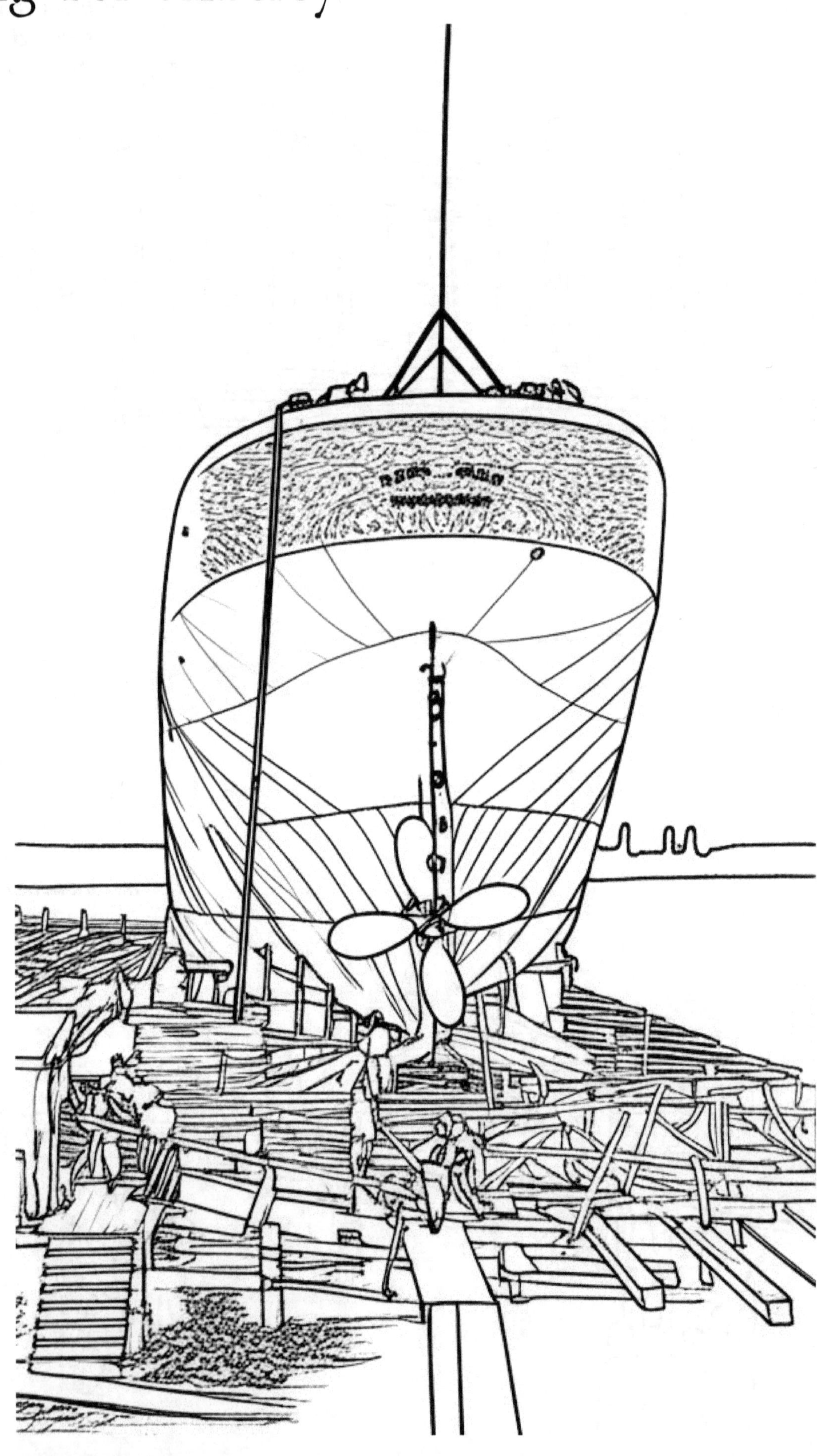

In both World Wars, shipyards on the Cape Fear River contributed to the war effort by building the Liberty and Victory ships that were essential to delivering the things American soildiers and their allies needed to defeat their enemies. Between 1918 and 1919, the Liberty Shipyard built and launched three experimental concrete ships into the Cape Fear River. During World War II, the N.C. Shipbuilding Co. in Wilmington built 126 Liberty ships, and another 117 of the larger and faster C-2 ships nicknamed Victory ships.

NC's Immortal Showboat

The *USS North Carolina* was built in the New York Navy Yard in Brooklyn in 1937, the namesake of a new class of fast battleships. The ship was the first battleship built by the United States in sixteen years, and underwent sea trials in time to make her available for duty just as the Japanese bombed Pearl Harbor. The ship was the first to sail into Pearl Harbor after the attack, inspiring U.S. servicemen still reeling from the Japanese onslaught. The *North Carolina* would go on to serve in every major battle in the Pacific, earning fifteen battle stars to become the most decorated American battleship of World War II. After the war, the *North Carolina* served as a training vessel for midshipmen before being decmissioned in the summer of 1947 and placed in the reserve fleet. A "Save Our Ship" campaign led by N.C. Governor Terry Sanford and the state's school children saved the ship from the breakers yard and brought her to Wilmington in October 1961. The ship has been there ever since, fulfilling its latest mission as a World War II musuem ship and memorial to the men who served, fought, and died in that war.

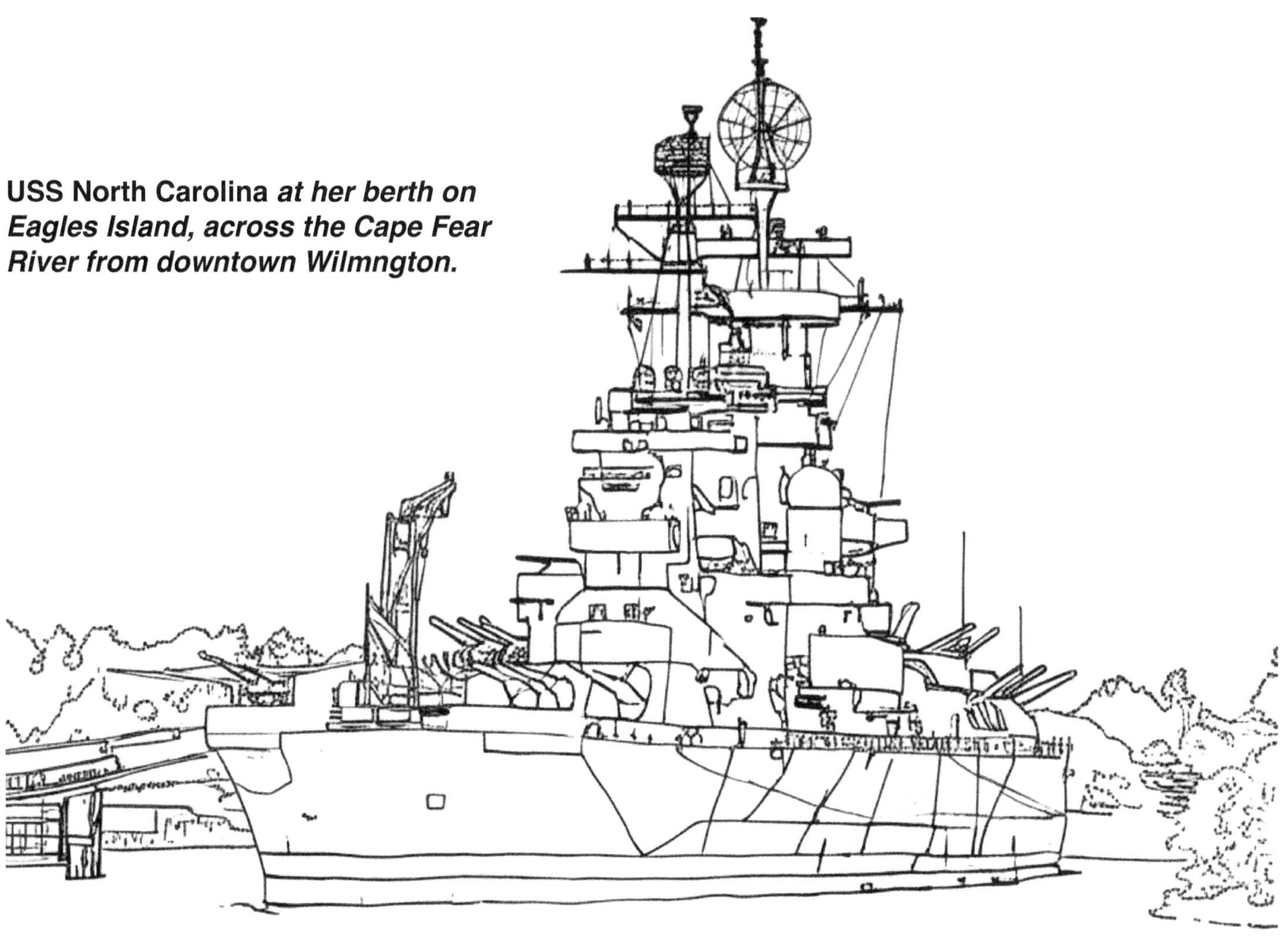

USS North Carolina ***at her berth on Eagles Island, across the Cape Fear River from downtown Wilmngton.***

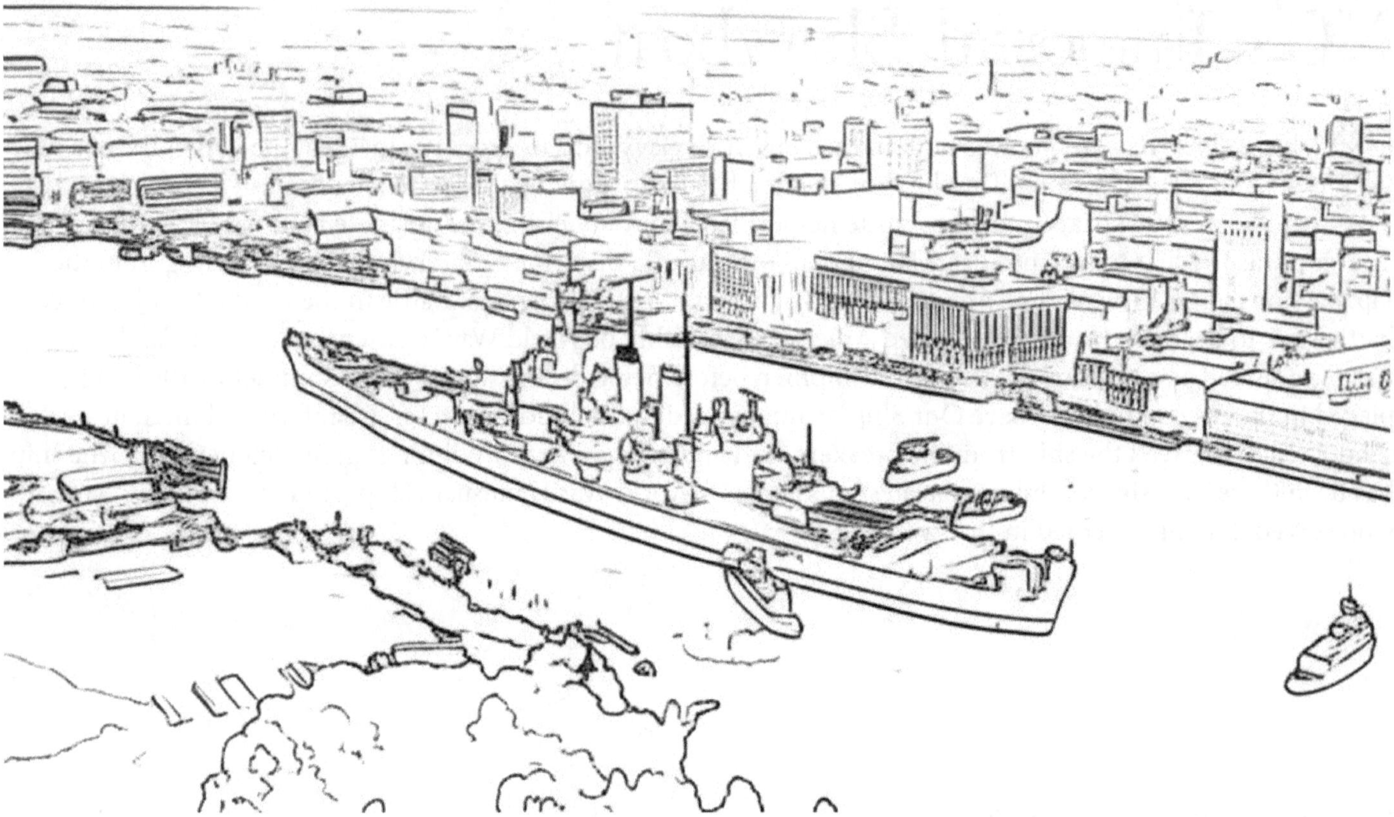

The **North Carolina** ***slowly made her way up the Cape Fear River with the aid of tugboats in October 1961 (above). As the tugs began turning the ship into the space dredged out for it on Eagles Island, the stern of the ship smashed into the Fergus Ark, a floating fish restaurant on the Wilmington riverfront (below).***

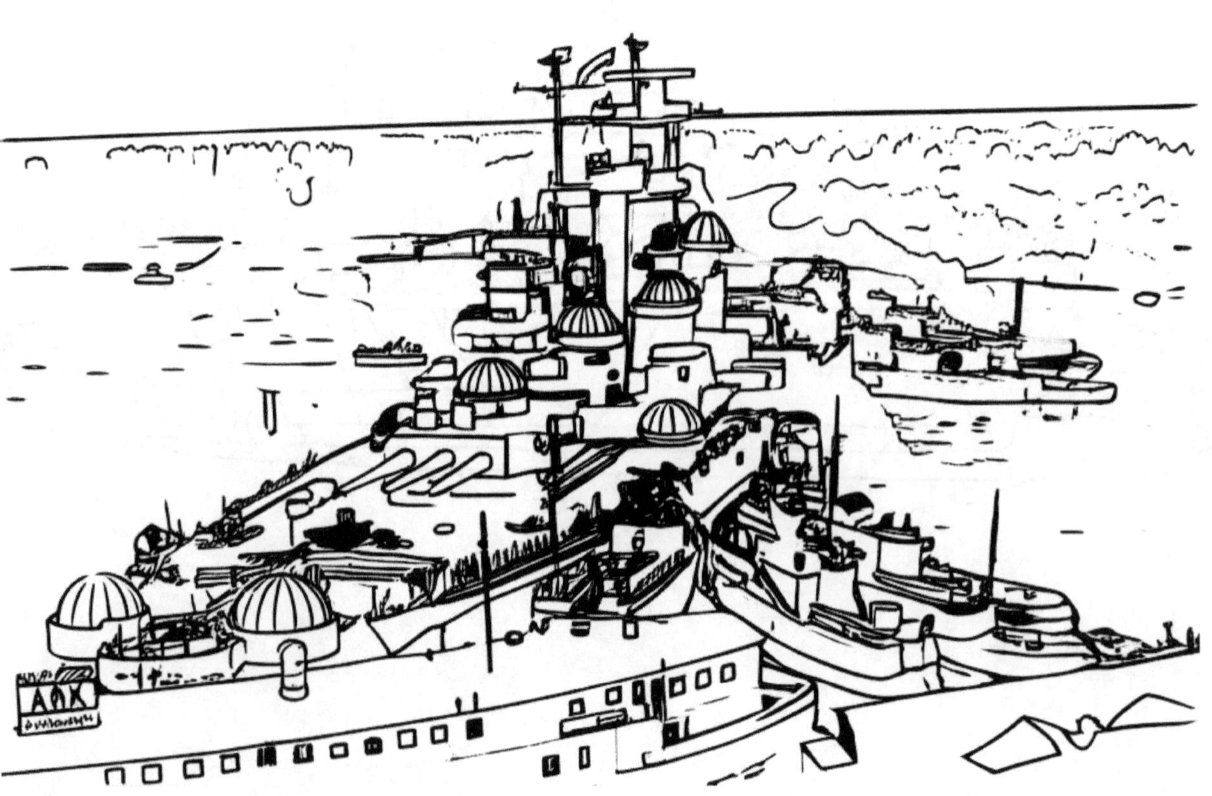

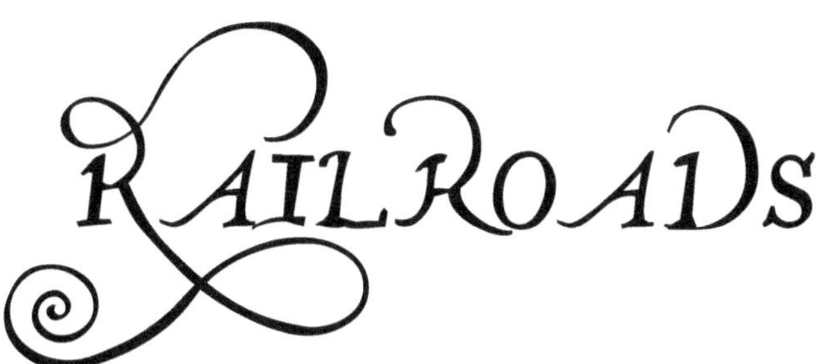
RAILROADS

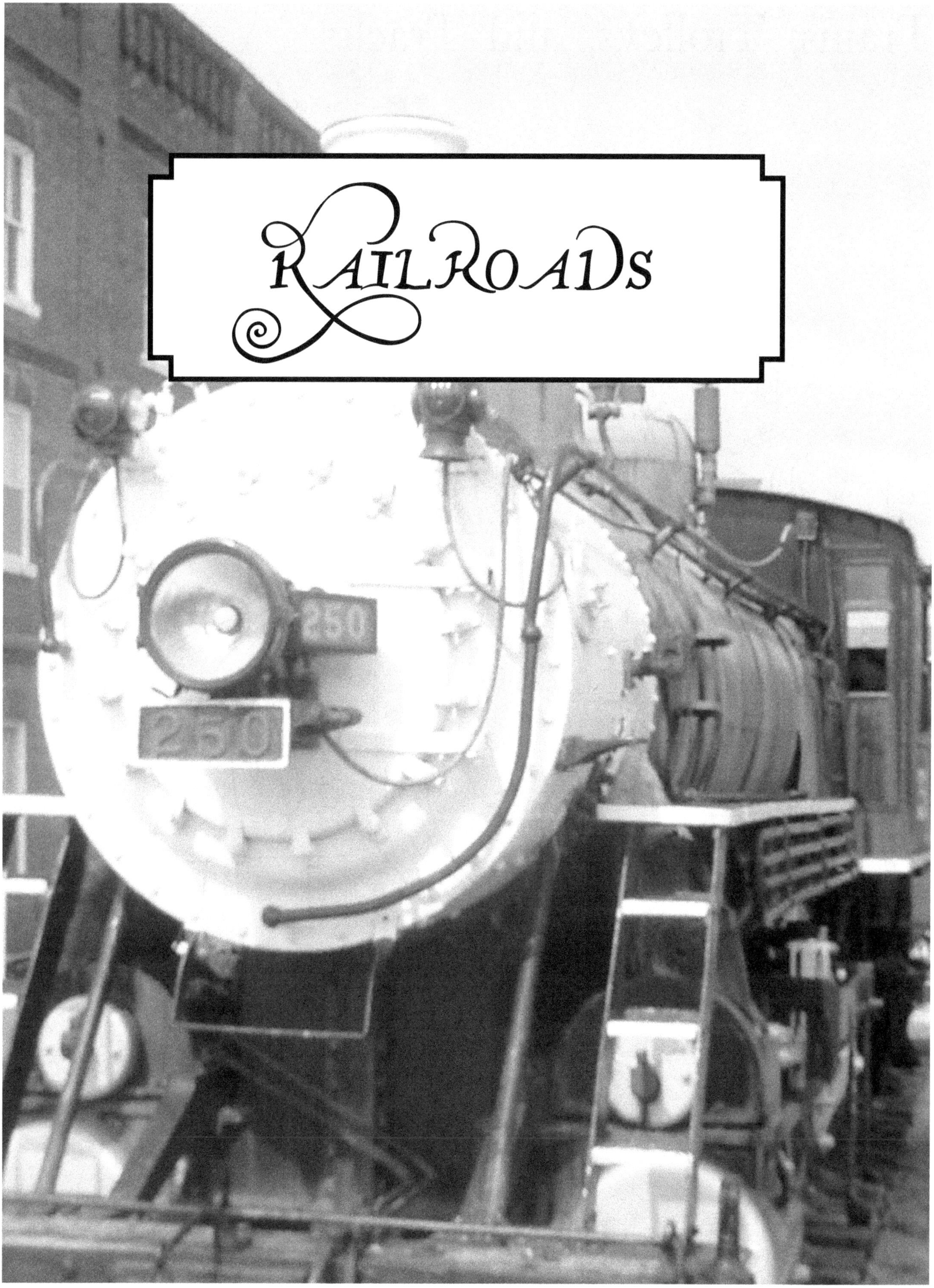

Trains, Trolleys, and Tracks

Trains have always played an important role in Wilmington's history. The port city had rail lines that carried cargo offloaded from arriving ships to points north, south, and west aboard trains that belched black smoke from coal and wood-fed boilers. Wilmington was home to the Atlantic Coastline Railroad, and the city was devastated by the ACLRR's move to Florida in 1960.

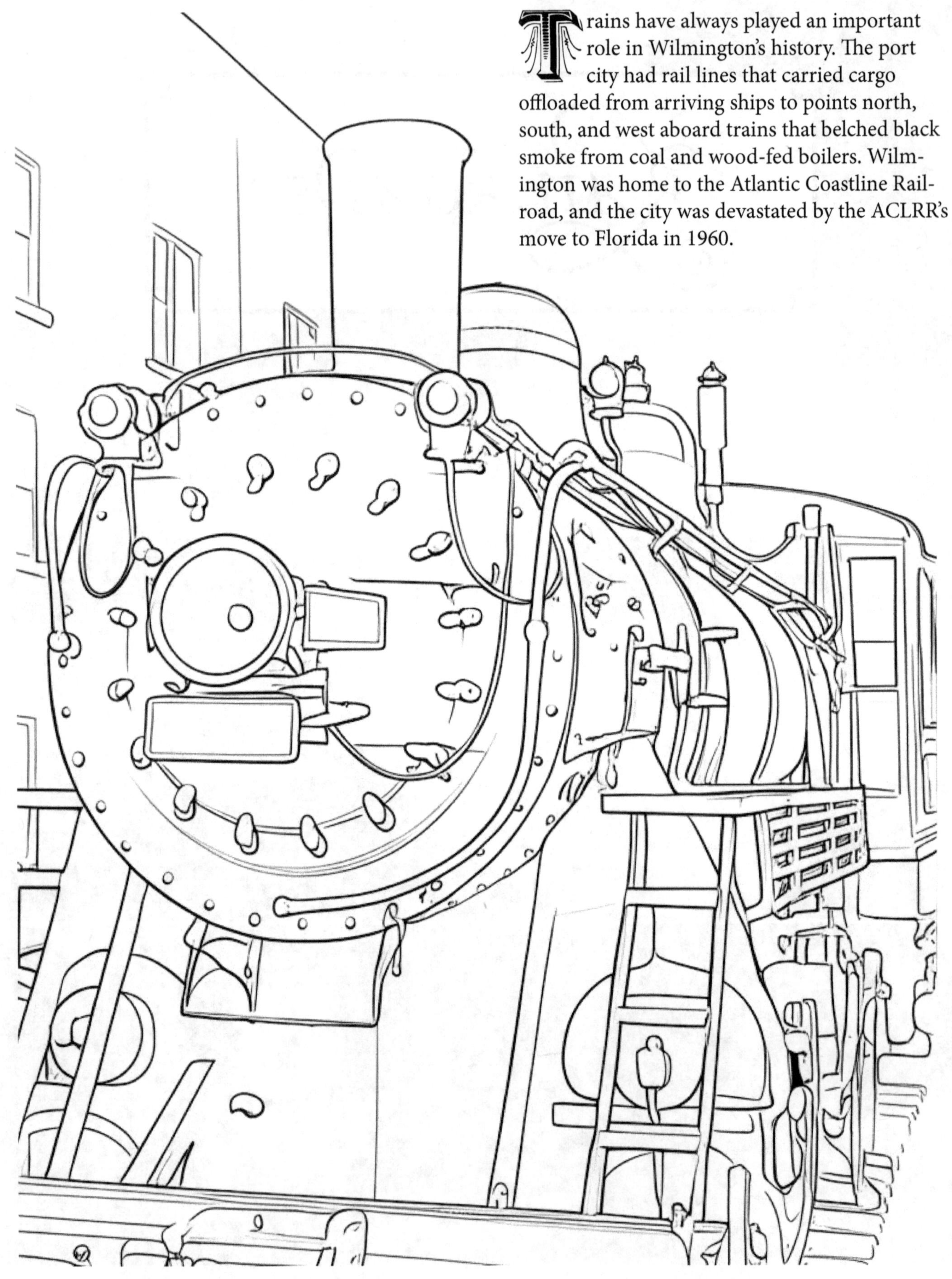

The Wilmington & Weldon Railroad

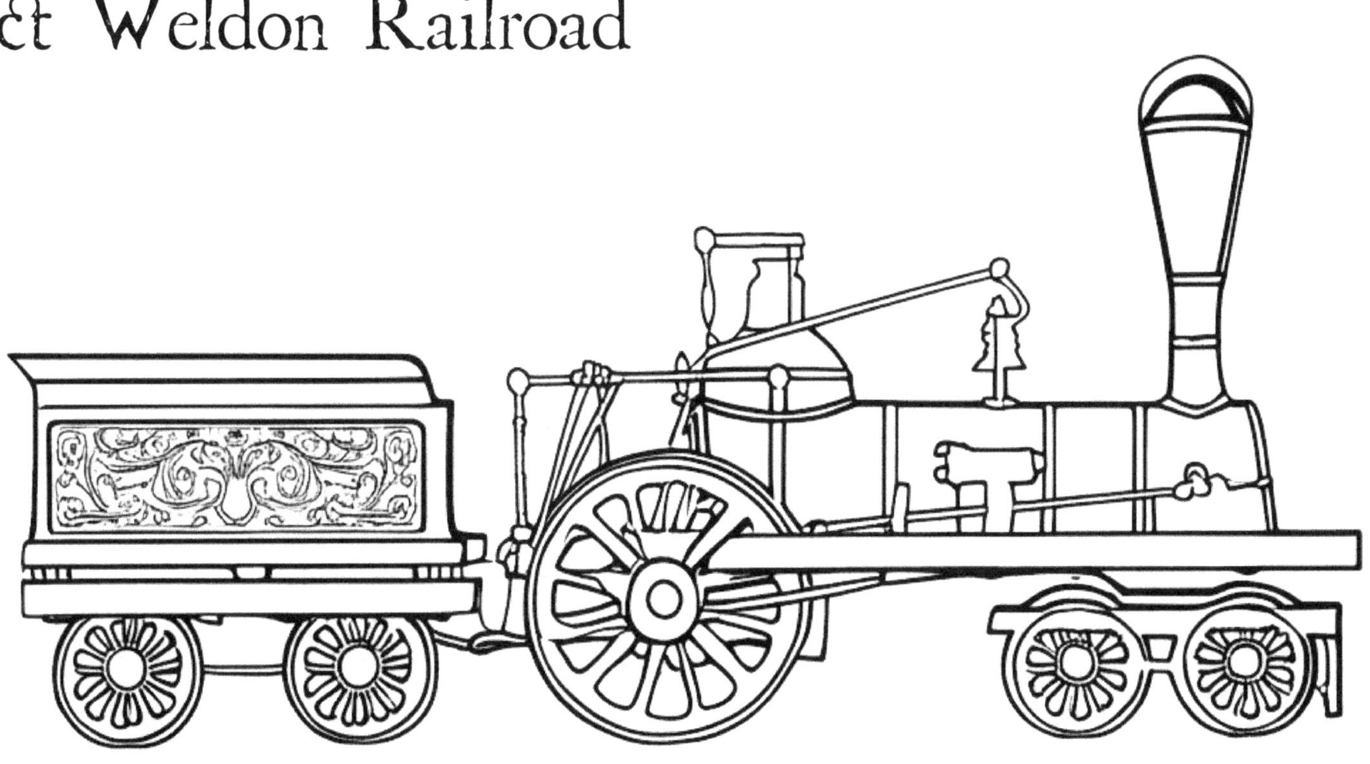

The Wilmington and Weldon Railroad was, at one time, the longest railroad in the world. Running from Wilmington to Weldon, N.C. the railroad ran north from the port city on the Cape Fear to connect with other lines reaching into Virginia. The value of the railroad to the Confederacy in the Civil War could not be understated. Robert E. Lee's Army of Northern Virginia depended on it to deliver the supplies his army needed to continue fighting, especially after the Union navy managed to close all the rebel ports except Wilmington. The picture above shows an early steam locomotive of the Wilmington & Weldon, while the picture below shows a locomotive and coal car of the Civil War era.

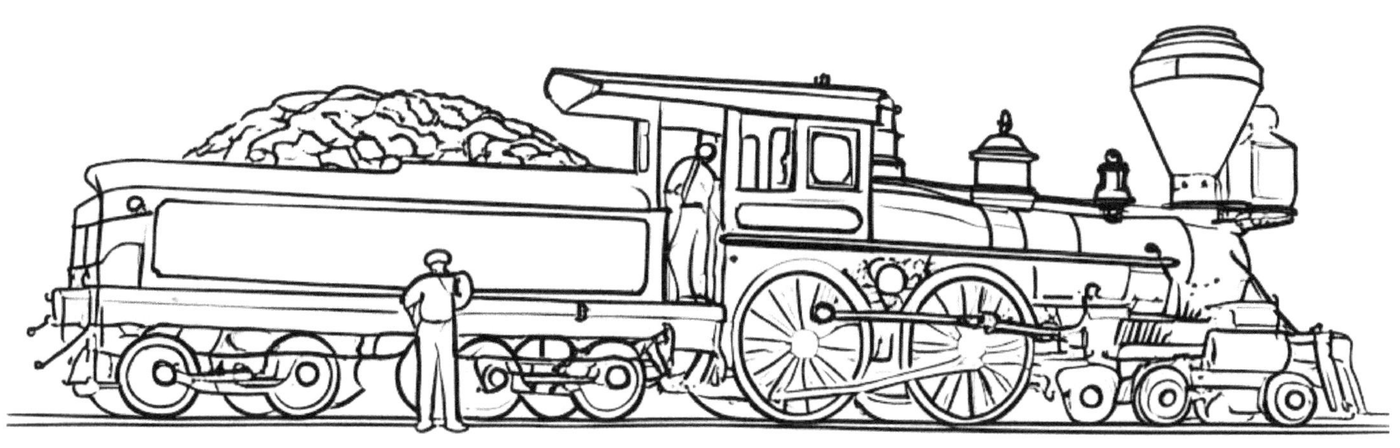

The Atlantic Coastline Railroad

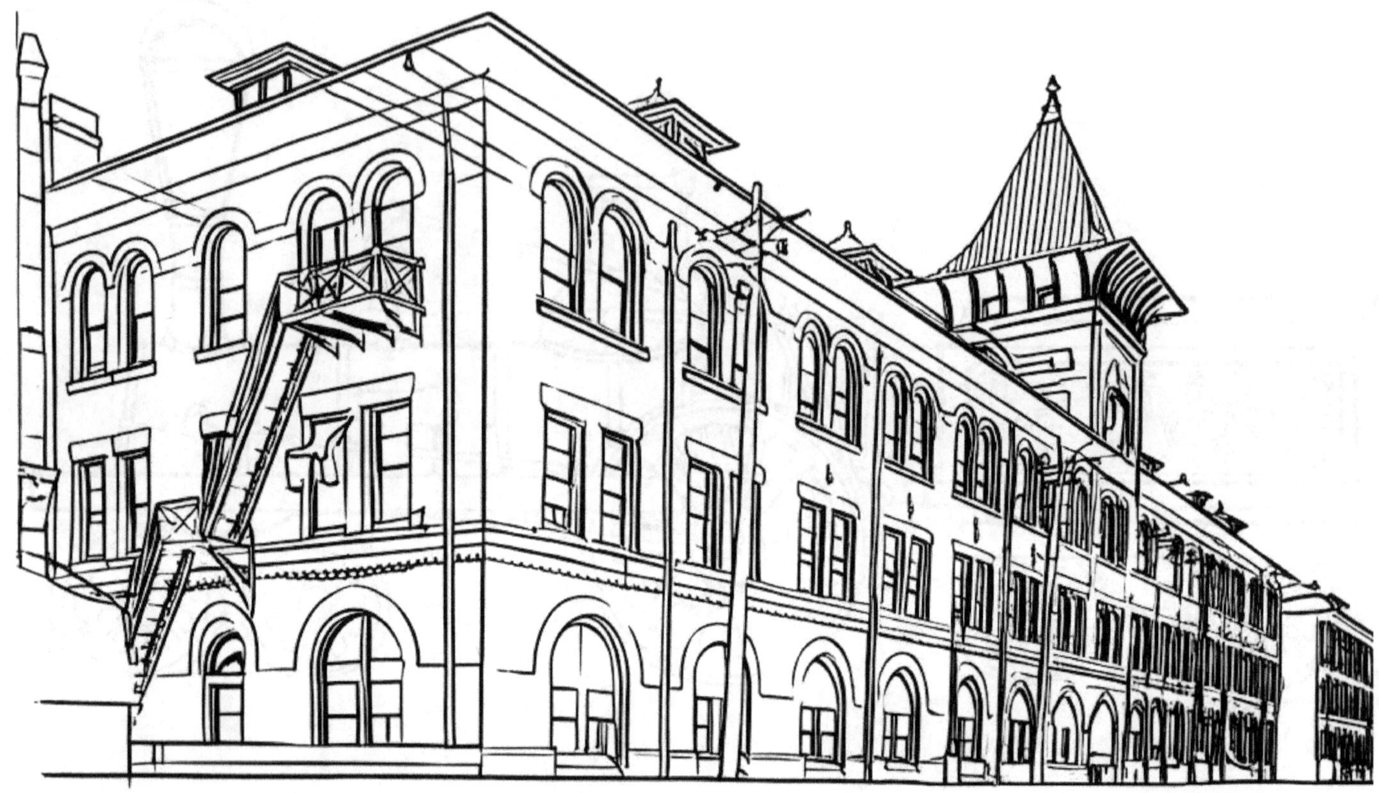

From 1900 to 1960, the Atlantic Coastline Railroad (ACLRR) was the major employer in Wilmington, N.C. Its headquarters there was largely thanks to the city's location midway between the railroad's lines running from Virginia to Florida. The ACLRR was formed when several smaller, earlier railroads merged to create the new railroad. The mergers meant the ACLRR inherited the rolling stock and infrastructure of the railroads it replaced. The oldest train yard the ACLRR inherited was the one at Wilmington, which dated back to 1840. The picture above shows the ACLRR headquarters at Wilmington, along the Cape Fear River. Below, the ACLRR's main rail yard. At the top of the opposite page, trains from around 1964 prepare for departure. At the bottom of the page, the demolition of the old ACLRR's Union Station is depicted.

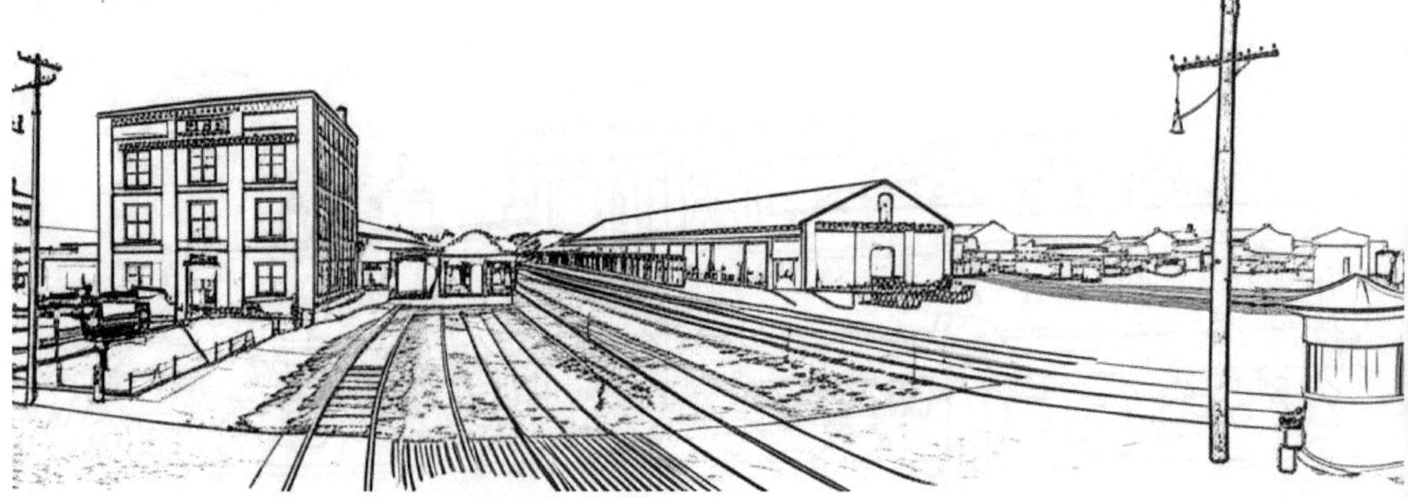

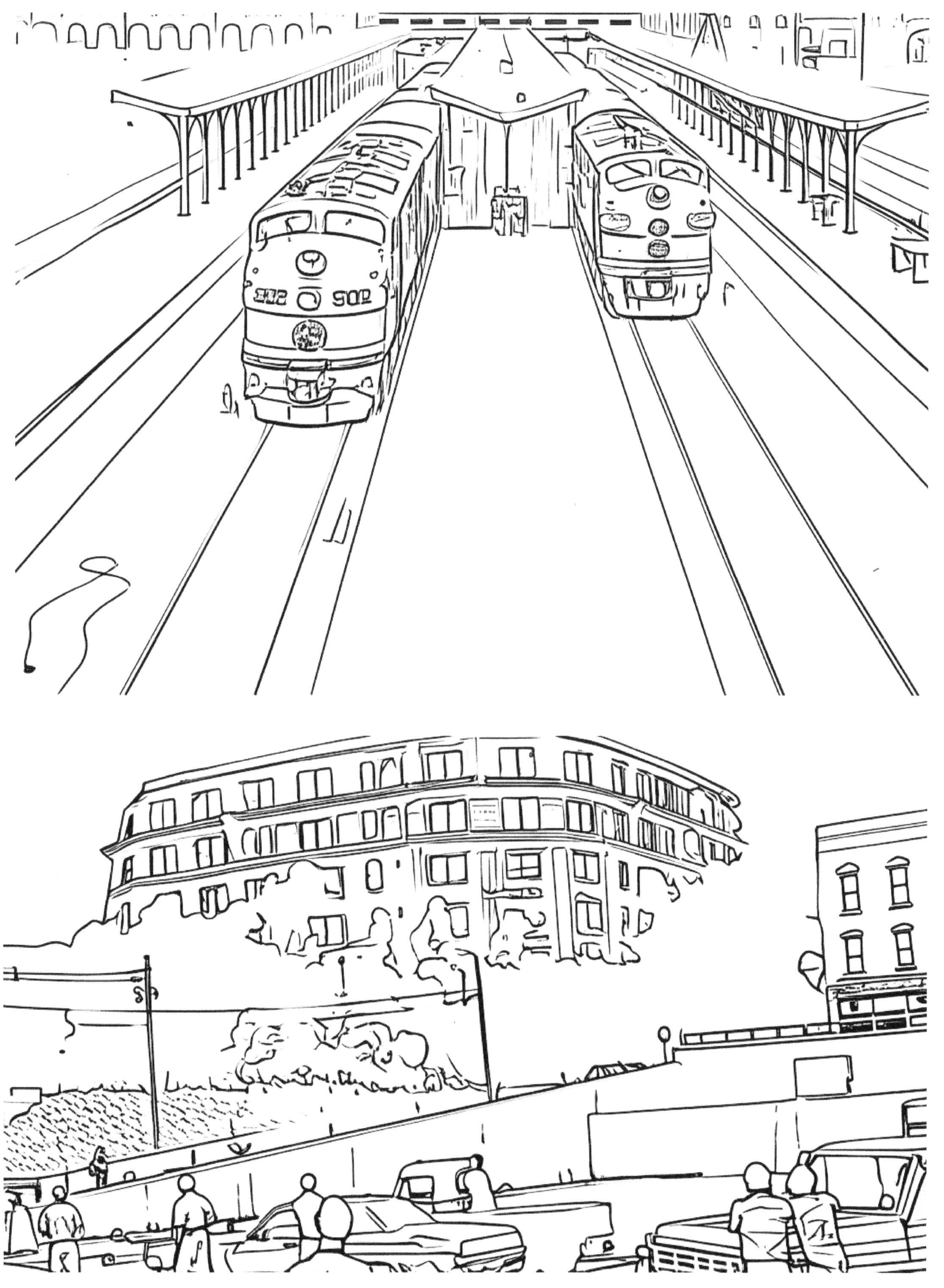

The Beach Trolley

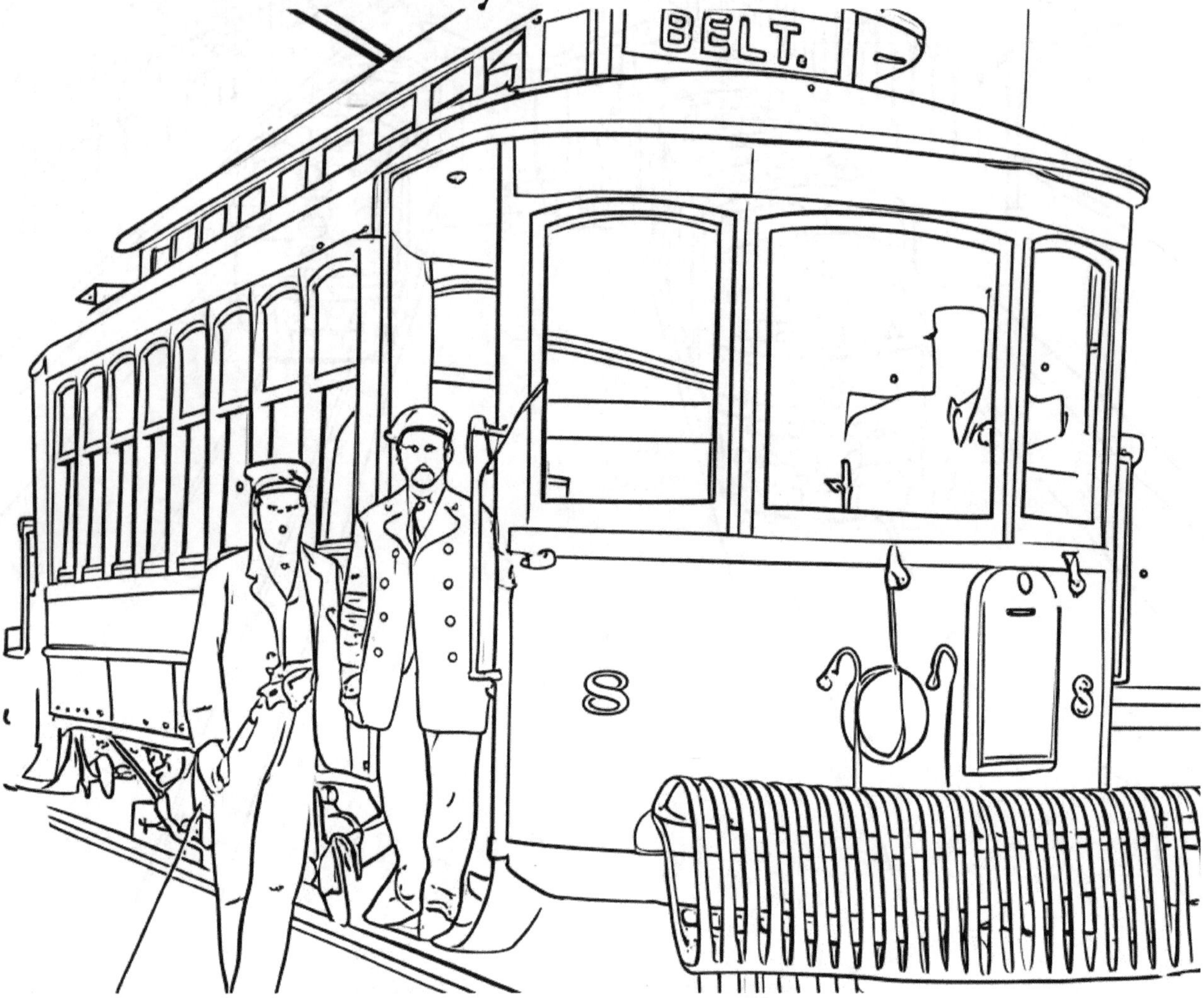

Trolleys once to carry passengers from Wilmington to Wrightsville Beach. The route followed down modern Wrightsville Avenue, to make a loop of the beach before returning to town. Stops included at Lumina Pavilion, and other stations along the beach.

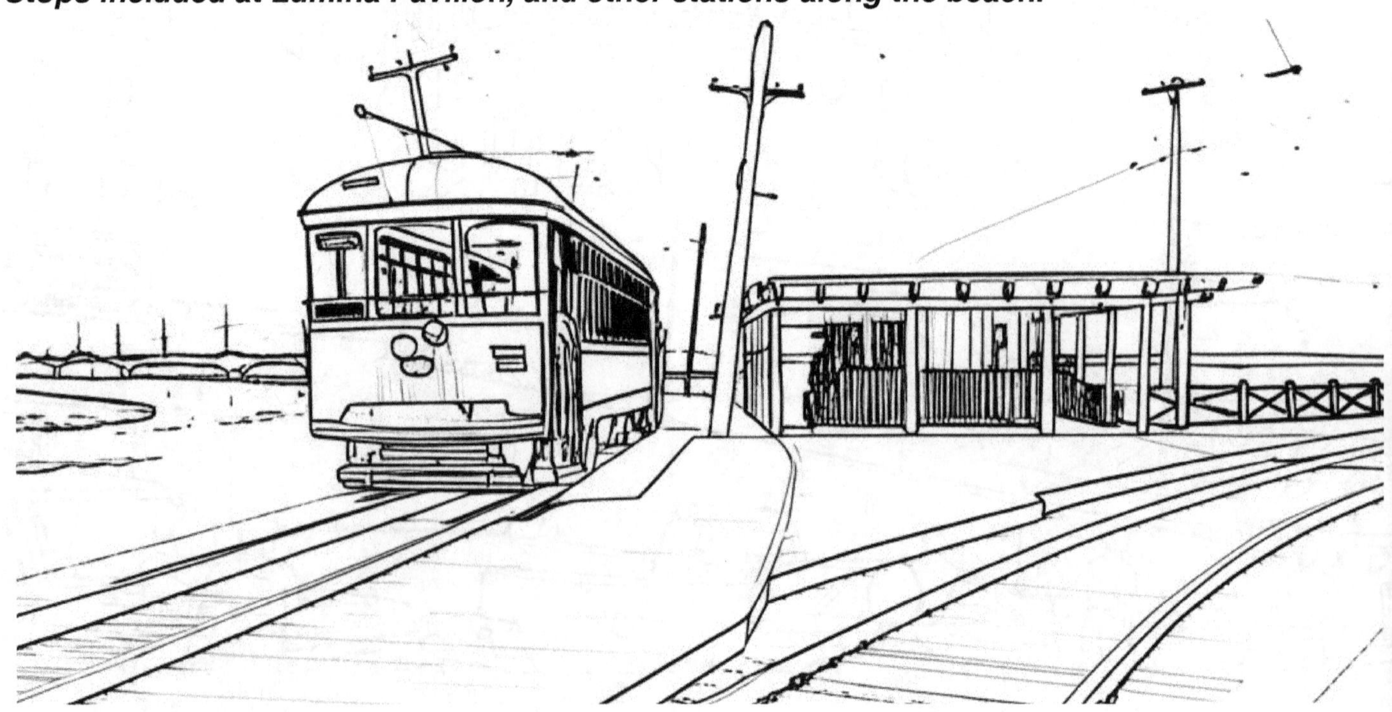

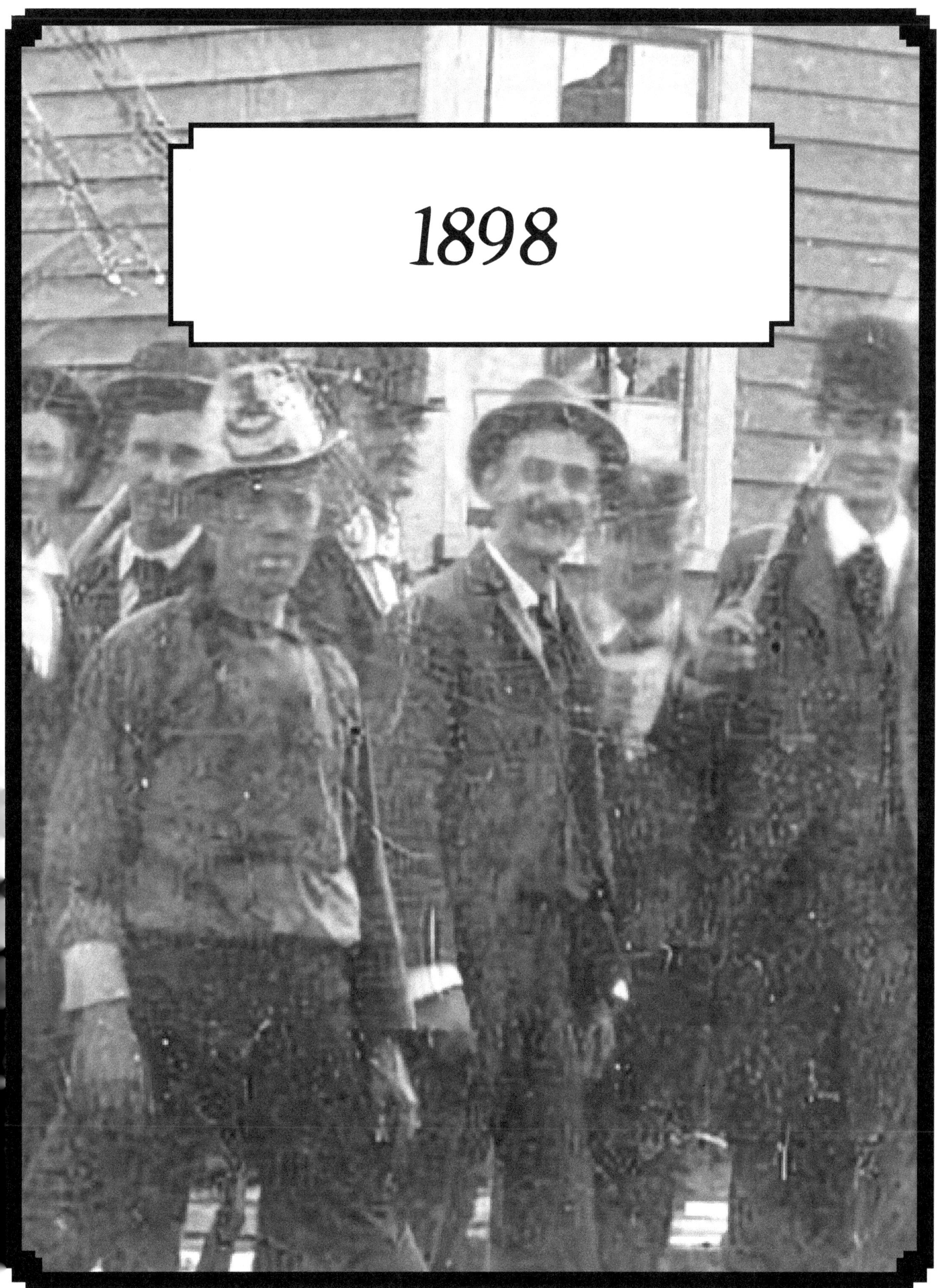
1898

Taking A City

The events of November 10, 1898 mark a dark day in the history of the Cape Fear. Over the course of several hours, huundreds of African-American citizens in Wilmington were murdered, chased out of town, or otherwise terrorized by a white mob determined to install a white supremacist government in Wilmington. The trigger was the response to a speech by a Georgia woman that called on white men to protect the virtue of their women from black men. Alex Manly (left), the editor of the Daily Record newspaper in Wilmington, pointed out in an editorial that perhaps black men should do the same for their women, as they were as likely to be at risk as white women were. In response, a mob incited by Alfred Moore Waddell (below) marched on Manly's newspaper and burned it to the ground. The mob, now as many as 2,000 strong, then marched into north Wilmington's Brooklyn community, shooting at any black person they saw. Sixty people were confirmed killed, but the number could be in the hundreds. The Wilmington riot of 1898 is the only successful coup d' etat in U.S. History.

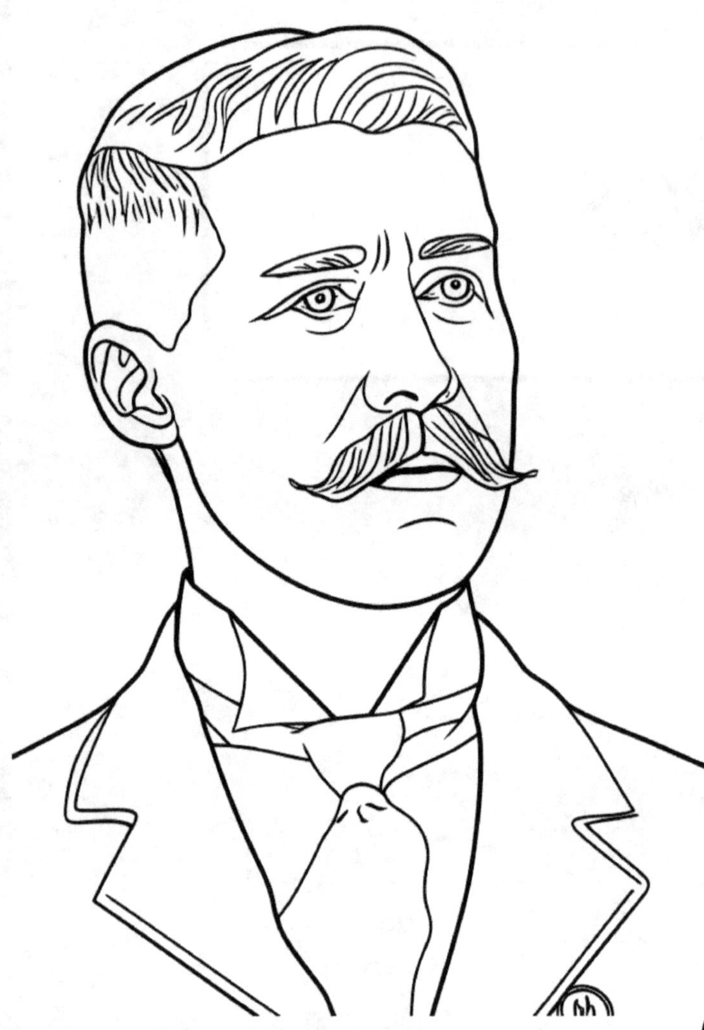

Alexander Manly (above) was the illegitemate son of former North Carolina governor Charles Manly and one of his enslaved women servants. Manly's light skin and Caucasian features allowed him to pass as white in most situations. He founded what at the time was the state's only black newspaper in Wilmington, a city with a thriving black middle class and professional community before the events of 1898. Alfred Moore Waddell (right) was a former Confederate army officer who saw an opportunity to use white supremacy as a way to counter the Fusion coalition that elected Democrats to office in the 1896 elections. Waddell used inflammatory speech to rile up the white mob he addressed at the John Taylor house on Market Street, sending them off to burn the offices of the Daily Record. He also issued an ultimatum that declared white men would never submit to black rule in Wilmington ever again.

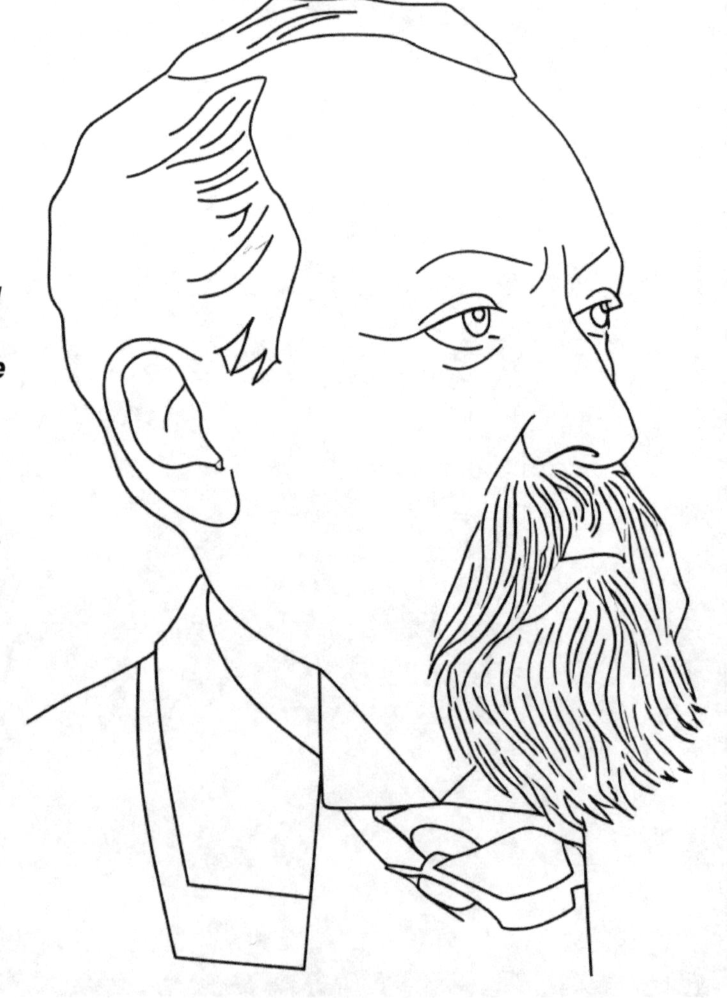

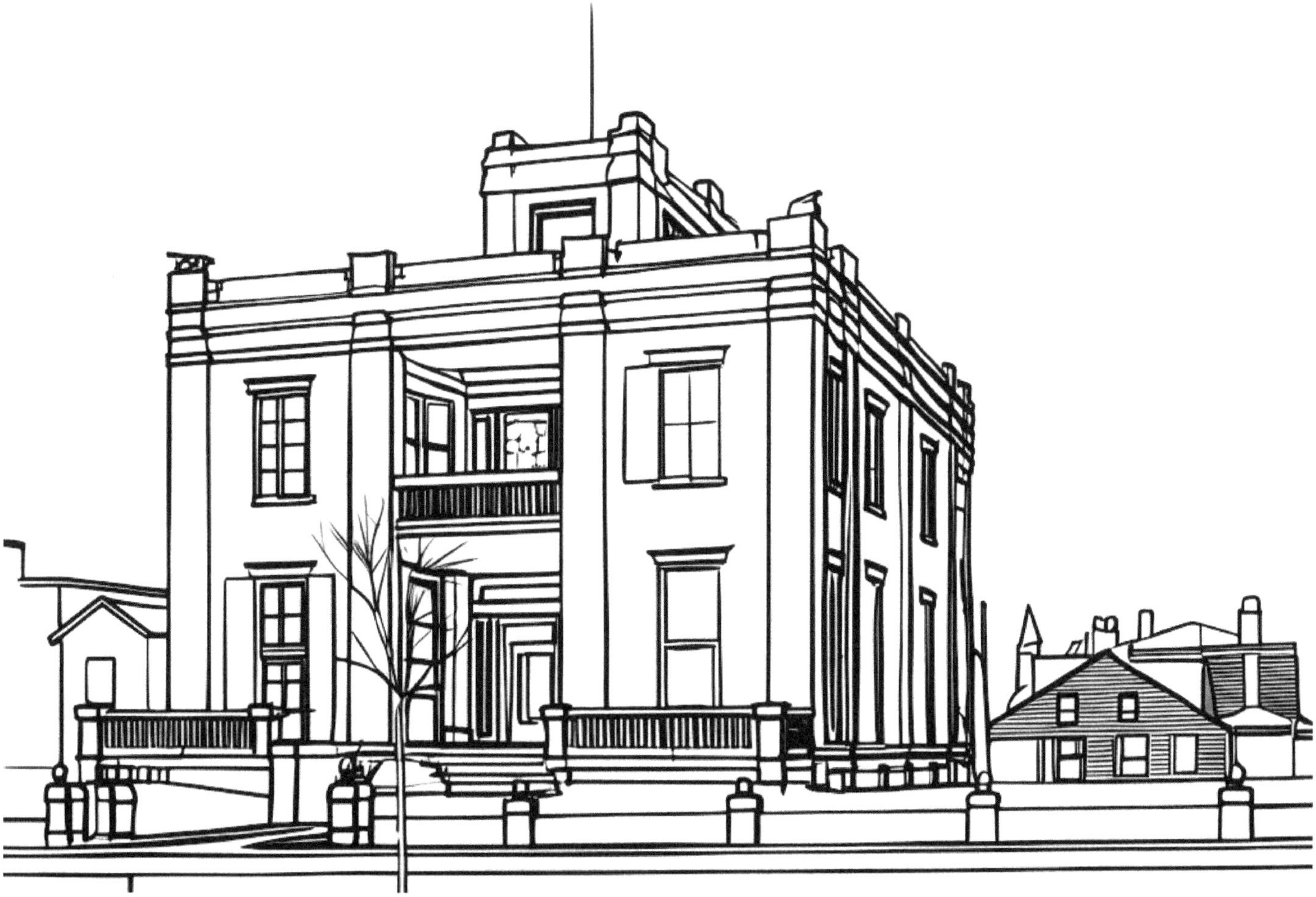

The John A. Taylor house on Market Street was also the home of the Wilmington Light Infantry militia. The group played a prominent role in the riots of November 10, 1898. It was from there that Alfred Moore Waddell sent the mob to burn the Daily Record office off Seventh Street. The result of that fire is seen below. The Daily Record offices were on the second floor of Love and Charity Hall. A black fire company a short distance away was prevented from responding to the blaze until the building and the press were total losses.

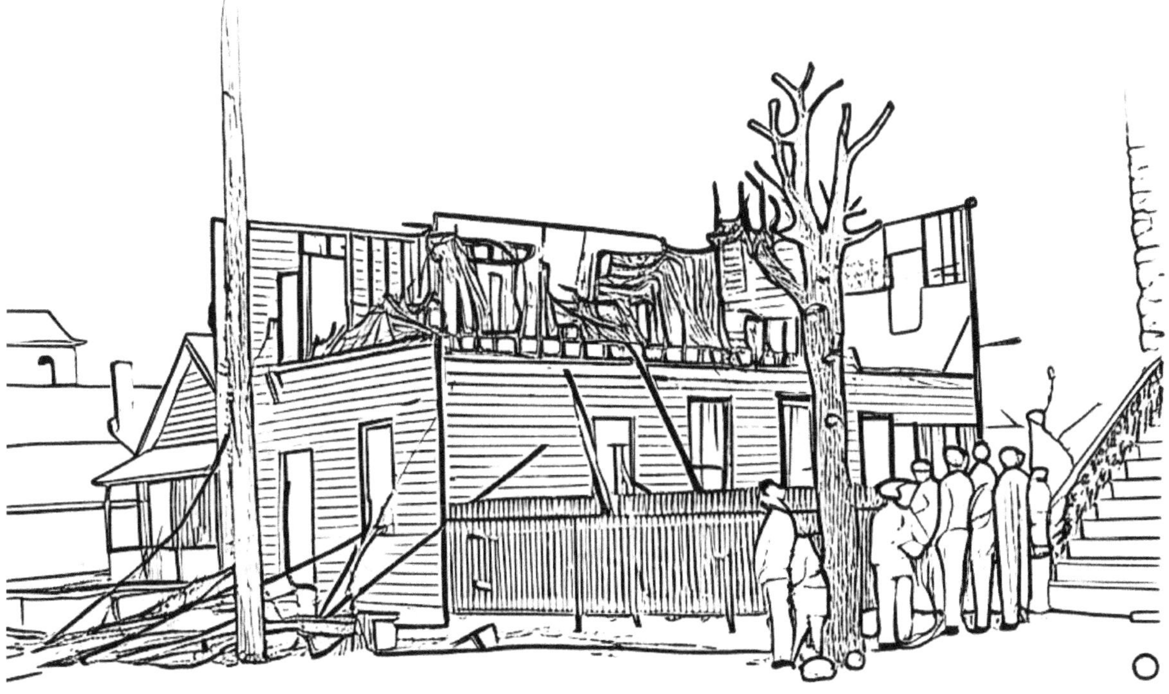

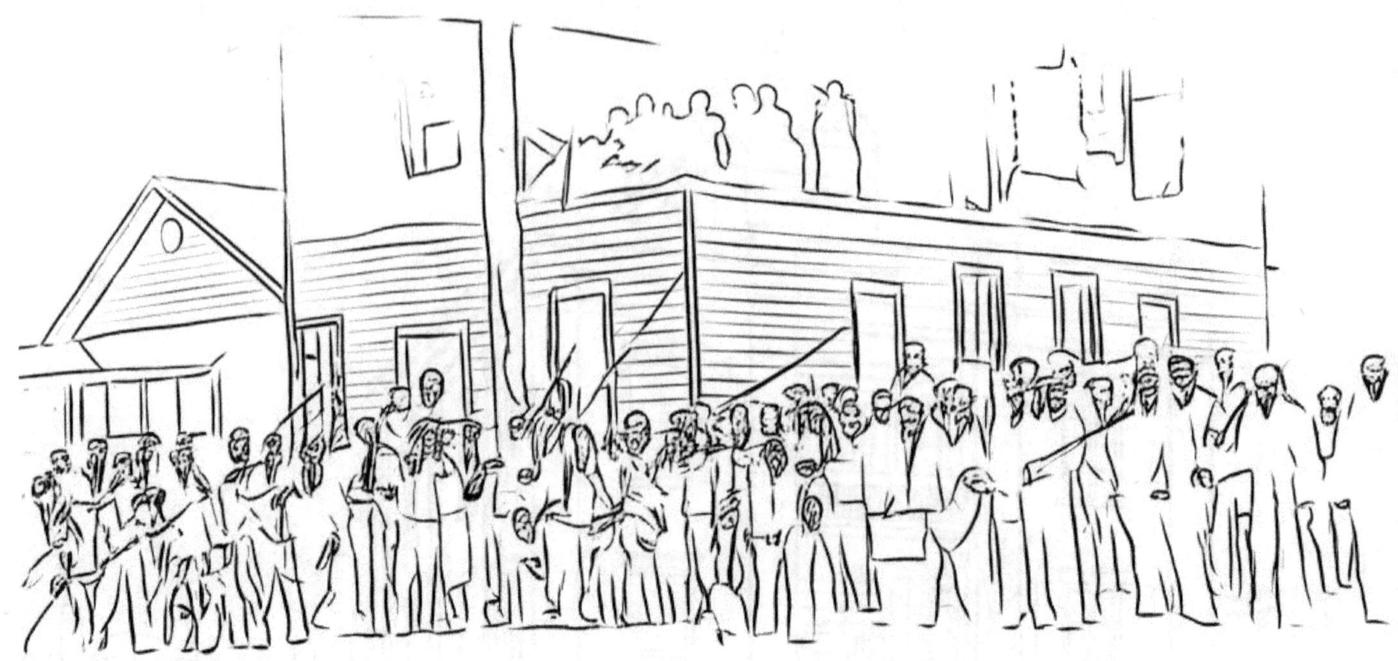

The above picture shows members of the arsonist mob in front of the burned remains of Love and Charity Hall. From there, they marched to North Fourth Street and began indiscriminantly shooting at black citizens. The store on the southwest corner of Fourth and Harnett Streets (below) is where the first victims fell. The rampage went on for hours.

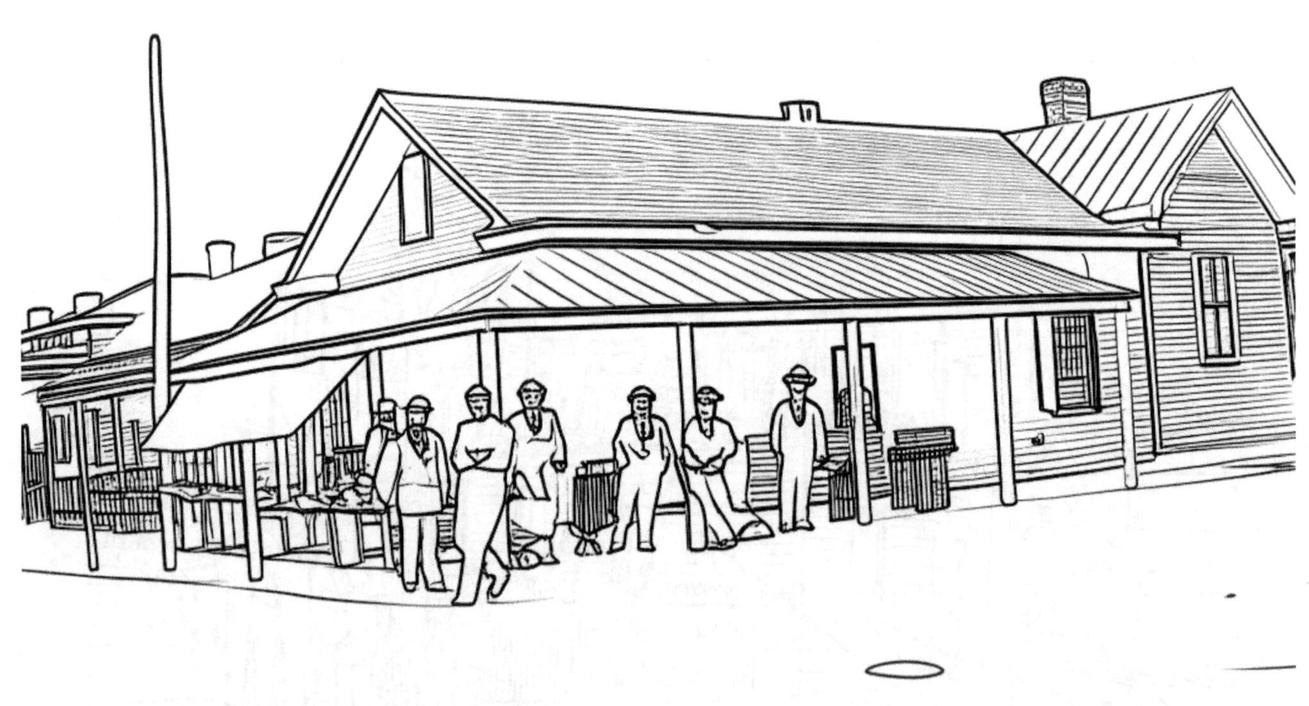

Alexander Manly and his brother, Frank, (right) escaped from Wilmington in a buggy the night before the killing began. Alexander made his way north, away from the danger represented by the white supremacists along the Cape Fear River. He never returned.

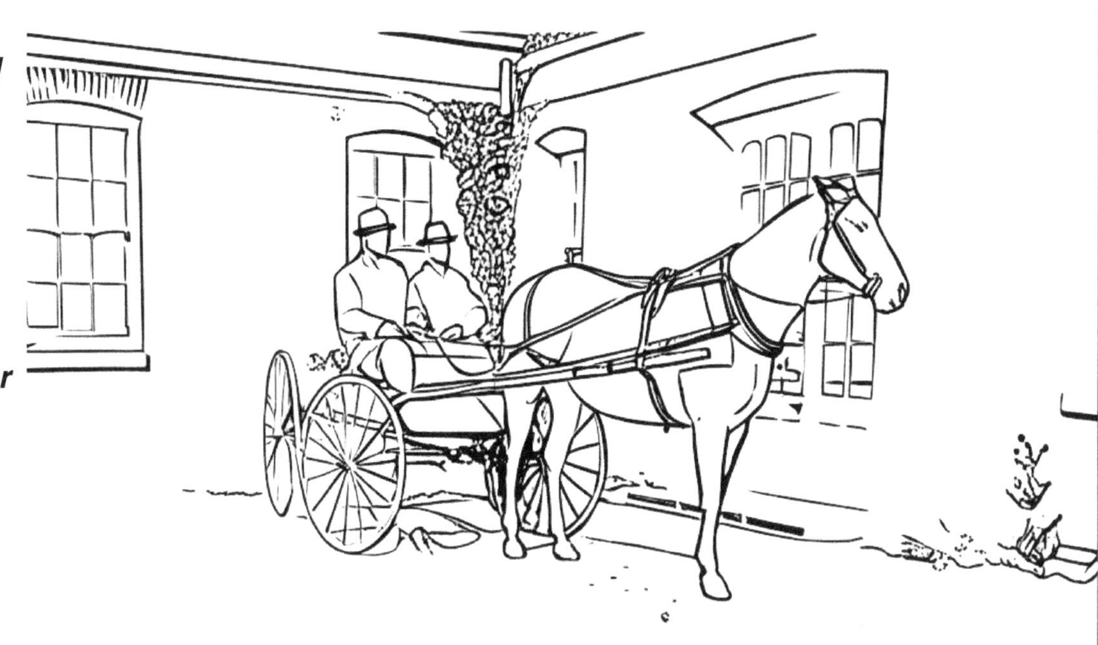

James Sprunt (right) brought his armed yacht close in to his Alexander Sprunt & Sons Cotton Compress to protect the black men who worked for him from the mob. Sprunt stood in front of the mob and threatened to fire on them if they did not disperse. Sprunt's actions were likely not based in altruism so much as economic necessity, as he needed the men to keep his compress operating.

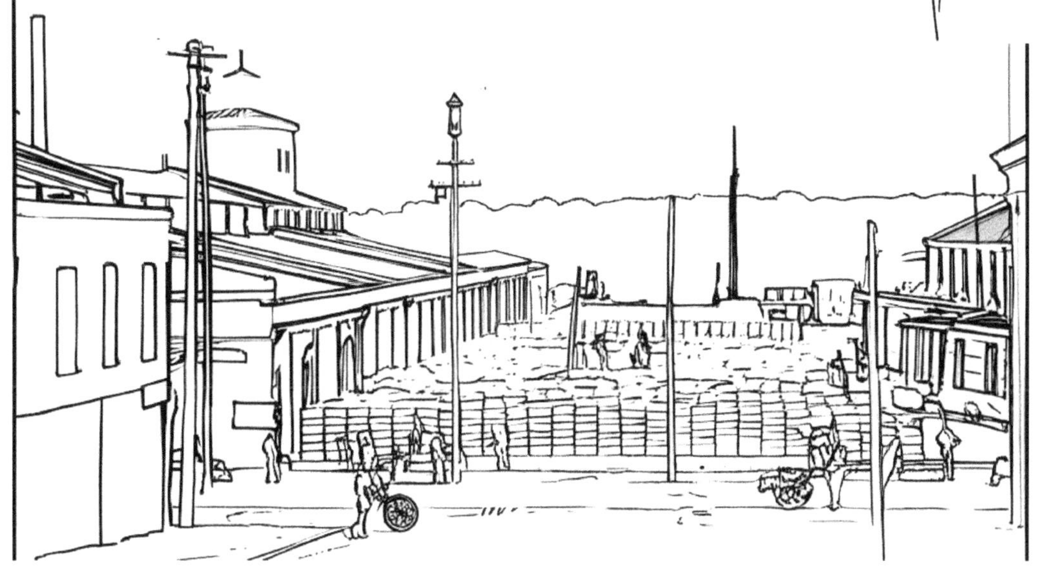

The Alexander Sprunt and Sons yards on the Cape Fear River (left), where today's Cotton Exchange is located. Sprunt's company became the largest cotton exporter in the world, and his African American employees were key to Sprunt's success.

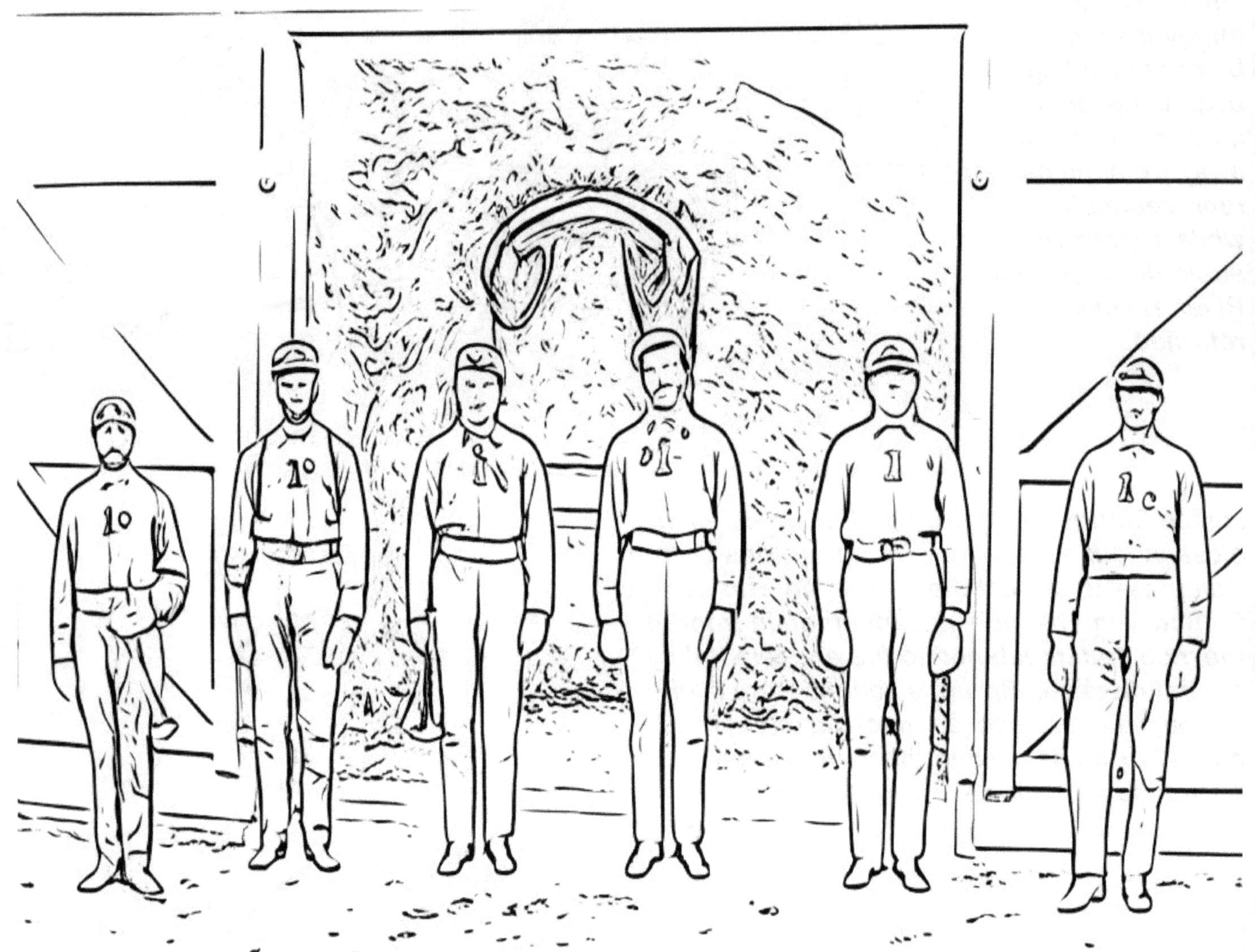

Wilmington had a thriving black middle class and professional class, including an all-black fire company (above). The firemen were located close by the fire at Love and Charity Hall, but were blocked from responding by armed white men until the building and Manly's press were a total loss.

THE REVOLUTIONARY ERA

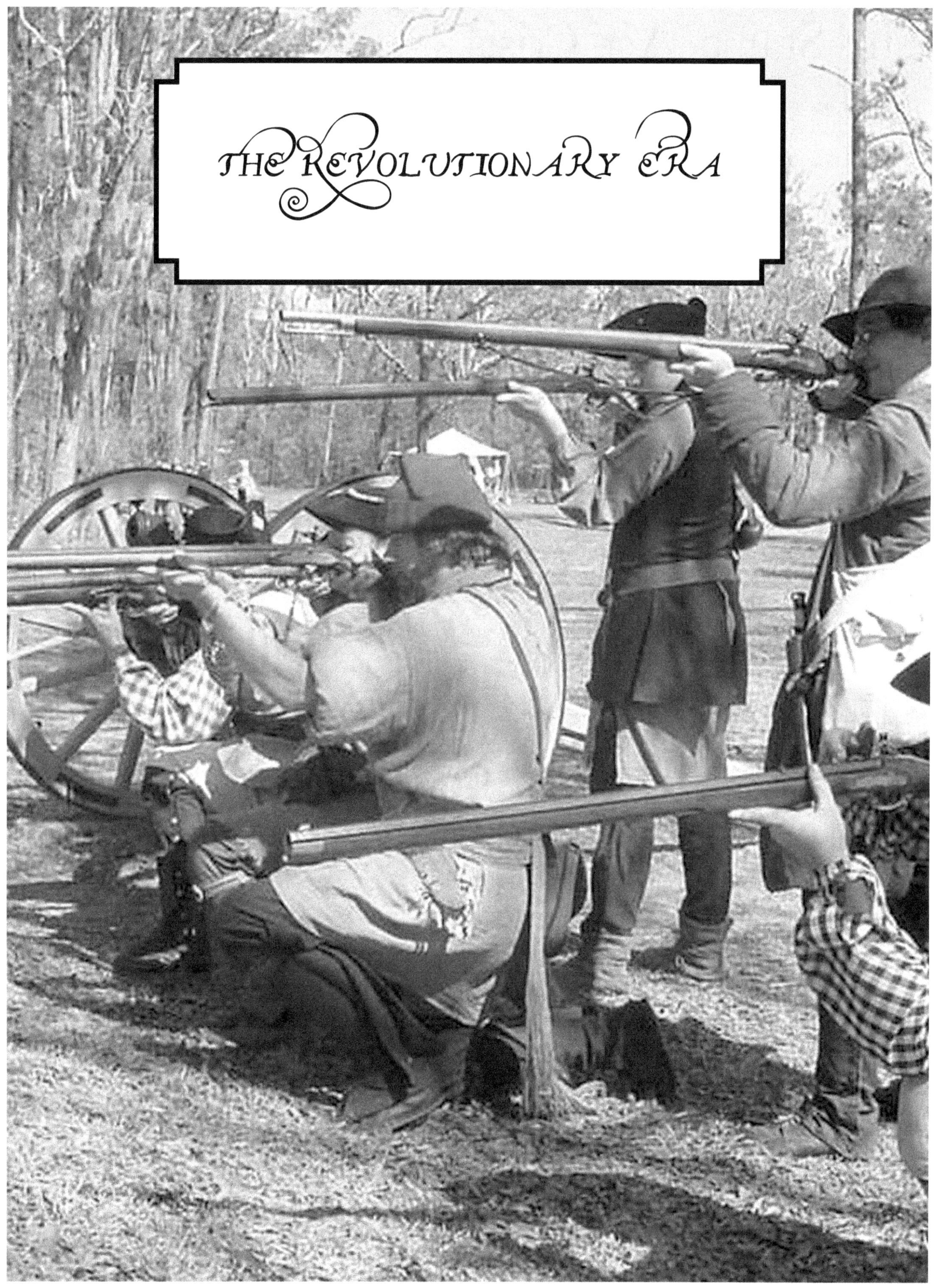

The Stamp Act Crisis

After the French & Indian War, Great Britain sought to generate income to pay its war debt by taxing all paper generated in the American colonies. The items taxed included everything from newspapers and legal documents, to playing cards. The American colonists rebelled against the tax on the grounds that they had no representation in the British parliament. On the Cape Fear River, the protests were especially strong, with violence always bubbling just below the surface. Of all the ports in British North America, the Cape Fear River is the only place where the British failed to successfully land any stamps.

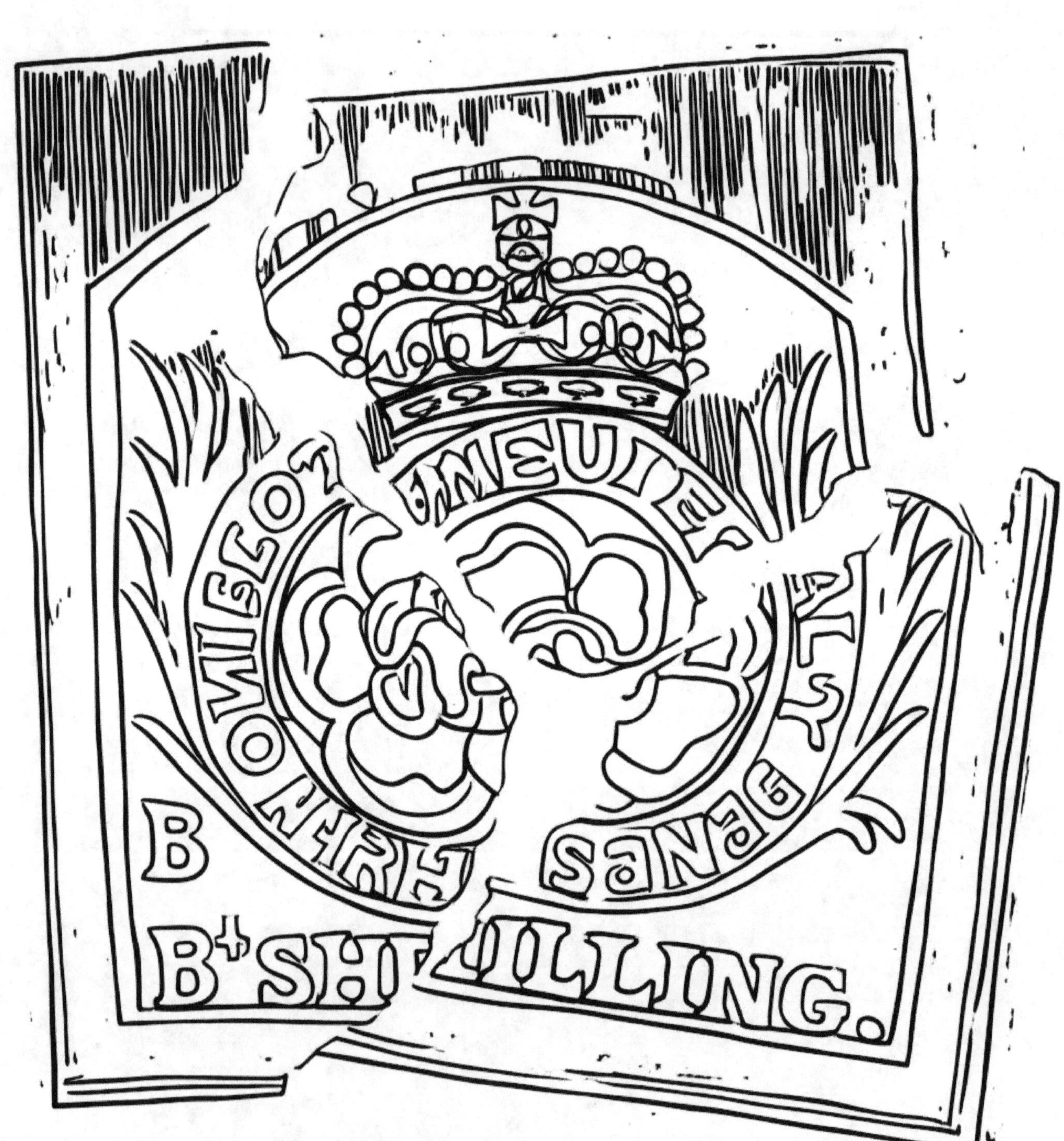

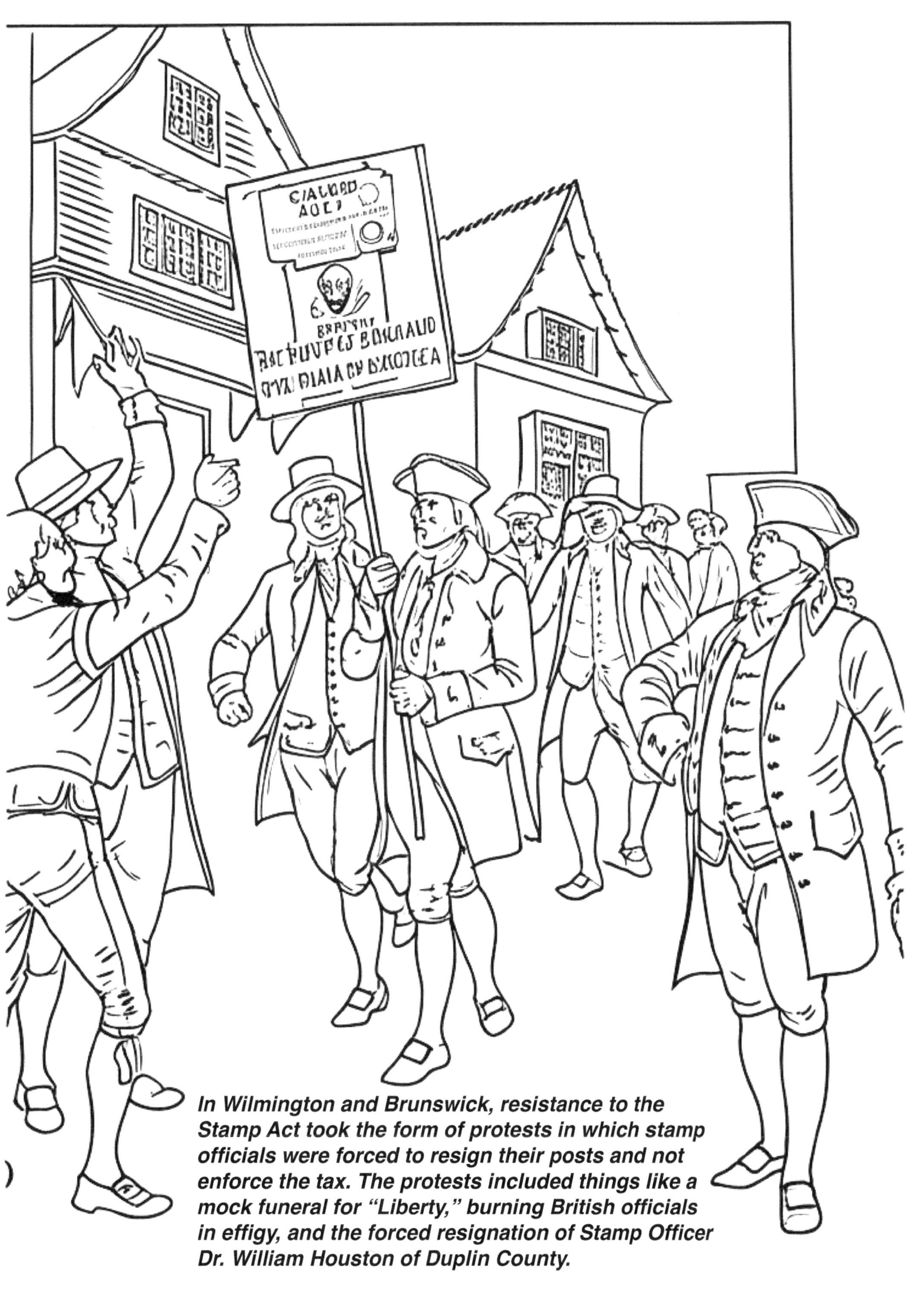

In Wilmington and Brunswick, resistance to the Stamp Act took the form of protests in which stamp officials were forced to resign their posts and not enforce the tax. The protests included things like a mock funeral for "Liberty," burning British officials in effigy, and the forced resignation of Stamp Officer Dr. William Houston of Duplin County.

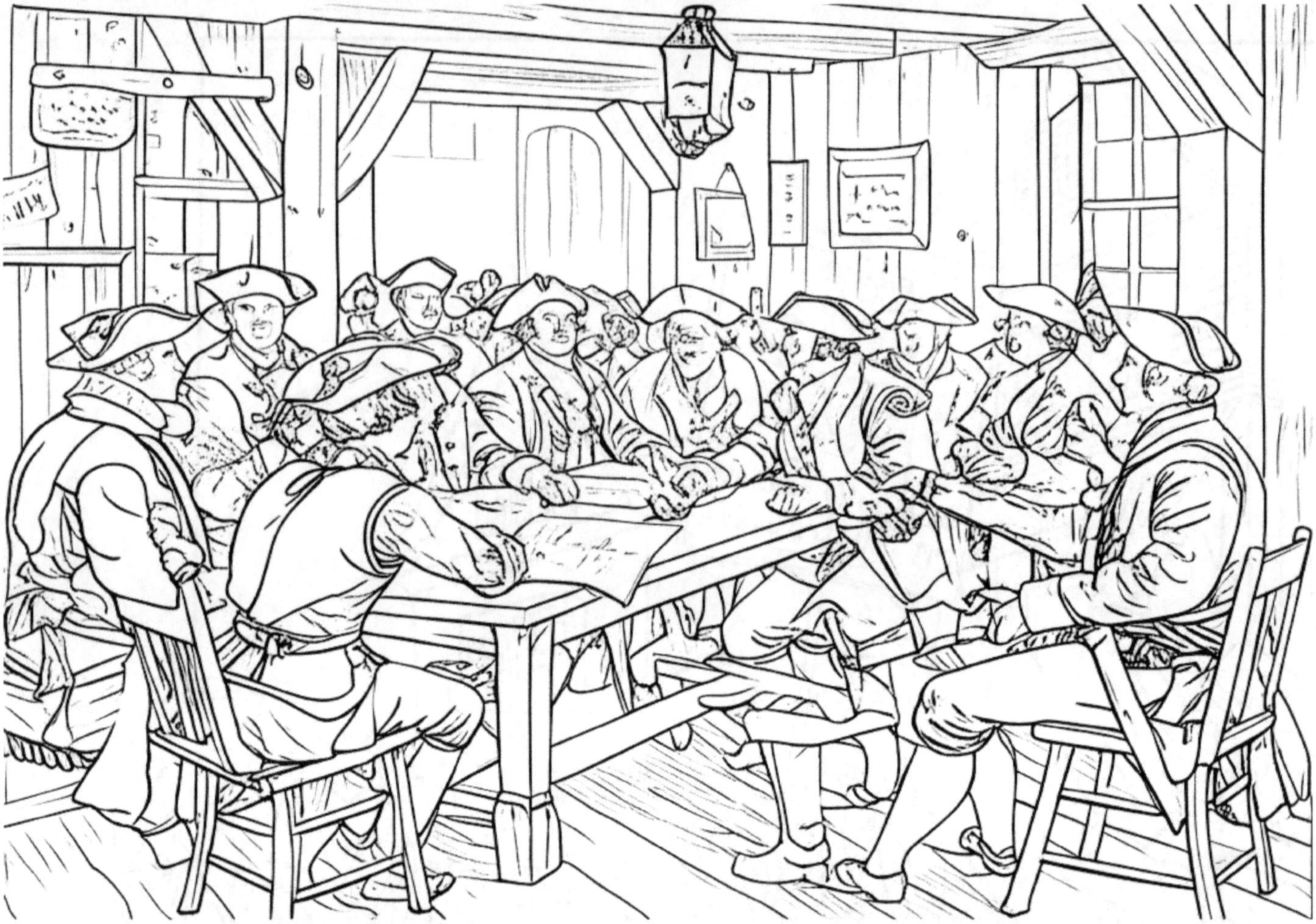

At the tavern in Brunswick (above), locals plotted their resistance to the Stamp Act. That resistance would see local men mount an armed opposition to the landing of the hated stamps (below).

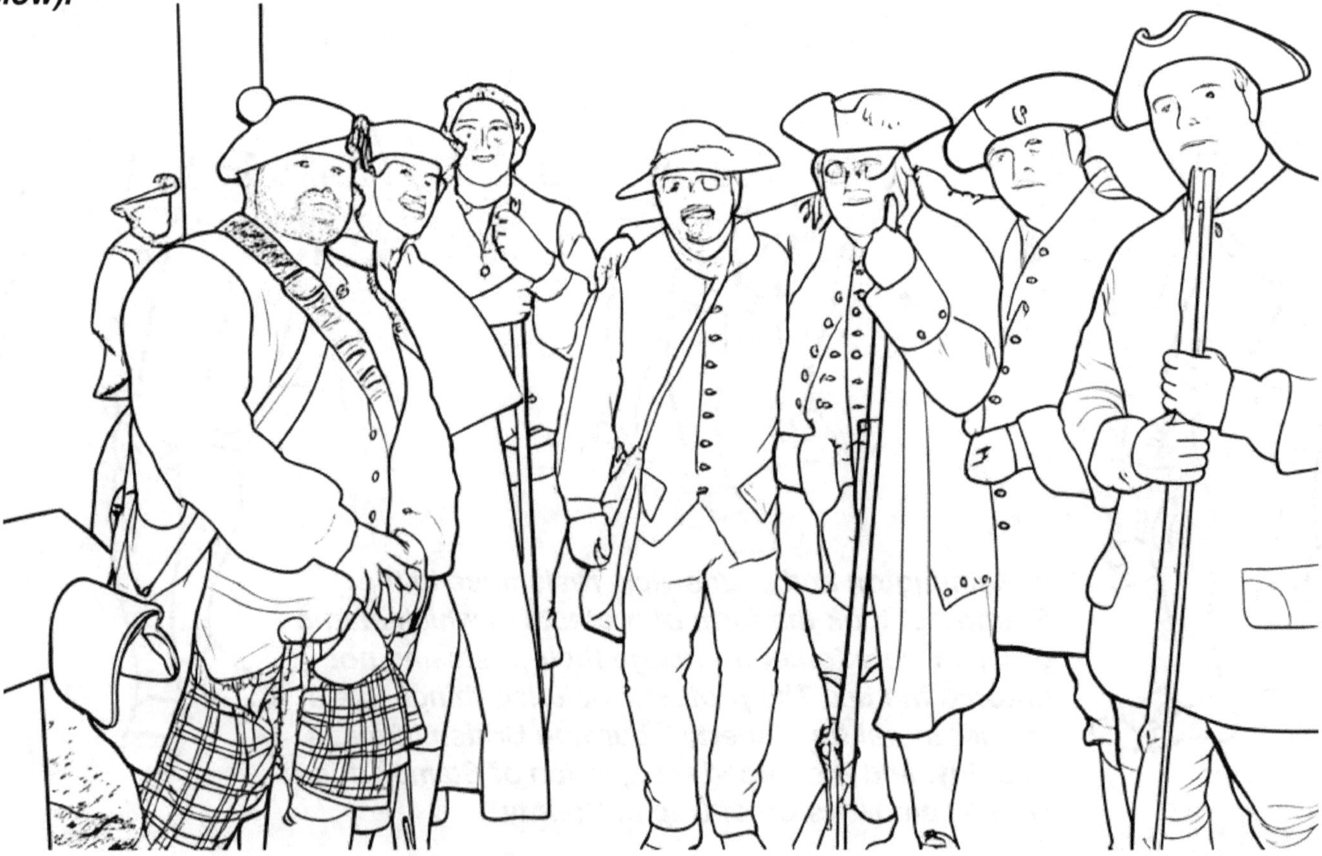

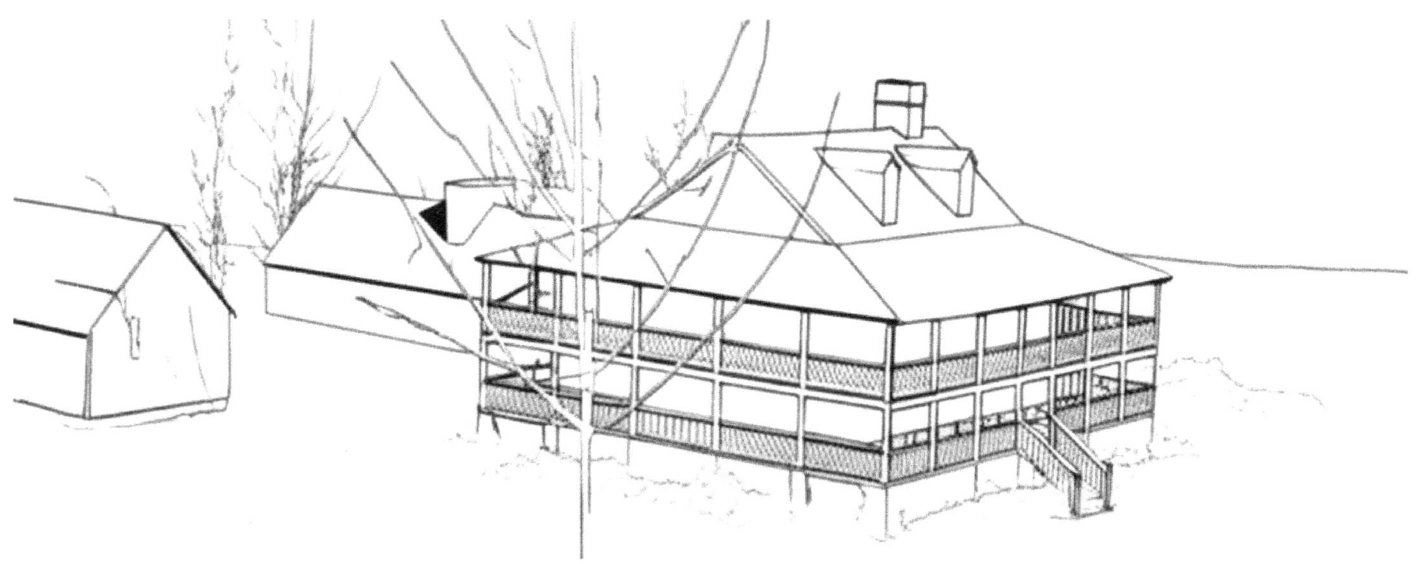

A British stamp officer named Pennington took refuge with Royal Governor William Tryon at the governor's Russellborough home north of Brunswick (above). One evening, several hundred armed men led by Cornelius Harnett, Jr., John Ashe, and Robert Howe showed up to demand that Pennington not enforce the Stamp Act. Tryon confronted the local men (below), outraged that they would challenge his authority on his own doorstep. Harnett and the others insisted on speaking with Pennington, so Tryon made the stamp officer resign his commission as a king's officer before allowing him to meet the rebellious locals. In doing so, Tryon avoided having to charge the locals with the serious offense of treason.

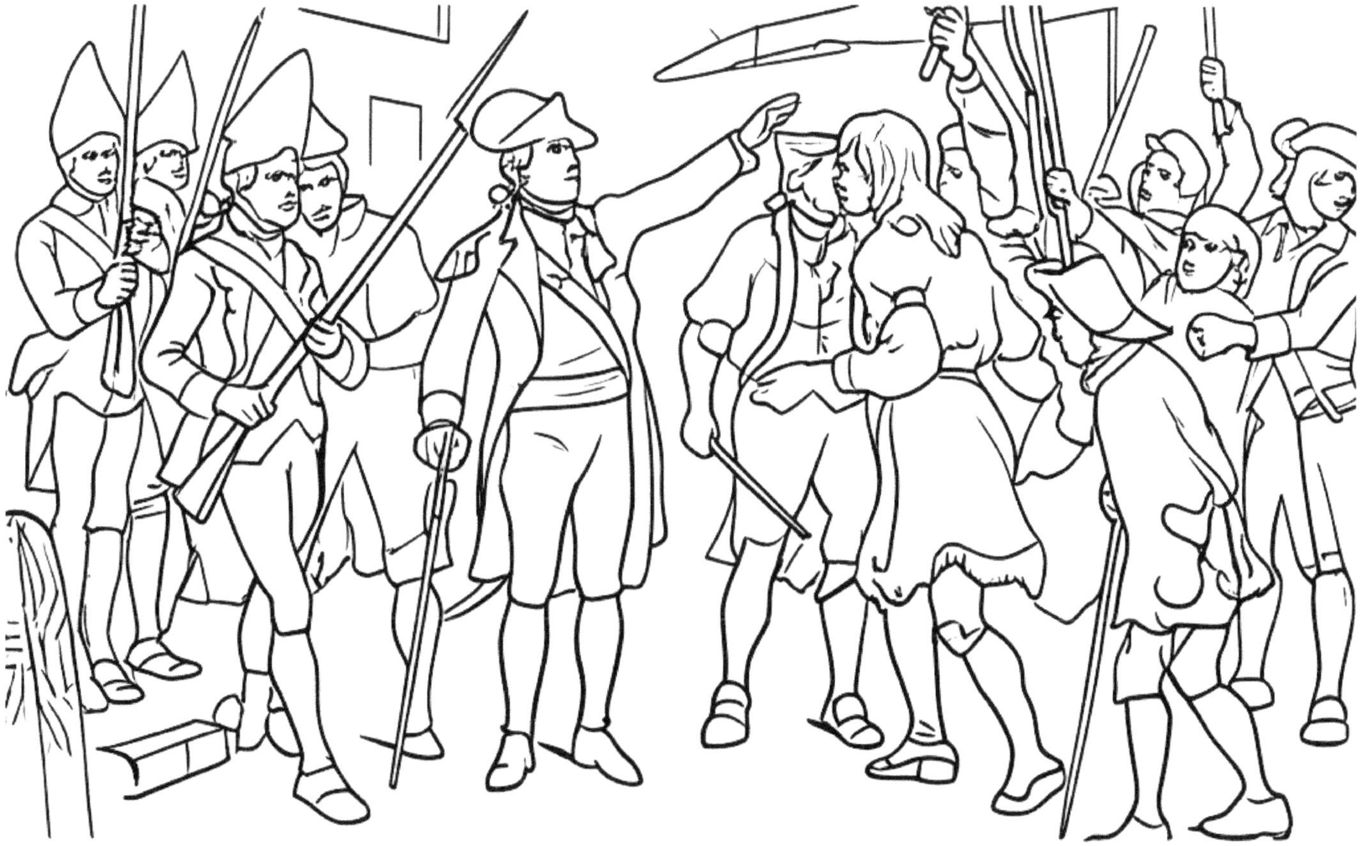

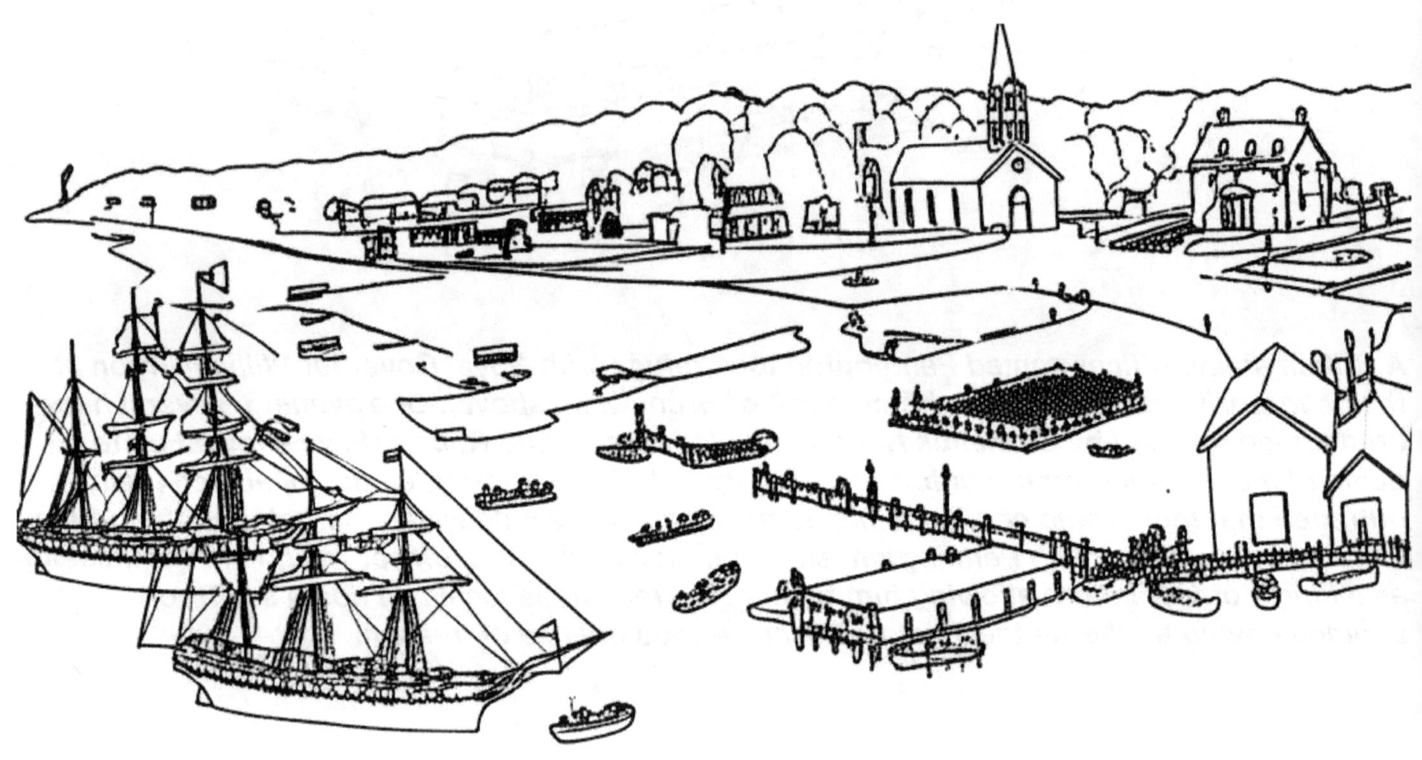

When the actual stamps arrived on the Cape Fear, nearly 1,000 men of southeastern North Carolina lined the riverbanks with their muskets to prevent them being landed. The local men did this eight years before the Boston Tea Party, and without the benefit of warpaint and feathers to disguise their identities. Parliament repealed the Stamp Act by 1767, but imposed other taxes on things like tea, coffee, and sugar to reinforce the idea that as British colonies, Parliament could tax the Americans as they saw fit. The Stamp Act crisis was the first steps the colonies made towards a break with Great Britain. A decade later, they would fight a revolution to complete that break.

The Battle at Moores Creek

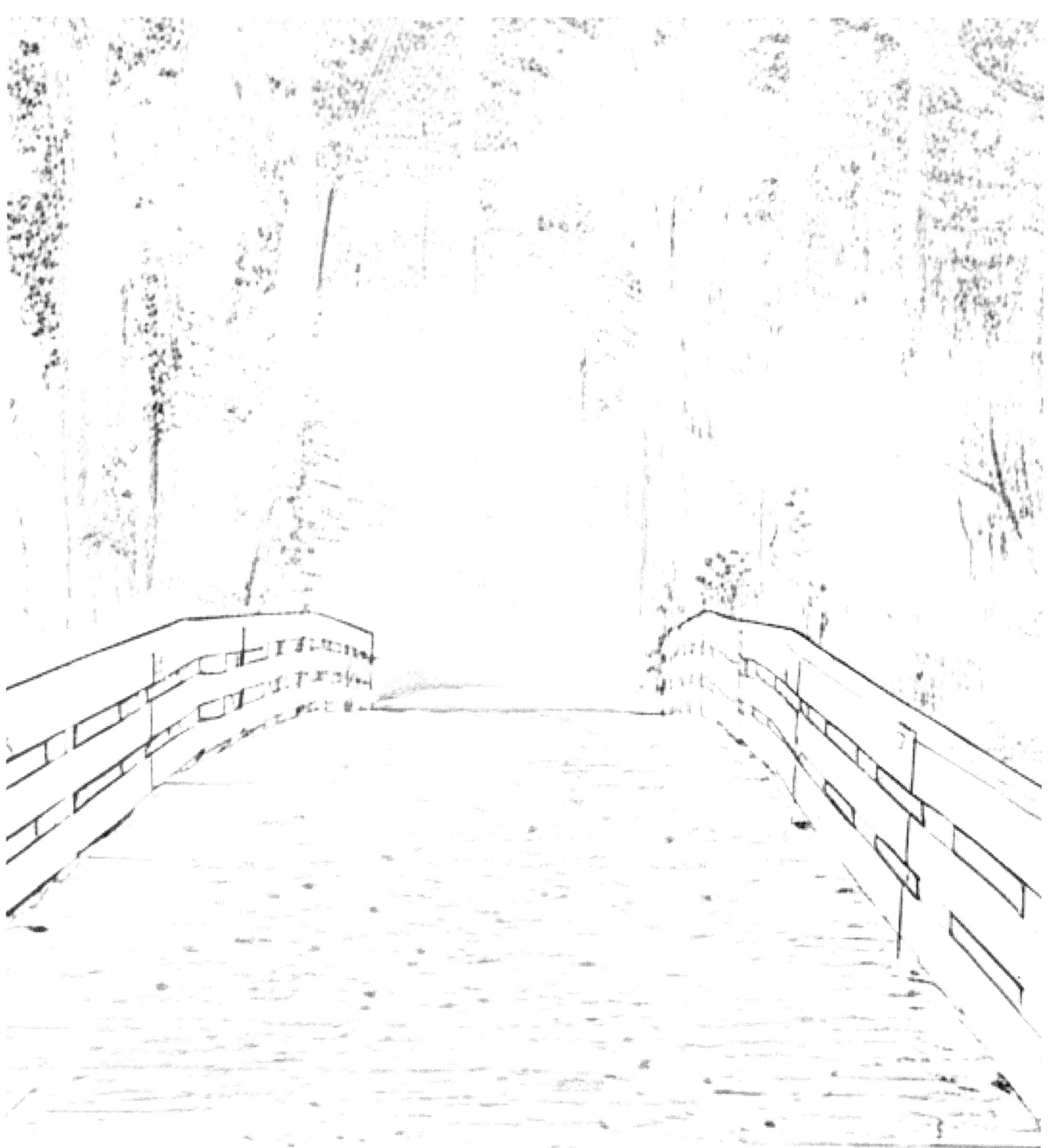

The bridge at Widow Moores Creek was the scene of a sharp, vicious fight that became the first Patriot victory at least in the South, if not the entire country. On the early mormning of February 27, 1776, Patriot milita under Richard Caswell and Alexander Lillington faced off with a column of Loyalist Highlanders at the bridge twenty miles northwest of Wilmington. The fight only lasted a few short minutes, but when it was over, Loyalist agitation in North Carolina came to a virtual standstill until Charleston, S.C. fell to the British in 1780.

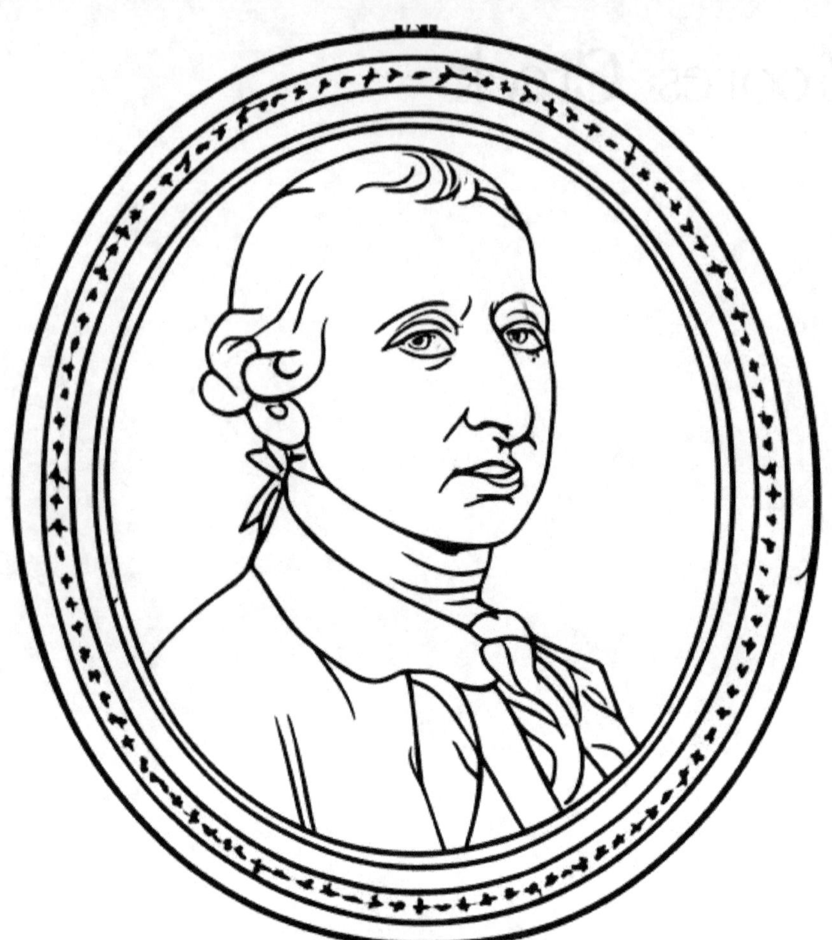

Royal Governor Josiah Martin (left) presented a plan to his superiors in London that called for the raising of a loyalist army from among the many Scots Highlanders and Regulators in the North Carolina interior. That army would be joined by regular British redcoats sent from Boston and Ireland to form a force that would reclaim the colony for King George III. The plan was approved.

To raise the loyalists, the British sent a veteran of the fight at Bunker Hill, a Scot named Donald MacDonald (right) to rally the troops. Martin and the British believed there was a vast force of new settlers just waiting to rise up in defense of their king because before those settlers had been given land grants in the N.C. interior, they had been required to sign loyalty oaths. They were right in that roughly 1,500 men responded to MacDonald's initial recruiting call.

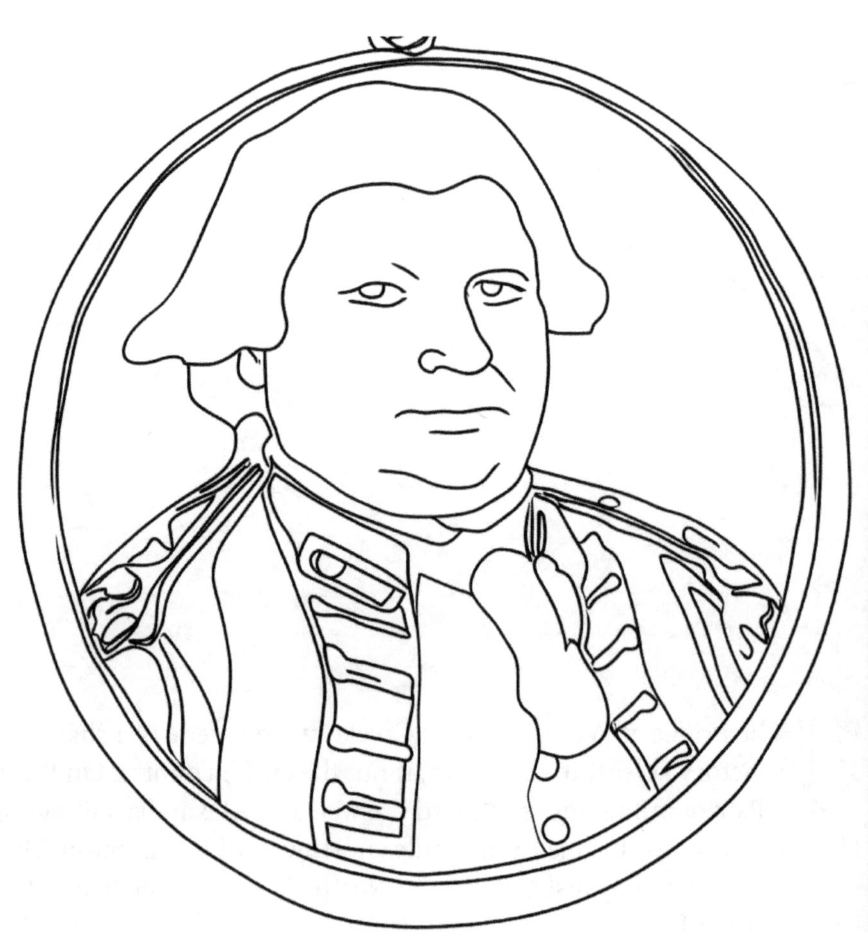

Martin did his planning aboard the HMS Cruizer*, a British sloop of war in the Cape Fear River stationed off of Fort Johnston. Martin had been in virtual prison abord the ship after fleeing the governor's mansion New Bern. What Martin did not know was that local Patriots were intercepting his messages from the* Cruizer*, and knew about his plan to raise a Loyalist army.*

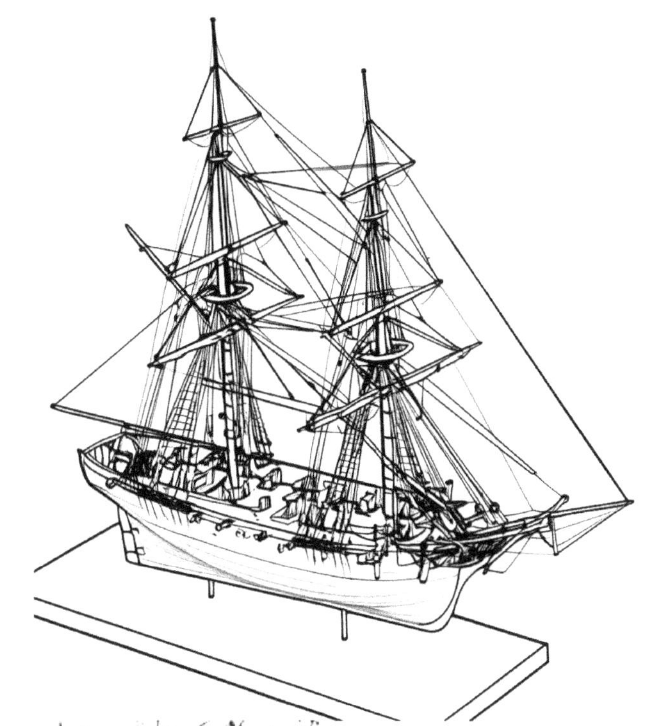

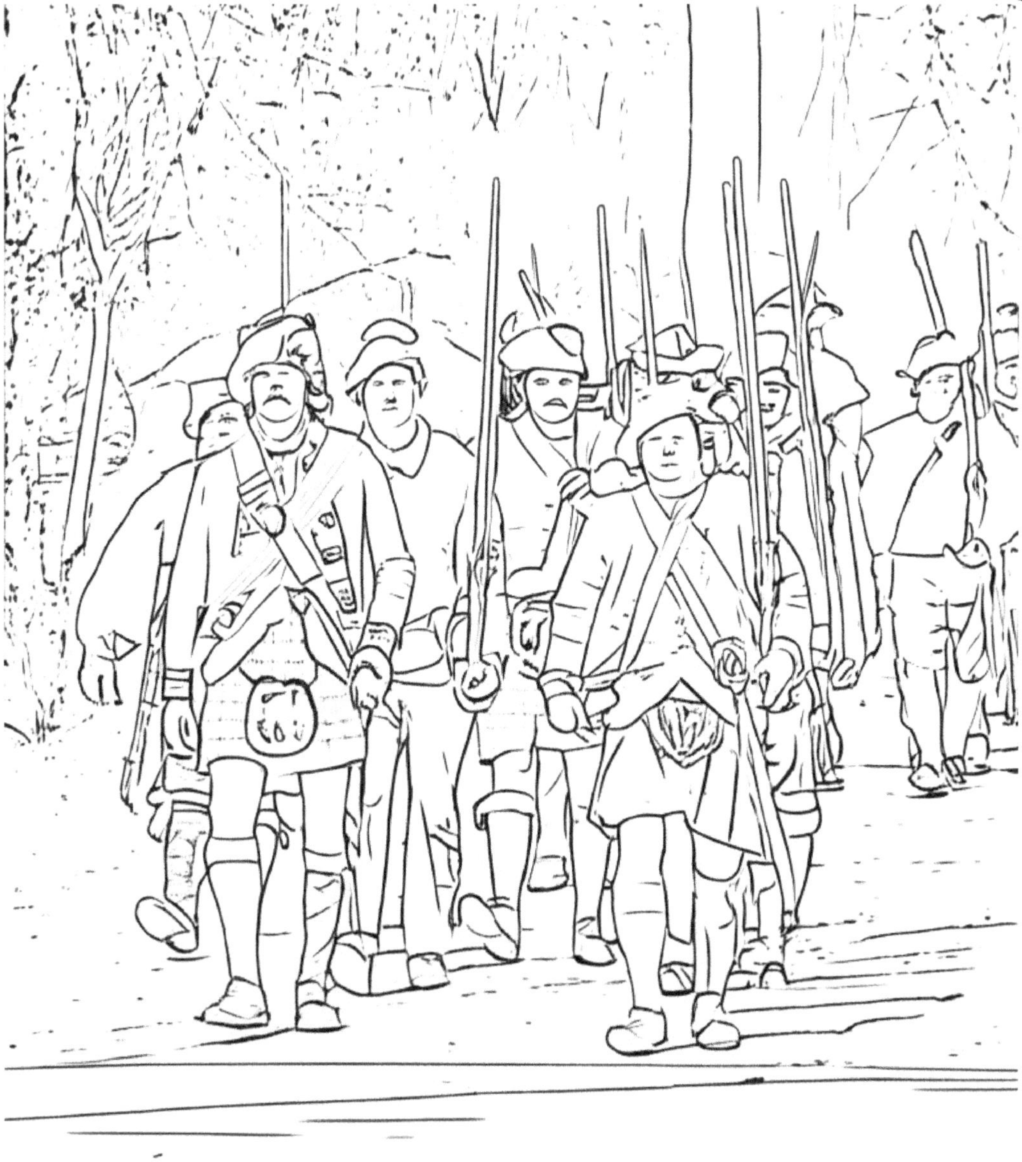

As MacDonald's Highland army marched out of Cross Creek (modern Fayetteville), they were met at Rockfish Creek by Col. James Moore's regiment of the North Carolina Continental Line. Moore's men were all armed, and even had several cannons with them. MacDonald's Highlanders lacked military firearms for the most part, so MacDonald opted to avoid a fight until he could reach the coast and link up with the British regulars being sent from Boston and Ireland.

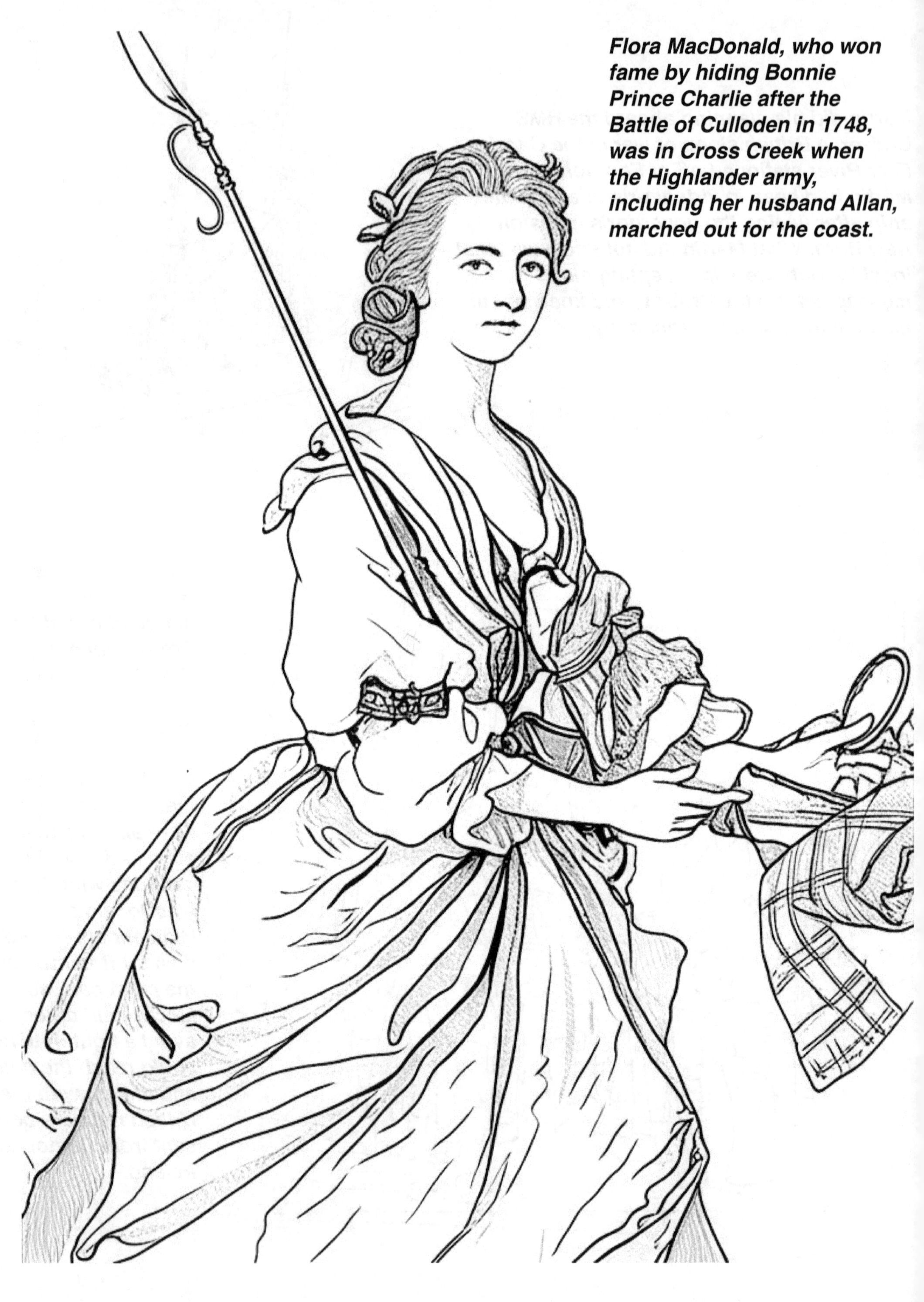

Flora MacDonald, who won fame by hiding Bonnie Prince Charlie after the Battle of Culloden in 1748, was in Cross Creek when the Highlander army, including her husband Allan, marched out for the coast.

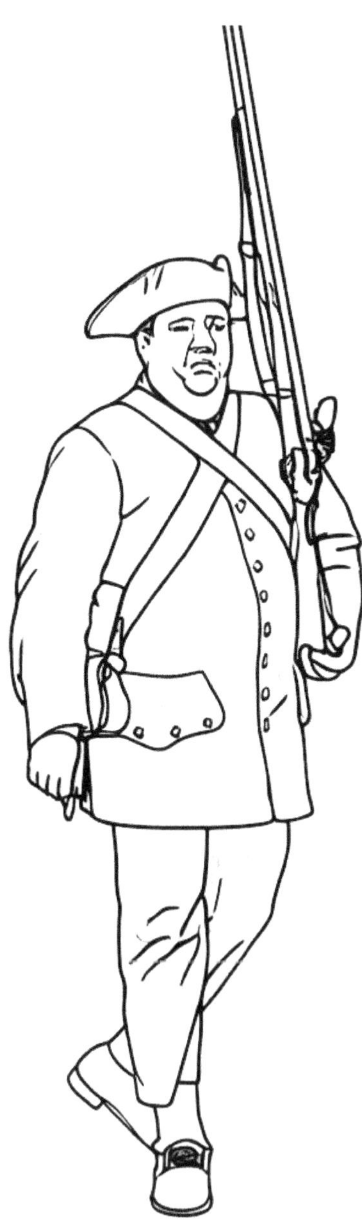

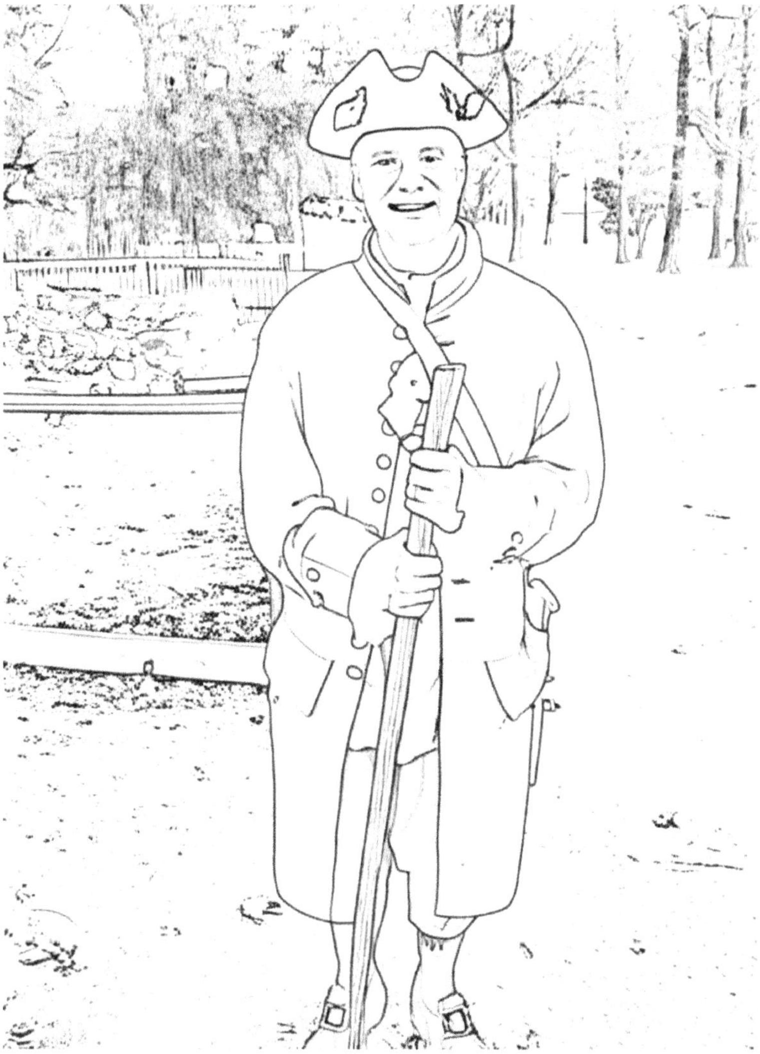

North Carolina militiamen like the ones above ranged in age from 16-60. They were responsible for having a firelock, twelve cartridges of ammunition, and two opposable teeth to bite the ends off the paper cartridges that contained the lead ball and powder for their muskets. It was men like these who lay siege to Fort Johnston (right) to deny its use to Gov. Martin and the British.

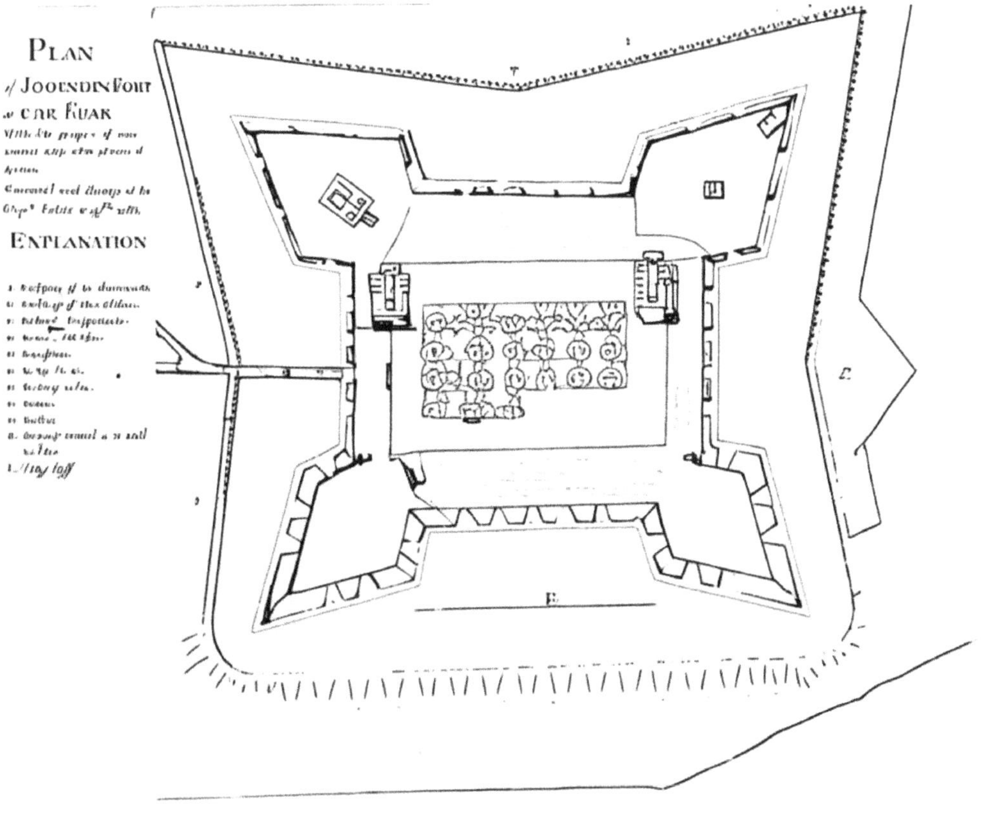

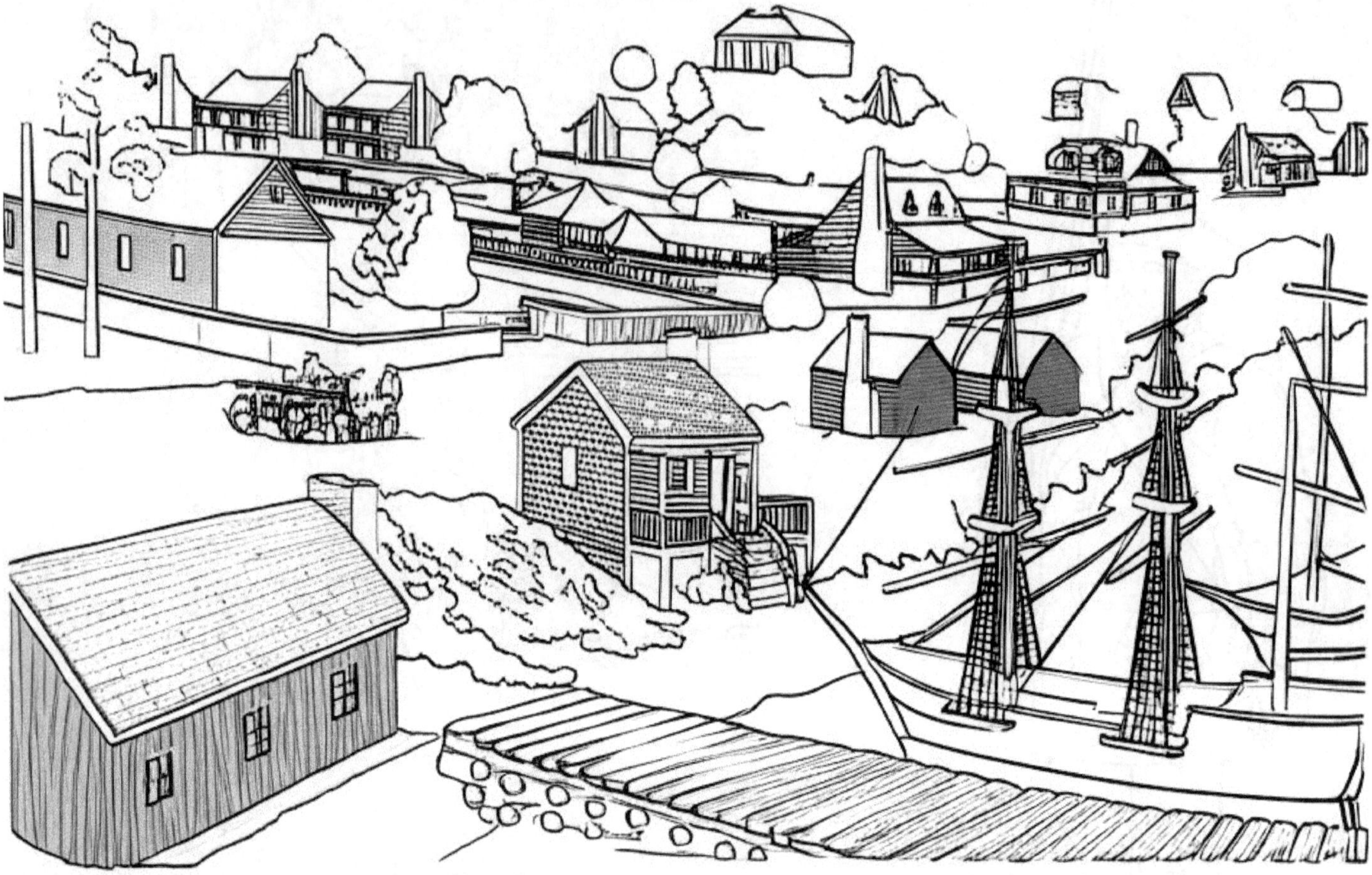

Colonial Brunswick (above, from a painting by James C. Horton), was the intended destination for MacDonald's Highlander army. But when Admiral Sir Peter Parker's fleet arrived in the Cape Fear River weeks after the fight at Moores Creek, there were no Loyalists there to greet them. The British contented themselves with raids up and down the river, attacking Robert Howe's plantation and sacking the nearly deserted Brunswick Town.

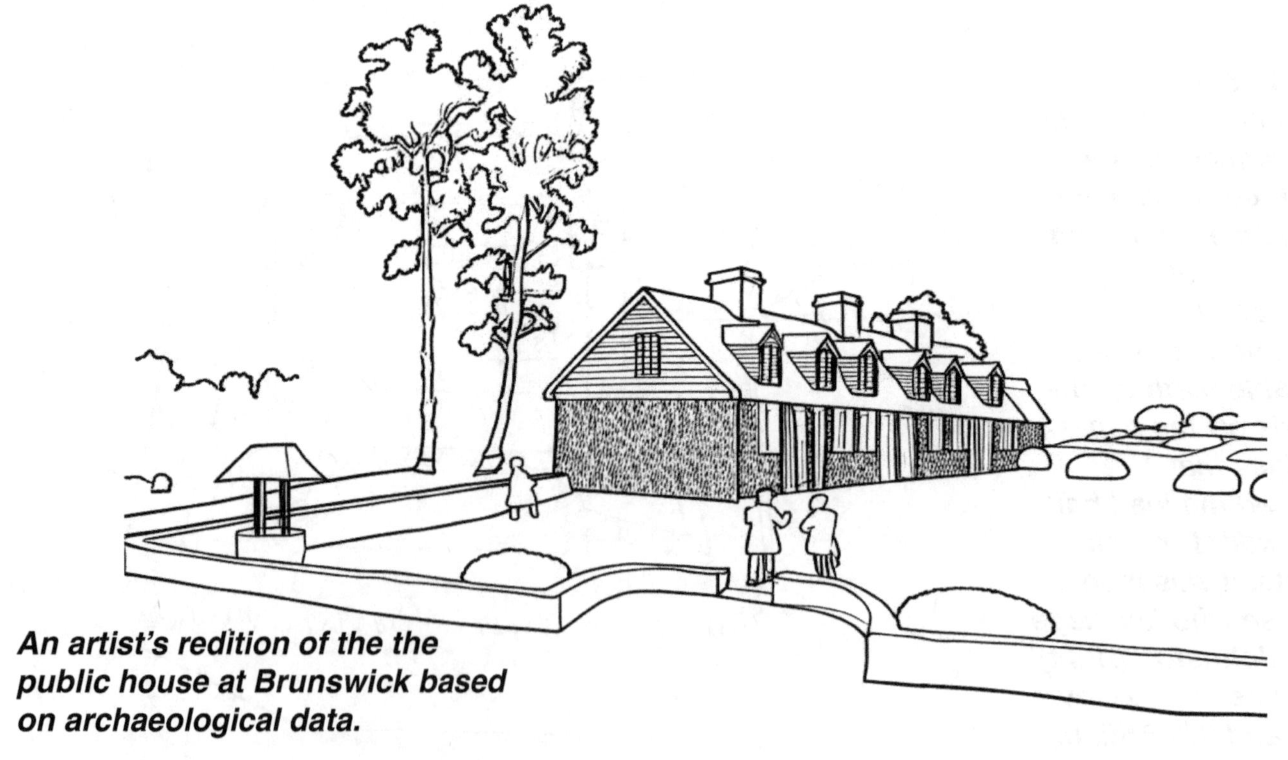

An artist's redition of the the public house at Brunswick based on archaeological data.

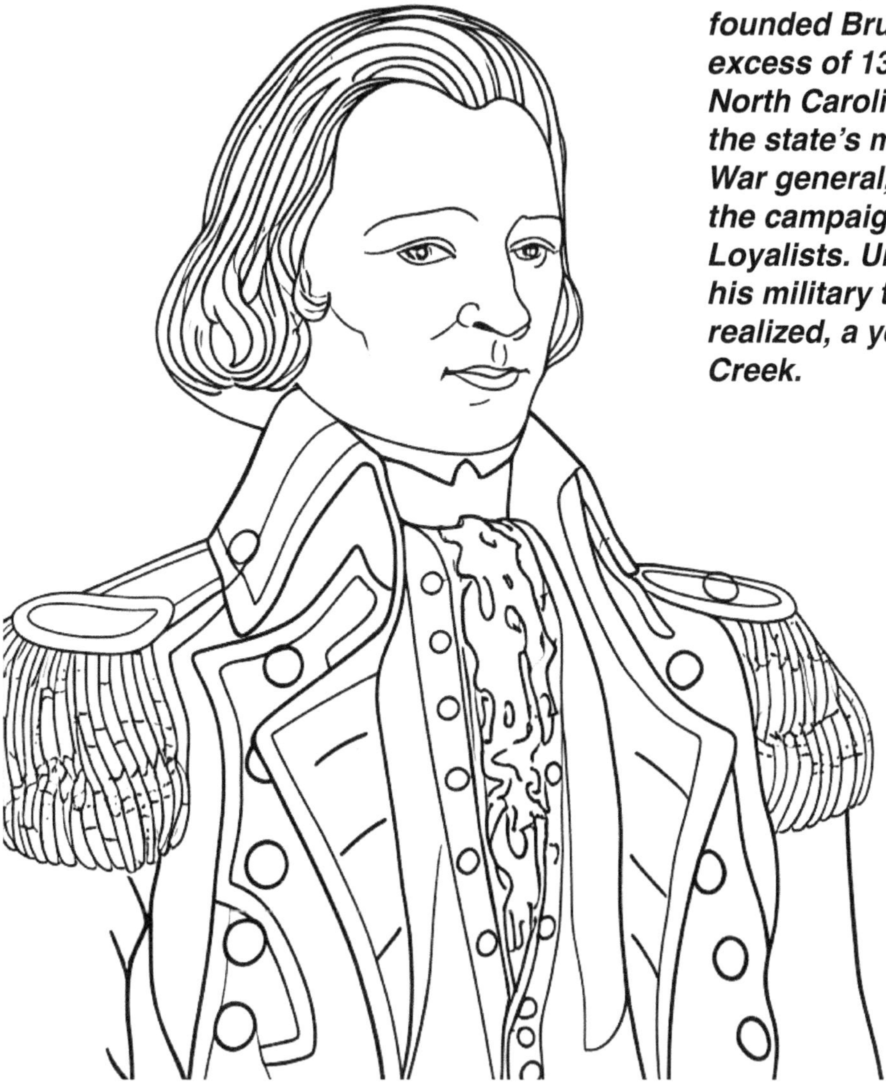

Col. James Moore was of the family that founded Brunswick and that owned in excess of 133,000 acres of southeastern North Carolina at one point. Moore was the state's most capable Revolutionary War general, and it was he who planned the campaign to stop the Highland Loyalists. Unfortunately, he died before his military talents could be fully realized, a year after the fight at Moores Creek.

Loyalist militia found the bridge before sunrise on February 27, 1776. While an advance element led by Donald MacLeod rushed down the causeway into the teeth of the Patriot defenses, others formed a firing line to return fire against Caswell and Lillington's men (below).

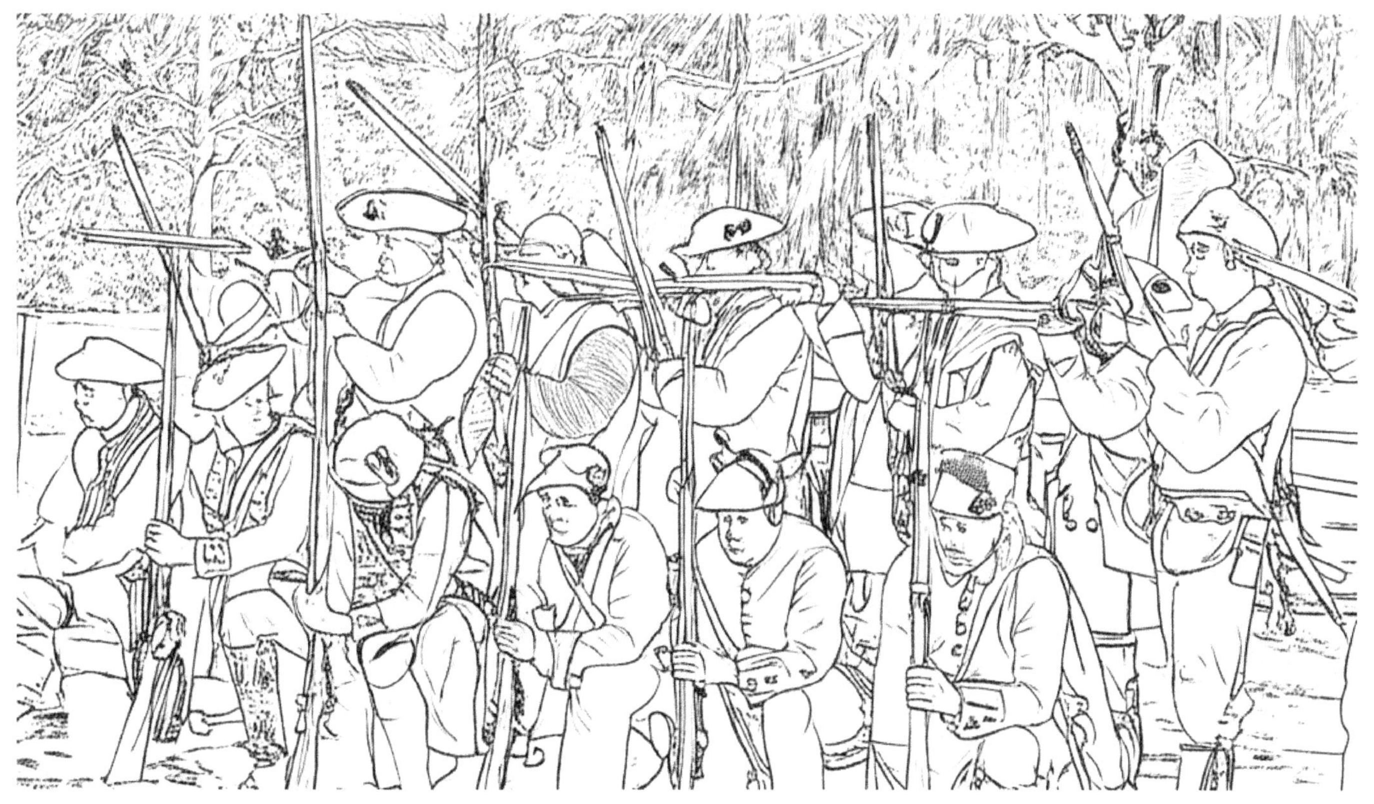

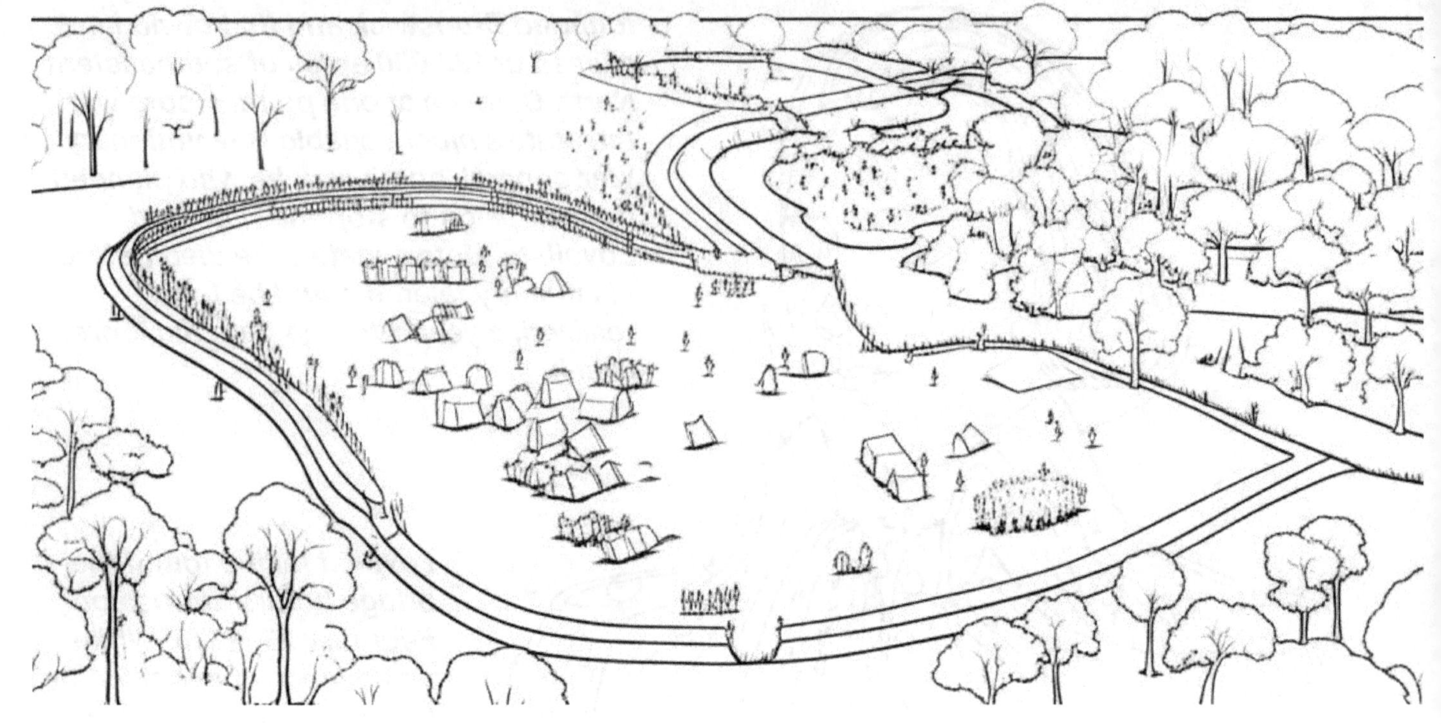

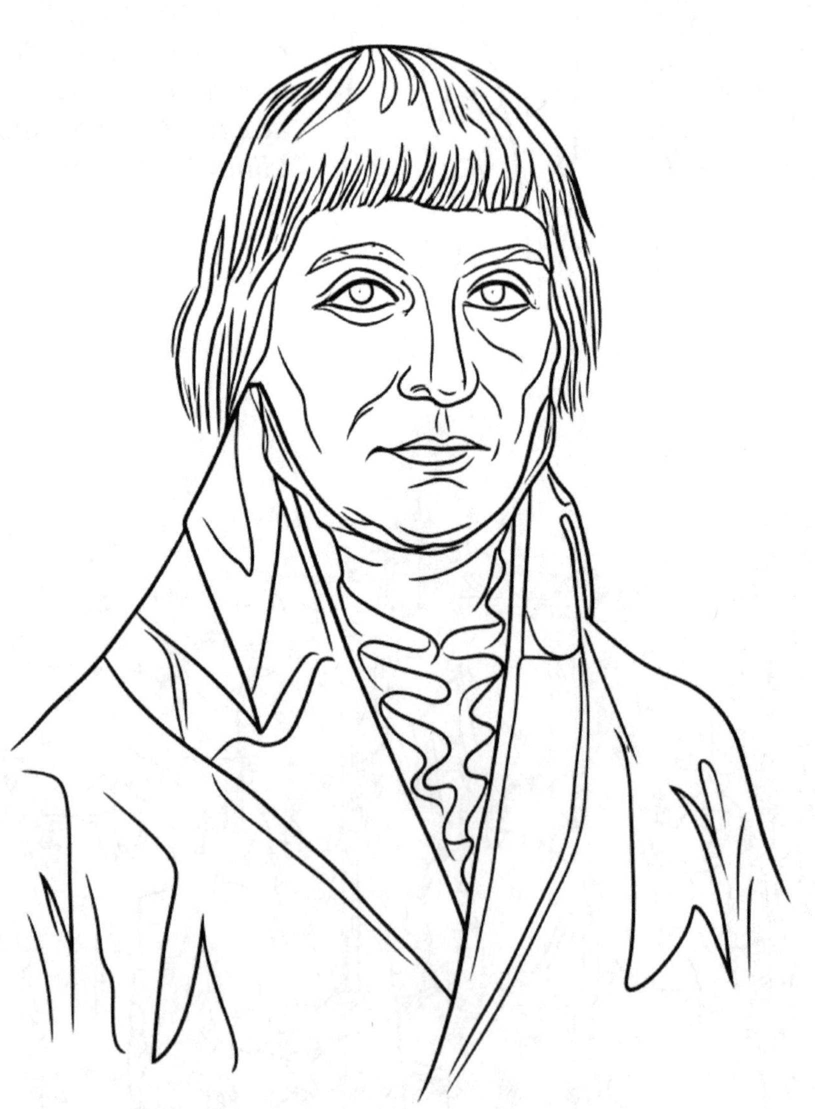

Col. Richard Caswell (left) ordered his men to build earthworks on the high ground east of the bridge, as seen in the drawing above. The Patriot militia, secure behind chest-high breastworks, waited until the Highlanders were just yards away before opening fire.

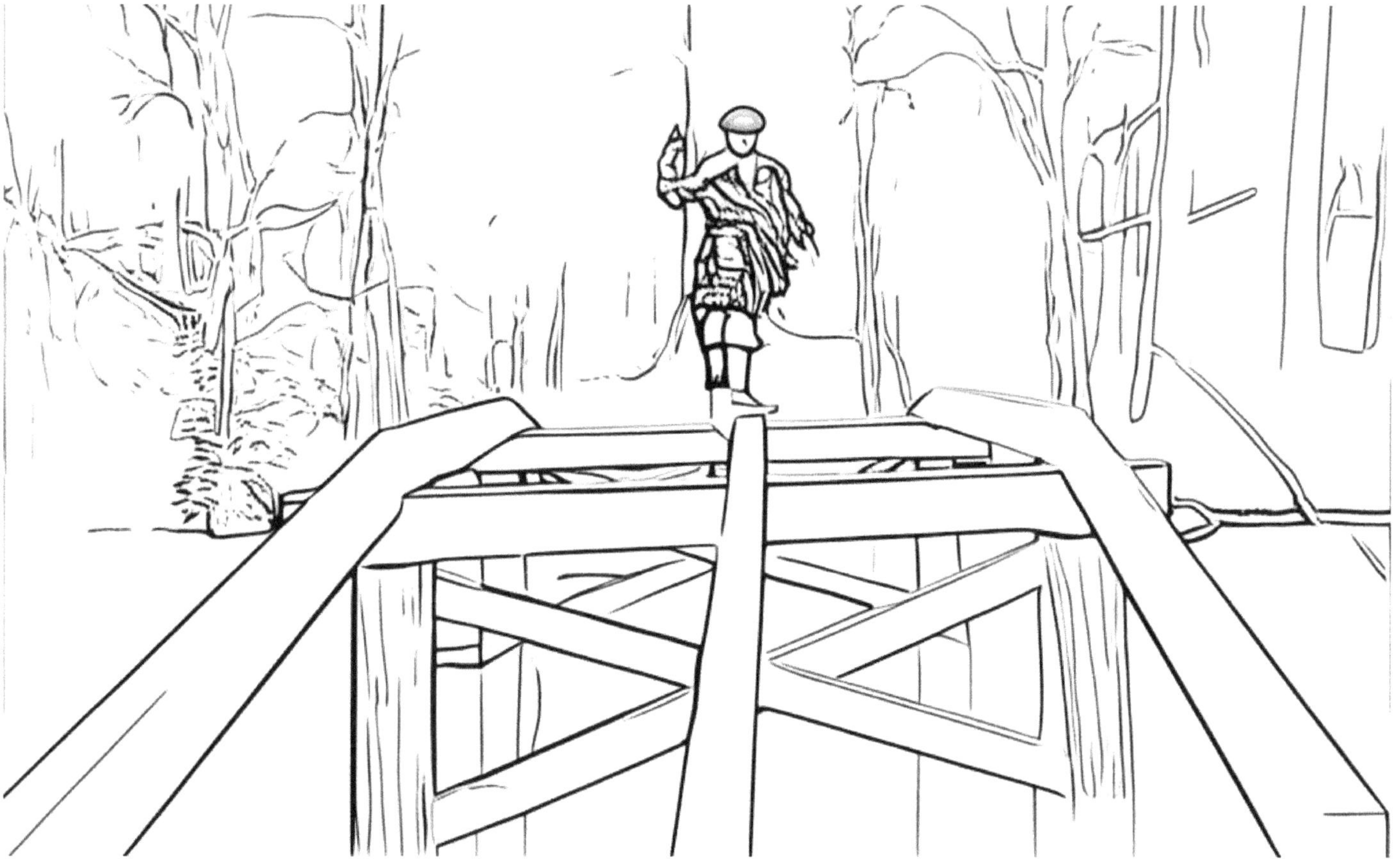

Caswell ordered the planks pulled up from the bridge, then greased the runners with tallow and soft soap to make getting across harder for the Highlanders (above). At the other end of the causeway that MacLeod's men eventually charged down, more than 900 militia waited behind chest-high breastworks with a three-pound dutch cannon called Old Mother Covington anchoring one end of the line (below), and a swivel gun anchoring the other.

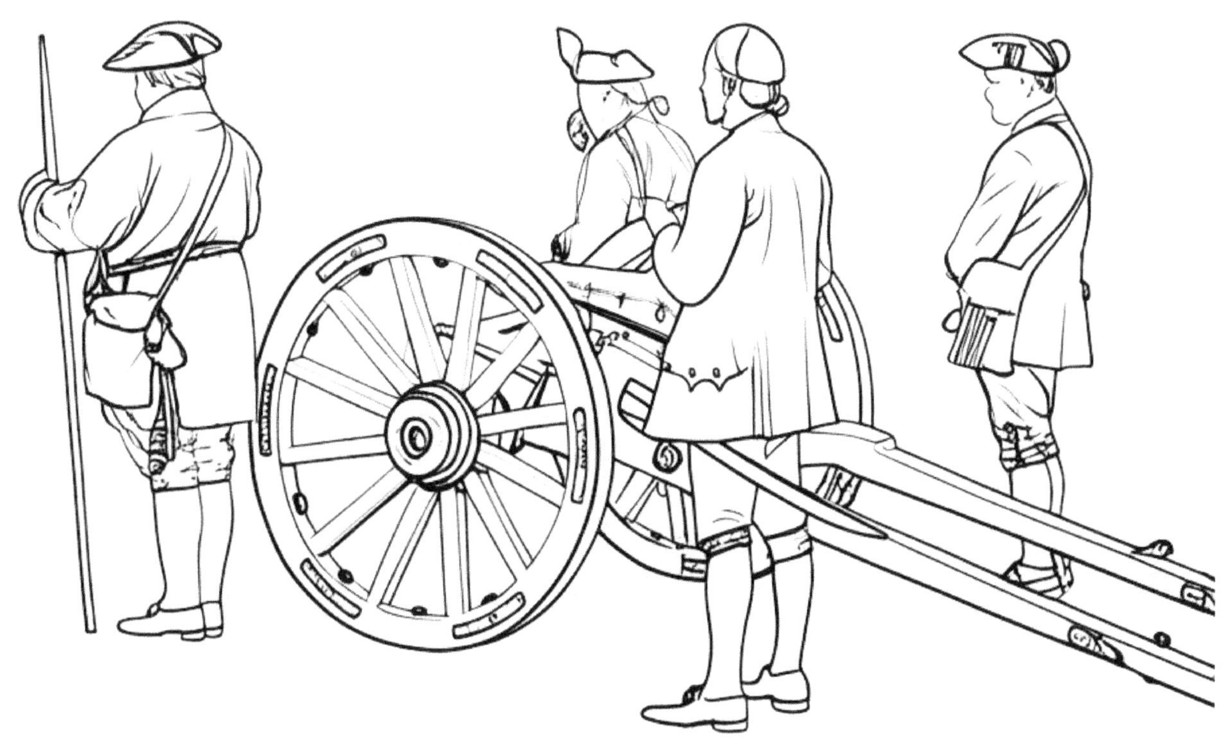

Swivel guns (right) were versatile weapons that functioned like big shotguns. Light enough to be easily moved about a ship or carried by troops in the field, swivel guns were loaded with everything from musket balls to rocks, nails, and broken glass. The effect on the charging Highlanders at Moores Creek was devastating.

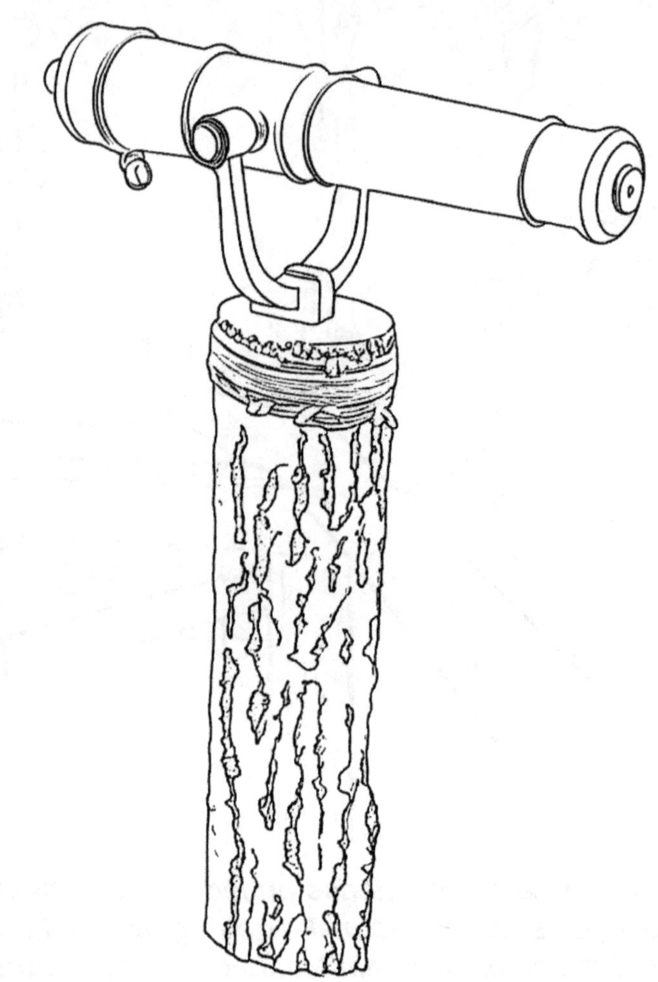

The Patriot militia at Moores Creek fired from behind thick, chest high breastworks that protected their torsos from enemy fire (below). As MacLeod's charging Scots raced up the causeway, screaming their war cry and brandishing their fearsome claymore swords, the Patriots waited until they were right upon them before firing.

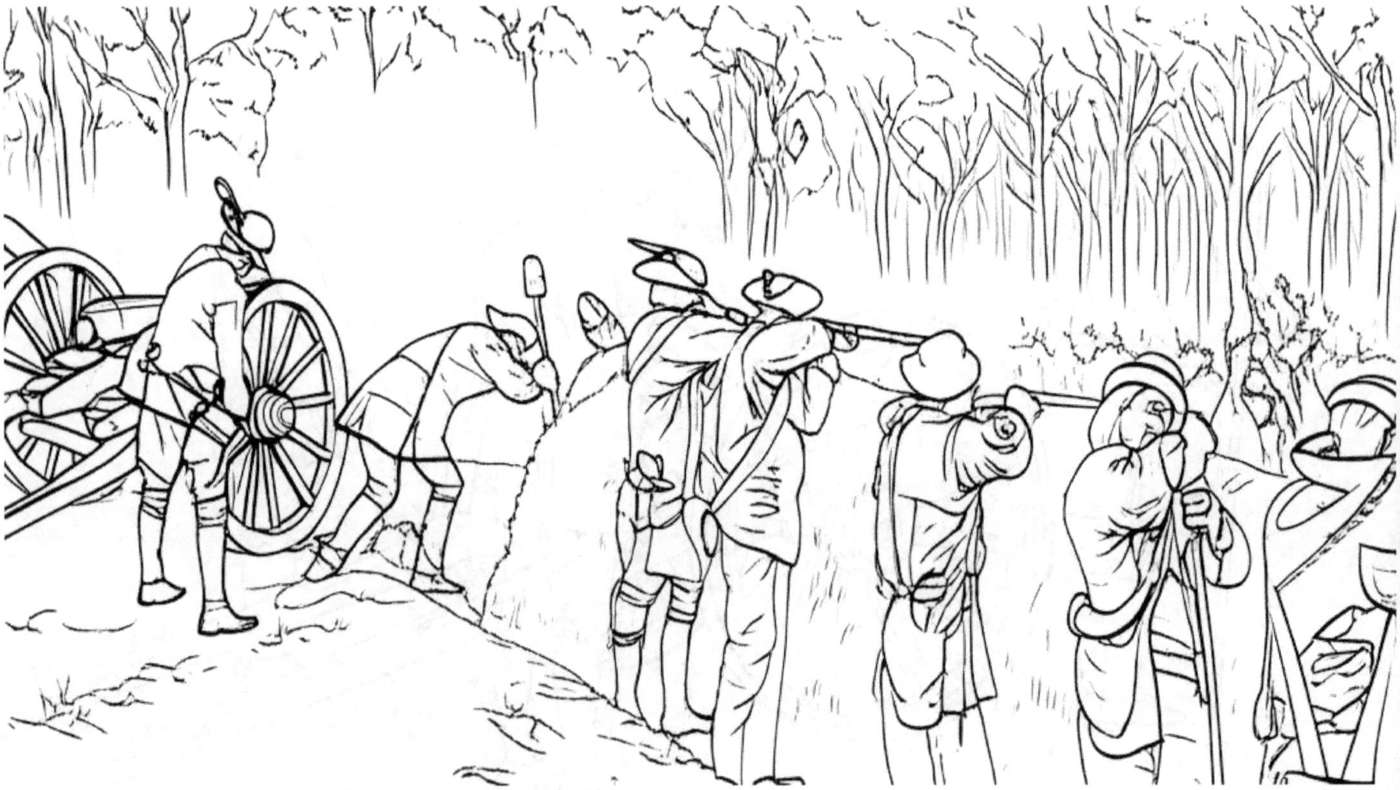

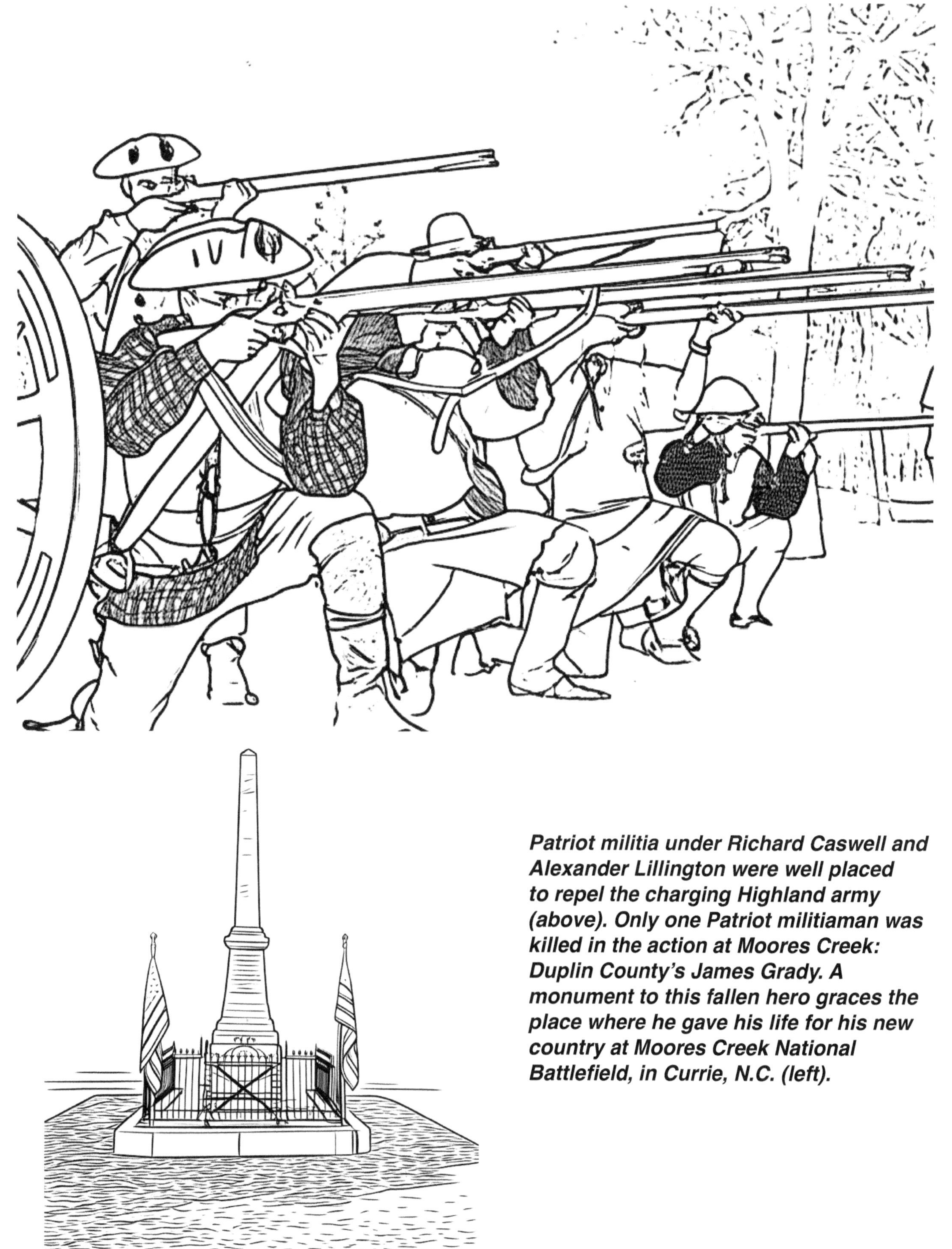

Patriot militia under Richard Caswell and Alexander Lillington were well placed to repel the charging Highland army (above). Only one Patriot militiaman was killed in the action at Moores Creek: Duplin County's James Grady. A monument to this fallen hero graces the place where he gave his life for his new country at Moores Creek National Battlefield, in Currie, N.C. (left).

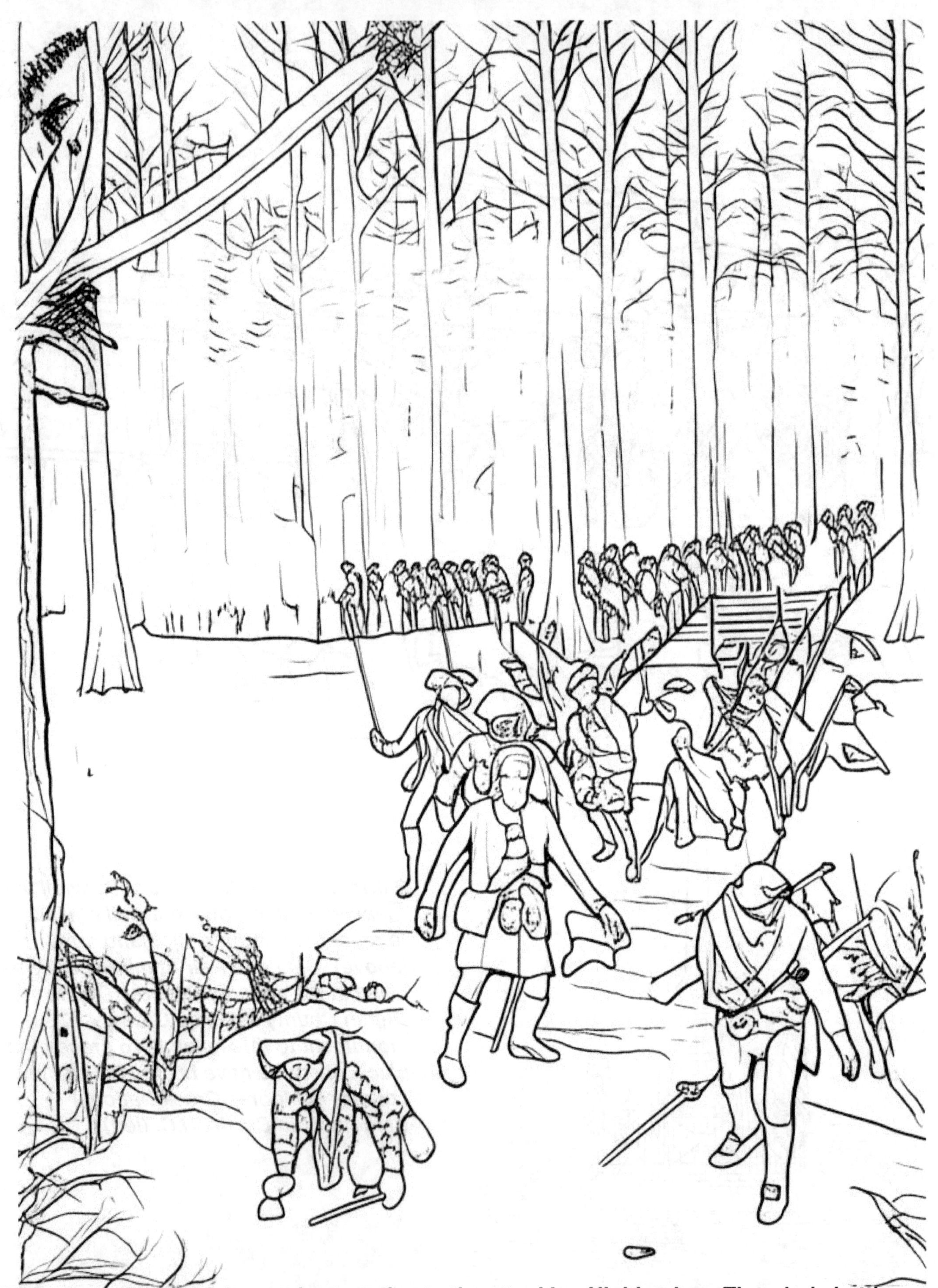

When the militia fired, it was devaastating to the attacking Highlanders. The whole battle was over in a matter of minutes, and Loyalist activity in the state was squashed.

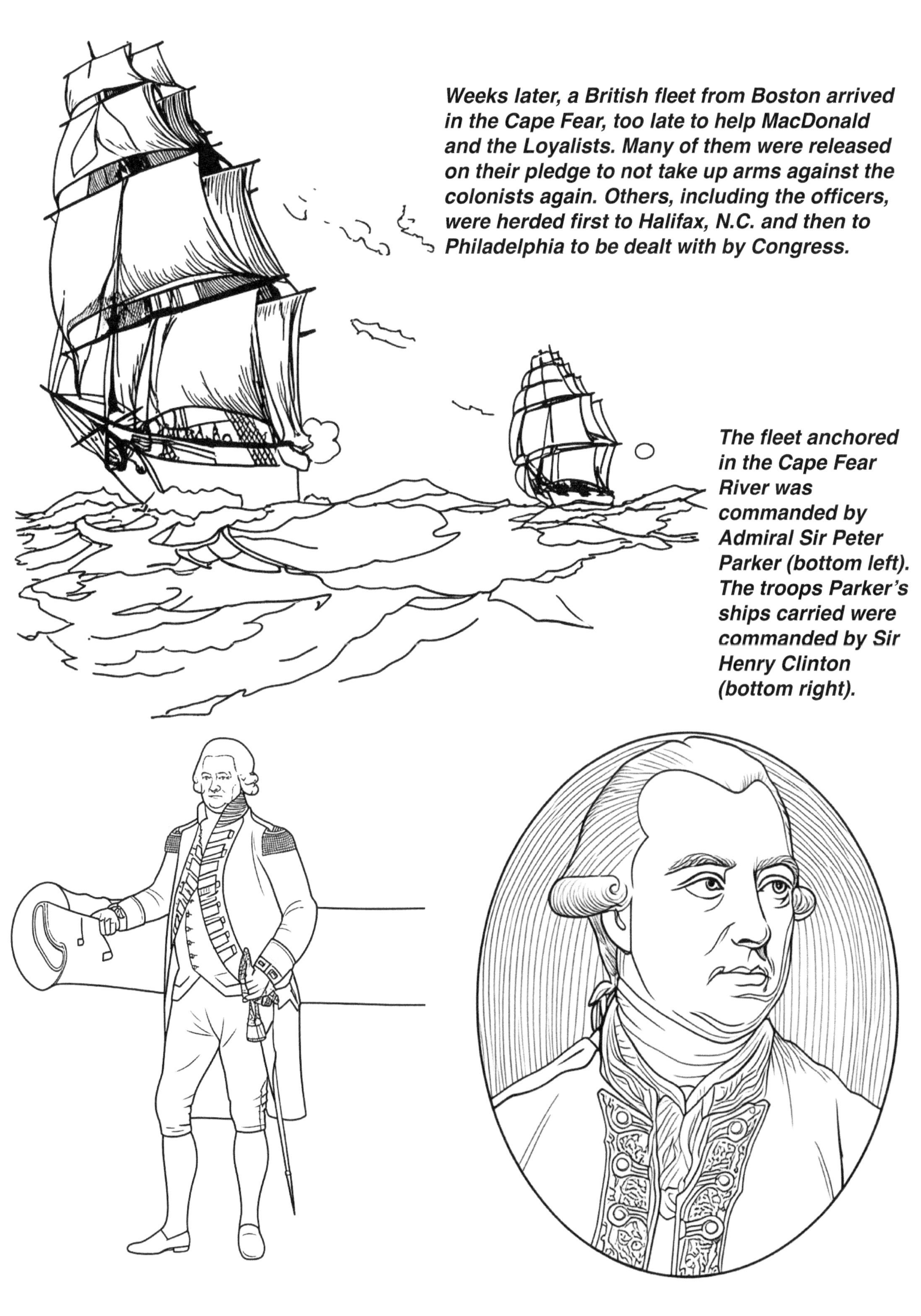

Weeks later, a British fleet from Boston arrived in the Cape Fear, too late to help MacDonald and the Loyalists. Many of them were released on their pledge to not take up arms against the colonists again. Others, including the officers, were herded first to Halifax, N.C. and then to Philadelphia to be dealt with by Congress.

The fleet anchored in the Cape Fear River was commanded by Admiral Sir Peter Parker (bottom left). The troops Parker's ships carried were commanded by Sir Henry Clinton (bottom right).

The British Occupation: 1781

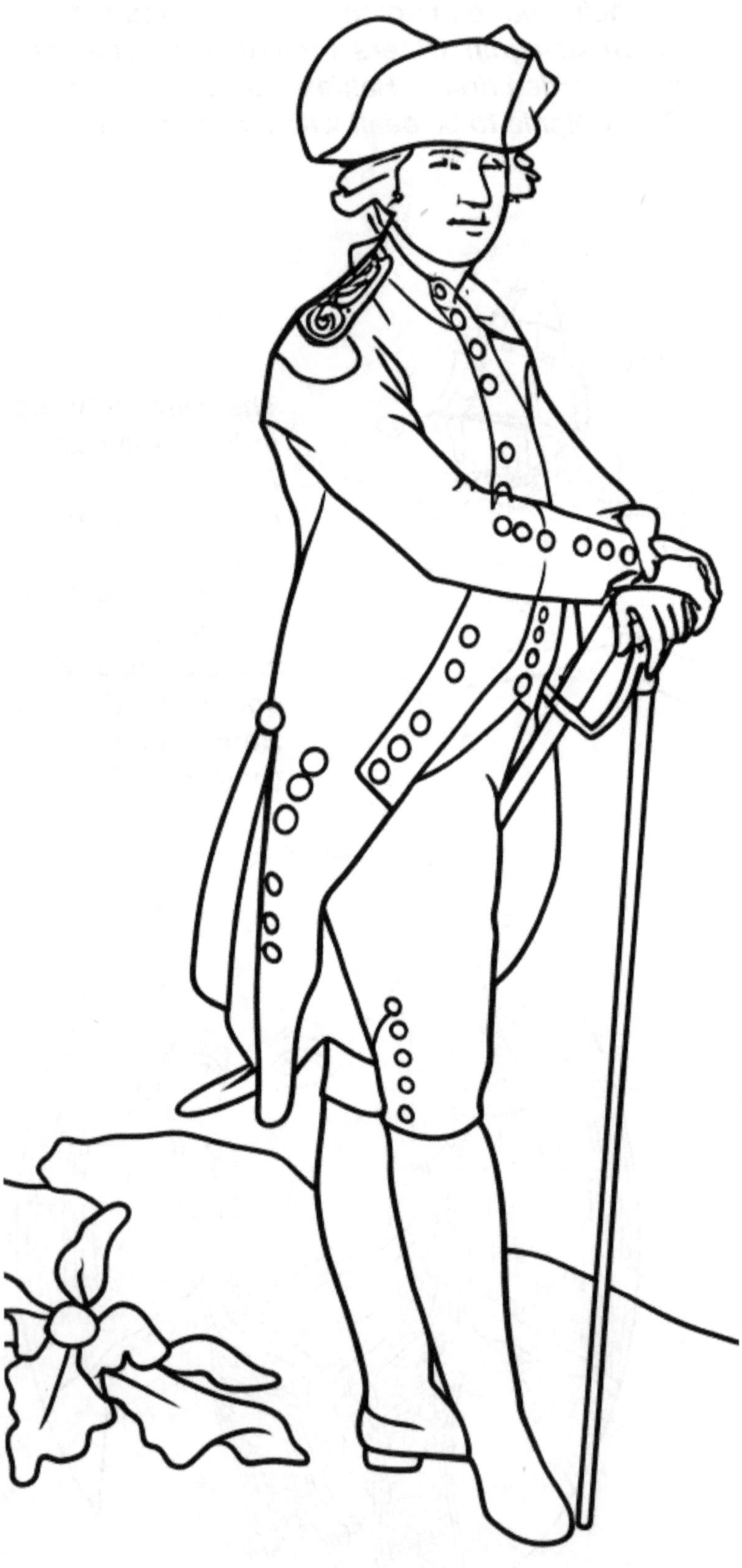

After Charleston fell in 1780, General Sir Charles Lord Cornwallis (left) conceived a plan for a campaign to take back all of the territory in the Carolinas that had fallen to the rebellious Americans. To resupply his forces while on the march, Cornwallis dispatched Major James Henry Craig (below) with the 82nd Regiment of Foot, a Highland regiment, to Wilmington. Wilmington controlled access to the Cape Fear River, running 147 miles into the interior. Craig's mission was to ferry supplies upriver to Cross Creek (modern Fayetteville) for Cornwallis to use when needed. But Craig was never able to complete his mission thanks to militiamen from the Cape Fear who blocked the river. After the battle at Guilford Courthouse in March 1781, Cornwallis was dismayed to find no supplies for his wounded and weary troops. It led to his march to Wilmington.

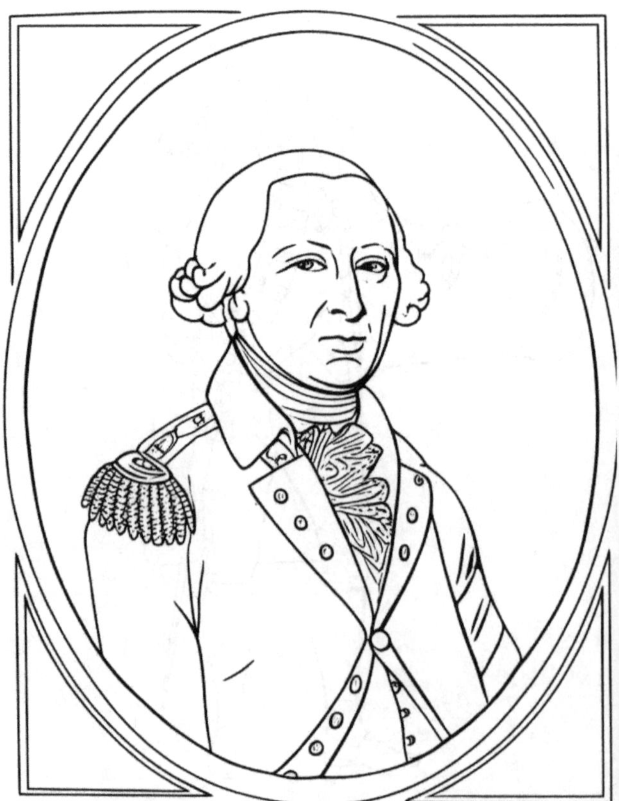

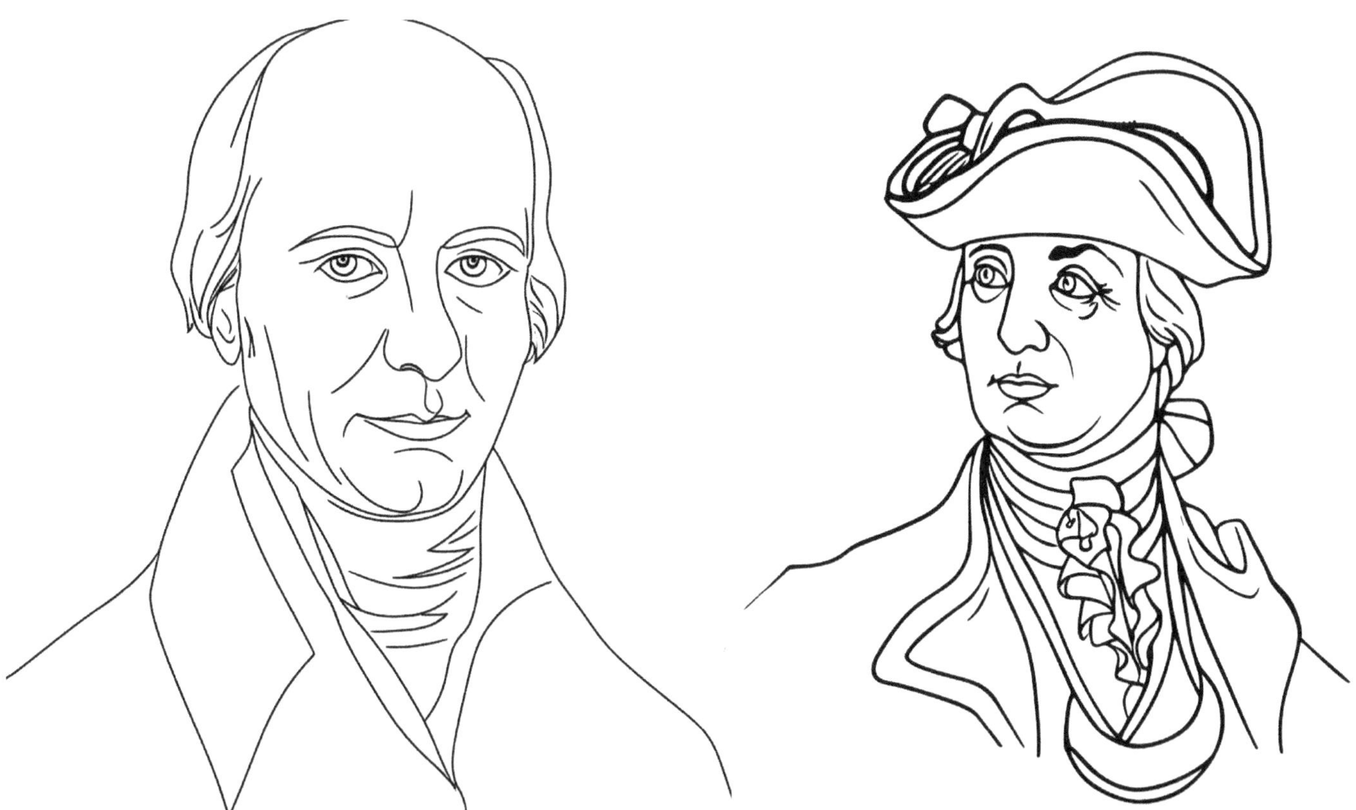

Maurice Moore (top left) was a leader of militia during the British occupation. Major General Robert Howe (top right) was on the list of wanted men Craig brought with him to Cape Fear, but he was not in the area when the British arrived. Redcoats landed south of Wilmington and marched to town (below), catching most people by surprise.

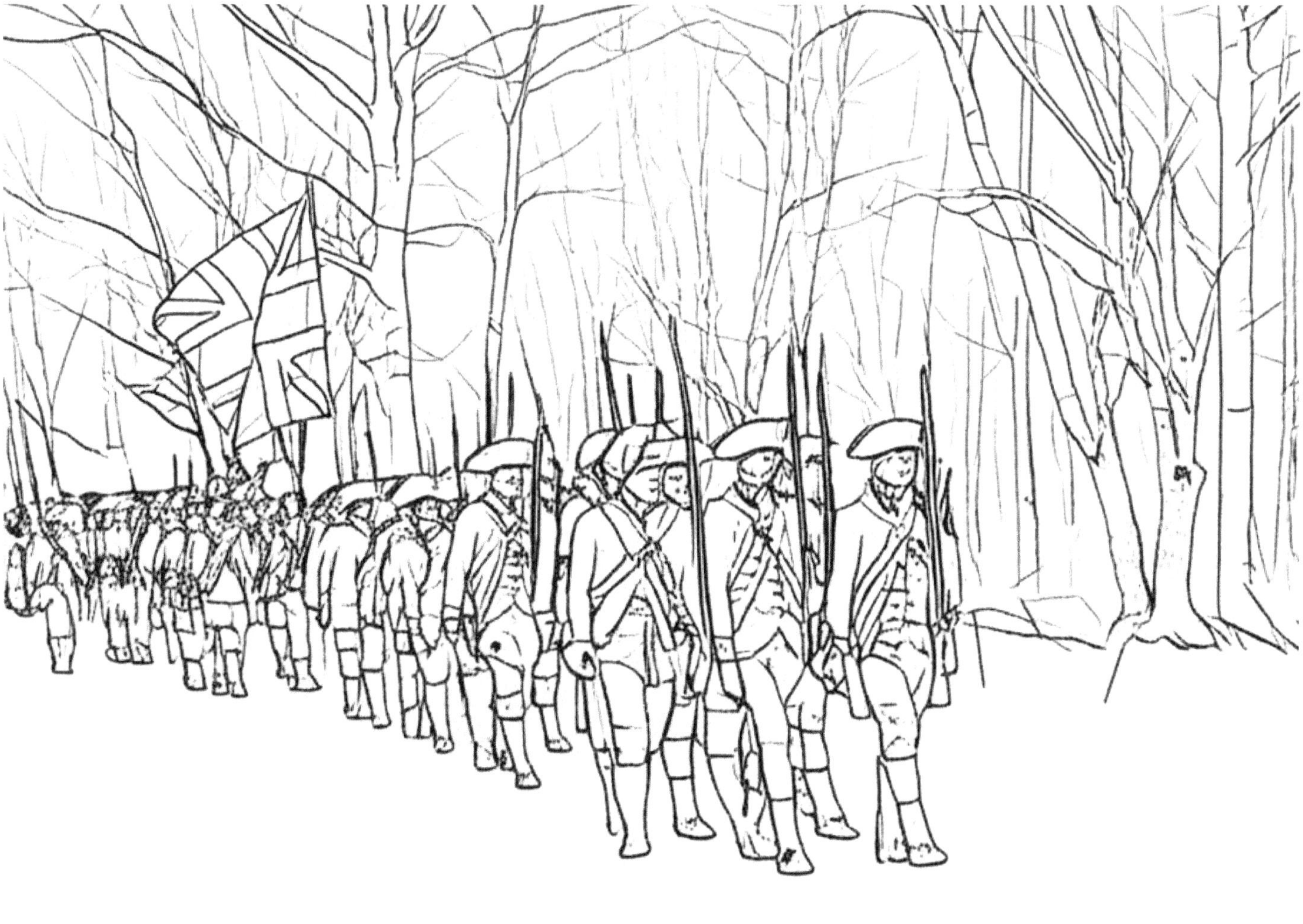

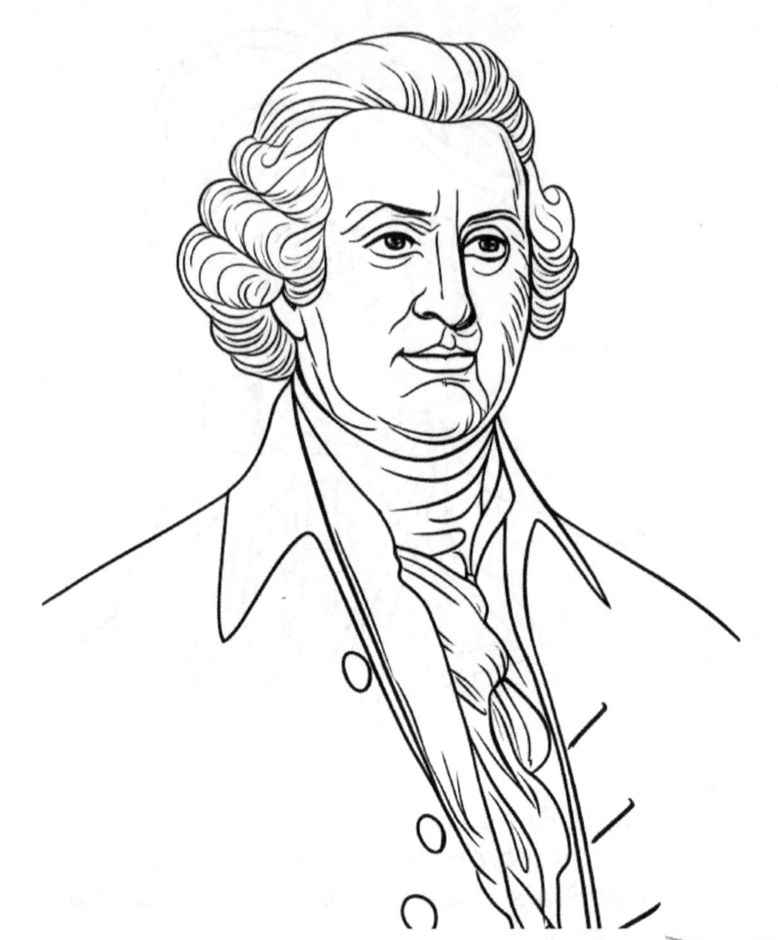

Wilmington's William Hooper (left) was at his home on Masonboro Sound when the British arrived. As a signer of the Declaration of Independence, he was another Patriot on Craig's capture list. Hooper fled to Hillsborough, and sent his wife and children into Wilmington in hopes they would be safe under the protection of British officers. He was wrong.

Mrs. Hooper found the British to be anything but gentlemen. Major Craig was finally convinced to release her and her children, but before they left he ordered them stripped of all their possessions except their underclothes. A Loyalist friend of the Hoopers interceded on their behalf, and was allowed to row Mrs. Hooper and her children across the Cape Fear River and put them into a wagon that took them to Hillsborough.

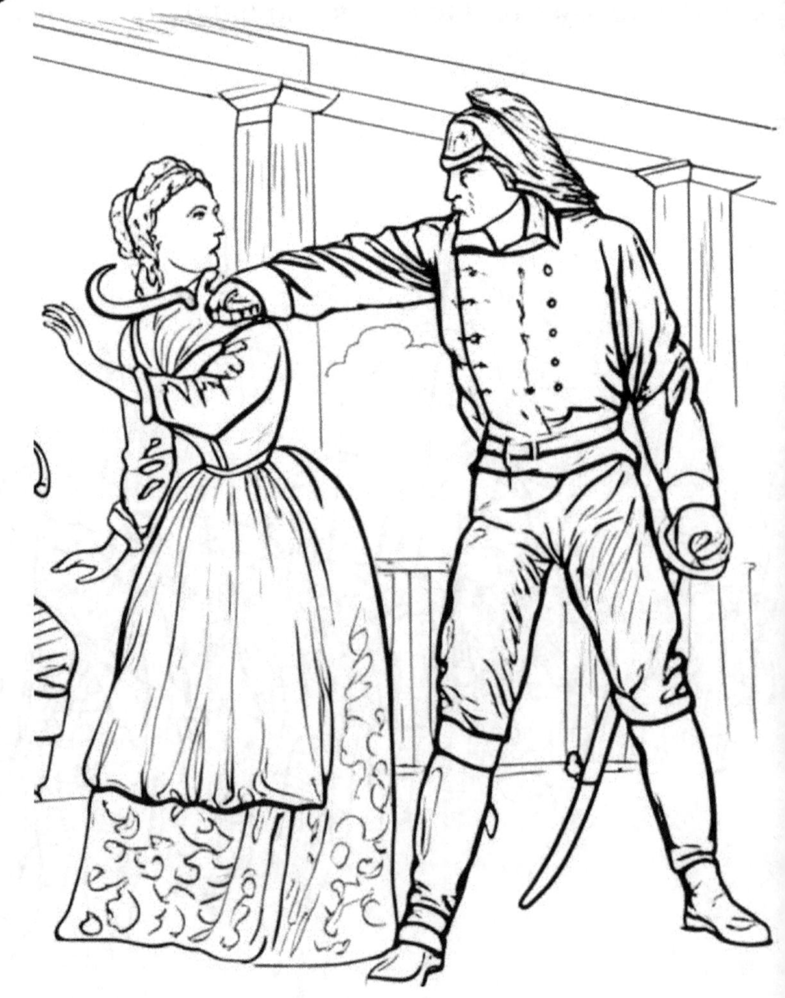

Patriot militia under Alexander Lillington fought two significant skirmishes with Craig's redcoats at Heron's Bridge, just east of where the bridge crosses from New Hanover to Pender County on modern I-40. It was the major chokepoint on the Northeast Cape Fear River. Craig's troops were never able to fully erase the militia presence at the bridge, and that failure led to the failure of Craig's larger mission: to resupply Cornwallis at Cross Creek.

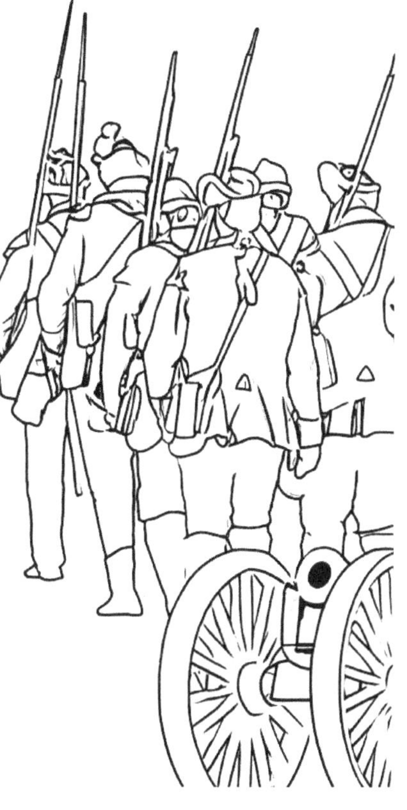

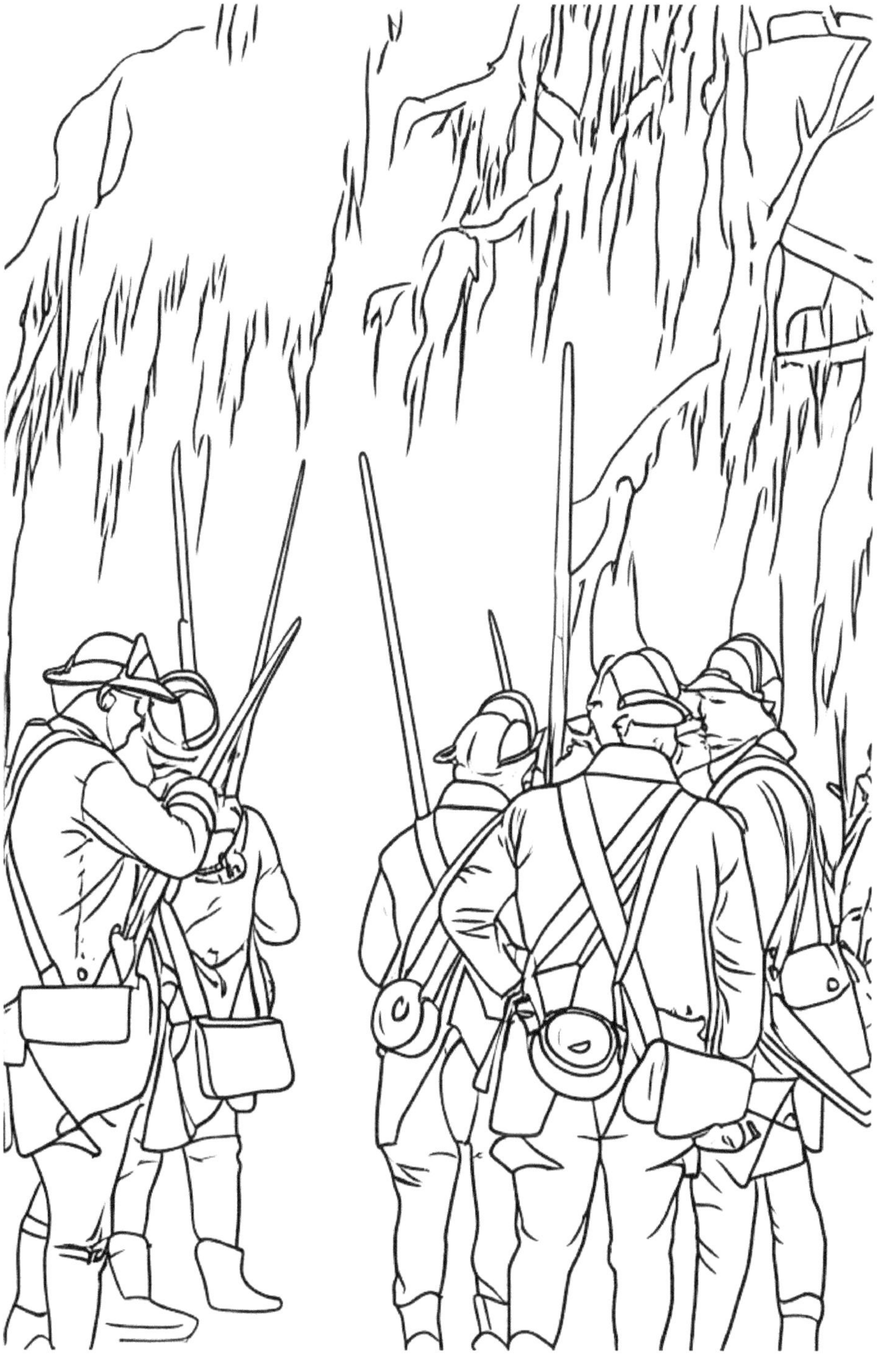

By November 1781, Continental troops under Gen. Griffith Rutherford had been dispatched to kick Craig and the recoats out of Wilmington. Rutherford's men engaged Craig's along the Northeast Cape Fear, while another column crossed over to Eagles Island and Brunswick County to pressure the British from the west.

The second battle at Heron's Bridge, from a painting by James C. Horton

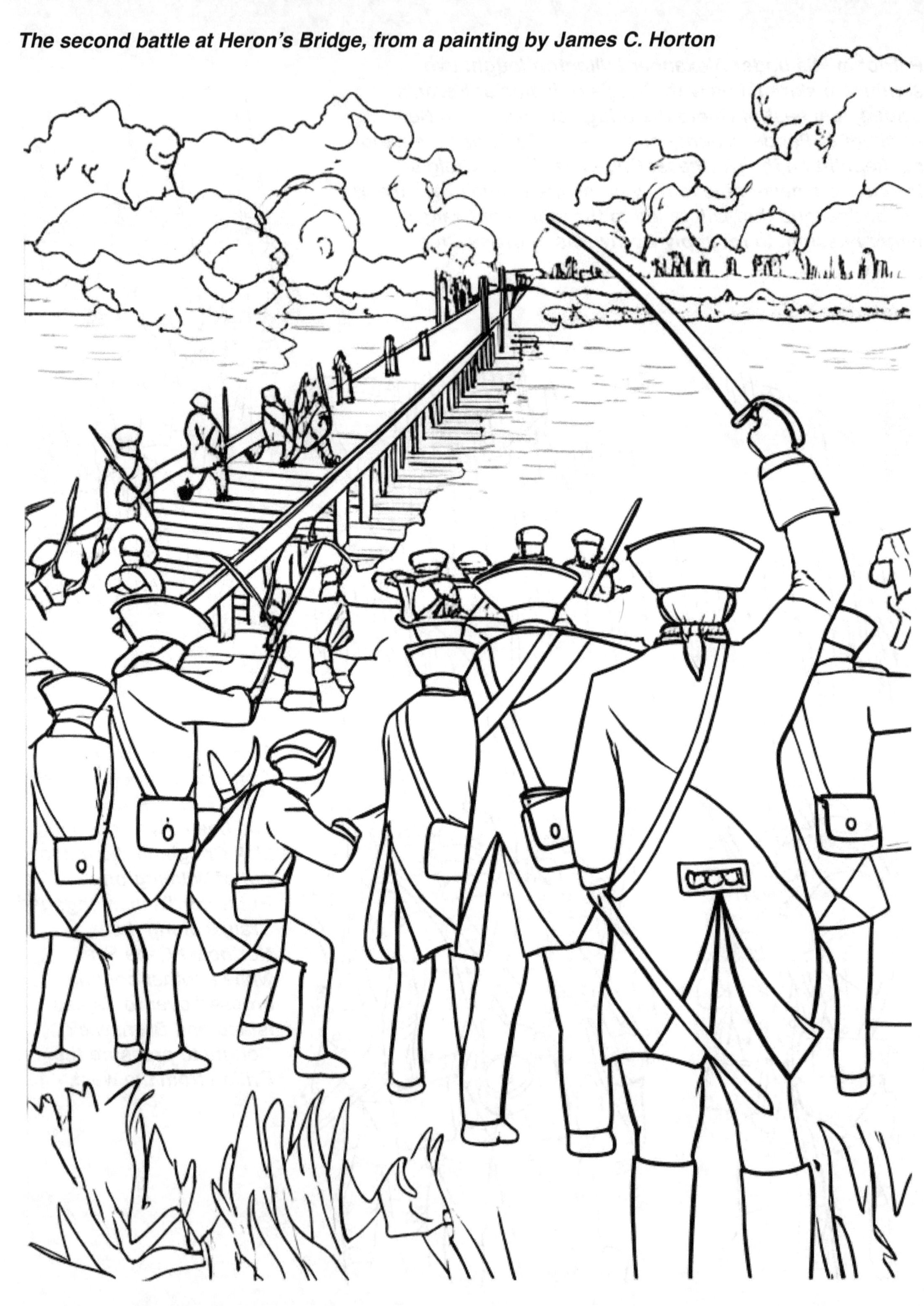

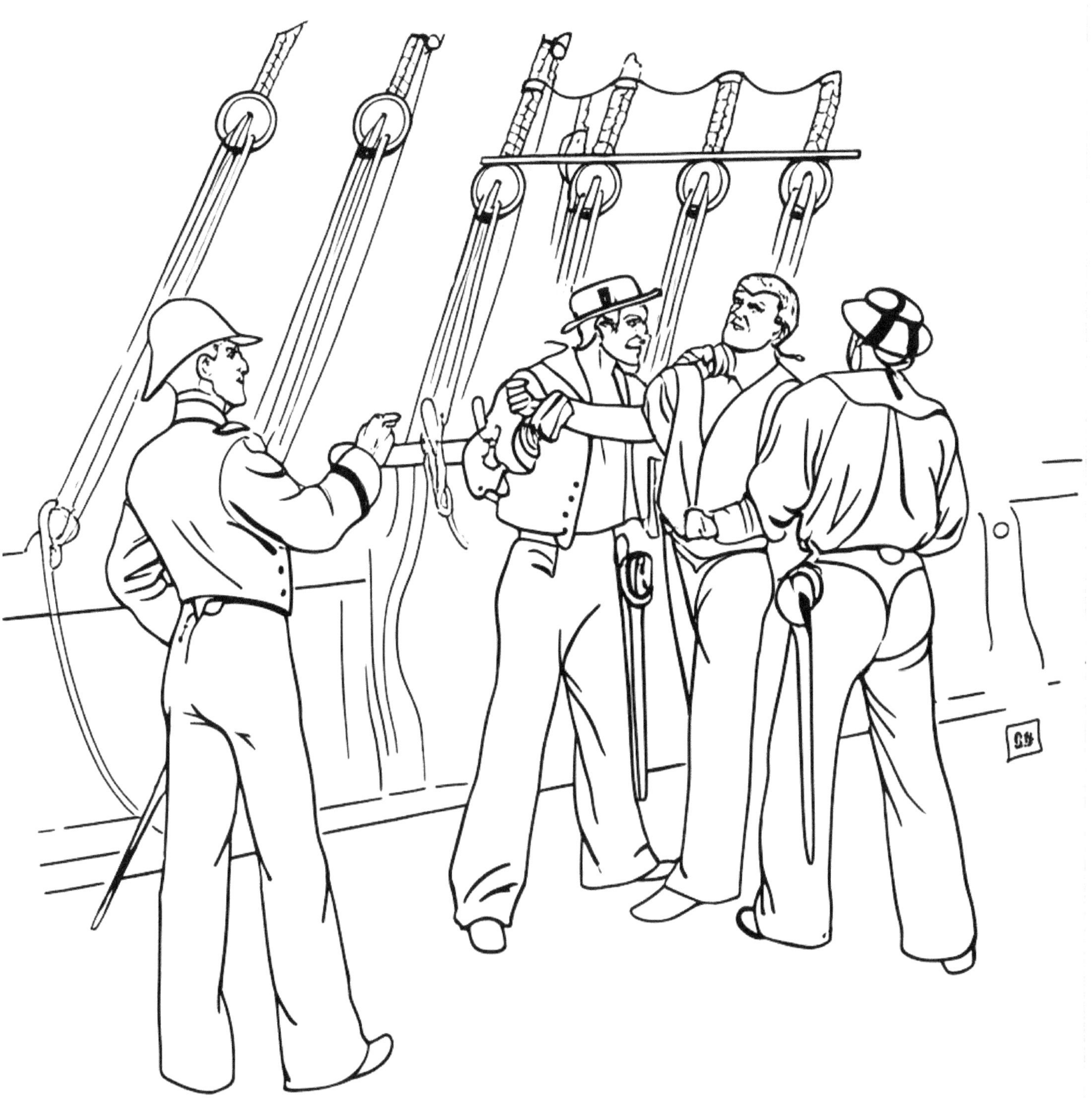

Brunswick Town blacksmith William Cain was captured by the British and sentenced to death as a spy while the redcoats occupied Wilmington. He was hanged from the yardarm of one of the British warships in the Cape Fear River, then his body was dumped overboard.

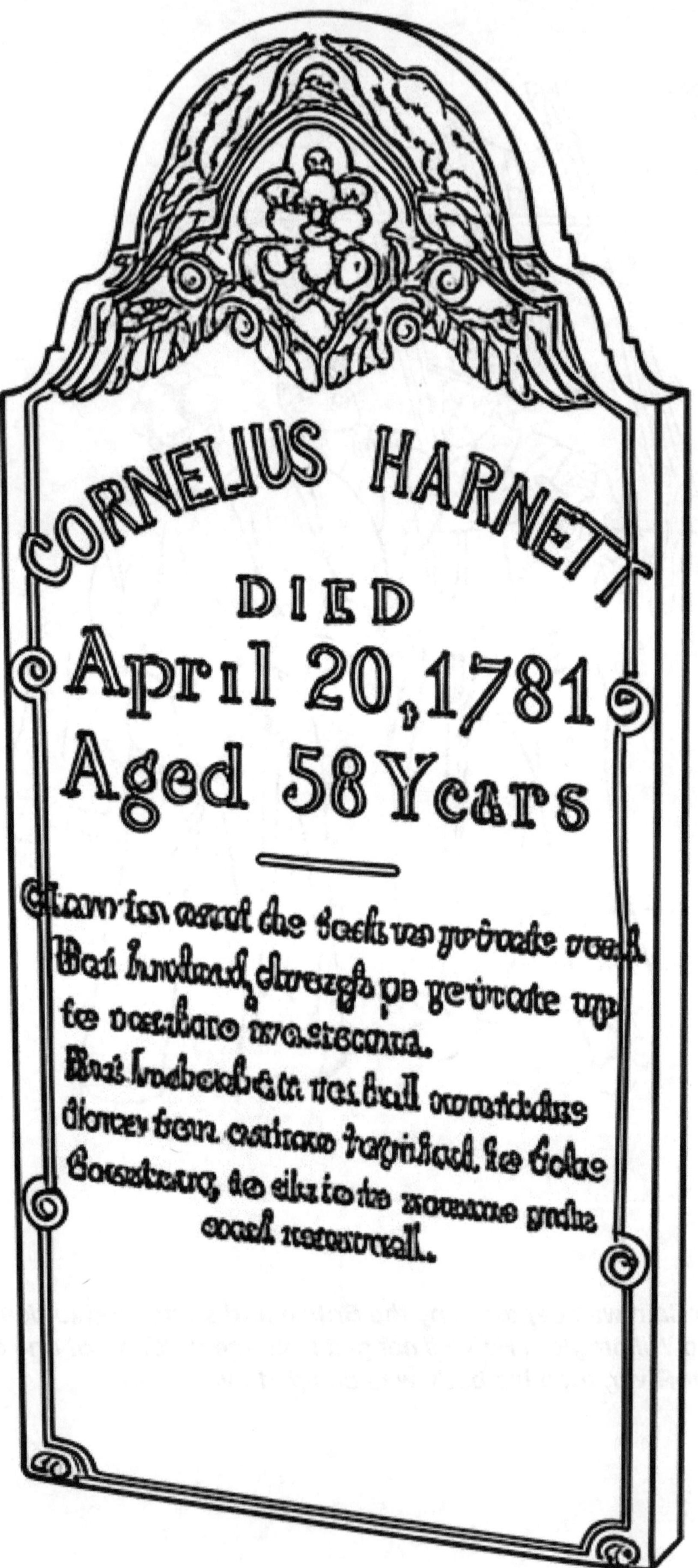

When the British arrived in Wilmington, they came ready to issue pardons for any rebel who took a loyalty oath to the king, and who promised to not fight anymore. There were two exceptions: Robert Howe and Cornelius Harnett. Howe was the highest ranking Southern general in George Washington's army, and was away from the Cape Fear when Craig's redcoats occupied Wilmington. Harnett, called by Josiah Quincy the "Samuel Adams of the South," fled when British troops entered the Cape Fear. Harnett came down with gout while on the run, and took refuge at the plantation of Col. John Spicer in Onslow County. Craig's troops found him there and dragged him from his sick bed, tying him across a horse like a sack of grain, and returned him to Wilmington. Held in an open air jail at Second and Market Streets called "the Bull Pen," Harnett got sick and died. He is buried in the graveyard at St. James Episcopal Church. His headstone (left) is visible from the sidewalk.

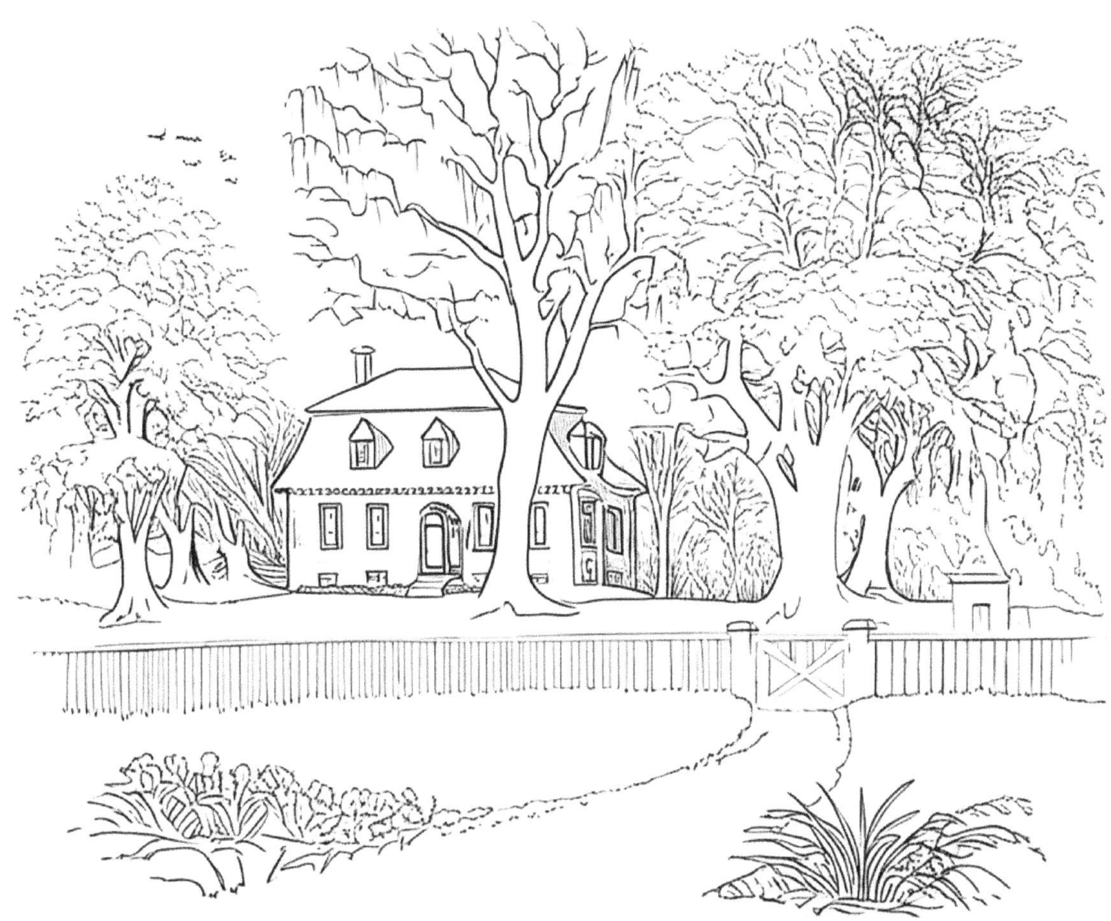

Harnett's home, first called Maynard, then later renamed Hilton, stood on Smith Creek where the Sweeney Water Treatment Plant in Wilmington is now. The above image is how Hilton looked in the colonial era. The bottom image is what it looked like just prior to demolition in the early 20th century.

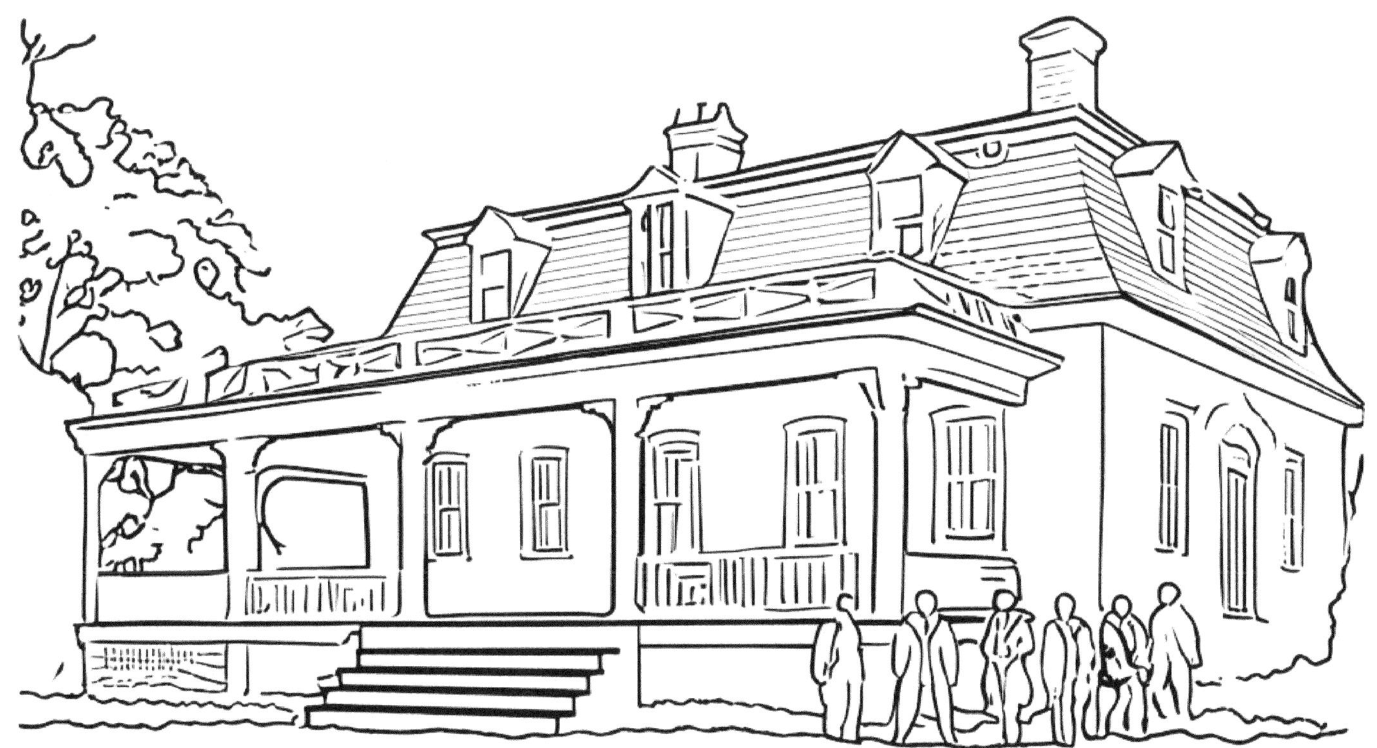

The Massacre at Eight Mile House

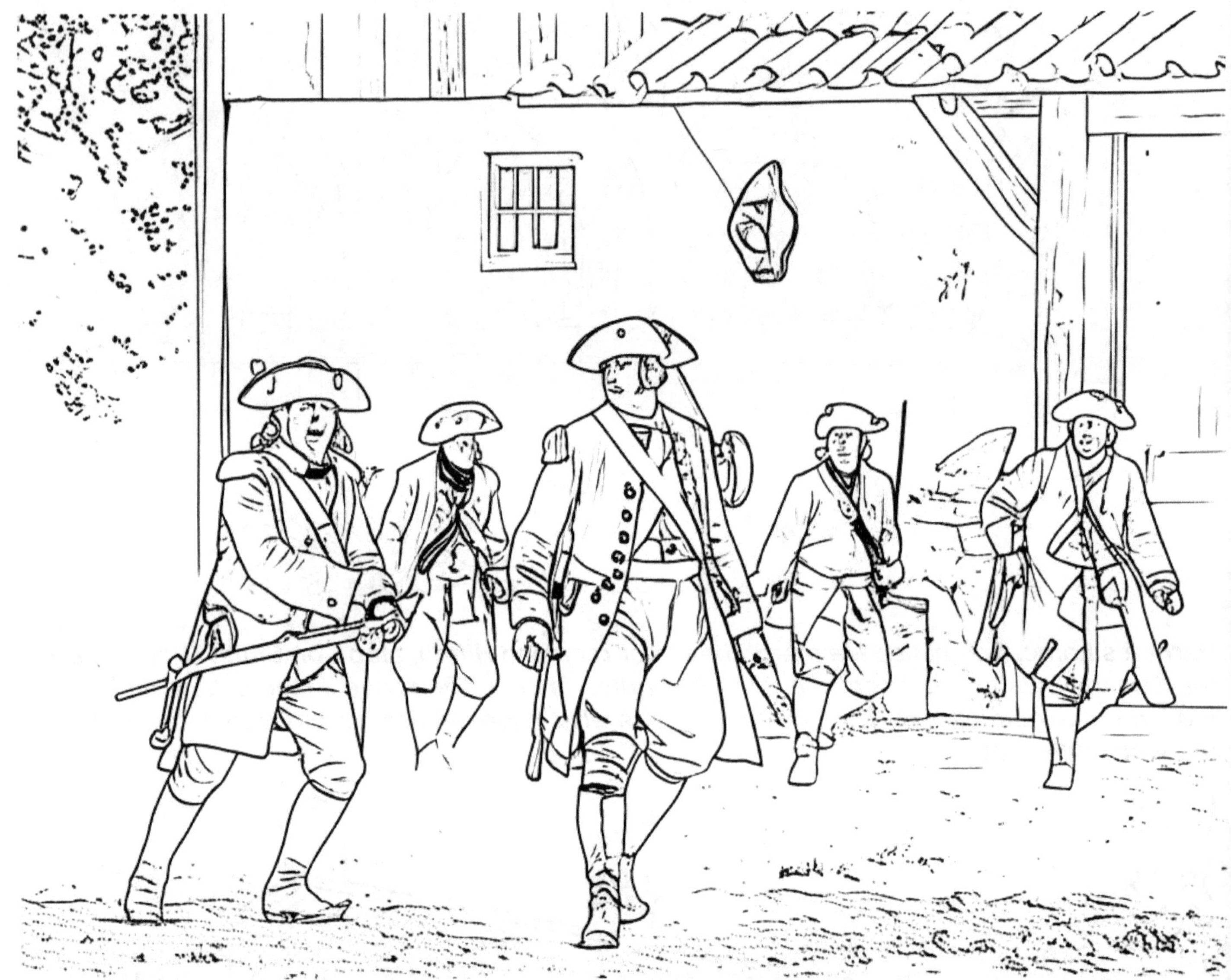

When Craig's British troops occupied Wilmington, Patriot militia kept an eye on them from outside the town. In what is now Ogden, N.C., there was a tavern. Known as Rouse's Tavern or Eight Mile House (because of its location eight miles from Wilmington), British troops caught a band of militia who, instead of being on guard, spent the night drinking. The militiamen slept off the night's revelries on the tavern floor until redcoats kicked in the door and put them all to the bayonet. Above, redcoat troops begin their assault on the tavern.

The Sniper of Point Peter

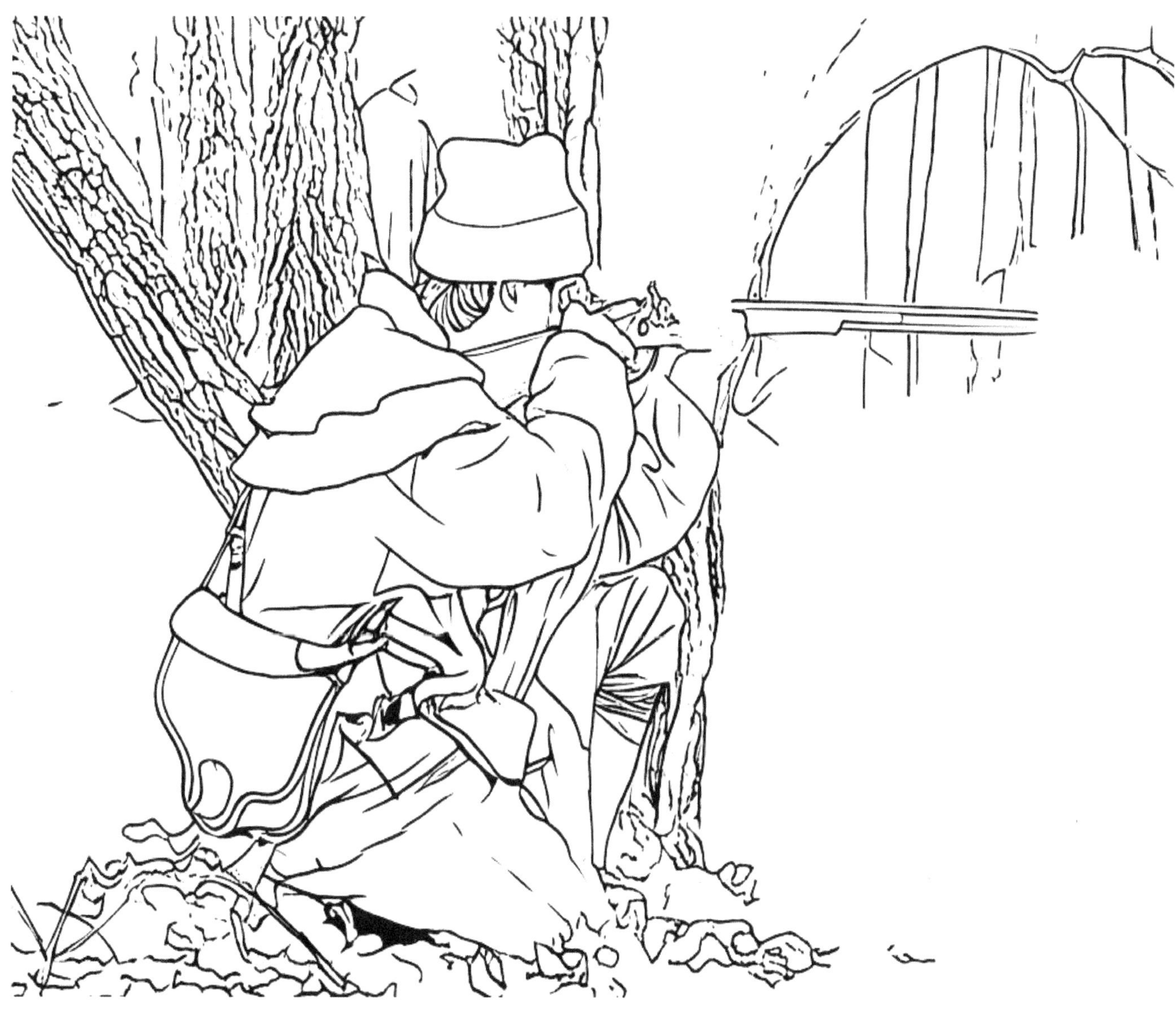

One story of the occupation by the British tells the tale of Thomas Bloodworth, a local tax official who tried unsuccessfully to prevent the redcoats from burning tax records and deeds when they came to town. Later, Bloodworth discovered a huge cypress tree on Point Peter, the place where the Cape Fear and Northeast Cape Fear Rivers split apart across from the Wilmington waterfront. The base of the tree was hollow up to a considerable height. Bloodworth, also a gunsmith, returned home and built a rifled musket capable of hitting targets along the Wilmington riverfront. He returned to the tree, bore a hole in the trunk to accomodate his rifle, and began shooting British soldiers across the river. Try as they might, Craig's redcoats could never figure out where the shots were coming from. While Bloodworth was suspected as the shooter, it was never proven.

Technically the British won the Battle of Guilford Courthouse, but suffered 25% casualties in doing it. Afterwards, Cornwallis was dismayed to find there were no supplies waiting for him at Cross Creek. He marched his army to Wilmington, where in April 1781 they spent two weeks resting and resupplying after the grueling Race to the Dan and Guilford Courthouse. While on the Cape Fear, he learned that British Gen. Phillips had landed a redcoat army in the Chesapeake. Cornwallis marched his army north to link up with him, and eventually found himself surrounded at Yorktown. The picture below shows Cornwallis reviewing his troops as the redcoats file into Wilmington past the Burgwin-Wright House.

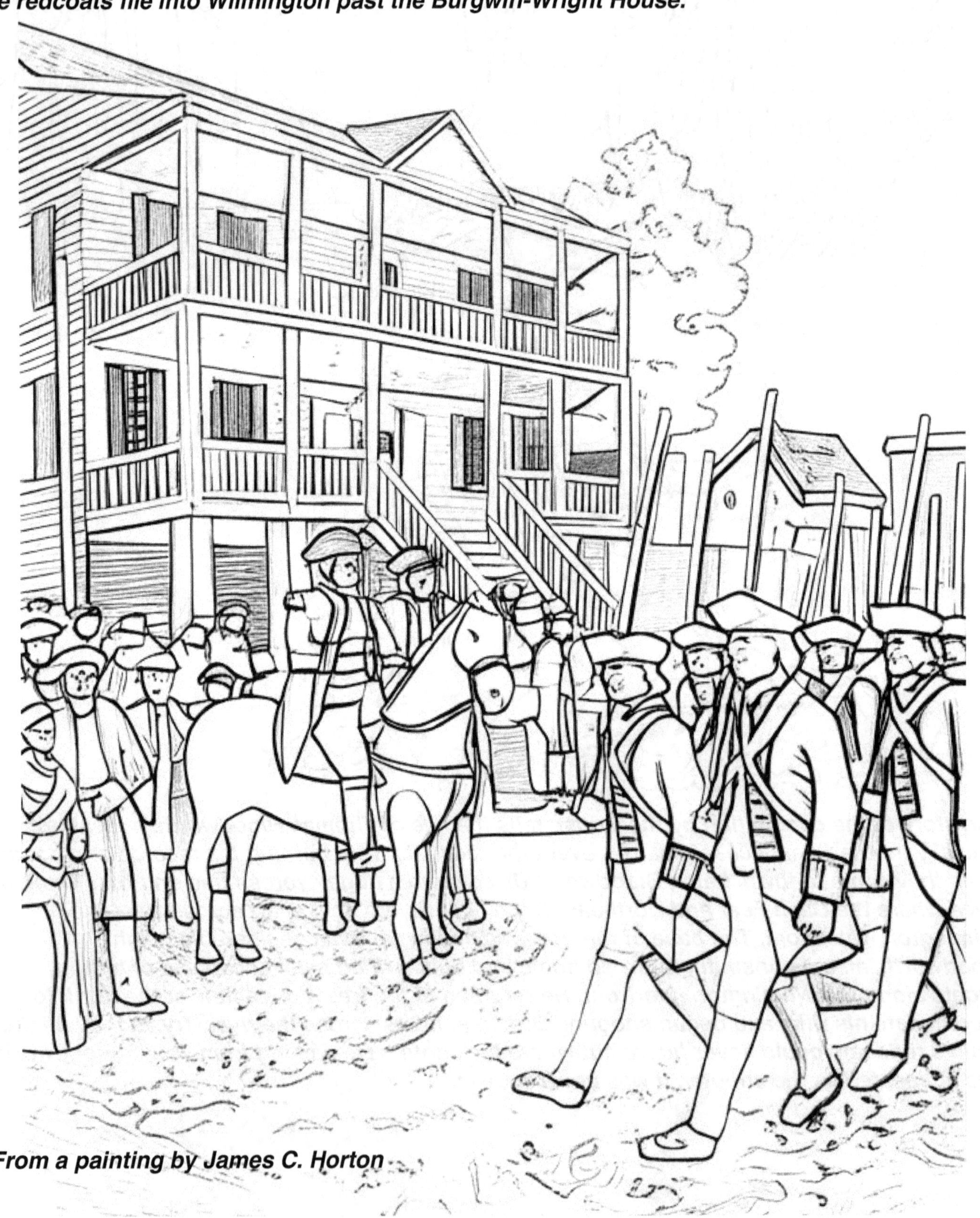

From a painting by James C. Horton

After Cornwallis surrendered at Yorktown, Patriot forces turned to ejecting Maj. Craig from Wilmington. Griffith Rutherford led Continental troops and militia against the redcoats in the town in November. As soldiers, loyalists, and slaves scrambled to evacuate aboard British ships, American cavalry raced down Market Street (right). The horse soldiers crashed into the crowds at the docks causing mayhem before withdrawing. As Patriot troops made their way into Wilmington, they could see the topmasts of the retreating British ships carrying the redcoats away at last (below).

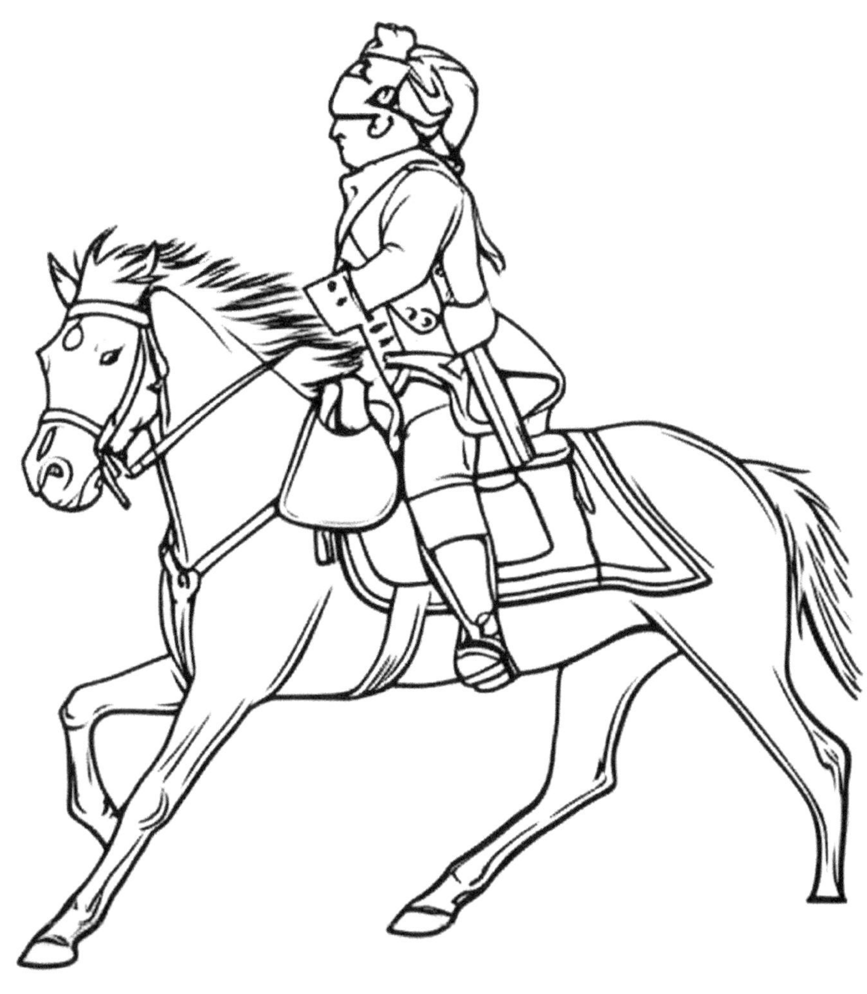

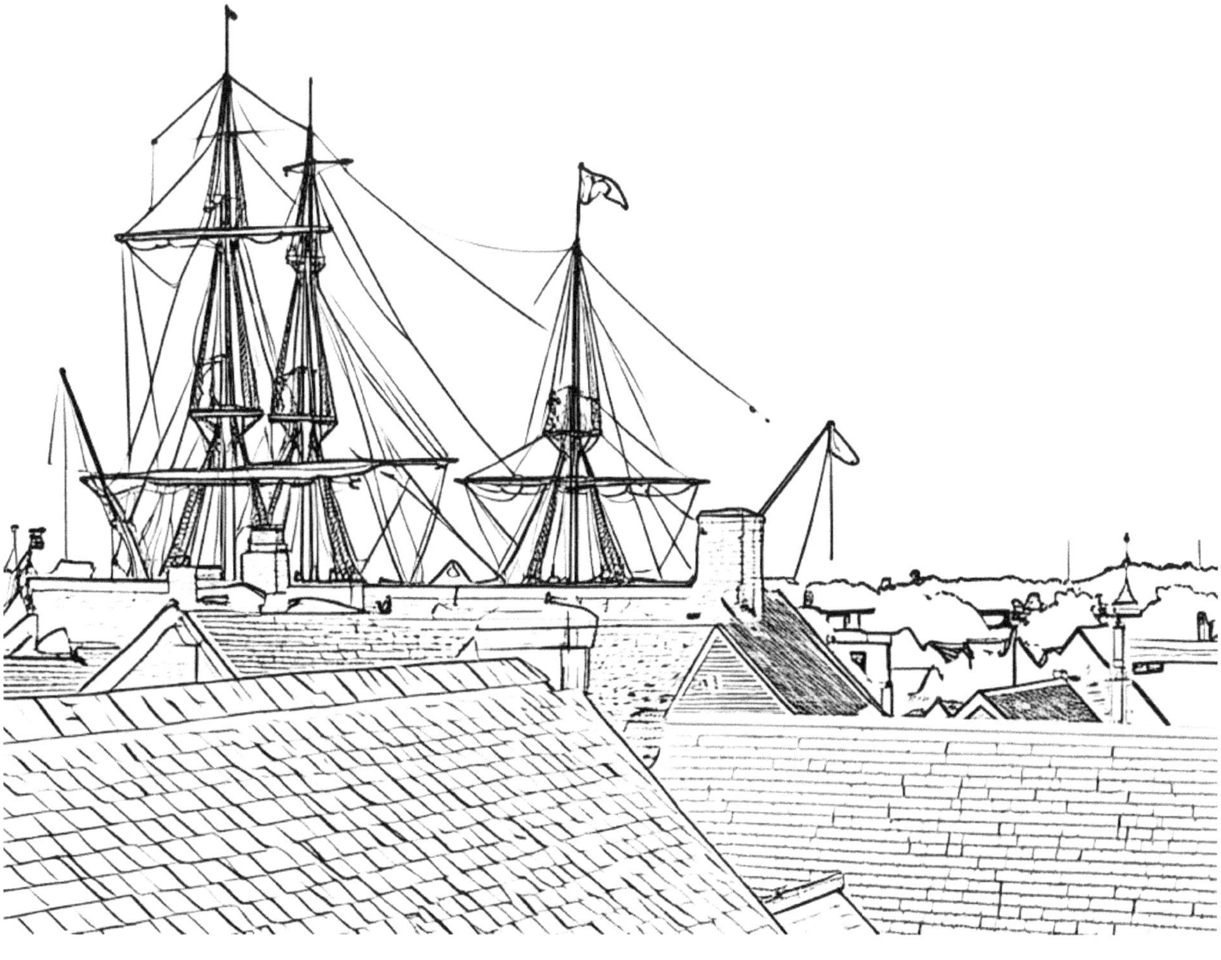

THE CIVIL WAR

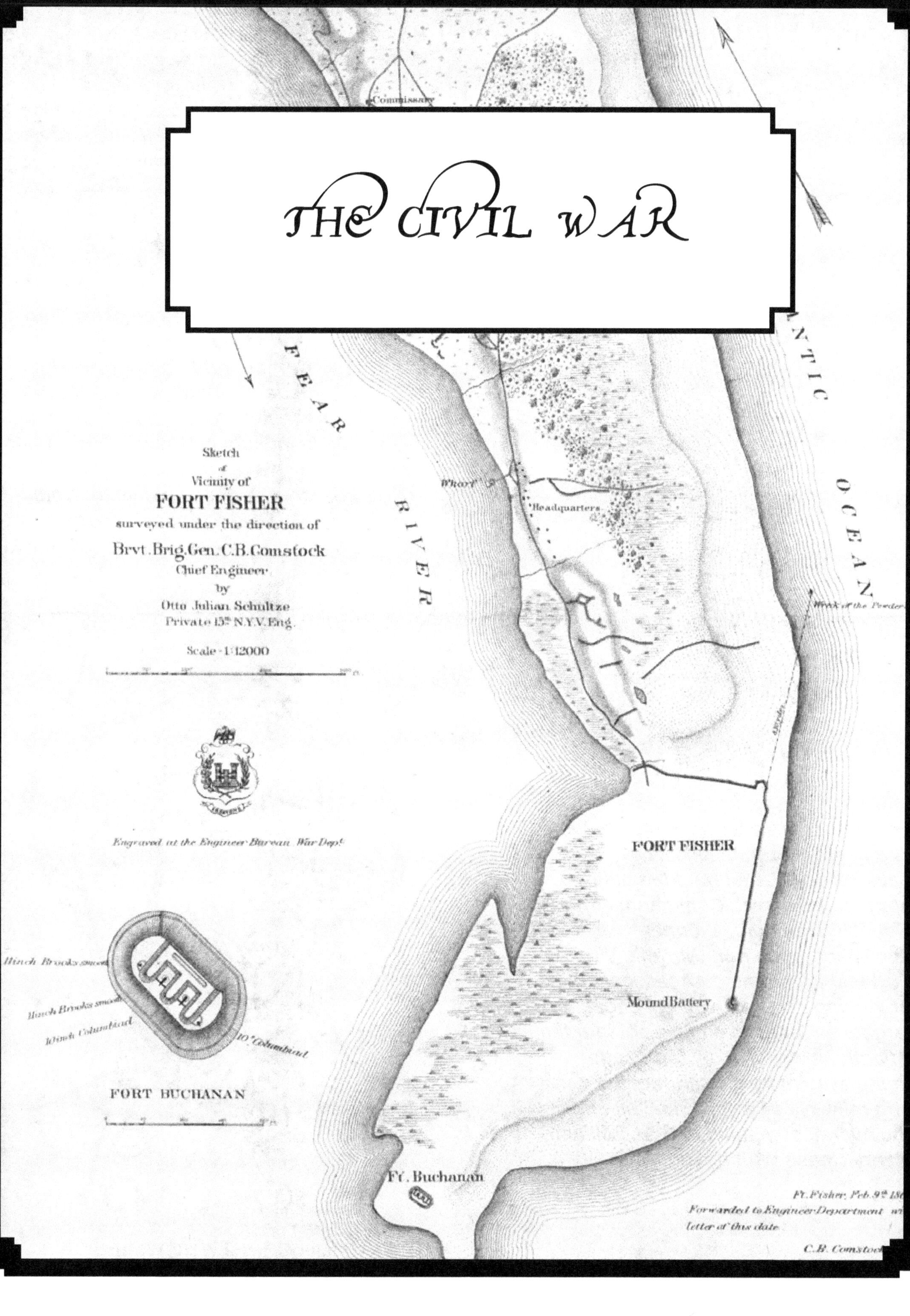

Commissary

FEAR RIVER

ATLANTIC OCEAN

Sketch
of
Vicinity of
FORT FISHER
surveyed under the direction of
Brvt. Brig. Gen. C.B. Comstock
Chief Engineer
by
Otto Julian Schultze
Private 15th N.Y.V. Eng.

Scale - 1:12000

Wharf

Headquarters

Engraved at the Engineer Bureau War Dep't.

FORT FISHER

Mound Battery

FORT BUCHANAN

Ft. Buchanan

Ft. Fisher, Feb. 9th 186
Forwarded to Engineer Department with
letter of this date
C.B. Comstock

Fort Fisher: The Rebel Gibraltar

Geography made the Cape Fear an especially tough nut to crack for the Union in the Civil War. With two inlets to access the river, separated by Frying Pan Shoals that ran 28 miles into the Atlantic, closing the port at Wilmington would be a tall order. The Confederates knew that. To protect the port, they constructed a series of eleven forts and batteries that any federal invader would have to deal with before it could get to the city. Fort Fisher was the lynchpin of it all.

Fort Fisher was massive, its land face stretching across the Confederate Point (formerly Federal Point) peninsula from the river to the sea. Its massive sand and earth walls were built by slaves and soldiers over the course of several years from 1861-1865 (opposite page).

Col. William Lamb

Fort Fisher grew from a single battery to a mighty fort shaped like a backwards "7" that ran for a mile south to New Inlet. Commanded by Col. William Lamb, a former newspaper man from Norfolk, Virginia, Fort Fisher mounted 47 seacoast guns of varying sizes, capable of engaging targets as far as five miles out into the Atlantic. It was the key fortification in the system built to protect the port and railways at Wilmington, all under the overall command of Gen. William Henry Chase Whiting (right).

Major General WHC Whiting

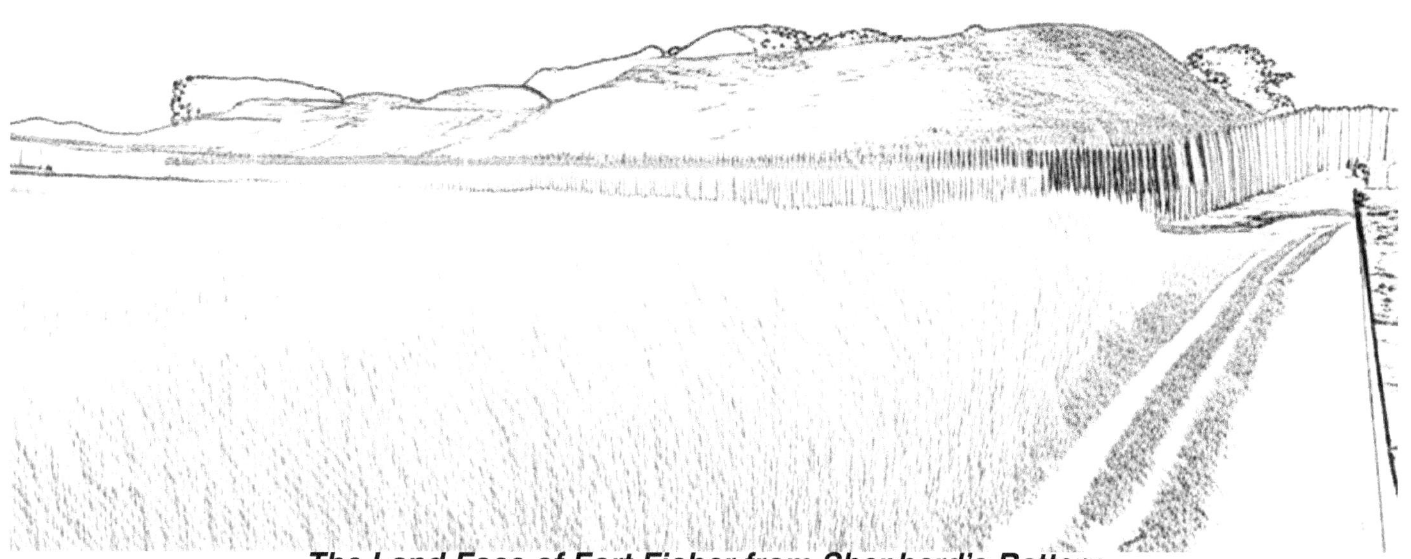

The Land Face of Fort Fisher from Shepherd's Battery

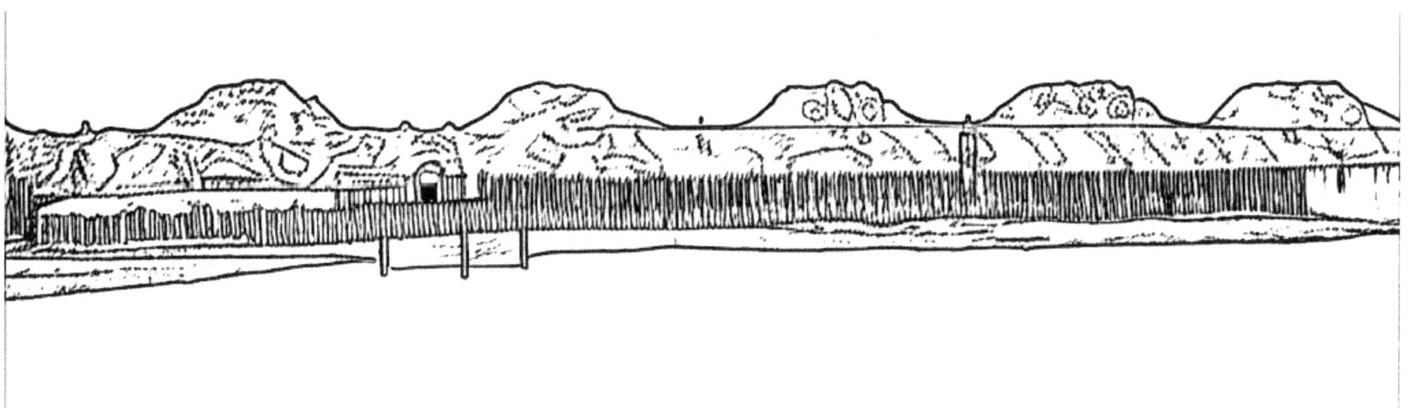

The Sea Face of Fort Fisher

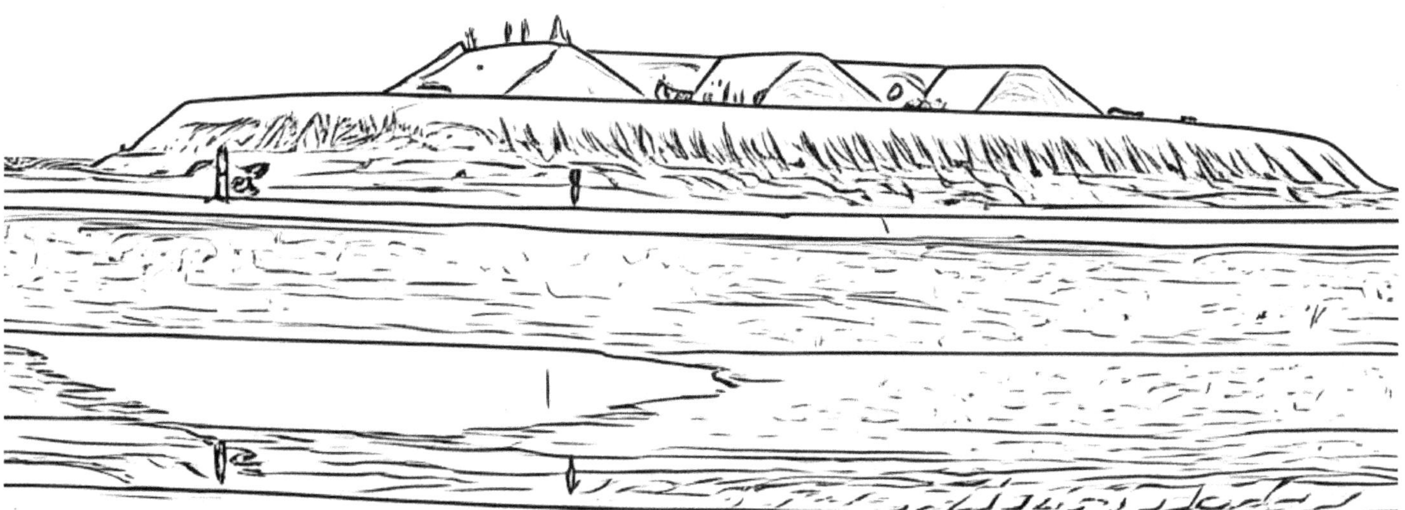

Battery Buchanan at the southern tip of the fort, overlooking New Inlet

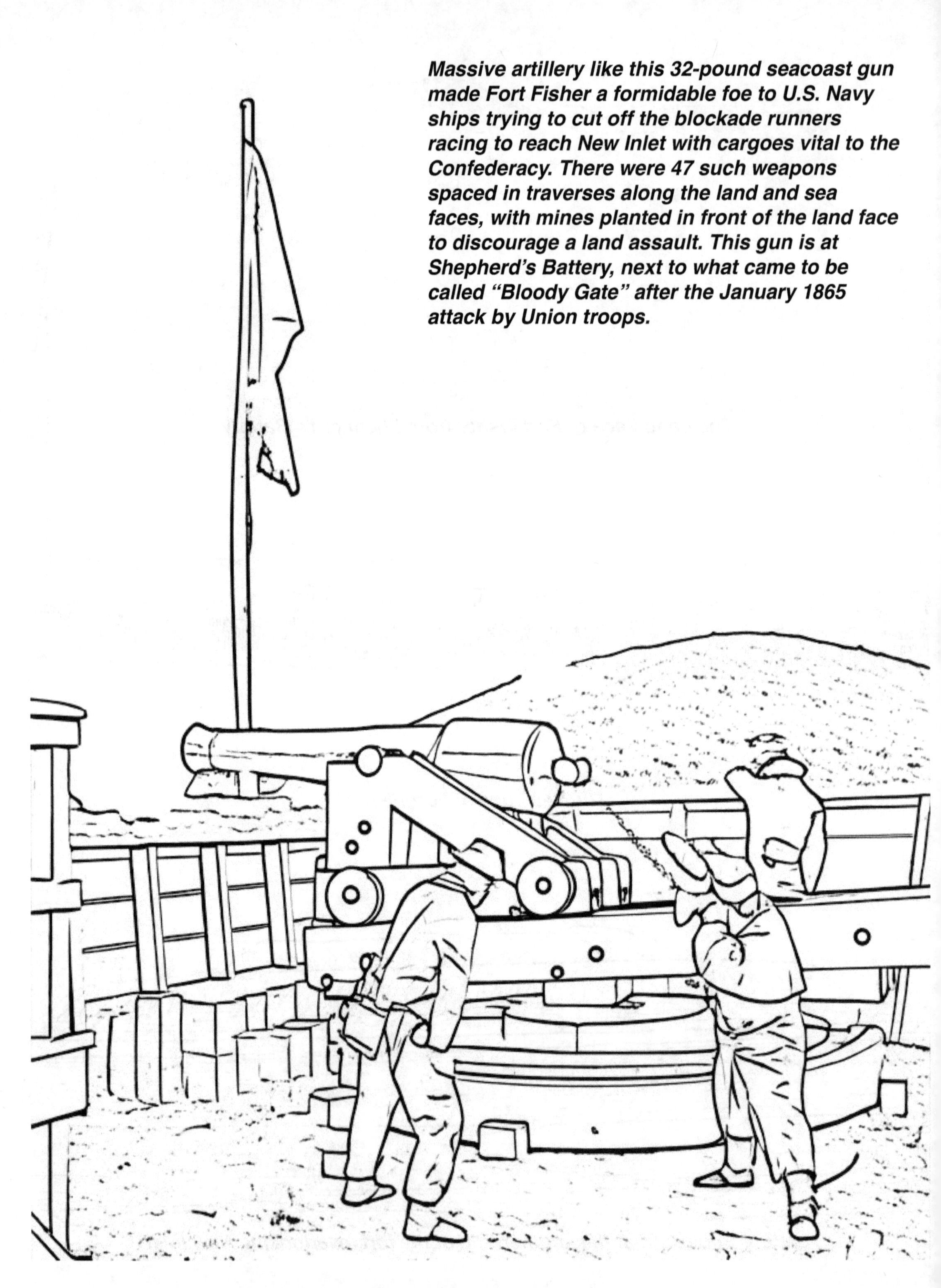

Massive artillery like this 32-pound seacoast gun made Fort Fisher a formidable foe to U.S. Navy ships trying to cut off the blockade runners racing to reach New Inlet with cargoes vital to the Confederacy. There were 47 such weapons spaced in traverses along the land and sea faces, with mines planted in front of the land face to discourage a land assault. This gun is at Shepherd's Battery, next to what came to be called "Bloody Gate" after the January 1865 attack by Union troops.

Running the Blockade

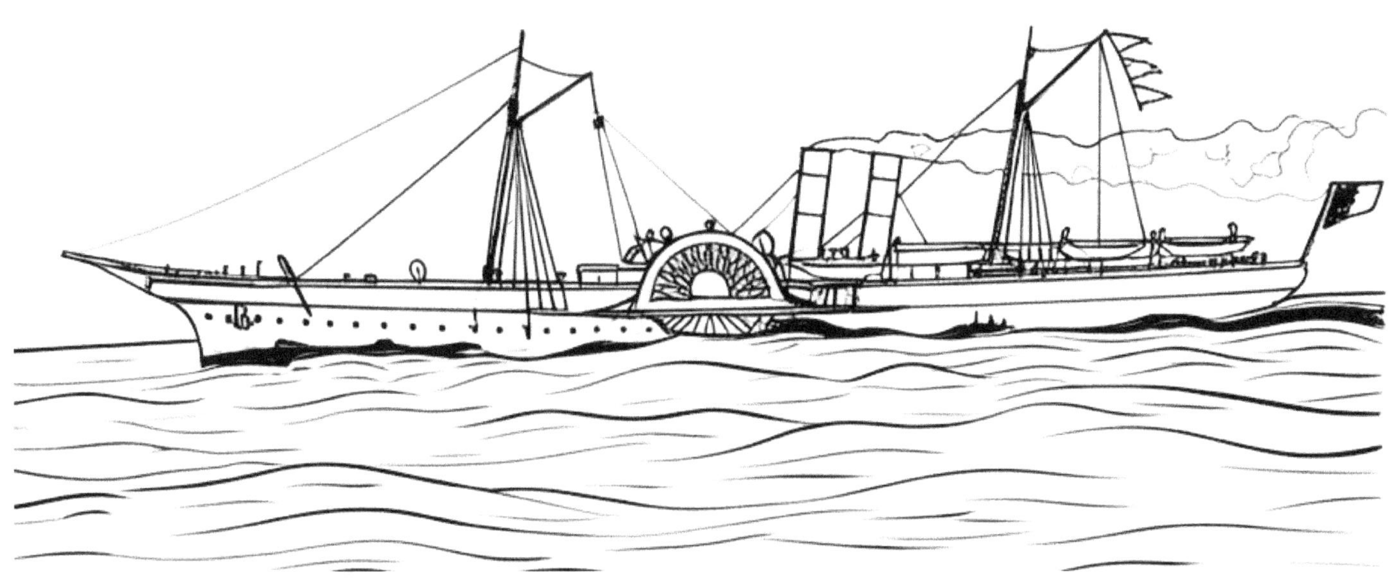

As the South had very little industrial infrastructure when the war began, virtually everything it needed to stay in the fight had to be brought in from overseas. That made sleek, fast, steam-driven blockade runners essential to the Confederate war effort. Ships like the **Ad-Vance** ***(above), and the*** **Modern Greece** ***(below) carried the bullets, weapons, medicines, and just about everything else required to keep an army in the field, and a civilian population ravaged by the destruction of war, alive. Blockade runners really were the lifeblood of the Confederacy. Without them, the Union would likely have been able to end the rebellion much sooner than the four years and 700,000 lives it ultimately took.***

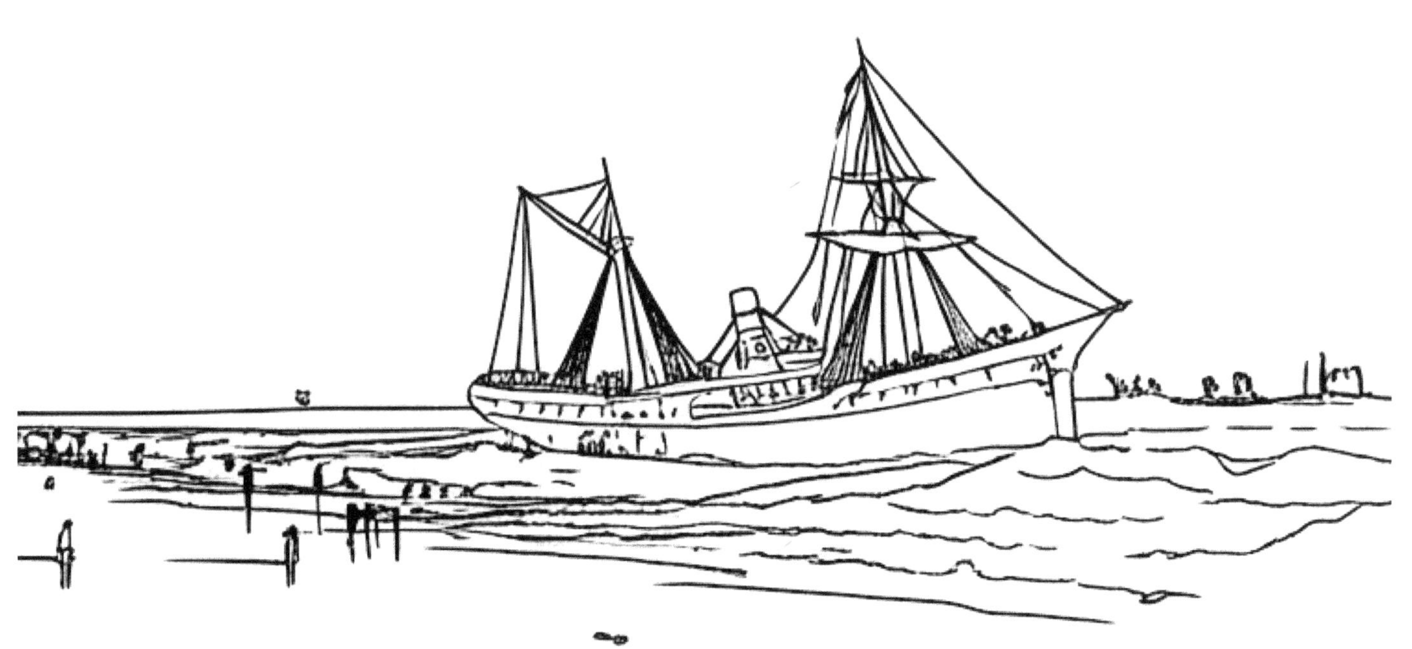

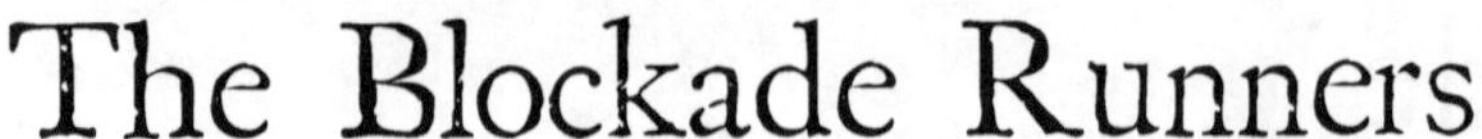

The Blockade Runners

Running the blockade required nerves of steel and more than a little courage. Men like the Cape Fear's own John Newland Maffitt (right) ran the blockade on fast, unarmed ships that deliverded essential cargoes to Confederate ports.

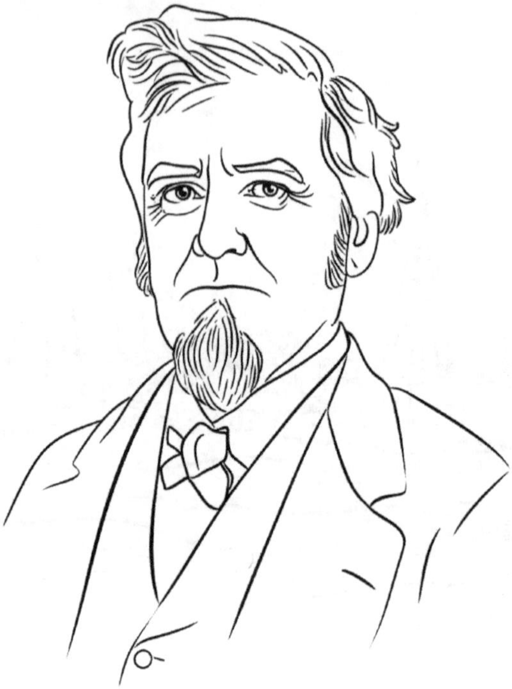

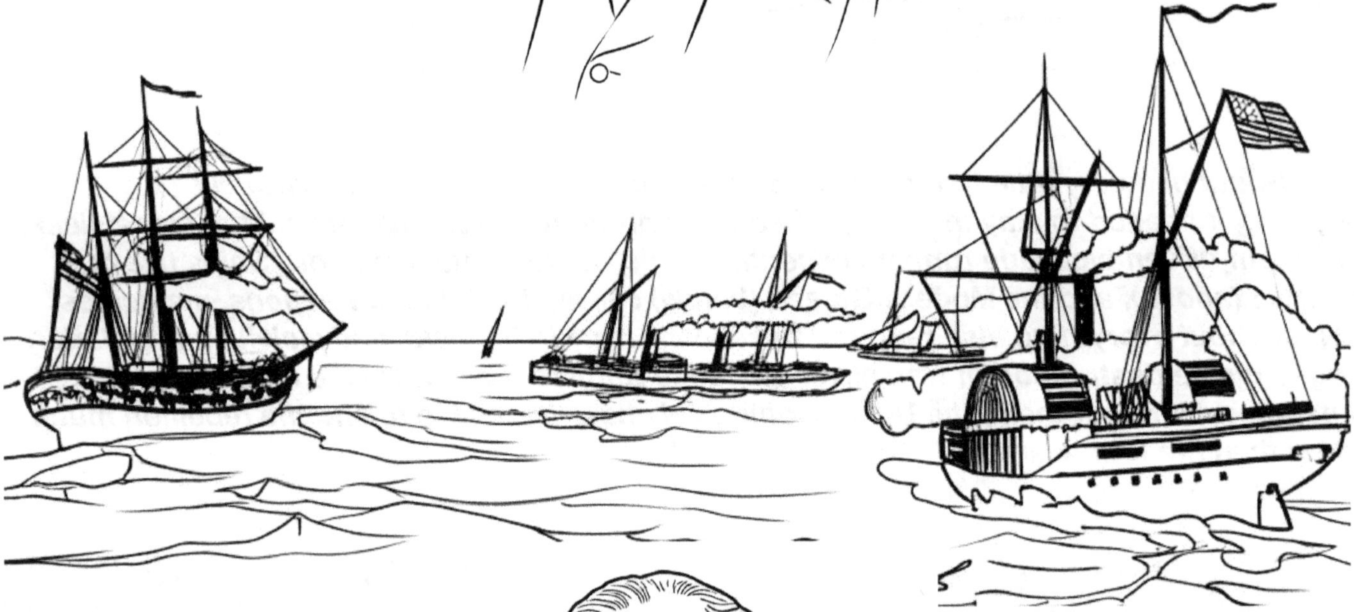

Above, the blockade runner* Lilian *threads the needle between two blockading federal warships off Fort Fisher.

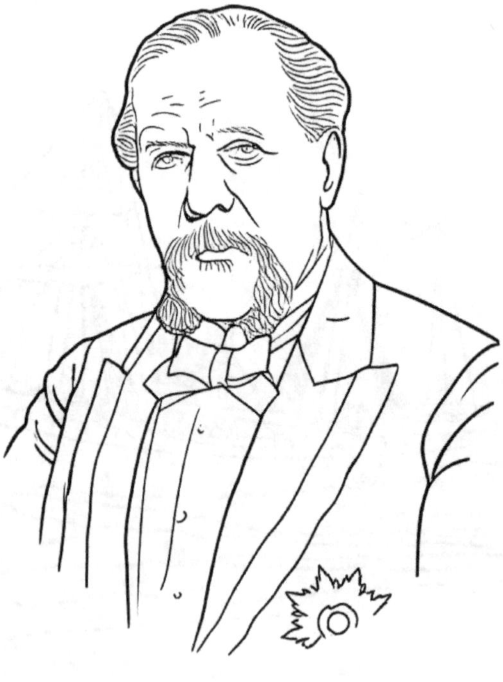

The cargoes carried by the blockade runners were so valuable that one or two trips could make a captain rich. So lucrative was it, several ship captains took leaves of absence from the British Navy to run the blockade and make their fortunes, before returning to their country's service. Among them was Charles Hobart Hampden (left).

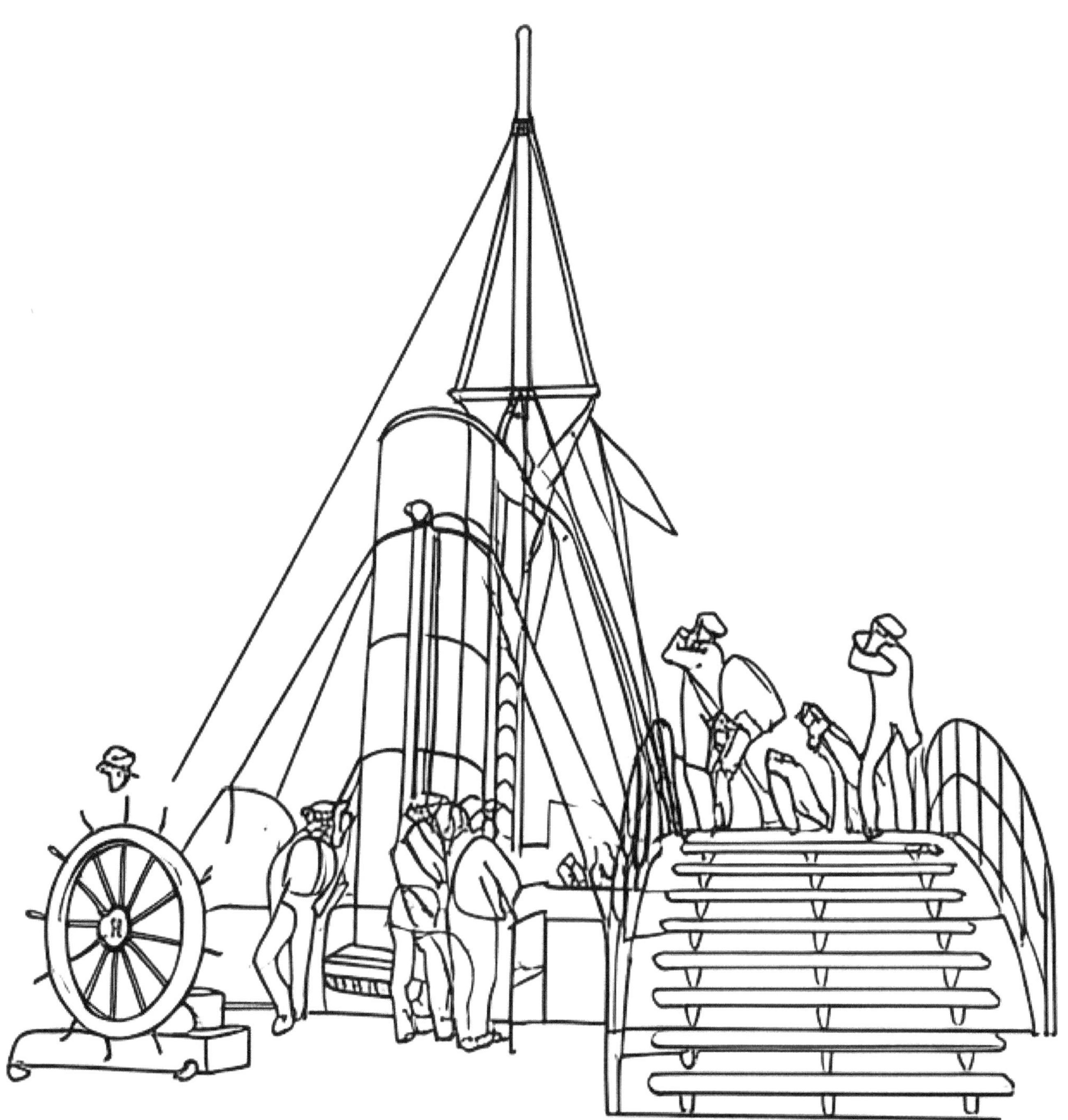

Running the blockade took a lot of nerve and courage. Blockade runners were unarmed so that if captured they could avoid a charge of piracy. That meant they had to use guts and guile to deliver their vital cargoes. The runners tried to wait for a moonless night to test the blockading cordon, slipping silently past two rows of Union blockaders. Sometimes they were so close they could hear sailors talking aboard the warships, or reach out and touch the sides of the looming enemy vessels. Lookouts on the paddle wheel housing of the steamers kept close watch for any sign that the blockaders had spotted them. When the Union ships did discover the blockade runners, flare rockets lit the night and alerted the rest of the blockaders that the chase was on. At that point, the blockade runners poured on the steam, the paddle wheels dug into the water at a furious pace, and the exposed blockade runner dashed for the safety of the guns at Fort Fisher.

The Port City

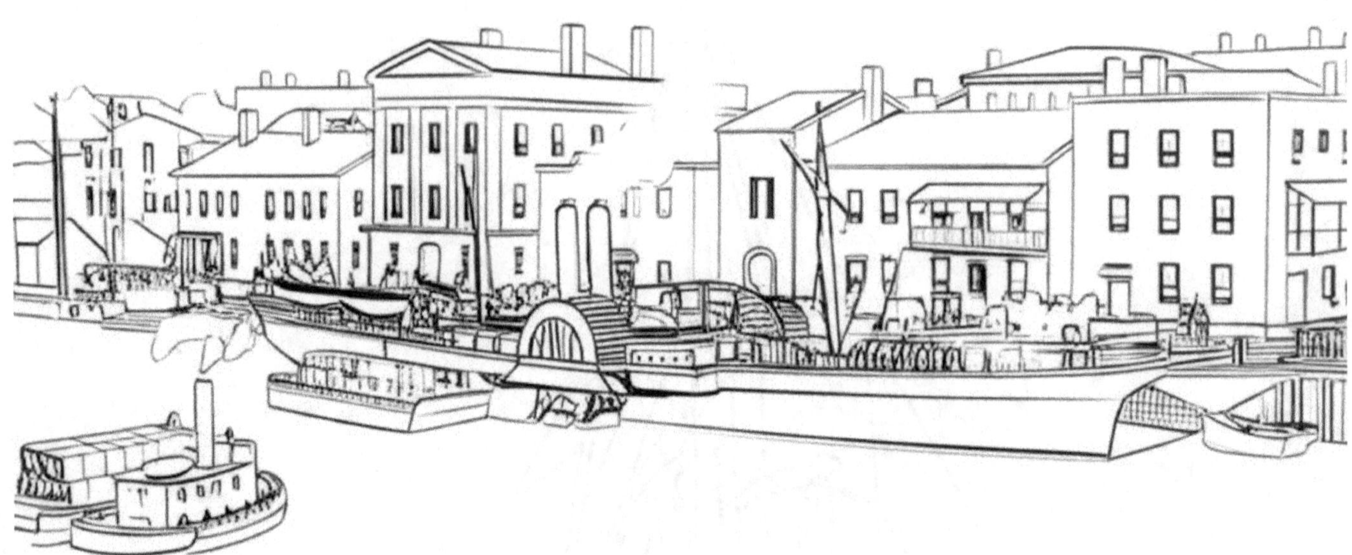

Wilmington became the most important port in the Confederacy. Because it sat on the river, 20 miles from the Atlantic Ocean, it could not be shelled from offshore. That meant to take it, Union troops would have to come up the Cape Fear River to make their attack. By 1865, Wilmington was the only open port left to the Confederacy. It was a thriving place full of soldiers, slaves, sailors, speculators, civilians, and railroad men. Above, the North Carolina-owned blockade runner Ad-Vance *loads at the foot of Market Street by the old Customs House.*

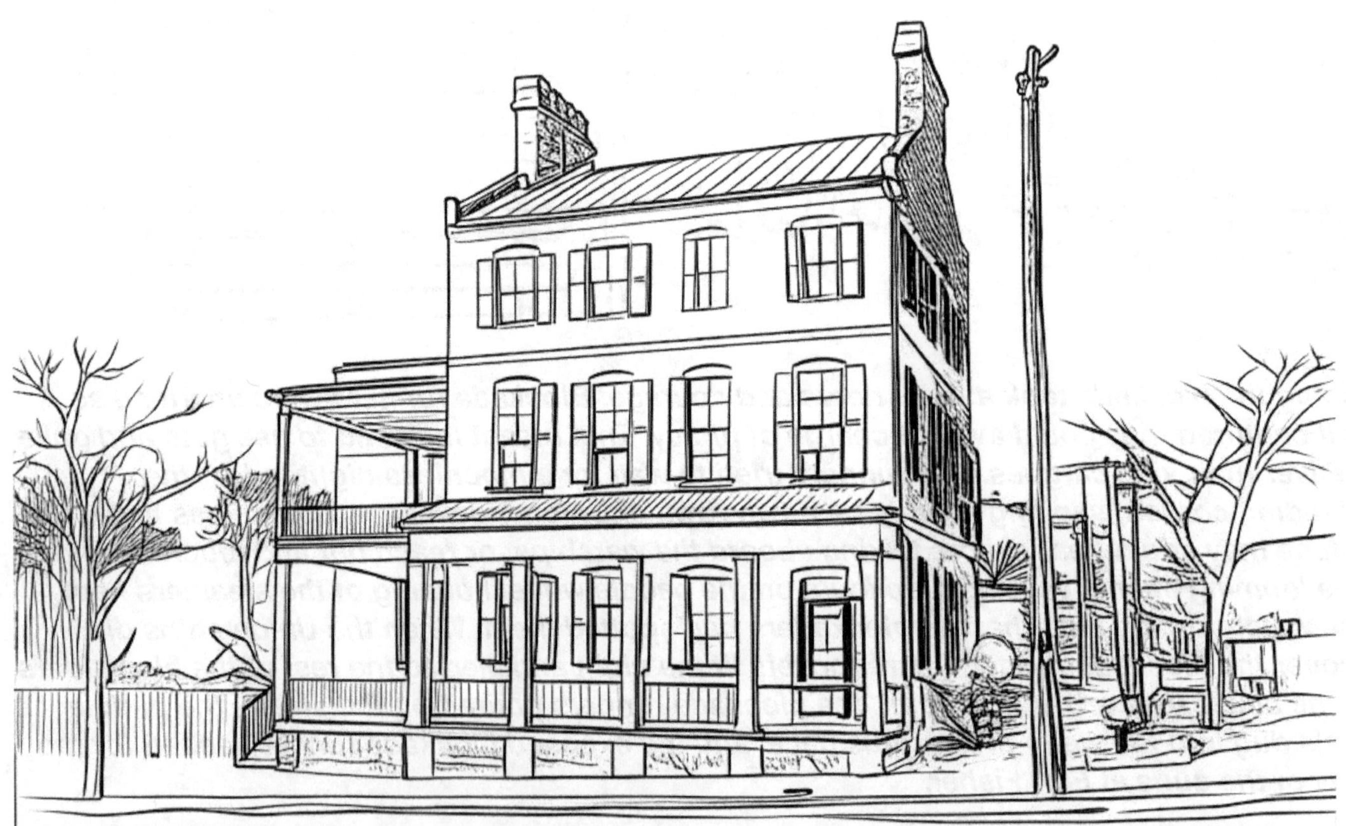

The DeRossett house sat across Market Street from the Burgwin-Wright house during the Civil War. The Confederate army used it as their headquarters. The house no longer exists.

Faces in the City

Major General W.H.C. Whiting (below) commanded the Cape Fear military district from the DeRossett House on Market Street. Though replaced by Gen. Braxton Bragg, Whiting lost his life rallying Confederate troops at Fort Fisher.

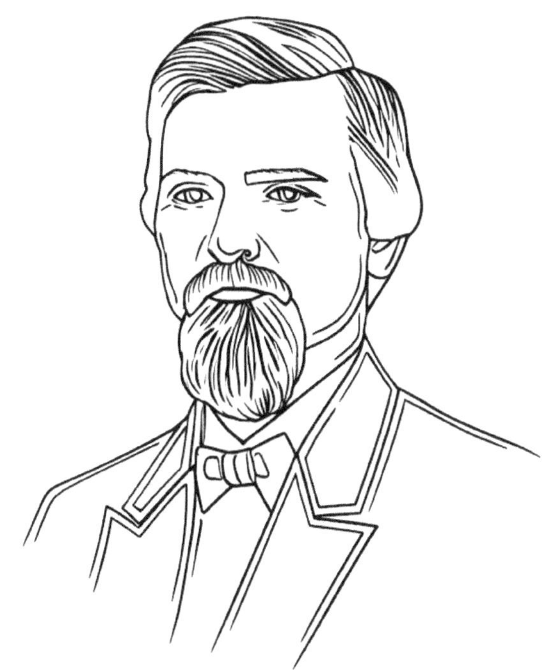

Reverend John Lamb Pritchard (above) oversaw the construction of First Baptist Church at Fifth and Market Streets in the years leading up to the Civil War. He was one of only three ministers who remained in Wilmington to tend to the sick during the dreadful yellow fever epidemic of 1862 that killed off a third of the city. The disease eventually killed him too.

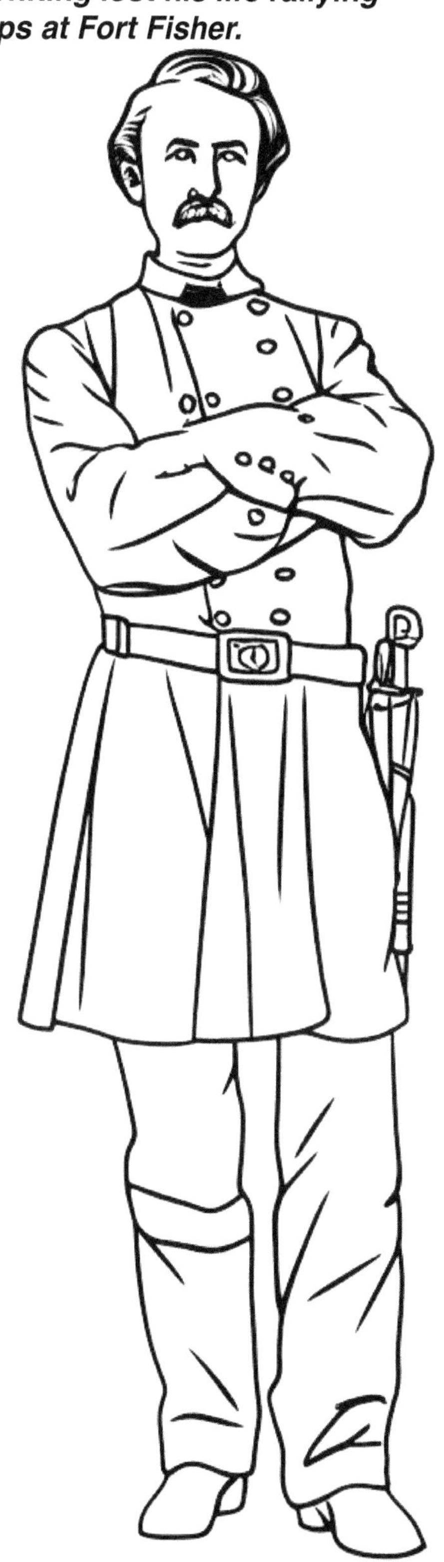

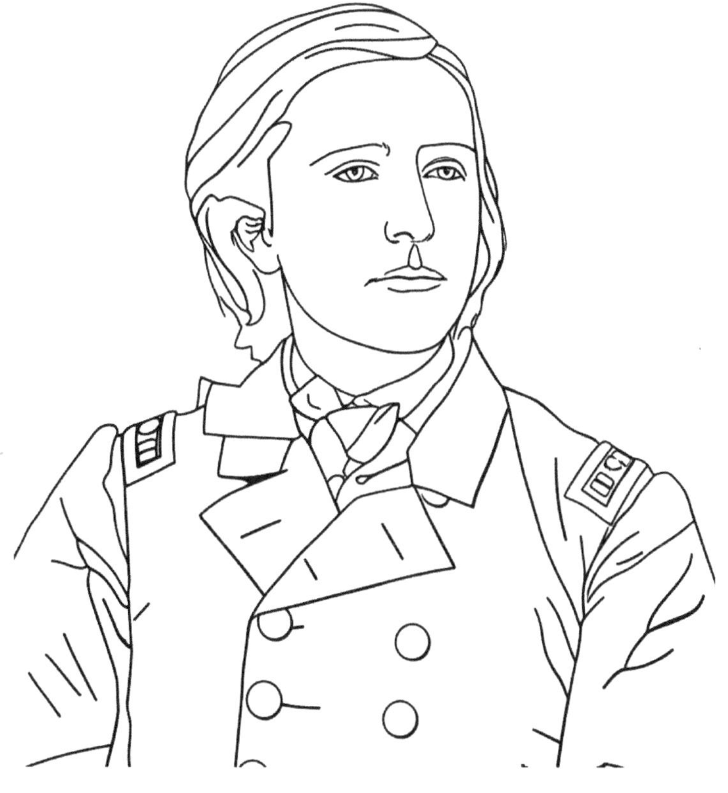

LtCdr. William B. Cushing (left), called "Lincoln's commando" for his daring escapades, made several raids on the Cape Fear, including one that saw him kidnap the second in command of Fort Johnston.

The Rose of the Confederacy

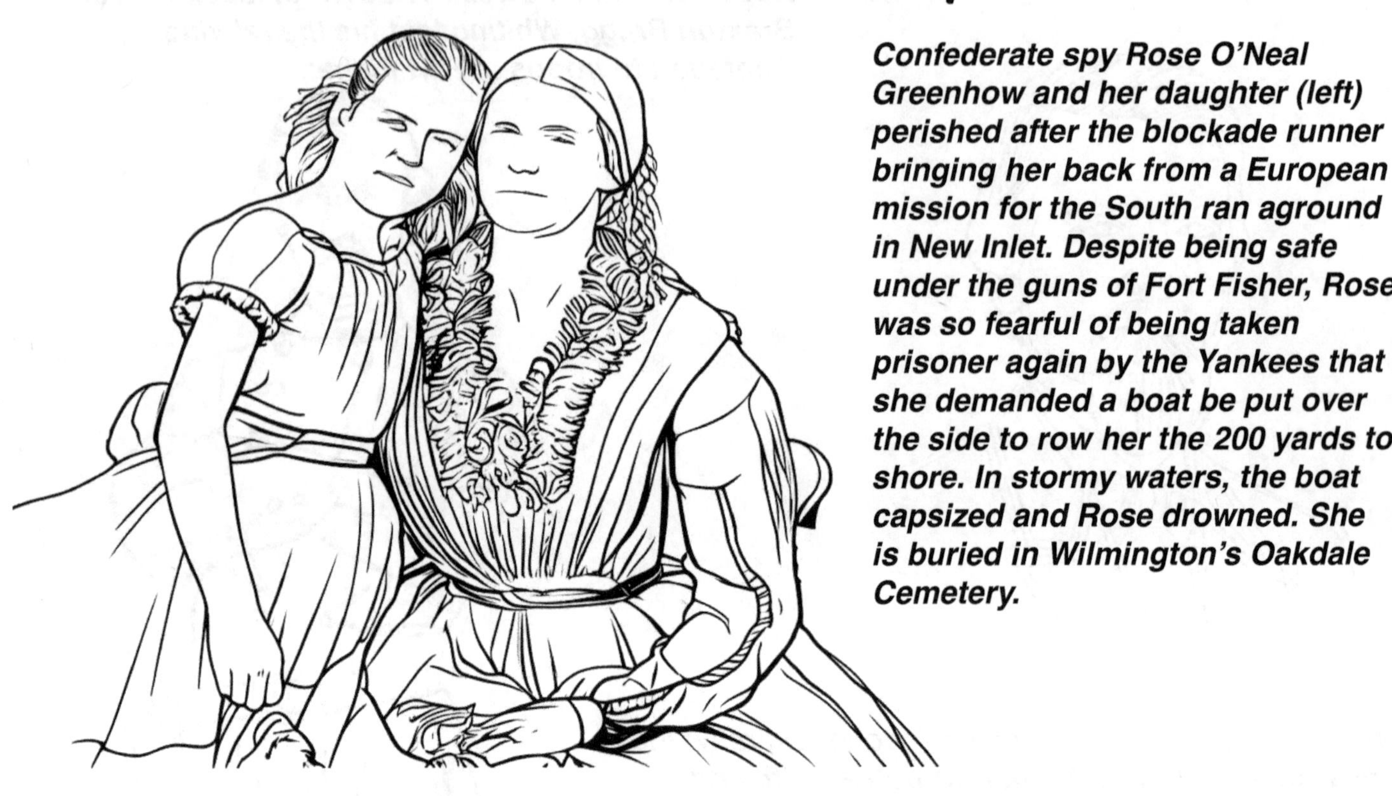

Confederate spy Rose O'Neal Greenhow and her daughter (left) perished after the blockade runner bringing her back from a European mission for the South ran aground in New Inlet. Despite being safe under the guns of Fort Fisher, Rose was so fearful of being taken prisoner again by the Yankees that she demanded a boat be put over the side to row her the 200 yards to shore. In stormy waters, the boat capsized and Rose drowned. She is buried in Wilmington's Oakdale Cemetery.

Rose O'Neal Greenhow's tombstone (lower left), and her disasterous climb into a waiting boat in the rough seas that killed her. (lower right).

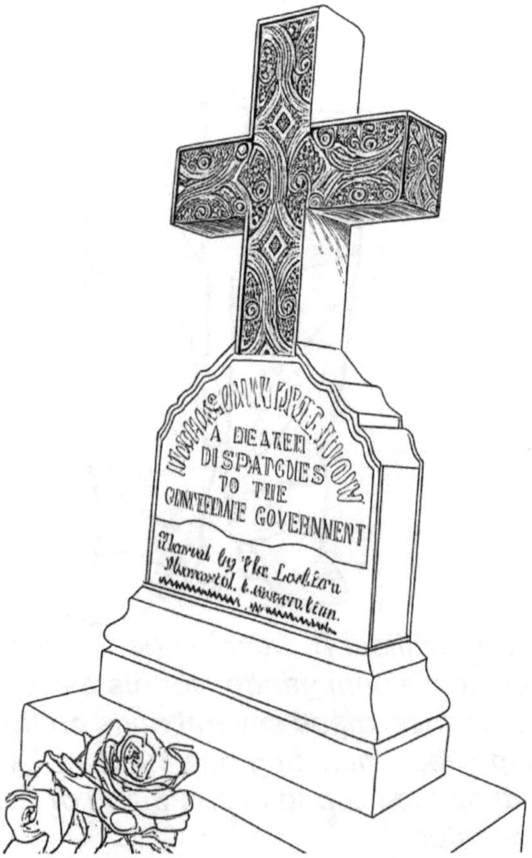

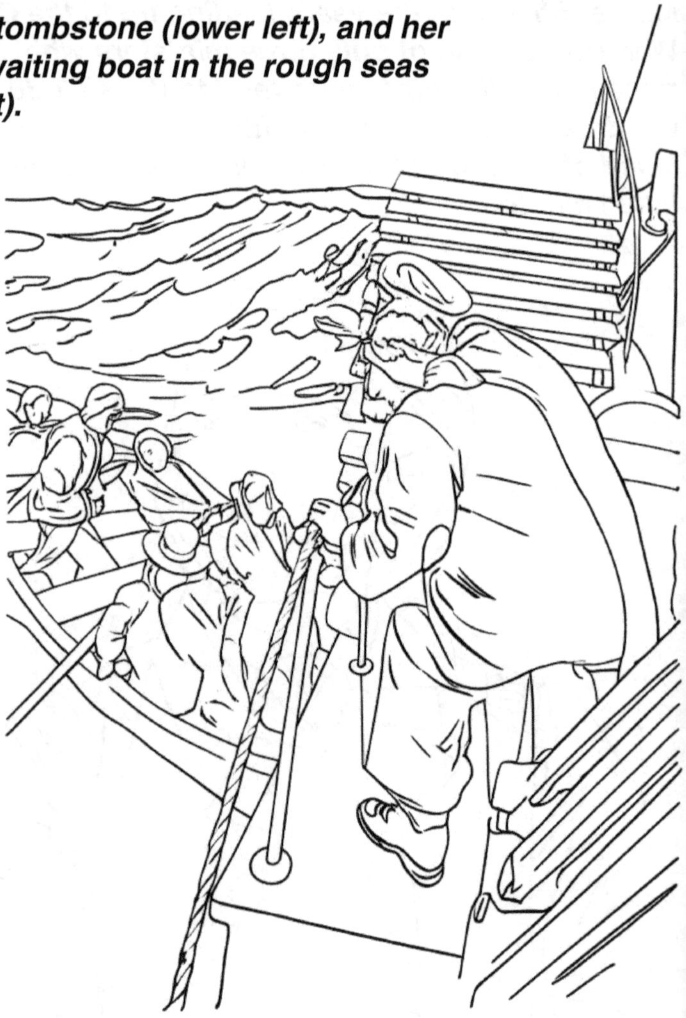

The Shipyards

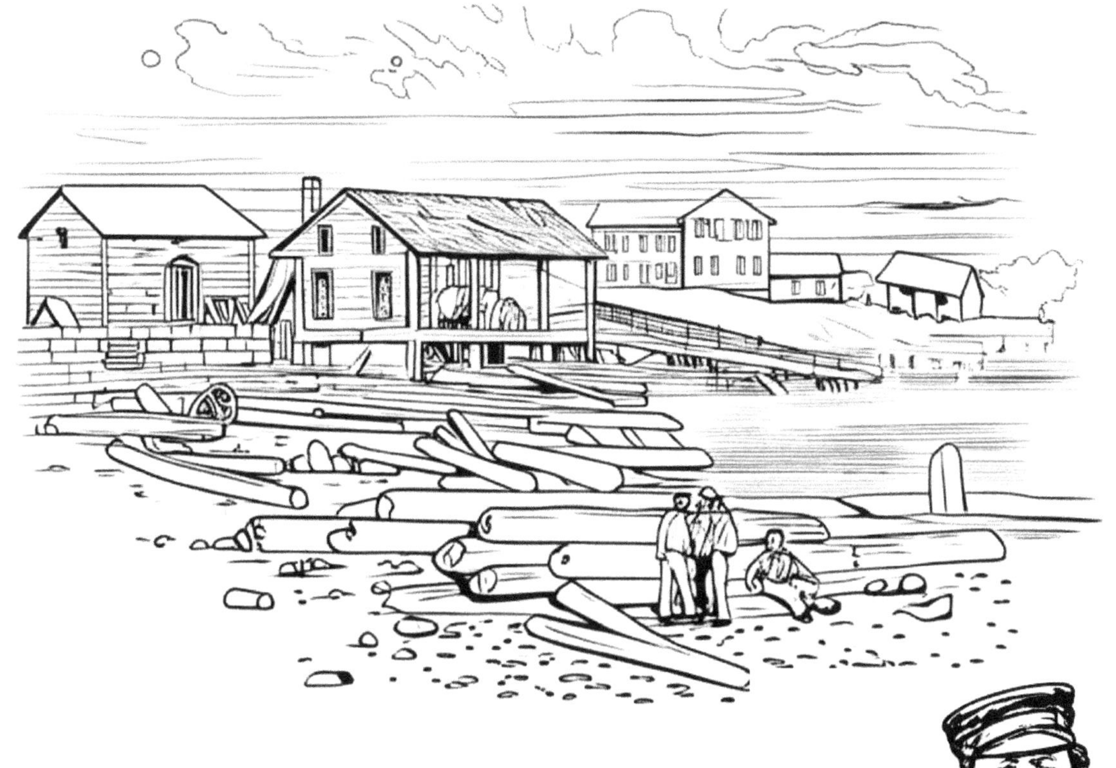

Cassidy Shipyard (above) sat just about where the foot of the Cape Fear Memorial Bridge in Wilmington is today. One of two shipyards in the port town during the Civil War, it turned out vessels and watercraft including the Confederate ironclad Raleigh*. Captain Benjamin Beery (right) operated a second shipyard on the other side of the river across from Wilmington, on Eagles Island. He and his brother, William, opened their yard in 1861 to build vessels for the Confederate Navy. One of his first jobs was to convert the seagoing tug* Mariner *into a privateer. Later, the Berrys built* CSS North Carolina*, a Richmond-class ironclad that never left the Cape Fear River.*

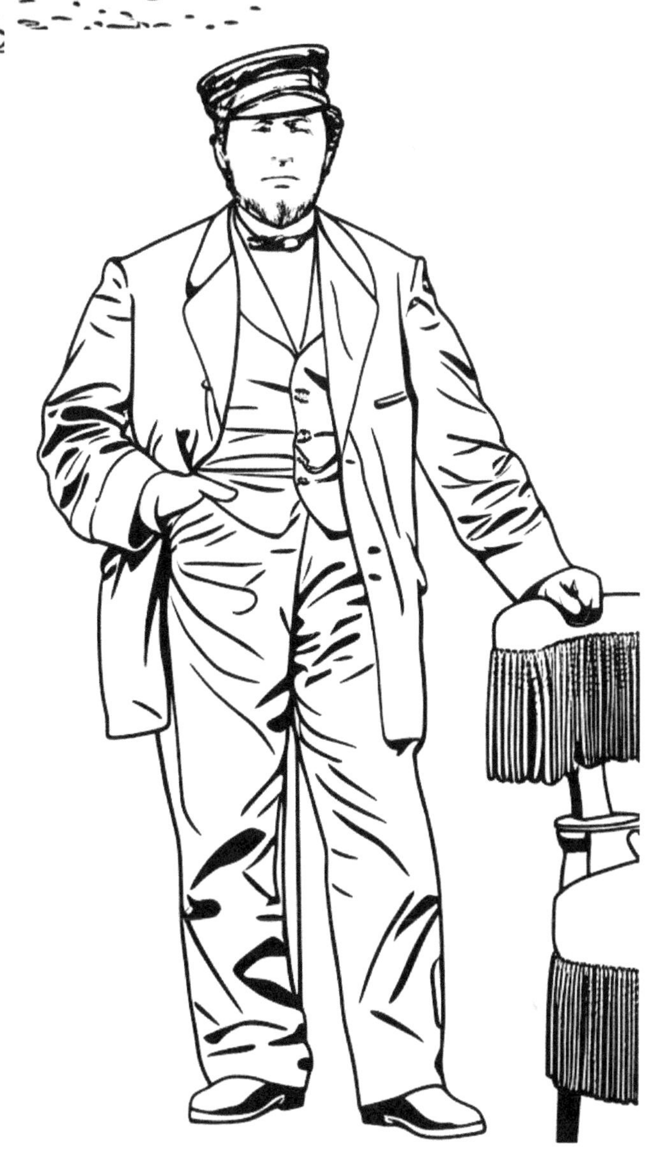

Wilmington's Ironclads

CSS Raleigh, *built by the Cassidy Shipyard, sallied out of New Inlet to challenge federal blockaders in May 1864.*

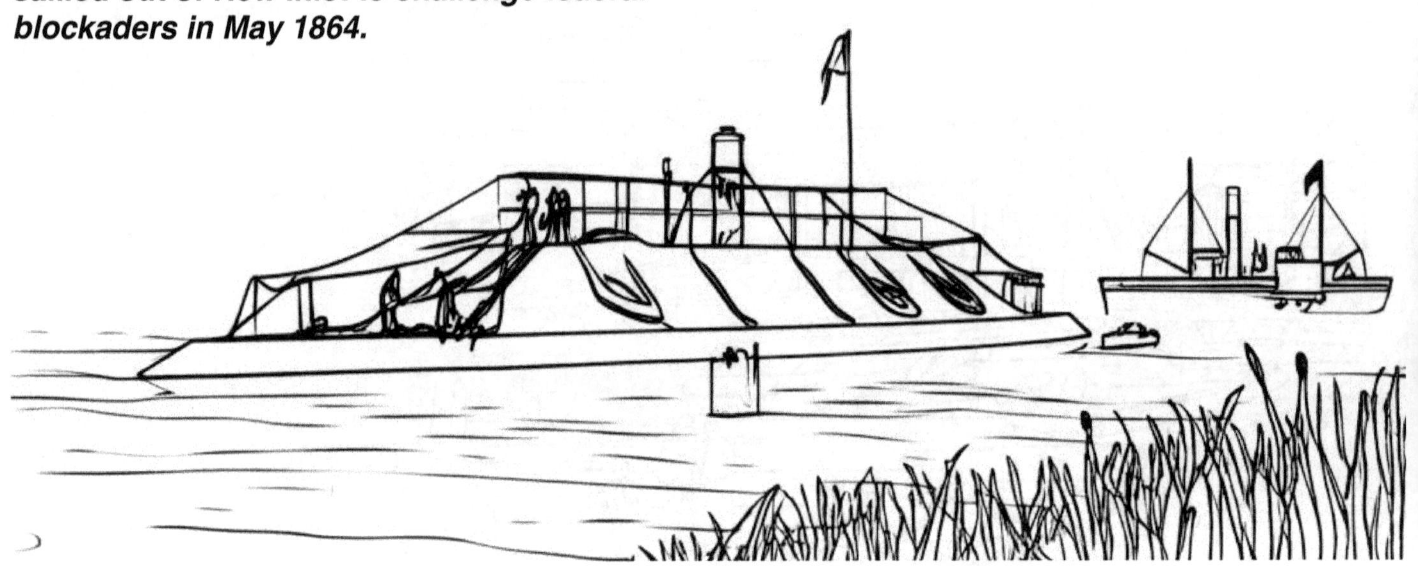

The two ironclads built on the Cape Fear River did not do very much to distinguish themselves. Both casemate-type ironclads, the Raleigh *and the* North Carolina *were out of service within a year of their commissioning. Because of a shortage of seasoned wood, the* North Carolina *was constructed with green wood that was soon infested with toredo worms that ate the bottom out of her. The* North Carolina *was tied off at Southport to serve as a guard ship until she sank at her dock and was towed over to Battery Island.* CSS Raleigh *at least managed to get into the war. On May 6, 1864,* Raleigh *sailed out of New Inlet in the company of two other Confederate escort ships and spent the day playing tag with federal blockading ships. The* Raleigh *was not fast enough to chase the enemy ships down, and the enemy ships could not penetrate* Raleigh's *armor, so it was essentially a big game of tag that ened with neither side being damaged. On the way back into the river,* Raleigh *ran aground on a sandbar off Zeke's Island known as The Rip and broke her back.* Raleigh *had been in service just one week.*

Made of green wood, CSS North Carolina *was tied up at Southport to serve as a sentry ship until she broke apart and sunk under her own weight.*

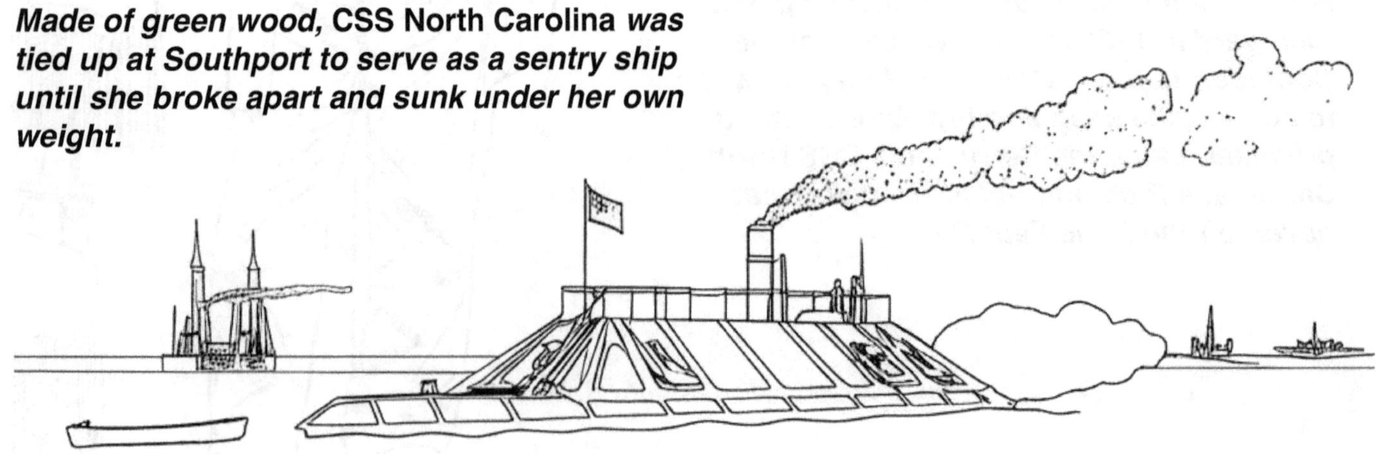

The First Fight for the Fort

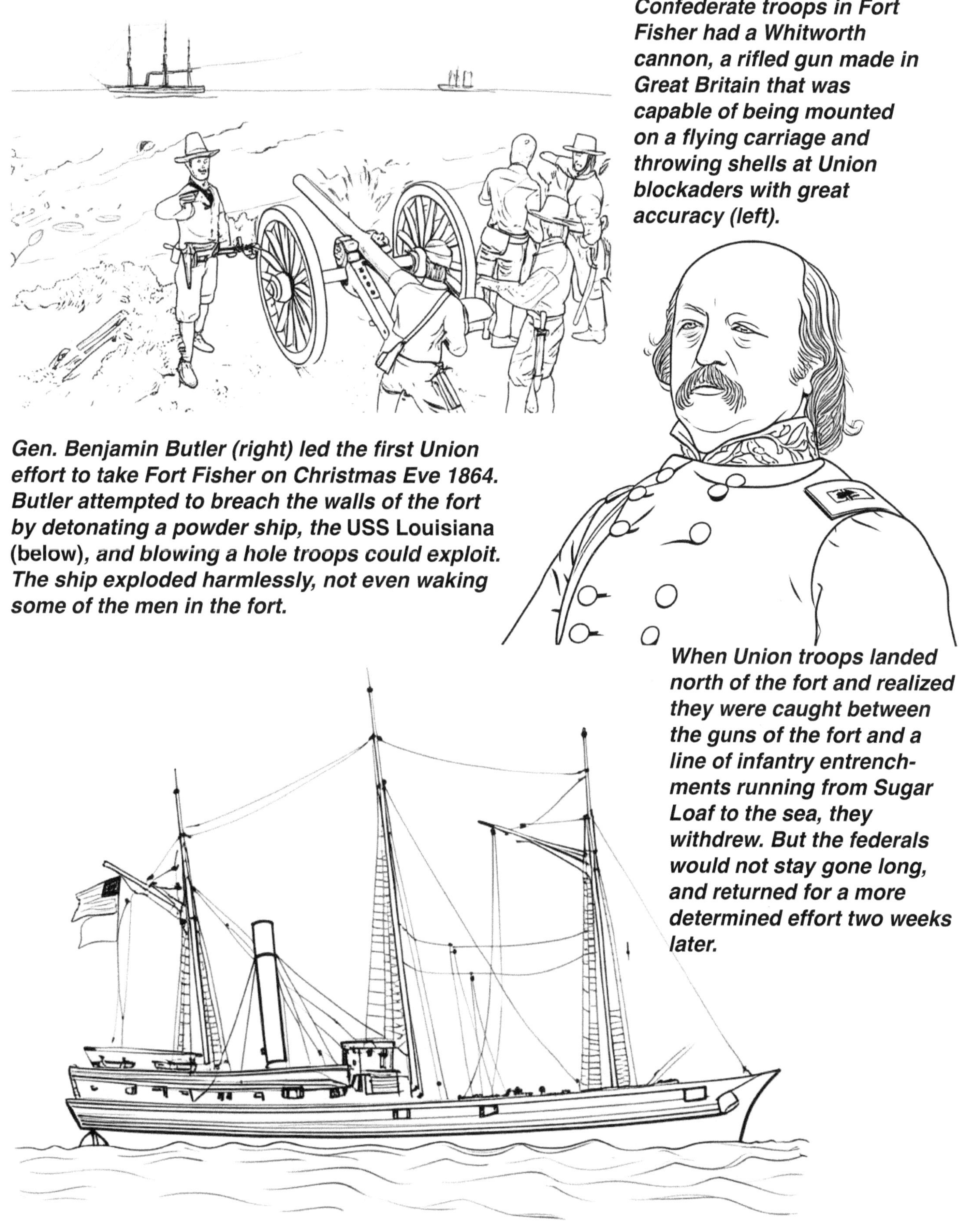

Confederate troops in Fort Fisher had a Whitworth cannon, a rifled gun made in Great Britain that was capable of being mounted on a flying carriage and throwing shells at Union blockaders with great accuracy (left).

Gen. Benjamin Butler (right) led the first Union effort to take Fort Fisher on Christmas Eve 1864. Butler attempted to breach the walls of the fort by detonating a powder ship, the USS Louisiana (below), and blowing a hole troops could exploit. The ship exploded harmlessly, not even waking some of the men in the fort.

When Union troops landed north of the fort and realized they were caught between the guns of the fort and a line of infantry entrenchments running from Sugar Loaf to the sea, they withdrew. But the federals would not stay gone long, and returned for a more determined effort two weeks later.

The Fall of Fort Fisher

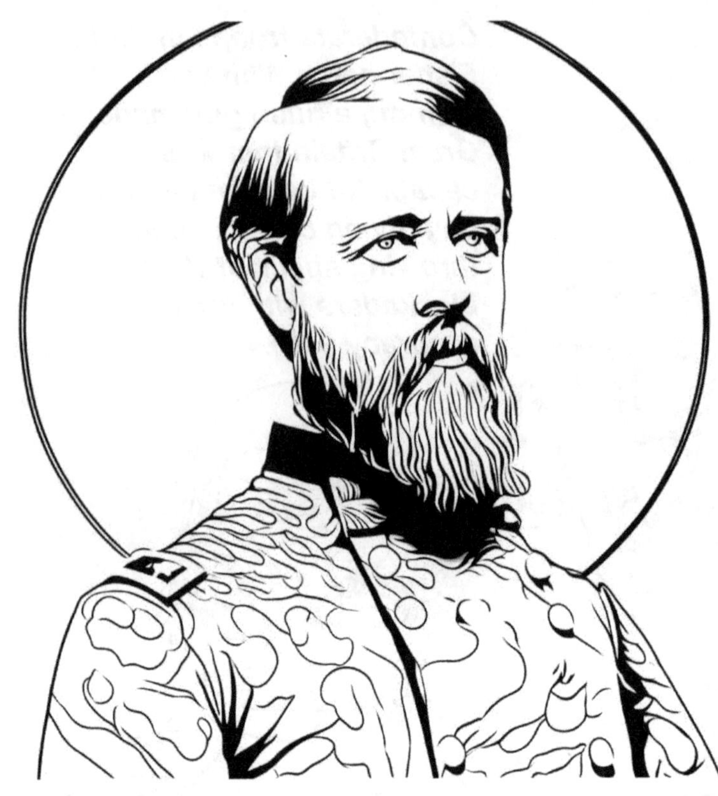

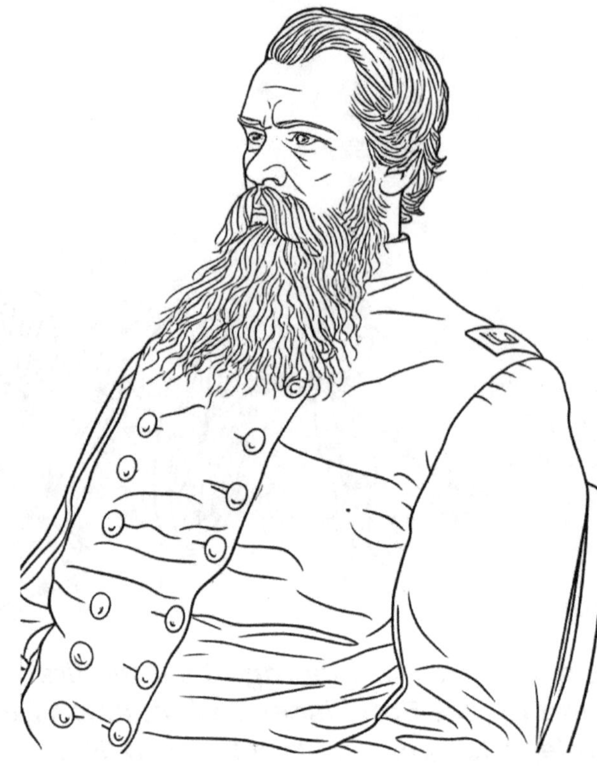

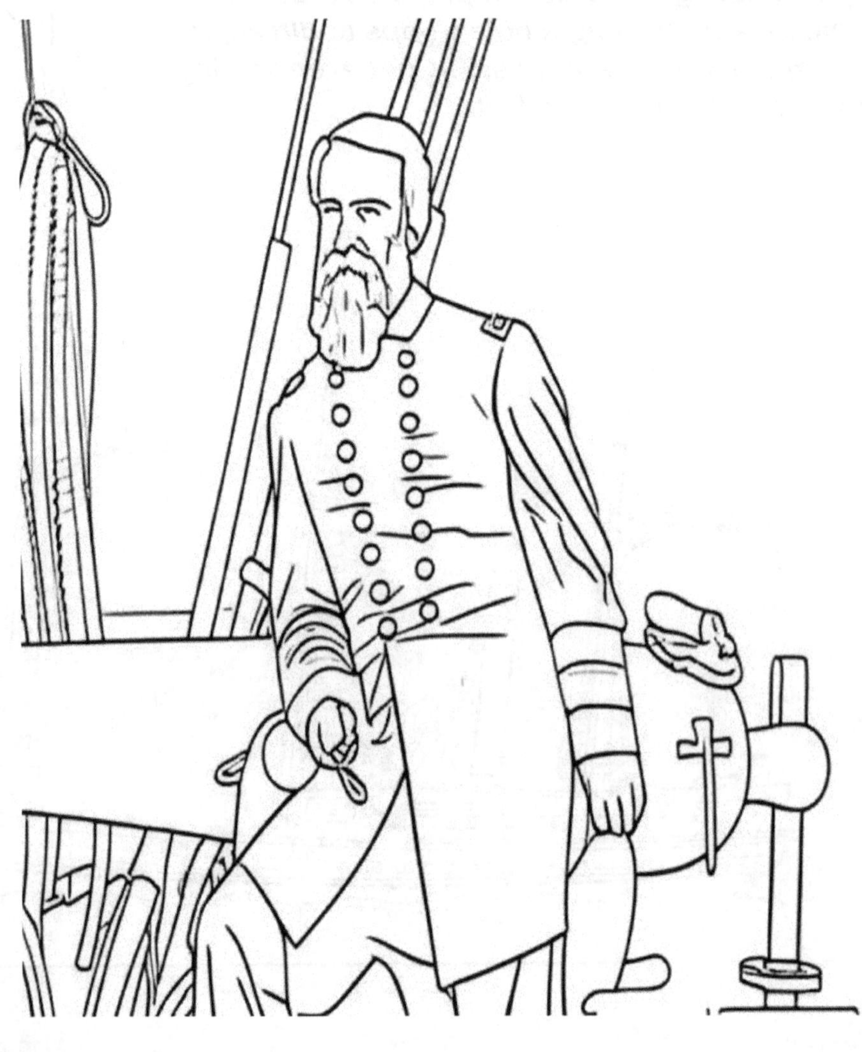

Admiral David Dixon Porter (right) led a flotilla of more than fifty ships carrying thousands of U.S. Army troops back to Fort Fisher in mid-January 1865. Under the overall command of Gen. Alfred Terry (above left), the federals landed to find the entrenchments that had been occupied by Confederate general Robert Hoke's men in the first attack, were now empty. That, and an attack by sailors and Marines on the Norhteast Bastion of the fort on the ocean side, distracted Col. Lamb's Confederates long enough for Newton Martin Curtis' (above right) men to force a breach at Bloody Gate on the river side and enter the fort. Curtis would win the Medal of Honor for his actions that day.

Col. Lamb's undermanned defenders did the best they could. Infantry rushed from bombproofs to fill the gaps between the heavy guns and repel the invaders (below).

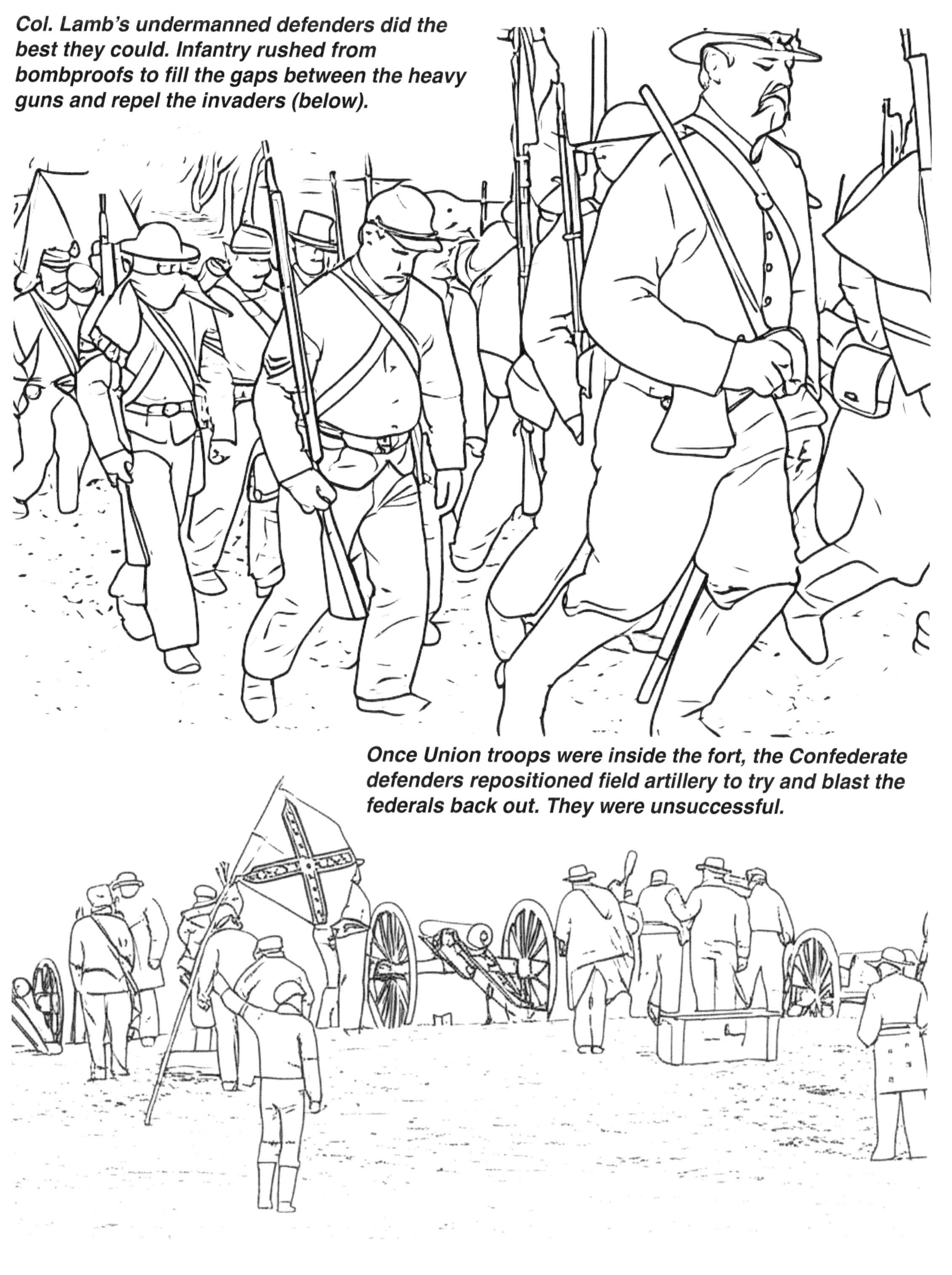

Once Union troops were inside the fort, the Confederate defenders repositioned field artillery to try and blast the federals back out. They were unsuccessful.

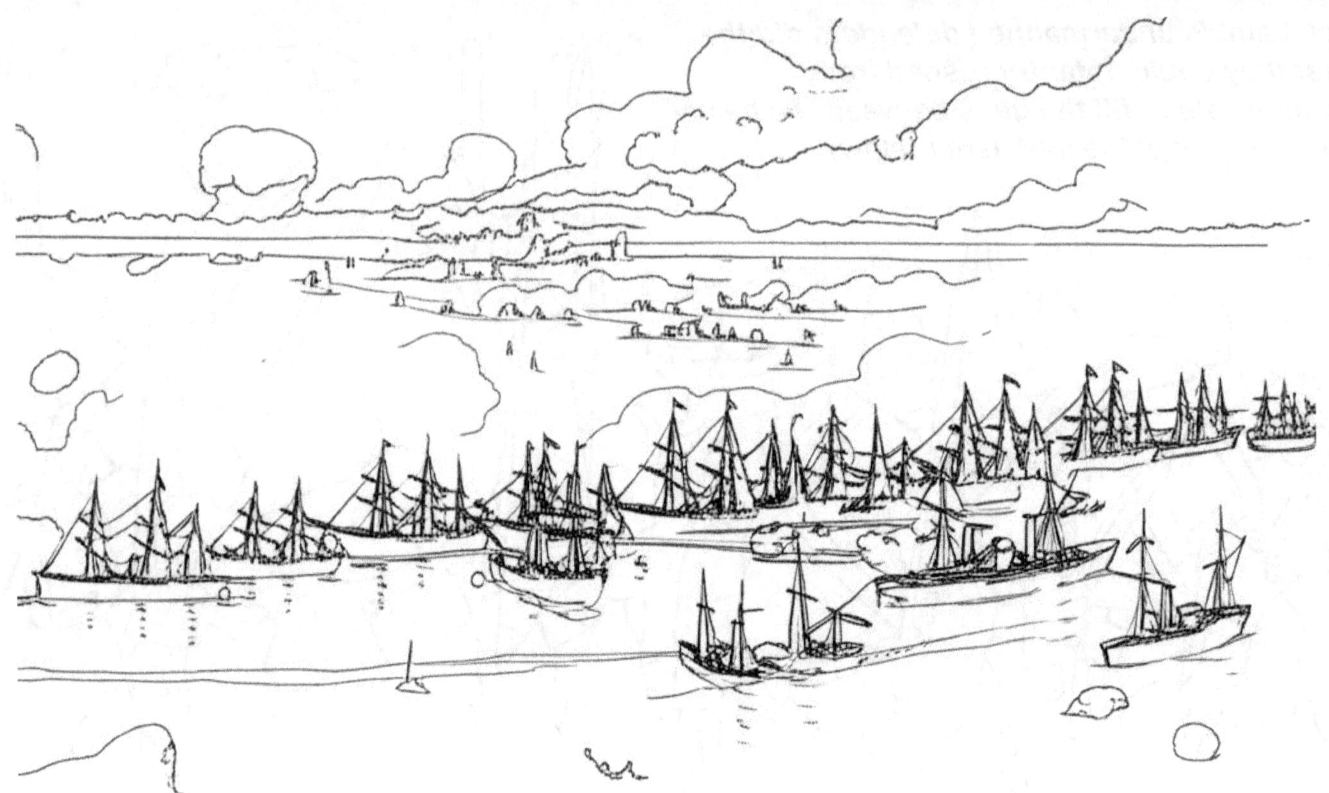

The flotilla of U.S. Navy ships gathered for the attack on Fort Fisher included monitors, converted blockade runners, and main battle ships. They delivered a barrage of over 19,000 shells on the fort over the course of two days before troops began landing (below). It remained the largest naval bombardment in history until World War II.

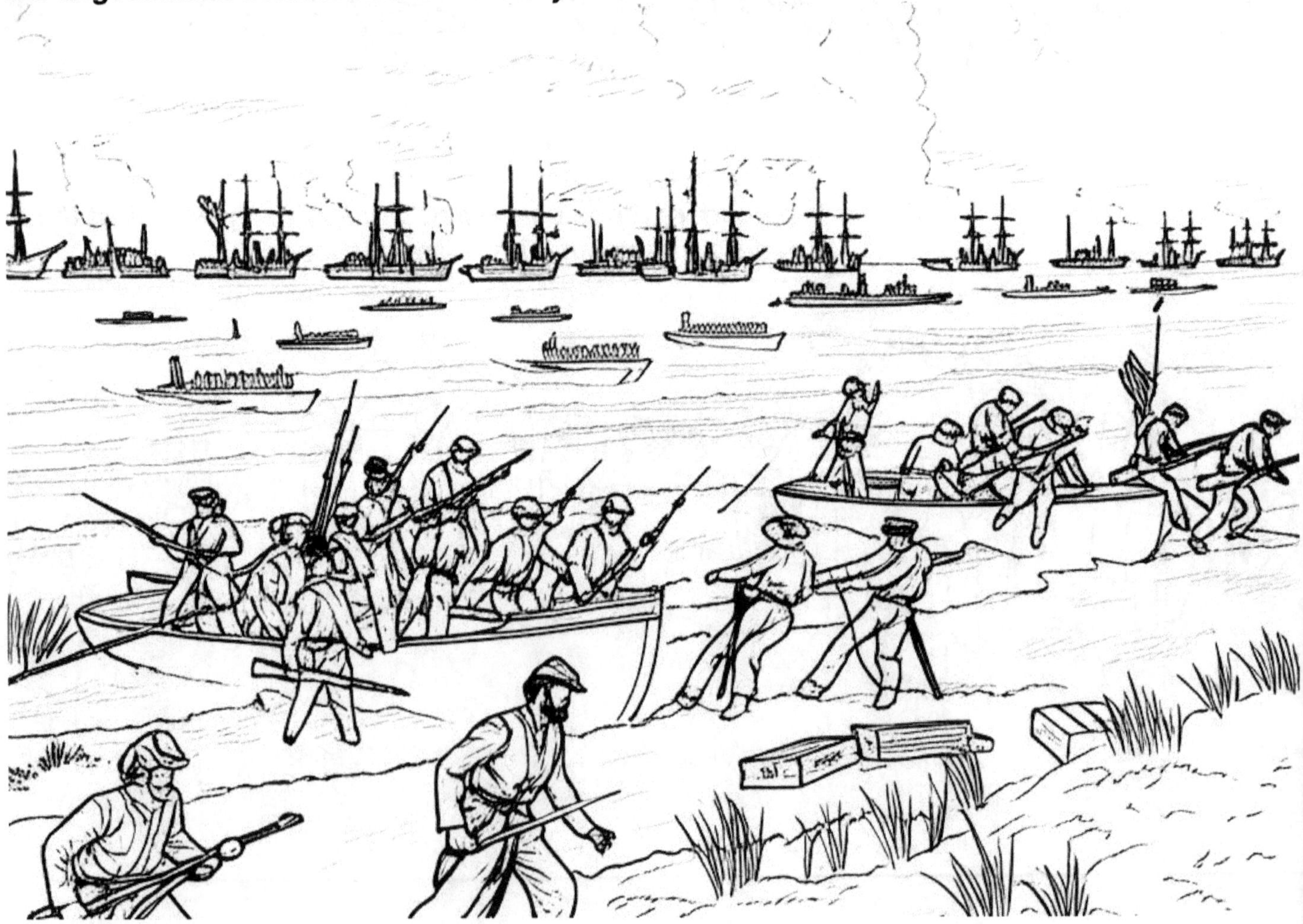

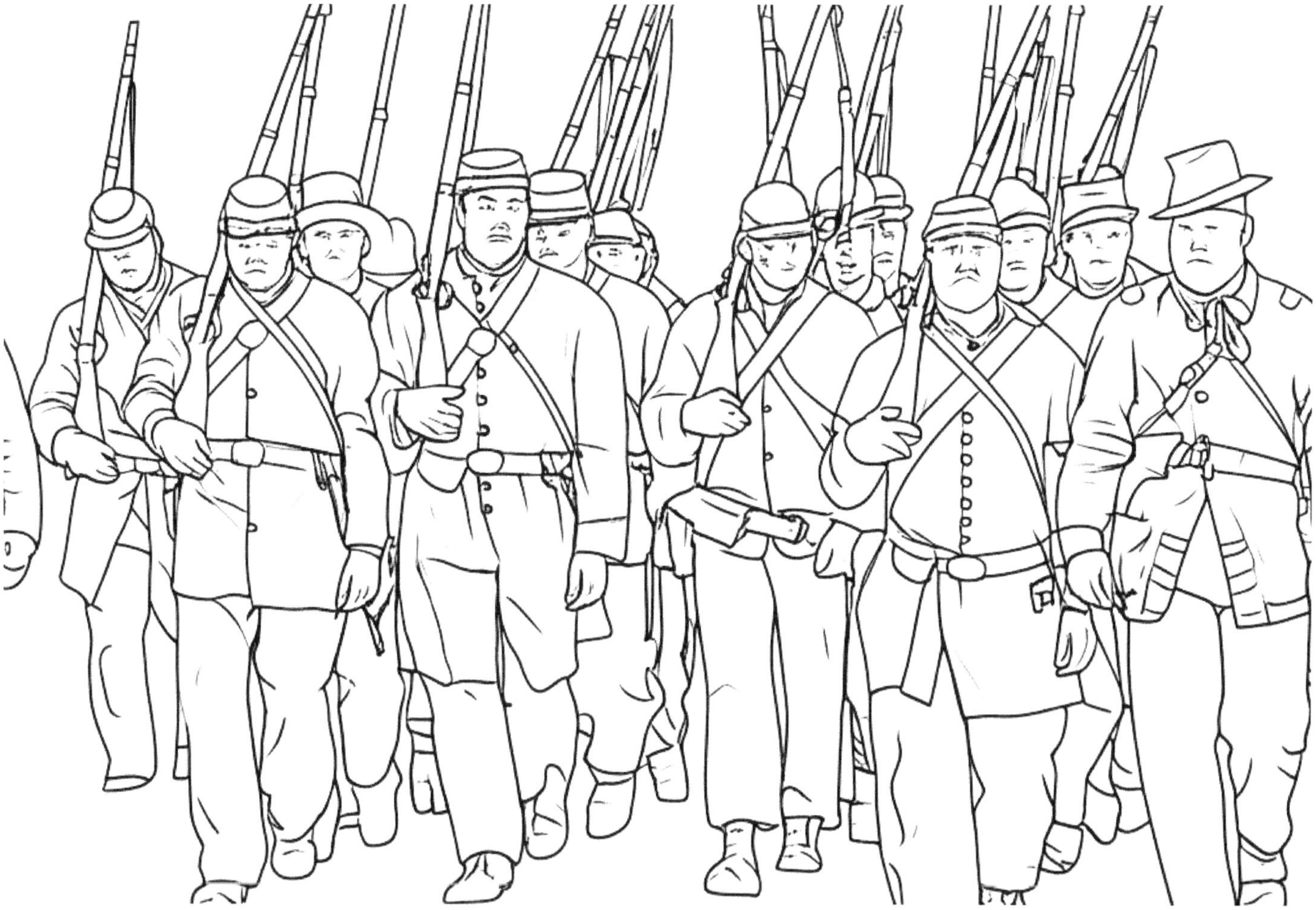

On the beach, federal troops marched to the river side of the land face (above). The army's attack was to go off at the same time a force of sailors and Marines attacked the ocean side of the fort's land face. Among the units mustered for the attack were U.S. Colored Troops, made up of freedmen and ex-slaves under the leadership of white officers. It was the USCTs who took the surrender of the fort after a day of vicious hand to hand fighting.

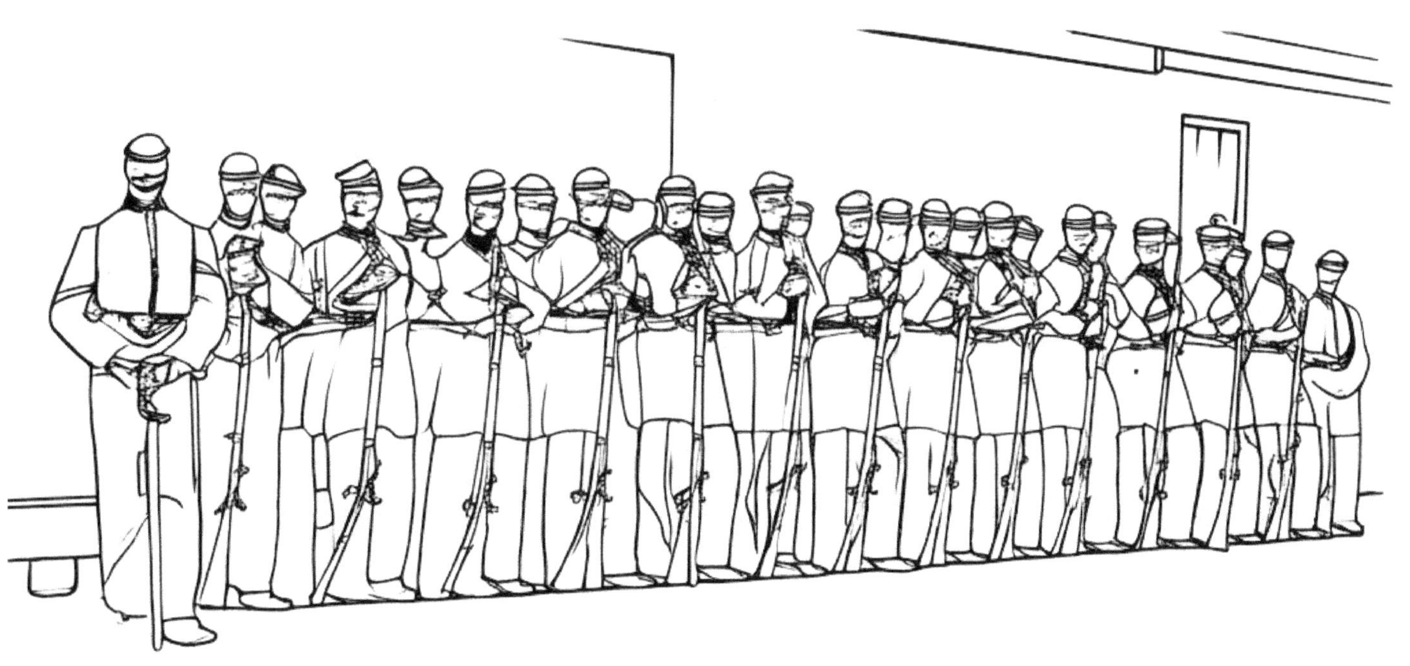

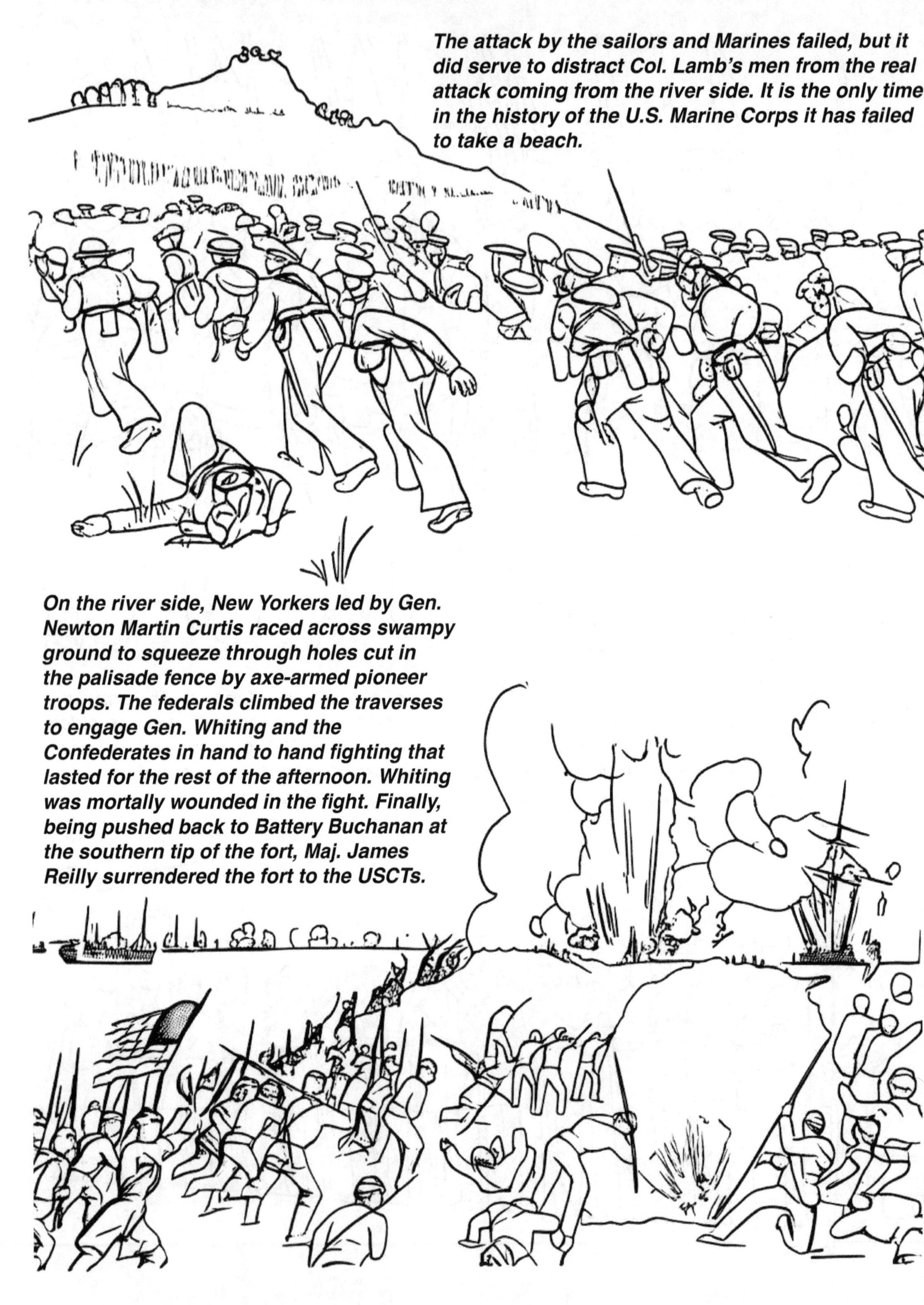

The attack by the sailors and Marines failed, but it did serve to distract Col. Lamb's men from the real attack coming from the river side. It is the only time in the history of the U.S. Marine Corps it has failed to take a beach.

On the river side, New Yorkers led by Gen. Newton Martin Curtis raced across swampy ground to squeeze through holes cut in the palisade fence by axe-armed pioneer troops. The federals climbed the traverses to engage Gen. Whiting and the Confederates in hand to hand fighting that lasted for the rest of the afternoon. Whiting was mortally wounded in the fight. Finally, being pushed back to Battery Buchanan at the southern tip of the fort, Maj. James Reilly surrendered the fort to the USCTs.

After the Battle

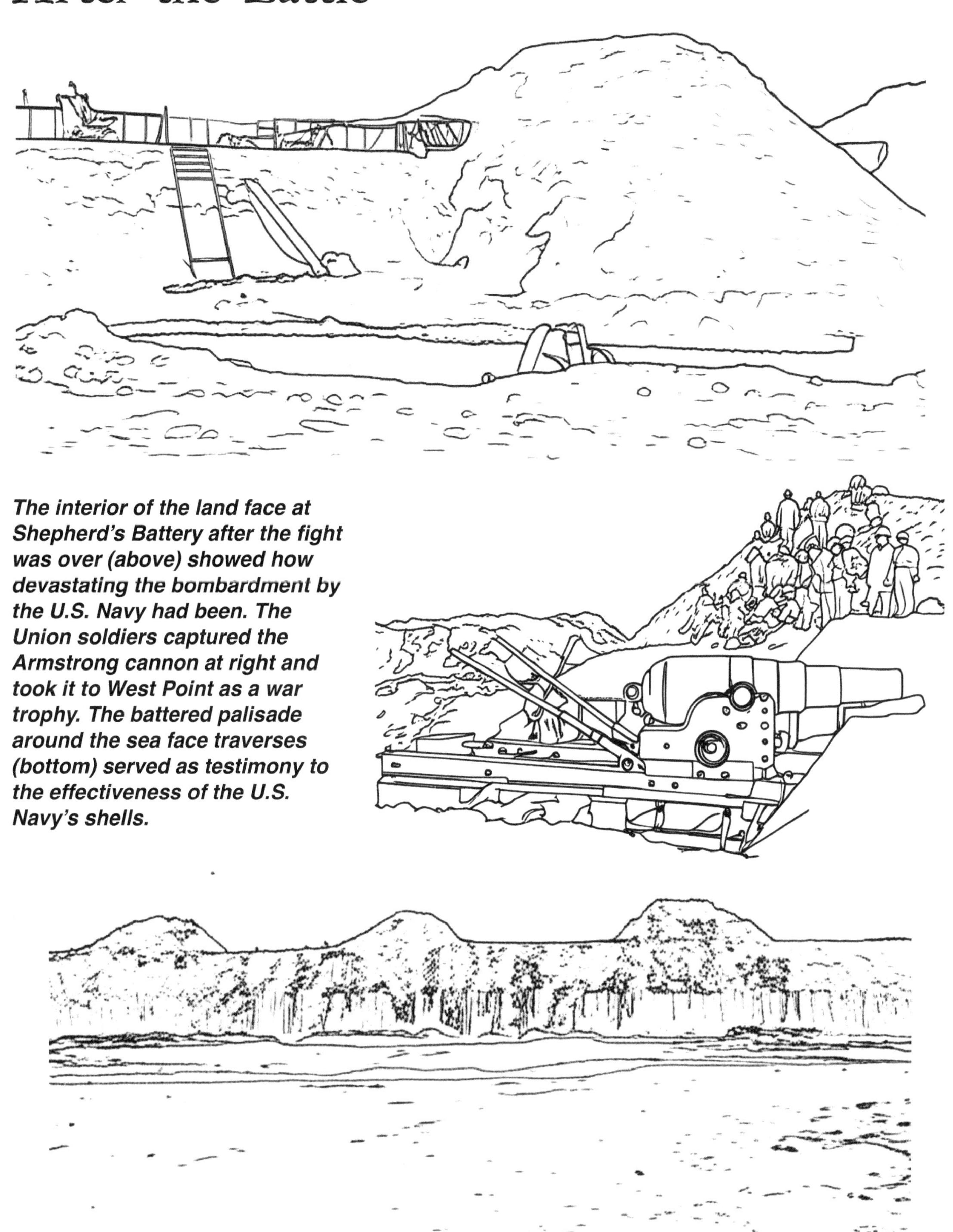

The interior of the land face at Shepherd's Battery after the fight was over (above) showed how devastating the bombardment by the U.S. Navy had been. The Union soldiers captured the Armstrong cannon at right and took it to West Point as a war trophy. The battered palisade around the sea face traverses (bottom) served as testimony to the effectiveness of the U.S. Navy's shells.

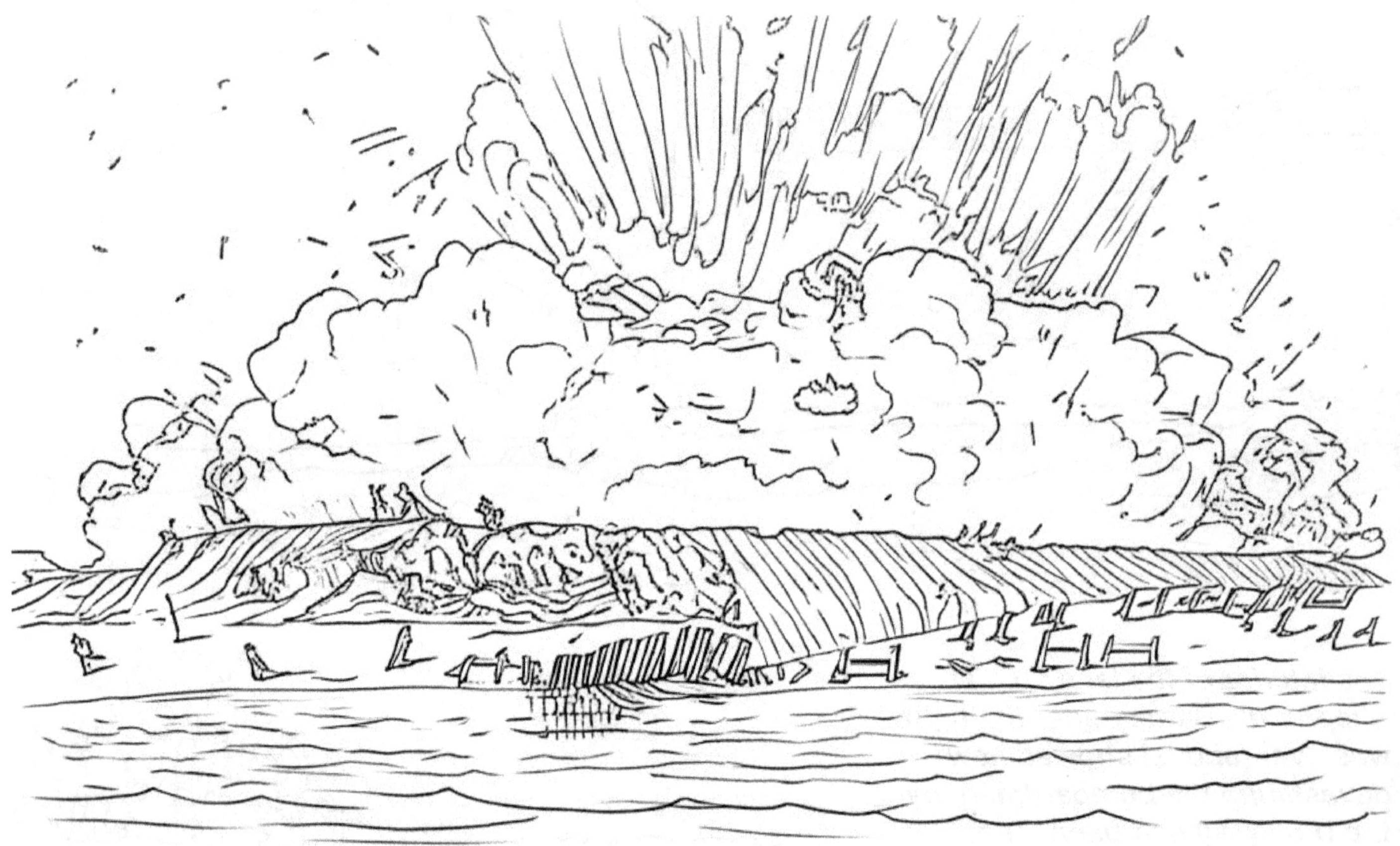

After the battle was over, Union troops occupied the defeated fort. In an accident that marred what had been a striking victory for the federals, a careless soldier caused the powder magazine at the Northeast Bastion to explode, killing many. The boom was heard as far away as Wilmington.

Fort Anderson

The second largest fortification on the Cape Fear River was Fort Anderson, built over roughly half the footprint of the old colonial town of Brunswick.

The interior of Fort Anderson's Battery A, facing the Cape Fear River, as it appears today.

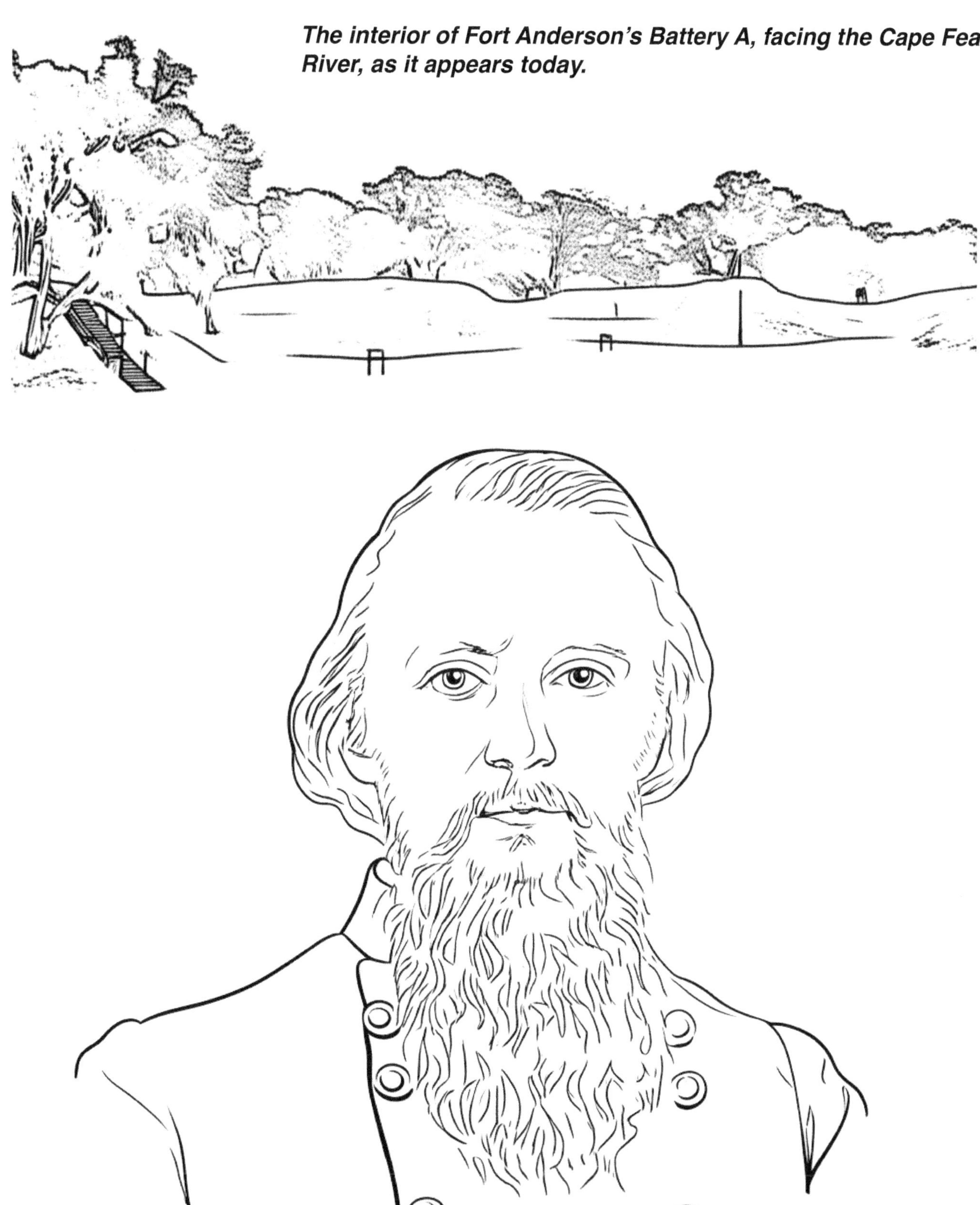

The fort was named after Brigadier General George Burgwyn Anderson, who died at the Battle of Antietam. Originally named Fort St. Philip after the colonial church ruins on the site, the name was changed to honor Anderson, a son of the Cape Fear, in 1863.

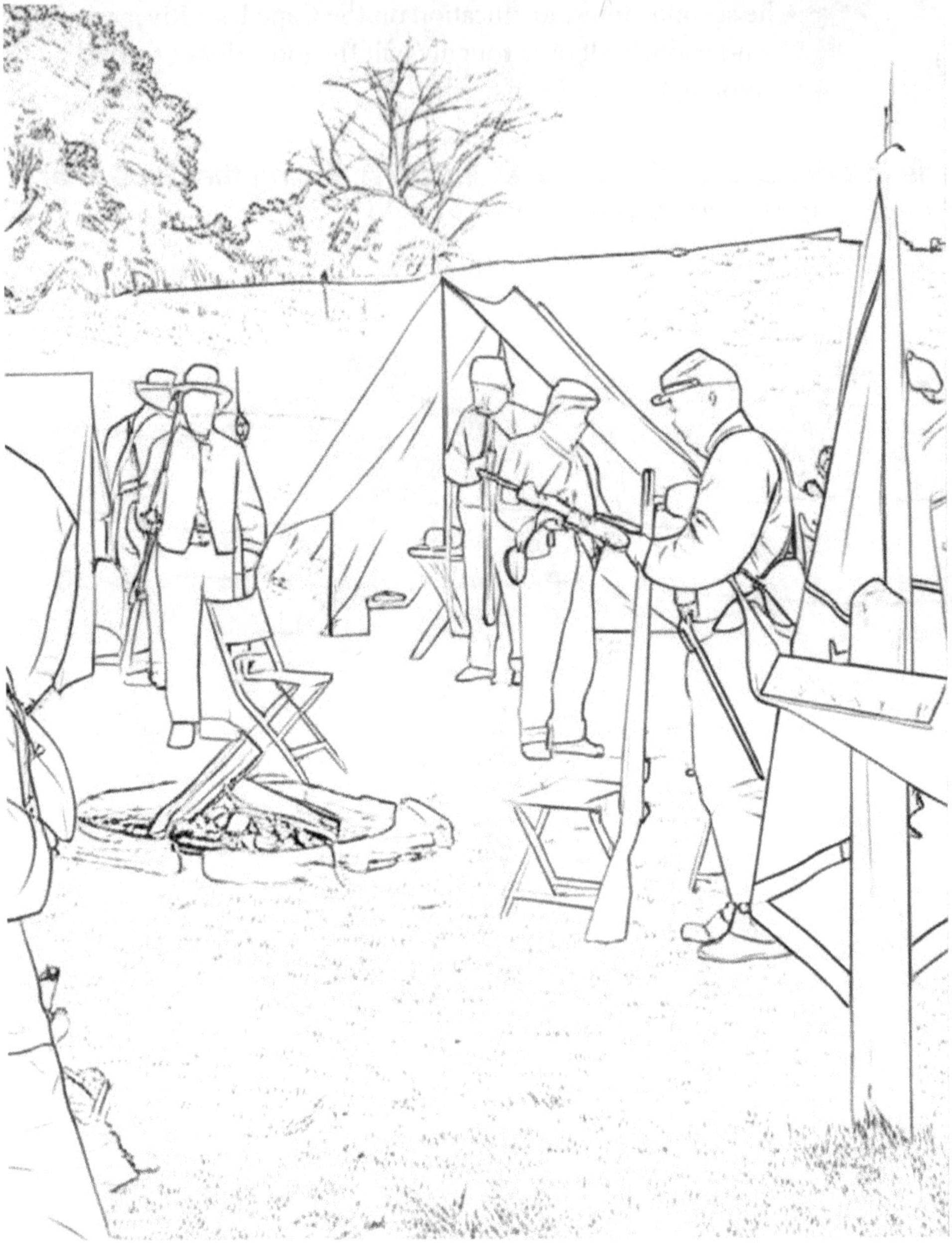

Troops in Fort Anderson knew that after Fort Fisher fell, they would be next in the crosshairs of the federal forces (left). The Union navy tried a bit of trickery by sending a fake monitor (below) upriver to lure the Confederates at Fort Anderson into detonating the mines in the river prematurely. The mission was led by William B. Cushing.

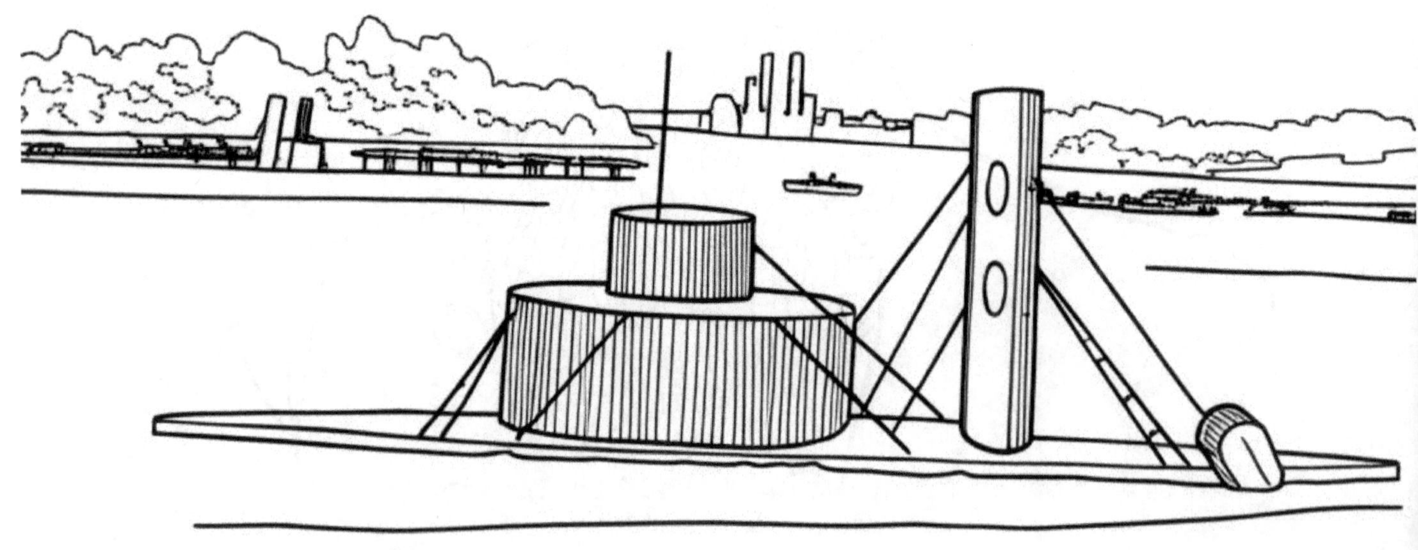

Ohio's Gen. Jacob D. Cox (right) landed his division at Southport in February 1865 and proceeded up the west bank of the Cape Fear River to converge on Wilmington. Enroute, his forces got behind the defenses of Fort Anderson by circling through a swamp anchoring the west end of the lines. When the Confederates realized Union cavalry was in their rear, they abandoned the fort and retreated towards Wilmington.

After Fort Anderson fell, the fort was used as a Freedman's encampment. Freed slaves lived in the fort until arrangements could be made to live elsewhere.

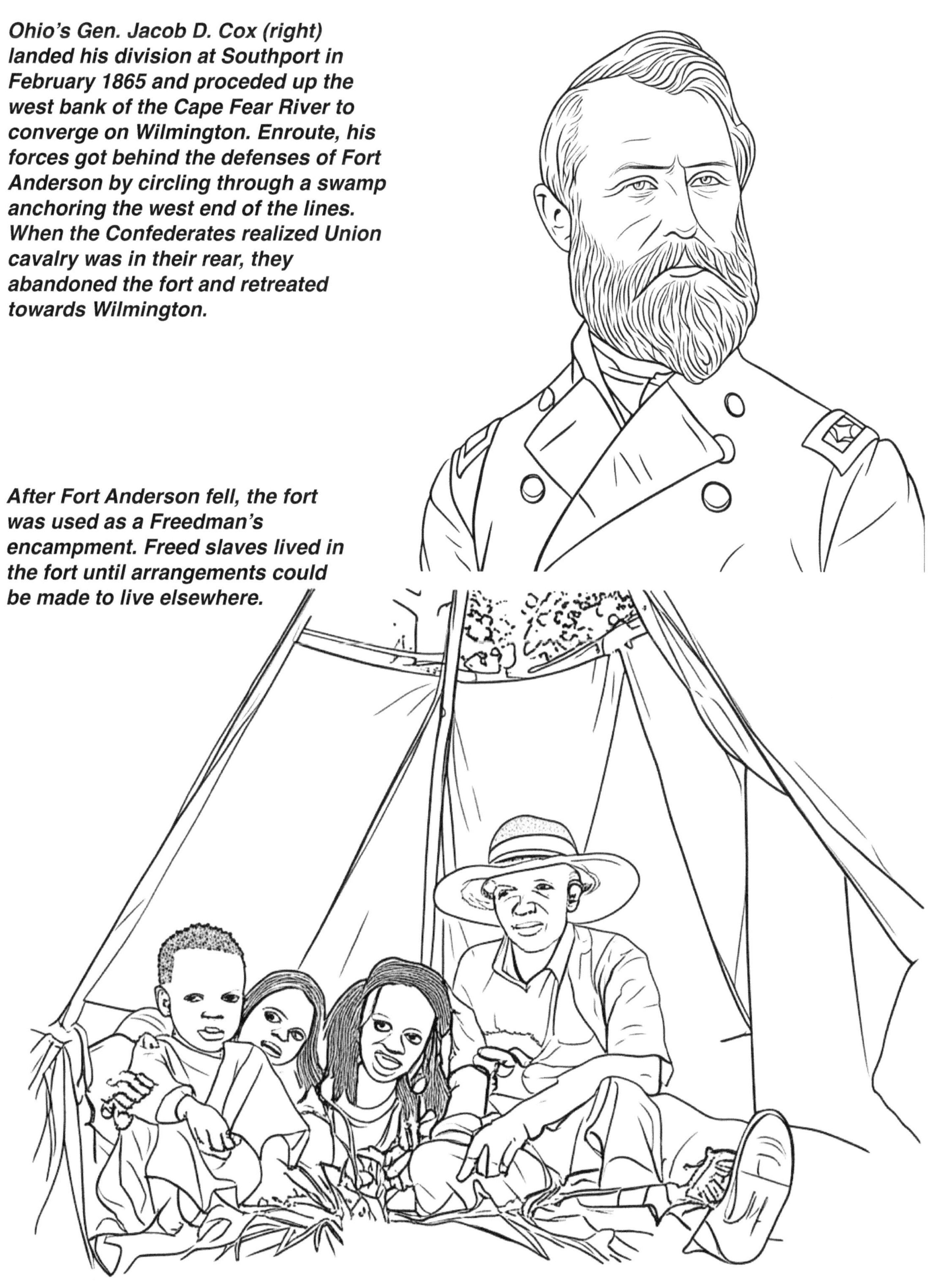

WORLD WAR II

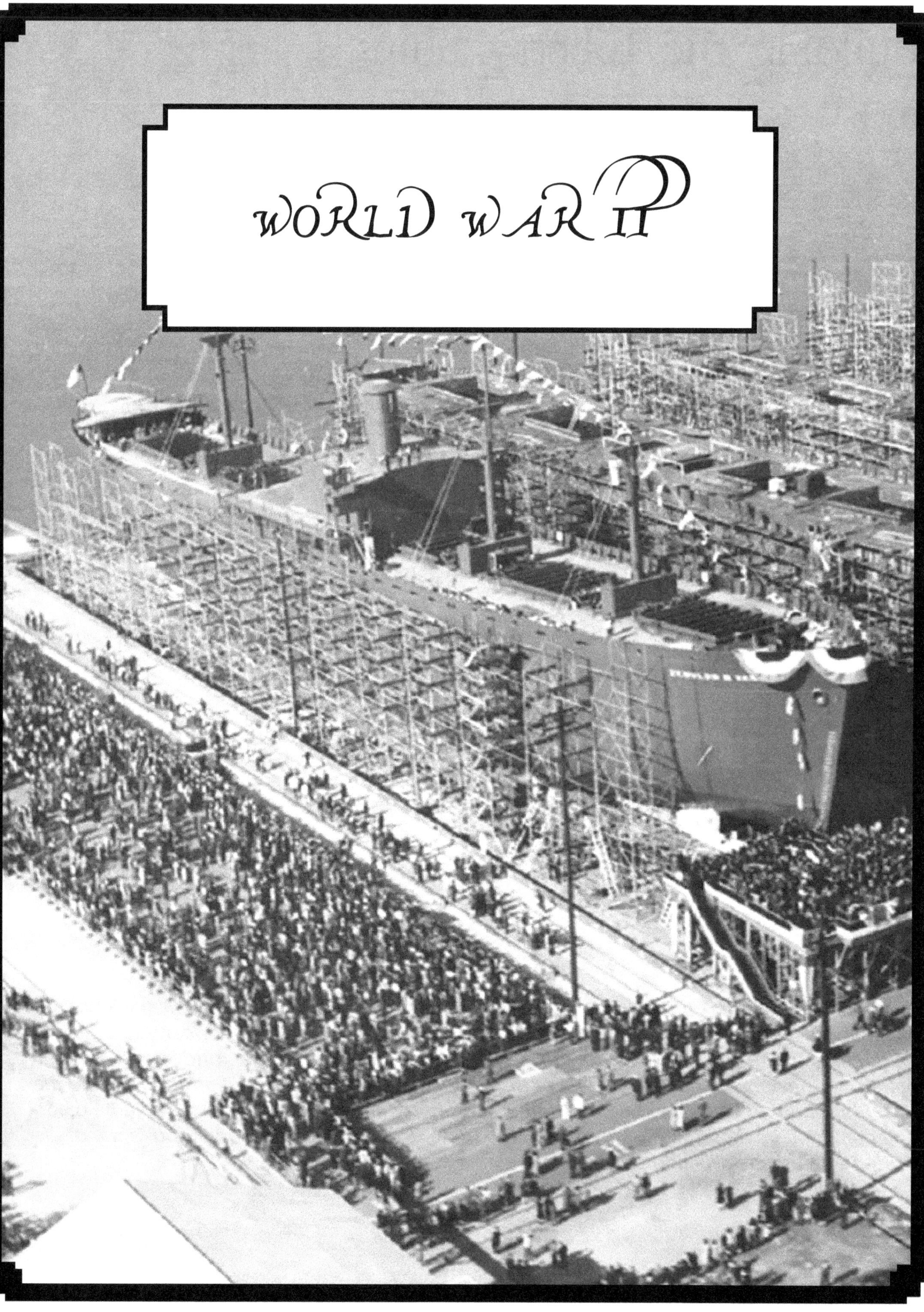

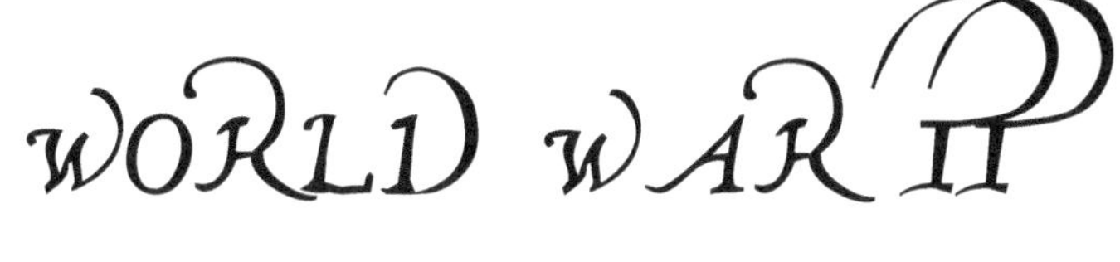

Building the Liberty Ships

Wilmington and the Cape Fear region played a significant role in the effort to win World War II. From shipbuilding, to training troops for overseas, to guarding German prisoners of war from North Africa, the war ushered in great changes.

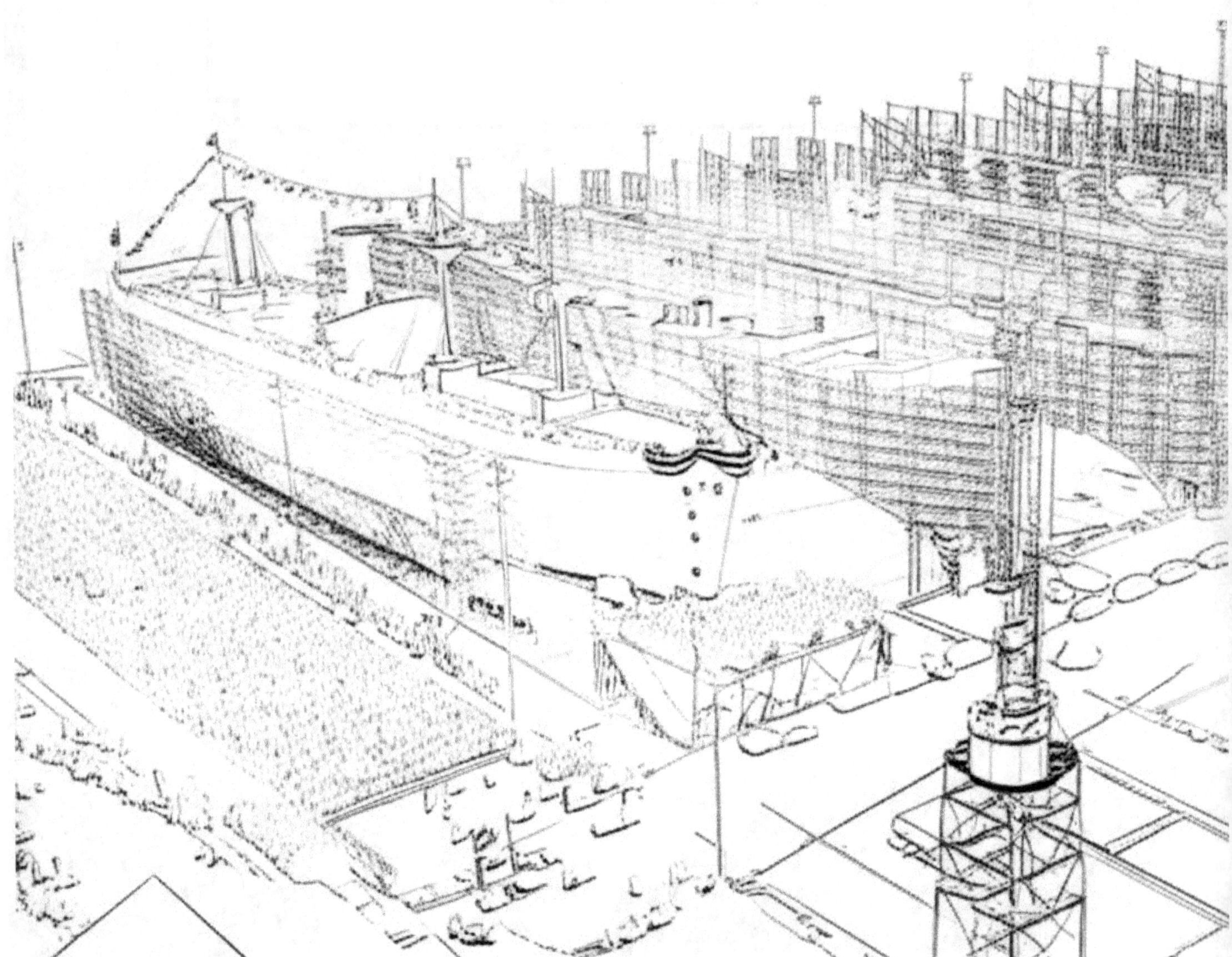

Even before the attack on Pearl Harbor, President Franklin D. Roosevelt knew the key to winning the war would be getting the supplies and armaments from American factories to the battlefields of Europe. To do that, a crash program of shipbuilding was undertaken to construct the vessels needed to deliver those goods. That included Wilmington, where the N.C. Shipbuilding Company began turning out Liberty ships as fast as they could be made. The company docks, roughly where the N.C. State Ports are now, drew in thousands of workers that made Wilmington a boom town.

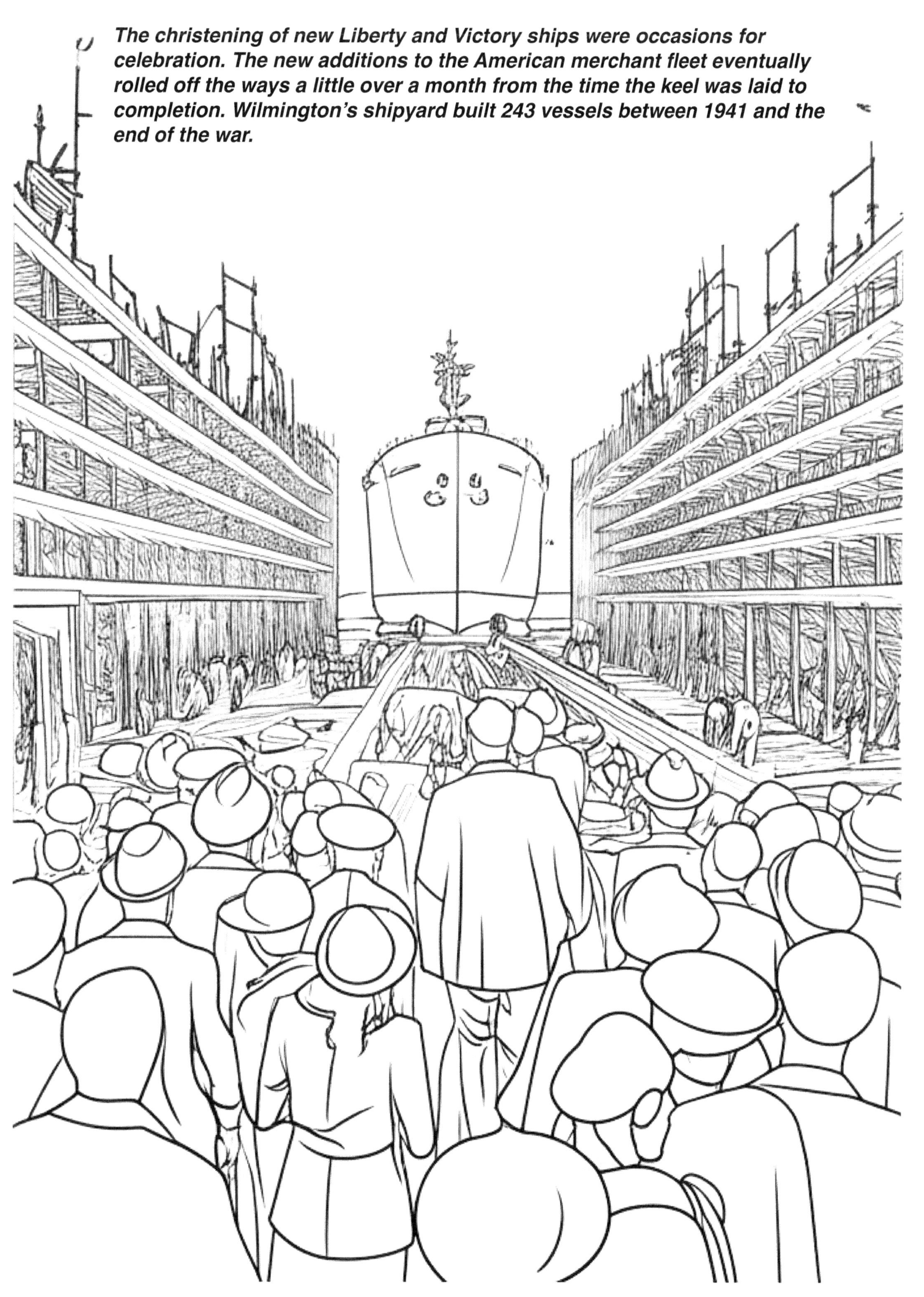

The christening of new Liberty and Victory ships were occasions for celebration. The new additions to the American merchant fleet eventually rolled off the ways a little over a month from the time the keel was laid to completion. Wilmington's shipyard built 243 vessels between 1941 and the end of the war.

On the Beaches

Along the East Coast, the threat of enemy saboteurs was a real issue. So was the threat of German U-boats. The U.S. Coast Guard used mounted patrols on the beaches to keep an eye on what was happening offshore of places like Bald Head Island.

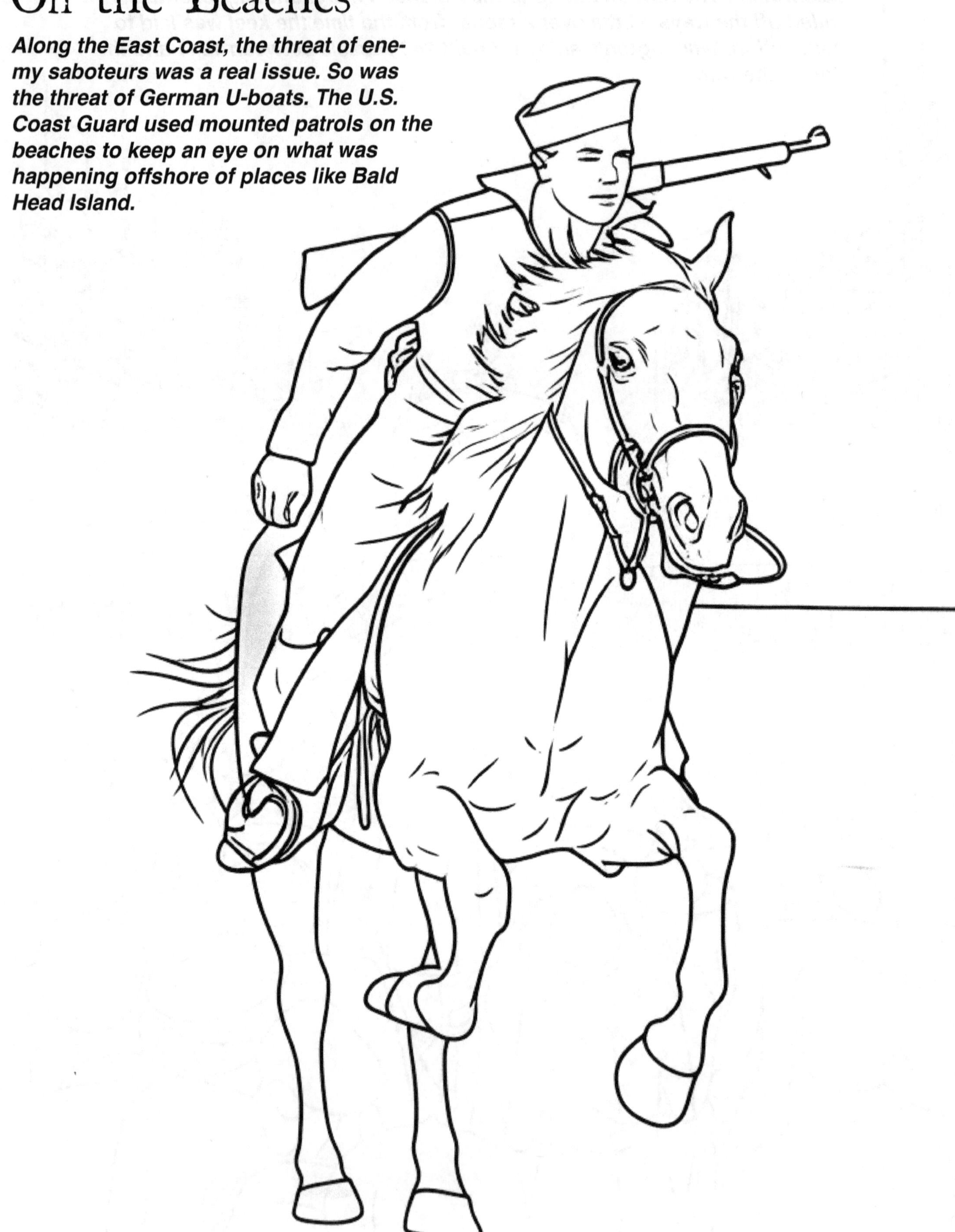

In the Battle Line

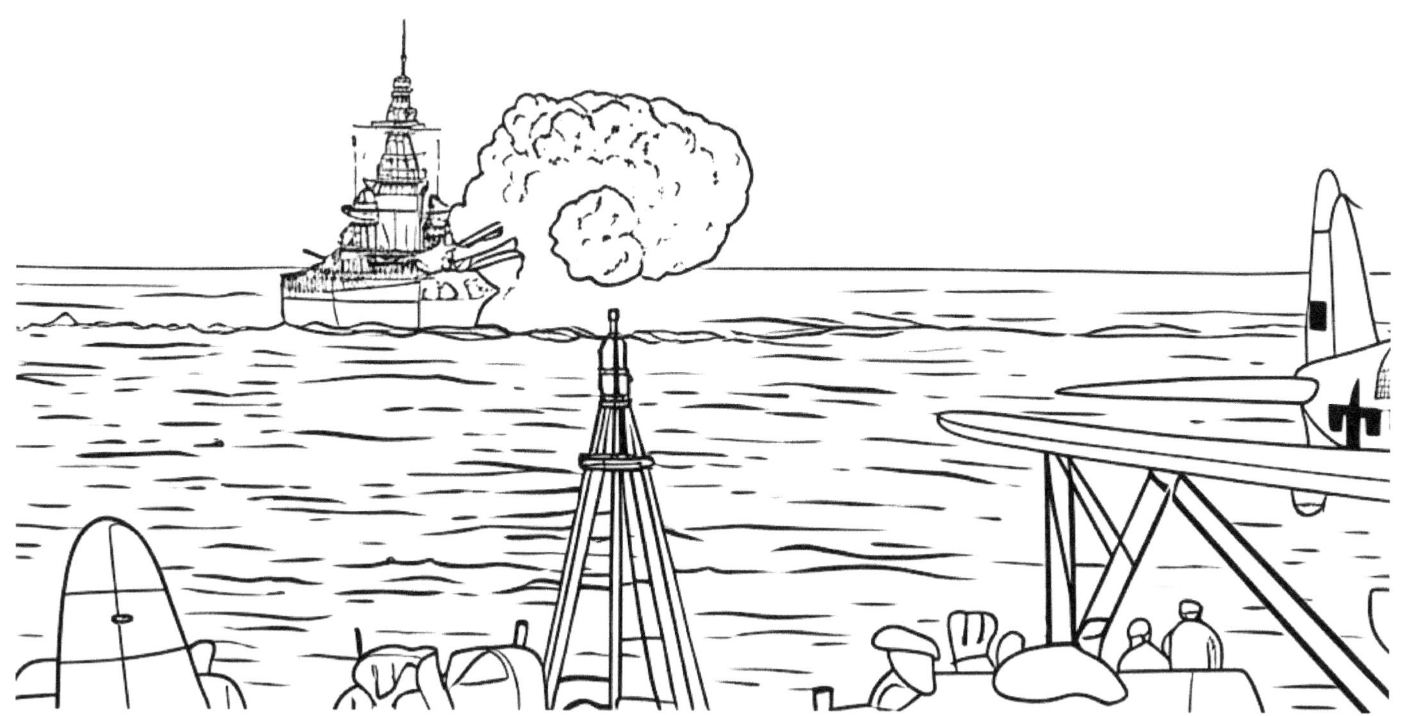

The USS North Carolina *delivering salvos from her 16" main guns in support of operations against Japanese controlled islands in the Pacific. The ship participated in every major campaign of the war in the Pacific Theater.*

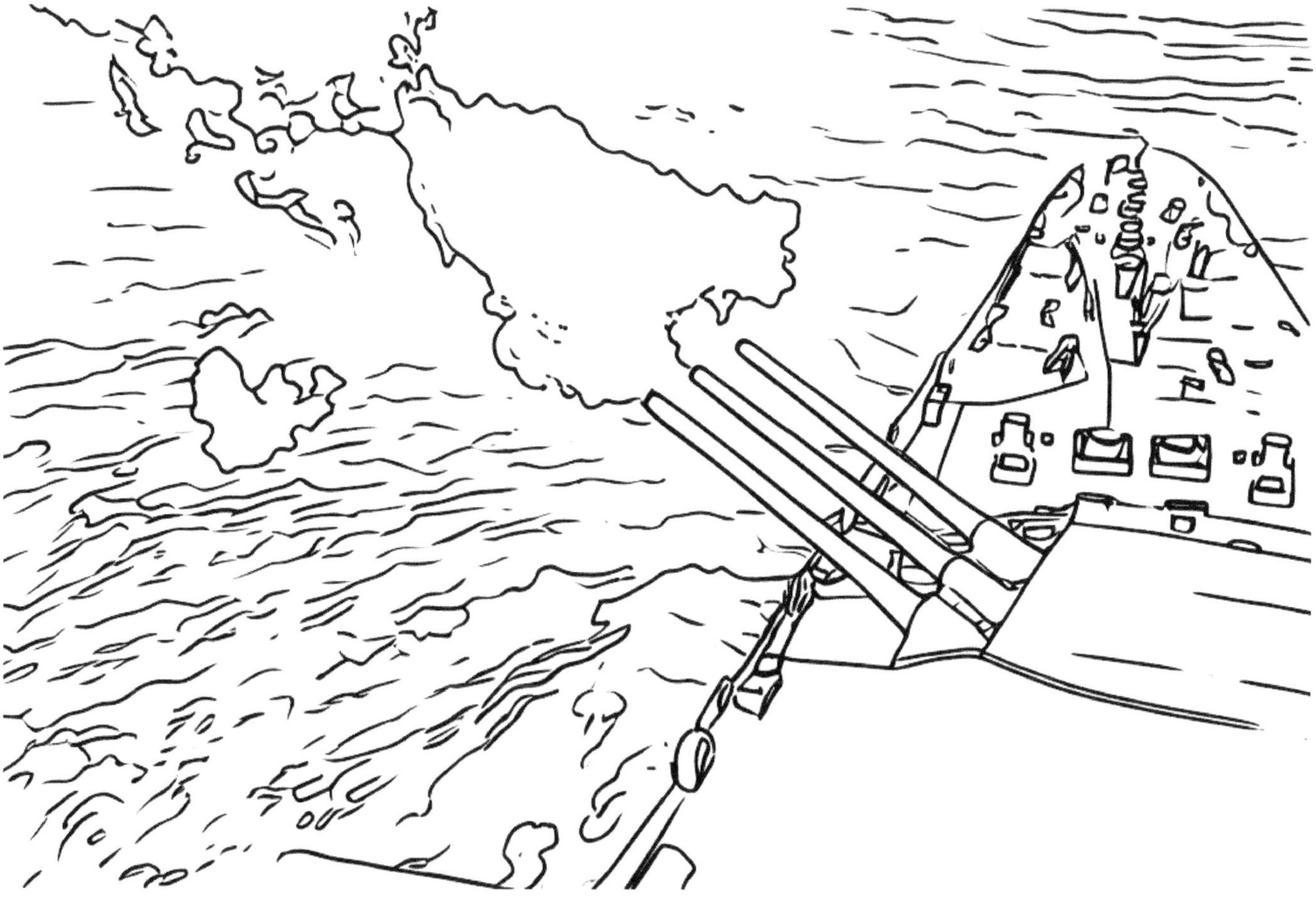

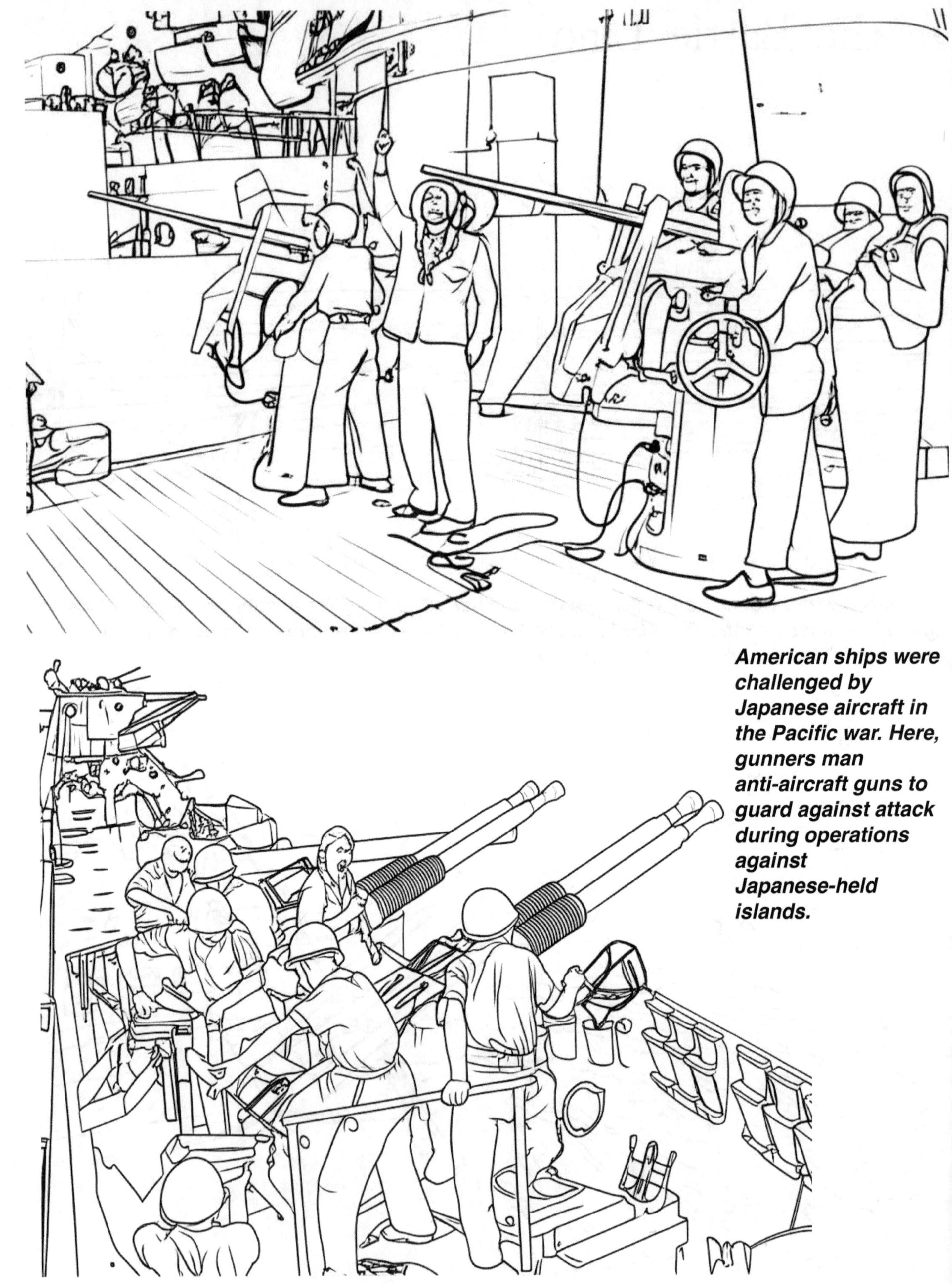

American ships were challenged by Japanese aircraft in the Pacific war. Here, gunners man anti-aircraft guns to guard against attack during operations against Japanese-held islands.

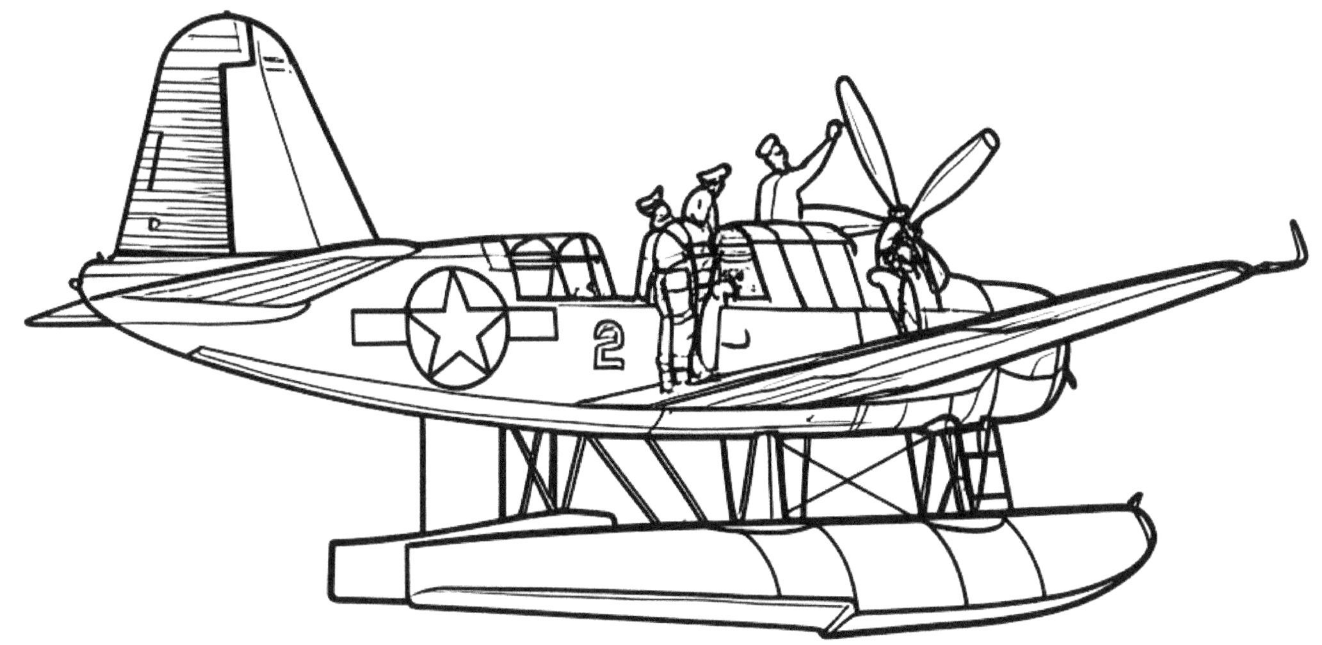

PBY patrol aircraft like the one above were carried on the the stern of the USS North Carolina, *extending its eyes beyond the horizon and providing a means of communicating with other units without resorting to radio. The plane was also useful for retrieving downed U.S. pilots who had crashed into the sea. Below, a lookout keeps a sharp eye out for the enemy.*

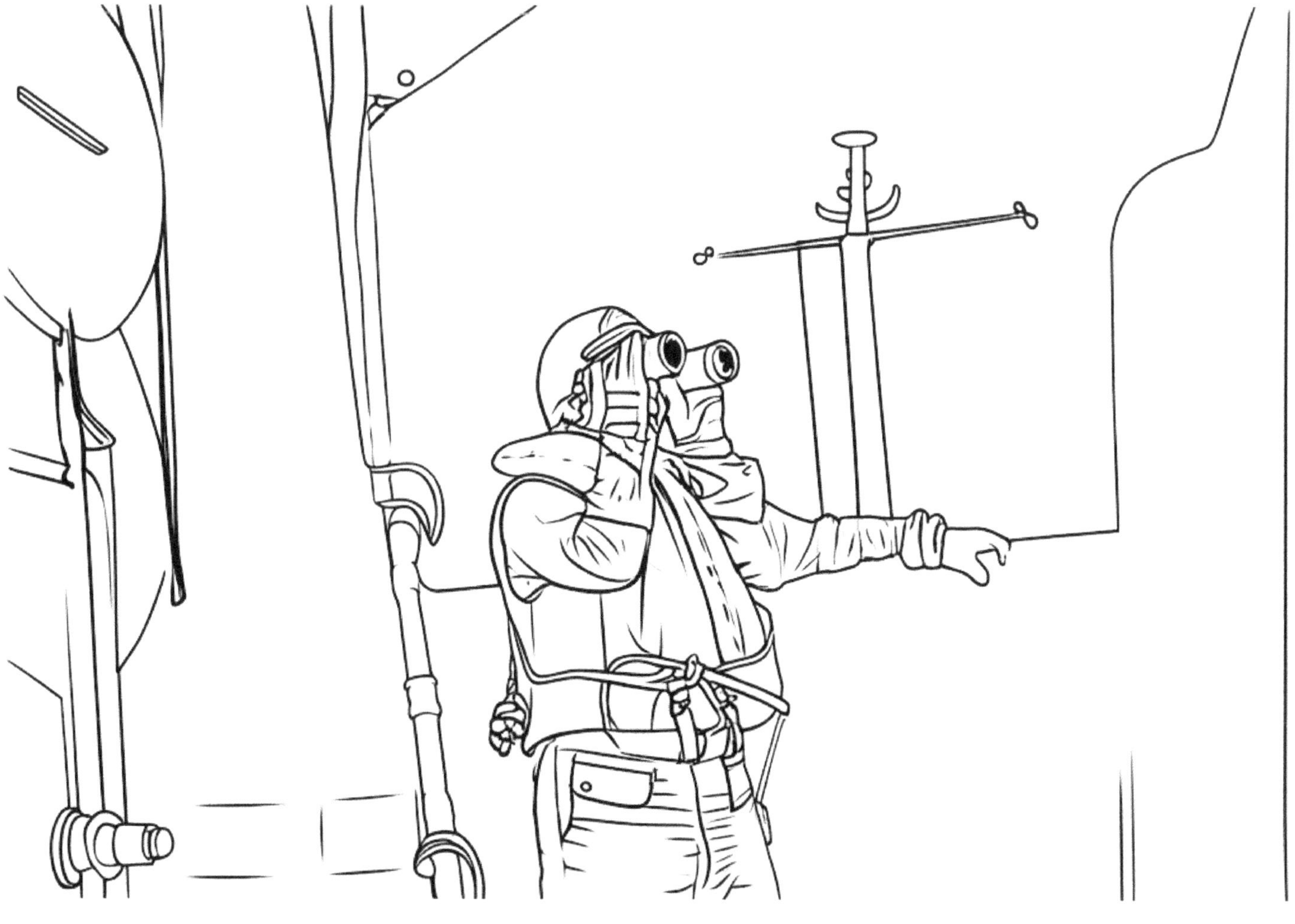

Training the Troops

Fort Fisher's mission in World War II was to train coastal artillery units from Camp Davis. The men trained on several different kinds of guns, from large cannons capable of engaging enemy ships, to mobile antiaircraft guns, to the fifty caliber Browning belt fed machine gun (opposite page).

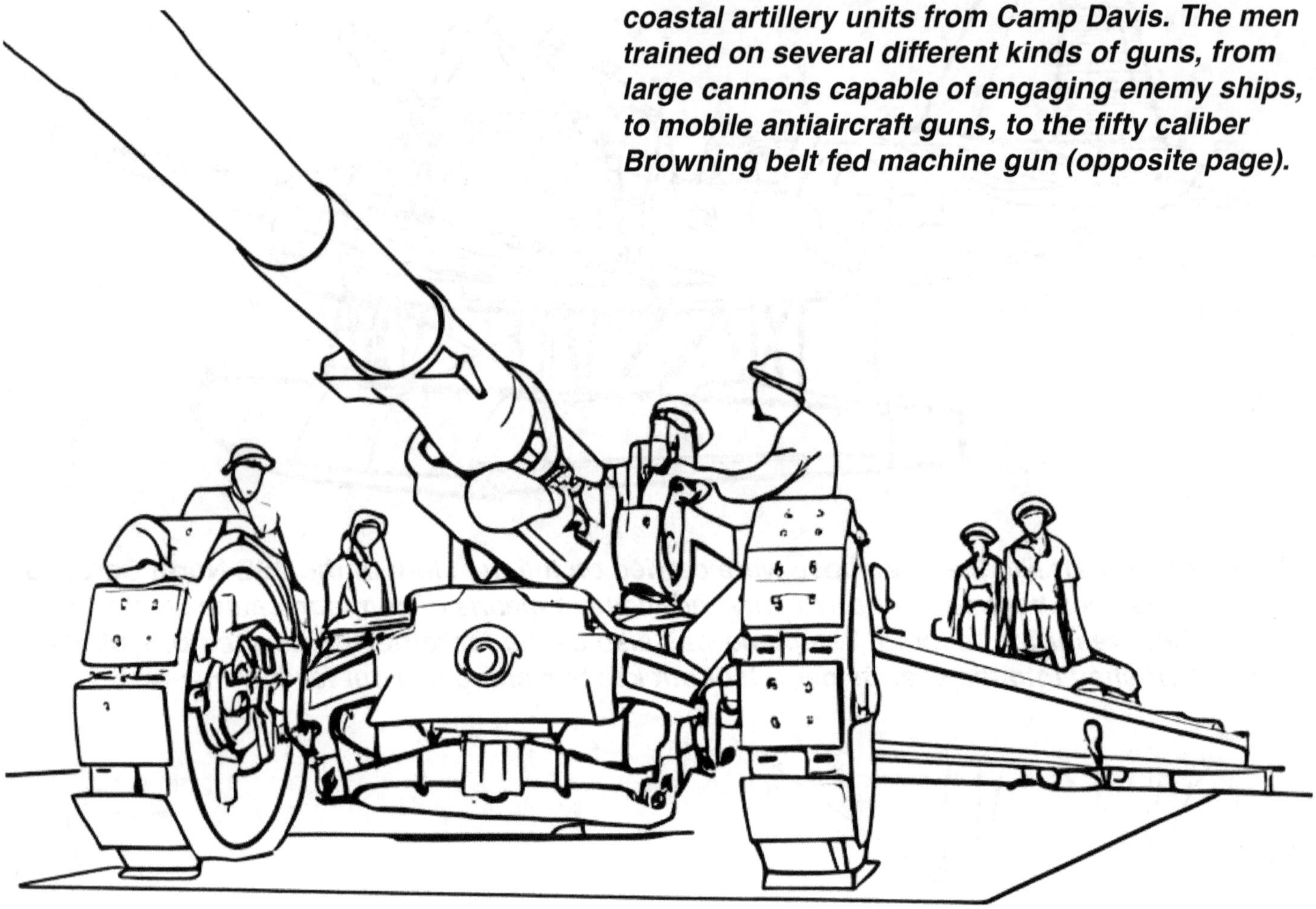

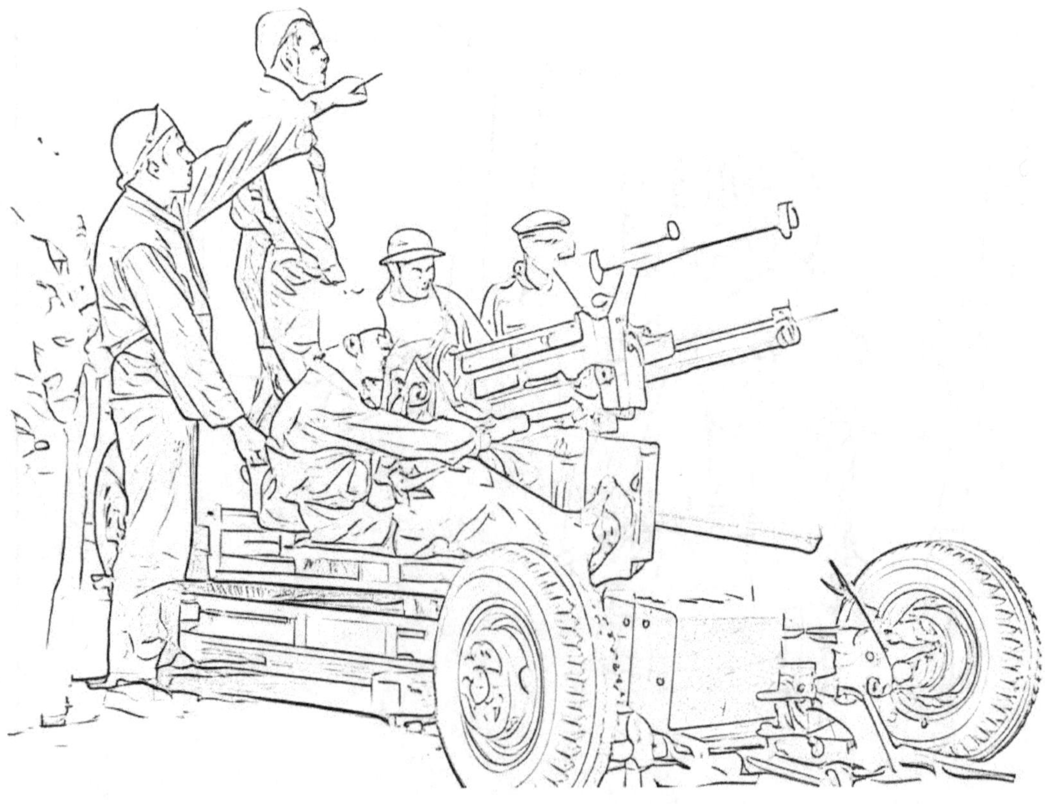

Soldiers training on the guns would practice by shooting at targets towed by Women Airforce Service Pilots, or WASPs.

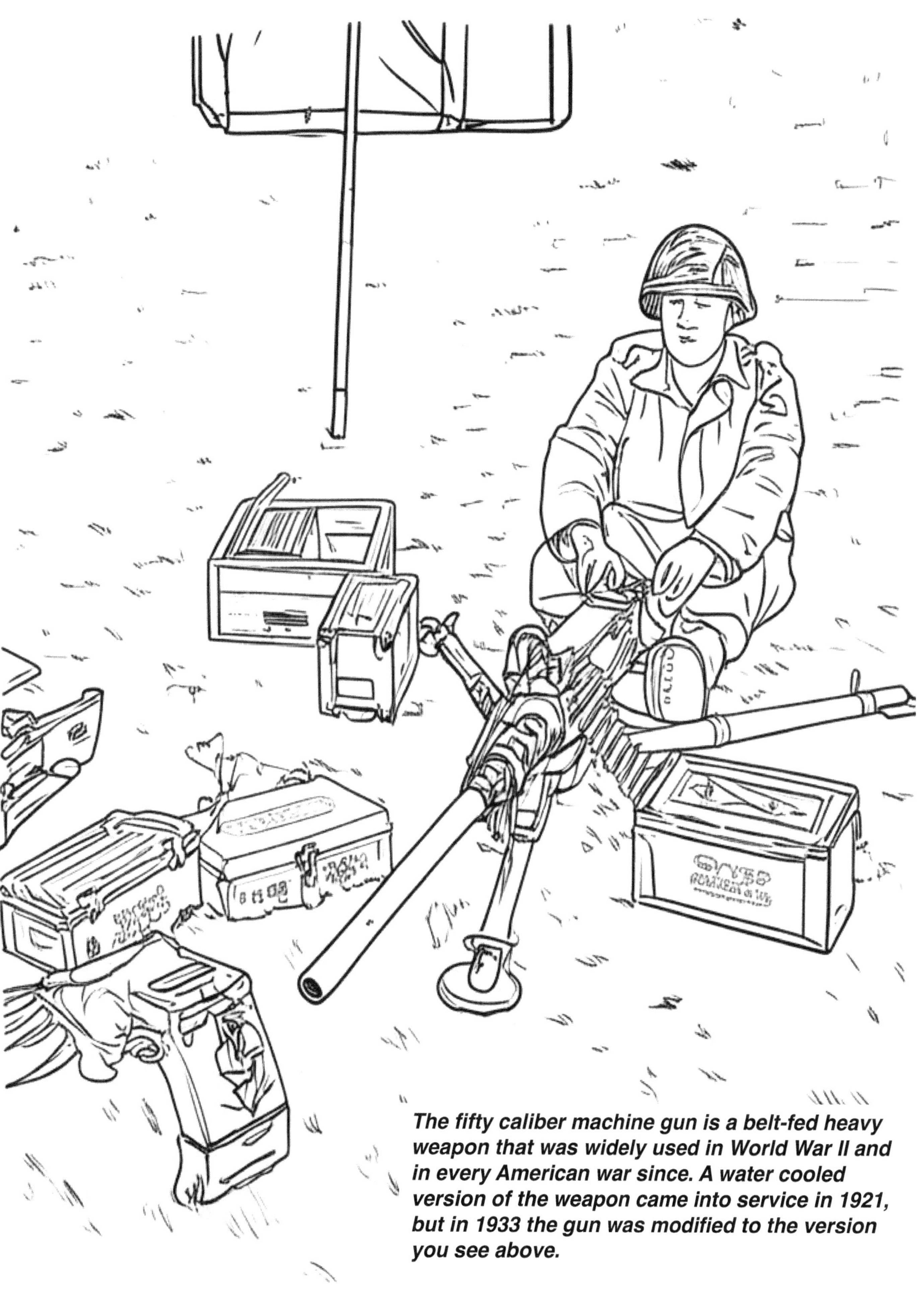

The fifty caliber machine gun is a belt-fed heavy weapon that was widely used in World War II and in every American war since. A water cooled version of the weapon came into service in 1921, but in 1933 the gun was modified to the version you see above.

Members of the Womens Army Corps (WACs) filled many duties that freed men up for combat, including acting as drivers (right) and doing administrative tasks. But women also served as pilots (below) ferrying aircraft from place to place, and towing targets for gunnery practice.

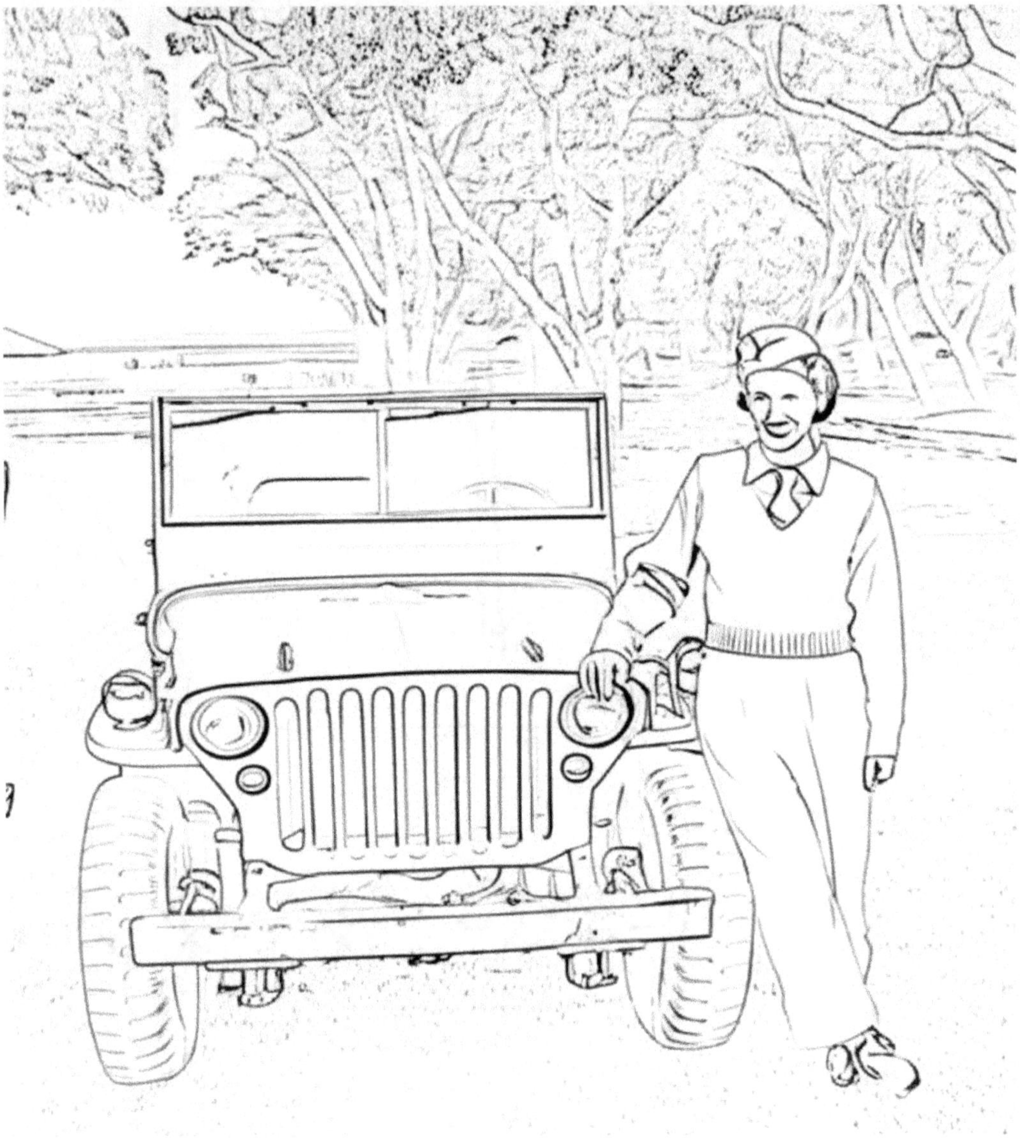

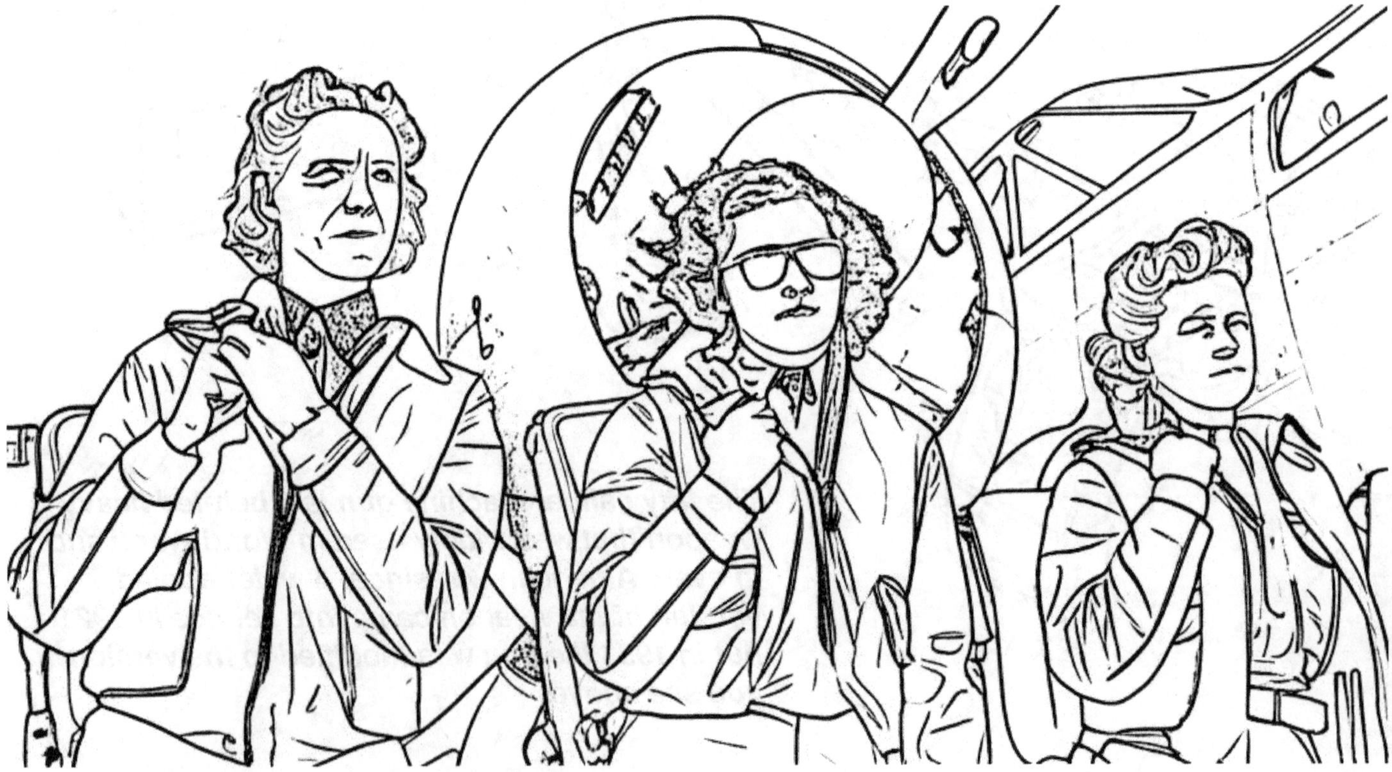

Men of Valor

Wilmington had two sons who earned the nation's highest award for valor in World War II. Charles P. Murray, Jr. (top right) earned his as a 1st Lieutenant in France, when he single handedly engaged Germans who were firing on a company of Americans from a hidden position. Murray threw grenades until he ran out, then crawled back to his platoon's position to retreive a machine gun and more grenades. Moving back to his position, Murray engaged the Germans again, killing 20 and wounding many more.

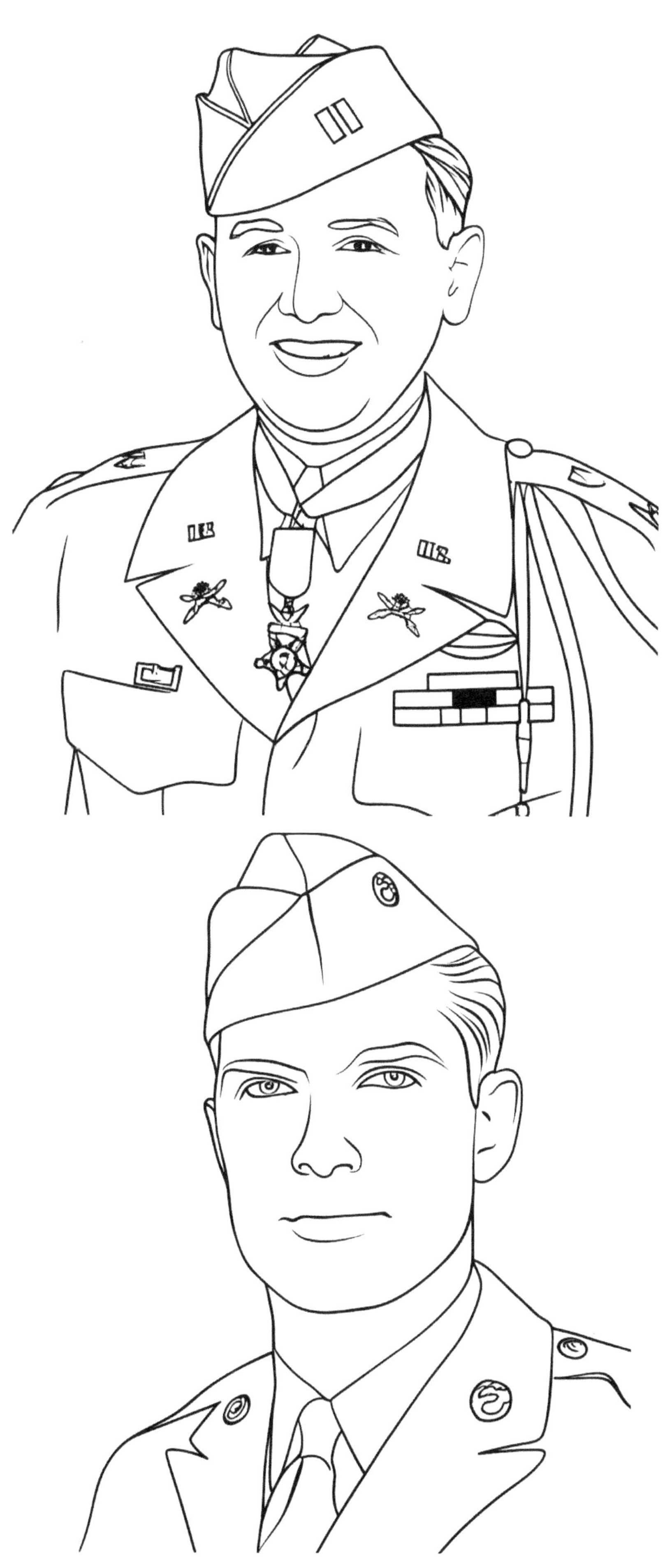

Navy Corpsman William "Billy" Halyburton (bottom right) earned his Medal of Honor on a battlefield half a world away from where Murray earned his. During the Battle of Okinawa, Halyburton landed with U.S. Marines. As Marines tried to cross a draw they called "Death Valley" because so many men had been wounded or killed trying to get across it, Halyburton saw men from his unit falling to enemy fire. The corpsman raced to the farthest wounded Marine and began giving aid. Machine gun, rifle, and sniper fire peppered the ground all around him. When the wounded Marine was hit again, Halyburton shielded him with his own body. The corpsman was hit too, but still tried to save the wounded Marine until Halyburton collapsed and died.

Fun Times Away From Post and Base

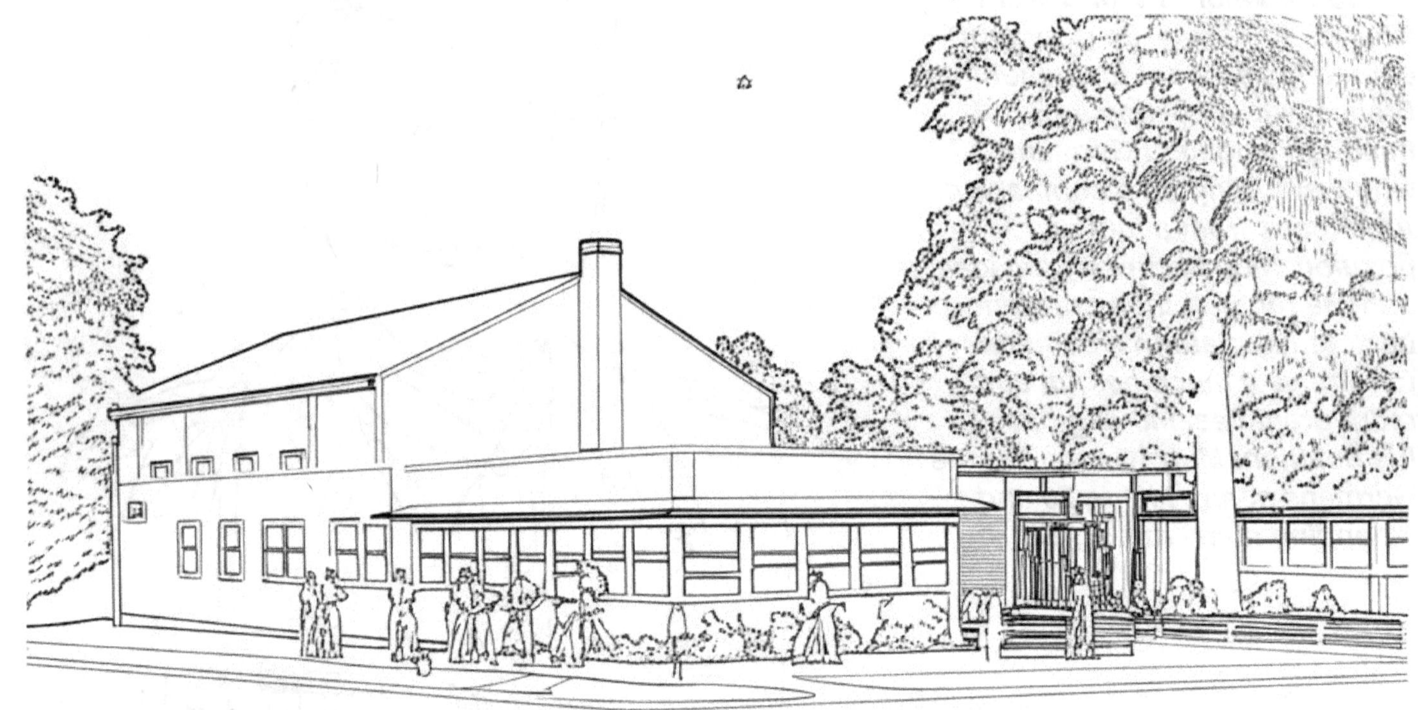

After a long week of field training, service members looking to blow off some steam and relax turned to the Wilmington USO Club (above). Inside, local women danced with soldiers and provided a much needed respite from the rigors of training for combat (below).

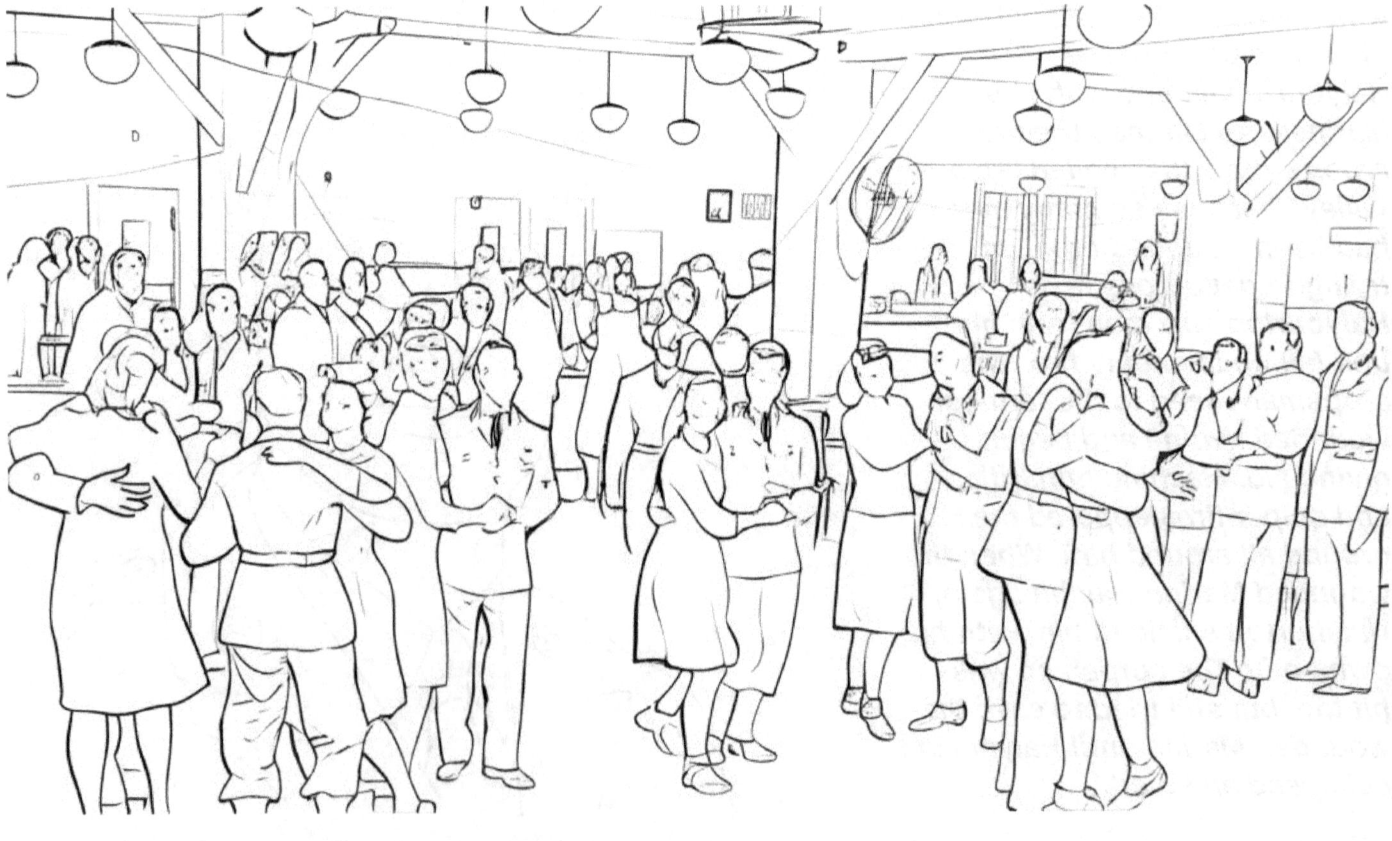

SPORTS ICONS

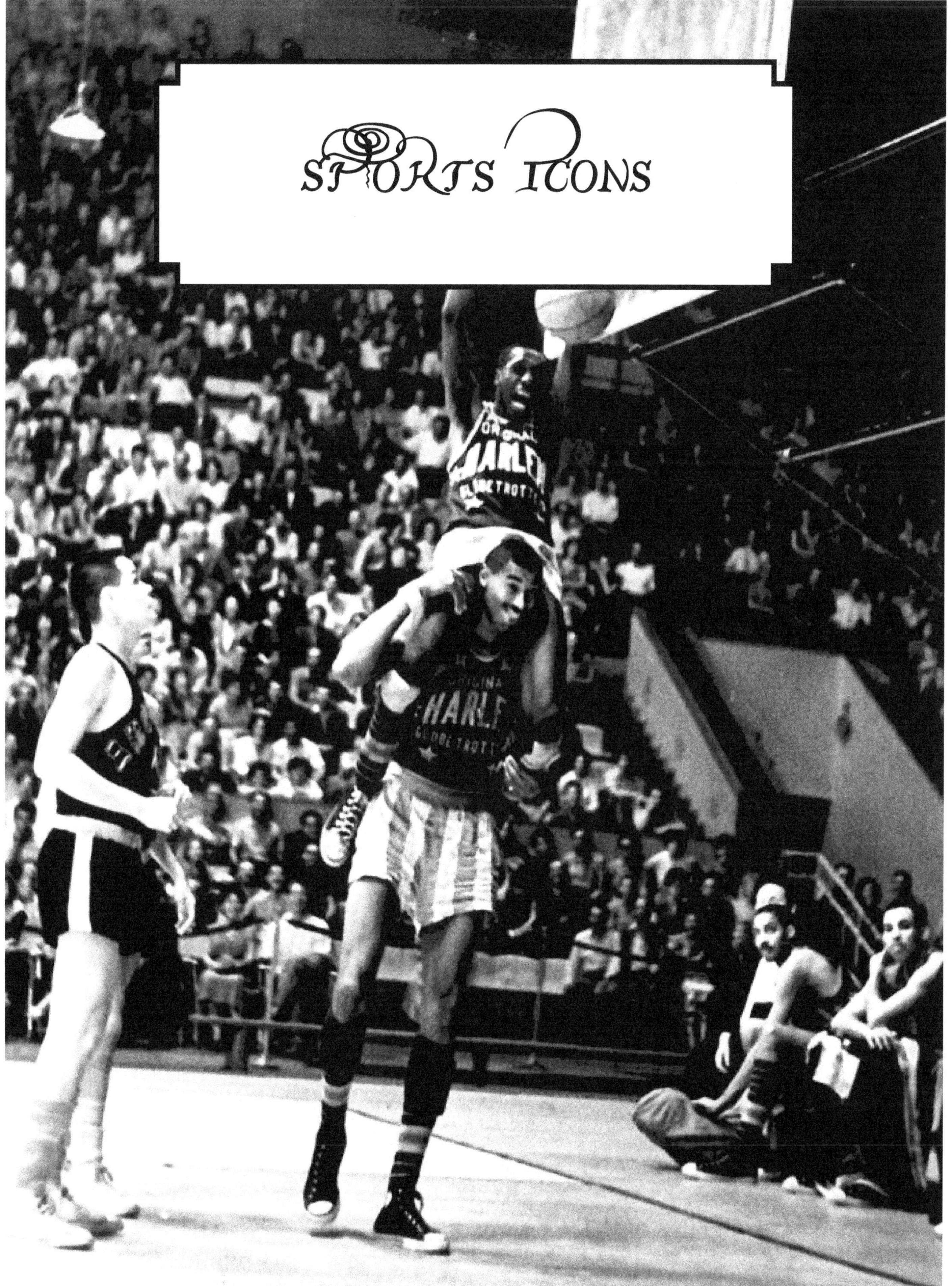

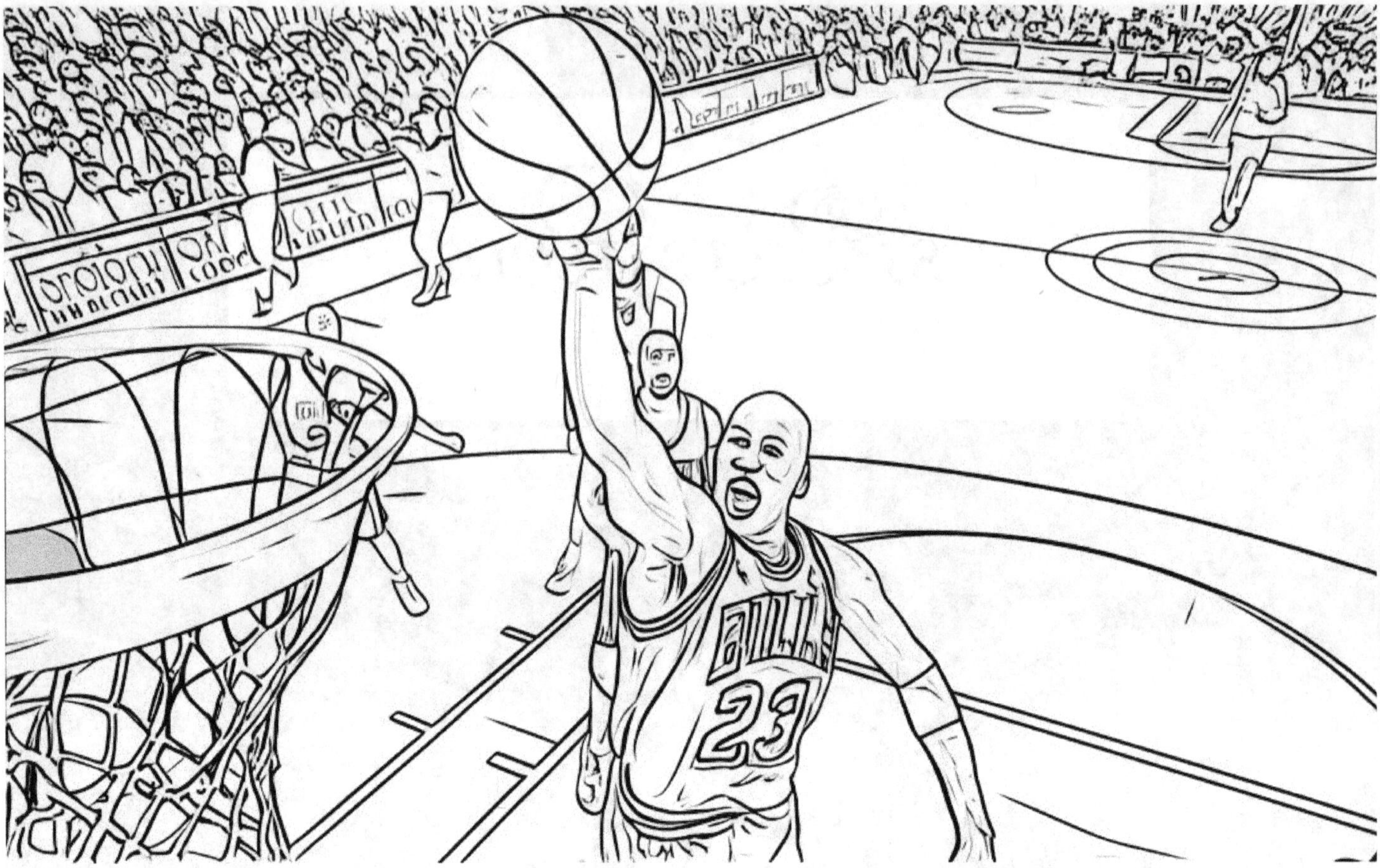

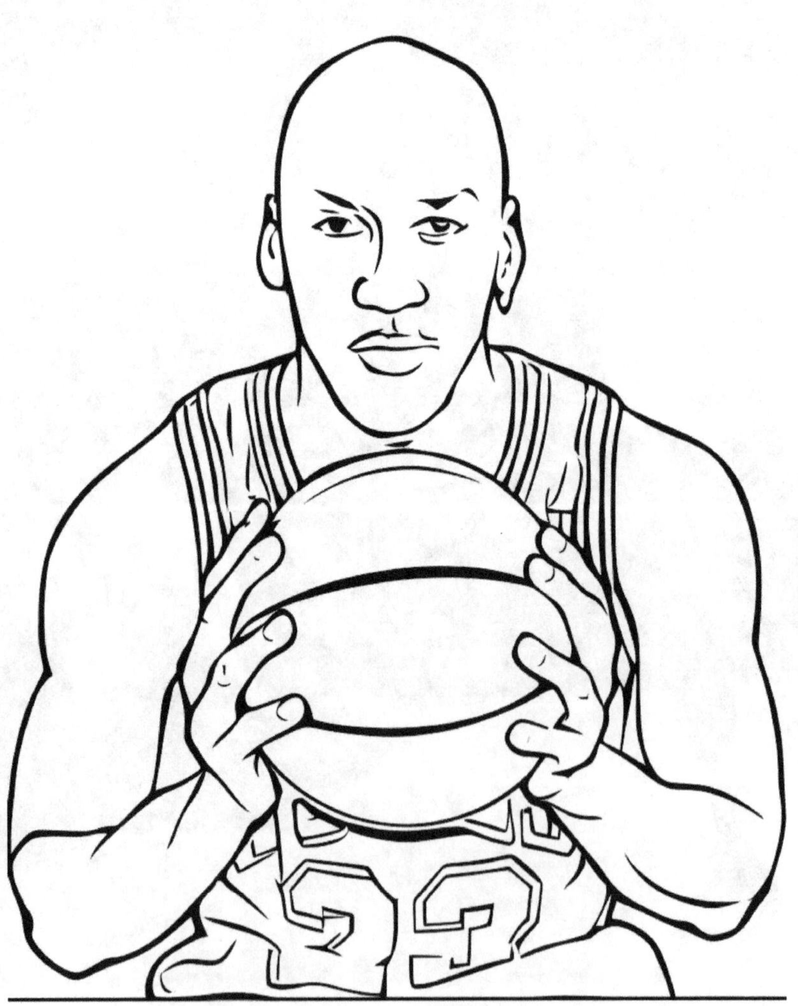

Wilmington's Michael Jordan is considered by most basketball fans as the best who ever played the game, though Jordan himself often points to greats like Oscar Robertson and Wilt Chamberlain as contenders too. But the facts speak for themselves. After taking to the court at E.A. Laney High School, then under the coaching of the great Dean Smith at the University of North Carolina, Jordan was drafted by the Chicago Bulls of the NBA. From there, he revolutionized the game, winning six championship rings and setting the bar for every other player who came after him.

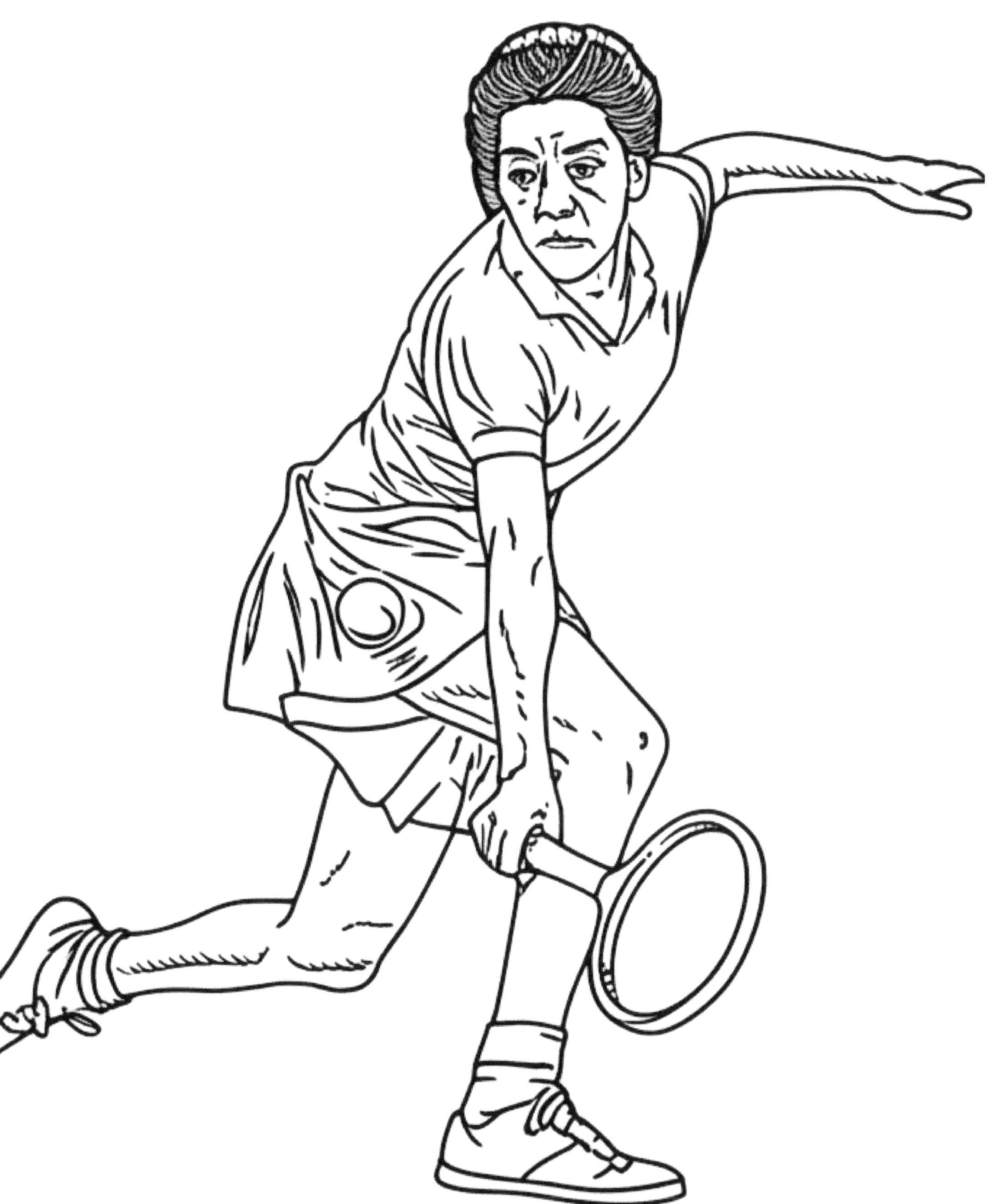

Althea Gibson lived with Wilmington's Dr. Hubert Eaton, who nourished her interest in tennis and helped her cross the color line in athletics. In 1956, Gibson was the first person of color to win a tennis Grand Slam event at the French Open. Before her career was over, she would win eleven Grand Slam titles: five singles titles, five doubles titles, and one mixed doubles title.

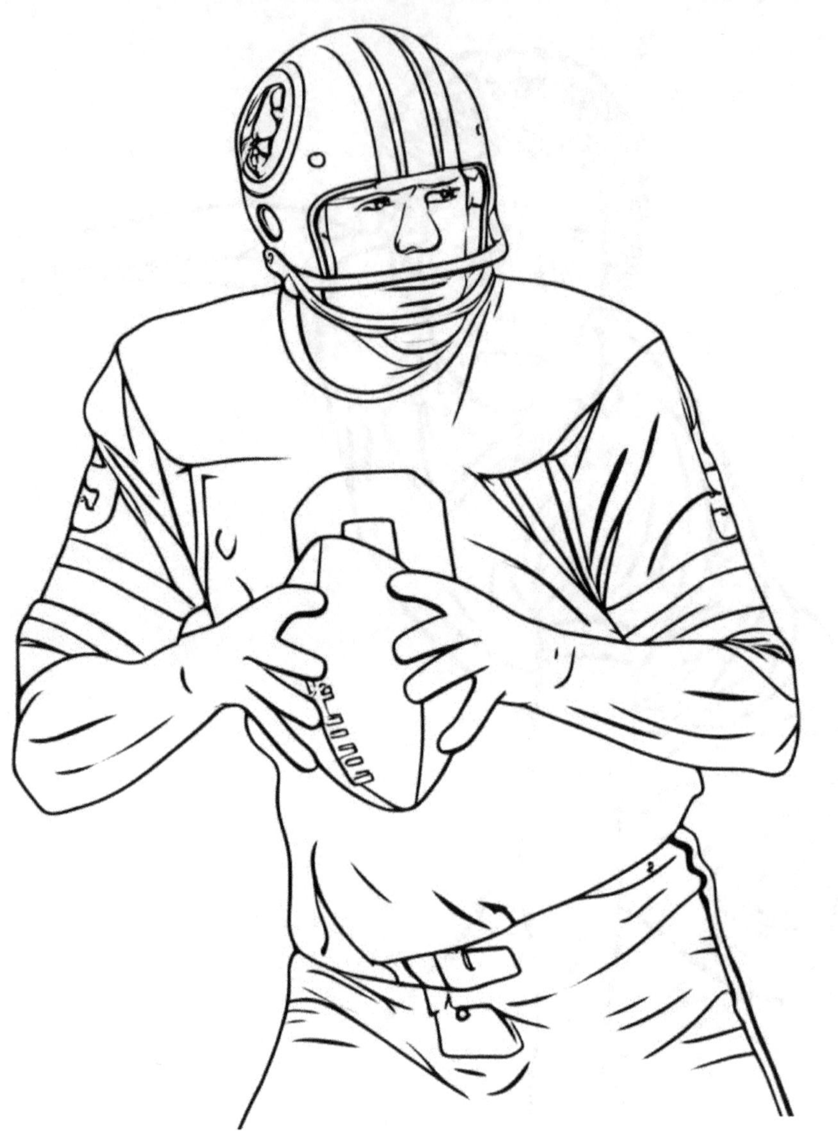

Sonny Jurgensen (left) was a graduate of New Hanover High School who went on to play quarterback at Duke University before playing in the National Football League with the Philadelphia Eagles and Washington Redskins. Jurgensen won a national title with the Eagles in 1960, the only time in his eighteen year career as a pro. He was inducted into the Pro Football Hall of Fame in 1983.

New Hanover High School's Roman Gabriel (right) played quarterback for North Carolina State University before being drafted by the Los Angeles Rams, where he played for eleven seasons. Gabriel then played five more seasons for the Phialdelphia Eagles before retiring. He was the first Filipino-American quarterback in the NFL, and the only Asian American to win the NFL Most Valuable Player Award as of 2025.

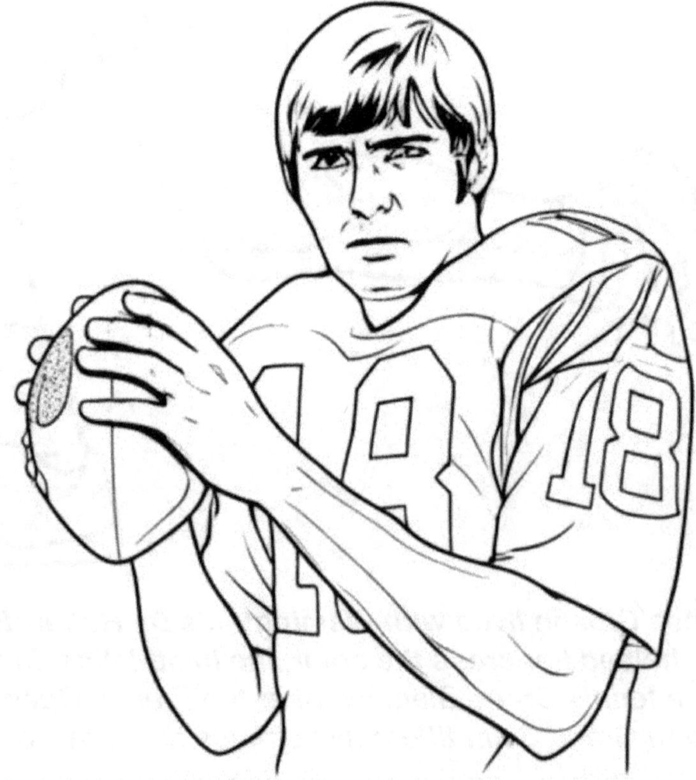

Clyde Simmons (right) was one of the most fearsome defensive ends to ever play the game. A product of Western Carolina University, the Wilmington native was a two-time NFL All Pro selection, and a two-time Pro Bowl selection with the Philadelphia Eagles. Simmons also played for the Cincinatti Bengals, Jacksoneville Jaguars, Arizona Cardinals, and Chicago Bears.

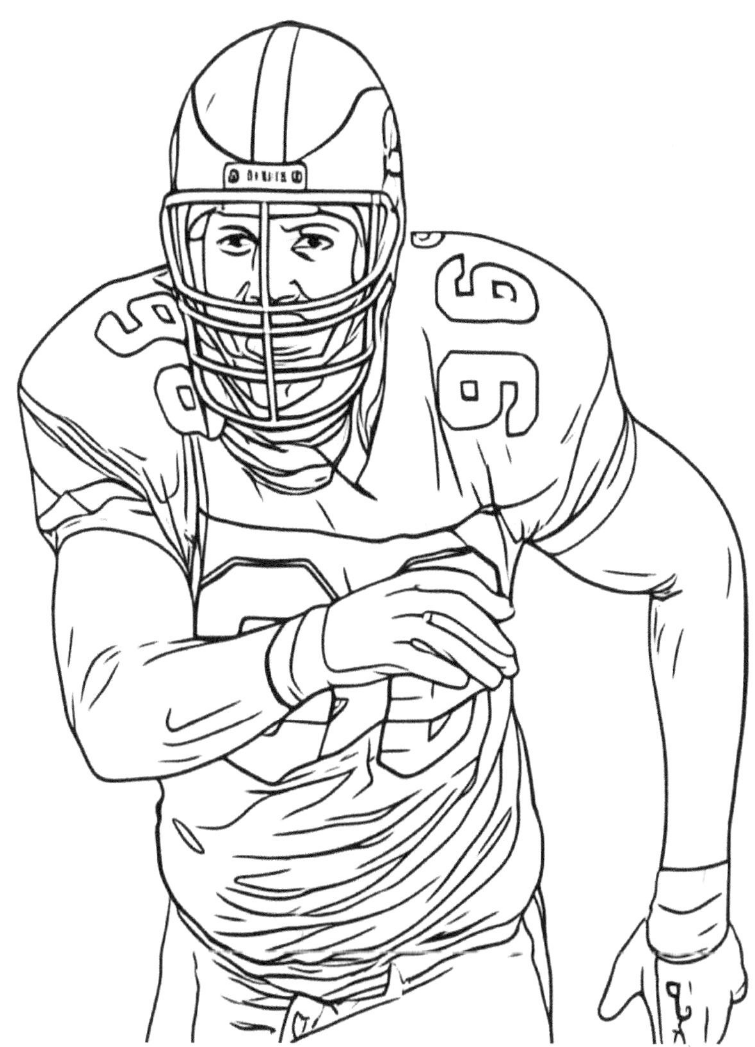

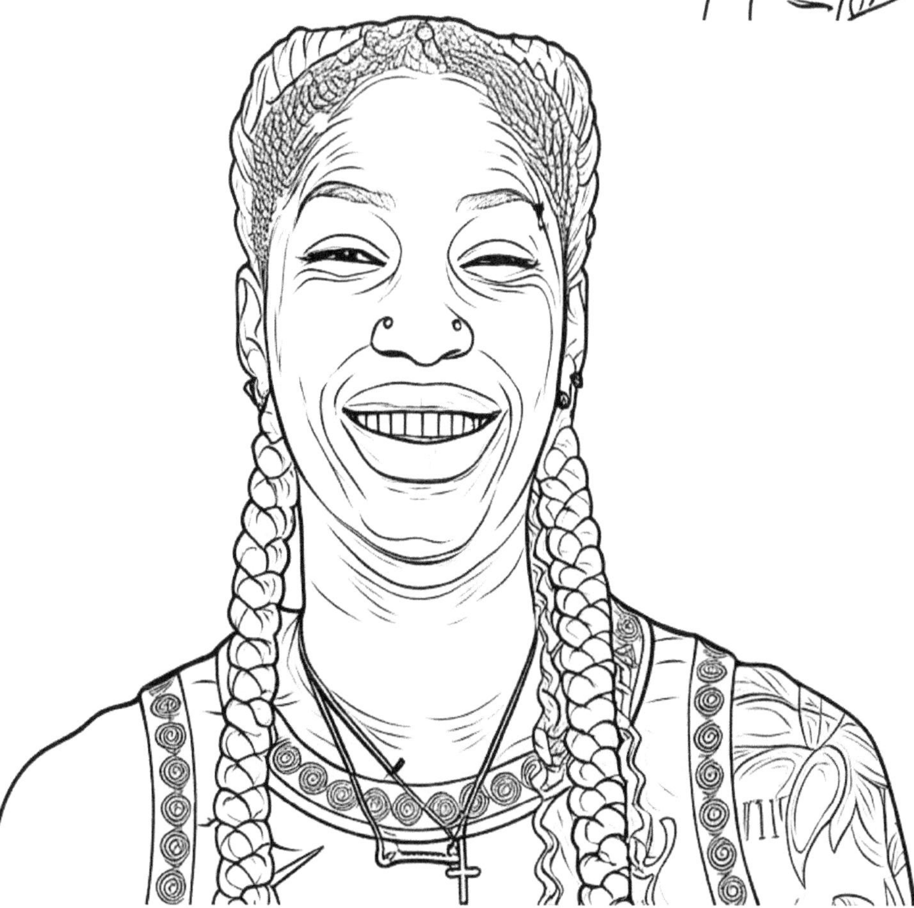

E.A. Laney and Ashley High School basket-ball's Saniya Rivers (left) played in college for the South Carolina Gamecocks when they won a national championshp, before transferring to North Carolina State University. In the 2025 WNBA draft, Rivers went to the Connecticut Sun, where she set rookie records in her first professional season.

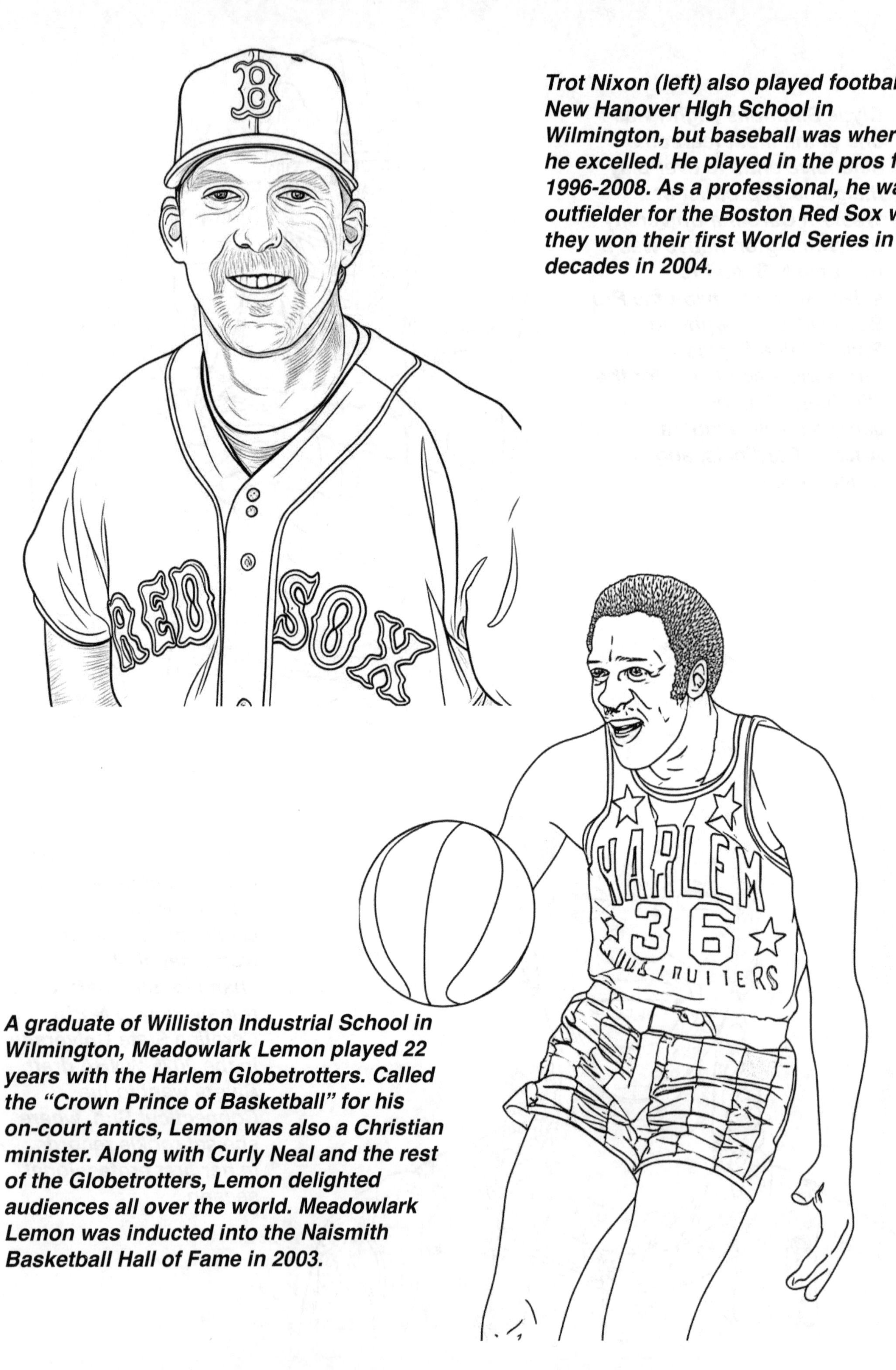

Trot Nixon (left) also played football at New Hanover HIgh School in Wilmington, but baseball was where he excelled. He played in the pros from 1996-2008. As a professional, he was an outfielder for the Boston Red Sox when they won their first World Series in decades in 2004.

A graduate of Williston Industrial School in Wilmington, Meadowlark Lemon played 22 years with the Harlem Globetrotters. Called the "Crown Prince of Basketball" for his on-court antics, Lemon was also a Christian minister. Along with Curly Neal and the rest of the Globetrotters, Lemon delighted audiences all over the world. Meadowlark Lemon was inducted into the Naismith Basketball Hall of Fame in 2003.

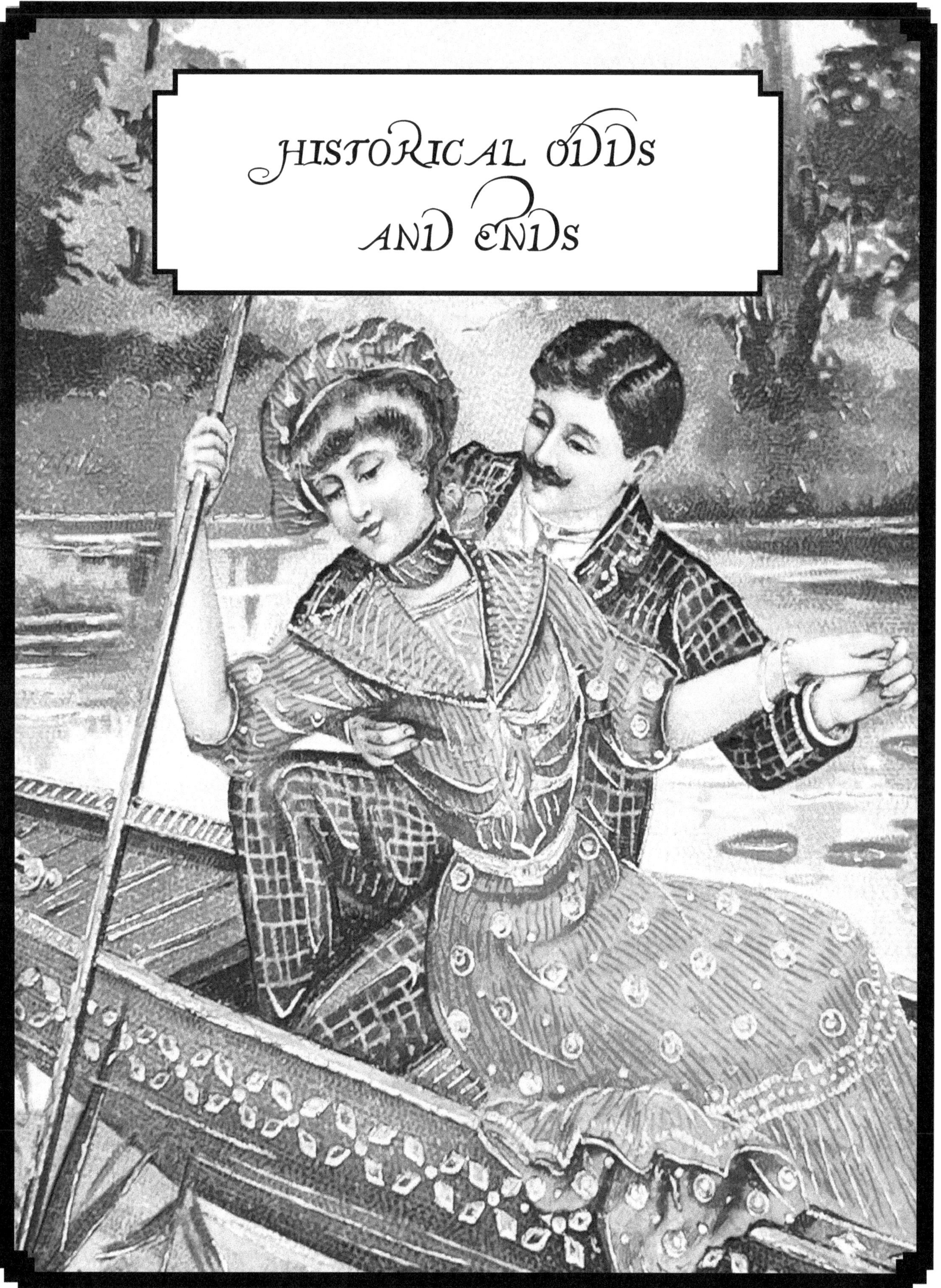
HISTORICAL ODDS
AND ENDS

Omar ibn-Said (right) was a African prince who was captured by an enemy tribe and sold into slavery in the United States in 1807. The Charleston, S.C. slave owner he was sold to was a cruel man, so Omar escaped and made his way north. Captured in Fayetteville, N.C., the county sheriff jailed him to await reclamation by his owner. The jailer noticed Omar using coal to write on the walls of his cell, and told James Owen, brother of N.C. governor John Owen, about him. James Owen bought Omar for himself and took him to his home in Bladen County, where he made him a house servant. Omar converted to Christianity, and attended services at First Presbyterian Church in Wilmington when James Owen was in town.

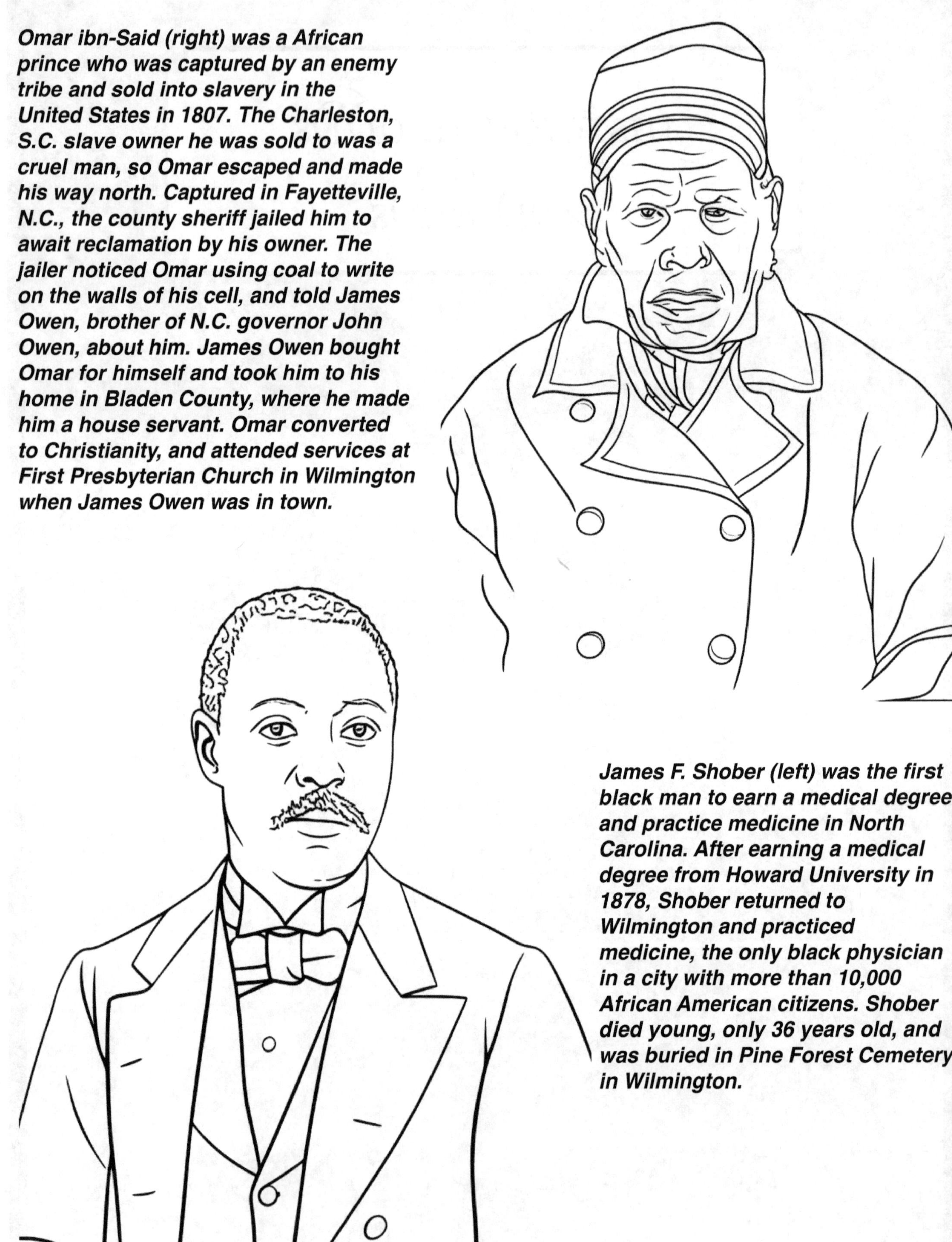

James F. Shober (left) was the first black man to earn a medical degree and practice medicine in North Carolina. After earning a medical degree from Howard University in 1878, Shober returned to Wilmington and practiced medicine, the only black physician in a city with more than 10,000 African American citizens. Shober died young, only 36 years old, and was buried in Pine Forest Cemetery in Wilmington.

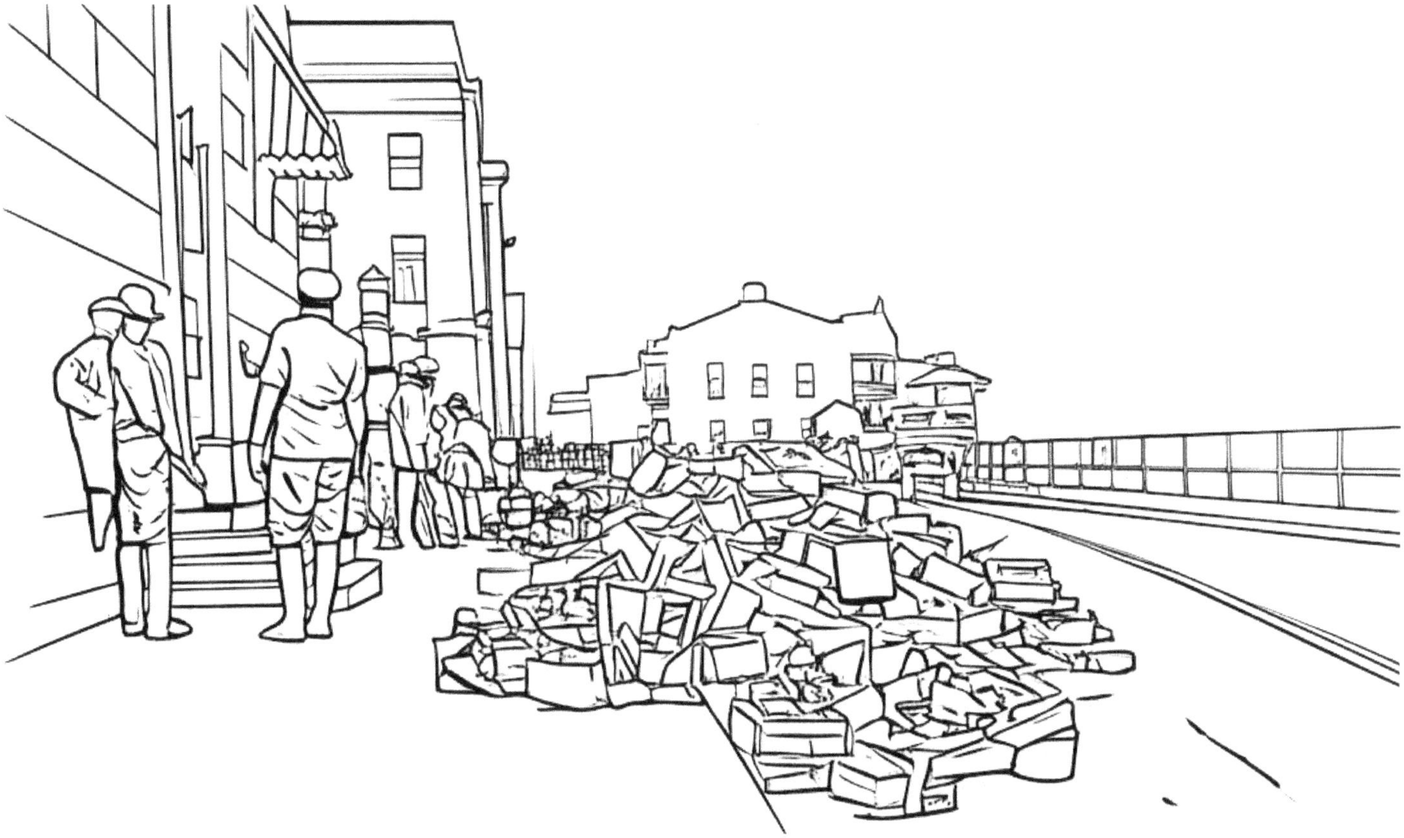

During Prohibition, revenue agents made public spectacles of their seizures of illegal alcohol. In the image above, crates and barrels of illicit liquor were smashed on Water Street in front of the Customs House, left to drain away into the sewers. The seizures did not stop the production of illegal alcohol, though.

Woodrow Wilson (right) lived in Wilmington from 1874-1882, when his father was the minister at First Presbyterian Church, on Third Street in the city. Known as "Tommy" in those days, the future President of the United States attended some classes at Tileston school, and was even tutored by the school's headmistress, Amy Bradley. But most of his early education was on his own. Woodrow Wilson is said to have been the first person to ride a two-wheel bicycle in Wilmington.

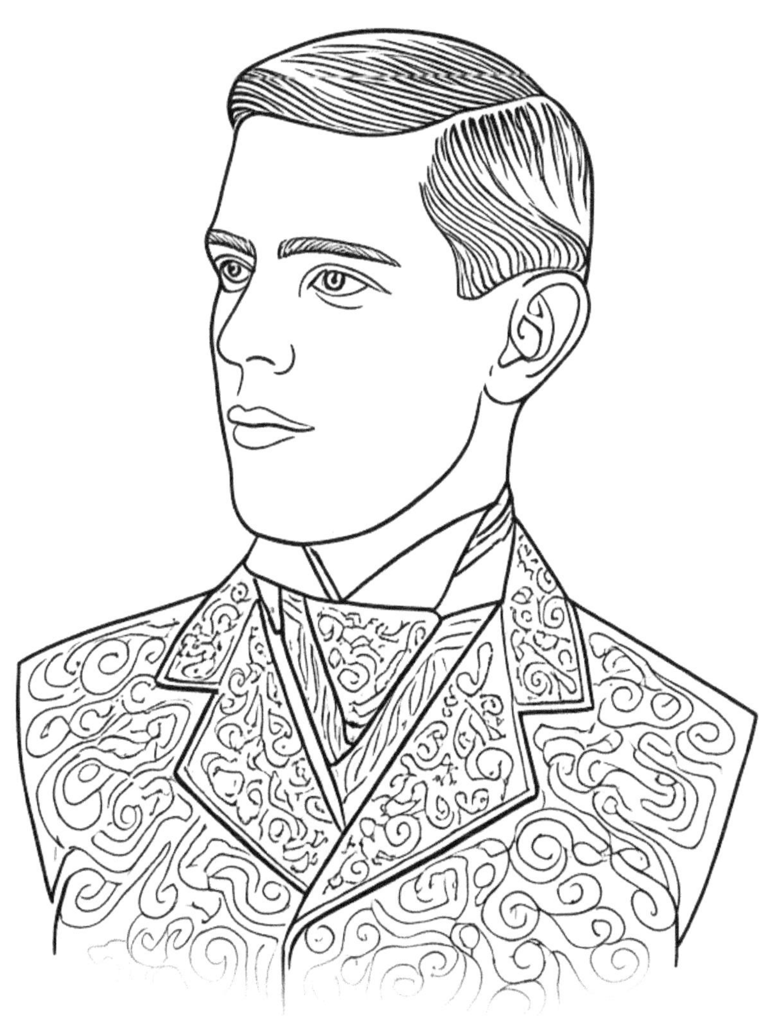

Anna McNeill Whistler (below) was the mother of artist James McNeill Whistler (bottom right), whose famous painting of her (right) has achieved iconic status. The daughter of a Wilmington physician, Anna decided to reside in England when the Civil War broke out and her husband entered Confederate service as a doctor. Anna and her son, James, ran the Union blockade off Wilmington aboard the Ad-Vance *blockade runner. She died while in England and is buried there.*

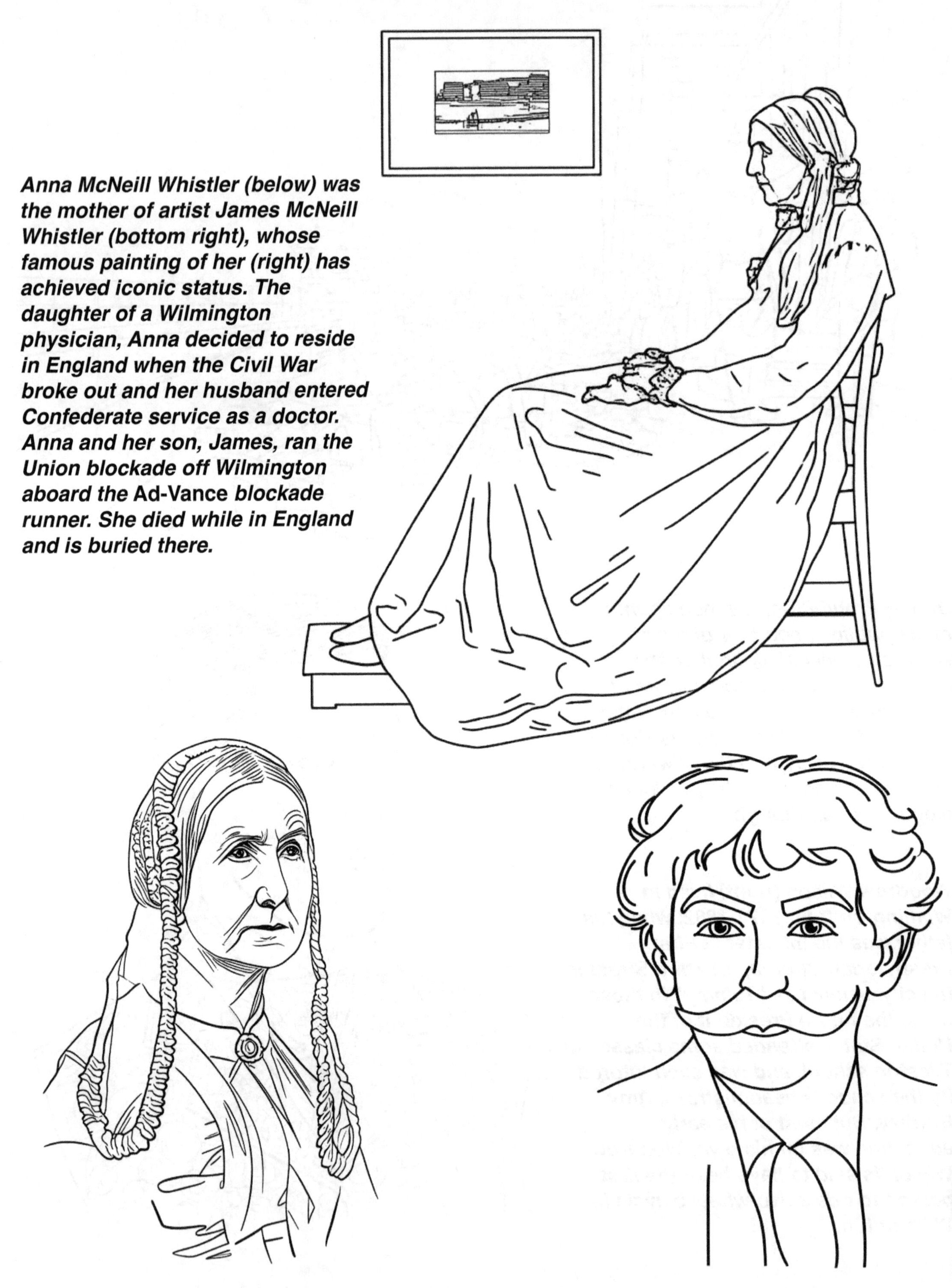

Firemen of 1899

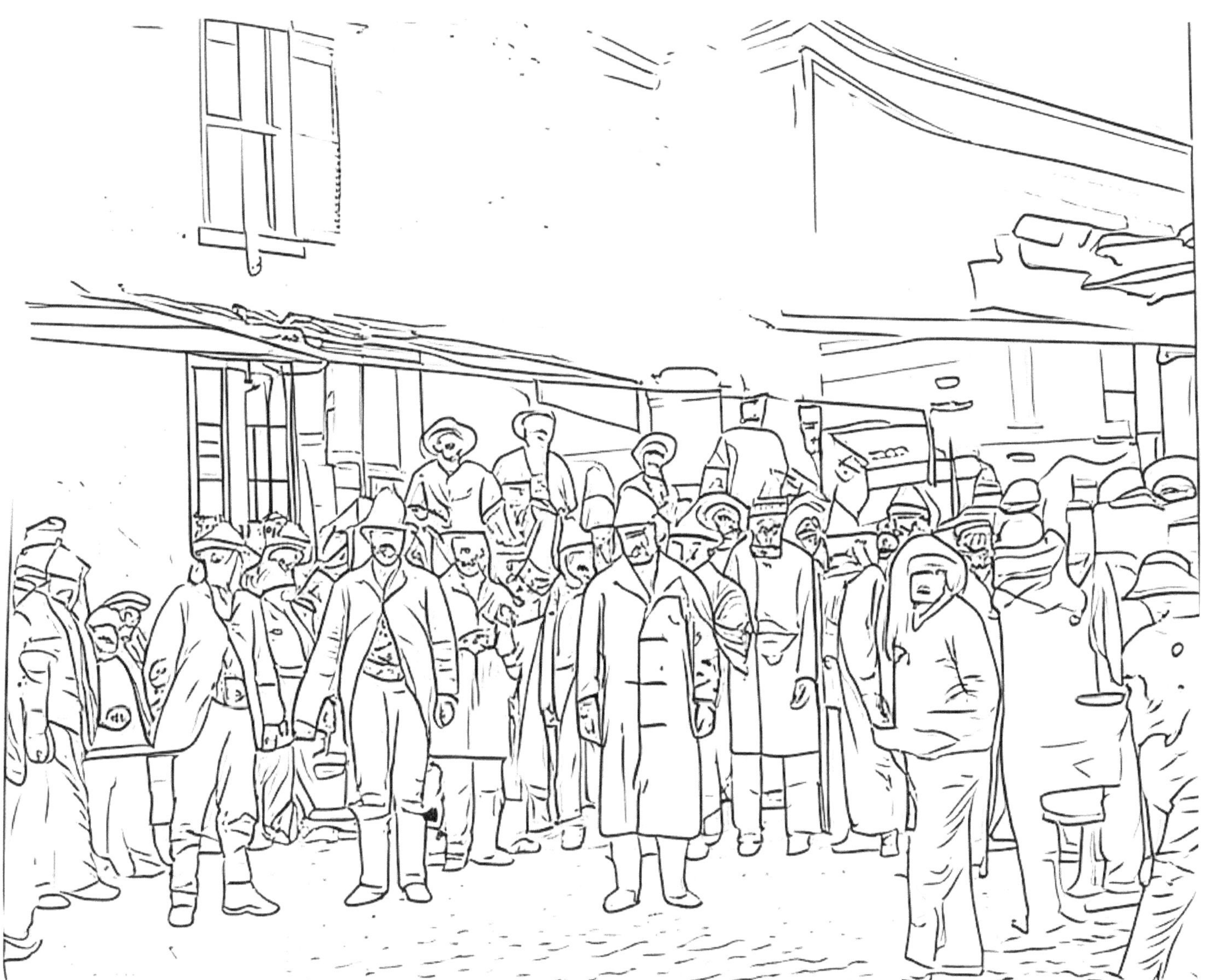

Over the centuries, the City of Wilmington has burned down at least three times. First Presbyterian Church once sat on the riverfront, but after burning down several times, it was moved a few blocks away from the dangerous cinders floating up from steamers tied up at the wharves. The image above shows firemen after a massive fire in 1899 that threatened to torch the city yet again.

The Colonel's Lady

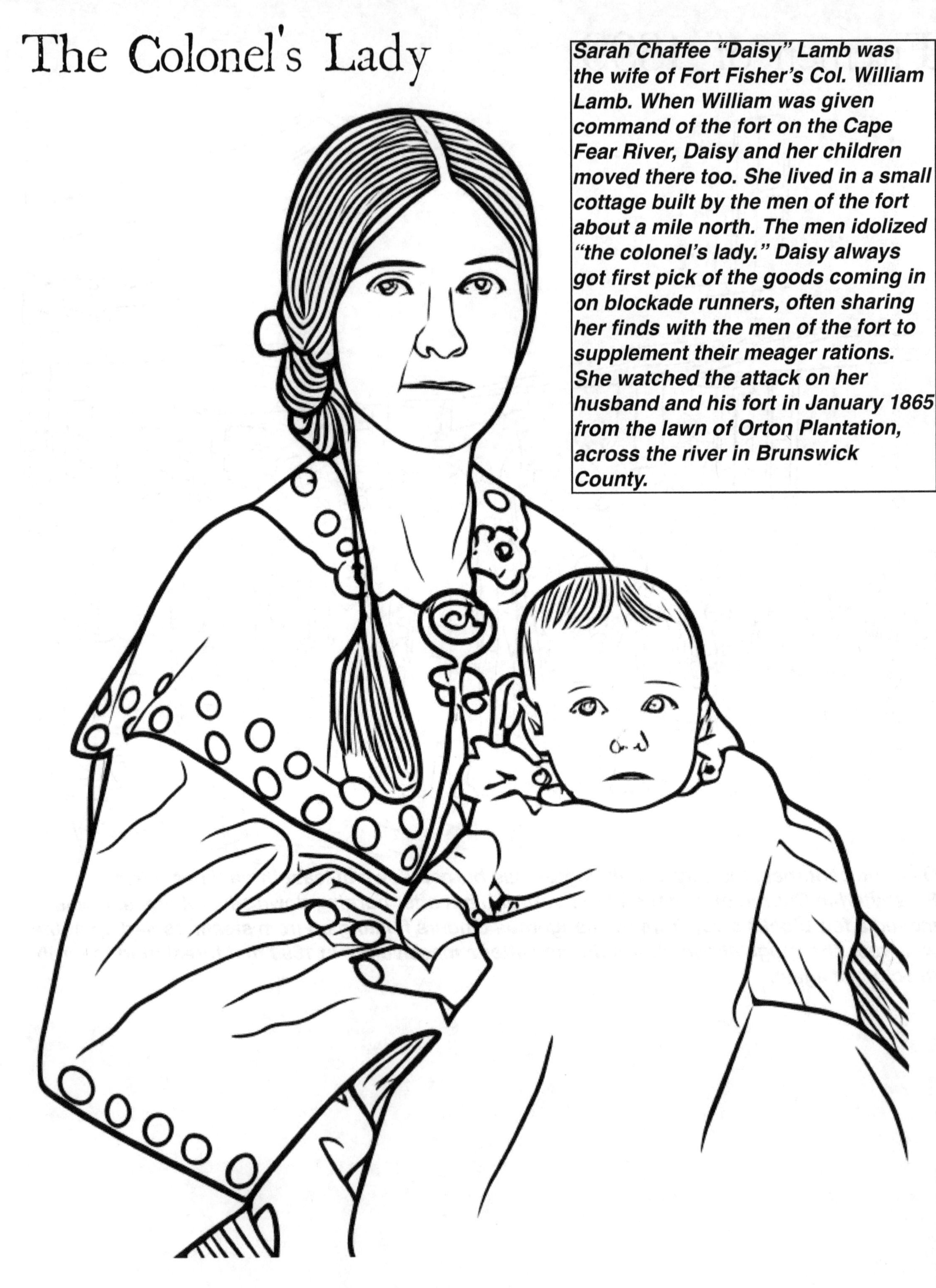

Sarah Chaffee "Daisy" Lamb was the wife of Fort Fisher's Col. William Lamb. When William was given command of the fort on the Cape Fear River, Daisy and her children moved there too. She lived in a small cottage built by the men of the fort about a mile north. The men idolized "the colonel's lady." Daisy always got first pick of the goods coming in on blockade runners, often sharing her finds with the men of the fort to supplement their meager rations. She watched the attack on her husband and his fort in January 1865 from the lawn of Orton Plantation, across the river in Brunswick County.

The Mothball Fleet

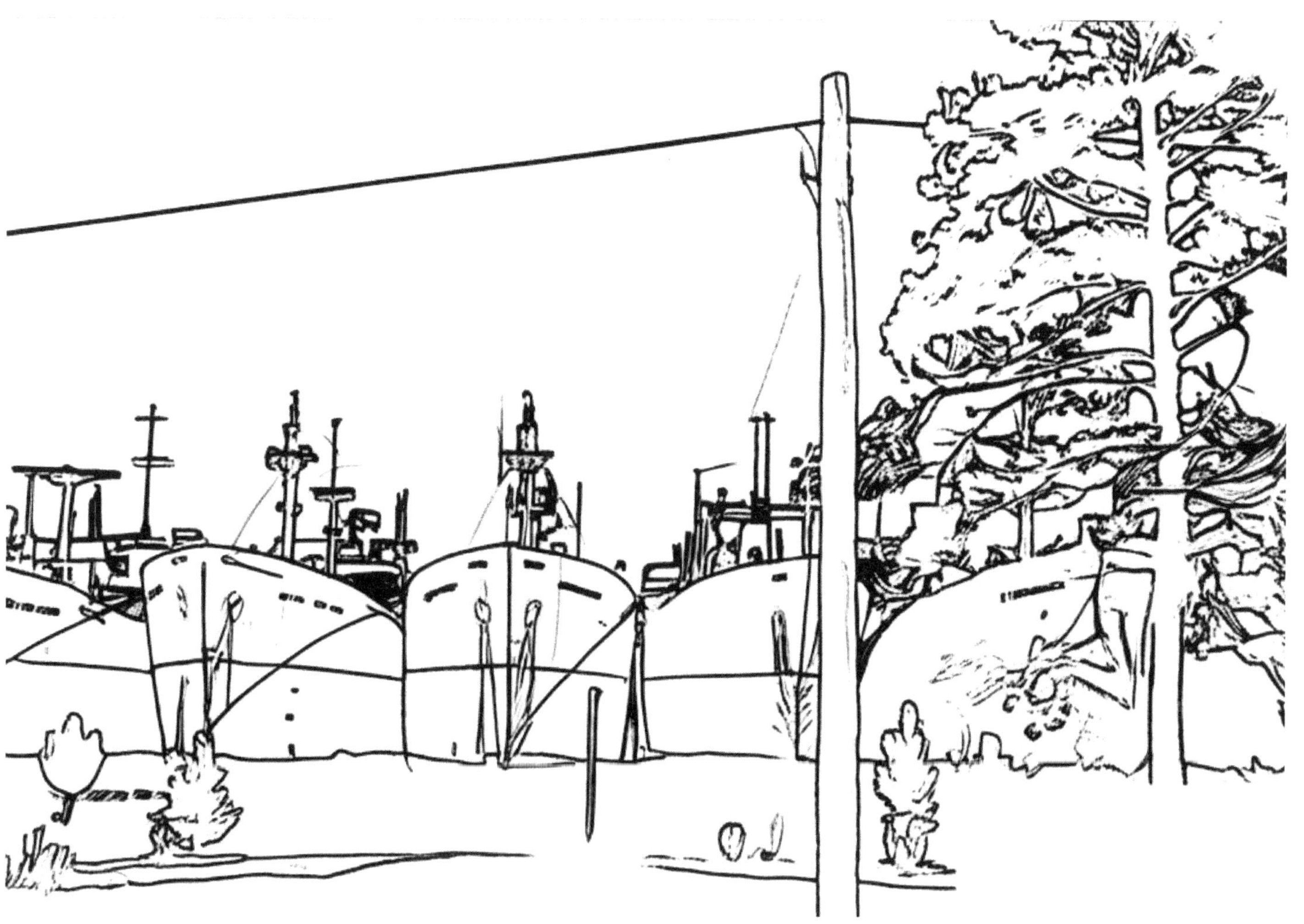

When World War II ended, the need for the hundreds of Liberty ships produced in yards like the one in Wilmington ended. Those surplus ships were decommissioned and put into mothballs, and kept in reserve at berths on the Brunswick River in case they should be needed again. As late as the 1960s, hundreds of the ships were visible to motorists crossing the Highway 17 bridge across the river at Eagles Island. Eventually, the ships were stripped of anything useful and towed out to sea. The ships were then scuttled to make artificial reefs. The image above shows some of those ships tied off along the riverfront on Eagles Island.

Sinking of the S.S. John D. Gill

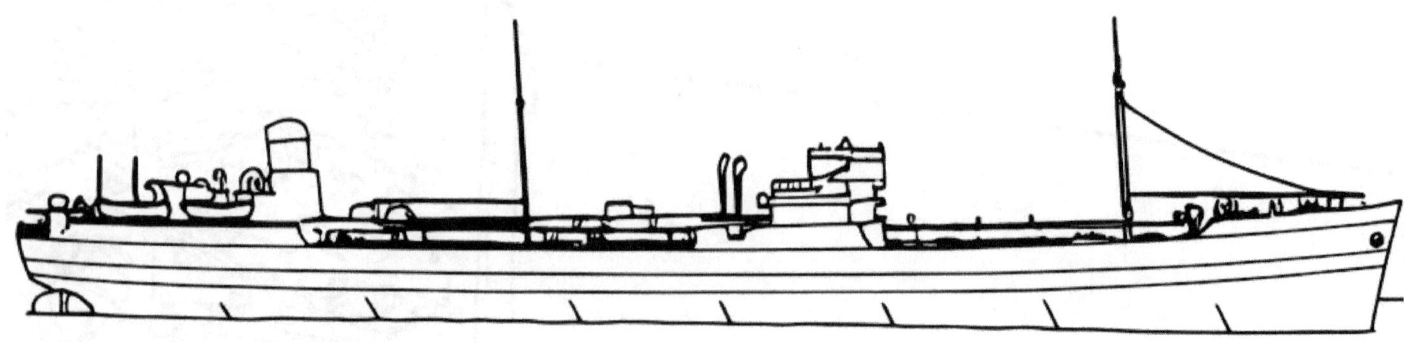

Three months after the bombing of Pearl Harbor, the American Oil tanker SS John D. Gill *(above) was torpedoed off Cape Fear in March 1942. Hit amidships, the tanker's load of 142,000 tons of fuel oil spilled into the Atlantic. A spark from the damaged ship set the oil soaked seas ablaze. People at the waterfront in Southport could see the blaze twenty-five miles away.*

The ship was torpedoed by the German submarine U-158 *(below). Only one lifeboat and one life raft escaped. Another tanker rescued the badly burned survivors and took them to Charleston. The U.S. Coast Guard rescued another 11 survivors and 16 casualties the next morning and took them to Southport, where they were treated at Dosher Hospital.*

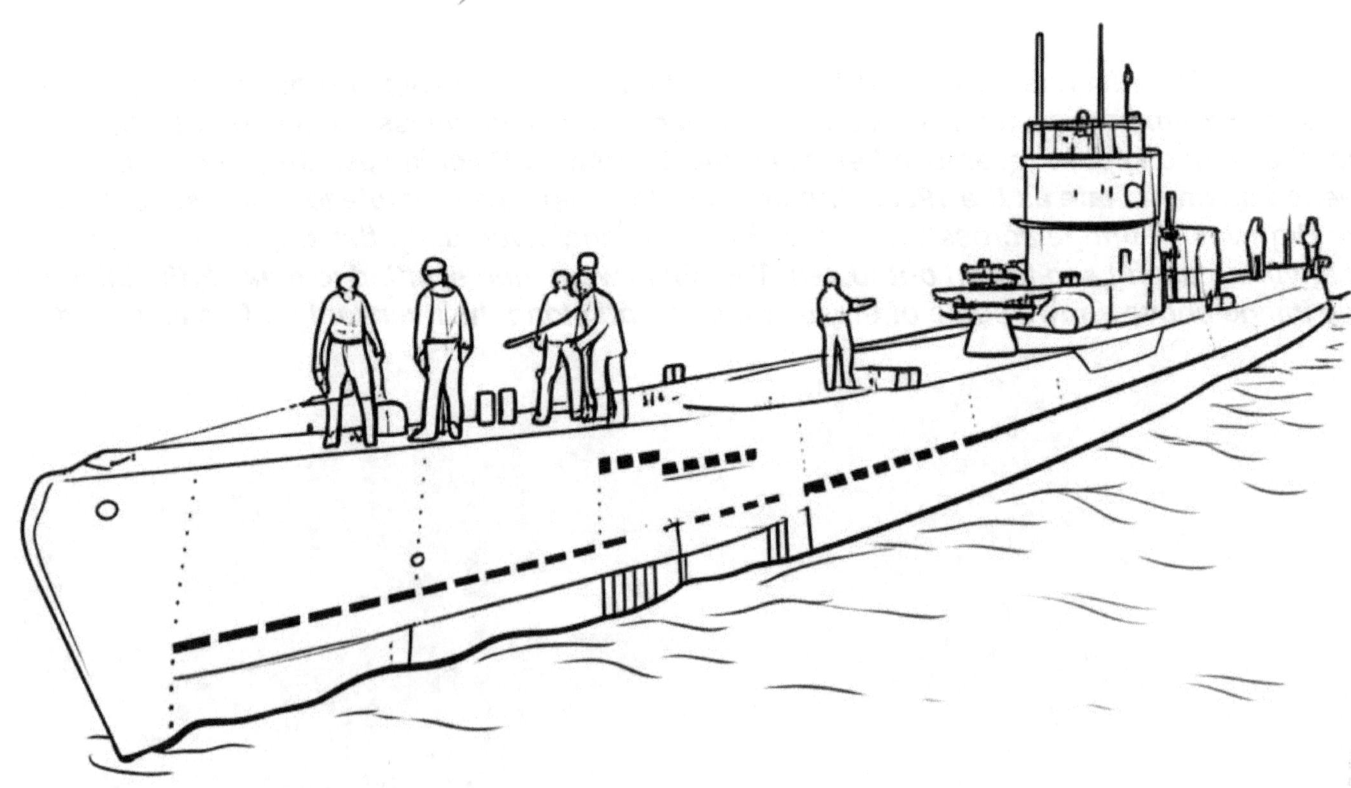

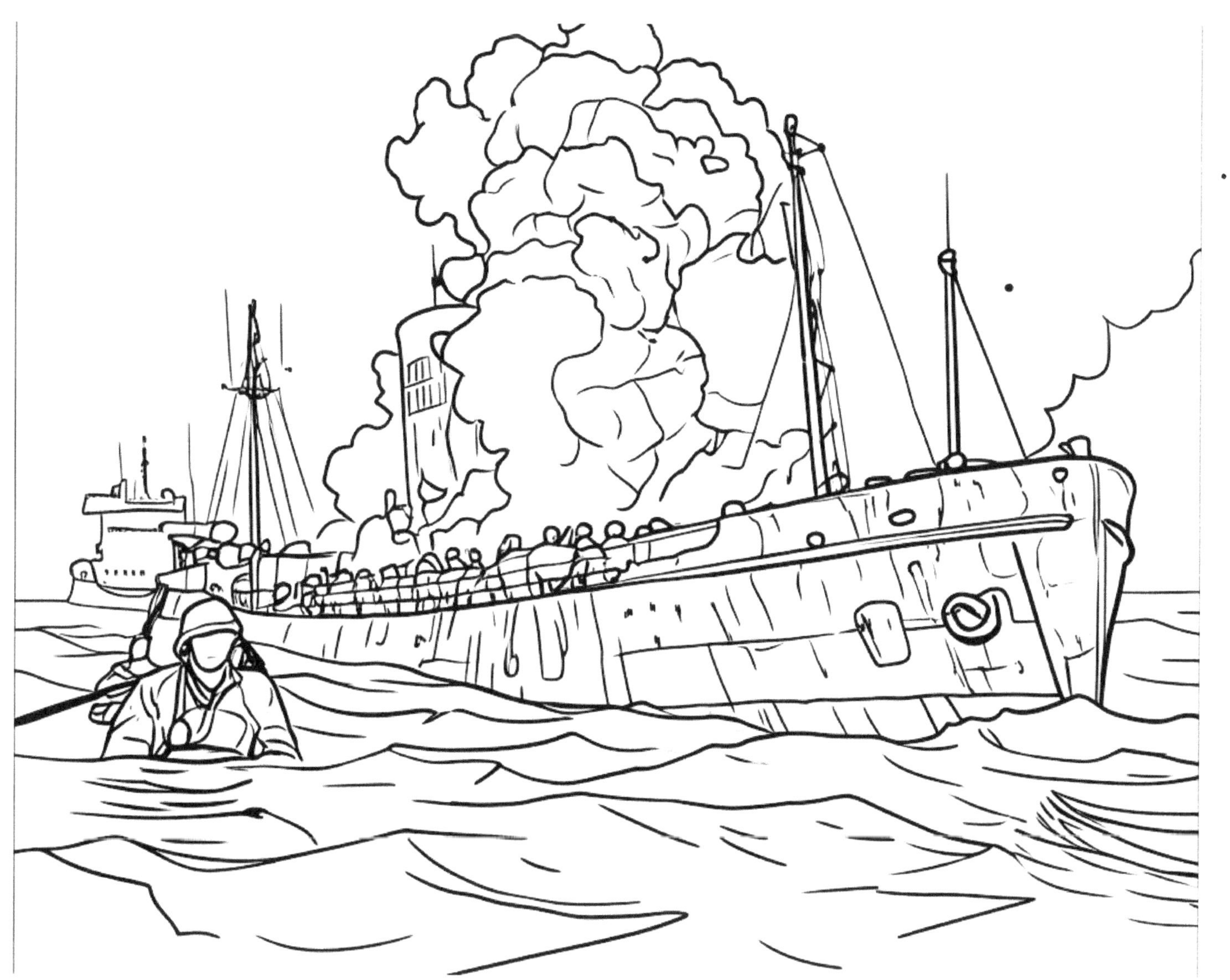

As the tanker John D. Gill *sank lower in the water, men threw themselves overboard to escape the torpedoed vessel. The ship and the water around it, thick with oil from the ship's ruptured holds, burst into flames. It was a horrible night for the crew of the* Gill.

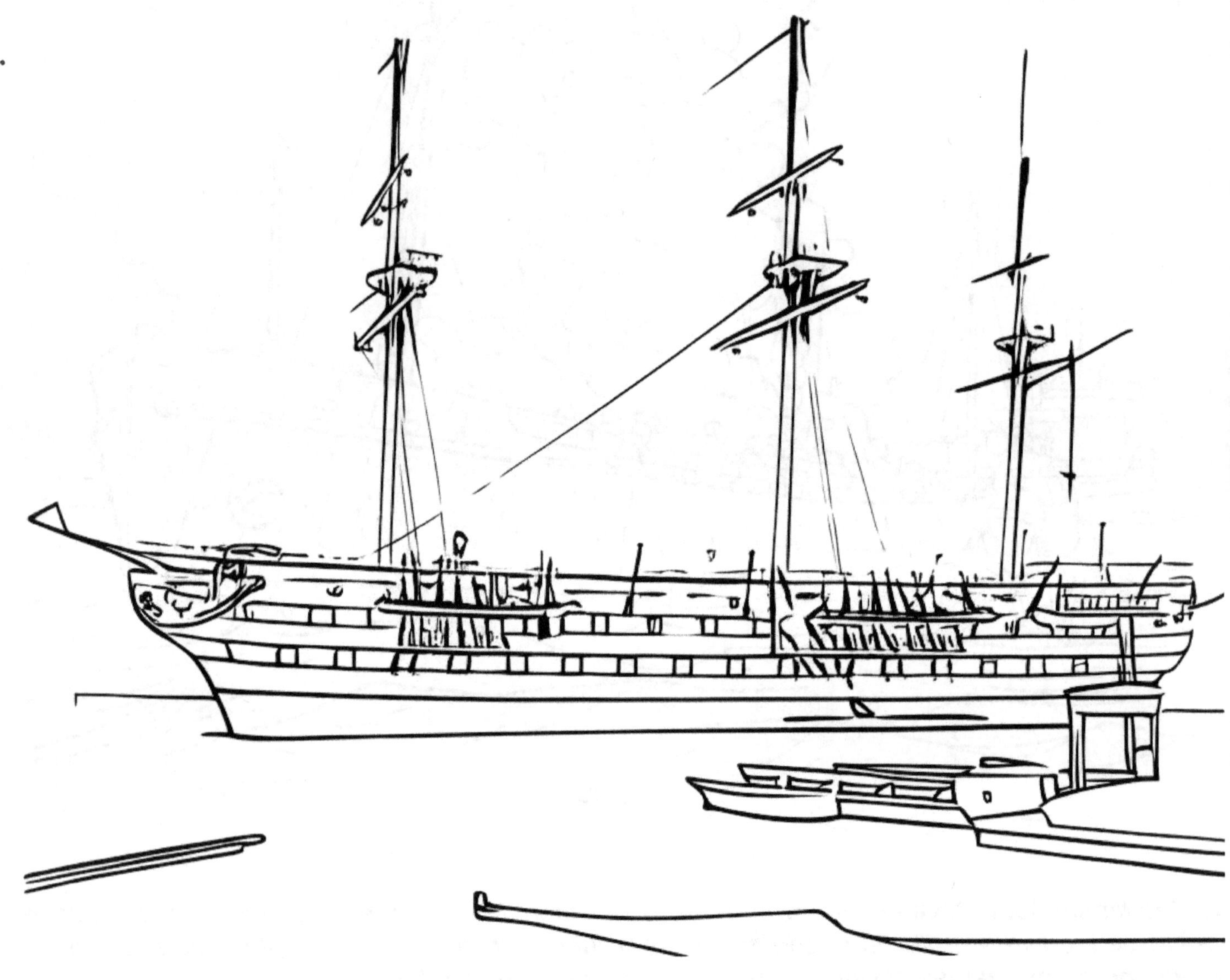

The World War II battleship moored on the Cape Fear River today was not the first to carry the name* North Carolina*. A ship of the line dating from 1820 was the first* USS North Carolina *(above). That ship was followed by a Tennessee-class armored cruiser of the same name in 1908. Today, the Virginia-class nuclear attack submarine* USS North Carolina *(SSN-777) carries the state's name.

In the Great Depression

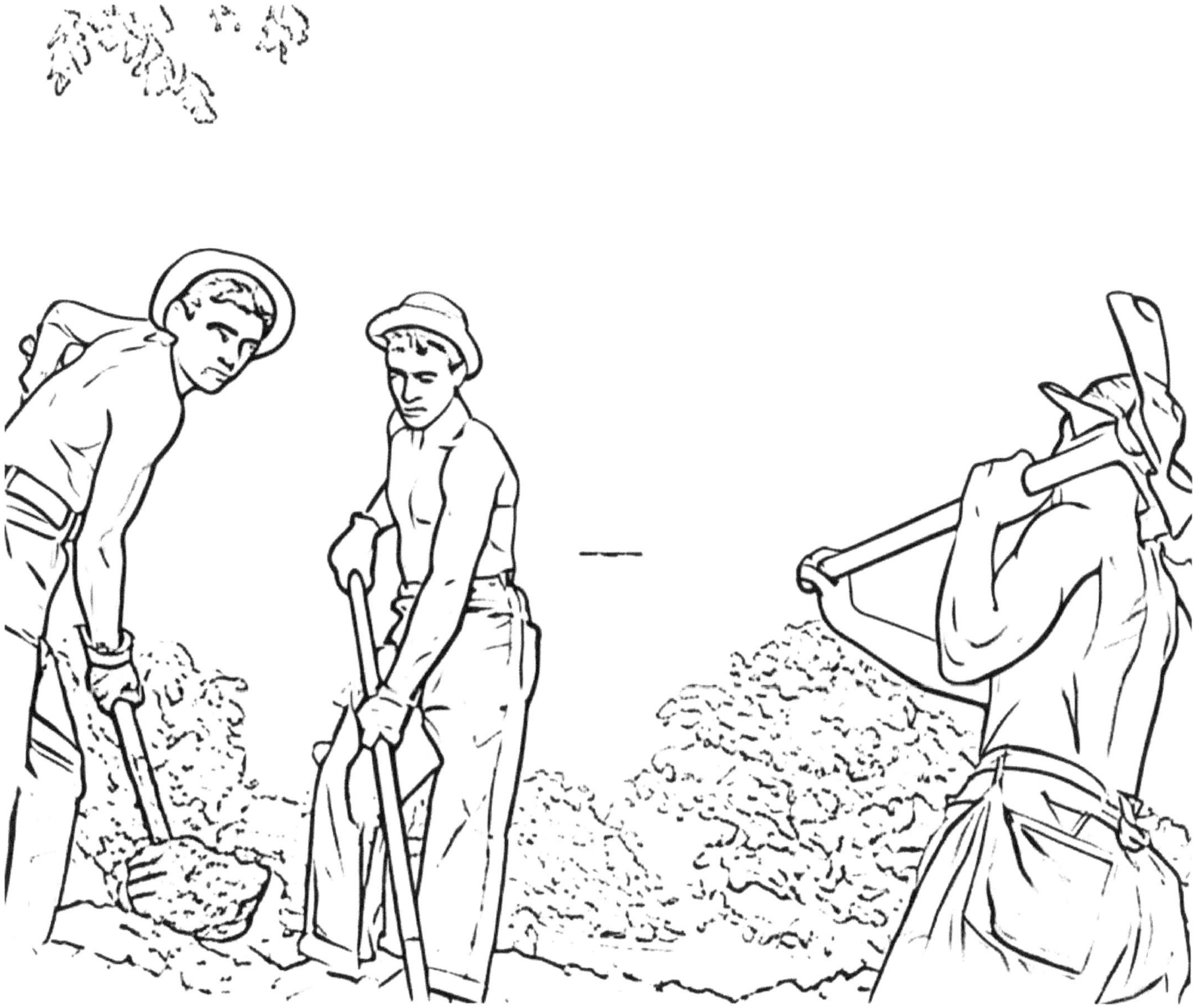

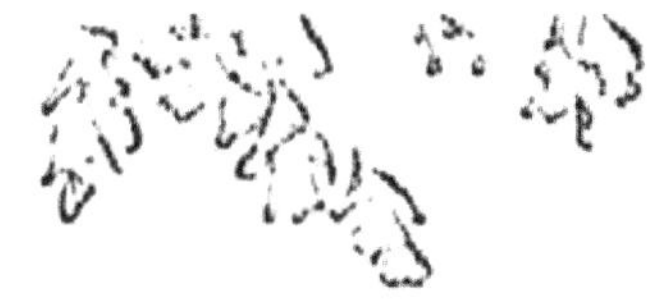

During the Great Depression, Franklin Delano Roosevelt's Civilian Conservation Corps was put to work doing infrastructure projects all over rthe country, including in the lower Cape Fear. One of the biggest was the construction of the road circling Greenfield Lake, and the construction of Legion Stadium.

About the Author...

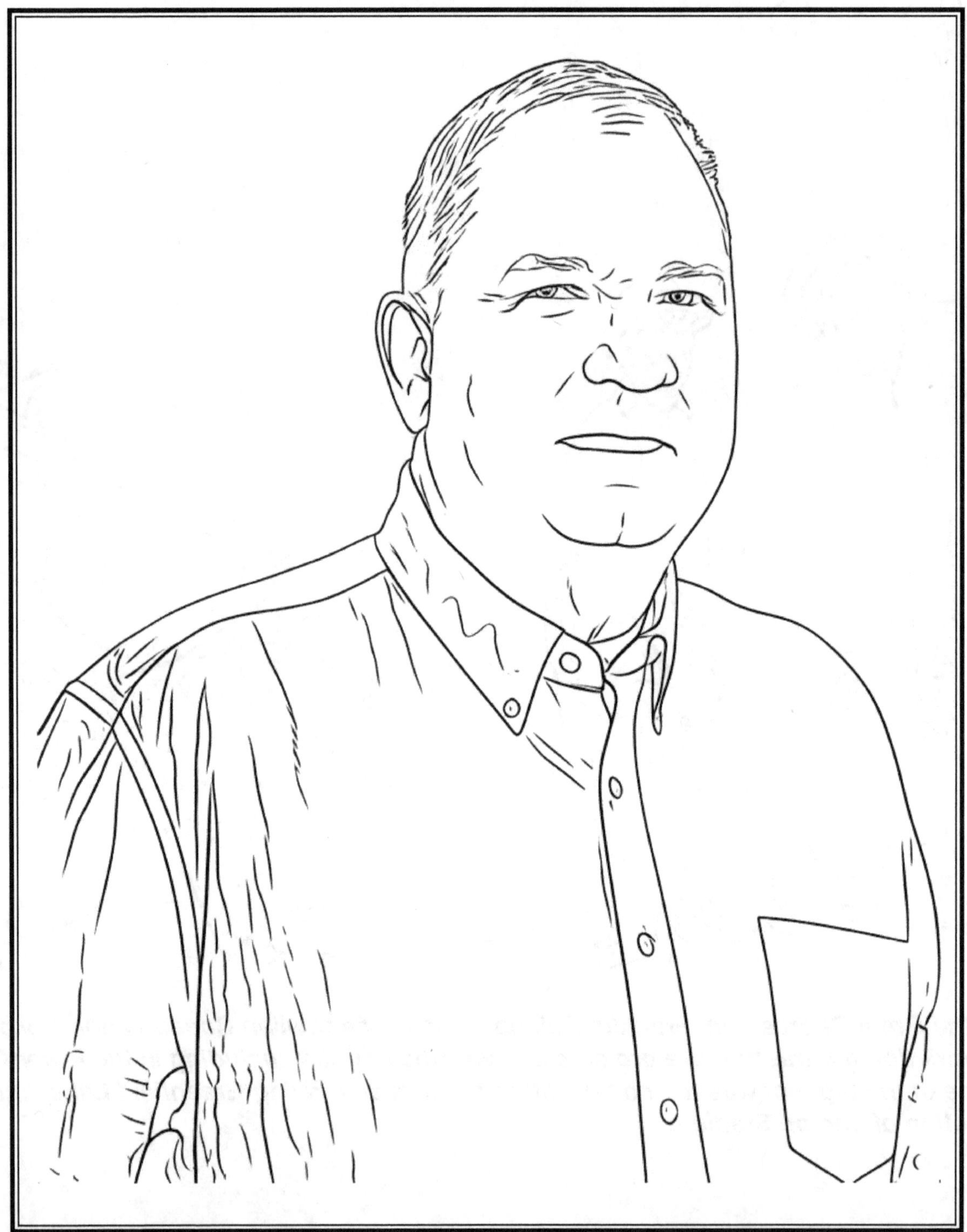

JACK E. FRYAR, JR. is the author or editor of more than 32 books of North Carolina and Cape Fear history. A native of Wilmington, N.C., he holds Masters degrees in History and Teaching from the University of North Carolina at Wilmington. He has taught high school and middle school history, and is a frequent lecturer on historical topics.

www.ingramcontent.com/pod-product-compliance
Lightning Source LLC
LaVergne TN
LVHW081402110826
845149LV00010B/1641

* 9 7 9 8 9 9 3 0 8 1 0 0 7 *